Managing America's Cities

ALSO BY ROGER L. KEMP
(AS EDITOR)

Economic Development in Local Government:
A Handbook for Public Officials and Citizens
(McFarland, 1995)

Strategic Planning for Local Government:
A Handbook for Officials and Citizens
(McFarland, 1993)

Privatization: The Provision of
Public Services by the Private Sector
(McFarland, 1991)

MANAGING AMERICA'S CITIES

A Handbook for Local Government Productivity

ROGER L. KEMP

McFarland & Company, Inc., Publishers
Jefferson, North Carolina, and London

British Library Cataloguing-in-Publication data are available

Library of Congress Cataloguing-in-Publication Data

Kemp, Roger L.
    Managing America's cities : a handbook for local government
productivity / Roger L. Kemp.
       p.   cm.
    Includes bibliographical references and index.
    ISBN 0-7864-0408-6 (library binding : alkaline paper) ∞
    1. Municipal services—United States—Management. 2. Government
productivity. 3. Municipal government—United States. I. Title.
HD4605.K447 1998
352.16'0973—dc21   97-24235
                                                          CIP

Manufactured in the United States of America

McFarland & Company, Inc., Publishers
  Box 611, Jefferson, North Carolina 28640

To Jill,
for many reasons

CONTENTS

ACKNOWLEDGMENTS

The author wishes to acknowledge the many professional, educational, and research organizations that provided the literature and bibliographic materials to make this volume possible.

PREFACE

City halls throughout America are undergoing a revolution in the manner by which municipal services are financed and delivered to citizens. Significant numbers of elected officials and public managers are striving to create more "user-friendly" organizations. Many public managers are embracing more flexible and adaptive management styles. Contemporary management practices are creating dynamic and responsive municipal organizations. These organizations are dynamic because they are accommodating change in a positive way. They are responsive because they are striving to improve the quality of their services. Citizens are also being empowered to coproduce public services. All parties—elected officials, public managers, and citizens—are now concerned about making their government more productive as well as holding down its costs.

The goal of today's local government is customer satisfaction at a reasonable cost. Citizen feedback instruments, process improvement techniques, improved planning practices, and the use of the new technologies have all helped to achieve this goal. Since organizations are mere legal entities, the employees that spend their working lives in municipal government should be recognized for embracing more positive service philosophies, work attitudes, and operational practices. To have effective government, roles must be clearly established and followed. Elected officials must adopt prudent public policies, city managers must hold department directors accountable for implementing these policies, and department managers must manage their employees to continually improve their operations and services.

Employee productivity has been greatly enhanced through the use of new computer hardware, software applications, and other technological innovations. It should be kept in mind that local government services have been and will always be labor intensive. While technologies may improve operations and services, they only assist employees in their efforts to better serve the public. For this reason, all technological applications are merely an instrument to help employees achieve the goal of improved customer satisfaction. Enhanced customer satisfaction means improving service quality and or reducing the cost

1

of these services. Unlike the private sector, the demand for public services is always high. Each public program has its own constituency, and these individuals continually desire to enhance the quantity and quality of their services.

The representatives of municipal government—elected officials, city managers, department directors, and employees—should never forget that their organization holds a monopoly over the public services they provide. If a citizen wishes to report a crime or a fire, or have a pothole repaired, they can only call their police, fire, or public works departments. For this reason, municipal employees should always strive to provide the highest quality services at the most reasonable cost. Some citizens feel that their municipal government should be operated like a private company, and that user fees are the answer to holding down property taxes. It should be kept in mind, however, that many citizens expect property-related services for paying their property taxes. For this reason, police, fire, and public works departments do not charge for many of their services. Other services, such as those provided by public libraries, have always had a tradition of free services. To charge for these services would alienate the very citizens they were intended to serve.

Municipal finance has also undergone drastic changes during the past decade. Many public services that only benefit selected users are now financed out of enterprise funds. This accounting arrangement treats certain public services as profit centers. User fees for these services are adjusted annually to cover their operating costs. Where appropriate, departmental user fees are being implemented and periodically adjusted to reflect the cost of doing business. In many sensitive public service areas, discounts are provided to young people, senior citizens, and families on fixed incomes. New financing tools such as development impact fees, utility connection charges, and assessment districts are being used to charge those who benefit from public improvements. It should be kept in mind that many citizens are willing and can afford to pay user fees for the public services they use.

Efforts to empower citizens to take responsibility for holding down the cost of their government are now commonplace. Recycling programs, conservation initiatives, neighborhood watch programs, medical screening clinics, fire and crime prevention services, and the like, all help to reduce the cost of public services. Citizens in many communities, for example, have significantly reduced their refuse collection and disposal costs through voluntary recycling efforts. Likewise, community crime and fire prevention programs have been successful in reducing the number of crimes and fire incidents. Citizens are increasingly aware that they can become active participants with their government in helping to hold down the cost of their public services. Citizen coproduction programs are increasing in popularity.

Since change is incremental, the future path of our municipal governments has already been charted and is firmly in place. While the goal of high quality services at a reasonable cost will not change, the multitude of avenues available to achieve this goal are presently in a state of transition. While the interface between a municipal organization and its clients will primarily remain one-on-one (employee to citizen), a variety of processes are now available to streamline and improve the manner in which these services are provided.

For the most part, public officials in each community are "doing their own thing" in the dynamic and changing field of municipal government. This volume describes the operations of a typical municipal government and takes stock of the numerous productivity trends being initiated in our city halls. The goal of this work is to codify this information and make it available to others who have an interest in this field. Elected officials will obtain an essential overview of municipal operations and departmental productivity applications. Local government professionals will find this information invaluable to improve their operations and services. Citizens will become educated about numerous innovative ways to improve the quality of their services, increase the productivity of their city hall, as well as reduce the cost of their government. Students wishing to enter this field, or merely learn more about it, will find this volume highly instructional and informative.

This volume currently represents the most comprehensive codification of knowledge available about the operations and productivity applications in our nation's municipal governments.

ROGER L. KEMP
Summer 1997
Meriden, Connecticut

INTRODUCTION

Evolution of Cities

The rapid growth of cities was largely the consequence of the development of new technologies and their application to the industrial and agricultural sectors of the American economy. The location of industrial facilities in our urban centers, and the surplus of labor brought about by agricultural advances in rural areas, provided the necessary labor supply for our industrial expansion. During the latter part of the 18th century, the United States witnessed a population migration of unprecedented proportions from rural to urban areas. Cities grew in size and flourished as this trend continued during the ensuing decades.

As our metropolitan areas flourished, a rapidly growing population base created the need to greatly expand the level of existing municipal services, as well as ways to finance them. One of the first local taxes—the municipal property tax—helped to generate the necessary revenues for local governments to finance property-related services. They typically include police, fire, and public works services. The rapid urbanization of America during the 19th century placed unanticipated demands on these municipal services. Local governments expanded services in these areas, and increased property taxes, in response to these new population demands.

New forms of taxes and fees evolved over the years to help finance a growing need for cultural and recreational programs. The decrease in working hours, evolving family patterns, and increased longevity created the need for new community programs in these nontraditional service areas. Communities, regardless of their size or geographic location, began to provide a full range of municipal services to their residents. The addition of these new services, and the expansion of traditional services, created the need for larger and more complex municipal service delivery systems. These factors led to the need for more professional management of America's cities to run the organizations that provided these services.

The magnitude of America's urban problems increased during the Great

Depression to the extent that local governments could no longer provide meaningful and workable solutions to their local municipal problems. The states, because of their restricted financial capability, were limited in the financial assistance they could provide to solve these problems. The federal government expanded its programs to fill this service vacuum. The central government began by providing direct programmatic, technical, and financial aid to cities to help ameliorate America's pressing urban problems. The height of federal involvement with localities, both operationally and financially, reached its peak during President Johnson's Great Society movement in the 1960s.

Federal aid to communities continued relatively unabated until the advent of the so-called "taxpayers' revolt" movement in the mid–1970s. Because of the mismatch between urban problems and municipal revenues, federal grant programs fulfilled the economic need of transferring tax monies from wealthier to poorer urban areas to balance the capability of local governments to cope with their urban problems. The growth of the taxpayers' revolt, Washington's preoccupation with balancing the federal budget, and the public pressure to eliminate the federal deficit all helped to form a change in the philosophical direction of the U.S. central government. Today, local problems mean local solutions. Local governments can no longer rely on higher levels of government for programmatic, technical, or financial support to tackle their urban problems.

This forced self-reliance has created the need for local elected officials to demand more of their management staffs, and for professional managers to seek out innovative and creative ways to reduce costs, increase productivity, and to maintain existing service levels. These tasks are particularly difficult in many urban communities that have witnessed an out-migration of their middle class population, an influx of low-income citizens demanding public services, and a declining property tax base. State governments, to some extent, have attempted to provide aid to their larger urban communities in an effort to counteract these negative trends. Because of limited state revenues, many pressing urban problems have gone unresolved, and are growing in both their enormity and complexity.

Changing societal trends and values over the past century have served to reshape municipal governments. As community governments grew in size to meet new service and population demands, three important national trends occurred simultaneously that facilitated our current form, structure, political processes, and administrative structures of America's contemporary municipal governments. These trends included the increasing popularity of business and corporate ideals, the progressive reform era, and the public administration movement. These three trends are briefly highlighted below.

Popularity of Business and Corporate Ideals. Businesspersons and the public concept of the corporation have been instrumental in determining public thought and values about community governments. The success of modern-day corporations in the private sector has had a significant influence on American political and administrative thought. Probably no political or administrative philosophy reflects business practices and corporate ideals more clearly than the growth of professional management in our nation's cities. Many citizens still compare the operation of their city government with that of the private corporation. The elected representatives are the board of directors, the city manager is the chief executive officer, and the citizens of the community are the stockholders of the government. Economy and efficiency, two primary values of the business community, are foundations of the movement towards the professional management of our municipalities.

Progressive Reform Movement. Many of the effects of rapid urbanization, particularly the early political machines and large monopolistic corporations, met with disfavor among many citizens, who were commonly called Progressives. These individuals, who formed a significant movement because of their large numbers, felt that the best interests of the public were frequently not being served by the existing political processes and some of the large corporations were perceived as being too strong and having too much power over common people. One of the most significant municipal reforms developed and supported by the Progressives was the council-manager plan. The management concepts embodied in the plan ideally suited the Progressive political philosophy of the time—a competent professional manager and public policy established by nonpartisan elected representatives. The manager's apolitical qualities suited the Progressive values, which favored impartiality and looked down upon personality politics and favoritism. Two key Progressive ideals—equality of participation in the political process and centralized administrative authority—were well balanced in this form of municipal governance.

Public Administration Philosophy. The modern city management profession also fit the emerging concepts of public management in the early 1900s. Many administrative scholars espoused a sharp division between policy determination and policy implementation. Highly respected scholars of the time drew a sharp distinction between "politics" and "administration." The council-manager plan incorporated the ideals of the separation of policymaking and the implementation of public policy. The elected representatives should be responsible for setting public policy, while the city manager should focus on its implementation. The separation of these two distinct tasks—policy setting and policy implementation—formed the basis of the emerging trend to separate community politics from the operation of the municipal organization. This widespread public administration philosophy facilitated the growth of professional management in America's cities.

As the Progressive reform movement emerged and spread, the prevailing philosophy of public administration at the time and the increasing popularity of business and corporate ideals provided the positive background against which professional municipal management blossomed into national popularity. All of these ideological and social forces provided the supportive environment in which professional municipal management spread from city to city across the landscape of America's local governments. The many changes and challenges currently facing our cities—increased service demands, fewer financial resources, citizen aversion to increased taxation, and fewer funds from higher levels of government—have tested the abilities of governing bodies to adopt policies to improve the condition of their cities and, at the same time, hold professional managers accountable for their proper implementation.

FORMS OF GOVERNANCE

There are several significantly different forms of local governmental structure that citizens can adopt to serve the needs of their community. The four most common types of municipal governance are the strong mayor form, the commission type, the mayor-council model, and the council-manager plan. Each structure's strengths and weaknesses are perceived differently by constituents, political officeholders, professional government managers, and the employees of the municipal organization. The particular form selected is not an easy decision for citizens to make. Elected leaders above all want to be responsive to their constituents. On the other hand citizens find equal treatment, an apolitical and objective service delivery system, and cost-effective government to be most important. The characteristics of each of these models of municipal governance are briefly described below.

Strong Mayor. In many large cities in the United States, the mayor is elected to "lead" the city, usually through partisan municipal elections. The mayor serves as the chief executive officer, while the city council serves as the legislative body. The mayor typically manages the municipal organization through mayor-appointed department managers. The mayor may have the authority to appoint a deputy mayor or chief administrative officer to run the daily operations of the city. This plan has its advantages and disadvantages, depending upon the qualifications of the person elected as the mayor. A good political leader is sometimes not a good municipal administrator. Hiring professionally trained administrators has served to overcome this shortcoming.

Commission. This form of government, which usually employs non-partisan, at-large elections includes a board of commissioners. Collectively they serve as the legislative body of their municipal government. Individually each commissioner serves as the head of one or more administrative departments (e.g., public works commissioner, police commissioner, and parks commissioner). The municipal reform movement in the United States has led to the near-demise of this form of local government. This model of municipal governance fuses policymaking with implementation, since both roles are performed by the same officeholders. The other major weakness of this model is obvious, since few elected leaders possess the necessary requirements to professionally manage large portions of a municipal organization.

Mayor-Council. This form has a legislative body that is elected either at-large, by ward or district, or by some combination of the two (i.e., some at-large and others by district). There are two distinguishing characteristics of this plan. The mayor is selected separately through at-large elections and his office is officially designated as the formal head of the municipal government. Depending upon local laws, the powers of the mayor may vary greatly from limited administrative duties to full-scale authority to appoint and remove department managers. The mayor sometimes has veto power over the policies adopted by the city council. The mayor frequently has authority to appoint a chief administrative officer to run the daily operations of the city. The city council typically must confirm this appointment.

Council-Manager. This form of government typically has a legislative body selected by popular vote through nonpartisan elections. Although council members are usually elected at-large, they are selected through some combination of at-large and district elections. They are responsible for setting policy, while the management of the municipal organization is under the direction of an appointed city manager. The city council appoints and removes the city manager by majority vote. The city manager has the power to appoint and remove department managers. The mayor, frequently elected by the city council, is a voting member of the governing body with no special veto or administrative power. The mayor is, however, the community's recognized political and legislative leader and represents the city at all official ceremonies as well as civic and social functions.

Nearly 4,000 cities in the United States operate under the council-manager plan, which separates the policymaking duties of elected officials from the administrative role of professionally trained managers. This is the most successful and popular form of government in cities over 10,000 in population. This form of government has been adopted on the average of one each week by citizens in cities and counties throughout the nation since 1945. Because of its popularity among citizens, it is the fastest growing form of municipal governance in America. For this reason, the references made in this volume to mayors, city councils, and city managers refers to this governmental structure, although other titles such as city administrator, chief executive officer, and business manager may commonly be used in other forms of government to refer to the duties of the city manager.

The form of government that the electorate of a community selects should best serve the needs of its citizens. Voters elect their representatives based on their confidence in them to set the right policies, and to ensure that these policies are implemented into programs and services to serve their needs. If the

council-manager plan best serves this goal, then it is the most desirable form
of government. If another model of local governance is adopted, it should
embody the type of governance desired by citizens. The form of government
best suited for a particular city should always be determined through the electoral process by popular vote. No system of municipal governance is perfect,
nor can any single system represent the wishes of all of the people all of the
time. When the form of local government selected represents the wishes of
the majority of the electorate, this is the form that best serves the democratic
process and the will of the people.

FORCES OF CHANGE

Dynamic changes are now underway in society that will have a dramatic
impact on cities from political, managerial, operational, financial, and technological standpoints. These changes have created trends that will require
local public officials to adapt and modify their municipal organizations in
order to meet the public's changing expectations of effective governing. The
milestone changes influencing cities throughout the country have been facilitated by political trends, demographic shifts, changing urban patterns, technological developments, and economic considerations. Many of these trends
are firmly in place, and will have a measurable impact on municipalities across
the nation for some time to come. They will also test the abilities of public
officials, both elected and appointed, as they strive to restore the public's trust
in their city government.

Gone are the more stable days for local governments. When revenues
were plentiful and public officials could merely adjust tax rates to balance budgets, life for public officials was relatively simple and routine. The outside
environment did not pose any significant challenges, opportunities, or threats.
Public programs were merely increased in response to citizen demands for
more services. When citizen demands could be met with existing revenues,
taxpayers were relatively complacent and did not get actively involved in the
affairs of their local government. Difficult economic times have fueled the
public's desire to hold down taxes, make government more accountable and
productive, and altered the traditional environment in which community governments function. In the future, both the scale and mix of public services, as
well as how they are managed and financed, will be reevaluated in response to
changes presently taking place in our society.

Traditional management practices, designed during more stable periods
of steady growth and routine change, are being replaced by a host of new management techniques. Without predictability, the common management practices of the past will be found to lack both reliability and credibility, especially in the eyes of citizens and the mayors and city councils they elect. How

public officials adapt to this new environment will reflect on their abilities to successfully cope with the future. Public officials are typically preoccupied with the present, and are usually reactive to change. Most of the time governments, at all levels, attempt to respond to change after the fact. Events are occurring now at such a fast pace that the traditional management styles, financial techniques, and technological practices of the past are quickly becoming obsolete.

To briefly explain the extent and magnitude of these changes, and to make them easier to understand, they have been grouped into five general categories. They include emerging political trends, changing demographics, evolving urban patterns, technological developments, and economic factors. The dramatic changes taking place in each of these areas and their influence on our public officials and their municipal organizations are summarized below.

Political Trends. More federal and state laws and court decisions of all types will greatly usurp the home-rule powers of local elected officials. Citizens demand more services, but do not want increased taxation, making it difficult for public officials to set program priorities and to balance their annual budgets. Public officials will stress economic development as a vehicle to raise revenues without increasing taxes. Responsibilities will continue to be shifted downwards from higher levels of government to municipalities. Financing these responsibilities will fall on the backs of municipal taxpayers. Because of the serious mismatch between revenues and problems, cities with low tax bases will have to resort to service reductions. Federal and state grant funds to communities will be limited, but not curtailed entirely. These grants will focus on achieving national priorities, such as crime reduction, affordable housing, and shelters for the homeless.

Demographic Changes. There will be a growing number of senior citizens who, because of their available time, will become more politically active. An aging population will increasingly demand more cultural, recreational, and social services. A greater number of smaller households will require more high-density residential developments, placing greater demands on existing public services, including police and fire protection. There will be a greater number of women in the workforce, and they will become more politically active in the workplace. Such issues as comparable worth and sexual harassment will increase in importance. A greater number of minority and immigrant groups will place new demands for specialized public services and more bilingual public employees. They will also demand greater representation in the political process through neighborhood, or district, elections as well as appointments to city boards and commissions.

Urban Patterns. Urban sprawl will be on the increase but will be located primarily along major vehicle transportation corridors and public mass transit routes. Cities will witness greater in-fill development in already urbanized areas. Land areas that once were marginal will be purchased and upgraded for new development. Older land areas, such as outdated industrial plants and aging commercial centers, will be upgraded and or retrofitted with new amenities to make them more profitable. In central city areas, continuing high land values will lead to increased gentrification, further exacerbating the need for affordable housing. New "ethnic centers" will evolve in metropolitan areas, with these residents desiring to maintain the cultural traditions, values, and customs of their homelands. Higher energy costs and greater traffic congestion will create more political pressure for public mass transit systems. Emphasis will be placed on multimodal systems which offer greater transportation options to citizens.

Technological Developments. There will be an increased use of microcomputers in the workplace, brought about by the more sophisticated systems, lower costs, and more user-friendly software. Information management will become increasingly necessary as computers make more information networks and databases available. Greater energy costs will continue to shape our building technologies. Computer management systems will become commonplace to monitor and regulate energy consumption in public buildings. More public meetings will be aired on public-access cable television stations. Programs will also be initiated to educate citizens on the key issues and problems facing their community. Advanced telecommunications systems, such as those with conference calling and facsimile transmission capabilities, will reduce the number of meetings and related costs. Because of expensive construction costs for underground mass transit systems, new light-rail systems will replace the underground subways of the past.

Economic Factors. The public's aversion to new taxes, and higher user fees and charges, will limit the growth of government services. Governing bodies will increasingly adopt new charges for selected users of public services, such as those fees charged to developers for the cost of public improvements. Public officials will attempt to get citizens more involved in holding down the costs of their public services. Such programs as recycling and composting, conservation, and volunteering to work for their community will increase in importance. Limited new revenues will be earmarked for those public programs with the highest payoff, both from a political and productivity standpoint. Federal grant programs will be limited, creating greater competition among cities for these funds. New grant programs will be earmarked for cities with low-income populations and related social, health, and housing problems. The public will continue to advocate for the "controlled growth" of government in order to hold down their taxes.

The magnitude of these changes will have a direct influence on the type of public services provided, how they are managed and financed, and the extent to which they fit the needs of the citizens being served. By being aware of the latest management, financial, and technological practices, as well as the numerous advances within with various functional and programmatic areas of cities, elected and appointed officials can create a smooth transition into the future for their community. If this does not occur, public meeting halls in cities across the country will become forums for debating citizen demands for greater government accountability, responsiveness, and change. While public officials in local governments must successfully adapt to these changes, it should be kept in mind that many factors external and internal to the municipal organization control the power and authority of public officials in all functional service areas, from conducting assessments to setting zoning regulations.

The various sources of power for public officials and municipal governments are created by selected federal, state, and local laws, as well as numerous court decisions. Conversely, the limits placed in these same powers are also influenced by different types of federal mandates, state regulations, local laws, and court decisions. The political and administrative environment of community governments is increasingly regulated by a number of conditions beyond the control of locally elected officials and their management staffs. While elected officials, city managers, and department managers may wish to implement new human resources practices, for example, existing employment laws, personnel regulations, and labor agreements may place restrictions on the use of such practices. Existing labor contracts, may place restrictions on privatizing or contracting for municipal services, as well as regulate the use of community volunteers. Figure 1.1 highlights many of the common sources and limits of power in our community governments.

Figure 1.1
Sources and Limits of Power in Municipal Governments

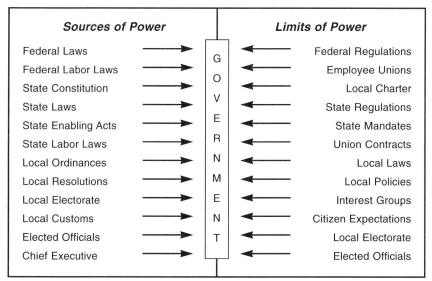

Sources of Power		Limits of Power
Federal Laws	G	Federal Regulations
Federal Labor Laws	O	Employee Unions
State Constitution	V	Local Charter
State Laws	E	State Regulations
State Enabling Acts	R	State Mandates
State Labor Laws	N	Union Contracts
Local Ordinances	M	Local Laws
Local Resolutions	E	Local Policies
Local Electorate	N	Interest Groups
Local Customs	T	Citizen Expectations
Elected Officials		Local Electorate
Chief Executive		Elected Officials

Municipal Organizations

Every city government has a governing body consisting of a mayor and city council. How the mayor is selected and the number of council members are determined by state laws for general law cities and by the electorate in charter cities. In many general law cities, for example, there are typically five council members elected at-large. The mayor is selected by majority vote of the governing body. In charter cities, on the other hand, the mayor is usually elected at-large, while the members of the council are elected through some combination of at-large and district elections. The number of council members in a charter city is usually seven or nine, but varies greatly and may even be based upon population. Some charter cities also require the election of other municipal positions such as the city clerk, treasurer, and auditor. The powers of the mayor, as well as these other positions, are set forth in the municipal charter. For the purpose of this study, the term governing body refers to the mayor and members of the city council. It is also assumed that the governing body sets policy, while the city manager implements this policy, and that all department managers, with the exception of the city attorney, are appointed by the city manager.

The typical municipal government provides a variety of services to its residents. These public services are provided by individual city departments, which are organized by function. Each department performs those services related to its function. Some departments perform a narrow function, such as police and fire departments, while other departments encompass broader functions, like public works and health and human services. The type of services a city provides depends upon a number of different factors. Communities on coastlines, for example, may provide small craft harbors and public beaches, while larger cities may have museums, zoos, and golf courses. Some cities have municipal airports and also provide public transit services. To make matters more confusing, some states require certain functions to be performed by counties, such as health, welfare, property assessments, and tax collection. In many urbanized areas, some services are provided by special districts. These services may include public transit, water distribution, and wastewater treatment. Furthermore, many communities contract for certain services from other municipalities and counties, as well as the private sector.

A municipal organization can also be divided into line and staff departments. Line departments provide a direct service to the public, while staff departments serve the organization to keep it operating smoothly. For these reasons, the external services provided by line departments are more visible to the public than those internal services performed by staff departments. Typical staff departments include city clerk, city manager, finance, and legal. Common line departments encompass fire, health and human services, library, parks and recreation, planning and building, police, and public works. Some departments, like city clerk, perform both line and staff functions. That is, they serve the public (e.g., the sale of public records, licenses, and permits) and also serve the needs of the organization (e.g., the preparation of meeting agendas, minutes, and staff reports, as well as the posting of public notices). Although the number of departments may vary from community to community, the above departments are so common that they are used to represent the typical municipal organization. Figure 1.2 graphically illustrates these departments.

Every department's operations can further be divided into specific programs, each related to a department's overall function. Each program represents a particular service and, taken together, these programs encompass those services provided by each municipal department. The number and types of programs in a municipal department may vary from department to department, as well as community to community. Variables that influence this phenomenon include each community's unique historical development, the privatization of services, the existence of contract services, and how each department director organizes their respective departmental operations. Individual municipal charters may also alter this program arrangement, but these changes would be the exception to the typical municipal organization rather than the norm. The chapters in this volume are organized around the typical municipal functions, or departments. The various programs indicated for each department are typical and common to its function. For these reasons, the programs shown in Table 1.1 represent the most common programs relating to each municipal department.

PRODUCTIVITY TRENDS

In the private sector, productivity occurs when an employee produces a good or performs a service in an effective and efficient manner. While private companies primarily produce individual goods and services in the general consumer marketplace, city governments perform a variety of services to citizens within the strict confines of their political boundaries. Most private managers have traditionally applied the following criteria when attempting to create a productive organization: Productivity = effectiveness + efficiency. Effectiveness refers to providing an improved service, while efficiency means performing the same service in a economical or cost-effective manner. Therefore, if managers do an excellent job but overrun their budget, they may be performing effectively but not efficiently. Conversely, if managers save budget funds at the expense of program quality, they may be performing efficiently but not effectively. In either of the above two examples, productivity does not exist using the traditional private sector definition of this term. Under this definition, for productivity to take place, managers must provide an improved level of service at a lower unit cost.

Figure 1.2
Typical Municipal Organization by Major Functions

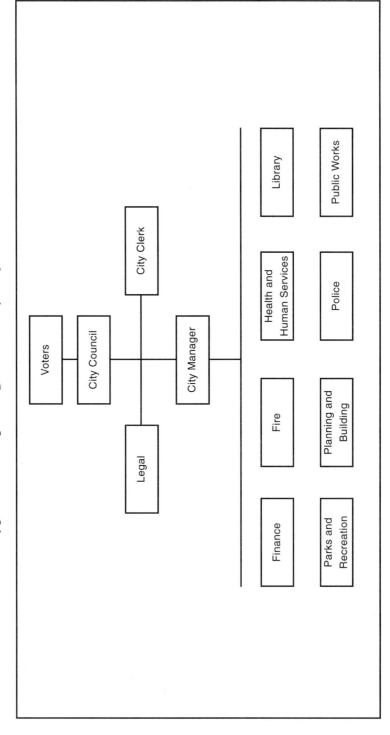

Table 1.1
Typical Municipal Organization
Major Functions and Programs

City Council
Office of the Mayor
Citizen Advisory Bodies
Financial Policies
Municipal Legislation
Legislative Advocacy
Standing Committees

City Manager
Administration
Organizational Develop-
    ment
Financial Management
Personnel
Labor Relations
Citizen Inquiries
Policies/Procedures
Special Assignments

City Clerk
Public Documents
Public Meetings
Records Management
Licenses/Permits
Vital Statistics
Election Administration
Registrar of Voters
Public Information

Legal
Legislation
Litigation
Legal Counsel
Legal Documents
Public Meetings
Safety and Risk

Finance
Treasurer
Comptroller
Debt Management
Revenue Management
Assessment
Budget Preparation
Purchasing
Data Processing

Fire
Fire Suppression
Fire Prevention
Fire Inspection
Emergency Services
Emergency Preparedness
Hazardous Materials

**Health and Human
Services**
Health Services
Health Education
Environmental Services
Code Enforcement
Community Clinics
Social Services

Library
Information Services
Technical Services
Children's Services
Community Services
Circulation Control
Literacy Programs

Parks and Recreation
Recreation Services
Parks Management
Youth Services
Senior Citizen Services
Community Events
Special Programs

Planning and Building
Land-Use Planning
Zoning Control
Development Regulations
Affordable Housing
Building Inspection
Code Enforcement
Economic Development
Capital Improvements

Police
Patrol Services
Community Policing
Investigations
Crime Prevention
Officer Training
Records Management
Dispatching
Police Auxiliary

Public Works
Engineering Services
Transportation Systems
Solid Waste Management
Water Resource Systems
Buildings and Grounds
Central Garage

For several valid reasons, the definition of the term productivity can be refined when it is applied to municipal organizations. City governments hold a monopolistic position in the marketplace for those services they provide. In the event of a fire, call-for-service is responded to only by the local fire department. When a burglary occurs, response only comes from the municipal police department. When roads are built or repaired, these services are provided only by the public works department. The consumer or taxpayer has no choice in who provides these services. These same service patterns generally hold true for most other municipal services. There are generally only two exceptions to this rule: for the services provided by public libraries and the programs available at park and recreational facilities. Citizens may use a neighboring city's library for services and may use the recreational facilities available in the parks of an adjacent community. In both cases, however, citizens are paying for these services through their local property taxes even if they choose not to use them in their own community. Since user fees are typically not charged for these services, citizens most likely will only pay once for these services through their property taxes.

Some of the services provided by city governments cannot be substantially improved or made appreciably more effective. For example, the issuance of building permits by a planning and building department cannot be improved substantially except for speeding up the issuance process itself. Likewise, a police or fire department's response is fairly routine and, in many cases, cannot be improved upon except by having it decreased. Citizens are satisfied to receive street sweeping services. This service can only be made more effective by performing it more frequently. The only way to improve the services of a municipal swimming pool would be to expand the number of hours it is open to the public. When the quality of a municipal service is fairly constant, such as in the above examples, the only way to increase productivity is to reduce the cost of providing the service, to speed up the time in which the service is provided, or to expand the number of hours that the service is made available to the public. In this volume, therefore, the term productivity relates to several factors, such as improving the quality of services, reducing the cost of services, and or improving internal operations to make employees more productive. Public employees accomplishing these goals are deemed to be improving the productivity of their municipal organizations.

Taking the swimming pool example cited above, the availability of the pool is the service provided to citizens wishing to use this facility. If this swimming pool was operated by part-time employees, rather than full-time employees, operating costs could be reduced. Likewise, if a city purchased its pool chemicals jointly with another city, achieving a lower unit cost because of economy of scale, additional cost savings would be realized. Similarly, if new pool equipment was purchased, this would reduce the energy costs of operating this facility. Also, if water conservation shower fixtures and energy conservation light timing devices were used, these efforts would further reduce the utility costs associated with maintaining this swimming pool. Further, if the department director did a cost/benefit analysis of contracting for pool maintenance, and it proved less expensive to have this service performed by the private sector, a further economy could be achieved by contracting for this service. Even though the quality of pool services has not been improved, all of these efforts relate to increasing the productivity of operating this municipal facility.

The term productivity is frequently used to refer to the performance of employees, supervisors, and department managers, as well as the entire municipal organization. For an entire municipal organization to be productive, its governing body and city manager must work together with their department managers to achieve a greater level of system-wide productivity. This effort must be continually communicated by the city manager to department managers, by department managers to supervisors, and by supervisors to individual employees. With continuing support from a governing body and city manager, the desire to achieve productivity improvements should be engrained in the culture of the organization. The more astute governing bodies and city managers have developed vision and mission statements for their municipal organizations to give positive direction to all employees within the workforce. These vision and mission statements are typically developed jointly between the city manager and department managers, and ultimately approved and endorsed by the city council. These statements are then distributed to all departments and displayed in a prominent place, making this information available to all supervisors and employees.

Lacking this organization-wide commitment, productivity may only be exhibited by some employees, supervisors, and managers in certain individual departments. For a municipal government to continually exhibit a high level of productivity improvement, the elected officials must hold the city manager accountable, the city manager must hold department directors accountable, department managers must hold their supervisors accountable, and supervisors must hold their employees accountable. Ideally, an organization's reward system should be tied to these productivity improvements. Such a compensation program is easier to implement at the city manager and department manager level. It is almost impossible to implement with individual employees because existing labor agreements and personnel practices typically preclude this practice. Since many municipal organizations lack this system-wide incentive, the task of productivity rests, by default, with the city manager and individual department managers. Also, when a governing body and city manager encourage the use of the latest technological developments in municipal departments, they encourage department managers to use computers, software applications, and other state-of-the-art equipment, to improve their operations. Although the number of employees may not be reduced because of these efforts, improved services and more effective internal operations will be achieved.

The various productivity trends examined in this volume have been broken down by department, program, and whether the trend is primarily internal or external to the organization. Internal trends generally relate to those productivity improvements made within individual departments, and primarily include financial, staffing, operational, organizational, and technological improvements. External trends relative to those productivity improvements initiated outside of a department's operating environment, such as using

Table 1.2
Departmental Productivity Trends

Internal	Departmental	External

CITY COUNCIL

City Clerk Services
City Manager Selection
Cost of Mandates and Decisions
Financial Management
Fire Services
Health and Human Services
Labor Relations and Personnel Issues
Legal Services
Library Services
Management/Union Relations
Organizational Downsizing
Parks and Recreation Services
Planning and Building Services
Police Services
Public Works Services
Use of Computers and New
    Technologies

Budget and Service Reductions
Budgeting Innovations
Coproduction of Public Services
Downtown Revitalization
Economic Development
Forms of Government
Growth Management Policies
Increased User Fees
Legislative Advocacy
Local Elections Systems
Privatization Concepts
Public Access Cable Television
Public Infrastructure and
    Development
Strategic Planning and Issues
    Management
Volunteer Programs

CITY MANAGER

Contemporary Finance Practices
Effectiveness of Elected Officials
Fiscal Impact Statements
Human Resources Administration
Management Information Systems
Management Merit Pay Programs
Management/Union Cooperation
Mission and Vision Statements
Organizational Downsizing
Public Liability Reduction
Real Estate Asset Management
Revenue Management Practices
Role of City Manager and Mayor
Total Quality Management
Use of Computers, Technologies,
    and Equipment

Benchmarking Techniques
Capital Improvement Plans
Contemporary Budgeting Practices
Contract Staff Services
Cost Containment
Customer Satisfaction Surveys
Economic and Downtown
    Development
Educating the Public
Growth Management Practices
Innovative Community Services
Privatization Practices
Public Service Impact Statements
Strategic vs. Traditional Planning
Volunteer and Student Internship
    Services
Working with the Community

CITY CLERK

Automated Cash Register and Receipting
    Systems
Computer Security
Computer Usage and City Clerk Services

City Clerk Internships
Contract City Clerk Services
Election Consolidations
Fixed Terms of Office

Internal	*Department*	*External*

Cross-Training of Staff
Fiscal Accountability
Ordinance Codification
Part-Time Employees
Records Management
Specialized City Clerk Training
User Fee Increases

Knowledge of City Clerk Resources
Licenses and Permits
Networking and Resource Sharing
Open Public Meeting Laws
Professional Certifications
Role of the City Clerk
Telephone Message Centers

LEGAL

Code Enforcement
Computer Usage and Legal Services
Conflict-of-Interest Issues
Cost of Municipal Mandates
Cross-Training of Staff
Labor Relations and Personnel Services
Liability Reduction Programs
Records Management
Safety and Risk Management
Settlement of Lawsuits
Specialized Legal Training

Claims Administration
Contract Computer Legal Services
Contract Legal Services
Knowledge of Legal Resources
Legal Internships
Model Ordinance Services
Networking and Resource Sharing
Outside Legal Services
Professional Certifications
Role of Legal Staff

FINANCE

Assessment Practices
Auditing Practices
Budgeting for Decision-Making
Capital Project Financing
Computer Systems and Software
   Applications
Creative Purchasing Practices
Debt Collection Administration
Financial Management Practices
Financial Monitoring
Financial Policies
Pricing Municipal Services
Revenue and Expenditure Forecasting
Revenue Management Practices
Special Fund Accounting
Tax Collection Practices
Treasury Management Practices

Contract Services
Development Impact Fees and
   Special Assessments
External Economic Conditions
Federal and State Grants
Investing Public Funds
Legislative Mandates
Privatization Considerations
Professional Certifications
Revenue Diversification
Revenue Surveys
Revenues Without Taxes
Sound Financial Practices
Taxes and Economic Development
User Charges and Regulatory Fees

FIRE

Budgetary Controls
Civilianization Practices
Evaluating Fire Services
Fire Prevention Practices
Fire Station Location Decisions
Fire Suppression Practices
Human Resources Management
   Practices

Contemporary Building
   Technologies
Code Enforcement
Codes and Regulations
Contract Services
Development Standards
Emergency Services Practices
Fire Service Master Planning

Table 1.2. Departmental Productivity Trends *continued*

Internal	*Department*	*External*
	FIRE *cont'd.*	
Incident Command Centers		Fire Station Closure Decisions
Interdepartmental Cooperation		Intergovernmental Cooperation
Management Information Systems		Professional Development
Occupational Safety and Health Programs		Public Education and Citizen Empowerment
Organizational Consolidation		Service, Disclosure, and Impact Fees
Use of Computers, Technologies, and Equipment		Use of Volunteer Firefighters
Work Shift Schedules		
	HEALTH AND HUMAN SERVICES	
Departmental Inspection Referrals		Community Resource Centers
Evolving Health Services		Contract and Coproduced Services
Evolving Human Services		Interagency Cooperation
General Assistance Programs		Private Cosponsorship of Public Programs
Hazardous Materials Disclosure and Enforcement		Professional Development
Human Resources Management Practices		Public Education and Citizen Empowerment
Innovative Public Services		Public Health and Human Services Master Planning
Knowledge of Available Resources		Sorting Out Responsibilities
Organizational Structures		State and Federal Grant Programs
Public Policies and Cost-Effectiveness		User Service Charges, Regulatory Fees, and Fines
Role of Elected Officials and Advisory Bodies		Working with the Community
Use of Computers and New Technologies		
	LIBRARY	
Evolving Community Services		Alternative Funding Sources
Evolving Information Services		Community Resource Centers
Evolving Technical Services		Contract Services
Financing Library Services		Library Service Master Planning
Human Resources Management Practices		Library Service Trends
Libraries and Children		Private Cosponsorship and Coproduction of Programs
Management Practices and Organizational Change		Professional Development
Organizational Structures and Advisory Bodies		Specialized Training and Citizen Empowerment
Role of Citizen Support Groups		User Service Charges and Fees
Staff Development and Internal Marketing		Working with the Community
Use of Computers and New Technologies		

Internal   *Department*   *External*

PARKS AND RECREATION

Cost-Containment and Increased
  Services
Evolving Community Events and
  Special Services
Evolving Parks and Open Spaces
Evolving Recreational Services
Financing Parks and Recreational
  Services
Financing Parks, Open Space, and
  Recreational Facilities
Management Practices and
  Organizational Change
Organizational Structures
Role of Citizen Support Groups
Staff Development and Internal
  Marketing
Use of Computers, Technologies, and
  Products

Alternative Funding Sources
Alternative Service Delivery
  Systems
Americans with Disabilities Act
  Compliance
Community Program Information
  Centers
Parks and Recreation Master
  Planning
Parks and Recreation Service Trends
Professional Development
Public Liability Reduction
  Programs
Service Philosophy of Elected
  Officials
User Fees and Service Charges
Working with the Community

PLANNING AND BUILDING

Affordable Housing
Capital Improvement Plans
  and Financing
Economic Development Planning
Evolving Building and Zoning Controls
Evolving Planning Services
Fiscal Impact Analysis
Human Resources Management
  Practices
Interdepartmental Code Enforcement
  Cooperation
Organizational Arrangements
Role of Elected Officials and
  Advisory Bodies
Use of Computers and Software
  Applications
Use of Economic Development
  Incentives

Comprehensive Community Code
  Enforcement
External Forces Influencing
  Planning
Financial Incentives
General Incentives and Assistance
Growth Management Techniques
Land-Based Incentives
Marketing Programs and Services
Professional Development
Public/Private Partnerships
Regional Planning Practices
Traditional vs. Strategic Planning
User Fees, Impact Charges, Special
  Assessments, and Fines
Working with the Community

POLICE

Budgetary Controls
Centralized Dispatching Services
Civilianization Practices
Evaluating Police Services

Budget and Service Reductions
Community Education and Citizen
  Empowerment
Contract Services

Table 1.2. Departmental Productivity Trends *continued*

Internal	*Department*	*External*

POLICE *cont'd.*

Internal	External
Evolving Community Policing Services	Coproduced Services
Evolving Crime Prevention Services	Financing Police Services
Human Resources Management Practices	Intergovernmental Cooperation and Resource Sharing
Management Information Systems	Police-Community Relations
Management Practices and Organizational Change	Police Service Master Planning
Organizational Consolidations	Police Service Trends
Use of Computers and Technologies	Professional Development
Workload Scheduling and Caseload Management	Working with Community Volunteers

PUBLIC WORKS

Internal	External
Capital Projects Planning and Programming	Americans with Disabilities Act Compliance
Cost Containment Practices	Bidding Practices
Costs and Benefits of Public Works Services	Contract Services
Human Resources Management Practices	Coproduced and Cofinanced Services
Management Information Systems	Outside Funding of Capital Projects
Municipal Financing of Capital Projects	Professional Development
Organizational Structures and Consolidations	Public Education and Citizen Empowerment
Real Estate Asset Management	Public Infrastructure Issues
Solid Waste Management Planning	Public Works Service Trends
Transportation Management Planning	State and Federal Grant Programs
Use of Computers, Technologies, and Products	User Fees, Service Charges, and Other Revenues
Water Resources Management Planning	Working with the Community

community volunteers, citizen service coproduction initiatives, seeking state and federal grants, privatization practices, contracting for services, and public/private partnerships, are listed alphabetically within these two categories for each department. Table 1.2 summarizes these departmental productivity trends. These external and internal productivity trends are described in each chapter of this volume in the same order in which they appear in this table. While some of the titles may be generic, the details of these various productivity improvements are geared to each individual department.

MUNICIPAL RESOURCES

The organization of each chapter is essentially the same throughout this volume. Each chapter starts with a brief introduction to the department, includes a description of its major programs, examines major departmental productivity trends, and concludes with an analysis of the future of these trends. This book commences with the city council and is followed by the staff departments (city manager, city clerk, legal, and finance). The line departments (fire, health and human services, library, parks and recreation, planning and building, police, and public works) follow and are listed in alphabetical order for ease of reference. This book also contains a listing of relevant municipal professional associations and organizations, as well as a comprehensive bibliography of literature related to municipal government.

The Municipal Resource Directory contains valuable information for readers wishing to pursue additional resources from various professional and research institutions. The following entries are made for each of these associations and organizations: name and address; telephone, FAX and toll-free telephone numbers; the name of the executive director (or related position); the type of organization or association, its membership audience, research topics, and resources and the mission of the group. Also included for each entry is the year in which it was established. This information has been compiled for nearly 50 major national and international professional associations representing the major membership, educational, and research institutions for each of the functional areas of municipal government. Table 1.3 lists these groups in alphabetical order by department. Those general municipal associations and organizations not specifically linked to individual functional areas are listed at the end of this table.

The bibliography represents a comprehensive compilation of relevant local government resource materials—primarily books, monographs, and professional journal articles. These bibliographic entries have been categorized under 20 separate headings and are shown in alphabetical order within each of these categories. There is a separate heading for each of the 12 functional areas of municipal government, plus 8 additional categories for other materials related to these functions. These additional headings include cities and society, economic development, forms of government, infrastructure, personnel, privatization, retrenchment management, and strategic planning. This bibliography represents an important codification of knowledge in these subject areas. This bibliography was developed to assist those readers wishing to pursue these topics in greater detail.

Many communities throughout the nation have initiated measures to increase the productivity of their municipal government and its various operational components. Others are in the process of developing and implementing similar productivity improvement programs. Many of these practices have

Table 1.3
Major Professional Associations
and Research Organizations
Serving Municipal Government
(by Function)

City Clerk
International Institute of Municipal
  Clerks

City Council
National League of Cities
United States Conference of Mayors

City Manager
International City/County Management
  Association
International Personnel Management
  Association
National Public Employer Labor Rela-
  tions Association
Public Technology, Inc.

Finance
Government Finance Officers Associa-
  tion
Institute of Internal Auditors
International Association of Assessing
  Officers
Municipal Treasurers Association
National Institute of Government Pur-
  chasing

Fire
International Association of Fire Chiefs
National Fire Protection Association

Health and Human Services
American Public Health Association
American Public Welfare Association
National Environmental Health Associ-
  ation

Legal
National Institute of Municipal Law
  Officers
Public Risk Management Association

Library
American Library Association
Special Libraries Association

Parks and Recreation
National Recreation and Park Association

Planning and Building
American Planning Association
Building Officials and Code Adminis-
  trators International
International Conference of Building
  Officials
International Downtown Association
National Association of Housing and
  Redevelopment Officials
National Community Development
  Association
National Council for Urban Economic
  Development
National Housing Conference

Police
International Association of Chiefs of
  Police
National Crime Prevention Council
National Criminal Justice Association
Police Executive Research Forum
Police Foundation

Public Works
American Public Power Association
American Public Works Association
American Water Works Association
Institute of Transportation Engineers
National Association of Flood and
  Storm Water Management Agencies
Solid Waste Management Association
  of North America
Water Environment Foundation

Others

Academy for State and Local Government	National Association of Towns and
American Society for Public Adminis-	Townships
tration	National Civic League
Institute of Public Administration	The Urban Institute

Note: Additional information concerning these associations and organizations may be found in the Municipal Resource Directory.

been diverse, fragmented, and piecemeal in their development and application. For the most part, municipal public officials—both elected and appointed—are "doing their own thing" in this dynamic, diverse, and rapidly evolving discipline. Politically and administratively sound productivity improvement initiatives must be developed to help ensure the public's confidence in their municipal government. This work represents the most comprehensive effort to date to document and explain the many evolving productivity trends in the various departments of a typical municipal organization. For these reasons, the goal of this volume is to help pull together the available knowledge in this new field of local government. This work should provide citizens, students, professionals, and members of governing bodies with the information needed to initiate similar productivity improvement programs within their own municipal organizations. Most of these productivity improvement applications are applicable to other city governments, regardless of their size or geographic location.

2

CITY COUNCIL

Every municipality has a legislative body consisting of a mayor and several members of the city council. In most cities the number of elected representatives ranges from five to seven, with the mayor serving as a member of the city council. Using the corporate analogy, the members of the governing body collectively serve as the board of directors for the municipal corporation; the mayor is the chairman of the board; and the citizens are the stockholders. Under this model the city manager serves in a role similar to that of president or general manager of a corporation. The primary role of elected officials is to serve as policymakers, as well as to officially approve existing staffing levels, programs and services, and to adopt the annual budget. Elected officials should not get actively involved in the daily operations of the municipal organization. Elected officials may also serve on one or more standing committees. Many elected officials usually do not spend a great deal of time at city hall since most hold other full-time jobs.

Citizens recognize their mayor as their chief elected official as well as the legislative leader of their community. Almost every municipality has come to recognize the special role that is performed by the office of the mayor. Citizens with problems, not knowing where to go within the organization to have them addressed, typically write, call, or visit the mayor. Even in communities where the mayor has limited ceremonial duties, citizens as well as the members of the management staff have come to respect the special role played by the mayor in serving as the interface between the municipal organization and the citizens it serves. For these reasons, the mayor has a special relationship with the city manager. It is essential that the mayor and city manager work well together to jointly achieve the goals of the city. The astute mayor turns over operational problems and issues to the city manager, who delegates them to department managers and holds them accountable for their resolution. The astute city manager, on the other hand, should adapt his or her management style to the personality of the mayor. This management style may change when a new person is elected to this office. The city manager should always keep in mind that it is the mayor and city council who hold the ultimate trust of the people.

In well-managed cities, the mayor works closely with the city council to set policies to resolve issues and problems within the community. The city manager and management staff should never make changes at the direction of the mayor if such changes require the approval of the city council. Many governing bodies are composed of individuals with strong personalities who represent diverse constituencies within the community. The mayor should respect the role of his or her colleagues on the city council and never try to undermine the policy role entrusted to these elected representatives. The city manager, in working with his or her management staff, should always be mindful that individual council members may make inquiries, process citizen complaints, and seek information about city operations and services. Many council members go directly to the city manager with their concerns, and hold him or her accountable for a proper response.

Every community has a host of permanent boards and commissions, some of which are mandated by charter and state law, such as the planning commission and zoning board. Many municipalities also have a number of committees frequently organized around specific issues such as beautification and neighborhood preservation. Some mayors create ad hoc committees or task forces to focus on current community problems such as juvenile delinquency, drug abuse, and gang prevention. Frequently the city manager may be asked to serve as staff liaison to some of these groups. In other cases, when these groups relate to a specific city function, the city manager will assign a department manager to serve in this capacity. For example, almost without exception, a city's planning director serves as the permanent staff liaison to a community's planning commission and zoning board. Staff members usually do not serve on these bodies; they merely provide organizational support. When they make recommendations, they are advisory in nature only. All of these groups, with few exceptions, are advisory to the governing body. While city councils frequently follow the recommendations of their advisory bodies, only the legislative body has the legal power to approve legislation.

In recent years, public officials in many communities have become more involved in legislative advocacy, primarily at the state level. Most municipalities belong to one state professional association, but maintain memberships in one or more national organizations. State associations organize state legislative advocacy activities on behalf of public officials in member municipalities. Similarly, national associations organize similar activities to influence federal legislation pending before the U.S. Congress. Many small- and medium-sized communities also conduct their own legislative advocacy with their state and federal legislative delegations. In recent years, city officials have spent a great deal of their time opposing state and federal mandates that impose operational requirements on city governments without providing monetary reimbursement. These same public officials also frequently lobby their state representatives for an increasing share of state revenues to help offset local property tax increases. As local budgets have become tighter, and citizens have increased their opposition to new or increased taxes, legislative advocacy efforts such as those described above have increased in both frequency and intensity.

An outline of the major programs performed by a city's governing body, including legislative advocacy, is shown in Figure 2.1.

DESCRIPTION OF PROGRAMS

Office of the Mayor. The members of the city council comprise the municipal corporation's governing body. The head of the city council is the mayor, who is the city's chief elected official. The mayor may be directly elected by the voters, selected by the members of the city council or, in some cases, the highest vote-getter of those candidates elected to the city council. The process by which the mayor is elected or selected is set forth by law. The mayor's duties are either defined by city charter or by state law, depending upon the type of laws governing the municipal corporation. In almost all cities there exists a separate Office of the Mayor. The mayor may also have certain appointing authority to municipal boards and commissions, set forth in the laws governing the city.

Regardless of the actual powers of the mayor, citizens usually perceive the mayor as the "head" or "leader" of their local government. Even in a city where the mayor has strictly limited ceremonial duties, the mayor is always considered the "legislative leader" of the city. Members of the city council typically have no special authority or powers, except their right to vote on municipal issues as members of the governing body.

Citizen Advisory Bodies. Virtually every city has several, sometimes even a dozen or more, citizen advisory commissions, boards, and committees. In addition to advising the legislative body, some of these advisory bodies have limited legal powers granted by state and local laws, such as planning commissions and zoning boards. Permanent commissions and boards are established by law, while committees and other ad hoc groups are usually established by a resolution or by motion of the governing body. City councils can create commissions and boards, while only a mayor generally has the power to create ad hoc committees. For example, while a governing body may establish a permanent city beautification commission, only the mayor can create a temporary beautification committee. It is not unusual for a mayor to establish temporary advisory groups, such as working committees or task forces, but these groups usually last only as long as the mayor that created them holds office.

The power to make appointments to regular municipal advisory bodies usually is vested with the governing body. The mayor alone, however, has the

Figure 2.1
City Council Major Programs

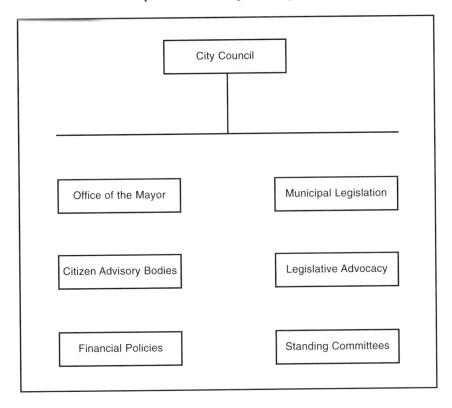

power to make appointments to temporary citizen advisory bodies created by the mayor. Mayors may also have further authority when it comes to making appointments to permanent municipal boards and commissions. This authority would be set forth in those laws which govern the city.

Financial Policies. The governing body usually has the exclusive power and authority over municipal finances. This includes the amount of funds allocated to each department during the annual budget process, along with the personnel authorized by these funds, as well as the amount of funding authorized for the entire city budget. Only the city council has the power to levy taxes to finance the general fund portion of the annual budget. The general fund represents that portion of the total municipal budget raised by local taxation. Also, only the city council has the power to accept grants and establish, or raise, user fees and charges. Once the annual budget is adopted, department managers are authorized to spend within the financial limits approved by the governing body. The city manager is responsible for oversight of the entire municipal budget. Any deviations from the authorized annual budget must be approved by the governing body. For example, new personnel requested by a department after the budget is adopted must be approved by the city council.

The city manager usually has the power to transfer funds during the year within limits established in advance by the elected officials. In no case, however, can these financial transfers exceed the bottom line of the budget approved by the governing body. Also, only the governing body has the power to incur debt on behalf of the municipal corporation.

Municipal Legislation. Within the limits set by state law, and locally adopted municipal charters, members of the legislative body may adopt or enact their own legislation. The official acts of local legislative bodies have legal power and authority only within the geographical confines of the municipal corporation. Hence, local laws may vary greatly from one municipality to another. Local legislation is usually passed in the form of approved resolutions or ordinances. An ordinance is typically a permanent law, mandate, or rule, while a resolution usually sets forth ministerial acts of a temporary nature or policy direction. For example, a permanent city commission would be established by ordinance, while a temporary committee would be created by a resolution. If the laws governing the municipal corporation do not provide for a distinction between ordinances and resolutions they may be used interchangeably. When local laws are adopted, state laws usually set forth the matter in which they are processed (e.g., public hearings, public notices, voting procedures, public readings, etc.).

In all cases, however, the laws of higher levels of government—federal and state—take precedence over locally adopted municipal laws. Also, land areas owned by the federal and state governments within a city's legal boundaries are generally subject to the laws of the government that owns the land.

Legislative Advocacy. Every municipal governing body frequently favors or opposes existing or proposed legislation being considered by the legislative bodies of higher levels of government. These public officials frequently attempt to influence or change state and or federal laws when there is a perceived benefit to the local community. For example, a local legislative body may favor a new state or federal grant program, or desire changes to the formula by which funds are allocated to cities. Also, new laws are continually being introduced by legislative assemblies at the state and federal level that would impact localities operationally and or fiscally. Generally, cities join forces to lobby and advocate for their position with other cities through mutual associations, such as the U.S. Conference of Mayors, National League of Cities, and various state leagues of municipalities.

Typically, the larger the city, the more likely a city council is to hire a professional lobbyist or legislative advocate to represent its interests in their state capital or Washington, D.C. While many larger cities may hire a legislative advocate to represent their interests in their state capital, only the largest of cities usually have such representation at the federal level of government. The larger the city, the more apt the governing body is likely to attempt to actively influence state and federal legislation. Also, most local legislative bodies frequently meet with their state and federal elected legislative delegations in an attempt to influence the legislative process.

Standing Committees. Every city has standing committees consisting of members of the legislative body. Smaller municipalities generally have fewer standing committees, while larger cities may have several standing committees. The number of standing committees that a legislative body has is, in part, dictated by its form of government.

Smaller municipalities may have a standing committee for a new program, such as recycling, energy conservation, or economic development. Larger cities, on the other hand, may have several standing committees organized around individual municipal departments or groupings of departments (i.e., related functional areas). For example, a public works committee would consider "public works" issues relating to the public works department, while a public safety committee would consider "public safety" issues relating to the police and fire departments. When these standing committees are created by legislative bodies, items appearing on the agenda of these legislative bodies for their consideration are usually referred to the appropriate committees for a recommendation to the full governing body.

In some states, these standing committees are authorized to hold public hearings before recommending proposed legislation to the governing body. In all cases, the number of members on any standing committee represents less than a quorum of the members of the entire governing body. These standing committees are frequently used to fine-tune issues relating administrative proposals and recommendations before they are formally considered by the entire legislative body.

PRODUCTIVITY TRENDS

The internal productivity improvements examined in this chapter include those related to both municipal staff and line departments. While elected officials would not implement these productivity-improvement and cost-reduction programs, they would adopt the policies and allocate the funds necessary to approve and finance them. For these reasons, they should have a working knowledge of these productivity trends. Because of their increasing importance, labor relations practices, personnel policies, and management/union cooperation efforts are also reviewed. These trends are especially important in light of limited financial resources and the continued downsizing taking place in many municipal organizations. The use of computers and other technologies have enabled workers to better service the public. Because of the important role played by the city manager in managing the operations of the organization, the desired qualifications of the person holding this position are also examined.

Many external productivity trends focus on improved budgets that help elected officials make important service and funding decisions, as well as ways to hold down expenses through volunteer and service coproduction programs. Almost without exception, elected officials are placing a high priority on economic development, and using it as a vehicle to raise revenues without increasing taxes. Also, older downtown areas are being revitalized to stimulate business activity, create jobs, and generate additional revenues. Growth management policies and practices are also discussed, given the reluctance of local elected officials to subsidize new developments within their communities. For this reason, creative ways to finance public improvements have been receiving increased attention. Elected officials have also taken a more active role in opposing legislation that increases the cost of their government, as well as advocating for additional revenues to hold down taxes. New forms of planning are taking center stage since public officials must now tackle tough issues and problems with fewer financial resources. Lastly, forms of government and local election systems are reviewed since they play an important role in equitable political representation, top level management continuity, and attracting and retaining qualified and competent municipal employees.

A complete listing of the production trends examined in this chapter—both internal and external—are highlighted in Table 2.1. While citizens must approve their local election process and form of government, elected representatives must approve many of the policies necessary to implement these programs. Elected public officials have a duty to plan for the future and, in so doing, adapt their municipal organization to the standards set forth by their electorate.

Internal

City Clerk Services. Most governing bodies recognize that their city clerk serves as the public information focal point for their community, and the importance of maintaining an up-to-date records management system. The city clerk department was one of the first agencies to use microfilm and microfiche, and is now on the cutting edge of using new technologies, such as microcomputers, computer networking, OCR (optical character recognition), CD-ROM (compact disk—read only memory system), and specialized computer software applications. Mayors and city councils know that the public not only expects but demands immediate access to public records of all types. The use of new technologies is frequently favored for the city clerk's office because of

Table 2.1
City Council Productivity Trends

Internal	External
City Clerk Services	Budget and Service Reductions
City Manager Selection	Budgeting Innovations
Cost of Mandates and Decisions	Coproduction of Public Services
Financial Management	Downtown Revitalization
Fire Services	Economic Development
Health and Human Services	Forms of Government
Labor Relations and Personnel Issues	Growth Management Policies
	Increased User Fees
Legal Services	Legislative Advocacy
Library Services	Local Election Systems
Management/Union Relations	Privatization Concepts
Organizational Downsizing	Public Access Cable Television
Parks and Recreation Services	Public Infrastructure and Development
Planning and Building Services	
Police Services	Strategic Planning and Issues Management
Public Works Services	
Use of Computers and New Technologies	Volunteer Programs

the recognized need to improve the management of their government's records as well as enhance citizen access to these public documents.

The use of other cost-saving measures, such as telephone message centers, automated cash register/receipting systems, contract code codification, and election consolidations are recognized as important ways to save money and improve services to the public. All of these trends, especially those dealing with the use of new technologies, will undoubtedly continue in the future.

City Manager Selection. The desired qualifications of local chief executive officers have changed over the past few decades. These qualifications may also vary depending upon the type of municipality. For example, when cities were rapidly expanding, many local officials hired former city engineers and public works directors as their city managers. These individuals were deemed to be qualified to oversee the physical development necessary to support the population growth of their municipality. This qualification may still hold true in some suburban cities that are still in their growth cycle. In more developed and highly urbanized centers, elected officials sought out city managers with people skills, who could mediate and negotiate between conflicting special interest groups. Generally, as cities became more complex, governing bodies advertised for city manager candidates with a Master of Public Administration (MPA) degree. With the advent of the taxpayers' revolt, locally elected officials sought out city managers with financial and economic development skills.

Most recently, mayors and city councils are seeking city managers with entrepreneurial skills, who cannot only handle municipal finance and economic development issues, but can also come up with new and creative ways to streamline and restructure their organization. As the environment and challenges facing cities change, so will the desired qualifications sought by elected officials in their chief executives.

Cost of Mandates and Decisions. Governing bodies are under increasing pressure for greater fiscal accountability by their constituents. To this end, mayors and city councils want to know the cost of their municipal decisions and legislative mandates. In the case of a decision for a new program, many public officials now require user fees to cover the cost of providing the service. In the case of new legislative mandates, they want to know the costs associated with their implementation and or enforcement. Gone are the days of making legislative decisions in a financial vacuum. Mayors and city councils frequently designate the city manager to make sure that fiscal impact statements appear on all of their agenda items. While the city manager may delegate the city clerk as the "gatekeeper" to ensure staff compliance with this request, the city manager is held accountable for the accuracy of these figures.

This trend is widespread in cities of all sizes and geographic locations. It is likely to increase in importance in future years as citizens demand greater accountability from their elected officials in an effort to hold down their taxes.

Financial Management. During the past several years, particularly since the beginning of the taxpayers' revolt of the late 1970s, governing bodies have focused their attention on several areas of financial management. Some elected public officials are now developing financial policies to ensure the long-term fiscal health of their municipality. These policies, usually approved unanimously by legislative bodies, typically may require minimum reserve levels, the preparation of annual capital project plans, debt ceiling limits, the use of revenue surveys, frequent user fee adjustments, multi-year financial projections, the use of life-cycle cost purchasing practices, and more informative and meaningful budgeting practices. Also, more frequent property reevaluations, business license tax collection and enforcement practices, and ways to enhance the collection of revenues from all existing sources, are getting increased attention from almost all governing bodies.

Most public officials also recognize the need to automate their finance, assessment, and property tax collection agencies to ensure timely billings and more prompt payments. These trends will continue in the future in all cities, particularly the trend to enhance the collection of taxes and fees due from existing revenue sources.

Fire Services. In the past, the goal of many governing bodies has been to reduce fire response times. Tight budgets and the public's aversion to increased property taxes has led many public officials to realize that they can only afford reasonable response times. Also, many new building technologies, such as new construction materials, sprinkler systems, and smoke detectors, have reduced the number of fire incidents in a community. More comprehensive fire inspection and fire prevention programs have facilitated this trend. Most communities have expanded their fire services to include responses to emergency medical, ambulance, and hazardous materials incidents. The trend has been to contract out ambulance and emergency medical services when the municipality can achieve a cost savings.

Elected officials also realize the costs associated with a new fire station. Once a fire station is built in a neighborhood, it is almost always politically impossible to close it down even if it is not needed. Hence, city councils usually only approve new fire stations when there is a demonstrated need, such as in rapidly expanding suburban communities with new residential areas. Also, because of hard economic times, it is usually less expensive to acquire a new fire apparatus through a lease/purchase plan, rather than to bond for this equipment. It is always more cost effective to pay cash for a fire apparatus if adequate funds are available. These trends are likely to continue in the future.

Health and Human Services. In many states, these services are performed by county governments. In some states, however, municipal governments perform health and human services. When these services are performed locally, every effort has been made to keep costs to a minimum, and to serve only the needs of a city's population. New programs such as community clinics, shelters for the homeless, treatment and counseling for AIDS victims, and workfare programs for general assistance recipients are generally financed by the state with federal grant funds. While many local officials believe that certain social services should be provided by the family, churches, and nonprofit agencies, the community's need for these services frequently exceeds the resources of these traditional support groups. Many citizens believe, and frequently demand, that these services be provided to maintain the quality of life for all of the residents in their community.

Traditionally, many of these services have been provided free of charge or for a nominal fee. Increasingly, health and social services are provided on a sliding-scale fee schedule based on one's ability to pay. Many cities have also established community information centers, making information available to citizens about the many health and social service programs provided by other levels of government, nonprofit agencies, and community groups. Health and human service officials are also typically designated to act as a clearinghouse for these services, referring citizens to other public, nonprofit, or community organizations for these services. Local elected officials frequently contract with private and nonprofit agencies to provide needed services not otherwise available in the community. These trends are firmly in place especially in those cities that must provide these services.

Labor Relations and Personnel Issues. Because of many state laws, the relationship between a city's elected officials and management staff to its employees is a very formal and legal one. Wages, hours, and working conditions are negotiated and set forth in lengthy documents commonly called labor agreements. Except for management employees, all employees within a municipality typically belong to a recognized bargaining unit. All of these employees have formal administrative processes for grievances, many of which require binding arbitration. Municipal employees are a microcosm of society and, as such, have increasingly been pursuing formal action to settle real and perceived disputes. The number of lawsuits, unfair labor practice complaints, workers' compensation cases, and grievances going to arbitration is on the increase. Also, a number of sensitive personnel-related issues exist, such as those involving substance abuse, sexual harassment, privacy rights, AIDS policies, the use of progressive discipline, and equal opportunity and affirmative action.

Almost all cities now have employee assistance programs, whereby personal counseling and advice is available on a number of different issues by merely making a telephone call to a hotline. It is not unusual for employee disciplinary problems arising out of alcohol or substance abuse to be treated as medical problems. Employee unions also typically use professional negotiators or lawyers to negotiate their labor agreements. For these reasons, elected officials in cities of all sizes are seeking the assistance of trained labor lawyers, professional negotiators, and personnel experts to represent their municipality on labor and personnel matters. Smaller municipalities frequently contract with specialists for these services. Larger cities frequently have trained experts in these fields on their staff.

Legal Services. Local governing bodies recognize the need to have a highly trained legal staff and, when necessary, to contract out specialized legal services to private sector attorneys. Chief legal officers and their staffs are increasingly being requested to develop comprehensive city codes to both enhance the quality of life and to improve the appearance of a city's neighborhoods. Many new codes are being adopted to regulate property maintenance and building aesthetics. City councils also require their legal staff to protect their municipality from public liability exposure, particularly since many cities are now self-insured. The use of safety and risk management programs, as well as hold harmless agreements and increased insurance requirements, are recognized as necessary tools to achieve this goal. Policymakers, especially in small- to medium-sized communities, are aware of the need to hire special attorneys for complex and lengthy contracts and franchise agreements. Councils are also aware of the need to use microcomputers for word processing, the development of databases, and for records management applications.

Public officials also realize that decisions to settle lawsuits are frequently made only for financial reasons. In the past, decisions to settle lawsuits were made on the legal merits of a particular case. Elected officials have recognized our changing legal environment, and these trends will no doubt continue in future years.

Library Services. The most rapidly expanding services of public libraries has been in the area of providing essential community programs. In order to enhance the value of municipal libraries, and to make their services available to a larger segment of the public, many mayors and city councils now recognize the importance of using their libraries to provide job information centers, computer training resources, business information services, and literacy training programs to their citizens. Public libraries are increasingly an important source of community information. It is common for municipal libraries to be designated as a city's community information center, making available public information about the services and programs available from other non-profit, community, and civic organizations.

Elected officials also recognize the importance of new technological innovations such as automated billing systems for overdue books, computerized check-out systems for books and other library materials, and computer security to prevent the theft of library materials. Many elected officials additionally realize the importance of their public library and its role in serving as the "window to the world" for their citizens, making books, periodicals, and other materials available from numerous sources via comprehensive computer databases and interlibrary loan programs. These community service, technological, and information resource trends will surely continue in the future.

Management/Union Relations. With the advent of state-mandated collective bargaining laws, and the development of lengthy and complex labor agreements between cities and their employee unions, elected officials recognize that they have limits on their authority. Clauses in labor agreements typically set forth salary levels, working conditions, and fringe benefit requirements. They may even include minimum staffing levels, regulate the use of outside student interns, and even contain no-layoff provisions. For these reasons, the organizational environment of municipalities is increasingly negotiated between management and labor. Therefore, many avenues to balance public budgets and make employees more productive require joint negotiations between management and labor. A new mayor and city council may find themselves limited in the number of ways they can alter their municipal organization.

For these reasons, many cities have developed collaborative and cooperative working relationships between their management personnel and their various employee bargaining units. In recent years, many cities have formed joint management/union productivity committees and or working groups in an effort to reduce costs and increase productivity. This trend is undoubtedly here to stay regardless of the size or location of a municipality.

Organizational Downsizing. Local governing bodies are aware that the two largest costs of government are for salaries and fringe benefits. Ergo, the easiest way to control the budget is through the number of positions authorized in the annual budget, and by lowering the level of fringe benefits provided to employees. The easiest and least disruptive way to reduce the number of personnel is to downsize the organization through employee attrition. Every municipal organization usually has an annual employee attrition rate of about 5 to 8 percent. The only problem with this policy is that there is no way to predict where or when vacancies will occur, and the fact that some service areas are more sensitive than others.

Since all vacant positions cannot be eliminated, city councils are asking their city manager and department managers to scrutinize positions and make recommendations concerning possible future vacancies. This has forced elected officials to debate the relative merits of different public services. Governing bodies are also approving changes in their employee health benefits. Many cities are self-insured, providing a managed care health plan, and frequently requiring employees to pay a portion of these costs. While the city council controls the number of positions funded in the annual budget, changes to existing health care benefits must usually be negotiated. These trends are likely to continue in many cities due to limited finances and the need to seek out cost-saving measures.

Parks and Recreation Services. Because of tight municipal budgets, parks and recreation services have been under increasing scrutiny by elected officials. In order to avoid service reductions, a number of different creative options are available to finance these programs. Many cities charge development impact fees to builders to finance the construction of new parks and recreational facilities. User fees are being used to generate revenues. When user fees are imposed or increased, discounts and or free periods are usually made available to young people and senior citizens. Rather than hiring new full-time employees, the use of part-time employees, seasonal workers, and contracts for services are now commonplace. All of these types of employees can be used when needed, do not receive fringe benefits, and have limited employment rights. Elected officials in smaller communities are also contracting with larger cities and counties for the use of their recreational facilities. City councils in many cities have privatized park maintenance, or contract with larger local governments for this service.

In some cities, sponsorship of recreational programs is sought from private companies as well as community civic associations. Many cities cosponsor city-wide celebrations and events, waiving their fees if these events are open to the entire community. Also, many specialized services, such as museums, zoos, golf courses, public arenas, and sports stadiums are operated as enterprise funds. Under this concept, these programs are not subsidized with taxpayer dollars. Instead, user fees are adjusted to cover their entire annual operating budgets. Some services are even being coproduced with community and nonprofit agencies. Under this arrangement the city may provide free space, but the service is actually performed by a private or nonprofit group. Most elected officials recognize the importance of small space development, such as tot lots, pocket parks, vest parks, and the need for linear parks and recreation trails. These established creative trends will likely be with us for some time.

Planning and Building Services. Many community master plans were developed many years ago when growth was common. These plans are being updated to reflect the reality of current economic conditions. Many elected officials have modified their city's master plan and have reduced the number of public roadways and facilities needed to sustain projected development and population growth trends. When these plans are updated, it is not uncommon to permit more flexible zoning patterns, such as mixed land uses (e.g., residential and commercial in the same building) and planned unit developments (e.g., flexible zoning regulations for large parcels of land). Many subdivision regulations are also being modified to require developers to dedicate land for planned public improvements when land is subdivided. Plans are also being amended to impose development impact fees on builders for the costs of planned public improvements such as schools, parks, open space, and arterial streets.

Many public officials also recognize the importance of providing affordable housing for citizens in their community. Although mandated by the federal government, city councils are developing a Comprehensive Housing Assistance Strategy (CHAS) to increase the number of affordable housing units within their communities. To achieve this goal, many cities now routinely provide development incentives such as low-interest development loans, first-time home buyer loans, waiving user fees, subsidizing on- and off-site improvements, streamlining development approvals, and granting density bonuses.

Most governing bodies routinely grant these development and financial incentives to stimulate the growth of affordable housing. These trends will no doubt continue in the future.

Police Services. Two somewhat opposing trends exist in the area of municipal police services. One is the trend towards community policing; the other is the trend involving the greater use of technologies to assist police officers in their crime-fighting duties.

Many governing bodies have favored a return to traditional walking patrols because of consistently high crime rates, citizen demands for safer neighborhoods, more requests for visible police services, and existing financial constraints. The police officers assigned to these duties solve neighborhood problems and actively solicit residents and merchants to become involved in neighborhood and commercial block watch programs. The goal of community policing is to be proactive by attempting to stop crime before it occurs.

City councils are also approving the use of modern technologies to put more officers on the street and to assist in the apprehension of criminals. These technologies include computerized 911 emergency response systems, the use of computers for the reporting and retrieval of crime information, as well as the use of mobile teleprinters and mobile data terminals. Laptop and hand-held computers are also used to increase the productivity of police officers. Video imaging systems are being acquired to free up police officers' time when booking prisoners.

These two trends—the back-to-basics of community policing and the use of new cutting-edge technologies—have enhanced the effectiveness of police departments and enabled public officials to improve services to their citizens. The civilianization of police officer positions, particularly those used for desk jobs and non-crime related activities, are on the increase due to the high salaries and fringe benefits received by sworn personnel.

Public Works Services. When municipal councils privatize public services and search for cost-saving measures, they frequently scrutinize those services provided by public works departments. In recent years, the privatization of public works programs has occurred in such areas as janitorial, landscape maintenance, refuse collection, recycling, engineering, and snow and ice removal services. Also, because of increased tonnage costs for solid waste disposal, many governing bodies have initiated municipal recycling programs. Some of these recycling programs have been mandated by state law. Since refuse disposal costs upwards of $100 per ton, municipal elected officials are attempting to remove as much recyclable material as possible from their municipal waste stream. This material includes paper products, tin cans, aluminum cans, plastics, glass jars and bottles, as well as leaf and grass clippings. Some cities have removed over one-half of the refuse from their traditional waste stream by implementing recycling programs, substantially reducing their tonnage disposal.

City councils also expect the development of multiple-year capital improvement plans for their community. These plans typically show the capital project needs of the community for the next five years, and are broken down by type of project and funding source. These plans have facilitated the development of grant applications, typically at the state level, for needed capital projects. Elected officials desire to know the capital needs of their community, even if they cannot afford to immediately finance them. Usually the first year of these plans is approved for funding, while the remaining years are approved in concept only. Also, rather than purchase unique or infrequently used pieces of equipment, elected officials expect their public works staffs to arrange equipment sharing plans with neighboring communities, or rent this equipment from the private sector. These trends will surely continue in future years.

Use of Computer and New Technologies. Most policymakers favor computerization and the use of new technologies, especially when their use can be justified to the taxpayers. Many mayors and city council members have felt that the cost of computerization had to be offset by a reduction in personnel. Experience has proven that this is frequently not the case. The use of mainframe and microcomputers are frequently approved in order to enable the existing city staff to better serve the public. In simple terms, the use of computers helps to make workers more productive.

When it comes to the use of new technologies, elected officials usually approve equipment when a reasonable payback period can be demonstrated—usually five years or less. For example, the cost of a new leaf composting facility would be compared against the annual tonnage costs to dispose of leaves. If the savings for the first five years is projected to pay for the entire leaf composting facility, approval would almost be certain. Computers and new technologies typically make the workforce more productive, provide a higher quality of services to the public, and hold down the need for additional personnel in the future.

External

Budget and Service Reductions. When governing bodies reduce public budgets and services they typically follow the same pattern, regardless of the municipality. The three expenses usually targeted first are accumulated reserves and contingency funds, capital project construction accounts, and monies budgeted for the maintenance of existing infrastructure improvements.

When it comes to reducing public services, police, fire, and public works services are typically spared the budget axe, while staff, museum, library, and recreation services are usually the first services to be reduced. This occurs because of the belief that so-called "hard" services must be maintained while "soft" services are expendable. This makes reducing public budgets difficult since police, fire, and public works services typically account for about three-fourths of a city's annual budget.

Instead of using this budget reduction philosophy, public officials should look at specific programs within the three largest service areas—police, fire, and public works—to determine which services may be reduced or eliminated. There is an increasing belief that, when budget and service reductions are necessary, that all departments should be equally scrutinized, not just the "soft" service areas. There is also a growing awareness among city councils that it is cheaper to maintain a city's infrastructure rather than replace it when it wears out.

The universal belief among politicians that their city's more visible public services should be maintained at all costs, since more votes are garnered during the next election by using this philosophy, is slowly changing. This trend is now being followed by more enlightened elected officials who believe that a city's quality of life should be safeguarded by maintaining all services—hard and soft alike. This trend will hopefully continue in future years.

Budgeting Innovations. Most cities, even today, use the traditional line-item approach to budgeting. This form of budgeting only shows what cities are purchasing with their tax dollars. Every organization has three distinct components—input, processing, and output. The line-item budget only shows the input side of the organization. The output side, describing what services are actually provided, and the processing side, measuring the productivity of these programs, have only recently been the focus of attention by elected officials. Every good municipal budget should describe the programs citizens are receiving for their taxes, as well as show those productivity measurements that are being used to determine the effectiveness of these programs. In small-to medium-sized communities, much of this work is delegated by the city manager to individual department managers. Larger cities, with separate budget offices and larger staffs, may have this budget work performed centrally.

Increasingly, mayors and city councils are demanding, in addition to showing the traditional budget line-items, the description of programs and the development of performance measurements to determine levels of productivity. In many cities, employee productivity is on the increase while the actual number of employees has decreased. Benchmarking techniques are also being used to develop standard measurements of performance. It is incumbent upon elected officials to show these positive trends to their taxpayers. The trend to develop program and performance budgets is on the increase in cities of all sizes.

Coproduction of Public Services. Many governing bodies now favor programs that empower citizens to lower the cost of their public services. They have done this by expanding their avenues of participation in the delivery of traditional municipal services. Some common examples include the use of neighborhood watch programs, citizen clean-up projects, adopt-a-park programs, municipal gift catalogs, citizen volunteer efforts and, most recently, recycling programs.

Since a city is limited in the number of police officers it can hire, neighborhood block watch programs enable citizens to assist in reporting suspected criminal activities to the police department. By using municipal gift catalogs, private companies, community groups, and citizens can donate items or monies to purchase goods needed by their city government. Under recycling programs, citizens have reduced their municipal waste streams by as much as one-half, thereby reducing their refuse to collection costs and property taxes. If a community organization desires a new municipal program, it is not unusual for the city to offer space free of charge if the organization agrees to provide the program.

Many cities have structured programs to assist in these community mobilization efforts. This trend has led to a decentralization of municipal authority and traditional avenues for service delivery. As public officials face future budget reductions, new and innovative ways for citizens to get involved in the coproduction of public services will be used to hold down the cost of government.

Downtown Revitalization. The efforts of elected officials to revitalize their downtowns have been on the increase for several years. These programs are so highly focused that they differ dramatically from a community's general economic development incentives. Nearly all cities have aging downtowns. Many of these downtowns have not aged so gracefully since retail trends, such as the development of regional shopping malls, have advanced to the point where major retailers no longer locate in older downtown areas.

Downtown revitalization programs are a matter of community pride, help create and foster a city's identity, and bring people back to the core of their community. A number of specific incentives have been developed to stimulate the rebirth of downtown areas. Common incentives include using enterprise zones, creating facade improvement programs, cleaning contaminated sites, identifying parcels of land for in-fill development, reforming zoning regulations, approving redevelopment areas, using tax increment funding, providing low-interest loans for small business development, allowing more flexible parking regulations, constructing of municipal parking garages, and developing specialized tax incentive and rebate programs.

Some cities are even hiring downtown managers to work with merchant associations and property owners to market their properties. Public-private partnerships are even being formed to specifically tailor these incentives to individual properties as well as for hard-to-develop parcels of land. The use of all of these incentives requires city council approval. Over time, the number and types of incentives used to attract development may decrease as vacancy rates decline. Many of these trends and innovations will be around for years to come.

Economic Development. The use of economic development incentives has become more popular in recent years because elected officials wish to hold down taxes and at the same time maintain an acceptable level of public services. A large number of incentives are now commonly available to entice private development to a community.

These incentives include financial inducements and land-based incentives, as well as other types of incentives such as enterprise zones, business incubators, and business retention programs. In addition to creating jobs and stimulating the local economy, new business and industry generates development fees, property taxes, business license fees, utility taxes, and sales taxes.

The number and types of incentives given to a developer should be compared to the long-term benefits accrued to the community by the proposed development. It must be kept in mind that many businesses and industries were started without these incentives. For this reason, the projected costs and benefits received by a municipality from a subsidized development should be financially defensible to local taxpayers. Other steps that can be taken to attract private investment include one-stop permit processes, streamlined development guidelines, flexible zoning and subdivision regulations, and a political philosophy that favors the use of prudent economic development incentives.

Generally, the more attractive the community, the fewer incentives that need to be provided. Conversely, less desirable communities usually provide more incentives to attract development. This same philosophy holds true for portions of cities. The less desirable the neighborhood, for example, the more incentives are made available to attract development. Elected officials must be careful to tailor these incentives to fit their community, and to only offer the minimum level of incentives needed to attract private investment. Incentives are always applied on a case-by-case basis. These trends are prevalent in communities of all sizes and geographic locations.

Forms of Government. While there are several quite different yet workable forms of municipal government, some of these forms have increased and decreased in popularity over the past several decades for different reasons. The four most common forms include the strong mayor, the commission, the mayor-council, and the council-manager plans of municipal governance.

Under the strong mayor form, the mayor appoints administrators and department managers. This form is most prevalent in larger cities, though some of these cities have changed over the years to the council-manager plan. The commission form is a vanishing system, the last vestiges found primarily in cities located in the northeastern states. This form, which combines policymaking and administrative duties in a single elected official, has its obvious shortcomings. The mayor-council plan has an elected mayor who generally appoints the chief executive officer and department managers with the approval of the governing body. A new mayor almost always brings in a new chief administrative officer along with several new department managers. The most popular and fastest growing form of government in small- to medium-sized communities is the council-manager plan. This plan places limits on the authority of the mayor, and vests the daily running of the municipality with a city manager, who is appointed by majority vote of the governing body.

Several societal trends have facilitated the growth of the council-manager form, including the rapid urbanization and complexity of our cities, the popularity of business and corporate ideals, the Progressive reform movement, and advancements in the practice of public administration.

Growth Management Policies. Growth management policies in municipal governments are not new. City councils have been controlling growth through the use of zoning, subdivision, and building regulations for decades. Public officials in most communities take a middle-of-the-road approach concerning growth. Most governing bodies desire to maintain the quality of life in their city, want to ensure that the proper public infrastructure is available to support growth, and insist that adequate funds will be available to properly finance public services to all of their residents. These concerns have led to the development of prudent growth management policies—ones that neither favor unmitigated growth nor unduly restrict growth. The development of growth management policies is based on rational decisions regarding future growth rates, the proper mix of land uses, economic development goals, provisions for public infrastructure and community services, as well as the protection of the environment.

Proper growth management practices can provide a positive framework for development, stimulate economic development, foster a positive business climate, and reduce many of the negative consequences of development and population growth. The establishment of growth management policies is an important and natural role for elected officials who must set public policies in light of competing and conflicting community interests. Many private sector companies place a high value on a community's quality of life, and their decisions to locate or relocate to a city are also based on these considerations. The use and refinement of practical growth management policies and practices will most likely continue in the future.

Increased User Fees. Many mayors and city councils, in an effort to make government operate more like the private sector, are adding new user fees as well as making more frequent adjustments to existing ones. This is being done for two reasons: to make sure that new services are cost-covering, and to ensure that user fees properly reflect the actual cost of doing business.

So as to not unduly restrict the use of public services by low-income citizens, particularly young people and senior citizens, two trends are prevalent when implementing or adjusting user fees. As fees are increased, "free use" periods are being provided during nonpeak activity periods. For example, if municipal pool entrance fees are increased to help offset operating costs, the pool may be open to the public free during the middle of the week—on the "slowest" day or days of the week. User fees may also be used to regulate peak activity periods at public facilities. If a municipal parking lot is filled to capacity on weekdays, a user fee may be imposed, providing free-use of this facility on weekends.

The adoption of sliding-scale user fee charges are also becoming commonplace. Under this plan, a variety of fees are charged to different types of users. For example, profit groups are charged the full amount, nonprofit organizations receive a discount, and programs cosponsored by the local government are not charged at all. These political "safety-valves" are frequently necessary when implementing new user fees or when adjusting existing ones.

Legislative Advocacy. In the past, mayors and city councils have been introspective concerning their legislative needs at the state and federal level. There is a growing awareness that federal and state mandates impose service requirements upon local governments without adequate, if any, financial reimbursement. In fact, much of what cities do is typically mandated by higher levels of government. Recent educational efforts by the U.S. Conference of Mayors (USCM), National League of Cities (NLC), and the International City/County Management Association (ICMA), have tried to relate this fact to mayors, city councils, and city managers.

Mayors and city councils in cities of all sizes now typically hold periodic legislative briefings with their elected federal and state delegations with the goal of informing them of these mandates, as well as their city's costs of compliance. Elected state representatives are increasingly passing legislation requiring that their mandates be accompanied by adequate financial reimbursement to local governments. Many locally elected officials are tired of having to cope with the costs of complying with state mandates, when they are faced with the annual problem of how to balance their own municipal budgets. These legislative efforts will definitely intensify and continue in the future.

In small- and medium-sized communities, city managers usually organize these meetings between governing bodies and their federal and state legislative delegations. Larger cities usually hire paid federal and state legislative advocates for this purpose.

Local Election Systems. For decades, citizens in most municipalities elected their local officials through at-large elections. Under this election system, all voters vote for all candidates on a city-wide basis. Over the years, cities with large immigrant and minority populations have changed to district, or ward, election systems. Under this system a city is divided into several different geographic areas for election purposes. Voters elect candidates for city council from their respective areas of the city. In reality, many cities use a combination of at-large and district council seats. A majority of council members are typically elected at-large with a minority being elected from districts.

The election method selected frequently depends on the socioeconomic composition of a particular community. The more homogeneous the community, the more likely it is to have at-large elections. Conversely, the more heterogeneous the city the more likely it is to have district elections. The problem arises when a city changes from a homogeneous to heterogeneous population base, and its election system does not reflect this population shift. Many immigrant and minority groups are successfully winning court battles to force a change to more district elections. Local election systems that do not reflect the wishes of the people—even if not the majority—will increasingly face successful court challenges in the future. This trend toward more district elections promises to continue.

Privatization Concepts. There has been a great deal of discussion about contracting with private sector companies for services traditionally provided by government. There are no studies available that prove positively that contracting out public services universally reduces the cost of providing the service. For this reason, privatization is not a panacea. Rather, it is an external service option that should be compared along with internal service options. In some cases, it may be less expensive initially to contract for a particular service, but future cost increases may make it more desirable to provide the service inhouse. For this reason, when a service is contracted to the private sector, safeguards should be placed into the agreement to justify future cost increases. Also, all contracts to privatize public services should be made with the goal of reviewing these costs at the end of the contract period to determine if the service can be performed less expensively by municipal employees.

Costs are only one variable in the complex equation of providing public services. Issues concerning the loss of political control, how to maintain public accountability, ensuring the quality of services, and how to handle citizen complaints are important factors to consider when making decisions to privatize public services. When considering alternative service options, elected officials should always keep in mind that citizens hold them responsible for the quality and cost of the service. Privatization options are here to stay, and the trend towards contracting out selected public services will continue.

Public Access Cable Television. Mayors and city councils cannot rely exclusively on the private media to provide coverage of their city's activities and events, especially positive news coverage. Nearly all private cable television companies, as part of their franchise agreements with municipalities, must dedicate at least one of their stations for public access. More sophisticated governing bodies are using this station as a vehicle to provide television coverage of city council meetings, board and commission meetings, and even forums on important community issues and events. Management staffs are increasingly being directed to provide public messages on this station concerning job announcements, meeting schedules, as well as the names and telephone numbers of department managers and other key management personnel. Other announcements may include how to make code complaints, who to contact for economic development information, how to volunteer to perform city services, how to register to vote, and the hours of operation of various municipal facilities. A few cities have even solicited community volunteers to read newspaper and magazine articles over this station to their blind citizens.

The above examples include only one-way cablecasting options. As this technology becomes more sophisticated and less expensive, two-way interactive cablecasting options will become more prevalent. The use of a city's cable access television station are many, and only limited by the creativity of elected officials and their management staffs.

Public Infrastructure and Development. Every community has a comprehensive or master plan showing future growth projections, including land uses, population projections, infrastructure improvements, and community facilities. Many public officials have adopted policies to ensure that future growth occurs in a planned fashion consistent with these approved long-range community plans. It is incumbent upon these officials to ensure that existing taxpayers do not pay for public improvement and community services that they do not use or benefit the community as a whole. For this reason, many governing bodies, in addition to controlling the type and timing of future development, are also now requiring private developers to pay for public facilities and improvements.

Development impact fees ensure that adequate funds are available to finance these pieces of the public infrastructure. For example, if a developer wishes to build a residential development before planned improvements are in place, the developer is required to pay for their costs. Some states have even adopted laws that require cities to ensure that the necessary supporting public infrastructure and community facilities are either in place or will be constructed by the time a development is completed. These development fees ensure that roadways, utilities, schools, open space, parks, and playgrounds will be constructed to properly serve the residents of new developments. When development fees are received they are typically placed in restricted funds that can only be spent for these purposes. The use of development fees is commonplace, particularly in high-growth communities. Their use will undoubtedly continue in the future.

Strategic Planning and Issues Management. There is a growing belief among elected officials that the traditional planning practices of the past are antiquated and no longer effective. Traditionally, city planners prepared community master plans and presented them to planning commissions and city councils for their consideration and approval. These plans, which frequently focused on goals rather than results, were almost universally approved. Even with these approved plans many important community issues remained unresolved. The belief in the traditional, top-down, planning model is slowly giving way to a realization that planning should be a bottoms-up approach which actively involves members of a municipality in identifying those issues facing their community.

New planning practices, such as strategic planning and issues management, have evolved to fill this vacuum. Many mayors, city councils, and city managers have initiated the development of strategic planning projects to identify the most common issues facing their community, with the goal of preparing action-oriented plans to resolve these issues. These strategic plans, while usually initiated by mayors and city councils, should be undertaken by community planning directors. As information in this new planning field becomes codified, it is expected that the strategic community planning practices will become institutionalized in municipal planning departments. Planning directors must be educated to the fact that their departments must plan for the future, and that this includes more than merely land-use related issues. Strategic planning and issues management are the newest planning practices to surface in cities in the past generation. It will take several years for these new practices to become routinized as common duties of municipal planning departments.

Volunteer Programs. During the 1980s, strapped with tight budgets, many elected officials approved the use of citizen volunteers to provide selected public services. Citizen involvement in the activities of their local government have often included such services as neighborhood watch programs, neighborhood clean-up programs, police explorer and cadet programs, neighborhood associations, citizen advisory committees, and providing assistance to senior citizens and the developmentally disabled. Volunteer and self-help programs enable a city to provide services to the public at no charge to the citizens. Due to issues of public liability and risk management, many cities only use citizen volunteers to provide nonessential and nonprofessional public services. Volunteers are usually not used to perform public safety services or the duties usually performed by regular municipal employees.

Many labor agreements restrict or prohibit the use of citizen volunteers. Public unions and employee associations typically do not mind their city using volunteers, if they are used to augment existing service levels and are not being used to displace regular city workers. The use of citizen volunteers is now commonplace, but sometimes their use is limited for these reasons. The use of citizen volunteers must be thought out in advance, and their services must be targeted to nonessential and nonprofessional areas of public services. Public officials must also make sure that adequate supervision is provided when volunteers are used. The trend towards the managed and targeted use of citizen volunteers is on the increase.

THE FUTURE

Several internal productivity trends because of their importance, warrant further discussion. The feelings of the electorate greatly impact elected officials. When local companies are reducing their operations and laying off employees, citizens expect their local government to hold down taxes and be more productive. In keeping with these broader trends, governing bodies are increasingly seeking city managers with people, negotiating, and economic development skills. They also want their chief executives to be entrepreneurial, constantly thinking of ways to conserve taxpayer dollars, improve services, and increase productivity. City councils expect the city manager to work with department managers to do the same with their respective departmental operations. Governing bodies also want to know the cost of their decisions, and are asking their staffs to note these costs on their departmental requests that require formal approval. Elected officials know that the largest expenses in government are for salaries and fringe benefits. Because of this they desire to downsize their organizations through attrition, minimizing the number of employee layoffs. Councils are also hiring labor lawyers to negotiate with those unions that use professional negotiators. When technology requests have a reasonable payback period, or when they improve services to the public, elected officials are approving these requests knowing that their organization must be leaner and more productive in the future.

The most important external trends deal with the relationship of city government to its taxpayers. Elected officials are demanding more rational decisionmaking approaches when reducing municipal budgets, since they desire to maintain the quality of life in their community. Program budgets are becoming popular since they can be used to equate dollar reductions with service reductions. Productivity measurements are becoming common as a vehicle to show program workload trends in individual departments. The desire to get citizens involved in lowering the cost of their government through service coproduction programs such as recycling, neighborhood watch, adopt-a-park, volunteerism, and related programs is on the increase. Almost without exception, city councils favor economic development incentives to generate jobs and revenues. Privatization practices and contracts for services are becoming more popular due to the high cost of government salaries and fringe benefits. Managing growth through the use of development impact fees ensures that proposed developments will pay their own way. Elected officials are adopting user fees and charges for programs that do not benefit the general public. Also, citizens have favored the council-manager form of government and district elections since they want to minimize politics in their government operations and improve community representation on their governing body.

Many elected officials favor new types of community planning that help set priorities, resolve issues and problems, and do so within a reasonable time frame. New planning practices, such as strategic planning and issues management, are being used to accomplish these goals. While traditional planning practices have focused on goals, these new planning models contain action plans that can achieve almost immediate results. It is not unusual that mayors and city councils have initiated these planning programs, given the length of their term of office and their desire for accomplishments during this period. Also, citizens now demand results from their government, not goals for the future. Elected officials should work with their city manager to initiate these progressive planning programs. Once these new programs have been instituted, they should be turned over to the city manager to keep them current. The city manager should delegate this function to the planning director, who has responsibility for community planning. Unfortunately, municipal planning practices have not kept pace with the expectations of elected officials. Multiple municipal priorities and limited finances will change these traditional community planning practices.

3

CITY MANAGER

Much of the responsibility for developing a responsive and economical organization rests with the city manager. It is his or her job to see to it that city council approved policies are implemented in a professional and cost-effective manner. In this regard, while the chief executive and department managers may make recommendations to the governing body, these recommendations are only advisory in nature. It is the elected officials that debate the issues, resolve them by majority vote, and turn their decisions over to the city manager and department directors for implementation. Even though there may have been a better solution, it is incumbent upon a municipality's professional staff to implement their governing body's directives as adopted. Many policies result from political compromise, creating policies that are less then perfect from a manager's perspective. While this sometimes upsets members of the staff, they must keep in mind that their job is not policymaking, but implementation. Most seasoned city managers and department managers recognize this reality and can separate their personal viewpoints from their professional responsibilities.

It is the city manager's job to develop department managers to ensure that city council initiated programs are carried out as designed. If a department manager cannot seem to "get with the program," it is the job of the chief executive to work closely with an individual to ensure his or her organizational performance. For this reason, the city manager may spend an inordinate amount of time with those few department managers that need assistance in this area. While performance suggestions usually resolve such problems, a reward system that ties performance to pay is the best vehicle to motivate a city's management staff. Lacking personal suggestions to improve performance, and providing monetary rewards for superior performance, disciplinary action is always available as a last resort to correct poor performance. On rare occasions, a city manager must discipline a department manager. In most cases, however, a department manager would rather "move on" rather than have a blemish on his or her career record.

This same pattern holds true for department managers and their subordinates.

Everyone in the municipal organization must be held accountable to accept-able standards of performance. The best way to ensure success is to have a well designed personnel system where all hirings and promotions are based on merit and past accomplishments. To accomplish this, examinations, oral interviews, and the ranking of all job candidates, as well as those employees seeking promotions, are critical to the long-term health of an organization. Other measures include psychological examinations for police officers, pre-employment medical examinations, and drug testing for job candidates for sen-sitive positions. Since top management jobs are usually exempt from these pro-cedures, it is incumbent upon city councils to use similar practices when hiring a city manager, and city managers to use such criteria when hiring a depart-ment director. While city councils serve as their own screening panel for city manager candidates, the astute city manager establishes similar screening pan-els when hiring department managers. When a person is hired, they should know that they were number one in the selection process. Likewise, an unsuc-cessful job candidate should know that the selection process was professional in all respects.

One of the most important annual tasks of the city manager is to pre-pare the proposed annual budget for the municipality. In this role, the city manager serves to reconcile departmental funding and staffing requests with a city's available financial resources. This task is critical, because all new posi-tions should be justified in terms of organizational need, and all new tech-nology requests should be based on their contributions to increased perfor-mance as well as possible cost-savings. Because many organizations are downsizing through attrition, the use of new technologies can frequently be justified since fewer personnel are available to work. New technologies can be used to increase performance and improve services to the public. Many munici-pal organizations have been able to maintain, even increase, their service stan-dards with fewer employees. All city managers know that municipal organi-zations are labor intensive and, because of this, the major expenses are for salaries and fringe benefits. Holding down these expenses is becoming increas-ingly important. For this reason, many city managers, with council approval, are using labor attorneys as professional negotiators when negotiating with for-mal employee unions.

One of the major breakthroughs in productivity has been the use of per-sonal computers for a host of office-wide productivity applications. Word pro-cessing, database management, graphics, and desktop publishing have revo-lutionized office automation over the past decade. Other office technologies such as photocopiers and facsimile machines have greatly increased employee productivity. All of these technologies are becoming more sophisticated and less costly at the same time. The city manager should advocate for the use of these technologies in all municipal departments. In the future, each worksta-tion is likely to have a personal computer, and each office will have its own photocopier and facsimile machines. Not long ago, few employees had computers and each floor of city hall had one copier and one facsimile machine.

The major programs undertaken in the typical city manager's office is summarized in Figure 3.1. The city manager usually has a small professional staff to assist him or her with these central administrative responsibilities.

DESCRIPTION OF PROGRAMS

Administration. The title of chief executive officer varies according to the type of government structure and, to a lesser extent, upon local customs and practices. While the charters in some large cities vest these duties with the mayor, most community charters require the hiring of a professionally trained executive, usually referred to as a city manager, city administrator, or business manager. The terms business manager and city administrator are most commonly used in mayor-council forms of government. The term city manager is used in nearly all council-manager forms of government.

One of the primary duties of the city manager is to run the daily operations of the city. In this capacity the city manager works with department managers, has frequent contact with a city's elected and appointed officials, and serves as an interface between the municipal organization and citizens in general. The city manager also organizes and coordinates all assignments and projects of an interdepartmental nature, deals with sensitive and complex issues not solved at the departmental level, and attempts to develop a team approach to the management of the municipal organization. The city manager is usually assisted by a small yet highly trained administrative support staff. As the focal point of the administrative organization, the city manager also serves as both the formal and informal liaison to citizen groups, merchant associations, the media, and governmental agencies.

Organizational Development. The city manager and his staff are responsible for the ongoing training and development of municipal employees. This usually involves leadership and management development training, productivity improvement initiatives, regular management staff meetings, and periodic department manager retreats. Frequently, retreats are held jointly between the elected officials and the top management staff (i.e., city manager, department managers, and possibly some of the city manager's support staff). The amount of time spent developing the municipal organization would depend upon several factors such as the level of commitment by the city manager, the qualifications of department managers, the size of the management staff, and available funds. If the city manager favored the extensive use of management training programs, and the governing body did not perceive this need, the necessary funds would not be provided.

Generally, the level of ongoing organizational development would depend

Figure 3.1
City Manager Major Programs

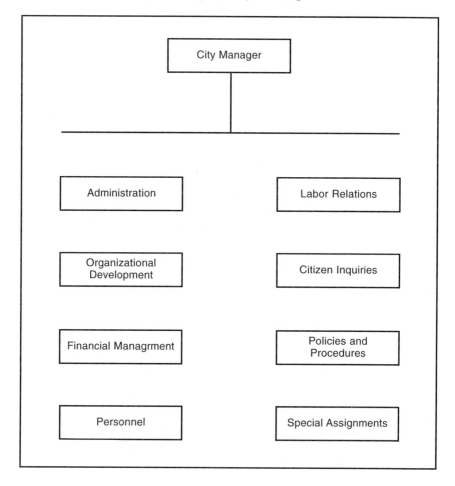

upon a desire by the city manager to improve the organization, ongoing funding by the governing body, and a willingness by the management staff to undergo training. At a minimum, middle management employees should receive training in supervisory skills and rank-and-file employees should receive training in their respective functional areas.

Financial Management. The city manager typically has the legal responsibility to prepare the annual municipal budget. While this task may be delegated to the finance director, budget officer, or another member of the staff, the city manager must submit the annual budget to the governing body for its consideration.

After the issuance of a budget directive, the city manager reviews all departmental budgets with each department manager before the proposed budget is completed. Once submitted to the governing body, study sessions are usually held, either with the entire legislative body or a subcommittee charged with reviewing the budget. During these study sessions each budget is reviewed in detail with the city manager and each department manager. Once all budgets have been reviewed and adjustments have been made, the entire city council must adopt the final budget. State laws usually require that a summary of the budget be published in the local newspaper, and that a public hearing be held to solicit citizen input on the budget before it is approved. At this stage of the process few changes are made to the budget document. Once adopted, the budget becomes the annual spending plan for the city.

Each department has an authorized budget, and the city manager monitors the budget to ensure that no department overspends its allocation. After the fiscal year has been completed, most state laws and municipal charters require that an independent financial audit be conducted which is then made available to the governing body and public for their review and inspection. The city manager also prepares and submits the proposed annual capital projects plan, which follows a similar process. Together, the operating and capital budgets comprise the entire annual municipal budget.

Personnel. The proper administration of the personnel function is one of the most important and sensitive areas of municipal management. Most cities have a merit-based personnel process, sometimes referred to as a civil service system.

The main characteristics of the civil service system include recruiting, selecting, and promoting employees based on merit (one's abilities, knowledge, and skills), and administering the personnel system without regard to race, color, national origin, sex, religion, or political affiliation. The merit system stresses the objective hiring of professionally trained employees without political interference. Where political patronage exists, as in some large cities, hiring and advancement depend upon relationships with key political leaders. Such governments exhibit high employee turnover when their political leadership changes. A job classification system, employee compensation plan, and performance evaluation process are essential to modern personnel practices. The salary structure of municipal jobs must always be internally equitable and externally competitive. Increasing emphasis is also being placed on the administration of fringe benefit and employee assistance programs.

The modern trend in personnel management is to centralize all personnel-related duties into a single division or department. Larger cities are likely to have an entire department devoted to this function. Small- and medium-sized communities usually place this function in the city manager's office.

Labor Relations. Most municipal workers, usually with the exception of top management, belong to a recognized bargaining unit—typically an employee association or organized labor union. Even in small cities, it is not unusual to have at least a half-dozen or so bargaining units. Larger cities may have a dozen or more formal bargaining units.

A labor contract exists between the municipality and each of these bargaining units. State and local laws typically set forth a city's relationship with its employee unions, as well as mandate the steps in the collective bargaining process. The city manager and the local government's personnel director or legal counsel are usually responsible for employee negotiations. The city manager can also select member of the management staff to serve on the city's bargaining committee. The trend for larger employee unions, such as police and fire unions, is to hire labor lawyers to conduct their bargaining. In such cases the city usually hires its own specialized labor counsel to serve as a member of their bargaining team. Specialized legal expertise is also frequently needed to interpret contract provisions and represent the city in complex grievances and allegations of unfair labor practices.

While labor contracts are negotiated by management, they must be approved by the elected officials, as well as the union membership, before they become effective. The administration of these labor contracts is a highly specialized and time-consuming task. As federal, state, and local laws, as well as the labor contracts themselves become more complex, this trend will continue.

Citizen Inquiries. In any city, regardless of its size, virtually hundreds of citizen inquiries and complaints are received during the year. These complaints are usually processed in one of three ways.

A member of the city manager's staff may be assigned to handle these inquiries and complaints on a part-time basis. Inquiries and complaints relating to functional areas of the municipal organization may be forwarded directly to respective department managers by the city manager. In larger cities a full-time ombudsman may be used to deal exclusively with citizen inquiries and complaints. If the second option is used, those inquiries and complaints that do not relate to specific functional areas would be assigned to a member of the city manager's staff for appropriate follow-up action. It is not unusual for disgruntled members of the public who have not received a satisfactory answer to their inquiry or complaint from the city staff to directly contact members of the governing body for a response. For this reason, most city managers place a high priority on handling citizen complaints and inquiries.

Computer software packages can track the processing of these inquiries and complaints within the organization, as well as generate letters back to citizens in order to document a written response for possible future reference. Lack of a prompt response to citizen inquiries and complaints is usually a sign of poor management practices.

Policies and Procedures. The members of the city council frequently

mandate new policies and procedures that must be implemented and monitored to ensure that they achieve their desired results. New policies and procedures are usually considered to resolve either community or organizational
issues and problems. They are generally of two types—those issues and problems relating to the organization's dealings with the public, and those issues
and problems relating to matters internal to the municipal organization. Some
policies and procedures require city-wide implementation, while others only
require departmental implementation. An example of the former includes a
requirement that user fees and charges be updated annually by all departments. An example of the latter might include the implementation of a community policing program within the police department.

Regardless of the type of policy or procedure mandated, it is the city
manager's responsibility to ensure that they are implemented to comply with
the mandate as well as ensure that the intended results are achieved. If the
desired results are not achieved, the city manager may recommend that already
adopted policies and procedures be amended to ensure that the intended results
are achieved. While the city manager frequently recommends policies and
procedures, especially those relating to the organization, it is not uncommon
for the legislative body to refer community issues and problems to the city
manager for review and recommendation on suggested new policies and procedures, or amendments to existing ones.

Special Assignments. Every municipal organization has many ongoing
special assignments and projects that must be completed throughout the year.
There are typically many special assignments generated by the governing body,
as well as those initiated directly by the city manager.

They generally fall into three major categories—those that are the responsibility of a single department, those that cross department lines, and those
that fall entirely within the city manager's office. A review of a municipality's
zoning regulations, for example, would involve only one department. The
development of a city-wide technology plan, on the other hand, would involve
all departments. An analysis of pending state legislation would only involve
the city manager and his or her support staff. The common chain of command
is for the governing body to hold the city manager accountable for the professional and timely completion of these tasks, and for the city manager to
hold department managers accountable—individually or collectively—depending upon the nature of the assignment or project involved.

Every city manager uses some form of tracking system to delegate these
assignments and monitor their timely completion. Some city managers incorporate these special assignments and projects into annual departmental performance objectives. The city manager would then use these annual objectives to evaluate the performance of individual department managers at the
end of the year.

PRODUCTIVITY TRENDS

The internal productivity trends described in the following pages encompass a number of ways to improve municipal organizations, both operationally and financially. They include the evolving relationship between city managers and their elected officials, as well as the use of organizational vision and mission statements to guide the behavior of employees towards desired goals. These trends examine both the human and technological components of municipal organizations. An effective human resources administration program is essential to attract and retain qualified employees. Likewise, an organization-wide management information system is critical to make department managers, their supervisors, and employees more productive. The use of total quality management (TQM) practices to improve service delivery, and the latest financial management practices, are also important. The latest technologies used to improve operations and public services are explored. Organizational downsizing and infrastructure management, two important considerations of city managers, are also highlighted. Additionally, the special roles of the mayor and city manager are discussed. Other cost-avoidance and cost-saving productivity techniques are reviewed.

External productivity improvements focus on using benchmarking techniques to improve public services, contemporary budgeting practices to assist policymakers in their budget deliberations, and ways to contain municipal costs, including privatization and contracting for services. One of the largest expenses in any municipality, its infrastructure, is reviewed from a long-term financial perspective. Economic development incentives, frequently overlooked in the capital planning process, are critical to attract and retain businesses. The value of downtown revitalization programs is also examined. Ways to generate revenues for future capital projects through such techniques as development impact fees are also reviewed. A host of new service-enhancement programs, including public educational campaigns, customer satisfaction surveys, volunteerism, and student internships are discussed. It is essential that city managers work with the community, as well as other city stakeholders, when developing future plans and programs. Since the city manager's office is a key link between the municipal organization and the community, citizen participation is critical in resolving issues and solving problems. The city manager can serve as a catalyst in this regard.

A complete list of the productivity trends examined in this chapter are summarized in Table 3.1. While the city manager must work with department managers to improve operational productivity, he or she must also work with the community to resolve major issues and problems. New planning techniques are also discussed that foster joint problem solving. The city manager must continually work with elected officials when undertaking these productivity improvement programs.

Table 3.1
City Manager Productivity Trends

Internal	External
Contemporary Finance Practices	Benchmarking Techniques
Effectiveness of Elected Officials	Capital Improvement Plans
Fiscal Impact Statements	Contemporary Budgeting Practices
Human Resources Administration	Contract Staff Services
Management Information Systems	Cost Containment
Management Merit Pay Programs	Customer Satisfaction Surveys
Management/Union Cooperation	Economic and Downtown Development
Mission and Vision Statements	Educating the Public
Organizational Downsizing	Growth Management Practices
Public Liability Reduction	Innovative Community Services
Real Estate Asset Management	Privatization Practices
Revenue Management Practices	Public Service Impact Statements
Role of City Manager and Mayor	Strategic vs. Traditional Planning
Total Quality Management	Volunteer and Student Internship Services
Use of Computers, Technologies, and Equipment	Working with the Community

Internal

Contemporary Finance Practices. The field of municipal public finance has changed drastically over the past decade. These trends may be broken down into several major areas, including the use of financial policies, budget and revenue projections, cash and treasury management practices, revenue administration techniques, innovative budgeting formats, advanced purchasing practices, and the trend from financial to performance audits.

If they do not already exist, city managers should recommend the adoption of sound financial management policies to their elected officials. Policies are used to establish debt limits, budget growth ceilings, set reserve and contingency criteria, require multi-year budget and financial projections, and mandate the development of annual capital project plans. It is now common to have three- to five-year budget and revenue projections in order to predict future financial problems. Computerized cash management practices are now commonly used to facilitate daily bank deposits. Treasury management software packages assist in tracking investments, conducting receipts/disbursements projections, and to forecast daily cash balances. Revenue administration techniques that enhance collections and ensure that user fees are periodically adjusted to reflect the cost of doing business are routine. Innovative budget formats, such as those used to identify programs and track program performance, are increasingly being used. Advanced purchasing techniques, such as life-cycle costing, joint purchasing with other agencies, purchasing from state procurement contracts, and centralized purchasing to achieve economies of scale should be routine. The field of municipal auditing now encompasses financial and performance audits. These types of audits not only compare budget appropriations against expenditures, but also compare program results to intended program performance goals.

Due to limited financial resources and tight budgets, these new financial practices and techniques are on the increase in all cities. It is incumbent upon a city's professional management and financial staff to ensure that these practices are used to optimize the use of local tax dollars.

Effectiveness of Elected Officials. One of the main responsibilities of the city manager, which usually does not receive enough attention, is to develop the effectiveness of a city's governing body. The city manager should set his or her priorities around the desires of the city council. The city manager should provide direction and delegate tasks to his or her staff and department managers, holding them accountable for effective performance. This frees up the city manager's time to work with the governing body to determine community and organizational priorities. The city manager should never forget that credit for resolving community issues and problems should always go to the elected officials. They alone are responsible to the citizens and maintain their office through the ballot box. The city manager is responsible only to the city council. City managers should never believe that it is their job to protect the public from the actions of their governing body. The future tenure of the city manager is almost always tied to the success of a city council.

City managers have a responsibility to develop the capabilities of elected officials and to make them aware of their roles and powers. Many elected officials seek office out of a desire for public service, with little or no past experience in municipal government or local politics. They serve part time, usually receive a modest salary, and typically do no have any personal staff support. In order for policymakers to make effective decisions, city managers must fully brief them on all facets of an issue before asking them to make formal public decisions. With fewer funds from higher levels of government, greater responsibility for solving community problems, and limited financial resources, city managers must work closely with their elected officials to solve community problems in increasingly innovative and creative ways. These demands of the profession will no doubt continue in the future.

Fiscal Impact Statements. City managers are under increasing pressure from elected officials, as well as tight budgets, to hold the line on costs and not exceed their annual budget appropriations. It is incumbent upon city managers to make their policymakers aware of the cost of their decisions. If not requested by elected officials, the city manager should issue a directive to all department managers to ensure that each staff recommendation contains a cost estimate and funding source. Some city managers have recommended policies requiring that all new costs must be accompanied by an appropriation, since it is technically illegal to overspend an adopted budget. Another common policy is that there will be no new programs or services unless they can be financed by user fees and charges. When such policies are adopted by governing bodies, it sends out a message to the taxpayers that they are concerned about their municipality's financial condition, and that they are being tough fiscal watchdogs.

Such policies serve as a safeguard against special interest legislation. The advocates of a particular program know that it will not be approved unless it can generate sufficient revenues to cover its costs. When requests such as those for new pieces of technology can be financed from internal savings, this information should be made a part of the fiscal impact statement. For example, rather than fill a personnel vacancy, a department manager may wish to purchase a new computer system. If the salary of this position is one-third of the cost of the computer system, the acquisition of this hardware would have a three-year payback period. This type of financial information must be made available to elected officials when they make decisions that have financial implications. The trend towards the use of fiscal impact statements has increased, primarily because of tight budgets and the efforts of city councils to contain municipal budget expenses.

Human Resources Administration. Sometimes referred to as personnel management, human resources administration includes the gamut of personnel-related services for employees from their initial hiring to their retirement, using a number of sophisticated personnel tools and techniques. Many state laws have impacted a city's relationship with its employees, since all employees except top management typically are required to belong to a recognized bargaining unit. The city manager must make sure that all labor agreements are administered uniformly by the personnel director. All hiring should be based on merit rather than patronage. Promotions are always open to all qualified applicants, and are made based on one's knowledge, skills, and abilities. All employees should receive annual performance evaluations. Discipline, when it is needed, must be documented and progressive, except in unusual cases. All employees, especially the rank-and-file, should have some degree of insulation from political pressures by external sources. Because of liability factors and potential labor relations problems, renewed emphasis is being placed on such practices as standardized testing, uniform job descriptions, position classification and compensation systems, comprehensive pre-employment physicals, drug testing, reference checking, and background investigations (for police and fire personnel).

City managers typically centralize all employee and organizational development programs, the administration of all fringe benefits, career development planning services, and retirement counseling under this function. When a personnel vacancy occurs, the trend has been to analyze each vacancy with the goal of achieving some kind of savings. Contract and part-time employees are sometimes being hired because they do not receive fringe benefits, and because they can be used on demand for special assignments and projects or during peak workload periods. Another recent trend is to civilianize police and fire positions when a non-sworn person can be used to perform their duties. Almost all cities have affirmative action goals, non-harassment, employee rights, and substance abuse policies, and must administer various state and federal mandates such as workers' compensation laws and the Family and Medical Leave Act. Some cities even centralize their daycare services, volunteer projects, and student internship programs under personnel.

Major trends include achieving economies through employee attrition, reducing employee fringe benefit costs, making workers more productive through training, and reducing a city's exposure to grievances, unfair labor practice complaints, and lawsuits. Existing labor agreements regulate many of these facets of human resources administration. Many small- and medium-sized communities use specialized personnel consultants to provide some of these services.

Management Information Systems. Management information systems, serving the needs of all municipal departments equally, is a recent phenomenon. Traditionally, data processing services started in finance departments. The typical applications were budget development, budget monitoring, payroll, and billing statements. As computer technology has changed to smaller, more powerful, less expensive, and more user-friendly systems, other department managers realized the importance of using standard software applications for their departments. Police, fire, and personnel applications followed. Departmental demands for computers services are now routine and must be addressed. It is not unusual for cities, especially medium-sized and larger ones, to have a separate management information systems departments. Slowly, the data processing function is being taken away from finance departments, which had been the primary user of computer services in the past. It became difficult for finance departments to serve the needs of all users equally since their financial applications were, in their own minds, the most important.

It is well worth the additional funds for cities to create management information systems departments. Astute MIS directors have a knowledge of management information systems, different computer technologies, software applications, and computer networking options. The current trend is moving away from departments having their own mainframe or mini-computers. A suitable city-wide system, with communications to all departments, can provide economies of scale and optimize the value of a city's investment in computer technology. Microcomputers, on the other hand, serve as office automation and personal productivity systems, improving the efficiency of workers and, at the same time, providing higher quality services to the public. Some cities, wishing to change their outdated computer practices, have developed computer master plans. These plans typically range from three to five years into the future and usually call for hiring an MIS director, purchasing a new host computer system, networking in user departments, purchasing microcomputers, and providing computer training to employees.

In most small, and in some medium-sized communities, the data processing function is still housed in the finance department. This trend is changing, and has been accelerated in recent years because of the computer hardware and software developments mentioned above.

Management Merit Pay Programs. Pay-for-performance plans tie the compensation of managers to the achievement of organizational objectives. These pay programs try to improve individual accountability and increase the level of organizational performance. Management merit pay programs consist of two components, a performance measurement system and granting salary adjustments based on measured performance. It would serve little purpose to evaluate employees subjectively and then attempt to apply merit pay adjustments. To work successfully, many city managers jointly develop annual performance objectives with each department manager. Each department manager's performance is then measured and evaluated annually. Managers are typically ranked according to their annual performance. After this task has been completed, salary adjustments are then made based on these performance rankings. Governing body approval is needed to establish pay-for-performance systems.

These compensation programs typically only work for city managers and department managers since many municipal employees receive annual step increases that are merely based on longevity. The ideal pay-for-performance program would be used to evaluate all employees within the organization (i.e., city manager, department managers, division managers, supervisors, as well as rank-and-file employees). Many labor agreements preclude the use of performance-based compensation plans for their members. To the extent that these provisions can be negotiated out of labor contracts, especially for professional and technical employees, this is an excellent way to tie the performance of these employees with their annual salary adjustments. In addition to rewarding and retaining outstanding employees, these compensation plans motivate employees to achieve higher levels of performance. The use of pay-for-performance plans is on the increase, especially for a city's top management employees. This trend will definitely continue in the future.

Management/Union Cooperation. City managers frequently get caught in the middle of the sentiments held by elected officials towards city employees, and the feelings of employees towards their city's governing body. The posture of elected officials usually reflects the typical feelings of taxpayers toward government in general (e.g., hold down costs, salaries are too high, fringe benefits are out of control, workers are not productive, and to "cut the fat" from the bureaucracy). When elected officials articulate these feelings, they alienate many city employees, making it difficult for labor/management relations. Also, most city councils and chief executives, to a great extent, have their hands tied when it comes to making change. This is due to increasingly voluminous labor agreements that regulate many aspects of wages, hours, fringe benefits, and working conditions. The work environment of municipalities, for these reasons, is increasingly negotiated. Constructive tension is good so long as it leads to productive ends. City managers must educate their city councils to the fact that it is essential to work with employee bargaining units when making change.

Those cities that excel in organizational change, making workers more productive and holding the line on costs, usually have positive working relationships with their employee bargaining units. Many city managers, with the support of their elected officials, have demanded joint union/management productivity, cost-cutting committees and or working groups. Hard economic times and tight budgets have demanded a close working relationship between a city's management and its unions. Both elected officials and municipal employees must recognize that they work for the taxpayers and should represent their best interests. Elected officials, management, and unions should not get in the way of working towards this goal. This trend is here to stay and will likely increase in importance in future years.

Mission and Vision Statements. A mission statement is used to define an organization's objectives and its methods of conducting business. Vision statements describe a desirable state that an organization wishes to attain in the future. Elements of mission and vision statements are often combined to provide a statement of a city's purposes, goals, and values.

In municipalities, typically the city manager, working with department managers, will write their city's overall mission or vision statement. Department managers, in turn, may prepare such statements for their individual departments. The city manager usually seeks governing body approval of those statements prepared for the entire organization. Department managers usually only require city manager approval for their respective departmental mission and vision statements. The typical process used involves several steps: the identification of a city's organizational culture and values, addressing the city's commitment to its key stakeholders (i.e., elected officials, citizens, and employees), seeking approval of these statements, and developing employee buy-in and support for these statements throughout the organization.

Mission and vision statements, once developed, are commonly used to guide management's thinking on strategic issues, inspiring employees to work more productively, guiding employee decisionmaking, and providing a cause around which employees can rally. Governing body and top management support is needed to make the use of these statements successful. It would serve little purpose, for example, for only one department manager to use these management tools without the proper organizational support. These statements have been used for many years in private companies, and are being used increasingly by city councils, city managers, and department directors.

Organizational Downsizing. City managers should make elected officials aware of the fact that in order to control the costs of their government they must not add new positions. The use of fiscal impact statements that show city councils the cost of their decisions has been a step in the right direction. Typically, three-quarters of a city's budget is comprised of salary and fringe benefit costs. Notwithstanding this factor, many governing bodies continually reduce operating budgets to the point where adequate supplies and materials cannot be purchased to maintain existing service levels. This is done because no one wants to lay off municipal employees and or reduce public services. Instead, the focus of reductions should be on lowering salary and fringe benefit costs. Hiring freezes and employee attrition plans are now commonplace to reduce the number of funded positions in a municipal organization. The improved management of health care and fringe benefit programs have also lowered expenses.

City managers must educate elected officials that all departmental budgets should be scrutinized when making reductions. It is not unusual for city councils to reduce the so-called soft service line departments (e.g., libraries, parks and recreation, museums, cultural activities) and the services provided by staff departments (e.g., city manager, city clerk, legal, personnel, and finance departments) since these departments are perceived as providing services to other municipal agencies. The recent catchphrase is "doing more with less," but it must be kept in mind that managing with less frequency means providing fewer services to the public. City managers and department managers frequently are caught in the middle of this dilemma during the annual budget process. City managers must also educate their governing bodies that there is a point of diminishing returns below which budget cuts will negatively impact desirable public services.

It is also incumbent upon chief executives to equate budget reductions with service reductions. The use of public service impact statements has helped to close this informational gap with the public. These trends will continue in the future until the public's attitude towards their city government improves.

Public Liability Reduction. Most city managers are aware of the exposure of their city and its operations to lawsuits from citizens. Municipal governments and their public officials no longer have total sovereign immunity. Many state laws and court decisions over the years have eroded these traditional rights.

Since cities are usually perceived by lawyers and some members of the public as having "deep pockets," chief executives are increasingly making their governing bodies aware of these issues, as well as the need to deal with them. Risk management, employee safety, and liability reduction programs are increasingly common in local governments. City managers should make sure that proper safeguards are in place to protect their city from unnecessary and frivolous lawsuits. The use of new techniques such as safety awareness and risk reduction training for employees, the insertion of hold-harmless clauses in municipal agreements and contracts, the utilization of specialized experts to review city facilities and services, and the institution of proper claims administration procedures all help to reduce the liability exposure of municipal organizations.

Many medium- and large-sized cities hire professional safety and risk managers to initiate these programs. Smaller cities may contract with specialized consultants in this field. While this function was initially housed in the central office or personnel department, it is increasingly common to assign such personnel to a city's legal department. This trend has evolved because of the close working relationship that exists between safety and risk management personnel and the duties performed by the legal staff in this technical area. The trend for municipalities to protect themselves from liability exposure will continue.

Real Estate Asset Management. All units of municipal government have a vast network of real estate assets, both improved and unimproved. These include parks, recreation facilities, streets and roadways, utility lines and plants, and numerous community facilities, to name a few. These taxpayer assets have seldom been properly managed. When municipal budgets are reduced, typically the first programs cut by elected officials are those for capital projects construction, as well as for the maintenance of existing capital facilities. Most all state and federal grant programs also favor new construction over the rehabilitation or maintenance of existing structures. In the private sector, for example, the useful life of an asset would be determined and a replacement fund would be established. This practice would make funds available to replace the asset at the end of its useful life. Not even the wealthiest of cities properly fund for the replacement of their capital projects. In fact, most cities do not even inventory their capital assets, let alone project their useful lives in order to know which asset should be replaced in any given fiscal year.

Most politicians want to fund more visible public services, as opposed to budget limited funds for capital replacement and maintenance. As one astute city manager once mentioned, while there are "friends of" groups for libraries, museums, and zoos, there will never be a group called "friends of the infrastructure." Nonetheless, it is incumbent upon city managers to have inventories of their city's capital assets prepared, showing the date of construction and projected useful life. Some cities are starting to do this with their street replacement programs. It is generally good planning practice to know what should be done even though it cannot be afforded. Some states now mandate that cities inventory and place a value on their capital assets. City managers should attempt to educate elected officials on the need to properly maintain their municipality's physical plant.

One recent book by the Government Finance Officers Association (GFOA) provides a step-by-step guide on how to initiate a community discussion about a city's infrastructure, and how to develop a consensus about which projects are needed and how to finance them. As more public pressure is brought by citizens to operate government more like the private sector, the use of these practices will become more common.

Revenue Management Practices. It is easier to increase revenues from existing approved sources than to have to resort to adopting new revenue sources to balance the annual budget. City managers have focused their attention on the need to optimize the collection of municipal revenues from existing sources. In the not-so-distant past, finance personnel would merely monitor their revenues as they came in to their city's treasury. Many cities are now reviewing their assessment and billing practices, collection and enforcement procedures and, most importantly, evaluating their collection performance. The enforcement component of the collection process has been lax in the past. Many cities with a business license tax, for example, have never even bothered to reconcile the yellow pages of their telephone directory against the list of those businesses actually paying this tax.

Many new tools are available to assess the amount and type of user fees and charges used by a municipality. The International City/County Management Association (ICMA), for example, publishes a revenue guide for local governments that includes an assortment of frequently used service fees and taxes, as well as common collection procedures; a manual for establishing the cost of services; and numerous monographs on how to maximize the collection of city revenues. The GFOA publishes a guide to municipal revenue administration, a catalog of public fees and charges (over 1,500 user fees and charges used in 178 cities in 38 states), as well as a guide on how to properly place a cost on public services. The use of revenue surveys is also becoming increasingly common. These surveys are used to compare revenue sources, the cost of collection, as well as collection rates, with other cities.

It is also common to adopt user fees to make new services cost-covering, as well as to make routine adjustments to existing user fees in order to make the provision of selected public services self-sustaining. New user fee techniques such as demand pricing, peak activity pricing, sliding-scale user fee, ability-to-pay user fees, and free-use periods, once thought to be sophisticated, are now routine. Many cities are also exploring new sources of non-tax revenues. The GFOA's Government Finance Research Center lists "alternative revenues" as the number one research topic requested by municipal governments. Specialized computer software applications are now available to enhance revenue management practices in local governments. All of these trends are on the increase and their use will become more popular in the future as city officials attempt to emulate the financial practices of the private sector.

Role of City Manager and Mayor. Much has been discussed and written about the roles of the mayor and city manager. The mayor should always be recognized as the chief political and legislative leader of the city, even though many city charters may restrict the role of the mayor to merely ceremonial duties. No mayor is totally comfortable with the fact that he or she is elected by popular mandate, yet can only perform limited duties essentially of a ceremonial nature. The astute city manger always knows that it is the mayor who holds the ultimate trust of the people—at least a majority of them. The city manager should never forget that he or she is hired by the mayor and city council.

The city manager can do several things to facilitate the role of the mayor. If the mayor wishes to be the spokesperson for the city, then press inquiries should be directed to the mayor. The city manager, in running the daily operations of the municipality, should strive to keep as many complaints, administrative issues, and personnel problems as possible away from the mayor. This frees up the city's chief elected official to perform those duties dealing with legislative advocacy, city council issues, and lobbying for the legislative interests of the city with higher levels of government. The city manager should periodically brief the mayor on important municipal problems and issues. The citizens look toward the mayor, not the city manager, as their ultimate municipal leader. When a conflict arises between the mayor and city manager, typically the city manager seldom wins since he or she is usually the outsider.

City managers should adapt their leadership and management styles to fit the politics of their governing body, including the mayor. The mayor and city manager should never be reaching for the microphone at the same time. City managers should help enhance the effectiveness, public perception, and role of their mayors. It is not unusual, when preparing letters to federal, state, and other local legislators, to have the mayor sign these pieces of correspondence. With these "caveats" in mind, city managers should have no problem in performing their roles and getting along with their mayors. These trends will continue among astute city managers.

Total Quality Management. Total quality management focuses on building a customer orientation within a municipal organization and building employee responsibility and capacity to produce quality services. Under total quality management, customer satisfaction and work unit evaluation and improvement are a continuous process. Employee work groups, organized around areas of public service, typically meet to evaluate customer feedback, review their work unit's activities and performance, identify problems, and correct these problems in a real-time manner rather than evaluating a service after it has been provided. Many labor unions initially thought that total quality management was a tool for management to reduce the number of employees.

For this reason, city managers typically work with unions when developing a total quality management process. The goal of this process is service improvement, customer satisfaction, and greater employee productivity. In short, total quality management involves decentralized decisionmaking on the part of employees, and management's willingness to make changes based on employee recommendations. Employee empowerment is critical to this process. This process is new to local governments.

Traditionally, service levels in cities are based on funding appropriations without regard to customer satisfaction. Under total quality management systems, customer satisfaction and work improvement are stressed, notwithstanding funding levels. It would be difficult, if not impossible, to expect customer satisfaction to increase when budget reductions are imposed on work units. It must be kept in mind that fewer funds usually mean fewer public services. For this reason, this process works best in organizations with a stable financial base. The use of total quality management practices will continue to be refined and increase in popularity as an important management tool to improve the quality of municipal services.

Use of Computers, Technologies, and Equipment. The single most dramatic change in the municipal workplace during the past decade has been the use of new computers, technologies, and innovative pieces of equipment. In the computer field, these items include open systems mainframe computers, the proliferation of microcomputers and laptop computers, local area networks (LANS), CD-ROMs, standardized and easy to use software applications, electronic mail, and document scanning systems. Even in the smallest of public libraries, for example, reference librarians virtually have a world of information available to their customers via the telephone modem on their computer system. Automated checkout systems, billing systems, and referencing systems are now commonplace in many municipal libraries. New, smaller, less expensive technologies include voice-mail message systems, facsimile transmission devices, and photocopying machines. Not long ago, each floor in a city hall had one large copier and one FAX machine. It is not unusual today for each department to have their own FAX machine and photocopier.

More sophisticated technologies now include parts inventory, energy monitoring, and fuel management systems, to name a few. Each department now has a host of sophisticated software available, many with specialized applications tailored to their unique work requirements. The days of hiring systems analysts and programmers is history for most municipalities. Ultimately, each work station in city hall will have a microcomputer. This technological revolution is in high gear in city halls throughout the nation. The use of these devices is increasing in popularity because, in most cases, a one-time investment can make workers more productive, hold down the need for new municipal employees, and enable the workforce to improve services to the public.

Frequently, smaller cities find it easier to use new computers, technologies, and new equipment, since they do not have a large investment in their existing systems. Larger cities with old computer systems, large inventories of aging technologies, and older equipment will find it more difficult and expensive to retrofit their work environment. These positive technological trends will definitely continue in future years.

External

Benchmarking Techniques. Benchmarking is a method of improving performance by identifying and implementing the best demonstrated practices in any given field. In the private sector, managers compare the performance of their products, services and processes against those of their competitors. The objective of benchmarking is to find examples of superior performance, understand the processes and practices driving that performance, and to adapt these practices to your own organization.

In local governments, city managers and department managers seek out the best programs and services in other similar cities, then adopt these practices to improve the quality of their own programs and services. Generally the steps involved include indicators, checking with other municipalities that excel in providing this particular service, analyzing the data collected and identifying opportunities for improvement and, lastly, adapting and implementing these best practices in your own organization. Both the quality and cost-effectiveness of services should be analyzed. There may be ways to maintain quality while reducing costs. The use of benchmarking techniques improves performance, reduces costs, and brings new ideas into the workforce and organization. Benchmarking techniques are important since cities typically operate in a vacuum.

While these techniques were developed in the private sector, they can be used with equal success by public managers in municipalities. Rather than reinventing the wheel, benchmarking practices can lead to the adaptation and implementation of the best practices in other comparable cities. The use of these techniques is new, but gaining in popularity as an important tool for local government managers to improve the quality and cost-effectiveness of their public services.

Capital Improvement Plans. Traditionally, many communities have neglected the preparation of comprehensive multi-year capital improvement plans. Since many city councils are preoccupied with balancing their annual operating budgets, elected officials have not wanted to incur additional municipal debt. It is incumbent upon city managers to educate elected officials that it is frequently cheaper in the long run to maintain pieces of the public infrastructure, rather than have them replaced after they deteriorate. Also, many city managers are recommending new planning approaches and growth management policies that link future growth to the availability of adequate public infrastructure and community facilities. Capital improvement plans usually project out a city's capital projects needs for a five year period.

These plans also link necessary public projects that are critical to a city's economic development goals. The neglect and deterioration of a city's infrastructure may deter new business and industry, may discourage the expansion of existing companies, and may facilitate companies leaving for more desirable locations. One of the most popular growth management tools is to link a city's future development to the availability of adequate public improvements and community facilities. This can be accomplished through the adoption of public facilities ordinances and development impact fees. Public facilities ordinances require that the necessary public infrastructure be in place before development occurs, unless the developer pays the cost for the infrastructure needed to support the proposed development. Development impact fees, on the other hand, require a developer to pay a fee representing a portion of the cost of new community facilities, such as parks, schools, libraries, utilities, and streets.

Even though capital improvement plans project capital needs several years into the future, usually the first year of these plans is approved and funded by the governing body. The planning commission is usually required to approve these plans before they are submitted to the city council. Financing should always be considered from other sources first, such as development impact fees and grants from other levels of government, before approving local funding. Most capital projects are financed through the issuance of general obligation bonds, which are typically amortized over the useful life of the projects. The trend is to have developers pay for their share of the cost of the public infrastructure required by their developments, except in cases where the public benefits clearly exceed the costs, such as for certain projects that help a city achieve its economic development goals.

Contemporary Budgeting Practices. Many city managers are now preparing their annual budgets in ways that assist elected officials in making important service and funding decisions. Under the traditional line-item approach to municipal budgeting, it was typical to mandate across-the-board budget reductions. The emphasis was on making budget reductions, frequently without knowing their impact on specific programs or public services. Many municipal budgets are now being prepared that describe departmental programs and their costs. These more sophisticated budgets, in addition to showing programs and their costs, also contain productivity measurements for individual programs. By linking policy decisions to programs, costs, and productivity, city managers can help their governing bodies make more informed budgetary decisions. Additionally, line-item budgets only show policymakers and citizens what is being spent, not what the taxpayers are receiving for their tax dollars. The contemporary budgeting practices described above help to close this informational gap.

Traditional line-item budgets are basically financial documents showing expenditures by department. These budgets, once adopted, are used for financial control purposes only. Program and performance budgeting enable public officials and management to use the budget as a management tool. Individual program costs can be controlled based on their productivity levels. While it is time-consuming to covert from a line-item to a program or performance budget, the time spent is worthwhile. Many governing bodies are now demanding these more advanced forms of budgeting. If not, it is incumbent upon city managers to prepare their budgets in such a way as to assist policymakers in their deliberations on the annual budget. The trend towards using more contemporary budget practices is on the increase, especially in medium- and large-sized cities that have adequate staff personnel available to devote to the annual budget development process.

Contract Staff Services. There are generally two types of municipal services: those provided by line departments and those provided by staff departments. Line departments (e.g. police, fire, public works) typically provide direct services to the public, while staff departments (e.g. city manager, legal, finance, personnel) usually serve the internal service needs of the organization. Staff departments have been reduced in recent years due to the budget balancing efforts of elected officials. Elected officials generally favor reducing staff services over more visible public services.

For this reason, it is now common for cities to contract with consultants and private companies for specialized staff services. These services may include safety and risk management, insurance, data processing, labor negotiators, specialized lawyers, engineering and planning, as well as the use of contract employees. Contract employees are usually hired on a part-time, full-time, or seasonal basis, do not receive fringe benefits, and have no employment rights. The use of contract services and employees have one primary benefit—the services can be provided on demand and used for only as long as necessary. Since personnel and fringe benefit costs consume a large portion of local budgets, elected officials have favored this trend. One word of caution is necessary: The cost of these services should be continually reviewed to make sure that they do not exceed the expense of hiring part-time or full-time employees to perform these services. In some cases it may be in the best interests of taxpayers to have in-house personnel perform these staff services.

Cost Containment. Frequently the budget-balancing philosophy held by elected officials differs from the views of their professional administrators. Members of a governing body, almost without exception, vote to retain visible public services. When budgetary savings must be achieved, the items to go first usually include reserve and contingency fund accounts, funds for capital projects, and funds for the maintenance of capital improvements. City managers, on the other hand, would most likely prefer some sort of budget reductions, coupled with user fee and minor tax increases. While city managers make budget balancing proposals, ultimately they must implement the wishes of elected officials. For this reason, the city manager has a critical role to educate elected officials on the financial and operational impacts of their decisions. In anticipation of financial problems, it is always more acceptable to have elected officials approve a city-wide hiring freeze. Such policies are usually modified quickly when too many police officers and firefighters leave the organization. Selected hiring freeze policies are more difficult to implement since they place a large burden on smaller departments.

The greatest benefit for future costs containment is through the use of new computer systems, labor-saving technologies, and more sophisticated pieces of equipment to make workers more productive. These practices help a city hold the line on personnel costs and at the same time improve services to the public. It must also be kept in mind that many citizens expect property-related services for paying their property taxes. Traditionally this has meant minimum acceptable levels of police, fire, and public works services. Selected programs within these departments should be scrutinized for cost savings, even though elected officials know that "deep" cuts would not be publicly acceptable. The trend is for city managers to recognize the importance of their role in educating their elected leaders on their budget balancing options, as well as to fully inform them of the possible impact of their decisions on a city's finances and public services.

Customer Satisfaction Surveys. Customer satisfaction surveys provide a vehicle to determine customer requirements, satisfaction levels, and to identify better ways to fulfill these needs. Such measuring instruments have been used in the private sector for many years, but are only beginning to be utilized as a management tool by public managers to municipalities. Even though the services provided by a city are not subject to competition—since each city has a monopoly for the services it provides to its citizens—there is a trend to treat taxpayers as customers.

These surveys basically are used to collect information from citizens and customers on a regular basis to understand their needs and satisfaction levels. Cities then use this information to improve customer satisfaction by identifying and eliminating the roadblocks to achieving improved customer service. The process of using these surveys includes actively soliciting input from customers on the level of satisfaction on particular services by using interviews, written and telephone surveys, and on-site visits. The results are then analyzed to determine opportunities for service improvement. The results of these surveys are then distributed to the appropriate managers to design changes to improve the satisfaction levels of their customers.

Traditionally, city employees, including many management personnel, have not treated citizens as customers. With increasing citizen skepticism of all levels of government, the public's aversion to increased taxation, and tax-payer demands for greater accountability, customer satisfaction surveys are one way to show citizens that their municipal officials care about the quality of their public services. The use of customer satisfaction surveys by city managers is on the increase. The use of these instruments will continue in the future as a vehicle to improve public services.

Economic and Downtown Development. Economic and downtown development incentives have evolved in a piecemeal fashion over the years. A host of tried and proven incentives are now available to public officials. City managers should always keep in mind that the package of incentives provided by a community should be tailored to achieve specific development objectives. Economic development incentives are provided to create jobs and generate additional revenues. Typical incentives include low-cost financing, tax incentives, waiving user and development fees, granting density bonuses, cleaning contaminated sites, relaxing zoning and development standards, providing for mixed land uses, and the public financing of off-site improvements.

Downtown development incentives, on the other hand, are usually provided to revitalize an aging central city district and to restore pride in a community. These incentives include the numerous tax benefits of enterprise zones; the creation of redevelopment project areas to assemble large parcels of land for development purposes; and a host of other incentives such as facade improvement loans, low-interest loans to stimulate business development, more flexible parking regulations, as well as municipal parking lots constructed at taxpayer expense.

City managers work closely with planning directors to tailor their city's incentives to achieve the development goals of their governing body. The type of incentives provided should be carefully selected and defensible to citizens, especially in poorer communities where citizens must in many cases finance many of these incentives with their hard-earned tax dollars. The benefits received by a community should always exceed the cost of the incentives provided to attract development. The use of carefully selected development incentives to attract private investment will surely continue in the future.

Educating the Public. Traditionally, citizens have used municipal services selectively. The public interface with local government is typically limited, and only occurs when these services are being used. Many citizens typically do not know the entire range of services provided by their government organization and its many departments. Since the taxpayers' revolt, public officials and employees alike recognize the need to improve their communications to citizens about the different facets of their government. For example, if citizens were made aware of their city's efforts to increase productivity, reduce costs, and maintain existing service levels with fewer budget resources, they may be more amenable to small property tax increases rather than budget reductions. Lacking this knowledge of their municipal organization, many citizens merely want to "cut-the-fat" in their city's budget. Cities cannot rely on local newspapers, radio or television stations to cover positive city activities and events. As most public officials know, most newspaper, radio and television news coverage is limited to important municipal issues, events, and, especially, problems.

For these reasons, city managers are attempting to educate citizens about their local government in a number of creative and technologically innovative ways. Public cable access television channels are being used to broadcast city council meetings, board and commission meetings, and to provide forums on important community issues. These same public access television channels are being used to provide community bulletin boards to communicate a wealth of information about a municipal government to citizens. Additionally, customer surveys are used to solicit feedback about public services from citizens in order to improve the quality of municipal services. The use of annual reports to showcase programs and services is also becoming commonplace. Traditional budget formats are being revised to show programs and productivity measurements. Public service impact statements are sometimes used to communicate the impact of budget reductions on public services to citizens. Some city managers and department directors are also actively marketing and promoting their community's services.

Whenever possible, elected officials should be actively involved in these public communication programs. The importance of these public information and educational programs is now recognized by all elected and appointed officials. The use of these positive communication tools will no doubt increase in the future.

Growth Management Practices. When growth management policies are desired by elected officials, city managers should work closely with their planning directors to ensure that the proper growth management techniques are recommended consistent with the goals of the governing body. These measures are highly controversial, tend to polarize special interest groups, and staff members should not engage in the public debate on growth management issues. The four basic growth management programs typically used by cities include growth phasing programs, the use of urban growth boundaries, rate-of-growth programs, and provisions for ensuring that adequate public facilities are available to accommodate new development. The specific planning tools include zoning designations, subdivision regulations, public facilities ordinances, development impact fees, and user fees for processing development applications, including inspections.

Current trends are against no-growth policies. Instead, most municipal planning practices favor planned growth and attempt to mitigate the undesirable impacts of development. These include preserving open spaces, protecting environmentally sensitive lands, controlling urban sprawl, and ensuring that adequate public infrastructure is available to sustain new development.

A city's legal department should closely review proposed growth management regulations since they may be subject to a lawsuit by one or more special interest groups. It is not unusual to hire special planning consultants to work with city managers and planning directors to specifically tailor growth rates and controls to a community. The specific growth management techniques used should be consistent with a community's desired economic development goals. Some governing bodies, because of the political sensitivity of proposed growth management initiatives, vote to place such measures on the ballot for the electorate to decide. Cities across the nation are favoring rational, phased approaches to growth, rather than extreme policy positions such as uncontrolled growth or no-growth policies. This more level-headed approach to controlling growth will likely continue in the future.

Innovative Community Services. Cities are being very creative in the way new programs are provided to the public. Many new services provide self-help resources for citizens, practical education programs, and actually involve citizens in the direct provision of public services. For example, some municipal libraries are providing job information centers, computer training programs, business information centers, and literacy training programs to their citizens. Many of these programs are being underwritten by friends of the library groups, private companies, and other non-traditional funding sources. Also, because of the many public services provided by educational institutions, community groups, and nonprofit organizations, some libraries are compiling listings of these services, and contacts for the desired service. This type of informational resource assists citizens as they seek out particular services to satisfy their personal needs.

The use of coproduction service strategies is also becoming more commonplace. Citizens can now routinely become actively involved in their government's municipal services through recycling programs, neighborhood watch groups, citizen clean-up projects, adopt-a-park programs, donating through city gift catalogs city "wish lists," and numerous other citizen volunteer efforts. Many cities also cosponsor community programs offered to citizens at public facilities. The city provides free space, its endorsement, and possibly some advertising, while the community group or nonprofit organization actually provides the service. All of these trends have led to a decentralization of service provision, and have drastically altered the traditional avenues available for the delivery of public services. The efforts of city managers to provide self-help resources, and to get citizens actively involved in providing public services have almost always received the endorsement of their governing bodies.

Most governing bodies endorse these new service concepts, and encourage their widespread usage in all municipal departments. These programs also help remove the traditional barriers between citizens and their city government. Other new and innovative methods to provide public services and hold down the cost of government will evolve in the future.

Privatization Practices. Traditionally, cities have held a monopoly on the provision of municipal services. All city services were usually always provided by the municipal government organization. Early privatization initiatives involved contracts for services with private companies when the local government did not have the internal capacity to provide the service. Examples of these services include refuse collection, recycling programs, buildings and grounds maintenance, vehicle towing and storage services, and the construction of public works projects. Rather than expand the municipal organization, services such as these could be provided by private companies for an agreed upon fee.

Elected officials and citizens deserve to know if the price of their municipal services is competitive with the private sector. Some city managers have even bid selected services and compared these bid prices against the municipal costs of providing the same service. Sometimes if a service can be provided less expensively by a private company, it may not always be in the best interest of taxpayers to contract for this service. Cost is not the only issue that should be considered. Current privatization practices include provisions for adequate safeguards to ensure service quality, maintaining public accountability, controlling costs, and requirements for handling citizen complaints.

Another trend is for cities to contract with nonprofit agencies for selected services not provided by the private sector. These programs may include services in the public health, social service, and recreational areas, to name a few. It is also not uncommon for smaller communities to contract with larger cities or counties for certain public services. A municipality's existing labor agreements may restrict or prohibit the use of privatization practices. The use of private companies and nonprofit agencies to provide selected public services is on the increase. The use of contractual safeguards to protect the public's interest should be a common practice.

Public Service Impact Statements. Budget reductions are often made without relating their impact on a city's public services. It is important to inform the public that, when budgets cuts are made, public services are negatively impacted. This practice helps to counteract the "cut-the-fat" mentality held by some taxpayers. Some elected officials and many citizens believe that taxes can be lowered merely by reducing unnecessary budget expenses. It is important that elected leaders help fill this knowledge vacuum through public informational techniques, such as the use of public service impact statements. City managers, when proposing budget reductions on their own, or when making them in response to elected official mandates, should always describe the impact of the proposed budget reductions on public services. Elected officials deserve to know the consequences of their decisions. Likewise, citizens should know the impact of proposed budget reductions on their community services.

Planning departments have long used environmental impact statements to describe the impacts of a proposed development on the environment.

Governing bodies and city managers should likewise use public service impact statements to describe the impacts of proposed budget reductions on existing service levels. Sometimes, when the impact of budget cuts on public services is made clear, citizens may be more amenable to implementing user fees, raising existing user fees, or favoring some form of modest tax increase. When user fee and tax increases are directly related to specific public services, the public can decide through their elected officials which options they prefer. Unless city councils and city managers educate the public in this important area, many citizens will continue to hold the belief that to balance budgets all you need to do is "cut-the-fat."

Strategic vs. Traditional Planning. Traditional planning practices in cities have typically been short-range, dominated by single issues, hierarchical in nature, and developed by city management with little or no citizen involvement. These plans also tended to have an operational focus and describe goals rather than stress results. Early strategic plans in the public sector were initiated almost exclusively by mayors and city councils.

With more than a decade of experience in this new planning field, strategic planning is becoming more of a science than an art form. Strategic planning practices are almost universally long-range, address multiple community issues, and involve many segments of a municipality in the planning process. Strategic plans have a policy focus and are results oriented. Every city should have a plan that addresses the major issues and problems facing a community. Some city managers were reluctant to initiate these plans at first because of the highly charged political nature of this planning process. It is incumbent upon city managers to recommend properly designed strategic planning projects to their elected officials. Many of the early, politically motivated strategic plans showed little in the way of actual results.

As city managers and planning directors become more involved in the use of strategic planning, the ultimate goal should be to have this planning process institutionalized in the planning department. Issues management, another form of strategic planning, is also being used to tackle community issues. Regardless of its name, new results-oriented planning practices designed to identify and resolve community issues are gaining in popularity in cities throughout the nation.

Volunteer and Student Internship Services. Citizen involvement in their government through volunteer and student internship programs has been on the increase for about the last decade. President Bush strongly advocated citizen volunteerism during his administration. Budget reductions at the local level have made the use of volunteers an attractive alternative to traditional methods of service delivery. City managers and department directors favor the increased use of student interns to perform specialized projects and services. While volunteers are not paid, student interns usually receive a small hourly wage for their services. Student involvement in public service is frequently required as a part of their degree program. Volunteers are typically older, possibly retired, and want to perform public service work or merely get more involved in the activities of their community. Students, on the other hand, participate out of a desire for college credit and to gain valuable work experience. Volunteers and student interns usually do not perform the work of regular municipal employees.

Existing labor agreements may restrict, even prohibit, the use of volunteers and student interns. For this reason, volunteers are typically used to augment existing city services, and student interns are used for special projects that cannot be performed by existing employees. While public unions have no fear of a city's use of student interns, they frequently feel that volunteers will be used to replace regular city workers. For these reasons, city managers should target the use of volunteers, making sure that they are used to augment existing municipal services, and are used in such a manner that they do not pose a liability to their public agency. The term "coproduction of public services" also includes the use of citizen volunteers. City managers should consult with their employee bargaining unit representatives when they place volunteers, making sure that adequate supervision is available from regular city employees.

The International City/County Management Association (ICMA) recently published the results of a national survey on the use of volunteers in providing municipal services, and a guidebook for directors of volunteer service programs. The selective use of volunteers and the number of student internship programs have increased in recent years and will continue to do so in the future.

Working with the Community. In the past, some city managers have made important decisions and developed critical policy recommendations in a political vacuum. With the increasing involvement of community groups, merchant associations, chambers of commerce, and other special interest groups, major decisions and policy recommendations should not be made introspectively.

For example, if a city manager works with a planning director on a new streetscape plan for a downtown area, it should not be presented to the city council for its consideration at this point. The astute city manager should make a list of the major stakeholders that have an interest in this plan, and seek citizen feedback on the proposal. In fact, such a plan should be presented as a "draft" proposal and not as a completed product. The final proposal presented to the governing body should be amended, within reason, to satisfy the needs of these major stakeholders. In this case, this plan should be presented to local merchant associations, community groups, the chamber of commerce, and any other significant stakeholder groups. When this plan is presented to the governing body, the accompanying report should mention that input on the development of the plan was received from those citizens whose lives and livelihoods are affected by it.

This advanced political processing will help win the support of elected officials. No single stakeholder or special interest group, however, should be allowed to unduly influence a significant proposal. The trend for city managers to actively work with major stakeholders and community groups is on the increase.

THE FUTURE

The most significant internal productivity trends have been the use of personal computers in the workplace, the development of management information systems, and the use of new office technologies. Three private industry trends have facilitated the use of these resources in municipal governments: more sophisticated computer hardware with greater storage capability, easy-to-use software applications, and decreasing hardware and software costs. Not too many years ago, personal computers were too expensive and, for this reason, only municipal engineers routinely used microcomputers. Also, the development of specialized software applications was cost-prohibitive. Many "canned" software applications can now be used to improve departmental operations. One of the most important tasks faced by city managers is making elected officials aware of the need to use these technologies. They should be presented as ways to increase employee productivity and improve public services. The same trends hold true for photocopy and facsimile machines. In the future, virtually all workstations will be equipped with a microcomputer, and each office will have its own photocopier and facsimile machine. City managers should prepare technology master plans for their organizations showing how to increase departmental productivity and improve services with these technologies.

The external productivity trend that has had the most profound impact on holding down the cost of municipal services has been the use of citizens to coproduce their public services. A minor trend only a few years ago, many standard citizen coproduction programs are available to help public officials hold down the cost of their government. Many communities are educating citizens of the importance of recycling programs (to reduce solid waste collection and disposal costs), neighborhood watch programs (to hold down crime and assist police officers), adopt-a-park and similar programs (to reduce maintenance costs), and water and energy conservation programs (to conserve water and energy and hold down their consumption costs). Citizen volunteerism has also helped to augment existing levels of services without having to hire additional municipal employees. Student internships have helped to provide young people with valuable job training and have helped departments complete many special studies and projects that would otherwise not have been completed. Some departments are even seeking private donations to help provide services, giving community-wide recognition to those companies participating in these programs. All of these programs represent positive ways for citizens to become more involved with their community government. Some of these programs expand services, others improve their quality, while others help reduce their costs.

One of the latest buzzwords in the lexicon of municipal government is "privatization," which is frequently confused with contracting for services. Under privatization, government gets out of the business of providing a particular service altogether. When a government contracts for a service, a private company performs the service for the government even though taxpayers may be the beneficiary of this service. For example, if a community quits providing refuse collection services and allows each property owner to acquire this service on their own from private haulers, then this service has been privatized. In this case government no longer performs or provides this service. If public officials want to do away with their own collection service for reasons of economy, they may contract for this service from a private company through the competitive bidding process. When the contract is awarded to the private company, the services are provided to citizens under contract with their government. In this case, while government does not perform the service, it is still responsible for providing the service now performed by a private company. There have been no studies conducted that prove that it is universally less expensive to contract for specific public services. A cost/benefit analysis must be developed for each specific service to determine its desirability for contracting whether or not the service is contracted or privatized, it behooves public officials to seek out private prices for their services and then compare them to their government's cost of providing this same service.

4

CITY CLERK

Some of the duties performed by city clerks are among the oldest responsibilities of municipal governments and are, almost without exception, universally provided by all communities. These traditional duties, many of which continue today, include maintaining a community's vital public records such as birth certificates, death certificates, marriage licenses, real property deeds, liens on real property, as well as important financial instruments. In some states, counties, or sometime the state, perform this function for all cities within their political boundaries. This has helped to achieve economies of scale since each city does not have to maintain its own records management system. Also when retrieving information, all that is necessary is to know the county in which the activity took place. In order to ensure continuity of record-keeping, virtually all states regulate what documents must be kept on file and for how long. When it comes to federal grants, the federal government dictates what records must be maintained and how long they must be kept on file.

In general law communities, state regulations usually require that the city clerk be an appointed position. In these cases, this position is usually appointed by the city manager. In charter cities, the city clerk may be an elective position. The rationale for having this position elected is that it performs a vital public service, and this service should only be entrusted to a citizen formally approved by the electorate. In either case, the city clerk is a department manager and is responsible for managing the city clerk function in a manner consistent with applicable local, state, and federal laws. When this position is elected, the city manager may have a tendency to treat the city clerk differently from other appointed department managers. It is a sound management practice, however, to treat the city clerk like all other department managers. Both appointed and elected city clerks follow the same policies and procedures that are followed by other municipal department managers. All city clerks should be considered a department manager and a part of the city's management team.

Internally, the city clerk is responsible for meeting all of the legal requirements for holding public meetings, and prepares meeting notices, agendas, and minutes for all meetings of the governing body. In this capacity, the clerk also maintains the official archives of the municipal government. All public documents, regardless of their nature, are filed and maintained for future reference. The city clerk makes sure that written information is available to the citizens prior to public meetings, and that copies of all official documents are available for inspection or purchase after these meetings. It is common practice for official records and documents to date back to when a municipality was first incorporated. The clerk is usually required by state law to obtain annual meeting schedules of all municipal boards and commissions. These schedules are posted to inform the public of these meetings. Some states require that these schedules be published in the newspaper. Certain items, such as proposed municipal laws and certain paperwork associated with federal grants, must also be published in the newspaper prior to being approved. This serves to notify citizens of pending city council action on these matters.

In many communities, the city clerk is responsible for the proper administration of local elections and is the registrar of voters. The administration of elections involves those activities necessary to conduct fair and impartial municipal elections, from the filing of all candidate petitions to the official certification of the final vote. In the capacity of registrar of voters, the city clerk maintains the official listing of qualified registered voters. All citizens wishing to vote must register their names with the registrar or deputy registrars, who are usually employees that work for the city clerk and have been trained to perform this task. While some city charters call for a separate registrar of voters, nearly all state laws require that the city clerk perform this function. Many communities now contract with their county government to administer their municipal elections. This ensures that the same election procedures and practices are consistent in all of the cities throughout the county. This also takes some of the politics out of having this task performed locally.

Many citizens go to the city clerk's office for information on how to resolve complaints, as well as to seek directions to other municipal departments. This is common since citizens are used to going to this department for a number of reasons, such as to review and or acquire official public records and documents. Additionally, many local and state permits and licenses are typically available from the city clerk. Those licenses or permits requiring departmental review or approval prior to issuance are forwarded to the responsible department for processing. For example, bicycle licenses may be issued directly by the city clerk, while taxicab permits would be forwarded to the police department to conduct a criminal records check on the applicant. The administration of local licenses and permits varies from community to community. State governments, however, usually designate the city clerk as the focal point for the sale of their licenses and permits. For these reasons, city clerk departments generate a significant amount of revenue compared to the size of their operations.

Figure 4.1 provides a detailed description of the eight major programs

Figure 4.1
City Clerk Major Programs

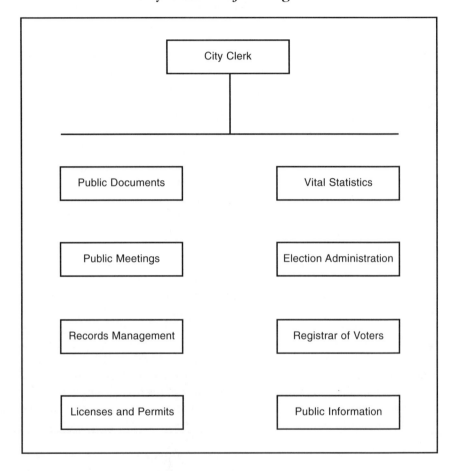

performed by the city clerk department. The city clerk supervises a clerical staff who assist in carrying out the various duties associated with these programs.

DESCRIPTION OF PROGRAMS

Public Documents. The city clerk serves as the official archivist in all municipal governments. All official documents are stored and kept on file for public review, reference, and inspection. These documents typically date back to when a municipality was first incorporated.

Some of the more common public documents maintained on permanent file in the city clerk's office include those relating to public meetings, agendas for all public meetings, minutes of all public meetings, vital statistics, municipal leases and agreements, ordinances and resolutions, the city charter, the city code, and other documents that are required to be saved by local, state, and federal law. While counties in some states keep records on vital statistics, it is not uncommon in many states for municipalities to maintain these records. The assignment of this function to either the city or county government would depend upon existing state laws. The destruction of old or obsolete records and documents always requires prior state approval. All public records and documents must be made available for public inspection upon demand. Without exception, copies of all public records and documents may also be purchased for a small fee approved by the governing body.

The city clerk also serves as the information center for inquiries from other cities, counties, the state, the federal government, as well as citizens in general. Additionally, the city clerk maintains copies of the official financial records of city government (e.g., annual budget documents, annual audit reports, and other financial instruments).

Public Meetings. One of the most important functions of the city clerk is to ensure that all public meetings are held in accordance with local and state laws. The city clerk also serves as the secretary to the governing body. This requires the preparation of all meeting agendas, minutes of all public meetings, and making sure that proper legal notification is provided to citizens in advance of all public meetings. In this capacity, the city clerk must ensure that copies of all agendas, reports, and other documents related to public meetings are made available to citizens and the press in advance of the actual meeting dates. Most state laws require that ordinances or resolutions be published in a local newspaper of general circulation. If a city has more than one such newspaper, the city council must designate one "official" newspaper in which to publish all legal notices and other public documents. The public depends upon the city clerk to provide timely and accurate information on all meetings.

Most states allow for closed, or executive, sessions to be held for those municipal matters pertaining to pending litigation, labor relations issues, and real estate negotiations. While agenda items relating to these matters may be considered in private, the official actions taken on these matters by the elected officials must be done in public. Most governing bodies meet twice each month, with their meetings held in the evening so the public may attend. Only the official public actions are recorded by the city clerk.

Records Management. As cities have grown in population and complexity, the number and types of public records maintained by city clerks has expanded accordingly. The systems used to maintain official public records and documents must have integrity, ease of reference, and must always be accessible to the public.

The city clerk must retain the originals of many official government documents. When copies of documents are given to the public they may be certified, if necessary, as being a true copy of the original. Legal requirements for citizen accessibility to official public records are set forth by state law. Federal and state laws also require that certain records be kept on file for public inspection for specific periods of time. Some records must also be kept in their original form. Refusing the public access to most records and documents is in violation of state and federal laws. Since storage space is limited at most city halls, the trend is to keep copies of many documents available on microfilm, microfiche, or magnetic tape. With the advent of more sophisticated and less expensive computer systems, more user-friendly software, and smaller computer units, records management systems have become more highly automated in recent years. Most city clerks have records retention schedules and purge their public records and documents annually. The destruction of official public records requires state approval in advance.

Effective records management systems are now essential and, although expensive, are necessary for the efficient use of limited office space, as well as the proper storage and retrieval of official documents which must be made available to the public upon demand.

Licenses and Permits. City clerks are also in charge of issuing municipal licenses and permits, which serve the dual purpose of regulating certain activities as well as generating revenues. Many city clerks collect fees for virtually dozens of licenses and permits. Some examples include dog and bicycle licenses, hunting and fishing permits, taxicab and limousine permits, bingo and raffle permits, and business licenses, to name a few.

Generally, the greater the possible damage or financial loss to the public, the greater the number and types of restrictions and qualifications placed upon the applicant prior to the issuance of the required license or permit. Increasingly, state laws regulate and impose requirements on many activities that require a municipal license or permit. When discretion is required in granting a license or permit, it is usually the governing body or an advisory body that decides upon and approves the granting of a license or permit.

It is also not uncommon for the state to impose licenses or permits and to designate city clerks as the point of fee collection and issuance. In such cases, only a portion of the revenues are kept at the local level, with the balance of the funds being remitted to the state. Almost without exception, the fees collected by the city clerk are deposited into the city's general fund. This fund finances the general operations of the city government.

Vital Statistics. The role of serving as the official keeper and "guardian" of vital public records has been a fundamental duty of the city clerk since colonial times. These records include, but are certainly not limited to, birth certificates, marriage licenses, death records, real property deeds, mechanics' liens, state and federal tax liens, and other real estate and financial documents.

Copies of the originals of these important records and documents are given a reference number, recorded into the public record, and maintained as a part of the permanent official records system. Also, the public recording function enables citizens to record other important documents such as military discharge papers, satisfaction of liens and mortgages, and other valued documents—especially those that may have possible future financial implications. Any document recorded may be immediately retrieved by using its reference number. Only copies of documents are kept on file; the originals are always returned to the citizen. How long these records must be kept and how they may be disposed of are matters regulated by state law. Guidelines governing the public's access to these documents is also set forth by state law.

The city clerk also maintains records on important local historic events, civic celebrations, time capsule information, and other municipal events. Increasingly, when appropriate, copies of records are being maintained on microfilm or microfiche to save space and lower storage costs. Vital statistics records are also part of the city clerk's overall records management and retrieval system.

Election Administration. Depending upon the state, the responsibility for election administration may be assigned to either the county or city government. In many areas, local, state, and national elections are still conducted by the city clerk. Election administration activities are closely regulated by state and federal laws, as well as numerous court decisions.

Basic election administration duties typically include maintaining official voter registration listings, handling all candidate petitions and filings, the publication and distribution of election materials to voters, including absentee ballots, the hiring and training of election workers, the printing and delivering of official ballots, tabulating the election results, and the final canvassing of those results. Election rules and regulations are designed to ensure the secrecy of ballots and to prevent voter fraud. When a vote recount is requested by a candidate, or when an election result is contested, it is the city clerk that recounts the ballots and approves the final results. The city clerk is also required to enforce state campaign laws, rules governing the size of campaign signs, as well as candidate financial disclosure requirements.

The national trend is to consolidate election administration duties at the county level of government. This is being done to promote the continuity of this function on a county-wide basis, to ensure consistent administrative activities, to achieve economies of scale, and to maintain the integrity of the election process in the eyes of the public.

Registrar of Voters. Most city clerks, by state law, are designated as the registrar of voters for their municipality. Every citizen wishing to vote must register in advance of the election though, some states provide for election day voter registration in an effort to enhance voter turnout.

Minimal residency and age requirements are established by federal and state law. Every citizen wishing to register to vote must provide a valid identification and verification of their residency. Duplicate voter registrations are against the law. In some parts of the country, citizens are required to register according to their political party affiliation. This generally qualifies them to vote in primary elections. Independent voters, for example, are not eligible to vote in partisan primary elections. In many states, postcard registration is available, eliminating the need to register in person. If a citizen's name is removed from the official voter registration rolls, he or she may challenge this action, and is entitled to administrative due process typically in the form of a hearing before the registrar of voters or one of his or her sworn deputies. City clerks frequently maintain extended evening hours before election dates to enable citizens to register to vote after their regular working hours.

Computers are now commonly used to maintain accurate and up-to-date voter registration rolls. The duties of the registrar of voters are critically linked to the election administration function since only registered voters may participate in elections.

Public Information. Because the city clerk is the official repository of all public documents, maintains information concerning all public meetings, keeps records of vital statistics, issues licenses and permits, and is the registrar of voters, it is not unusual for members of the public to view the office of the city clerk as the main information focal point for their municipal government. Also, many citizens, not knowing where to direct an inquiry or complaint, frequently go to the city clerk. The city clerk usually responds to citizen inquiries in one of three ways. First, the city clerk may have the information on hand and respond immediately to the inquiry. Second, the city clerk may obtain the information or answer from another department to satisfy the inquiry. Third, the city clerk may refer a citizen to the appropriate department or individual within the municipal organization for a response.

While the position of city clerk is frequently an elected office, it is usually not a highly political office. Unlike some mayors and council members, city clerks usually have long tenures due to low election turnover. It is also not unusual when one city clerk retires to have another deputy city clerk run for the position of city clerk. The retiring city clerk frequently endorses this person for city clerk. This continuity has made the office of the city clerk one of the most stable positions in U.S. city government.

PRODUCTIVITY TRENDS

Many of the following internal productivity trends describe how computer hardware and software applications, as well as other office technologies, are being applied in city clerk departments. When microcomputers were expensive and software had to be specially designed for specific applications, the cost of office automation was prohibitive. This was especially true for city clerks in smaller communities. Other new office technologies such as document scanners, compact computer storage disks, and automated cash register and receipting systems are also being utilized. Not too long ago, the city clerk's staff maintained their records manually. Cash transactions were even recorded in the same manner. All monies received from over-the-counter transactions is now turned over to the finance department daily for deposit to optimize interest earnings. Since the primary role of the city clerk is document preparation, storage, and retrieval, new software applications have revolutionized the records management function in this department. These new technologies have led to greater cross-training of staff, as well as an increased number of formal training programs offered by universities and professional associations. Other productivity improvements center on fiscal accountability. These include informing elected officials of the cost of their decisions, as well as making more frequent adjustments to their fees.

External productivity improvements include contracting for specialized services, increased networking and resource sharing, and a general increase in the level of professionalism among city clerks. Because of the technological explosion taking place, and the tendency to contract for some services rather than hire additional staff, a knowledge of the private sector resources available in this field is critical. In their ongoing search for ways to save scarce funds, many city clerks are contracting with their county government for elections administration. One of the most important roles performed by city clerks is to ensure that their municipal government is "open" to the public. In this respect, city clerks have been given responsibility for complying with "sunshine" laws, such as making all official documents available for inspection by the public and press. City clerks, because of their position of public trust, have also been charged with the task of making sure public officials comply with financial disclosure laws and ethics regulations. For these reasons, the city clerk department, in the eyes of the public, is one of the most visible and trusted arms of any municipal government.

A listing of the productivity trends reviewed in this chapter are set forth in Table 4.1. The city clerk, like other department managers, must seek governing body approval of any new programs and services. This usually occurs during the annual budget approval process.

Internal

Automatic Cash Register and Receipting Systems. Manual record-keeping for cash and the issuance of receipts is quickly becoming a practice of the past. Sophisticated and relatively inexpensive automated cash register and receipting systems are now commonly used to properly account for all of the cash and check payments received on a daily basis. This technology also facilitates

Table 4.1
City Clerk Productivity Trends

Internal	*External*
Automatic Cash Register and Receipting Systems	City Clerk Internships
Computer Security	Contract City Clerk Services
Computer Usage and City Clerk Services	Election Consolidations
Cross-Training of Staff	Fixed Terms of Office
Fiscal Accountability	Knowledge of City Clerk Resources
Ordinance Codification	Licenses and Permits
Part-Time Employees	Networking and Resource Sharing
Records Management	Open Public Meeting Laws
Specialized City Clerk Training	Professional Certifications
User Fee Increases	Role of the City Clerk
	Telephone Message Centers

making daily bank deposits, which increases the amount of interest earned on these collectibles. It also does away with the need to prepare manual receipts for each transaction. The more sophisticated systems store all transactions on a computer database, doing away with the need to maintain physical documents and records. Because of the importance of keeping information on all financial transactions, back-up disks or tapes are also commonly used for record-keeping purposes.

Computer Security. As the cost of computer hardware decreases and software applications become more user-friendly, the increased use of computers in the workplace has given rise to the need for enhanced computer security. Security precautions are needed to safeguard databases against unauthorized computer entry to prevent the loss or unauthorized use of valuable public information. Secured areas with limited access and the use of passwords for specific software applications are now commonplace in city clerk departments. Back-up disks and tapes are also frequently used to guard against the inadvertent destruction or loss of important municipal clerk records and information.

Computer Usage and City Clerk Services. As personnel in city clerk departments become more computer literate, and the cost of microcomputer systems decrease, the use of smaller personal computers has become an efficient way to perform routine administrative, technical, and clerical tasks, such as word processing, the preparation and management of documents, information storage and retrieval records management, access to departmental databases, and the issuance of permits and licenses to the public. Inexpensive office networking systems are also available to interconnect all microcomputers within a department. This reduces software costs and facilitates the development of common officewide city clerk databases. The advent of more sophisticated, inexpensive, and user-friendly software has facilitated this trend. Cumbersome software instructional manuals and the long hours of training are no longer necessary for employees to become computer literate.

Cross-Training of Staff. In order to stretch scarce budget allocations, many municipal clerks are cross-training their personnel to perform a variety of clerk-related services. Rather than having to rely on a single staff person or persons to perform a particular type of service, cross-training permits a greater utilization of existing personnel to perform a variety of city duties and services. The availability of computer networks, access to city clerk databases, and common officewide systems for information storage and retrieval have assisted in the cross-training of both professional and clerical personnel. Existing labor agreements may limit or restrict the use of cross-training practices, especially at the secretarial and clerical level, if more than one union represents these municipal employees. Employee cross-training reduces labor costs by holding down the need for additional personnel. It also enables employees to fill-in for common staffing shortages in the workplace created by vacation, sick leave, and maternity leave.

Fiscal Accountability. Mayors and city councils are increasingly requesting that their city manager and department managers place the cost of all new programs, expansion of existing services, and proposed mandates on all reports going to the governing body for its consideration. In the not-to-distant past, many elected officials would frequently make decisions in a financial vacuum, not knowing the fiscal impact of their decisions on the municipal budget. Now, however, more and more governing bodies are demanding information regarding the cost of their public decisions. The task of checking all staff reports and requests for legislation frequently rests with the city manager. It is common for the city manager to delegate this task to respective department managers and appoint the city clerk as the "gatekeeper" to ensure compliance with this requirement. This trend is widespread in cities of all sizes, regardless of their location.

Ordinance Codification. This labor-intensive task is frequently contracted to a private professional municipal code codification company. The annual codification of municipal codes enhances the storage and retrieval of public information; it also enables city clerks to better serve the public. This task is necessary since city codes are constantly being updated with the passage of new legislation as well as amendments to existing laws. At the end of each year, a city's existing code is amended to incorporate all changes made throughout the year. Many code codification companies use state-of-the-art computer systems with sophisticated word processing and desk-top publishing applications to complete this task. Many cities do not have adequately trained staffs and lack the specialized computer hardware technology and software applications to properly undertake projects of this nature. It is most cost-effective for a municipality to use a single code codification company for a number of years since these companies store municipal codes on a database, making annual changes less expensive.

Part-Time Employees. Many city clerk departments have increased their usage of part-time employees to assume the duties of regular personnel who are either on vacation or extended sick leave. This trend has reduced the number of full-time employees, thereby reducing the size of their staffs at a considerable savings in overtime and fringe benefit costs. Salary costs are reduced by one-half since existing personnel would receive overtime payments of one and one-half for each hour worked. Also, part-time employees typically do not receive fringe benefits, usually estimated to be one-third of salary costs. Therefore, the use of part-time employees is usually about one-half the cost of using full-time employees. Part-time employees are not used to take the place of regular full-time employees. As the routine workload expands or personnel are needed to undertake special projects, part-time employees may be utilized with success for these purposes. Existing labor agreements may govern the use of part-time employees in the workplace.

Records Management. City clerk records frequently must be kept on file for a number of years. Some records, such as vital statistics (e.g., birth, death, and marriage certificates) must be maintained as a matter of public record indefinitely. Many city clerk departments, due to limited office and storage space, are converting these records to microfilm, microfiche, and or computer database storage. Two new technologies—OCR (optical character recognition) and CD-ROM (compact disk-read only memory system)—have assisted city clerks in the automation of their municipal records. The use of OCR hardware has enabled city clerks to scan and store public documents on a computer database. The CD-ROMs, because of their large storage capacity, are now being used for document storage and retrieval systems. These new technologies not only enhance the management of municipal documents, but also improve both the storage and retrieval of public records. If the city clerk and legal departments are part of the same computer network, the city clerk may print a hard copy of a legal document merely by accessing it directly from files stored on a common computer database.

This type of computer networking reduces duplicating costs and provides real-time access and printing of legal documents. It also speeds up the preparation of city council agendas. In addition to saving money, state-of-the-art records management practices improves services to elected officials, other municipal departments, and the public.

Specialized City Clerk Training. The municipal clerk profession is becoming more complex and specialized. It is now common to budget funds for training in order to develop staff expertise in new technical city clerk areas such as computer hardware options, office automation systems, records management programs, and specialized software applications, to name a few. Because of the increasing number of laws and regulations in this field, especially those mandated by higher levels of government, as well as advances in computer hardware and software applications, specialized training is necessary for personnel to keep abreast of the latest hardware and software developments in this field. National and statewide professional associations frequently provide up-to-date training in these, and other specialized and expanding areas of city clerk departments.

User Fee Increases. Every effort is being made to make more municipal services cost-covering, and city clerk services are no exception. The fees charged for notary services, the issuance of various public records and documents (such as for birth, death, and marriage certificates), and licenses and permits are now being adjusted to reflect the actual cost of providing these services. Free or inexpensive costs for services are quickly becoming a thing of the past. These increased revenues are typically used to maintain existing operations and services, as opposed to having to resort to unacceptable service reductions. Also, the trend has been to adjust user fees annually. In the past, user fees were adjusted infrequently, creating political opposition to such fee increases. When user fees are adjusted more frequently, like prices in the private sector marketplace, they are more politically acceptable to governing bodies as well as the public.

External

City Clerk Internships. Some city clerk departments are using student interns from local colleges and universities on a part-time basis to assist the regular staff in performing selected city clerk-related duties. This trend not only provides valuable training to students who may wish to enter the municipal clerk field, but also assists the full-time staff with some of the more routine duties associated with city clerk matters. Student interns are also frequently used to perform special projects of a limited duration. City clerk interns typically receive a hourly wage or minimum salary and do not receive fringe benefits. City clerk interns seeking a general exposure to the municipal clerk field typically work in smaller communities; those wishing to work in more specialized areas of this field usually work in larger cities. Existing labor agreements may govern the use of these internship arrangements.

Contract City Clerk Services. Many city clerks are contracting out selected services, especially those of a specialized or technological nature, to the private sector. This is desirable when a service cannot be provided by the existing staff, or when it is less expensive to have the work or service performed by an outside company. Municipal code codification, the selection and installation of computer hardware, the development of software applications, and placing existing public documents and records on microfilm and microfiche are examples of this trend. In the case of transferring records and documents to microfilm and microfiche, it may be less expensive not to purchase the specialized equipment necessary to perform these services.

A city clerk would compare the cost of this equipment against the cost of having this service performed by a private company. In the case of the selection and installation of computer hardware and the development of software applications, it is almost always cheaper to hire outside consultants to perform these services. It is incumbent upon city clerks to ensure that proper quality controls are in place when contracting out a service to the private sector.

Election Consolidations. The trend in recent years has been for municipalities to contract with their county government in order to consolidate city and county elections to achieve economies of scale. Many smaller municipalities now contract with county governments to conduct their local election services. Since many counties perform election services for many cities within their political boundaries, these larger units of government frequently have more sophisticated election equipment, can purchase election supplies in large quantities, and can conduct election training on a countywide basis. More sophisticated election equipment, much of which is computer-based, is also made available to cities within the county. This equipment frequently makes voting easier for the public and leads to a quicker compilation of the results once the polls are closed. Also, the printing of sample ballots and the preparation of ballots in different languages (which is required in many states) is more cost-effective if it is performed for many cities on a countywide basis.

Another major trend is for communities to change their election dates to coincide with state and national elections, since counties frequently provide these election services. This lowers election costs for a municipality. The downside of this practice is that local ballots can become overshadowed by state and national election issues and offices.

Fixed Terms of Office. Since municipal clerks are sometimes political appointments, many states have implemented fixed terms of office and permanent tenure arrangements after a set number of years in office. When the city clerk is an elective office, the term of office is usually four years. The term of office, job tenure rights, and the length of the term of office for an elective city clerk are usually mandated by the state, set forth in city charters, or made a part of municipal codes. These trends have enhanced the continuity of city clerk operations and has provided job stability to professionals in this field. Even in many cities with the council-manager form of government, the city clerk is frequently an elected position. This goes back to the basic role and purpose of the city clerk—to ensure the integrity of public records, guarantee public access to these records, and properly inform citizens of all public meetings. For these reasons, of all municipal department manager positions, the city clerk is the most likely one to be held by an elected official.

The national trend towards fixed term limits for elected officials may serve to undermine some of the advantages of tenure rights and professional certifications for those citizens (and municipal employees) wishing to seek this office. Fixed terms may preclude a career interest in this field because of the limited number of years one may hold this elective office.

Knowledge of City Clerk Resources. Many private sector consulting companies now provide a number of different hardware systems, software applications, and code codification services in the city clerk field. Also public nonprofit professional associations assess these systems, applications, and services at their conferences and in their trade journals. Having a working knowledge of these private and nonprofit sector resources is essential, especially in smaller city clerk departments with limited budgets, staff expertise, and technical resources. State regulatory agencies and state-side professional associations also provide valuable information on the use of new computer hardware and software technologies. As more of these services become available in the private marketplace, it is essential to have a thorough knowledge of the most cost-effective systems available.

In larger cities, city clerks may wish to hire specialized consultants in these fields before making decisions on which hardware systems, software applications, and codification services to purchase. The marketplace is changing so quickly that a system or service only a few years old may now be obsolete.

Licenses and Permits. The city clerk department is the municipal focal point for the issuance of most licenses and permits granted by a local government. In the case of city-initiated licenses and permits, every effort is being made to make the issuance of these items cost-covering. The city clerk also issues many state licenses and permits. In this case, much of the revenue collected goes to the state government. Local governing bodies and state city clerk associations are increasingly lobbying their state legislators to make sure that the amount of local revenues retained is sufficient to make the issuance of a particular license or permit cost-covering. In the past, state mandates were forced upon municipalities, including city clerk departments, with little or no revenue to cover the cost of providing these services. With increasingly tight municipal budgets, city clerks are seeking equitable fee sharing arrangements with their state governments. This trend is likely to continue in the future.

Networking and Resource Sharing. Because of new and more sophisticated computer systems and easy-to-use software applications, many city clerk departments are well on their way to complete office automation. The phrase "paperless office" certainly applies to trends in this field. Rather than learning from costly mistakes, city clerks are increasingly using their state and national professional associations to share information about new technologies, products, and services. This professional networking and information sharing is critical in a highly competitive marketplace with numerous consultants and private companies selling these service innovations. The decision on which computers to use, what software packages to purchase, and the costs and benefits of various lease or purchase options, are easier to make if a particular product or service is being successfully used in another similar community.

Sometimes less expensive products require more upfront and ongoing employee training. It may be less expensive in the long run to purchase more costly, higher quality products. For this reason, the use of life-cycle costing methods may be more prudent than merely accepting the lowest bidder.

Open Public Meeting Laws. Most states mandate complicated and strict open public meeting laws. In the absence of state laws, many city charters and municipal codes contain their own regulations and requirements regarding open public meetings. The enforcement of all of these laws is usually the legal responsibility of the city clerk. A knowledge of these laws and their proper implementation is essential to properly conduct a government's business. These requirements typically include the proper posting of meeting notices in public places, advertising meeting notices in a local newspaper of general circulation, and reading statements at all public meetings that the city is in compliance with these requirements. Closed or executive sessions, where the public is not invited, may usually only be held on personnel matters, real estate negotiations, and to discuss pending litigation. These laws vary from state to state. When a legal question arises concerning a public meeting law, the city clerk usually seeks the legal advice of the municipal attorney.

Copies of all contracts, resolutions, ordinances, and other public documents appearing on a public meeting agenda must also be made available to the public prior to actually holding the public meeting.

Professional Certifications. Some state governments, state and national professional associations, and educational institutions are providing formal programs leading to professional designations and certifications in the city clerk field. This trend has helped to increase the level of competency in this field, as well as setting a standard when seeking new personnel to fill professional vacancies. For example, the International Institute of Municipal Clerks (IIMC) has established a Professional Certification Program to provide formal recognition for the experience, training, and expertise of its national membership.

Some states mandate that a professional certification be received within one year after appointment. Many elected municipal clerks, once they take office, pursue professional certification programs. Such certification may help them gain re-election or facilitate their efforts to find another city clerk position if they are not re-elected.

Role of the City Clerk. Traditionally, the city clerk has always been a focal point of public contract for citizens in their dealings with municipal governments. When a citizen does not know who to contact with a inquiry, question, or complaint, they frequently go to the city clerk to ask for directions. Also, with the increasing level of public awareness and involvement of citizens in the affairs of their government, including a greater number of citizens attending public meetings, and the desire of taxpayers to know more about their city government, the public role of the city clerk has escalated in importance in recent years. The city clerk has an increasing level of responsibility to the public in providing access to public records, preparing and making available the agendas of city council meetings, as well as the documents to be acted upon, and complying with open public meeting laws. For these reasons, the public role performed by the city clerk is one of the most vital functions in any municipal government.

Telephone Message Centers. Many sophisticated telephone systems and services are now available in the marketplace at a reasonable cost. Since many telephone inquiries are of a routine nature, it is now possible to program telephones with standard responses to citizen inquiries. These typically include answers to such questions as the hours of operation; who to contact for specific services; how to obtain birth and death certificates, land records, as well as marriage licenses and other routine public documents. Other innovative telecommunications services such as menu-driven telephone directories and voice mail also assist city clerks in improving the quality of their services to the public. All of these telephone systems and services help to free up the time of existing personnel to perform other essential job duties.

THE FUTURE

One of the most significant internal productivity improvements made in city clerk departments has been in the field of automated records management. Due to the many types of public records and documents that must be kept on file, the number of years they must be maintained, and the fact that both the city staff and public desire immediate access to this material, it was only natural that city clerks would automate this aspect of their operations. The automation of the preparation, storage, and retrieval of these records and documents has enabled city clerks to greatly improve the quality and timeliness of their services to citizens as well as other municipal departments. This department will be one of the first to have personal computers at each workstation, linked together via a local area network to a common database. For these reasons, the employees in this department are among the first municipal workers to be computer-literate. These automated records management practices have reduced the number of "hard" files and records that must be maintained and, at the same time, have significantly reduced the traditional file cabinet storage requirements of this department. Since the public has access to many of these documents, computer security has taken on an increased importance to safeguard against the inadvertent destruction of these databases.

The most important external productivity trends include the number of technical resources available to this field in the private marketplace, an increased awareness of the importance of personal networking and resource sharing, and the greater proliferation of professional training and certification programs. A growing number of private consultants and companies provide a variety of services to assist city clerks to improve their operations. This has led to the increased need for personal networking between city clerks to learn about these new technologies, products, and services. Since many of their colleagues have used these resources, valuable insight can be gained on the success of these applications in similar departments. Because of the increasing complexity in this field, and the need for professional development, many educational and certification programs are now available from state governments, educational institutions, and professional associations. These programs have increased the level of competency in this field. These professional designations are also helpful when hiring or electing new city clerks.

Most importantly, the role of the city clerk has increased significantly over the years. While the types of functions and programs provided by a local government may vary from community to community, every municipality has a city clerk. Many city clerks also perform the same basic types of services, regardless of the size of a community or its location. The city clerk, in performing his or her role as municipal archivist and official repository of public records and documents, must provide all members of the public with equal access to this information. For this reason, the person holding this position must exhibit the utmost integrity, honesty, and fairness in their dealings with citizens. All citizen requests for public information must be responded to in a timely and accurate fashion. The many productivity improvements examined in this chapter represent ways for city clerks to improve the quality of the services they provide to the public. The use of modern office technologies and professional certification programs have facilitated these productivity trends.

5

LEGAL

Without exception, every community has a chief legal counsel to advise the city council, boards and commissions, and department managers on municipal legal issues. In most cities this position is called city attorney, although other titles such as legal counsel and corporation counsel are used in communities in different parts of the country. While informal verbal legal opinions may be provided on-the-spot at public meetings, all formal legal opinions are always provided in writing. It is common for city attorneys to routinely provide legal opinions at the request of the mayor, city council members, the city manager, and department managers. Department managers usually must request these opinions through their city manager. The opinions of the city attorney are advisory in nature to the governing body. Although usually followed, a governing body does not have to abide by these legal opinions. Legal opinions are frequently requested by the staff on a number of different operational matters. Almost without exception, these opinions are followed by the city manager and his or her department managers. The city attorney, like the city manager, is usually appointed and serves at the pleasure of the governing body. Because the city attorney's duties are strictly limited to legal matters, this job is not as politically vulnerable as a city manager's position. Hence, city attorneys usually have a longer employment tenure than city managers.

While smaller communities may contract for legal services from private attorneys, these attorneys almost without exception are specialists in municipal law. Private attorneys specializing in this field typically have several clients, usually consisting of a number of smaller cities and special districts. The growing trend in medium-sized communities is to hire full-time municipal attorneys. All larger cities have full-time attorneys. Generally, the greater the population of a municipality, the larger the size of its legal staff. Also, while contract municipal attorneys tend to be generalists in their field, larger cities have a number of members on their legal staff that specialize in different areas of municipal law. For this reason, smaller communities usually contract with private attorneys for many specialized legal services. Because of the increasing number of claims and lawsuits filed against communities, there is a trend for all cities to contract out their litigation and other specialized legal services to private attorneys. Small- and medium-sized communities usually always contract out their specialized legal services, such as those involving litigation, since one case could consume a staff attorney's time for several months.

Because of the likelihood of litigation against a city's adopted legislation and policies, the city manager, as well as most department managers, always forward copies of proposed policies and laws to the city attorney for review and approval before they are formally submitted to the governing body for its consideration. While the management staff may draft simple policies and legislation, complex matters are routinely referred to the city attorney for preparation by the legal staff. They are then reviewed and approved by department managers to ensure that they serve their intended purpose. The city attorney performs this role because this position is entrusted with the duty of limiting a municipality's public liability exposure. In this capacity, all leases, contracts, and agreements, regardless of their nature, now have special legal clauses that limit a city's exposure to public liability. As a further hedge against liability exposure, many cities have liability insurance policies to pay for settlements over a certain monetary threshold. One of the major trends in recent years is to settle individual lawsuits before they go to court, since the costs of litigation are so expensive. Increasingly, the decision as to whether or not to settle a claim or lawsuit against a city has become a financial decision rather than a legal one. Unfortunately, the dollars saved through out-of-court settlements have come to mean more than the legal merits of these cases.

One of the most rapidly evolving specialties in municipal government is safety and risk management services. While this function may be located in the personnel office in some cities, many communities are placing this program in their legal department. This is due to the close working relationship between the safety and risk manager and the duties performed by the city attorney relative to limiting a city's liability exposure. The person holding this position usually investigates all claims filed against a community and makes recommendations to the legal staff for their settlement. Claims with smaller monetary settlements are usually settled administratively, while claims requiring larger monetary settlements require governing body approval. In this regard, safety and risk managers and the legal staff have the same goal of limiting a city's liability exposure and settling claims in the most cost-effective manner. Safety and risk managers also attempt to reduce a city's liability exposure through formal employee safety and municipal risk-reduction programs. The larger the city the more likely it is to have a full-time safety and risk manager. Smaller communities usually contract out this service to private consultants specializing in this field.

The major programs provided by the legal department are described in Figure 5.1. Although the city attorney is appointed directly by the city council,

Figure 5.1
Legal Major Programs

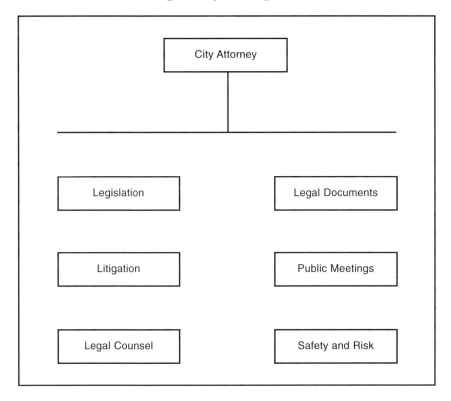

he or she is a regular department manager and is always considered a valuable member of a city's top management staff.

DESCRIPTION OF PROGRAMS

Legislation. The members of the governing body may adopt or enact their own legislation, subject to the requirements and limitations set forth in local charters and the state law. Local legislation is typically passed in the form of approved resolutions and ordinances. An ordinance is usually used to enact laws, mandates, or permanent rules. Resolutions, on the other hand, are used to approve ministerial acts and to set forth policy direction. If the local and state laws do not provide for a distinction between the two, they may be used interchangeably.

Before ordinances and resolutions are placed on the agenda for consideration by the governing body, they are usually prepared by the legal staff of the municipality. In some cases, department managers draft such legislation, subject to the review and approval of the legal staff. In all cases, proposed ordinances and resolutions are approved in advance by the city attorney before being placed on the agenda for consideration by the elected officials. State law sets forth the manner in which all legislation is adopted (e.g., public hearings, public notices, voting procedures, public readings). If legislation is adopted that does not follow these legal guidelines, it may be declared invalid and unenforceable. It should be kept in mind that the legal staff is only advisory to the governing body, and their advice may not always be followed.

Also, it is not uncommon for a governing body to "fine tune" proposed legislation before it is formally adopted. Whatever legislation is finally adopted must be defended by the legal staff if court action is brought against the municipality.

Litigation. The legal staff represents the municipality against all lawsuits and claims filed against the city, its departments, or any of its public officials — elected or appointed. While most legal cases are handled in-house by the existing legal staff, some cases requiring specialized legal expertise may be assigned to private-sector lawyers when it is deemed to be in the best interest of the city. It is also not uncommon to assign cases that require a great amount of time to private attorneys, usually on an hourly fee basis. Claims are also frequently filed against a city for alleged or actual injuries or damages sustained by individuals, as well as their real and personal property. In these cases, the legal staff works closely with a municipality's safety and risk management experts prior to settling these claims.

All lawsuits and claims are reviewed by the legal staff before making a final settlement. In most cities, the legal department can settle claims on their own below a financial limit previously approved by the governing body. All proposed settlements in excess of this amount must receive the approval of the elected officials. Closed sessions are held to discuss the details of these cases, but the final vote to settle a case must be done in the public meeting.

Legal Counsel. One of the city attorney's basic duties is to serve as the in-house counsel to the governing body, boards and commissions, city manager, and department managers. Verbal and written legal opinions are given, usually upon request, to answer legal questions that may arise in relation to the duties and responsibilities of these public officials.

The city attorney is appointed by the governing body, and like the city manager serves at their pleasure. In this capacity, he or she attends all meetings of the governing body and other boards and commissions as designated by the charter, or by local custom and practice. The role of the legal counsel is to attempt to facilitate the actions and policies of the governing body. On occasion, the city attorney may advise the governing body that a proposed law, regulation, or policy is questionable, if not illegal. All legal opinions provided by the corporation counsel are advisory in nature. As such, they do not have to be followed at all times by the governing body. They are usually always followed, however, by the city's management staff. It is not unusual for the city attorney or other member of the legal staff to attend board and commission meetings upon request.

Department managers typically request legal opinions through the city manager. Other employees may request legal options through their chain of command. The advice of the corporation counsel is usually sought before or during the decisionmaking process—prior to officially adopting resolutions, ordinances, and other legal documents.

Legal Documents. The municipal legal staff prepares and reviews all city-related legal documents prior to their consideration and adoption by the governing body. These legal documents include, but are not limited to, leases, contracts, franchise agreements, ordinances, and resolutions.

In many states, the use of the initiative and referendum are alternative ways to enact ordinances and laws. An initiative authorizes a specific number of voters to propose changes to existing ordinances and laws which are then either accepted or rejected by the electorate. An affirmative vote of the electorate on such measures is binding upon the governing body. A referendum allows voters to consider and either accept or reject proposals set forth by the governing body. These ballot measures are only advisory upon the governing body. Municipalities are empowered by their state constitution to adopt their own laws. A legal document for a purpose beyond the scope or legal authority of the local government is not valid. All legal documents involving the expenditure of public funds must have a budget appropriation authorizing the expenditure of these funds.

All legal documents, once approved, are filed with the city clerk for public inspection and future reference. The public may purchase copies of all legal documents for a small fee, usually to cover the cost of duplication. This fee may be adjusted by the governing body as expenses increase.

Public Meetings. The city attorney attends all meetings of the legislative body, and other board and commission meetings as designated by the municipal charter or by local custom and practice. The city attorney also may be required to attend the meetings of other legal entities created by the governing body, such as a redevelopment agency or economic development corporation. The legal staff may also be called upon to attend city council committee meetings when legal expertise is needed for an item on their agenda. A governing body also holds periodic study sessions in which important topics or proposed programs are discussed. The city attorney may be called upon from time to time to attend these meetings.

At the meetings of the legislative body, the role of the city attorney is to answer any questions of a legal nature that may arise during the meeting. The attorney may also be asked on occasion to render legal opinions on potential conflicts of interest prior to taking a vote on a particular agenda item. For example, if a spouse of a member of the governing body works for a private company with a proposed contract for services with the city, there may be a conflict of interest. The city attorney would be called upon to render a legal opinion in such a situation. Sometimes the governing body designates the city attorney as their parliamentarian. In this capacity, he or she may be called upon to answer questions concerning Robert's Rules of Order.

The duty of the city attorney to attend public meetings is important and appropriate, since a city's legal staff prepares all resolutions, ordinances, and other legal documents for the governing body's consideration.

Safety and Risk. The safety and risk management function in municipalities has increased in importance in recent years, particularly with the erosion of the rights protecting cities under the doctrine of sovereign immunity. Many state laws and court decisions over the years have eroded and restricted these rights.

Due to the litigious nature of society, the high financial exposure of public liability lawsuits, and the fact that cities are frequently perceived as a "deep-pocket," many legal departments are taking steps to limit the liability exposure of their public agencies. Common steps include reviewing existing and proposed written policies and procedures, seeking legal counsel before making selected decisions, safety awareness and risk reduction training, ensuring the equal rights of employees and citizens, and using outside experts to update policies and procedures in technical areas where there is a high degree of liability exposure. When public officials perform ministerial duties they may be personally liable for the injury or damage caused to others by their incompetency or mistakes. When public officials make discretionary decisions, however, they are usually immune from personal liability unless corruption, malice, or willful neglect can be proven.

In recent years, states have been adopting laws to limit the liability of municipal public officials. Examples of these mandates include laws governing limited immunity, monetary ceilings on public liability claims, limiting settlements to compensatory damages, and precluding settlements for punitive damages. The role of the legal staff has increased in recent years as this function has expanded in importance.

PRODUCTIVITY TRENDS

Internal productivity trends in this department, because of already limited staffing, have focused on ways to reduce liability as well as costs in other areas of municipal government. Using members of the legal staff to assist management in labor negotiations, efforts to limit a community's public liability exposure, employee safety and risk management programs, and the early settlement of claims and lawsuits to avoid expensive litigation are all examples of this trend. Many governing bodies now require that a "price tag" be placed on proposed laws before they are considered for implementation. This has helped elected officials to make more informed decisions. The legal staff may work with the finance director or other department managers on this task, depending upon the nature of the legislation being proposed. A greater number of laws now have due process provisions to enable citizens to appeal the decisions of code enforcement and inspection personnel. This has also helped to reduce the number of lawsuits and claims filed against a municipality. All of these efforts have been facilitated by the use of personal computers, specially designed legal software, and advanced training in the many complex areas of municipal law.

Due to limited staffing, many departments are now contracting out specialized legal work to private attorneys. Other departments are contracting out selected legal services to avoid increasing the size of their existing legal staffs. Many online legal services are available with the use of personal computers, specialized software packages, and inexpensive telephone modems. Legal research can now be performed without having to spend many hours in local law libraries. A model ordinance service is also available to review those laws adopted in other communities. These laws can then be adapted and adopted to fit the unique legal needs of a municipality. The number of private sector legal resources available to cities has increased dramatically in recent years, making a knowledge of these resources essential to operate a state-of-the-art legal department. City attorneys have shared information about these new services through local networking opportunities as well as programs provided by their national professional associations. The effort to reduce public liability has led to a host of special contract clauses and other legal safeguards to protect a community against lawsuits.

Table 5.1 highlights these, and other, legal department productivity trends. This department has traditionally provided internal staff services, but its external role has increased in importance in recent years as the legal staff continues its ongoing efforts to protect their municipal government from potential legal costs arising from public liability issues.

Internal

Code Enforcement. Many municipal governments have taken an aggressive stance towards code enforcement. Comprehensive codes and standards frequently exist in the areas of building, health, housing, planning, and zoning. More specialized codes regulate landscaping, signage, parking, outdoor storage, occupancy limitations and, increasingly, acceptable levels of property maintenance. These codes ensure the public safety and welfare of a community by requiring orderly development, preventing neighborhood deterioration, and

Table 5.1
Legal Productivity Trends

Internal	*External*
Code Enforcement	Claims Administration
Computer Usage and Legal Services	Contract Computer Legal Services
Conflict-of-Interest Issues	Contract Legal Services
Cost of Municipal Mandates	Knowledge of Legal Resources
Cross-Training of Staff	Legal Internships
Labor Relations and Personnel Services	Model Ordinance Services
Liability Reduction Programs	Networking and Resource Sharing
Records Management	Outside Legal Services
Safety and Risk Management	Professional Certifications
Settlement of Lawsuits	Role of Legal Staff
Specialized Legal Training	

safeguarding life and property. The staff must ensure that these codes are legal, enforced in a uniform manner, that proper appeals processes exist for violators, and that penalties are standardized among the various codes adopted for enforcement. Department personnel who prepare these codes now routinely have them reviewed by the legal staff for these reasons.

Computer Usage and Legal Services. As legal staffs become more computer literate, and the costs of microcomputer systems decrease, the use of smaller personal computers has become an efficient way to perform routine administrative, clerical, and technical tasks such as word processing, the preparation and management of documents, information storage and retrieval, records management, and access to regional and national legal databases. Laptop computers enable lawyers to work at home and while attending conferences. These databases can be downloaded either directly from a laptop computer or via computer modem to the office microcomputer for storage or to receive a hard copy. More sophisticated and user-friendly graphics software is also being used to prepare court exhibits. Inexpensive office networking systems are also available to interconnect all microcomputers within a department. This reduces software costs and facilitates the development of legal databases. The advent of more sophisticated, inexpensive, and user-friendly software has facilitated this trend.

Conflict-of-Interest Issues. Many states and cities have mandated strict conflict-of-interest laws and codes. These regulations typically require the disclosure of information to the public and standards for preventing dishonesty by public officials—both elected and appointed. When one of these rules is not clear, it is increasingly common for public officials to consult with or seek a legal opinion from the legal staff before voting on an issue. In the case of management personnel, advice is frequently sought before making a recommendation for consideration by the governing body when a possible conflict-of-interest may exist. Severe penalties exist for violating these statutes, including the invalidation of public contracts, the possible removal of public officials from their office, as well as criminal prosecution. Public officials in particular and citizens in general are increasingly sensitive to ensuring the integrity and honesty of their local government and its operations.

Cost of Municipal Mandates. Increasingly, because of limited revenues and tight budgets, city attorneys are noting the cost of decisions for items they place on agendas for consideration by their governing bodies. Elected officials should be made aware of the cost of their decisions and the legislation they adopt. The downside of this trend is that decisions are increasingly being made for financial reasons, rather than on actual need or merit of a new law or program. Increasingly, legislation may not be adopted if its costs exceed the expected revenues. Also, public officials want to be made aware of the operational cost associated with the enforcement of these proposed legislative mandates. This precaution has reduced the number of new mandates in municipal governments.

Cross-Training of Staff. In order to save scarce budget dollars, city attorneys are cross-training their personnel to perform a variety of different legal tasks. Rather than relying on a staff person or persons to perform one type of a service, cross-training permits a greater utilization of existing personnel to perform a variety of legal-related tasks and services. The availability of computer networks, access to legal databases, and common officewide databases for information storage and retrieval have assisted in the cross-training of professional and secretarial personnel. Existing labor agreements may limit or restrict the use of cross-training practices, especially at the secretarial and clerical level if more than one union represents these municipal employees.

Labor Relations and Personnel Services. Legal staffs are increasingly providing valuable counsel to local government policymakers, chief executives, and personnel directors on labor relations and personnel matters. Personnel and labor relations laws and issues are becoming more numerous and complex. The number of employee grievances, personnel-related lawsuits, and arbitration hearings are increasing at an exponential rate. Elected officials, city managers, and personnel directors no longer make these decisions in a vacuum due to the potential exposure of time and expense that may result from making the wrong decision in a particular case. The trend is to have trained in-house legal expertise in labor relations and personnel available to assist policymakers and top management when making labor relations and personnel decisions.

Smaller communities may contract with qualified private attorneys for these services. Larger cities usually have one or more staff attorneys with expertise in these areas.

Liability Reduction Programs. Due to the litigiousness of our society many municipal contracts, lease and franchise agreements, licenses and permits, and proposed legislation are now likely to be reviewed with the goal of limiting the liability exposure of public agencies. The use of binding arbitration, conflict resolution specialists, special liability insurance requirements, and hold-harmless provisions are now commonplace. Many cities have formalized employee safety and risk reduction policies and programs that require a review of proposed legislation and programs prior to their being considered by a governing body for implementation. Public officials are increasingly cautious when allowing private groups the use of public property. They want to ensure that adequate safeguards exist to protect their municipal government and its taxpayers from exposure to public liability.

Records Management. Many legal records and documents must frequently be kept for a number of years. Many legal departments, in order to save scarce office space, have converted their "hard copy" records to microfilm, microfiche, and or computer database storage. This enhances records management and information retrieval. In addition to saving money, this also improves the quality of legal services to the elected officials and city staff. An example of this new technology is OCR (optical character recognition), a process in which documents are scanned, stored, and retrieved on a computer database for future reference. The CD-ROMs are now being used for storage and retrieval systems, as well as to file and save entire legal documents, because of their inherently large storage capacity. If the legal and city clerk departments are a part of the same computer network, the city clerk may be able to print a hard copy of a legal document merely by accessing it directly from files stored on the computer database.

This type of computer networking reduces duplicating costs and provides real-time access to legal documents. It also speeds up the preparation of city council agendas.

Safety and Risk Management. The increased attention by public officials to reduce public liability claims has given rise to the need for personnel with expertise in the rapidly evolving field of employee safety and risk management. These personnel are frequently called safety or risk managers. While they are usually not trained as lawyers, they may be assigned to the legal department because of their functional and operational responsibilities. They typically investigate claims and make recommendations to the legal staff on their settlement. Safety and risk managers also establish ongoing employee safety and municipal risk-reduction programs.

Smaller cities may use outside management and legal consultants to perform this function. Larger cities are more likely to employ full-time trained experts in this field.

Settlement of Lawsuits. Two factors have led to a surge in the number of out of court settlements in lawsuits against municipalities: the high cost of litigation and the unpredictability of jury verdicts. In some cases, an out of court settlement costs less than the projected expenses to litigate a particular case. In other cases, the nature of the lawsuit may result in an excessive jury award. Chief legal officers are increasingly recommending out of court settlements to their governing bodies based on financial factors, rather than the actual legal merits of a particular lawsuit. These decisions are so numerous that many settlements bear no relationship to the actual guilt or innocence on the part of the municipality or its employees. It is important for public officials and citizens to realize that lawsuits are frequently settled for financial reasons rather than legal considerations.

Specialized Legal Training. The municipal law field is becoming increasingly complex and specialized. It is now common to budget funds for training in order to develop staff expertise in new technical legal areas such as environmental and health laws, the Americans with Disabilities Act, the Family and Medical Leave Act, state workers' compensation laws, risk management, and municipal growth management initiatives, to name a few. Because of the increasing number of laws and regulations in these fields—especially those mandated by higher levels of government—specialized legal training is necessary to safeguard a public entity from potentially costly and time-consuming litigation. National and statewide professional associations frequently provide up-to-date legal training in these as well as other specialized and expanding areas of municipal law.

External

Claims Administration. Due to escalating insurance premium costs during the past decade, many municipalities are now self-insured for their monetary exposure to public liability. In the past, when insurance coverage was commonplace, claims against a city would be referred to its insurance carrier for resolution. These claims are now referred to the legal department for disposition. This trend has given rise to the need for more specialized personnel such as safety and risk managers and municipal attorneys trained in this field. These personnel usually administer and investigate claims, negotiate settlements, and make recommendations for final disposition of claims against a municipality. It is not unusual for claims below a certain monetary threshold (e.g., $3,000 to $5,000) to be settled administratively. The settlement of larger claims, however, requires approval of the governing body. The larger the city, the more likely it is to have full-time expertise in this specialized field.

Contract Computer Legal Services. In recent years, with the advent of more sophisticated, user-friendly, and less expensive computer systems, many computer software packages have been developed to better serve the needs of municipal legal departments. Examples of these state-of-the-art program applications include legal information centers, legal databases, case management, and litigation support services. These online computer services provide immediate access to higher court decisions, appellate court opinions, state statutes, and state regulations. Cases, abstracts, and transcripts—both full and condensed versions—are now available real-time via inexpensive computer modems. These modems are now standard equipment with most state-of-the-art computer systems. Many of these services are now available on CD-ROM for a modest monthly fee. Computer networking is also available, complete with e-mail and direct access to the latest opinions in many specialized areas of the law—including municipal law. A recent publication is devoted exclusively to the field of law office computing, related legal software applications, and various online services.

Contract Legal Services. Many departments are increasingly contracting selected legal services to the private sector. Unique and specialized legal opinions, the defense of unusual public liability lawsuits, sensitive personnel-related cases, the preparation of complex leases and franchise agreements, and other specialized services that may not be available from the existing legal staff are examples of this trend. Time constraints and the workload of the existing legal staff may also warrant using private attorneys. Outside legal counsel may also be used for politically sensitive cases such as those involving ethics violations, employee terminations, sexual harassment, and lawsuits against a municipality by local taxpayers or community groups. Due to the high cost of litigation, many lawsuits are settled out of court to reduce anticipated legal expenses associated with the defense of a particular case. It should be noted however that this contracting-out may not always reduce costs.

Knowledge of Legal Resources. Many private sector consulting companies now provide a number of different hardware systems, software applications, and online information services in the municipal law field. Also, public nonprofit professional associations assess these systems, applications, and services at their conferences and in their trade journals. Having a working knowledge of these private and nonprofit sector resources is essential, especially in smaller legal departments with limited budgets, staff expertise, and technical resources. State regulatory agencies and state-wide professional associations also provide valuable information on the use of new computer hardware and software technologies. As more of these services become available in the marketplace, it is essential to have a thorough knowledge of the most cost-effective systems available.

In larger cities, chief legal officers may wish to hire specialized consultants in this field before making decisions on which hardware systems, software applications, and online services to purchase. The marketplace is changing so quickly that a system only a few years old may now be obsolete.

Legal Internships. Some legal departments are using legal interns from local law schools on a part-time basis to assist the regular staff in performing legal duties. This trend not only provides valuable legal training to law students who may wish to enter the field of municipal law, but also assists the full time staff with some of the more routine duties associated with municipal legal matters. Legal interns typically receive an hourly wage or minimum salary and do not receive fringe benefits. Legal interns seeking a general exposure to municipal law typically work in smaller communities. Legal interns wishing to work in more specialized areas of municipal law usually seek internships in larger cities. Existing labor agreement may govern the use of these internship arrangements.

Model Ordinance Services. The National Institute of Municipal Law Officers (NIMLO) provides a Model Ordinance Service to municipalities throughout the nation. These model ordinances not only cover the traditional subjects of local legislation, but also include new legal topics such as juvenile curfews, aggressive panhandling, cable television and fiber optics franchise agreements, and the American with Disabilities Act (ADA), to name a few. This service also includes supporting legal analyses and case law citations for each of these model ordinances. The case law citations cover both state and federal court decisions that relate to these ordinances. This database is also available in computer disk form, allowing cities to adapt these ordinances for their own use without having to spend many hours of legal research. This service not only saves valuable time but reduces the likelihood of successful litigation on newly adopted municipal laws. This service will soon be available in CD-ROM format to facilitate model ordinance searches at a reduced cost.

Networking and Resource Sharing. Many legal departments throughout the nation are now linked electronically to regional, statewide, and national legal databases. Smaller regional databases are being linked together with new software in order to create larger and more sophisticated legal databases. This is being done to assist attorneys in their legal research to help them make more informed legal decisions and opinions to better serve the public. This trend is being facilitated by more sophisticated computer hardware and software, larger amounts of computer storage, and lower processing costs. Many private online computer services are also available that provide access to specialized legal databases. In this regard, law departments are on the cutting-edge of the evolving national "information superhighway."

Outside Legal Services. The use of private attorneys to provide traditional municipal legal services is becoming more commonplace. Savings are realized because these private attorneys do not receive fringe benefits and because their services can be used only when needed. Such services are typically used when specialized legal expertise is required, or when the existing staff time is not available to work on either complex or time-consuming legal issues. Examples of these services include lengthy court cases, specialized labor negotiations, the preparation of complex contracts and franchise agreements, and the settlement of unique claims and lawsuits against a municipality. Smaller cities are more likely to contract for specialized legal services because of the minimal size of their professional legal staffs.

Professional Certifications. Some states, professional associations and educational institutions are providing structured programs leading to professional designations and certifications in the field of municipal law. This trend has helped to increase the level of competency in this field, as well as set standards when seeking new personnel to fill professional vacancies. For example, NIMLO is establishing a Municipal Fellows Certification Program to provide formal recognition for the experience and expertise of qualified municipal attorneys.

Role of the Legal Staff. The traditional role of the legal staff has been to advise the city's governing body, city manager, and department managers on legal matters. All proposed legislation is usually reviewed by the legal staff before being forwarded to the city council for consideration. Increasingly, the city manager and department managers are seeking legal advice on proposed programs and resolutions to issues before presenting them to the governing body for their consideration. The chief legal officer and his or her staff are also more active in dealing with the community, such as when settling citizen claims against the municipality, negotiating insurance and other legal requirements with community groups, and answering taxpayer questions on existing and proposed pieces of legislation, programs, and services. With the increased emphasis on code enforcement, the legal staff is frequently called upon to ensure that all codes are enforced uniformly. The external role of the legal department has become increasingly important and time-consuming in recent years.

THE FUTURE

The most popular internal productivity trends include those programs that have the goal of either cost reduction or cost avoidance. Cost reduction programs include preparing legislation that includes the cost of its implementation. Once these operational costs are known, it may be possible to alter proposed legislation to reduce these expenses. Negotiations for the early settlement of claims and lawsuits helps to reduce litigation expenses. Litigation costs for time-consuming and complex jury trials are prohibitive, even if these are contracted out to private attorneys. When municipal lawyers review proposed legislation, contracts, agreements, and other legal documents to reduce a city's public liability exposure, they help reduce the cost of government. Even though this figure is not quantifiable, it holds down the number of liability suits against a community. Employee safety and risk management initiatives also help a city government hold down its internal operating costs. The city council, city manager, and department managers are increasingly relying on the services of the legal department in these important areas.

One of the most dramatic external productivity trends has been the proliferation of private sector services available in the municipal legal marketplace. The use of online computer legal services illustrates this trend. These programs provide real-time access to higher court decisions, appellate court opinions, state statutes, as well as other legal services. Several of these services are even available nationally. The popularity of these services has led to the need for personal computers with specialized software applications to access these legal programs. This has facilitated the need for city attorneys to network with their colleagues and share information about these programs and services. The sophistication of these services has increased so dramatically in recent years that a system only a few years old may now be obsolete. Advanced computers with expanded memory capabilities have facilitated the number of these online services. The city attorney may not be a computer expert, but he or she can survey their peers to find the best programs available and then adapt these services in their own legal departments.

The use of contract legal services from private attorneys has increased dramatically in a number of different legal areas for several valid reasons. Legal departments in small- and medium-sized communities seek these services out of necessity due to the small size of their professional staffs. Also, infrequently needed or highly specialized legal expertise may not be available in smaller communities. Even in larger cities, many time-consuming and or complex legal issues may be beyond the expertise of the in-house legal staff or may require so much time to perform that other legal work may suffer. Many private attorneys now provide such specialized services as labor relations, redevelopment, condemnation, franchise agreements, and environmental law. Some private attorneys are sole practitioners in the field of municipal legal services, providing contract legal services to small communities that do not want to finance their own full-time legal department. The use of private attorneys to perform public legal work is becoming common for these reasons.

FINANCE

The traditional duties performed by the finance department have been greatly expanded in recent years in the areas of budgeting and financial management. Citizens are demanding more services but do not want to pay additional taxes. In response to this reality, elected officials are making an all-out effort to hold down budget expenses and property taxes. Further, the number of federal and state grant programs for cities, as well as their funding levels, have been significantly reduced over the past decade. Both elected and appointed officials face a difficult dilemma—how to maintain existing service levels without raising taxes. As inflation and salary increases eat away at municipal budgets, it is an extremely tedious task to maintain services without raising some revenue sources. A host of innovative financial practices and budgeting techniques have evolved to cope with these problems. City managers and department managers are told by elected officials to keep their costs down and, at the same time, not to reduce services. Finance directors are caught in the middle of this issue. Improved budgeting and financial management practices have evolved in response to these political and financial pressures.

The operations of the finance department have a dramatic impact on all other municipal departments. This department collects revenues and controls expenditures, recommends debt and manages debt limits, assesses taxes and collects them from citizens, manages existing revenues and seeks out new revenue sources, and reports and manages expenditures. Finance directors also control purchasing practices to ensure the competitiveness and integrity of the public bidding process. At the same time, department managers want to award contracts based on professional qualifications and experience rather than costs. The data processing function has been refined to report budget appropriations as well as to warn department managers of pending budget problems. This dual role of optimizer of revenues and controller of expenditures has dramatically enhanced the importance of the finance department as an integral function of local government. Finance directors are charged with the dual responsibilities of collecting revenues from existing sources and holding down municipal

116

expenses. For this reason, finance directors and their staffs receive increasing pressure from all sides—from elected officials wanting to maintain services and lower taxes to department managers wanting additional revenues to maintain services. Finance directors have responded creatively to this challenge.

New innovative operational practices have emerged to satisfy these difficult financial and budgetary demands. To enhance revenues, the finance director now adjusts assessments more frequently when improvements are made to property, attempts to collect all revenues when they are due, vigorously pursues citizens to collect revenues from past due accounts, and invests municipal funds to seek the highest rate of return consistent with sound investment principles. To improve budgeting practices, department managers are being asked to prepare program budgets to equate their expenditures with public services, and to develop performance measurements to show the productivity of their programs. Increasingly, the revenues generated by departments are compared to their expenses, showing the net general fund requirements of all departments. To close this gap, new user fees and charges are being assessed and efforts are being made to periodically adjust existing service charges to reflect the cost of doing business. Budget directives now require that available revenues be calculated before determining departmental expenditure levels for the coming year. In the past, departmental expenditure levels were determined first, then taxes were adjusted to meet these spending requirements. This practice is no longer politically acceptable.

The area of revenue management, out of necessity, has received a great deal of attention by finance directors. It is becoming a common practice to inventory all municipal revenues sources, compare user fees and service charges to those charges imposed by other similar communities, and to make adjustments to ensure the competitiveness of a city's fee structure. The criteria used for determining user fees have become more sophisticated. Indirect costs and overhead charges are being included in user fee formulas to truly make selected services cost-covering. Finance directors are also comparing their internal collection practices with those of other communities with the goal of streamlining their collection procedures as well as reducing their costs. Elected officials are adopting numerous financial policies to ensure the long-term financial health of their governments. These policies include municipal debt ceiling limits, restrictions on long-term borrowing, minimum reserve requirements, annual adjustments to user fees and service charges, capital project planning requirements, and requiring long-term revenue and expenditures projections to warn of impending gaps between municipal revenues and departmental expenditures. Enterprise funds are also being established to treat certain public services as profit centers. Under this concept, user fees are adjusted annually to make these services totally cost-covering.

Figure 6.1 illustrates the eight major programs usually performed by the typical finance department. In some areas of the country certain functions

Figure 6.1
Finance Major Programs

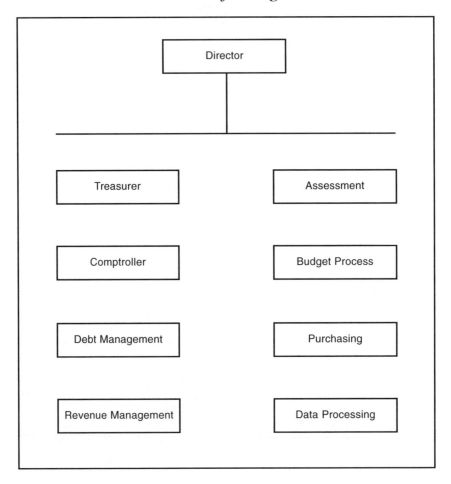

such as property assessments and tax collections are performed by counties. Also, it should be kept in mind that state laws regulate many aspects of municipal finance, and these regulations may vary greatly from state to state.

DESCRIPTION OF PROGRAMS

Treasurer. The treasurer collects all property taxes, special assessments, utility bills, user fees and charges, and other taxes and revenues due to the city. He or she also administers delinquent property tax sales, maintains custody of all city funds, plans the cash flow, and disburses city funds for the payments of bills owed by the municipality. One of the key roles of the treasurer is to invest available funds to ensure their greatest possible return to the city. A good treasurer also always attempts to minimize debt expenses and financial service costs. A sound treasury management system is based on bringing in revenues as quickly as possible and postponing expenditures, consistent with receiving discounts on payments when available.

Idle funds—those not needed for immediate cash flow purposes—are invested to secure the maximum rate of return for the taxpayers. Idle funds are typically those funds not needed to pay operating costs within a 30-day period. The treasurer usually checks with several banks for the best available "financial package"—including checking, borrowing, and investment services. To the extent possible, and consistent with a competitive rate of return on investments, it is not unusual to favor local banks whenever possible. If higher rates of return are available from other banks, however, it is in the best interest of taxpayers to place municipal funds in these financial institutions.

The treasurer serves as the official custodian of the city's general fund— where all local taxes, assessments, utility payments, user fees and charges, and other locally generated revenues are deposited.

Comptroller. The municipal comptroller is in charge of the division of accounts. In this capacity he or she preaudits all purchase orders, receipts, and disbursements; prepares the employee payroll, prepares and issues checks, sometimes called warrants; maintains the general accounting records of the city; and maintains and supervises all cost accounts. While individual departments collect revenues for their respective fees and user charges, the comptroller is responsible for the collection of all property and other tax bills, special assessments, utility, and other service charges not collected at the departmental level.

The comptroller also maintains up-to-date inventory records of all municipal property. While some cities in some states do not maintain a municipal property inventory, many states require that this inventory be maintained to show the estimated value of all municipal-owned real estate and improvements. In some cities, the property tax billing function is delegated, typically by city charter, to a tax collector. In some states, counties perform the property tax billing function for municipalities within their boundaries, charging each city a small percentage of the revenues collected.

In most small- and medium-sized communities the treasurer and comptroller function rests with the same person, typically the finance director.

Debt Management. This activity of municipal finance deals with the acquisition and use of borrowed money. There are two types of debt obligations—short-term and long-term. Short-term debt includes borrowing funds to cover a shortage of money, financing items of equipment under lease or purchase agreements, and borrowing funds in anticipation of future revenues.

The later category of borrowing involves the use tax anticipation notes (TANs). Obviously, short-term loans obtained against future revenues should never exceed the amount of the expected revenues.

Long-term debt, used to generate funds for large capital project, falls into one of two categories—general obligation bonds and revenue bonds. General obligation bonds are backed by the "full faith and credit" of the municipality. It is common when financing smaller projects to issue bond anticipation notes (BANs) until enough debt is incurred to issue general obligation bonds. Revenue bonds, on the other hand, are repaid by the revenues generated from a particular municipal project. These revenues are collected from user fees and charges paid by customers and users. Typical local government projects that generate revenues are sewer treatment and water purification plants.

Interest rates are lowest on general obligation bonds since their payment is assured by the city government. Interest rates are slightly higher on revenue bonds since they are dependent upon a future revenue stream. The dependency on a future revenue stream has an element of risk since natural or manmade emergencies and or disasters may interrupt this income stream. For this reason, general obligation bonds have a lower default rate and revenue bonds have a higher default rate. Hence, the slight difference in interest rates between these bonds.

Managing debt involves those activities associated with borrowing, monitoring, and repaying funds received using the above debt instruments.

Revenue Management. This function includes the inventorying of all revenue sources, estimating annual revenues from each source, making periodic billings and receiving collections, accounting for all revenues received, monitoring their usage, and ensuring that all revenues are spent according to a city's annual financial plan. There are nonrestricted and restricted revenue sources.

State, federal, and other grants are usually legally earmarked for specific purposes. Hence, the use of these funds is restricted. Nonrestricted revenues are deposited into a municipality's general fund. The general fund includes all locally generated taxes and user service fees. Property taxes, sales taxes, and user fees comprise the largest share of general fund revenues. These funds are used to finance the general operations of a municipal government. Nonrestricted or discretionary funds are under the direct control of the governing body, while restricted or nondiscretionary funds must be allocated for those programs for which they are legally designated.

It is not uncommon to make frequent adjustments to user fees and charges to make them reflect the cost of doing business. Revenue surveys are also used to make sure that local user fees are in line with the charges made by neighboring communities. Due to the public's aversion to increased taxation, the proper management of existing revenues is an increasingly important function of municipal finance.

Assessment. Property taxes are the major source of revenue of all municipalities—albeit the most unpopular one. The primary base of this tax is the value of real property (i.e., land and improvements) and personal property (e.g. vehicles, equipment, and fixtures). Property is inventoried and assessed in all municipalities. This process provides a definitive tax base and stable revenue source for local governments.

The assessor typically makes studies of property values for assessment purposes, prepares and maintains property maps and records, prepares assessments for all properties (real and personal), and establishes the annual assessment rolls upon which tax rates are applied. The assessor also administers special assessments for selected improvements to public property (e.g., parks, utilities, sidewalks, and in some cases schools). All other local taxes use a predetermined collection rate, and the amount collected varies according to the tax base. The three major variables used to determine property taxes include the amount of the annual budget, the value of all property assessments, and the tax rate. In some states, counties perform the property tax assessment and billing function for cities within their boundaries, charging each city a small percentage of the revenues collected.

The property tax was one of the first taxes levied to finance local government. This was appropriate since property taxes go to finance many property-related municipal services—police, fire, and public works. This tax is desirable since it is broad-based, uniformly applied, locally administered, and provides a steady and reliable source of revenues. All states provide owners with a legal vehicle to make property assessment appeals.

Budget Process. The budget process consists of five steps: the issuance of a budget directive, the receipt of departmental budgets, an administrative review of each budget, the review and approval of the annual budget by the governing body, and an annual audit to compare budget allocations with expenditures to ensure that all funds were spent as authorized. Many state laws and municipal charters require that the annual audit be performed by an independent outside accounting firm.

The budget directive, typically prepared jointly by the city manager and budget officer, goes out under the signature of the chief executive officer. The budget officer then collects all departmental budgets, usually reviewing them for compliance with the budget directive. The city manager and budget officer then sit down with each department manager to review their proposed spending plan. The budget document is then prepared and presented to the members of the legislative body for their consideration. They typically hold budget review sessions with the city manager, budget officer, and each department manager. They usually make changes to the proposed budget during this process. Once this process has been completed, the legislative body is legally required to hold a public hearing on the proposed budget. After this public hearing, the governing body considers and officially adopts the annual budget.

The elected officials hold the ultimate power when it comes to the budget. They can make any changes they want until they are satisfied with the level and quality of municipal services and, once adopted, the budget becomes the annual financial plan for the municipality. Department managers are then authorized to incur expenses within the adopted budget for their respective departments. All municipal operating budgets include three cost components—expenses for personnel, operation and maintenance, and capital outlay. Capital outlay expenses include personal property such as furniture, calculators, computers, and other nonconsumable items. The total municipal budget includes both the operating and capital components. It is not unusual for the annual capital budget to be prepared separately from the operating budget.

Once the budget is adopted it is continually monitored to ensure compliance with approved spending plans. The city manager holds individual department managers accountable for their respective budgets, and the governing body holds the city manager accountable for compliance with the entire municipal budget. In many small- and medium-sized communities, the finance director performs the duties of the budget officer. In larger municipal organizations, the budget officer is a separate position within the finance department. The size of the budget staff depends upon the magnitude and complexity of the municipal budget.

Purchasing. Over the years, many communities have centralized most of their purchasing activities under a purchasing officer. Local councils have also established formal purchasing limits, over which all goods and services must be competitively bid—with contracts being awarded to the lowest responsible bidder. Professional, scientific, and technical services are usually contracted for, based on a request-for-proposal, since experience and qualifications, not cost, are the most critical selection factors. These limits vary from city to city, but usually range from $5,000 to $20,000. Below this threshold, usually three informal bid quotes or cost estimates are required. Department managers may purchase goods and services below this limit, with all requests for goods and services above this limit being coordinated by the purchasing officer. State laws and local charters typically set forth how the purchasing function is handled.

Regardless of the size of a community, all purchasing responsibilities should be centralized in a single office. This provides for cost-savings through bulk purchases, savings for smaller purchases, and control over existing inventories. Every effort should be made to reduce favoritism towards individual vendors, to encourage greater competition for the acquisition of goods and services, to ensure standard specifications for commonly used goods and services, and to obtain all goods and services at the lowest possible cost. In this respect, the purchasing officer is the guardian of the public trust. He or she must ensure that the best quality product is purchased at the lowest possible cost.

Many smaller cities cooperate when purchasing larger items—such as equipment, vehicles, and computers—to achieve economies-of-scale. Almost without exception, the greater the quantity of an item purchased, the lower the unit cost. Many communities participate in joint purchasing programs with neighboring cities, school districts, and or the state. Even the smallest of communities have a purchasing officer because of the importance of the duties performed, and the possible savings to a municipality and its taxpayers.

Data Processing. Not long ago, most cities only had a single mainframe computer, which was usually located in the finance department. The typical applications included payroll, budget, and billings and collections. During the past decade, four major trends have occurred simultaneously in the field of computer technology—computer hardware has become more sophisticated, smaller, and less expensive, and software has become more user-friendly.

These trends have revolutionized the daily operations of cities across America. Mainframe computers have become smaller, yet more powerful, and the applications and databases available are frequently networked to individual departments via computer terminals or microcomputers connected with electronic cable or telephone modems. Contemporary municipal computer applications include the budget process, budget analysis, finance and revenue, purchasing, property assessments, billings and collections, personnel, public safety, and geographic mapping services. There has also been a proliferation of microcomputers in the workplace—both horizontally and vertically within the organization. Ultimately all work stations will have a microcomputer available. Not all microcomputers need to be connected to the mainframe. Many microcomputers serve as stand-alone systems simply making workers more productive. It is frequently a common practice to standardize all computer hardware, software applications, and station configurations.

In many small- and medium-sized communities, the mainframe computer is still housed in the finance department. In most larger cities, a separate data processing department frequently exists. The current trend in larger cities is to have a separate department of management information systems (MIS). This trend is filtering down to many medium-sized communities. The goal of this technology is to serve the information needs of all departments equally, enabling employees to better serve the public in the process.

PRODUCTIVITY TRENDS

The internal productivity trends reviewed in this section include new financial planning techniques, politically acceptable ways to increase revenues, innovative budgeting practices, and ways to hold down municipal expenditures. Creative financial planning practices include multi-year expenditure and revenue forecasting, the preparation of long-range capital project plans, and the use of timely financial reports to monitor departmental expenditures. Multi-year forecasts can be used to keep expenses in line with revenues, to project revenue shortfalls, or to prompt elected officials to alter the composition of these variables to balance future budgets. Capital planning can be used to show the long-range annual expenses of larger projects, provide sufficient time to explore alternative funding sources, and assist a community in qualifying for available federal or state grant programs. Sophisticated financial reports are distributed at the beginning of each month to assist department managers in monitoring and controlling their budget expenses.

Other operational productivity trends include ways to generate additional revenues without increasing taxes. This goal is being accomplished through a number of different initiatives such as adopting user fees and service charges, treasury management techniques to increase interest income, tax collection procedures to facilitate prompt payments, and enhanced municipal debt collection procedures. All of these trends represent ways to increase revenues from existing sources. Finance directors, working in conjunction with their city managers, are using program budget formats along with performance measurements to track the productivity of individual programs. To properly account for revenues and expenses, a number of new funding options are being used, such as enterprise funds, special revenue funds, and internal service funds. New financial software applications, combined with more sophisticated computer hardware, have facilitated these trends. Joint purchasing programs are also being initiated to achieve lower unit costs. New performance auditing practices include monitoring the effectiveness of individual departmental programs.

External productivity trends have focused on fighting government mandates, privatizing and contracting for services, the creative financing of capital projects, and revenue enhancement and stabilization initiatives. Local elected officials are now opposing dictates from higher levels of government that do not provide proper financial reimbursement. Contracting for certain services is now commonplace, especially when these services are only used infrequently and or reduce the cost of providing the service. Privatization options should always be explored to ensure that departmental programs are cost-effective. Before privatizing a program, consideration should be given to a number of non-economic factors. New financial techniques for capital financing include development impact fees and special assessment districts. Revenue enhancement practices include optimizing a city's return on idle funds and using revenue surveys to ensure the integrity of a city's user fee calculations. Long-range financial stabilization practices include monitoring key external economic variables, local revenue diversification efforts, and using sound financial planning practices. While a municipality cannot control its external economic environment, it can be proactive in anticipating adverse impacts and take internal measures to mitigate these external economic threats.

Table 6.1
Finance Productivity Trends

Internal	External
Assessment Practices	Contract Services
Auditing Practices	Development Impact Fees and Special Assessments
Budgeting for Decision Making	
Capital Project Financing	External Economic Conditions
Computer Systems and Software Applications	Federal and State Grants
	Investing Public Funds
Creative Purchasing Practices	Legislative Mandates
Debt Collection Administration	Privatization Considerations
Financial Management Practices	Professional Certifications
Financial Monitoring	Revenue Diversification
Financial Policies	Revenue Surveys
Pricing Municipal Services	Revenues Without Taxes
Revenue and Expenditure Forecasting	Sound Financial Practices
	Taxes and Economic Development
Revenue Management Practices	User Charges and Regulatory Fees
Special Fund Accounting	
Tax Collection Practices	
Treasury Management Practices	

The financial productivity trends identified and discussed in this chapter are listed in Table 6.1. The use of these financial practices will vary greatly from city to city depending upon the size of a community, its socioeconomic composition, existing state laws and charter requirements, and the willingness of elected officials to plan for the long-range financial health of their city government.

Internal

Assessment Practices. While many county governments are mandated by states to perform the assessment function, cities in some states, primarily in the northeast, perform this task. Several major trends are taking place in this field. Many assessors are contracting for specialized legal and appraisal services when real property assessments are appealed. Since this work is seasonal (i.e., during the appeals period), these services can be handled more cost-effectively by contracts with private providers. This is especially true in small towns with limited staff and technical resources. Many smaller cities now contract with counties to conduct their property assessments. Savings can result because of the economies of scale achieved by consolidating these services under a county government. Specialized computer software is also available for property valuation, assessment, and appraisal applications, saving considerable time and money over traditional manual systems. Most states mandate property revaluations, forcing communities to periodically update their real property assessments. Specialized revaluation companies now routinely perform this work for municipalities, since it would be counterproductive to hire inhouse personnel to perform this infrequent task.

Another recent area of concern for assessors is the impact of economic development decisions on a community's property tax revenues. When property tax concessions are granted to attract private investment, this shifts the property tax burden to other citizens. This is because a city's revenue requirements are constantly expanding and, if one source is reduced, other areas of the property tax revenue base must be increased. Assessors should make sure, for this reason, that such incentives are used judiciously. Public officials should make sure that the benefits received from new development outweigh the lost property tax revenues from using this incentive.

Traditionally, professional societies have offered certifications and designations for assessors. Increasingly, states are requiring professional qualifications for their local assessors. This trend has helped to increase the level of competency in this field, as well as set standards when seeking new personnel to fill professional-level vacancies.

All of these trends are on the increase, especially those concerning the use of contract services, new computer technologies, specialized software applications, professional designations, and uniform assessment practices.

Auditing Practices. Local government audits are legally required to ensure that a city's annual expenses are consistent with the council's approved budget appropriation. Audits are performed at the department level then added together to compare a city's total annual expenses against its appropriation. An annual audit report contains recommendations on ways to improve budget accountability, financial controls, cash management, and other aspects of municipal finance. Each grant required its own audit until the federally mandated Single Audit Act of 1984. Even though a municipal organization does not spend all of its money, it does not mean that all of its agencies, departments, or programs are fulfilling their mandates or doing a good job. Management or performance audits have evolved to fill this informational vacuum. While financial audits are performed citywide, performance or management audits are conducted on specific work units within the organization.

One of the problems with integrating these two audits is that financial audits are prepared using commonly accepted professional standards, while the criteria used to conduct performance audits must be developed for each organizational work unit audited. For performance audits to be effective, specific program expectations and objectives should be set forth when a program is initially approved. The use of sunset legislation, whereby a new program or service is evaluated at the end of a specific time period, is increasing in popularity. Rather than have a program automatically continued, it may be continued based on the results of a performance evaluation. While the finance director is primarily concerned with expenses, elected officials and city managers are concerned with departmental performance results.

Finance directors should recommend policies that require all new programs and services to be evaluated after one year, prior to being considered for funding for the following fiscal year. The use of such policies has been increasing, especially when new programs are expected to generate enough revenues to make them financially self-sufficient.

Budgeting for Decision Making. For the past several decades, most municipalities prepared their traditional annual line-item budgets showing only expenses. These budgets did not describe departmental programs or measure their productivity. Also, because these line-item budgets only showed departmental expenditures, all departmental revenues were typically deposited directly into a city's general fund.

With the advent of the taxpayers' revolt, limited new revenue sources, and the desire of citizens to hold down their taxes, finance directors together with their city managers have undertaken new and innovative budgeting approaches to meet the financial challenges. Rather than having to rely on cost-cutting policy directives from elected officials to make across-the-board budget reductions, program budgets were developed to describe departmental programs and show their costs. Additionally, performance measurements have been developed to assess the productivity of individual programs. It is now common to show program revenues next to program costs.

These more sophisticated budgets force city councils to evaluate costs, productivity, and revenues for individual departmental programs. This has led to a more focused review of municipal services during the annual budget process based on these variables. Elected officials, for example, may wish to reduce expensive, low-performance programs that do not generate sufficient revenues. By comparing program costs against revenues, elected officials also know the extent that taxpayers in general are subsidizing individual programs. This has led to a desire to adjust user fees, thereby increasing revenues, to help make many programs more financially self-sustaining.

These innovative budgeting trends, while not commonplace, are being increasingly used to assist city councils in making difficult budget decisions. Rather than wait for elected officials to mandate an update to their city's outdated budgeting practices, finance directors should incorporate these changes into their regular annual budgetary process.

Capital Project Financing. When preparing a city's capital improvement program, the finance director should always be consulted to determine short-term and long-range financing options for individual capital projects. The number of capital financing options may be numerous. Prior to considering taxpayer financing of capital projects, the availability of funding from higher levels of government should be explored first. While federal grant funds for infrastructure development have diminished greatly over the past decade, some federal loans (e.g., for sewer and water treatment plants) and grants (e.g., for community development) for selected capital projects are still available. Some states also have economic development funds, low-interest loans, special grants, and dedicated revenues such as gasoline and motor vehicle taxes (i.e., for major street projects), state bond funds for specific purposes (e.g., parks, open space, and historic preservation), and state bond banks to enable smaller cities to obtain funding at reduced interest rates.

If federal and state funding is not available, the finance director should then consider alternatives. Short-term financing options include bond antic-ipation notes, grant anticipation notes, and commercial paper, to name a few. Long-range financing options include the use of general obligation bonds, revenue bonds, industrial development bonds, tax increment bonds, and spe-cial assessment bonds. Various sale or leaseback and privatization options are also available depending upon the nature of the project. The field of capital financing has changed so rapidly that the finance director should explore financing options at the time a project is being considered. Because of the com-plexity and the changing nature of capital financing, specialized consultants are frequently hired to provide assistance to public officials in determining the most cost-effective financing alternatives available. The use of specialized financial consultants for larger capital projects is now commonplace.

Capital improvement plans should not be presented to elected officials for their consideration until suggested funding sources are made concerning the projects contained in the plan. Because of fewer federal and state grant funds for capital projects, the trend toward using creative capital financing alternatives will no doubt continue in the future.

Computer Systems and Software Applications. Traditionally, the first users of computers in city governments and municipal data processing services in general were finance departments. These financial applications included budget development, execution, and monitoring; the calculation and generation of employee payroll checks; and the preparation of municipal billing statements.

As computer technology advanced to smaller, more powerful, less expen-sive, and more user-friendly systems, the number of financial applications increased. Now it is not uncommon to have all finance department worksta-tions connected to the host computer via a local area network (LAN). Other municipal departments are commonly connected to the budget database to facilitate the periodic monitoring of their annual budgets. Several innovative financial software applications are now on the market dealing with the prepa-ration of annual financial reports, the issuance and management of municipal bonds, as well as cash and treasury management services. The latter software applications help finance directors forecast short-term cash investments, estimate their daily cash needs, and track municipal investments.

Most medium-sized and larger cities have their own computer systems and software applications. Many smaller communities share computer systems or contract with computer service bureaus. The advantage of using a computer service bureau is that no initial investment is needed for computer hardware, and customized state-of-the-art software is provided by the vendor. Automated cash register and receipting systems are also commonly used to account for cash received, issue receipts to the public, and assist in making daily cash deposits to the bank. Safeguards to ensure computer security—such as restricted access to the host computer, the selective networking of microcomputers to the mainframe computer, and the use of designated access codes to restrict entry to the financial database—are now commonplace in many communities. Many of the budget and revenue projections, monitoring of financial trends, as well as other financial calculations and projections have been facilitated by the use of computers and specialized software applications.

As mainframe computers, microcomputers, and software applications become less expensive and more user-friendly, other innovative financial applications will be developed in the future. These computer hardware and software trends will facilitate this trend.

Creative Purchasing Practices. All purchasing activities within a city should be centralized. By consolidating purchasing practices and by using competitive bidding procedures, cities can achieve economies of scale that will stretch their limited budget dollars. There are several major trends unfolding within the purchasing field. These include the use of purchasing professionals, cooperative purchasing, diversified purchasing, life cycle costing, value management, value engineering, and value incentive contracting.

Most cities now routinely hire professional purchasing agents and buyers, frequently with nationally recognized designations such as Certified Purchasing Manager (CPM). Life cycle costing includes an analysis of the total lifetime costs of purchasing and operating an item (as opposed to selecting the lowest bidder). It may be less expensive to purchase a more expensive item when quality, maintenance, training, and operating costs are taken into consideration. Value management involves the use of a multidisciplinary study team to evaluate a project with the goal of reducing costs while maintaining quality. It is typically used for larger construction projects prior to placing the project out for competitive bidding. Value engineering typically involves the hiring of a construction manager during the design phase of a project to review the project, place components of the project out to bid, rather than the entire project, and negotiate with contractors to receive the best possible price for each project component. Incentive contracting involves the use of specialized contract clauses when a project is put out to bid. The successful bidder is rewarded for recommending cost-saving alternatives that will not impair the quality of the project. If these suggestions are accepted by a community, the cost savings are shared with the contractor according to the predetermined formula in the contract.

While many of these creative purchasing practices are relatively new, they are being increasingly used to enhance the quality and cost-effectiveness of the municipal purchasing functions. As more professional purchasing agents and buyers are hired in the future, these cutting-edge trends will become common practice.

Debt Collection Administration. Enhancing municipal debt collection is one way to raise revenue without increasing taxes. Simply stated, municipal debt collection administration can be described as getting the money that is already due and payable to a community from existing revenue sources. Finance directors should make an all-out effort to maximize their city's return from all of its existing revenue sources.

While most citizens routinely pay their taxes, some citizens do not pay them for one reason or another. It is incumbent upon finance directors to make sure that enhanced collection efforts are undertaken. This will reduce the need to impose additional property taxes on taxpaying citizens. Frequently, non-payment occurs in the areas of real and personal property taxes, as well as for public utility, business license, and parking citation fees. Finance directors need to manage their city's accounts receivable as they do in the private sector. Finance directors are now beginning to measure their collection performance, compare their collection rates against those of other cities, use collection avenues available in small claims courts, as well as use outside third party debt collection services. The collection of municipal debt from existing revenue sources represents an opportunity for finance directors to maximize their city's return from existing revenue sources.

Enhanced municipal debt collection procedures are preferred by elected officials over having to resort to new taxes and user fees, increases in existing taxes and user fees, or having to resort to undesirable service reductions. For these reasons, the trend towards the collection of revenues from existing municipal revenue sources will undoubtedly continue in the future.

Financial Management Practices. A number of contemporary practices have emerged to promote the financial self-sufficiency of cities. At the governing body level, financial policies are now being routinely adopted to regulate many areas of municipal finance. These policies provide consistent guidelines for the future and can only be changed legislatively. City councils are also requesting fiscal impact statements to make them aware of the financial implications of their decisions. Many finance directors now monitor and report annually on financial trends in their community—both external and internal to their municipal organization. Revenue and expenditure projections are now common for three to five years into the future, providing valuable signals on possible future budget and revenue problems.

At the operational level, program and performance budgets have assisted decisionmakers in their annual budget-balancing process, helping them to make more informed decisions. In addition to improving operating budgets, capital project planning and budgeting practices have improved. Multiple-year capital project plans are now routine. Development impact fees provide the financing source for many of these projects. Department managers are also being educated on how to price their public services, leading to more realistic user fees and charges and more frequent adjustments to these revenue sources. This practice has facilitated the trend of citizens paying for the services they use, if these services do not benefit the general public. Special accounting funds are increasing in popularity to treat targeted public services as cost centers, to earmark selected revenues for specific purposes, and to allocate internal costs to operating departments to more accurately reflect the true cost of providing these services. Many of these innovations have been made possible through the use of computers and sophisticated software applications.

Finance departments have taken on increased importance in recent years. While some of these practices reflect cutting-edge innovations in the field of public finance, they will become more common in the future as finance directors assist their cities in achieving a greater level of fiscal self-sufficiency.

Financial Monitoring. Finance directors know that financial troubles are based on several factors, some of which are external to a city's operations. Internal problems may arise because of a decline in revenues, an increase in expenditures, decreasing cash and budgetary surpluses, a growing debt burden, an accumulation of unfunded liabilities, as well as the deterioration of a city's infrastructure. External factors include a general decline in a city's tax base, an increased demand for public services, adverse external economic conditions, the decreased availability of grant programs from higher levels of government, and uncontrolled events such as natural disasters and emergencies. While a municipality cannot control these external variables, every effort should be made to periodically evaluate and assess their impact on the community.

Financial factors under the control of the legislative body should also be monitored. These financial variables include revenue and expenditure trends, a city's operating position (e.g. fund balances, reserves, liquidity), short- and long-term debt obligations, the level of unfunded liabilities, and the condition of a city's infrastructure. Even though elected officials cannot control negative external factors, they can make efforts to place their city on a sound financial footing, thereby minimizing the adverse impact of these external influences. Sound legislatively adopted financial policies lead to fiscally prudent management and financial practices.

The astute finance director monitors these external and internal financial trends, recommends sound financial policies to the governing body, and implements these policies to ensure the long-range financial health of their municipal organization.

Financial Policies. Governing bodies continually adopt policies to establish new programs, procedures and regulations. Public finance is one of the few areas of municipal government that has few adopted policies to guide decisionmaking. Finance directors should work closely with their city managers to propose financial policies to their governing bodies in order to develop a common set of expectations when making future financial decisions.

Typical debt management policies regulate a city's debt limit, confine long-term borrowing for specific purposes, and place limits on the duration of new debt. Capital improvement policies may include mandating the development of a multi-year capital projects plan, showing the operational cost impact of all proposed capital projects, requiring the staff to explore grant funding sources for all projects, and not to approve any capital projects during the year unless they are contained in the plan. The most common revenue policies include the goal of maintaining a diversified revenue base, the requirement for long-range revenue projections, to keep all property assessments as a set percentage of market value, limits on the amount of uncollected property taxes, the requirement that user fees and charges be periodically adjusted to reflect the actual cost of providing a service, and the establishment of enterprise funds to ensure that selected services are cost-covering.

The use of sound financial policies enhances the public's confidence in their municipal government; requires city councils, city managers, and finance directors to think about ways to enhance their city's financial well-being; and improves the continuity of decisionmaking on issues relating to municipal public finance. If these policies do not already exist, they should be proposed by the finance director. Many cities are now developing financial policies to govern different areas of municipal finance. In the future, more sophisticated legislative policies will be developed to guide the decisions of elected and appointed officials as they strive to improve their city's financial self-sufficiency.

Pricing Municipal Services. Charging for municipal services is frequently a desirable alternative to mandating service reductions. With the trend towards charging citizens user fees for municipal services, department managers are being asked to place a unit price on the cost of the services they provide to the public. Since many department managers have not been trained on how to properly cost-out their services, finance directors should issue a procedure explaining exactly how to calculate these costs.

These instructions must include direct, indirect, as well as central overhead expenses. Direct costs include salary, material, and supplies expenses. Indirect costs, on the other hand, typically include fringe benefits, pension expenses, and insurance costs. Although most user fees are based on direct and indirect costs, to be totally reflective of a city's operating costs they should include central overhead charges (e.g., administration, finance, personnel, purchasing, et cetera). Most department managers, out of a lack of understanding on how to accurately cost-out their municipal services, only include direct operating expenses. Many cities are now starting to add their indirect costs to their user fees. Few cities, however, calculate the cost of their central service overhead expenses and incorporate them into their user fees.

Finance directors, through their city managers, should explain these cost components to elected officials. The ultimate decision on how to charge for municipal services rests with the governing body. Once accurate unit costs information has been determined, it can be used to set user fees, compare a city's costs against those of a private contractor, and for budgetary purposes (i.e., to compare the costs and revenues of specific public services). Although unit costs reflect quantity, careful attention should be paid to maintaining the quality of municipal services.

The trend to price public services, initially brought about by financial pressures, is now a common practice. This practice enables public officials to charge those citizens who use a service for the cost of the service, eliminating unnecessary taxpayer subsidizes for many public services. Those services that benefit taxpayers in general—such as police, fire, and public works services—generally do not have a user fee associated with the service. This is because citizens expect certain property-related services for their property taxes. The trend towards charging for municipal services is common, and is increasing in popularity as a reasonable alternative to reducing public services.

Revenue and Expenditure Forecasts. Most finance directors usually only project a municipality's revenues and expenditures for one year at a time. Because of this, elected officials only have a short-term perspective on their city's financial condition. Relatively few finance directors undertake multiyear revenue and expenditure forecasts.

Short-range forecasts (up to one year) are used to prepare the annual municipal budget and to manage cash flow. Medium-range forecasts (two to five years) are used to project expenditures and revenues and to identify future fiscal gaps between the two. Long-range forecasts (five years or more) are used to determine early warning signs for major fiscal problems in the future, to develop financial policies, and to make important land-use decisions.

Future revenue projections are based on a city's current revenue structure. Future expenditure projections are based on a continuation of current service levels. For these reasons, multiyear expenditure and revenue forecasts yield important information on the adequacy of service levels and the level of revenues needed to maintain these services. If gaps occur between the two projections, usually some combination of future revenue enhancements or service reductions will have to be considered by elected officials to balance future annual budgets.

Finance directors should routinely conduct medium-range expenditure and revenue projections to make elected officials aware of possible future budgetary problems. Governing bodies are increasingly demanding these multiyear projections. The use of long-range financial projections in cities will likely increase in the future.

Revenue Management Practices. Many cities are seeking long-term revenue stability through tax diversification, the adoption of revenue policies,
promoting self-sufficiency, optimizing revenues from existing sources, increasing their user fees and charges, and controlling the costs of revenue administration. These goals are being accomplished in a number of difficult and creative ways.

Many municipal finance directors have updated their assessment practices, streamlined their property tax collection procedures, taken a more aggressive position on debt collection, as well as refined their treasury management
practices to optimize their investment returns. Long-range revenue projections are now being used to forecast future revenue needs. Many cities are using
special funds to earmark selected revenues for specific expenditure purposes.
Development impact fees and negotiated exactions are frequently used to
finance capital improvement projects. Equally important is the trend to modify municipal budget formats to show specific programs costs and revenues,
informing elected officials of the extent of taxpayer subsidies required for individual departmental programs. Some governing bodies have even adopted
policies mandating that they will not consider new programs unless a revenue
source can be identified in advance, such as user fees or charges, to finance the
program being requested.

Finance directors believe in recommending financial policies to their
elected officials in order to promote sound fiscal practices that will enhance
their city's long-range financial self-sufficiency. Few finance directors believe
that grants from higher levels of government should be considered as a stable
revenue source. Rather than continue a program after the expiration of a grant,
which has been common in the past, many cities are now eliminating these
services when grant funds have been exhausted. Some of the most creative
financial practices of the last decade have been in the area of revenue management. These trends will undoubtedly continue in the future.

Special Fund Accounting. In order to improve internal financial management, budget practices, and accounting procedures, many cities are using a
number of special accounting funds. The most commonly used funds include
enterprise funds, special revenue funds, and internal service funds.

Enterprise funds are used to treat certain government services as profit
centers. For example, it is not unusual for finance directors to recommend, and
for governing bodies to approve, establishing enterprise funds for sewer and
water services, refuse collection services, golf courses, museums, convention
centers, arenas, and zoos. When these funds are established, the revenues from
these services are adjusted annually to cover both operating and capital
expenses. These services are totally financially self-sustaining and do not
require a taxpayer subsidy. Special revenue funds are used to earmark specific
revenues for selected public services and projects. For example, special revenue funds are used to account for development impact fees, funds generated

by "friends of" groups, and special tax levies designated for specific public services or projects. When these funds are established, the revenues generated from these sources can only legally be spent for their designated purposes.

Internal service funds are being used to show the true costs of operating a unit of government. They are used for departments that provide internal services to other departments on a user fee basis. For example, internal service funds are frequently used to allocate costs for central garage services, janitorial services, duplicating services, the cost of utilities, and to allocate telephone expenses. The use of these funds allocates centrally budgeted expenses to other departments to show the true cost of providing public services. The costs charged to other departments through internal service funds should be competitive; otherwise, user department managers may advocate to privately contract for these services.

The use of enterprise, special revenue, and internal service funds are on the increase. These budgeting and accounting practices make municipal governments more accountable to everyone—elected officials, taxpayers, and department managers.

Tax Collection Practices. During the past decade, due to tight budgets and efforts to optimize existing revenue sources, a number of major changes have taken place in the traditional practices used to collect property taxes. A city's tax collection efforts can be divided between current taxes and delinquent taxes.

To enhance the collection of current taxes, tax collectors are frequently updating the design of their tax statements to make the public aware of how their property taxes are calculated, mailing out reminder notices to citizens before these statements are mailed, making an all-out effort to maintain current mailing addresses, providing extended office hours and multiple collection points, and commonly adding interest rates and penalties to encourage prompt payments. Strategies for collecting delinquent taxes include immediate notification of the delinquency, the attachments of rents upon those properties for which the owners have not paid their taxes, and contracting out the collection of delinquent taxes if payments are not made by a certain date. Some cities even publish the names of delinquent taxpayers in the local newspaper and pursue minor delinquencies in small-claims court. In order to avoid delinquent accounts, some cities offer a payment plan, typically for a one-year period. Two recent collection efforts include the withholding of payments to contractors with delinquent property tax accounts, and not issuing building permits to property owners who have not paid their property taxes.

When all collection efforts have failed, a lien is placed on the real property for the amount of outstanding property taxes and, if not paid within a specified time period, foreclosure action is taken to sell the property to recover the amount of the delinquent taxes. Prior to a municipality taking title to a property, because of many state environmental laws, efforts should be made to make sure that the property is not contaminated with hazardous materials, since the owner of record must legally absorb the costs of clean-up. Many states require counties to perform property tax collection services. Some cities contract with counties for the collection of their property taxes. Many states require professional certifications for their tax collectors. Nearly all states have laws regulating overall tax rate limits, as well as impose tax limits on selected types of proportion.

Some communities are even selling their delinquent property tax liens to private investment companies. In a first-time offering, which includes past due accounts going back several years, it is not uncommon for a municipality to receive a percentage of these past due accounts. The investment company receives the balance on each account, plus accrued interest, until the point of payment. Careful attention should be given to the impact of such sales on a city's future property tax collection rate. The greater the value of the past-due accounts sold, the lower the percentage of future collections on this category of accounts. A few states permit municipalities to contract out their tax collection services. The additional up-front revenues received are obtained because the city will have no delinquent accounts. If a community wishes to switch back to in-house collections, property tax revenues must be decreased by the amount of these delinquent accounts.

All of these trends, especially those to enhance the collection of revenues from property taxes, are on the increase. As finance directors and tax collectors become more creative, additional measures will be taken to increase property tax collections. Municipal tax collection procedures in many cities now reflect state-of-the-art collection practices used in the private sector.

Treasury Management Practices. Forced to deal with financial constraints, fewer grants from higher levels of government, and the public's distaste for additional taxes, finance directors have refined and improved their treasury management practices. Treasury management includes the collection of taxes, maintaining custody of municipal funds, planning a city's cash flow needs, the disbursement of city funds and the investment of available municipal funds.

Recent objectives for these activities include collecting tax revenues as soon as possible, maintaining only the minimum cash flow needed to cover short-term expenses, delaying disbursements as long as practical (consistent with receiving discounts, when available, for prompt payments), and optimizing the return on the investment of municipal funds. To facilitate these trends, the treasury management function is usually centralized under a single person, typically the finance director, although larger cities may have a separate treasurer. In order to gain higher interest rates, different funds may be pooled together and placed in only a few bank accounts yielding higher interest rates (as opposed to in many individual smaller accounts). Rather than having each city invest its own funds, some states offer their municipalities state-administered investment pools. These programs, because they aggregate funds from many units of local government, enable cities to receive a higher return on their investments.

Increasingly, finance directors are also attempting to minimize their city's debt and financial service costs. Debt costs are minimized by limiting the size of debt and the length it is financed. Financial service costs are being reduced by checking with several banks for the least expensive package of financial ser-vices (e.g., checking, borrowing, and investing). In some cases, external money managers are being used to manage a city's short-term funds. Professional money managers offer cities the opportunity to diversify their investments, optimize their return, and reduce their internal costs. Specialized software applications are available to assist finance directors in performing these trea-sury management duties.

All of these trends, designed to minimize costs and optimize investment returns, will become increasingly common in the future as finance directors improve their treasury management skills.

External

Contract Services. Municipal finance is a highly technical and special-ized field. In light of recent budget reductions, many finance departments have been forced to contract out selected services to the private sector. Some of the more common services provided by contract include the preparation of annual financial audits, the compilation of fixed asset inventories, city-wide property assessment revaluations, and specialized data processing services. Addition-ally, it is not unusual for a finance department to use private companies to conduct actuarial studies for employee pension funds and, when the assess-ment function is performed inhouse, to use private attorneys and real estate appraisers to defend the city's assessment decisions when they are appealed by property owners.

Other common contract services include the use of bond counsels, finan-cial consultants, and rating agencies for the issuance of municipal debt. Some recent contracts for services, which reflect state-of-the-art financial manage-ment practices, include the use of management consultants to conduct per-formance audits, contracting for debt collection services, hiring external money managers to optimize the return on short-term investments, and to compet-itively seek financial services from banks in order to reduce the cost of these ser-vices. Small- and medium-sized communities usually contract for more finan-cial services because of the limited size of their staffs and technical resources.

Generally, the larger the city, the less the need to contract for specialized financial services. For example, smaller cities may establish interlocal service agreements to share computer services, contract with larger cities or counties for these services, or contract with a computer service bureau. These con-tracting arrangements are preferred because of the low initial investment needed to initiate these services, the fact that hardware will not have to be replaced every few years, and that no advanced funding is needed for the development of specialized financial software applications. Larger cities typically perform many of these services with their existing staffs.

The trend to use outside companies and consultants for specialized financial services is on the increase and will no doubt continue in the future.

Development Impact Fees and Special Assessments. Cities in high population growth areas are increasingly using development impact fees to offset their capital improvement costs. Specifically, in addition to dedicating land for public facilities, developers are being required to pay a share of the construction cost for these community facilities. This is especially true when these improvements only benefit the residents of new development, as opposed to providing a benefit for citizens in general.

For example, development impact fees are being used to finance local streets, parks, open spaces, and schools, as well as public utilities, such as the expansion of existing water systems and increasing the capacity of wastewater treatment plants. City councils typically do not wish to finance these improvements with general obligation bonds and have all taxpayers absorb the costs of the community facilities. Special assessments, another form of benefit-based financing, enables cities to assess property owners for the cost of certain public improvements. The rationale for using special assessment districts is that the improvements made increase the value of the properties, and that these property owners should pay because of the increased value added to their real estate. Special assessments are typically made for street improvements, water and sewer lines, and recreational facilities, as well as for off-street public parking lots and municipal garages.

While impact fees are generally collected prior to construction, special assessments are collected after a project is completed. Upon completion of the project, property owners have the option of paying off their assessment in full or making installment payments over a specified number of years. Both of these financing tools—development impact fees and special assessment districts—shift the costs for capital projects to those citizens benefiting from these improvements. While the administration of development impact fees has a low overhead cost, since these fees are merely collected and deposited into a special revenue fund, special assessment districts require annual billings to property owners and extensive record-keeping. For this reason, some states permit municipalities to add these overhead costs on to each property owner's annual assessment.

The use of development impact fees and special assessment districts has increased in recent years. They each provide a valuable legal vehicle to finance capital projects without increasing property taxes overall.

External Economic Conditions. Some finance directors are using financial monitoring techniques to track important trends both internal and external to their municipal organization. When performing this type of analysis, special attention should be paid to selected external conditions and variables such as inflation, employment, economic wealth, and business activity.

While these conditions are beyond the direct control of a city's policy-makers, negative trends can be anticipated and positive steps can be taken to mitigate the undesirable impacts of these external economic factors. A diverse revenue base, for example, can protect a community from the negative consequences of a national or regional economic recession. Likewise, a diverse business and industrial base with stable markets and job levels can protect a city from regional and statewide downward business cycles. Also, competitive municipal tax levels and sound economic development incentives can help a city maintain its competitive edge in the local economy. Prudent financial management practices can assist policymakers and public officials cope with negative economic conditions.

If not already in place, finance directors should recommend that policies be adopted to limit the use of one-time revenues to balance their municipal budget, not to defer current costs (e.g., such as infrastructure maintenance and pension liabilities), and to assess the long-range costs of a liability (e.g., to purchase capital assets without knowing the costs of operating and main-taining these assets). A governing body should have approved financial poli-cies in place to preclude such negative financial practices. These policies guide the decisions of current and future governing bodies, the city manager, finance director, and management staff, and provide long-term financial stability to the municipal organization. If sound financial policies are not already in place, finance directors should recommend such policies to their city councils through the city manager. The professional staff must assist elected officials in safeguarding their community from the negative consequences of external eco-nomic conditions.

While public officials cannot control these external circumstances, they can mitigate their negative influence on their community's financial condition. Practices to monitor these external economic conditions are on the increase. The development of sound financial policies to help cope with an uncertain economic environment, while yet not commonplace, is gaining in popularity.

Federal and State Grants. Federal and state grants used to be considered a stable source of annual municipal revenues. They could be counted on each year to provide valuable public services—both operating and capital—and allow cities to minimize their general fund expenditures for these services.

Under President Johnson's Great Society there were over 1,000 categor-ical grants available to local governments. While President Nixon's New Fed-eralism streamlined the grants administration process, federal funds were still available for many public services and capital projects. Many federal grant programs favored giving money to the states. The states, in turn, would admin-ister these grant programs, making funds available to their cities. Over the years, local officials, both elected and appointed, have become skeptical of these grant programs for several reasons. For example, many of these grant programs were earmarked for the construction of capital projects but did not provide funds for their operation or maintenance. These costs fell upon local governments. Additionally, when these programs were terminated, as was the case with the Comprehensive Employment and Training Act (CETA), many city councils had to allocate general fund monies to continue the public services provided by these programs.

During the mid– to late–1970s many larger cities built up an artificial reliance on these grant programs. In many cases federal and state grants comprised about one-fourth to one-third of their entire budget. Throughout the 1980s, and continuing to the present, the number of grant programs decreased in number while the remaining programs became victims of severely reduced funding levels. During this time, many local governing bodies built up an artificial dependency on these "outside" funding sources. This led to a loss of fiscal autonomy and financial self-reliance.

Most governing bodies and especially finance directors now believe that their community should be in charge of its own financial destiny. Because federal legislators are preoccupied with balancing their own budget and reducing the national debt, these feelings are likely to continue in future years.

Investing Public Funds. A great deal of negative publicity is typically generated by the loss of invested public funds, or when a municipality defaults on a general obligation bond. All municipal treasurers invest a portion of their liquid funds in a portfolio of marketable financial securities. Municipal investment options are usually limited since nearly all states restrict the type of securities in which treasurers can invest their public funds.

Although municipal treasurers have some leeway when investing, the legal list of investment options is usually limited to U.S. treasury securities, U.S. agency securities, and bank certificates of deposit. One of the most important factors to consider when investing public funds is the degree of risk involved—that is, the possible loss of principal and interest of invested funds. Since treasurers are custodians of public tax dollars, they should always strive to make sound risk-free investments even if the interest yield is lower than other investment alternatives. When the services of professional money managers are obtained, careful attention should be paid to constantly monitor and evaluate the money manager and the investment portfolio. Adequate internal controls should also be established to require periodic financial reports and proper accounting procedures to account for all invested funds and interest income.

All cities should have an investment policy setting forth their specific investment objectives. The use of active investment practices enable treasurers to have more control over their investments. Passive investing practices, on the other hand, lead to a loss of operational control over a municipality's financial investments. In order to assist smaller- and medium-sized cities, many states are forming statewide investment pools, administered by the state to provide greater returns on local funds consistent with risk-free investments. The investing of public funds is one area of public finance where cities should not be allowed total local autonomy. New state laws and regulations concerning the investment of public funds will surely continue in the future. While this represents a loss of municipal home-rule control, these mandates are typically welcomed by taxpayers, as well as many elected officials and finance directors.

Legislative Mandates. Local elected and appointed officials, including finance directors, are increasingly concerned about the financial impact of legislative mandates from higher levels of government. Three major trends, facilitated by limited financial resources and tight budgets, have emerged over the past decade. First, local governing bodies increasingly want to know the cost of their own proposed mandates before they are implemented. To this end, they have required that all agenda items for their consideration contain a fiscal impact statement, along with proposed funding sources. Second, federal and state governments are increasingly approving mandates upon municipalities without proper reimbursement. The lack of municipal financial resources has left many cities in violation of these laws since they cannot afford the cost of compliance. Third, local governing bodies, together with their state and national professional associations, have undertaken intensive lobbying efforts to limit the number of unfunded mandates. Many state municipal leagues, as a part of the services they provide to their member cities, are now cataloging these mandates, estimating compliance costs, as well as monitoring proposed pieces of legislation to determine their impact upon municipalities.

A recent publication by the National League of Cities (NLC), highlights and examines anti-mandate legislative strategies. This publication even provides a sample state constitutional reimbursement requirement. Another report provides a comprehensive bibliography on state and federal mandate studies, listing over 60 such studies in nearly 30 states. As the political pressure intensifies against these mandates, finance directors are frequently being requested to provide the cost of their city's compliance on a mandate-by-mandate basis. This financial information is being used to fight the battle against federal and state mandates without proper reimbursement. As local elected officials cope with their own financial problems, they do not want to increase taxes to finance the cost of mandates imposed by higher levels of government.

The lobbying efforts of city councils have led to more frequent meetings with their federal and state legislative delegations. This trend will continue because of the prevailing philosophy that local taxes should only be used to finance municipal services.

Privatization Considerations. The national trend towards contracting for selected public services has continued unabated. The number of services contracted to the private sector is on the increase. The trend to place a cost on public services for user fee purposes has also provided valuable cost information upon which to base privatization decisions. Finance directors have been instrumental in educating department managers that their user fees should be developed based on direct, indirect and central overhead expenses.

The initial "rush" to privatize public services, however, has made public officials cautious for several reasons. When contemplating private contracts for public services, costs should not be the only consideration. Other important factors such as loss of control, ensuring service quality, maintaining public accountability, controlling future costs, and providing requirements for handling citizen complaints should also be considered. When all of these factors are taken into consideration, it may not always be in the public's interest to contract for a service merely because it is less expensive. Before a municipality makes a contracting decision, the finance director should review the internal costs of providing the service to make sure that they are accurate. The finance director, who oversees the purchasing function, should also develop procedures to ensure that proper safeguards are included in all requests for proposals, bid awards, and actual contract agreements. The finance director should also educate elected officials and other management personnel on the need for proper contractual safeguards to make sure that the public's interests are protected.

Even before contracts with private providers became popular, many communities were already contracting for selected public services with county governments, other municipalities and local nonprofit organizations. The trend for municipalities to contract with other units of government and nonprofit agencies is also on the increase. A community's existing labor agreements may restrict, even prohibit, the use of certain privatization practices. These agreements should be reviewed before undertaking efforts to privatize municipal services. The use of contracts to provide public services, especially those with the proper legal safeguards to protect the public's interests, are on the increase.

Professional Certifications. The number of professional designations and certifications in the field of municipal finance is on the increase. Many states frequently provide technical training leading to certifications for finance directors, tax collectors, and assessors. Many states mandate that when new personnel are hired to fill these positions that they possess these credentials or obtain them within a specified time period after they are hired, typically one year from the date of appointment. Many public universities and professional associations are also providing certifications to verify competency levels in these technical fields. Some public universities provide a certificate in municipal finance or financial management upon completion of a prescribed program of study (typically several courses). These programs usually provide graduate-level study in this field for working professionals who already have or do not wish to pursue a master's degree.

The Government Finance Officers Association (GFOA), the leading professional association for finance directors, in addition to providing many technical training courses for mid-level finance personnel, offers advanced training for finance directors. The Advanced Government Finance Institute, an intensive one-week training program, is specifically designed for top-level finance managers. In addition to providing certifications for finance professionals, GFOA provides a "certificate of achievement for excellence" in financial reporting and budget presentation. These trends have helped to increase the level of competency in the municipal finance field, as well as establish standards when recruiting new personnel to fill professional vacancies.

All of these educational trends are positive for a number of different reasons. They have led to the implementation of advanced financial management practices, increased existing levels of employee productivity, and have expanded the usage of computers and sophisticated software applications.

Revenue Diversification. The type of taxes, service charges, development impact fees, and regulatory fees used by a community should reflect the socio-economic composition, values, attitudes, and perceptions of citizens. This premise also holds true for the type of grants applied for from federal and state programs. The types of revenue sources, as well as their amount, should be perceived as equitable in the eyes of most taxpayers.

To accomplish this goal, a city's revenue base should be politically acceptable to citizens, establish financial stability, generate enough revenues to balance the annual budget, lead to long-range financial self-sufficiency, and be administered in an economical manner. The type and amount of city revenues needed to finance the annual budget is subject to public hearings, and elected officials must determine if these revenues are politically acceptable to their constituents. The type of revenue sources used should be reasonably reliable over time, and should not fluctuate greatly from year to year. Needless to say, the type and amount of revenues collected should not be more than is needed to balance the annual budget, except in unusual cases which must be explained and justified to the public.

Governing bodies have learned not to rely on state and federal grants as a stable revenue source. The financial self-sufficiency of a city should be paramount in determining the mix of those revenue sources needed to provide an acceptable level of public services. The collection of revenues should be centralized, cost-effective, and designed to achieve economics of scale. In many regions of the country, states and counties collect certain revenues since this collection process is less expensive to the taxpayers. Elected officials, frequently upon the recommendation of their finance director, have adopted financial policies to help achieve these revenue goals. Revenue diversification is essential if public officials—both elected and appointed—wish to promote and achieve the long-range goal of financial self-sufficiency for their community.

With fewer state and federal grants, and the public's aversion to increased taxation, a city's revenue structure should be the subject of public discussion and debate, rather than merely having elected officials reacting to the annual financial crises faced by many communities. Increased attention is now being placed on the types of municipal revenue sources, as well as their suitability to finance public services on an ongoing basis.

Revenue Surveys. Most communities establish their user fees, and charges for permits and licenses, in a vacuum, without regard to the competitiveness of their pricing or the cost of collection. While competitive pricing is common in the private sector, it has only recently been used by local governments.

The use of revenue surveys, an instrument for comparing user fees and charges among similar cities, assists in evaluating the adequacy of a city's revenue structure, as well as identifying possible new revenue sources. Revenue surveys can also be used to collect cost information to determine the most effective methods of revenue collection. Revenue surveys include a listing of all of the fees and charges used in a municipality, the criteria used to develop them, and the cost of their collection. Because of the great number of fees and charges used by a municipality, the finance director may wish to limit the number of revenue sources included in a revenue survey. Once developed, this survey should be distributed to similar cities, giving consideration to socio-economic, economic, geographic, and population factors. The final report accompanying the revenue survey should recommend adjustments to existing fees and charges, suggesting new revenue sources, and discussing the need for possible changes in revenue collection procedures.

The use of revenue surveys focuses public attention on the importance of user fees and charges, demonstrates the commitment of elected officials to proper financial planning, and enhances the integrity and cost-effectiveness of a city's revenue sources and collection policies. The use of revenue surveys is growing in popularity. If not already in use, finance directors should recommend the periodic use of revenue surveys for these reasons.

Revenues Without Taxes. With fewer state and federal grants available, and the public's aversion to increased taxes of any kind, all municipal officials now favor the opportunity to raise additional revenues without increasing existing taxes. This philosophy serves to minimize the need for future budget and service reductions by allowing elected officials the opportunity to maintain existing levels of public services without having to resort to tax increases.

Several contemporary financial practices demonstrate this fiscal philosophy. Many governing bodies, for example, have adopted policies to make developers pay for the cost of community facilities, are establishing assessment districts to charge property owners for improvements that benefit their property, are using economic development incentives to expand their tax base, and are imposing and raising user fees and regulatory charges to help offset the cost of providing public services. Under pressure to expand their city's revenues from existing sources, finance directors have also responded to this challenge in a number of creative and innovative ways. They have, for example, updated and modernized their assessment practices, implemented cost-saving purchasing techniques, enhanced their debt collection and revenue management programs, and updated their treasury management practices to increase their return on municipal investments. Recent financial policies, such as those requiring user fees to pay the cost of new services and developers to pay for capital projects, have served to facilitate this trend.

Elected and appointed officials have responded to this revenue challenge in many different and positive ways. Additional state-of-the-art legislative policies and financial practices to raise revenues without increasing taxes will evolve in the future as public officials respond to this political challenge.

Sound Financial Practices. The annual municipal budget balancing process is always a difficult task. Several negative decisions are commonly made by policymakers with respect to balancing their annual budgets.

The first is to reduce or eliminate "rainy day" municipal contingency funds and accumulated reserves. Contingency funds, for example, used to be funded at about 1 percent of the total budget. It is not unusual now to budget these emergency funds at only a fraction of this amount. Many municipal budgets are so tight that special appropriations are frequently needed for even the smallest unforeseen expenses. If funds are not available for special appropriations because they have been eliminated to balance operating budgets, governing bodies must approve emergency appropriations, which are added to the subsequent year's tax levy. Second, budgets for the maintenance of the municipal infrastructure are almost always eliminated, even though it is cheaper to maintain and repair public facilities rather than to have them replaced. Third, funds allocated for needed capital projects are frequently eliminated since elected officials almost always favor funding the most visible public services. Not funding needed capital projects frequently has a negative impact on a city's economic development programs and ongoing efforts to maintain the existing quality of community life.

Finance directors must teach elected officials that usually three-quarters or more of a municipal budget consists of personnel costs—salaries and fringe benefits. By controlling salaries and fringe benefit costs, elected officials can hold down expenses and make it easier to plan for the future. When operational budget reductions must be made, all departments should be treated equitably. It is not a sound practice, for example, to spare police, fire, and public works services at the expense of smaller line and staff departments. Pieces of larger programs in these departments should also be scrutinized when making budget reductions. Also, it is incumbent upon finance directors to link budget reductions with service reductions to counteract the "cut-the-fat" mentality frequently held by some members of the public. Public service impact statements, which describe the operational impact of budget reductions, are one technique being used to fill this public informational vacuum.

As elected and appointed officials gain more experience at balancing their annual budgets with limited resources, the use of such sound financial practices will become common practice.

Taxes and Economic Development. Many communities now routinely provide tax incentives to attract private investment. Cities gain by receiving increased taxes for improvements made to real property and for new equipment, as well as by expanded employment opportunities. The private company gains by paying lower taxes, thereby reducing its overhead costs and increasing its profitability.

Two downfalls of using these incentives include governmental interference in the private marketplace, and the fact that the jobs taken by residents of neighboring cities are paid for by the taxpayers of the city in which the plant is located. In reality, the level of municipal taxes is of secondary importance when making business decisions. Most relocation decisions are based upon space availability, labor costs, energy rates, and transportation expenses. If these factors are equal in two locations, then tax incentives may play a part in a company's decision to relocate to one community over another. If a city offers too many tax incentives, which ultimately shifts the tax burden to residential property owners, they face the possibility that these property owners may move to neighboring municipalities with lower taxes. The types of incentives provided should be only those necessary to attract private investment. Many states now provide tax incentives, thereby spreading the cost of these incentives over their entire tax-paying population.

For these reasons, it makes sense for city councils to adopt policies dealing with the type and level of incentives provided to attract private investment. Public officials in many cities—especially those that are economically depressed—tend to provide too many incentives, increasing the tax burden of their citizens. It is incumbent upon finance directors to recommend sound economic development incentives. The "package" of incentives offered should be analyzed and considered on a case-by-case basis, and only after carefully evaluating the increased amount of net real and personal property taxes, and number of jobs generated.

Economic development incentives should be considered a form of municipal investment. Like all investments, the return should be calculated and evaluated before offering incentives to private companies. The trend towards the prudent use of economic development incentives will continue in the future.

User Charges and Regulatory Fees. User charges and regulatory fees represent the fastest growing revenue sources for communities. As the reliance of cities on property taxes has decreased, user charges and regulatory fees have increased to balance the revenue equation. While enterprise funds are used to establish selected city services as profit centers, user fees are designed to raise revenues to offset department operating expenses. For example, certain public health activities have a community-wide benefit, while certain health clinics only benefit the citizen using this service.

The trend has been to charge a fee, even if not totally cost-covering, to offset the cost of providing municipal services. Trends in the area of user fees include charging fees when only individuals benefit from a specific service, making annual adjustments to make these charges reflect the actual cost of providing the service, using sliding-scale fees based on age and or income factors, providing discounts to certain groups such as young people and senior citizens, and offering free use periods for economically disadvantaged citizens. Several of these trends provide elected officials with political "safety valves" when user fees are initially imposed or subsequently increased.

The use of regulatory fees, which typically include charges for licenses and permits, is also on the increase. These charges are frequently made for numerous permits (e.g., building, sidewalk construction, curb cuts, elevator, and parades) and licenses (e.g., business, marriage, bicycle, dog registration, and food handling). The purpose of these fees is to cover the cost of regulating the activity for which the fee is charged. These regulatory fees are also periodically adjusted to reflect the increased cost of providing these services. The degree to which some fees cover service costs depends upon the extent to which a particular service benefits the general public. Certain fees, by their nature, will never be totally cost-covering. User fees, whatever their level, for example, will never offset the cost of providing many municipal services, such as those provided by library, health and human services, public works, police, and fire departments.

The role of fees has been to regulate the demand for public services, to establish proper service levels, to charge those citizens who benefit from services, and to decrease reliance on less desirable revenue sources such as the property tax. Most elected officials, finance directors, city managers, and department heads favor the use of reasonable service charges and regulatory fees. They represent one of the most equitable vehicles to offset operating costs by generating additional revenues without raising taxes. The imposition of user charges and regulatory fees has gained in popularity in recent years for these reasons.

THE FUTURE

The most important internal productivity trend includes efforts to increase a community's revenues from existing revenue sources. This is popular with elected officials because it provides a more politically acceptable alternative than increasing taxes. Several areas of a finance department's operations are impacted by this revenue goal. Assessment practices have been modified to include more frequent revaluations, and property tax collection practices have been improved to help a community speed up the payment of individual tax bills. In both of these cases, computers equipped with specialized software have made these revenue-enhancement practices possible. Municipal debt collection procedures have been improved to increase collections from numerous existing revenue sources. Also, pricing municipal services has evolved from an art form to a highly technical scientific methodology. User fee calculations now frequently include provisions to capture not only direct and indirect costs, but also a municipality's central overhead expenses. Treasury management practices have also been improved to increase interest income from municipal investments. Local legislative bodies are approving various financial policies that require their management staffs to achieve these financial goals.

A significant and dramatic external trend has been to charge citizens for the public services they use. This is especially true when these services benefit only specific segments of the community and not the general public. While police, fire, and public works services generally benefit all taxpayers, many of the services provided by other municipal departments only benefit the citizens using a specific service. As an alternative to eliminating or reducing a particular program, elected officials are frequently approving the implementation of user service charges. City managers, finance directors, and department managers have endorsed this trend. When looking at the "big picture" this practice is reasonable since many citizens want government to reduce those services that they do not directly use. Public officials must not forget that services are used by different segments of the community, and all services are valuable to the citizens that use them. The use of development impact fees to charge developers for the cost of future roadways, utilities, and community facilities is another example of this trend. Special assessment districts are becoming increasingly popular as a financial vehicle to charge those property owners who benefit from specific public improvements. Gone are the days when taxpayers subsidized services that only benefit a few property owners.

One internal financial trend, which also directly impacts many users of services, is the creation of municipal enterprise funds. Under this accounting practice, selected public services are treated as profit centers. Examples of these services include golf courses, public auditoriums and arenas, municipal zoos and museums, sewer and water services, refuse collection services, convention centers and specific tourist attractions. The rationale for this practice is that these services do not benefit the general public; they only benefit the particular citizens that use these services, and taxpayers in general should not pay to construct and operate these types of facilities. Elected officials are also using revenue bonds to finance the construction of these facilities, since they generate a guaranteed future income stream through admission fees or service charges. This income stream is generated solely by those citizens who pay for these services. The trend to build these facilities with revenue bonds and to establish enterprise funds to finance their operations fits with the evolving political philosophy of holding down taxes and making users pay for those services that do not directly benefit the general public.

7

FIRE

The traditional role performed by early volunteer fire departments was fire suppression. When a fire broke out, the alarm was sounded, and water, and firemen arrived at the scene to extinguish the fire. The biggest problem was transporting the water necessary to extinguish the fire. Horse-drawn wagons with water containers were used. Another problem was having enough wagons and horses to make sure that enough water could be transported to the fire so it could be extinguished. Now, volunteer fire departments exist primarily in rural areas of the nation. Almost without exception, all urban areas now have professional fire departments. As our nation becomes more urbanized, the number of volunteer fire companies has decreased while the number of professional departments has increased. Changes in building codes and the adoption of fire safety codes have helped to reduce the number of structural fires. Over the years, fire inspection and fire prevention activities have increased in importance. During this time, the duties performed by fire departments have evolved from a loose art form to a precise science.

For fire departments to be effective today, they must have a developed database of common incidents and effective responses, a citywide communications system, the ability to provide the latest response techniques, and respond with the proper fire suppression materials to properly extinguish fires. The goal of fire suppression is to limit personal injury and property loss. Having a sufficient number of trained personnel, and the latest firefighting equipment and technologies are essential to properly serve the public. Having a sufficient number of fire station locations is also essential for providing acceptable response times. The number and location of fire stations in a community is determined by a combination of criteria, including response times, geography, and ability to pay. Once a fire station has been constructed, it must be properly staffed—24 hours a day, every day of the year. It must also be outfitted with fire apparatus, fire suppression equipment, and a suitable communications system. Politically, once a fire station exists, it is almost impossible to close it, even if its location is determined to be ineffective because of subsequent residential and commercial development patterns.

149

Professional firefighters in contemporary fire departments spend a great deal of their time performing other activities, such as conducting fire prevention programs and providing fire inspection services. Fire prevention programs include the elimination of known fire hazards, requiring the latest building technologies to make buildings fire resistant, and educating the public on the proper handling and storage of hazardous materials. Adequate building codes and fire prevention codes have helped achieve these community fire prevention goals. Specially trained fire inspectors review plans for proposed buildings and perform on-site inspections to make sure that property owners and contractors comply with these code requirements. A new building cannot be occupied until it has passed a fire code inspection. These personnel also conduct inspections of older buildings and issue violation notices to enforce corrective action. Some cities have adopted smoke detector requirements for residential structures. In many cases, the titles to these properties cannot be transferred until smoke detectors have been installed and fire inspectors have verified this fact. A major part of fire prevention involves citizen education on how to prevent fires. Many of these programs are provided to children in elementary schools.

Most fire departments are now involved in a number of other related activities such as providing emergency services, performing emergency management duties, and responding to hazardous materials incidents. Emergency services include performing search and rescue operations, providing ambulance services, and having personnel trained as emergency medical technicians. Emergency management duties include having emergency response plans, conducting periodic simulated emergency exercises to test these plans, and being able to respond to any emergency situation that may arise in a community. Federal and state laws require that municipal fire departments perform this service. Municipal codes regulate the handling, storage, disposal, and inspection of many hazardous materials. These services are provided by specially trained fire personnel. Local fire departments have also been given the responsibility to respond to all hazardous materials incidents. As the number of calls-for-service for fire suppression responses have declined over the years, these other duties have been expanded and have increased in importance. Many urban fire departments provide all of these services.

The six major programs performed by municipal fire departments are shown in Figure 7.1. These services may vary, since some communities contract out their emergency ambulance services and some cities contract with their county government for hazardous materials enforcement. In the course of performing these services, fire departments cooperate with a number of other municipal departments, including police, planning and building, health and human services, and public works.

Figure 7.1
Fire Major Programs

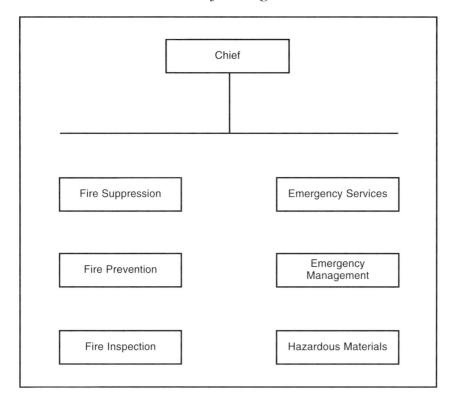

DESCRIPTION OF PROGRAMS

Fire Suppression. The traditional role of the fire department has been fire suppression. The days of firefighters merely "waiting for the bell to ring," and responding with an adequate supply of water, are gone forever.

Effective responses to calls-for-service require information about predictable incidents, a state-of-the-art communications system, the latest response techniques, proper fire suppression materials, and having a sufficient number of locations to properly respond to such emergencies. Properly trained personnel, the latest equipment, and the use of new techniques and technologies are critical components of fire suppression. Modern fire departments maintain a database of the most common types of fires and emergency responses. The type of training provided, desired staffing levels, the equipment and technology available, and the response techniques used are based on maintaining an appropriate level of readiness to respond to common fires and emergencies.

Response times, as opposed to distances, are commonly used to determine the location of fire stations within a community. Geography may also be a key factor in determining the location of fire stations. For example, a portion of a city may be only a short distance from a fire station, but if it is on the other side of a mountain, without access, this area may warrant having its own fire station. There is always a trade-off between minimizing response times, the number of fire stations in a municipality, and costs.

During the past decade, much of the emphasis has been placed on controlling, if not reducing, costs. To this end, fire prevention and inspection activities have taken on increased importance in reducing the number of fires and emergencies.

Fire Prevention. Fire prevention activities typically include those tasks necessary to reduce the danger of fires by reducing or eliminating potential fire hazards, requiring the latest building technologies to make buildings fire resistant, and the proper storage and handling of hazardous materials.

In general terms, fire prevention includes having adequate fire prevention codes, building codes, proper code enforcement through periodic inspections, and educating the public on how to prevent fires. All states mandate a minimum level of fire safety codes to prevent fires. Fire prevention has evolved as a separate division within fire departments. These fire personnel frequently enforce state and local regulations dealing with the proper use, storage, handling, and transportation of potentially explosive and flammable materials. In addition to regulating these materials, fire prevention personnel also distribute information to the public on how to respond to the potential dangers and how to protect themselves in times of emergencies.

Much of this work requires coordination with other city departments such as building, planning, zoning, code enforcement, health, public works, and police. A close working relationship is also maintained with representatives of local hospitals, schools, factories, warehouses, commercial buildings, as well as with the general public.

Fire Inspection. Fire inspection requirements have taken on increased importance in recent years. Although a fire prevention activity, it is so important that specialized fire personnel are required to perform these inspections. Most communities adopt fire regulations as a part of their comprehensive building code requirements. For this reason periodic revisions and modifications to the fire code must be coordinated with building or planning department officials as a part of their regular building code update.

Fire codes typically set forth regulations concerning the use of fire-resistant building materials, including electrical wiring and heating sources, the proper storage of hazardous materials and chemicals, the number and location of fire exits, special requirements for public assembly halls, and legally required on-site fire detection, protection, and suppression equipment. These codes frequently require smoke detectors and automatic sprinkler systems for certain types of buildings. All of these codes are designed to save lives, minimize personal injuries, and reduce the amount of property damage caused by fire. Effective fire prevention requires a comprehensive code enforcement program.

Typically, for routine violations, a written warning is given to first-time violators. If the code violation is not corrected within a specified time period, strict penalties can be imposed, ranging from a fine to restrictions on the use and occupancy of the building to court action that legally forces code compliance. When new developments are proposed, fire inspection personnel routinely review these plans for compliance as a part of a municipality's plan review process.

Emergency Services. Fire prevention and inspection programs have proven to be successful, enabling fire personnel to respond to other types of emergency situations. Since fire personnel have always responded to emergencies, it was only natural to expand the types of emergency situations to which they respond.

All fire departments have some type of emergency response vehicle to perform basic search and rescue operations. Ambulance services, on the other hand, may be provided by the local fire department or contracted out to the private sector. When a fire department provides ambulance services, a municipal ambulance is directly dispatched in response to the call. If the service is a contractual one, the dispatcher calls upon the private ambulance service to respond. In many emergency situations the call for service is to the fire department. In this case fire fighters respond, assess the situation, and call the private ambulance service.

Most calls for service are now for emergency medical services. Many fire personnel receive training as emergency medical technicians (EMTs). This duty is frequently voluntary and an additional salary stipend is received for having this qualification and for performing this duty. The number of firefighters trained in providing medical assistance and the level of their training depends upon who performs the service. All fire departments perform a variety of emergency response services as a part of their basic operations.

Emergency Management. Federal and state laws require cities to respond to emergencies and disasters—natural or manmade. The law not only requires that a municipality respond, but it also mandates that it be properly prepared to respond, including having an up-to-date emergency operation plan. Emergency operation plans should include common responses to the most likely emergencies and disasters. Almost without exception, every city conducts mock emergency and disaster exercises to properly test and evaluate their plan before an actual incident occurs.

Emergencies typically can be handled with local community resources, while disasters frequently require the assistance of higher levels of government. The Federal Emergency Management Agency (FEMA) requires that cities, counties, and state governments provide assistance before the resources of the federal government can be used by a municipality. For example, when city resources are exhausted, municipal officials may call upon the county government for assistance. When county resources are exhausted these officials may call upon the state government for assistance, and when state resources are exhausted these officials may call upon the federal government for assistance. Mutual assistance agreements usually exist between neighboring communities. These agreements enable a city to provide an immediate response with resources far beyond what it alone could provide.

There are four phases of emergency management operations: preparedness, mitigation, response, and recovery. Every city must have an emergency management coordinator to coordinate these activities. In most small- to medium-sized communities, this function is usually assigned to the fire department.

Hazardous Materials. Fire prevention codes regulate the usage, handling, storage, and inspection of hazardous materials in a municipality. When an emergency occurs, it is always the fire department that responds. Possible emergency situations arising from known hazardous materials should be included in a city's emergency operation plan.

Many states now require cities to prepare inventories of hazardous materials by company and location. Such listings are useful since many chemical fires may not respond to traditional fire suppression efforts. Other firefighting measures may become necessary to extinguish industrial fires. A response to a release of poisonous gases would also require a highly specialized response. The National Fire Protection Association (NFPA) publishes several guidebooks for responding to fires and emergencies caused by dangerous chemicals, gases, liquids, and other industrial materials. Many municipalities are also adopting new fire prevention codes to regulate the usage, handling, and storage of flammable and combustible chemicals and gases within their political boundaries. These codes also typically mandate strict storage requirements and periodic inspections by fire department personnel.

Although fire department personnel respond to these incidents, those personnel involved in these responses must have the proper information, equipment, and training. Typical equipment used ranges from protective clothing, the possible use of self-contained breathing apparatus, to heavy equipment that may be needed to control hazardous materials. As the public's awareness of hazardous materials has increased, calls for service have risen accordingly.

Productivity Trends

Many of the recent internal productivity trends in fire departments include an increased emphasis on fire prevention practices, the automation of departmental records, and ways to reduce budgetary expenses and improve employee productivity. Fire prevention programs are popular because they are proactive rather than reactive. Helping citizens prevent fires should be more important than responding to fires. Citizen education is one of the cornerstones of an effective fire prevention program. Most fire departments are using computers to automate their existing records, developing new databases, and creating local area networks (LANs) to link fire headquarters with neighborhood fire stations. Many cities are developing hazardous material inventories, itemizing these inventories by individual addresses, and using this information to properly respond to industrial fires. Initiatives are also being implemented to increase employee productivity, such as the use of new technologies and equipment, the formation of incident command centers during emergencies, measures to improve the safety and health of firefighting personnel, and shorter work shift schedules. Scientific criteria have even been developed to determine the best location for new fire stations.

External productivity trends have focused on new building technologies, the use of modern municipal codes, citizen education programs, and the adoption of user fees and service charges. New building technologies include fire resistant construction materials, fire detection systems, and fire alarm and signaling systems, to name a few. Municipal codes are being updated to include fire prevention measures to protect citizens from the hazards of fire, chemical spills, and other emergency situations. Departments are also focusing their attention on citizens' education with the goal of empowering citizens to protect themselves against fires, as well as how to properly respond to fires. A variety of new instructional materials are available to educate and empower citizens in these areas. Fire departments have traditionally had few user fees and service charges. New fees and charges are being implemented for false alarms, fire inspections, plan checking, ambulance services, and emergency medical services. Many cities are requiring private companies not only to provide a hazardous materials inventory, but also charging a fee after its provision. The fees cover the costs of incorporating the information provided into the fire department's database. This gives firefighters a "head start" when responding to emergencies as these locations, thus limiting the loss of life and property damage. Some communities have adopted service charges for augmented levels of fire services for larger buildings such as high-rise residential developments. Nationally, the use of fire volunteers is on the decrease. This trend has been facilitated by the urbanization of the nation's cities and state training requirements for new firefighting personnel.

A listing of the productivity trends examined in this chapter is shown in Table 7.1. Fire departments usually have one of the largest budgets, next to police departments, in most municipalities. Because of this, fire chiefs have been under increasing pressure to reduce their costs and improve employee productivity.

Table 7.1
Fire Productivity Trends

Internal	External
Budgetary Controls	Code Enforcement
Civilianization Practices	Codes and Regulations
Evaluating Fire Services	Contemporary Building Technolo-
Fire Prevention Practices	gies
Fire Station Location Decisions	Contract Services
Fire Suppression Practices	Development Standards
Human Resources Management	Emergency Services Practices
Practices	Fire Service Master Planning
Incident Command Centers	Fire Station Closure Decisions
Interdepartmental Cooperation	Intergovernmental Cooperation
Management Information Systems	Professional Development
Occupational Safety and Health	Public Education and Citizen
Programs	Empowerment
Organizational Consolidations	Service, Disclosure, and Impact Fees
Use of Computers, Technologies,	Use of Volunteer Firefighters
and Equipment	
Work Shift Schedules	

Internal

Budgetary Controls. Fire department budgets typically have one of the largest annual appropriations of all municipal departments. The majority of a fire department's budget goes to finance salaries and fringe benefits. Salary budget accounts include, but are not limited to, wages, overtime, longevity pay, and callback time. Fringe benefits typically include expenses for retirement, insurance (life, health and dental) and a uniform allowance, to name a few.

Several types of budgetary controls have evolved over the years to monitor expenditures in fire departments. The most common types of budgetary controls include the monitoring of line-item expenses, monthly budget reports, percentage deviation reports, periodic budget allotments, and controls on filling authorized and funded positions. Monthly budget reports compare the budgets of individual line-items against their expenditures and encumbrances at the end of each month. They typically show the balances for each line-item budget account. Percentage deviation reports show line-item expenditures and encumbrances as a percentage compared to the budgeted appropriation for each line item. Allotment budgeting, not commonly used, includes making a portion of an annual budget available on a monthly or quarterly basis. Seasonal differences in expenditure rates are included when making allotment budgets.

Management controls are also frequently imposed on the filling of authorized and funded positions since personnel expenses make up the largest share of any municipal budget. By not filling existing vacancies immediately, or by delaying the filling of vacancies created throughout the fiscal year, considerable savings can be achieved. In tough budget times, a policy not to fill vacant authorized positions for three months can save 25 percent of annual salary and fringe benefit costs. The development of "tight" departmental budgets and the use of various budgetary control and monitoring techniques are becoming common. The use of these techniques to control expenses—primarily personnel and fringe benefit costs—will undoubtedly continue in the future.

Civilianization Practices. The proper mix of staffing has received increasing attention because of the high costs of salaries and fringe benefits for uniformed personnel. Not too long ago, almost all of the employees in fire departments (except possibly at the clerical level) were uniformed fire personnel. Over the years, the mix of uniformed versus civilian staffing has changed dramatically.

Many positions are now held by civilians for several reasons, the primary of which is for economy. Many aspects of fire service operations have become so complex that they are no longer attractive to the average firefighter. Civilian employees are now frequently used to perform specialized work such as code enforcement, fire inspections, dispatching, emergency medical services, disaster preparedness, buildings and grounds maintenance, public education, and certain training functions. Also, many firefighting personnel prefer their longer work schedules as opposed to working five eight-hour days. For this reason, it is sometimes difficult to recruit uniformed personnel to perform those jobs that have regular weekday work schedules.

When civilianization practices were originally initiated, the goal was to free up the time of uniformed personnel to fight fires rather than reduce their numbers. Now, the goal is to hire civilian personnel for reasons of economy since they typically receive a lower salary and fewer fringe benefits. Existing labor agreements may restrict the use of civilian employees. The use of civilian positions in the fire service is on the increase. This trend will continue in the future as attention is focused on additional ways to balance fire department budgets.

Evaluating Fire Services. There are several reasons for elected officials, as well as fire chiefs, to want to evaluate their community's existing types and levels of fire services. Such baseline information should be developed when conducting a fire service master plan, and may be necessary when administrations change, or may be desirable by a newly appointed fire chief who wishes to "take stock" of what the fire department presently provides to the public in the way of municipal fire services.

The services and factors that should be evaluated include existing risk levels, average response times, the types and number of available apparatus and specialized equipment, the levels of services for fire prevention programs, and existing code administration programs. This assessment should also include the current levels of emergency and fire suppression service capabilities. Since there are no uniform standards for a fire department's service levels, the results desired must be compared to the funds available to finance these services. The level of services will vary from community to community depending upon the existing tax base of a city, the service levels desired, as well as the willingness of taxpayers to pay for these services.

The development of this type of baseline information is helpful for both financial as well as operational planning. Elected officials, for example, when making budget decisions in fire services want to know the impact of possible budget reductions on public services. This type of information is also essential to keep city councils and citizens informed about the quality of their fire services. Once a service evaluation has been conducted it should be periodically updated to reflect any changes that may have taken place since the initial assessment was undertaken. Benchmarking techniques are also being used to compare inhouse fire service practices with those programs provided by other recognized and well-run fire departments.

The National Fire Service Accreditation Program, sponsored by the International Association of Fire Chiefs (IAFC), recently published a self-assessment manual for fire management personnel. Criteria are being developed by which to nationally accredit fire departments. For this reason, the use of self-assessment practices to evaluate a community's level of fire services, as well as review internal operating procedures, will surely increase in the future.

Fire Prevention Practices. Fire prevention programs encompass all efforts taken by uniformed and civilian personnel to reduce the number and magnitude of fires by reducing known fire hazards, making structures fire resistant, minimizing the dangers of hazardous materials, and by providing for the prompt and safe evacuation of people from burning buildings.

Almost all cities have an adopted fire prevention code, many of which are adapted from model codes from nationally recognized organizations such as the NFPA. These codes, once adopted, become part of community's building code requirements. Typical elements of a successful fire prevention program include public education, fire investigation, the enforcement of fire codes, preconstruction plan reviews, and property inspections to ensure compliance with established fire prevention laws and regulations. One of the newest additions to fire prevention programs are regulations concerning the use, storage, and disposal of hazardous materials. Fire prevention personnel also report suspected code violations to other municipal departments for follow-up enforcement action. They work closely with other department personnel in planning, building, zoning, health, and police to ensure code compliance with the goal of limiting the loss of life and property due to fires.

In medium-sized and larger cities this function is usually centralized into a fire prevention bureau or fire marshal's office. In small communities fire prevention duties may be assigned to a single person within the fire department. The most successful fire prevention programs reduce the need for fire suppression services. The use of comprehensive fire prevention techniques, especially those involving public education, are on the increase.

Fire Station Location Decisions. The single largest fire department–related expense in any city is the cost of a new fire station. While the capital expenses reflect a one-time cost, the annual operating costs go on in perpetuity. The cost to outfit a new fire station with apparatus and equipment is also substantial.

The largest long-term expense is hiring the firefighting personnel to properly staff the new station. This is an annual cost that goes on forever. For this reason, the decision to construct a new fire station should not be taken lightly by a governing body. A fire station should not be located in an area merely based on politics or the vocal demands of area residents. It is common for fire chiefs to recommend to their city managers that a professional consultant be hired to determine the location of a new fire station. Several factors must be considered when making a decision to locate a fire station. These criteria commonly include average response times, known hazard potentials, existing building densities, and a city's planned population growth. It should also be kept in mind that it is usually less expensive to retrofit and modernize an old fire station than it is to construct a new one.

Traditionally, city councils have issued general obligation bonds to finance new fire stations. This financing mechanism spreads the cost of a new fire station over a city's entire taxpaying population. For this reason, the trend has been to adopt impact fees to assess developers a share of the costs associated with building a new fire station. The rationale for this fee is that the demand for additional fire services is created by the new population added by residential growth. The use of development impact fees to finance new fire services is gaining in popularity.

Fire Suppression Practices. Historically, the role of fire departments was to extinguish fires. A successful response was one in which the fire was put out quickly, thereby limiting the loss of life and property. Now, however, firefighters must have a knowledge of different suppression techniques, methods for handling hazardous materials, and rescue operation procedures, as well as how to treat medical emergencies.

Fire chiefs, along with their top management personnel, now routinely evaluate their department's response efforts with the goal of identifying shortcomings and making service improvements. A tracking system to record aggregate fire patterns, as well as their causes and relationships, is critical to this evaluation process. Microcomputers and specialized software applications have been developed for this purpose. The results of these evaluations are also used to improve existing community fire prevention programs. In order to assist in properly responding to fires, many fire departments have developed site-specific hazardous materials inventories. These inventories are usually updated annually. When a response is made to an address, known hazardous materials may be identified by retrieving this information from a common city-wide computer database.

A department's apparatus and equipment needs are usually organized around the most likely incidents to occur in any given area. Hence, the numbers and types of apparatus and specialized equipment may vary from fire station to fire station in any community. Fire chiefs also routinely test the readiness of their fire personnel through constant evaluations, drills and exercises, and by continually testing and inspecting their fire apparatus and equipment. A department's fire suppression efforts are no longer an art form. These efforts represent a predetermined comprehensive mix of apparatus, equipment, staffing, and expertise, based on the type of incident.

The use of incident command centers for larger responses have streamlined and improved the coordination of interdepartmental and multiagency responses to emergency situations.

Human Resources Management Practices. The field of human resources management is becoming increasingly complicated, especially for those departments with uniformed personnel. Many state and federal laws, court decisions, and local labor agreements have greatly influenced municipal personnel practices.

Some of the new issues that must be continually addressed include affirmative action, sex discrimination, drug abuse and drug testing, test validation, and the use of legally sound hiring practices. Legislatively, the Fair Labor Standards Act (FLSA), Occupation Health and Safety Administration (OSHA), the Age Discrimination and Employment Act (ADEA), and the Equal Employment Opportunity Commission (EEOC) regulations have served to both standardize and complicate personnel practices in local governments. Local labor agreements are also more complex, with many fringe benefits being tailored to meet the individual needs of firefighters and their families. Most cities now have employee assistance programs (EAPs) to provide 24-hour assistance to their employees and families on a number of different health, medical, and social issues. Many cities now have mandatory pre-employment medical examinations and drug testing for all new employees.

Most medium-sized and larger communities have centralized and integrated these new requirements into their human resource programs. Smaller communities may hire outside consultants to provide many of these human resource services on a fee basis. The trend has been to integrate all of the traditional aspects of the personnel function (i.e., recruitment, selection, training, career planning, performance appraisals, and retirement counseling) with the evolving human aspects of the workplace (i.e., health, safety, employee rights, affirmative action, sex and age discrimination, drug testing, and other forms of employee assistance). The trend in human resources management is to serve the entire range of needs of employees and their families. This trend is becoming commonplace in cities of all sizes.

Incident Command Centers. When municipal fire departments respond to disasters and emergencies, state-of-the-art management practices favor the use of incident command centers (ICCs). The incident command system represents a temporary organization that is formed for one reason—to manage all resources assigned to a specific incident.

While originally designed for major multi-jurisdictional responses, it was later adapted by cities to improve local incident responses. Resources from a number of different municipal departments (e.g., fire, police, health, planning, building, and public works) are coordinated by an on-scene commander. The on-scene commander is in charge, notwithstanding his or her regular job title, lines of authority or levels of responsibility. Typical incident command centers are responsible for one common organizational structure for each incident for the entire duration of the response. This temporary organization includes the functions of command, operations, planning, logistics, and finance.

If an incident crosses jurisdictional boundaries, a unified management team is formed to represent the interests of all participating agencies. The lead agency is usually the city in which the incident has taken place. It is not unusual for communities to hold annual mock disaster exercises to test their incident command center skills. The trend is for fire departments to be the lead agency when forming incident command centers, and to have the on-scene commander coordinate all departmental responses and resources for the incident. The on-scene commander, for larger incidents, would report directly to the emergency operations center (EOC).

These emergency response practices have been tested over the years and been found to be the most effective way in which to organize a community's response to major incidents. The use of these modern management techniques has improved the coordination of resources and enhanced the effectiveness of a city's response to emergency situations.

Interdepartmental Cooperation. Throughout the years, as municipal organizations became more diversified and complex, specialized departments evolved to provide additional public services. Fire chiefs now know that their efforts to respond to emergencies and disasters require the cooperation of several municipal departments.

For example, for a small fire, public works employees may be needed to turn off utilities and block off streets, while police officers would be needed to divert traffic, provide crowd control, and assist in arson investigations. For larger incidents, other departments would provide personnel to assist (e.g., the city manager's office would provide public information, the planning and building department would estimate damages, and the health department would arrange for medical services and temporary lodging). Additional assistance may also be requested from neighboring communities, as well as the county, state, and or federal government. The rule of thumb is that the resources of one level of government must be totally exhausted in responding to the emergency before going to the next higher level of government for assistance.

The response to major disasters and emergencies is so complex that many communities now hold annual emergency exercises in order to practice and refine their response skills involving interdepartmental, intergovernmental, and nonprofit agency coordination. These exercises typically focus on the most likely emergencies or disasters to occur in a given community. Emergency assistance agreements are also common among neighboring municipalities as well as between cities and their county government. Interdepartmental, intermunicipal, and intergovernmental cooperation is common when responding to major emergencies and disasters. Fire chiefs are usually the motivating forces behind these trends, all of which are on the increase.

Management Information Systems. The use of computers and specialized fire department software applications have revolutionized the way information is collected, analyzed, and used to make management decisions. Specialized software applications are frequently used to track calls-for-service, the number and types of fire incidents, fire prevention inspections, equipment maintenance schedules, site-specific hazardous materials and inventories, as well as to monitor departmental budgets.

The reports generated assist fire personnel in detecting patterns of incidents, the number and types of arson investigation, and the effectiveness of fire prevention and other fire-related programs. By analyzing the type and number of fire incidents, for example, fire chiefs can use this information to update existing fire prevention and suppression programs. Computer reports are also used to provide real-time information to on-scene incident commanders. Fire chiefs, when designing their data requirements, should make sure that the data collected is compatible with state and national fire data collection systems. The development of common information will lead to statewide and possible national standards in this field in the future.

Many fire departments are linked to centralized mainframe computers while others use stand-alone minicomputers. It is becoming common for each fire station to have one or more microcomputers linked to a central fire department database. Special online interactive services are also available to fire departments from their professional associations. Many fire and building codes are available in computer disk form, eliminating the need to purchase many code books for individual employees. The LANs are commonly used to connect departmental microcomputers.

The increased use of microcomputers, modems, and easy to use specialized software applications, as well as online services, have facilitated these management information systems trends.

Occupational Safety and Health Programs. Federal and state regulations mandate minimum levels of safety and health standards for firefighters. These standards include the type of clothing and equipment used for fire suppression, the use of protective equipment for hearing and vision, minimum lighting requirements, minimum apparatus and equipment standards, and the use of self-contained breathing apparatus (SCBA). Most states now require that SCBA equipment be used by fire personnel when responding to certain types of fire and hazardous materials emergencies. Proper training and supervision is also required for employee safety and health programs.

The IAFC recently published a communicable disease exposure control plan which provides guidelines for fire departments on safety precautions that should be undertaken by uniformed personnel when providing emergency assistance to individuals. The NFPA also publishes nationally accepted standards for responding to hazardous materials incidents, dealing with industrial fire hazards, and for the handling of flammable and combustible liquids.

With the increasing emphasis on air quality, many fire departments have purchased new exhaust filtering systems to retrofit older fire stations and make them safer for their employees. Old diesel filtering devices are quickly becoming outdated by these new ventilation systems. These new stationwide systems may be cheaper in the long run than retrofitting individual pieces of apparatus with smoke filters. Both the number and types of regulations dealing with the safety and health of uniformed fire personnel are increasing.

Organizational Consolidations. While much publicity has been given to consolidating fire and police departments into public safety departments, fewer than 50 cities throughout the country have actually consolidated these functions. Most of these consolidations have taken place in smaller communities.

The much more common practice is for cities to contract with their county government or for smaller communities to contract with a larger neighboring city for selected fire services. Typical contracts with other governments are generally for hazardous materials responses, emergency medical services, emergency management assistance, code administration and enforcement, and for centralized dispatching services. Many of these services are beyond the financial capacity of smaller cities, or the number of incidents is so infrequent as to not justify an inhouse response capability. There is a trend towards consolidating fire services among smaller cities and fire districts. Some cities in certain areas of the country, primarily in the south and west, have merged two or more fire departments to provide multijurisdictional fire services. These consolidations have occurred primarily in high population growth areas.

The greatest economies of scale have resulted from regional fire service consolidations. These economies have been achieved by centralizing management functions; centralized dispatching and communication networks, as well as support services; improving services because of increased resource levels and more specialized equipment; and by standardizing fire prevention codes. The primary disadvantage of regional fire service consolidation is the perceived loss of local control. Many local elected officials have opposed fire service consolidations for these reasons. While fire and police consolidations and regional fire service consolidations are not a major trend, contract fire services among cities and between cities and counties are gaining in popularity. These trends are likely to increase in the future, especially in smaller and medium-sized communities with limited staffs and technical resources.

Use of Computers, Technologies, and Equipment. Many advances have been made in the fire service field over the years. Most fire department headquarters, as well as neighborhood fire stations, are now routinely equipped with microcomputers. Microcomputers at fire headquarters may be interconnected via LANs. Some fire headquarters, as well as fire stations, are connected to a citywide host computer via microcomputers equipped with modems.

Microcomputers with modems have opened up new online services, such as ICHIEFS, a nationwide fire department networking service complete with key-word research capabilities. Uniformed management personnel can now provide direct input into IAFC's legislative advocacy program as well as access the latest vendor products and services. More than one thousand fire departments subscribe to this online service. The use of microcomputers has become a common way to perform routine administrative tasks such as incident reporting, tracking vehicle maintenance records, performing word processing, maintaining training schedules, issuing permits, preparing hazardous materials inventories, and maintaining building inspection records. The NFPA has various types of codes available on computer disks. Also, new types of emergency medical equipment, hazardous materials response technologies, ventilation systems, self-contained breathing apparatus, and extrication devices have helped to make significant advances in fire services during the past few years.

Although faced with tight budgets, fire chiefs have generally advocated for more sophisticated technologies and equipment to improve their operations and services. All of these trends have helped make uniformed fire personnel more productive. These trends will no doubt continue in the future.

Work Shift Schedules. Many different shift options are used for uniformed fire personnel. Some departments use shifts based on 24-hour periods, while others use shorter shifts ranging from 8 to 14 hours in length. The type of shift used by uniformed fire personnel is often determined by labor agreements. For this reason, the shift patterns used may not be altered by management unless they are renegotiated. When management and fire unions make changes to existing working conditions contained in these agreements, these changes must be approved by the city council.

In recent years, because of limited municipal financial resources, the trend has been for fire unions to bargain for 24-hour work schedules rather than salary increases. From a management perspective, this is a negative trend since departmental productivity decreases as firefighters are fatigued by their longer work schedules. These shifts are typically preferred by uniformed fire personnel because it provides more time to pursue outside part-time employment opportunities. Fire headquarters staff and fire prevention personnel almost always work the same hours as regular city hall employees. This makes it more difficult for fire chiefs to recruit qualified staff employees who must change their working hours, increasing the number of days per week that they must work. More equitable and shorter work shifts make it easier to recruit and retain valuable staff employees. The trend towards 24-hour work schedules has led to the use of more civilian employees in fire department staff positions.

The trend towards the greater use of civilian employees to fill what have traditionally been uniformed staff positions will inevitably increase in the future because of these factors.

External

Contemporary Building Technologies. During the past decade, many technological advances have taken place in the development of fire-resistant building materials, fire detection systems, fire alarm and signaling systems, private fire suppression practices, and other high technology devices designed to prevent and extinguish fires.

Most cities now require built-in automatic sprinkler systems in all new commercial and industrial buildings. Many cities are also mandating the installation of smoke detectors in all new residential construction. In the case of older residential units, many cities have adopted laws that require the installation of smoke detectors before the title to the property can be transferred to a new owner. Because of advances in private sector construction practices, most states periodically update their building code requirements, which are frequently mandated upon municipalities. When cities have the discretion to adopt their own building codes, careful attention must be made to these technological advances to make sure they are incorporated into local building code requirements.

Changes in the field of new building and fire safety technologies are constant, as well as complex. For this reason, the NFPA recently published a 1,200-plus page technical handbook setting forth guidelines for fire protection engineering and fire safety standards. This book is being made available to engineers, architects, designers, manufacturers, and private sector safety personnel. Other recent NFPA publications include topics and issues relating to fire alarm systems, employee signaling technologies, the use and installation

of smoke detectors, state-of-the-art fire extinguishers, and automatic sprinkler and standpipe system options. Private sector executives have also taken
a keen interest in improving fire prevention and fire safety standards for their
companies, both in the layout and design of new facilities as well as in
retrofitting existing facilities when they are updated.

These technological advances, as well as increased private-sector awareness of fire mitigation and fire safety practices, will increase in the future.
These trends will lead to fewer fires and a decreased number of calls-for-service, making more time available for uniformed fire personnel to get involved
in other aspects of fire department operations, such as code enforcement, fire
prevention, emergency medical services, and hazardous materials disclosure
and enforcement programs.

Code Enforcement. One of the basic features of fire prevention programs
is to ensure proper code enforcement. Because a typical municipality has many
codes regulating many facets of the community, interdepartmental cooperation is required for the effective administration of these codes.

Those departments involved in code enforcement refer suspected code
violations to the appropriate department for follow-up enforcement action.
Fire inspectors, for example, may report possible building code violations to
the planning department. Likewise, building inspectors refer fire code violations to fire inspectors. The trend is to cross-train inspectors in the most common codes, and for all departments to cooperate with each other in their
respective code enforcement activities. It is not unusual for one department
to withhold the issuance of a municipal permit until other departmental code
inspections have been conducted. For example, building, zoning, and health
permits may not be issued until fire prevention code compliance has been
certified.

Code violation penalties usually include fines, withholding occupancy
permits, restricting or denying the use of the property, and possible jail sen-
tences. Many cities have increased their monetary fines to facilitate code compliance. Some cities have substantially increased their fines for repeat violators, or for those property owners or occupants who do not correct code
violations in a timely manner. The trend toward increased fines and penalties
for violations will continue in the future.

Codes and Regulations. The purpose of cities is to promote and protect
the health, safety, and welfare of its citizens. In order to accomplish this mission, a number of different codes and regulations have been adopted over the
years to protect citizens from the hazards of fire, chemical spills, and emergency situations.

Traditionally, the typical municipal codes regulate building construction,
fire prevention requirements, health conditions, housing standards, land-use
regulations, and environmental pollution laws. Building codes are used to establish fire safety and structural safety standards. Fire prevention regulations set

forth minimum protection features such as alarm systems, sprinkler systems, occupancy limits, and means of ingress and egress. Health codes set standards for sanitary conditions. Housing standards set forth requirements for property and building maintenance. Land-use and zoning regulations limit the type of improvements to real property, as well as legally allowable building densities. Environmental laws commonly regulate the use and storage of hazardous materials.

The number of specialized codes and regulations have increased dramatically in recent years. The NFPA alone has nearly 300 model codes and standards, ranging from automotive and marine service station codes to the proper storage and handling of numerous chemicals, gases, and fuels. The types of codes and regulations adopted by a municipality must be tailored to meet the fire safety needs of the community. Highly urbanized industrial cities, for example, may have dozens of specialized codes, while rural communities may only need a few general codes.

The trend is for fire chiefs, and their support staffs, to assess the unique needs of their city and recommend those codes that they feel are appropriate. The use of more sophisticated and specialized codes is on the increase, particularly in larger cities and communities in highly urbanized areas.

Contract Services. The use of contract services in fire departments is on the increase. Computer consultants are frequently hired to select computer hardware, design LANs, and install computer systems. Software vendors and consultants may be used to select the appropriate software applications, or to design or modify existing software packages to fit the management information needs of departments. Many cities also use contract employees to coordinate their emergency management programs.

Some communities hire management consultants when conducting departmental assessments to determine the adequacy of existing fire services. When making decisions on the possible location of new fire stations, or determining the adequacy of existing fire station locations, specialized fire service management consultants are commonly used to assist local public officials in making these important decisions. Financial consultants may be used to develop equitable development impact fees and the procedures to administer the collection of these revenues. When forming assessment districts to finance fire stations, it is common to hire specialized financial consultants to determine the proper allocation of assessment costs to individual property owners.

While the trend is toward performing ambulance and emergency medical services with existing fire personnel, some cities are contracting out these services to private ambulance companies. Many smaller communities are contracting with larger cities or counties for selected fire services, especially hazardous materials enforcement programs. The use of these contract services by fire departments is on the increase, especially in smaller communities with limited staffs and technical resources.

Development Standards. In these financially difficult times, many cities are trying to increase their property tax revenues and provide additional jobs by offering economic development incentives. While growth and jobs may be a desirable goal from a revenue standpoint, the impact of such growth on existing fire services should be assessed.

At some point, a new fire station and or additional types of fire apparatus may be needed to properly service new types of industry or population growth. While development impact fees are being used to offset the capital costs of new fire stations, all taxpayers must finance their annual operating expenses. Local elected officials also have the power to alter many types of development standards, such as parking requirements, lot coverage limits, height limitations, and building setbacks, to name a few. These requirements may be waived or lowered by majority vote of city council. Additionally, many local governments are offering increased dwelling unit densities to attract private investment. While the number of dwelling units may be increased, these greater building densities may negatively impact upon the existing levels of fire protection and suppression services. Greater building densities may also generate the need for new fire apparatus to properly respond to calls-for-service.

For these reasons, fire chiefs should be asked to review and comment on proposed economic development incentives before they are approved. This information should be provided to elected officials as a part of their decisionmaking process when considering the use of these incentives. The trend is to assess the impact of proposed incentives on fire services before making economic development policy decisions

Emergency Service Practices. The role of fire departments in providing emergency services has been expanding over the years as the risks and needs of communities have changed. Emergency medical services, rescue operation services, hazardous materials enforcement, and the extrication of accident victims are now commonly provided by uniformed fire personnel.

Since the original mission of the fire service was to respond to emergencies, these additional duties fit nicely within the fire service organizational framework. Also, more advanced building technologies, fire sprinkler regulations, and smoke detector requirements have resulted in fewer calls for service in the area of fire suppression over the years. This trend has made more time available for fire personnel to deal with evolving emergency services. Even in smaller communities, fire suppression duties have changed from extinguishing simple house fires to providing specialized services to large developments as well as high-rise office and residential structures. For this reason, even fire departments in small communities have a need for training in multiagency incident response management practices. Cities of all sizes must stand ready to respond to hazardous materials incidents.

When Congress passed the Superfund Amendments and Reauthorization

Act (SARA) in 1986, they mandated additional responsibilities on municipal governments. For example, property owners or building occupants are required to notify state planning committees of selected hazardous materials, including materials on hand in excess of legally established limitations. If an emergency occurs, the fire departments that have jurisdiction over these properties must be prepared to properly respond to these types of incidents. Also, the Emergency Planning and Community Right-to-Know Act mandates the public disclosure of certain hazardous materials. This information must be made available to the public upon request. It is not unusual for local newspapers to acquire this information and publish it for their readers. This media exposure serves to make industries aware of the negative impact that hazardous wastes have on their company's public image.

Fire Service Master Planning. Most fire departments are faced with increasing citizen demands for their services. Their financial resources, however, have been limited because of citywide revenue limitations, a sluggish economy, and the public's disdain for additional taxes. Rather than make arbitrary cutbacks in fire services, many fire chiefs are recommending the development of fire service master plans. Typically these plans are used to develop desired service levels, analyze the most cost-effective manner in which to provide these services, and require periodic service evaluations to ensure that acceptable standards of service are maintained. It is not unusual for planning committees to consist of a combination of internal and external stakeholders. Internal stakeholders typically include representatives from the fire, building, planning, police, and public works departments. External stakeholders usually include representatives from the public, the board of education, private sector companies, and appropriate regional, state, and national organizations.

When the planning committee is formed, it should evaluate the changing environment (e.g., political, financial, and technological), define the types and number of issues and problems that must be addressed, identify possible solutions, and provide an action plan to resolve agreed-upon issues and problems. These plans should then be given to the governing body in order to assist them in establishing satisfactory levels of community fire services and the funding required to support these services. This is a form of strategic, or issues management, planning. The planning group should meet periodically after the plan is completed to periodically assess progress toward the plan's goals, as well as to continually scan the external environment to determine if any new issues have emerged. As old issues are resolved, new issues that must be addressed should be included in the plan. Since fire service master plans are technical by nature, it is desirable to have a planning advisory committee to determine direction, as well as a planning team to actually implement the plan. The leader of the planning team should also serve as a member of the advisory committee. This person serves as a link between the policy and operation aspects of the master plan.

The use of fire service master planning is on the increase. It is a good management practice to undertake the development of these plans even if a community is not facing financial problems.

Fire Station Closure Decisions. Many fire stations evolved piecemeal as cities developed and grew in population over the years. Because of this long-range trend, some cities may have more fire stations than they actually need to properly service their community. When contemporary fire station location factors are considered, the existing number of fire stations may be excessive. When budget reductions are considered, a sizable savings may result from closing a fire station. This is especially true because of the annual maintenance costs, energy expenses, and the fact that fire stations are staffed 24 hours a day, 7 days a week. While the savings in maintenance and energy costs represent one-time savings, the salaries and fringe benefits saved will last forever.

When fire chiefs wish to explore the possibility of closing a fire station they typically use private fire management consultants to perform consolidation studies because of the politics involved in the location (and closure) of fire stations. As any city council member can attest, closing a fire station is a highly charged political decision. It is not unusual for the "word" to spread quickly about the possibility of closing a fire station. Many citizens who live near the fire station targeted for possible closure show up in mass at public meetings. This places intense political pressure on elected officials, who typically wish to please citizens, not anger them. For this reason, an outside consultant can be used to explain all of the factors considered at these public meetings.

One common rule of thumb is that it is easier not to build a fire station than to have to close an existing fire station. Fire unions, for obvious reasons, typically oppose closing fire stations. The trend has been to base fire station closure decisions on scientifically developed criteria, rather than merely cost-saving considerations.

Intergovernmental Cooperation. During the past several years a number of positive intergovernmental relationships and contract service arrangements have evolved in the area of fire services. At the municipal level, many departments routinely share specialized personnel and equipment resources. Examples would be the sharing of technical experts such as arson investigators, and unique pieces of fire apparatus such as fire trucks with aerial capabilities. Many cities have joined forces in their purchasing practices, with some cities jointly purchasing with county and state governments. The goal of these joint purchasing efforts is to achieve economies of scale (i.e., the greater the quantity purchased, the lower the unit price). Also common are jointly owned fire training facilities, or contracts between smaller communities and larger city or county governments to use their training facilities. Many smaller neighboring cities are also combining their police and fire dispatching operations. In some cases, smaller municipalities are contracting with larger cities for these services. Many small- and medium-sized communities are also contracting with larger cities or county governments for specialized fire services, such as hazardous materials enforcement services.

Most cities have developed or are developing mutual aid agreements to memorialize their intent to cooperate and share resources when responding to public disasters and emergencies. Many of these agreements are also being made with county governments. In the area of emergency and disaster planning, the trend is for communities to hold annual simulation exercises to test their response skills. When these exercises are held, they typically involve representatives from other communities, county and state government, as well as a host of local public and nonprofit organizations, such as school districts, hospitals, and the Red Cross, to name a few. One of the most important functions of a fire chief is to develop and nurture the relationship between a municipal fire department and these other public and nonprofit organizations. Having a knowledge of the resources available from these other organizations is essential when responding to large-scale emergencies and disasters.

All of these intergovernmental relationships provide vehicles to increase the effectiveness of local fire services, as well as expand a fire department's access to important resources, without increasing the departmental budget. All of these trends, especially those involving the intergovernmental sharing of resources and services, will continue.

Professional Development. A number of professional associations, technical resources, and training programs are available to uniformed fire personnel. At the national level, the National Fire Academy provides specialized training in a number of technical areas of the fire service. The IAFC recently published a self-assessment manual leading to departmental accreditation through the National Fire Service Accreditation Program. This is the first program of its type in the country, setting forth uniform standards leading to national accreditation. The ongoing training and professional development of fire personnel are a part of this program.

Those firefighters involved in special assignments, such as providing emergency medical services, advanced paramedic and lifesaving support, and hazardous materials enforcement usually receive a salary stipend for performing these services. The fees generated by these special services help offset the cost of these salary stipends. Training programs and annual salary stipends can be used to improve morale by offering career advancement for fire service employees. The funds spent for specialized training are usually offset by increased levels of productivity. This is especially true in small departments where career advancement is limited because of the lack of promotional opportunities.

Public Education and Citizen Empowerment. One of the main cornerstones of an effective fire prevention program is public education and citizen empowerment. The goal of these efforts is to educate the public on how to protect themselves against fire hazards, as well as how to react appropriately when a fire occurs.

The NFPA has numerous fire safety educational programs available for school children of all ages. Instructional materials, videos, and pamphlets are also available from numerous sources on how to use home fire extinguishers, how to select and where to install smoke detectors, and recommended fire safety guidelines and checklists for homeowners and renters. Specialized training programs and videos on fire safety are also available for private companies on numerous topics such as fire safety procedures for employees, how to properly evacuate buildings, and fire safety recommendations for specific establishments such as high-rise buildings, hotels and motels, health care facilities, and convalescent homes.

All of these public informational programs help to educate and empower citizens to protect themselves from the hazards of fire. When citizens take an active role in preventing fires, they directly reduce the cost of their municipal fire services, not to mention their insurance premiums. The trend for fire departments to educate and empower the public on issues related to fire safety is on the increase, and will surely continue in the future.

Service, Disclosure, and Impact Fees. A community's governing body, as well as its taxpayers, generally feel that municipal fire services should be financed from annual property tax revenues. The rationale for this common belief is that fire services are a basic property-related service.

Over the past decade, however, the trend has been to charge users of specific fire programs for the cost of these specialized services. A growing number of user fees are now common in cities through the country. These include charging a fee for multiple false alarms, fire inspections, plan checking, standby services at public events, ambulance services, and emergency medical services. Many cities even charge private companies a fee for the development of site-specific hazardous material inventories, as well as the cost to annually update these databases. Some communities have initiated annual charges to property owners for augmented fire services to protect larger buildings with excessive service demands. Also, some cities are charging property owners for salvage work at fire scenes, as well as for fires caused by neglect or by hazards created by property owners or building occupants. These service fees are designed to offset fire department operating budgets.

New fees are also emerging to help finance capital improvements that only benefit new residents in recently developed areas of a community. One of the largest fire-related expenses for communities is the cost of a new fire station. New fire stations are usually constructed to meet new service demands created by urban growth. Development impact fees are one way to charge new residents (since these costs are passed on in the form of increased sales prices) for the cost of fire stations. The trend is to make selected services cost-covering, and to annually update these fees to reflect the increased cost of doing business.

Use of Volunteer Firefighters. There are three common staffing patterns in fire departments: only paid employees, a combination of paid and volunteer personnel, and strictly community volunteers.

The type of staffing pattern a community has is influenced by a number of different variables, such as land size, population density, geographic region, and form of government. Generally, volunteer fire departments are most prevalent in the Northeast, while paid departments are most common in the West and South, including the Southeast. The greatest pressure for change has been in cities with fully volunteer fire departments. The national trend is toward the use of paid fire personnel for two primary reasons: those cities that have volunteer fire services have had higher than average rates of fire loss, and volunteer fire departments have experienced a decline in their memberships in recent years. Other factors include an increased citizen demand for additional fire services and more stringent training requirements. Some cities limit the use of fire volunteers, fire reserves, and fire auxiliaries to rural areas. In some cases, these rural areas had volunteer fire departments at the time they were annexed into a contiguous municipality.

Most cities have emergency planning councils that include citizen representatives. Many fire departments also have internship training programs (for prospective firefighters) and fire cadet programs (for high school students wishing to explore careers in the fire service). The trend is away from the use of community volunteers towards the utilization of full-time professional fire personnel to provide fire services. The use of internship and cadet programs in fire departments is on the increase.

THE FUTURE

Internal productivity improvements made in the area of fire suppression services demonstrate major achievements in fire departments throughout the country. This has been the basic type of service provided by fire departments throughout the years. In the past, a fire that was extinguished quickly, and limited the loss of life and property, was the common goal of fire chiefs. Many fires require a more complex and comprehensive response. Firefighters must now have a knowledge of various fire suppression techniques, procedures for handling hazardous materials, the latest rescue operation practices, and training in the treatment of medical emergencies. Fire chiefs routinely evaluate their department's response to fire incidents with the goal of improving their response performance to subsequent emergencies. The use of contemporary fire apparatus and equipment, modern building technologies, a host of new codes and regulations, coupled with improved code enforcement, have helped to reduce the number of fire emergencies. A department's fire suppression efforts now require the proper mix of apparatus, equipment, staffing, and expertise, based upon the most common types of incidents. These variables are now being reviewed and tailored to each fire station based on the most likely emergency responses.

In addition to providing an effective response to fire incidents, a major emphasis is now being made on public education and citizen empowerment programs. The most significant external productivity trends deal with fire prevention programs, rather than fire responses. This proactive effort has been made possible by numerous citizen educational programs. These programs include the proper use of home fire extinguishers, how to select and install smoke detectors, and recommended fire safety checklists for homeowners and renters. Programs are also available for businesspersons such as fire safety procedures for employees, how to safely evacuate buildings, and specific fire safety recommendations for special developments such as high-rise office buildings and residential condominium projects, hotels and motels, and health care facilities and convalescent homes. Many fire prevention programs are also being provided to schoolchildren. When citizens, businesspersons, and children take an active role in preventing fires, and knowing how to properly respond to emergency situations, they reduce the need for a response from their local fire department. Proactive programs such as these have helped to control, if not reduce, the costs of municipal fire services.

One productivity trend, while receiving a great amount of publicity, has not achieved much widespread popularity. This involves the consolidation of traditional fire and police departments into public safety departments. Almost without exception, only a handful of smaller communities throughout the nation have consolidated these historically separate municipal functions. This lack of popularity is based on the reluctance of elected officials to integrate these departments because of opposing forces—existing police and fire unions, the different types of employees in these two departments, and the distinct difference between these separate municipal services. A much larger trend, and one that receives little in the way of publicity, has been for smaller communities to contract with larger cities and for cities to contract with their county government for selected fire services. These contracts for services usually involve hazardous materials response, emergency medical services, code administration and enforcement, and centralized dispatching services. In many cases, these fire services are beyond the financial capability of many smaller communities. In other instances, the number of incidents is so infrequent that the expense of developing an inhouse response capability cannot be publicly justified. Contrary to popular opinion, contracts for services among cities and between cities and counties are much more popular than the creation of public safety departments that consolidate municipal police and fire services. The use of these contract services not only improves services but frequently reduces their costs to the taxpayer.

8

HEALTH AND
HUMAN SERVICES

Some states require their county governments to provide health services. In these states, when human service programs have been initiated, they have frequently been added on to county health departments. Some communities in these states have grafted on human services programs to their recreation departments. Some of these agencies have been appropriately renamed recreation and human service departments to reflect these additional duties. In those states where cities are required to provide health services, human service programs have typically been placed in municipal health departments. Many human services programs have been added at the municipal level in recent years in response to federal and state budget cutbacks. Still other programs have been tailored to fit the needs of individual communities. In many of these cities, the number of human services programs have increased in recent years to the extent that these agencies are now known as the department of health and human services. While the number and types of programs provided by health and human service departments may vary from city to city and state to state, the most common programs are examined in this chapter.

Many municipal health services are required by state law, although elected officials may expand these services to fit the needs of their community. All that is necessary to do this is a governing body's agreement on the types of services desired, and their willingness to fund these services. Many human services, on the other hand, are somewhat more controversial. This stems from the belief on the part of some elected officials that social programs should not be the responsibility of municipal government. The personal philosophy of many public officials is that these services should be provided by families, churches, and other nonprofit community organizations. There is a growing belief, however, that these existing services are not sufficient to address the growing human service needs of many communities. The professional management staff in many municipalities are conducting community needs assessments inventorying available services to meet these needs, and making recommendations to their elected officials on ways to provide for these unmet service needs. The health and human service needs of communities may increase in the future because of the limits being placed on general assistance payments and health benefits to low-income citizens. When these benefits end, some of these needy citizens will seek these services from their municipal government.

The implementation of user fees in these service areas are somewhat limited since the imposition of a fee may preclude low-income citizens from using these services—the very market they were intended to serve. For this reason, when user fees are approved, they are usually intended to only offset a portion of the operating costs of these programs. Some communities are even basing their user fees on ability to pay. Under this concept, the greater one's income the larger the fee and, conversely, the smaller one's income the lesser the fee. The trend is generally to charge some type of fee, even if it is only a modest one based on ability to pay. For these reasons, many health and human services are financed from property tax revenues. Citizens in more affluent communities frequently recognize that these services indirectly benefit the general public. Taxpayers in many poorer municipalities tend to feel that their city government should play a limited role in financing these services. This attitude stems from the feeling that many citizens do not want to pay for services that they do not directly use. Since the elected officials represent the values held by their constituents, heated debates frequently occur on whether property taxes should be increased to finance these types of services.

Most health and human services departments provide an assortment of public health services, community health education programs, and community clinics to their citizens. The types of services provided are tailored to the needs of the community. For example, communities with younger populations may provide well-baby clinics, while municipalities with aging populations may provide exercise and nutrition programs. Environmental and code administration services are also common. Environmental services include ensuring acceptable standards of air and water quality, regulating landfills, modernizing underground fuel storage tanks, removing lead-based paints from residential structures, and removing asbestos from public buildings. Code administration services include the enforcement of health and sanitary codes. Health inspectors and sanitarians are responsible for providing these municipal services. These inspectors frequently refer many violations to other departments for follow-up enforcement action. Social services are also provided by health and human services departments. The number and types of services provided vary greatly from community to community, based on need and ability to pay.

The most common programs performed by health and human services departments are listed in Figure 8.1. While these services may be fairly common in many municipalities, other services may also be provided depending

Figure 8.1
Health and Human Services Major Programs

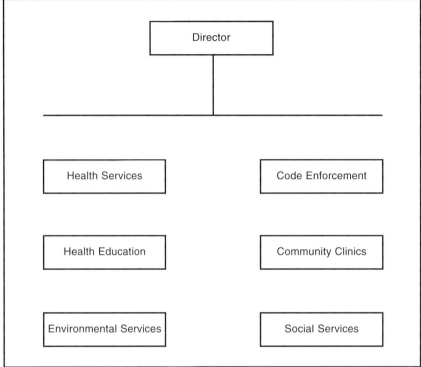

upon state laws, charter requirements, and the service needs of a community as expressed by its elected officials.

DESCRIPTION OF PROGRAMS

Health Services. Most municipalities provide some level of health services to their residents. In some states health services are provided by county governments. Notwithstanding the level of government that provides these services, they are primarily mandated by the state government, secondarily by the city charter.

In recent years, health-related programs have increased in importance at the municipal level, especially those services related to environmental health issues. The traditional areas of concern include the prevention and control of communicable and chronic diseases and the health concerns of young people and senior citizens. Environmental health issues currently on the local agenda include exposure to hazardous materials, the promotion of safe drinking water, and programs relating to clean air.

In many older communities, exposure to lead-based paints, asbestos contamination, exposure to radioactive wastes, and senior citizen diseases are of primary concern. In newer, more suburban communities, health care issues relating to infants, children, and adolescents are of primary importance. These services include educational programs concerning proper nutrition and immunization (for infants); disease prevention and control (for children); and alcohol, drug abuse, and the prevention and control of sexually transmitted diseases (for adolescents).

Community-based health service programs designed to prevent these diseases are now commonplace in most cities. Many health-related programs are funded by the state and federal governments, safeguarding them from the budget-cutting decisions of local governing bodies.

Health Education. Health education programs provide citywide community awareness and information on the prevention of illnesses and diseases before they become a reality, rather than spending limited local funds on medical treatment after health problems develop.

For example, public campaigns on the proper immunization of children prevents future—and more costly—adult health care treatment solutions. Similarly, community health educational programs help to reduce the level of health concerns and problems in a community, preventing future expenses associated with more costly medical responses. Community health education in recent years has focused on antismoking programs, the promotion of proper exercise and nutrition, the proper and responsible use of alcohol, antidrug initiatives to prevent future criminal and social problems, an awareness of the recognition and treatment of mental illnesses, as well as how to prevent sexually transmitted diseases such as AIDS. Many of these programs are promoted and funded by the federal and state governments. These educational activities are an essential component of health programs in cities—the level of government closest to the people. In many municipalities, federal funds such as those provided under the Community Development Block Grant programs enable local public officials to allocate monies to community nonprofit agencies to handle some of these important community health education and prevention programs.

Environmental Services. Traditional health-related services in cities have been primarily concerned with the prevention and control of selected community health problems, primarily through public educational programs. Over the past decade, many environmental health issues have increased in importance.

Many environmental regulations and standards are now mandated upon cities by their state government, with enforcement being delegated to local public health officials. Recent state-mandated environmental health laws and regulations include safeguarding the public from contaminants, managing hazardous materials, ensuring proper air and water quality standards, regulating landfills, modernizing underground fuel storage tanks, removing lead-based paints from residential structures, and eliminating asbestos from public places. The focus on these issues has changed from being strictly educational and reactive, to taking a more positive and proactive stance in safeguarding the public's health.

Health inspectors and sanitarians spend a great deal of their time managing these environmental health issues through comprehensive inspection programs and strict follow-up enforcement actions. Local public health officials also work with other special districts, as well as other levels of government, in dealing with these issues. For example, reported violations are commonly referred to special districts, state departments, and federal government agencies for follow-up action. Large monetary fines and strict compliance requirements, traditionally limited to chronic offenders, are now routinely imposed upon first-time violators.

Code Enforcement. All local public health agencies are responsible for enforcing both the state and municipal public health codes. Most local public health regulations are patterned after their state public health code. Local codes may be more comprehensive than their state codes, with state codes setting forth the minimum public health requirements. If the local code does not address a requirement, the state code must be followed.

Public health codes require the reporting of certain communicable diseases to the state, such as cases of rabies, sexually transmitted diseases such as AIDS, and other selected diseases relating to public health issues. Typical health code inspection and enforcement actions include sanitary conditions in restaurants, complaints of rodent infestation, swimming pool inspections, and numerous nuisance complaints. Nuisance complaints include those violations relating to high noise levels, the accumulation of garbage and debris on public and private property, and stray and wild animal control. Health inspectors also review proposed building plans for all food service establishments. These typically include restaurants, cafeterias, fast-food establishments, hotels and motels, hospitals, public and private schools, and convalescent homes.

Local health officials also jointly cooperate with other municipal departmental code enforcement programs, which are typically administered by the planning, building, and public works departments. These departments also routinely forward health code complaints to health inspectors for follow-up action.

Community Clinics. Municipal health agencies are increasingly offering a greater number of clinics to the public in an effort to provide screening, early detection, and prompt medical treatment for many common yet potentially serious health problems. The number and types of clinics varies greatly. Their need is usually determined by conducting a community needs assessment, preparing an inventory of a city's existing public and private health resources, and determining health care "gaps" in the community.

Typical clinical programs include screening and testing services for high blood pressure, proper dental hygiene, high cholesterol levels, impaired hearing and eyesight, and providing immunization against common childhood diseases. Some cities also provide well-baby clinics, skin cancer screening services, smoking cessation programs, exercise and nutrition classes, and weight loss counseling. While these services typically have been provided free in the past, many cities now charge a nominal cost-covering fee for their services. Many programs for young people and senior citizens are still free of charge. Many clinical programs geared for young people are provided through the local school system. Many other programs are offered in the evening for the convenience of working adults. Some cities also provide health fairs to emphasize personal wellness and disease prevention. Community clinics are also provided for animals, such as those for rabies inoculations and spay and neuter services.

In an effort to save limited funds, many cities have gone to using part-time contract physicians and other health care professionals. Referrals for follow-up treatment are usually made to local doctors on a rotating basis.

Social Services. As human services have increased in importance over the years, they have typically been assigned to a community's health department. Some cities have even renamed their health departments to reflect the importance of this new function. Human services are those public services designed to confront and ameliorate a community's social problems. These programs usually serve low-income and disadvantaged citizens.

Typical human services include those programs dealing with such issues as juvenile delinquency, low income senior citizens, racial prejudice, housing discrimination, unemployment, affordable child care, mental illness, the physically disabled, alcohol and drug abuse, and poverty. While many people believe that these services should be provided by the family, churches, and nonprofit organizations, the community need for these services frequently exceeds the ability of these traditional support groups. Even though the federal and state governments provide many social services or grant funding for these services at the local level, many cities must frequently meet the remaining citizen demand for human services. Most cities provide a combination of federal, state, and locally approved and financed social service programs.

Many citizens believe, and frequently demand, that these services be provided to maintain the quality of life for all residents of their community. Typically these services are provided free of charge, for a nominal fee, or for a fee based on one's ability to pay. Local public officials also frequently serve as a clearinghouse for social services, referring citizens to other public and nonprofit agencies as appropriate.

Productivity Trends

The types of programs provided by health and human services departments have been expanding in recent years. A number of internal productivity trends are examined herein to illustrate this trend. Recent health services have included the expansion of the number of health-related community clinics. These clinics have been tailored to the unique needs of a community's population. New human services have included programs specifically designed for young people, low-income persons, and senior citizens. Examples of these services should include drug prevention and education programs for young people, employment counseling and job skills development for low-income persons, and free lunch programs for senior citizens on fixed incomes. General assistance payments, called welfare payments in some states, involve monthly payments to qualifying individuals and families. Workfare, job development, employment counseling, and day care services are now provided to those persons receiving these public payments. Because of the sensitivity of the issues and problems facing a community in these service areas, many governing bodies have created citizen advisory bodies to review service alternatives and recommend the best way to provide services in these areas. Inexpensive computers and specialized software applications have assisted in tracking clients, their needs, and the services provided to these citizens.

External productivity trends have emphasized ways to expand services without additional local funding, using local nonprofit agencies to provide contract services, and increasing interagency cooperation to assist those citizens in need of these services. In order to hold down costs, many department directors have sought private funding for their services. Rather than duplicate their programs, many communities are contracting with local nonprofit organizations to provide specialized health and human services. Another important trend is for health and human service professionals to cooperate in interagency referrals. These efforts have helped to direct citizens to those agencies that can provide assistance for their particular needs. Frequently, so many programs are available from other local nonprofit agencies that a knowledge of these external resources is essential to properly refer citizens to these outside agencies. Many departments have initiated public education and citizen empowerment programs to assist citizens in solving their own personal problems before they require government intervention. Because grant funds have been reduced in these service areas, many cities have initiated user fees, typically based on one's ability to pay.

Those internal and external productivity trends examined in this chapter are highlighted in Table 8.1. While the number of services has been expanding, the creative efforts of department managers have helped to hold down expenses by cooperating with other government agencies, as well as the many local nonprofit organizations that provide health and human services.

Table 8.1
Health and Human Services Productivity Trends

Internal	External
Departmental Inspection Referrals	Community Resource Centers
Evolving Health Services	Contract and Coproduced Services
Evolving Human Services	Interagency Cooperation
General Assistance Programs	Private Cosponsorship of Public Programs
Hazardous Materials Disclosure and Enforcement	Professional Development
Human Resources Management Practices	Public Education and Citizen Empowerment
Innovative Public Services	Public Health and Human Services Master Planning
Knowledge of Available Resources	Sorting Out Responsibilities
Organizational Structures	State and Federal Grant Programs
Public Policies and Cost-Effectiveness	User Service Charges, Regulatory Fees, and Fines
Role of Elected Officials and Advisory Bodies	Working with the Community
Use of Computers and New Technologies	

Internal

Departmental Inspection Referrals. Several municipal departments have highly trained inspection personnel. These inspectors typically work in the functional areas of building, fire, housing, public works, zoning, and health. State laws usually require separate certification programs and specialized qualifications for these employees.

In more progressive municipal organizations, these inspection personnel are being cross-trained to the extent that they are made aware of the general code requirements in each of these functional inspection areas. For example, health inspectors routinely refer other possible code violations to the appropriate departmental inspection employees for follow-up enforcement. Likewise, other departmental inspectors routinely refer possible health, environmental, and health-related housing code violations to health inspectors for follow-up inspections and proper enforcement action. While state laws, labor agreements, and job descriptions may restrict the inspectional duties of these employees, the trend is towards greater interdepartmental cooperation in referring possible code violations to other municipal departments.

This trend has served four important purposes. It has increased the work productivity of all municipal inspection employees, has facilitated a more comprehensive approach to the enforcement of city codes, and has enhanced interdepartmental cooperation in this important area of local government. Most importantly, it sends a message to the public that their municipal government is actively concerned and involved in the enforcement of all city codes. City managers have encouraged this trend since it reflects the efforts of departments to cooperate with the goal of improving services to the public. Elected officials have endorsed these efforts since they hold down the need to hire additional departmental inspection personnel. These trends are on the increase in communities of all sizes and geographic locations.

Evolving Health Services. The types of programs provided in the health service area are frequently mandated by state statute. Additional health services, when they are provided, have evolved over the years to fit the unique needs of those citizens being served. In recent years, environmental health issues such as air and water quality and those programs promoting increased sanitary standards have been high on most municipal service agendas.

In older communities, issues surrounding senior citizens such as disease prevention, medical diagnostic clinics, and early treatment services are of primary concern. In younger communities, issues concerning infants, children, and young adults are of primary importance. The types of community clinics being provided are also tailored to fit a municipality's needs. In communities with aging populations, blood pressure, hearing and eyesight, cholesterol level, skin cancer screening, smoking cessation, weight loss, and exercise and nutrition clinics are frequently provided. In newer suburban communities, childhood immunization, dental hygiene, drug prevention, sex education, and well-baby clinics are being made available to younger families and residents.

Municipal health services in recent years have increasingly focused their attention on community health education programs concentrating on disease prevention, medical screening, and early treatment programs. The numerous health clinics provided are designed to both educate the public as well as diagnose and direct citizens into early treatment programs. Many health-related clinics are provided free of charge by local area doctors. In some cases, departments contract with area physicians and dentists to provide these clinic services. While most health services have been provided free in the past, there is a trend to charge a modest fee for clinics and other services that only benefit specific users.

Evolving Human Services. While many public health programs have been established for some time, the number of human services offered to citizens have been expanding in recent years. With fewer grants from higher levels of government, elected officials and local administrators have assumed more of the role of servicing the needs of low-income and disadvantaged citizens in their communities.

A host of special programs have evolved to serve the needs of young people, families, and senior citizens. Typical youth programs include juvenile and gang prevention services, sex and drug education programs, youth employment services, drop-in centers for teenagers, and the establishment of safe houses for runaways. Specialized programs for senior citizens frequently include affordable housing assistance, free lunch programs such as those provided by Meals-on-Wheels, and handicapped access programs. For families, including single adult households, affordable child care services and family counseling programs are commonly provided. In addition to these specialized services, a number of general programs are now being provided for the benefit of the entire community. These programs include, but are certainly not limited to, mental health counseling, alcohol and drug abuse counseling, the prevention of racial prejudice and housing discrimination, discount transportation services for the young and elderly, employment and training development, consumer protection, tenant rights, and crisis intervention.

Many of these services are coordinated with other public and nonprofit community organizations. When a municipality does not offer a specific service, referral services are provided to direct citizens to these other agencies. There is a trend among cities to contract with other public and nonprofit agencies for some of these services. The trend in the past has been to provide these services free of charge. Now it is not unusual to impose a modest fee based on one's ability to pay. Many of these services are still provided free to young people and senior citizens. Local elected officials and administrators have been faced with the difficult dilemma of having to confront increased service demands in the face of limited financial resources. For this reason, the human and social services provided by a municipality must be prioritized and specifically tailored to met the service demands of citizens at a reasonable expense.

General Assistance Programs. Many state laws vest county governments with the responsibility of performing services to citizens on public assistance, including the distribution of general assistance payments to qualified low-income citizens. Some state laws require city governments to perform these services. Cities throughout the nation have been highly innovative in the implementation of new programs to hold down both the administrative costs of these programs, as well as to limit the number of citizens receiving general assistance payments.

While these cities must operate within the parameters set by state law, many of these laws have allowed communities to design and operate creative workfare, job development, and employment counseling programs, as well as place durational limits on the length of general assistance payments. Workfare programs have required many general assistance recipients to work a set number of hours per week in order to qualify for and receive general assistance payments. Exclusions are usually granted to some recipients for medical and other specific reasons. Job development programs have been designed to instruct public assistance recipients on resume preparation, how to seek out employment and make job applications, and ways to enhance their personal interview skills. Employment counseling services have educated these citizens on how to use local job banks and available educational programs to enhance their employability. Some cities have even developed their own job banks in order to facilitate the placement of general assistance recipients in local jobs that fit their skills and interests. Other cities have approved durational limits on the number of months that a citizen may receive general assistance payments. General assistance programs with durational limits on benefits are most successful when combined with workfare, job development, and employment counseling services.

This service area is presently in a state of transition. The outcome of the exact nature of services ultimately provided will be determined by federal legislation as well as individual state laws. The national trend in local governments is to develop new and innovative programs to help general assistance recipients to end their dependency on government aid as a way of life. These programs have been especially popular with politicians and taxpayers, and have helped to hold down the cost of municipal government. All of these trends are on the increase and are likely to be around for many years in the future.

Hazardous Materials Disclosure and Enforcement. Public health officials, because of their specialized qualifications and functional responsibilities, are oftentimes assigned duties relating to hazardous materials disclosure and enforcement. For example, virtually all states have mandated "right-to-know" programs upon their municipalities due to federal requirements concerning the content disclosure of all hazardous materials used in the municipal workplace. Each department must inventory, label, and make instructions available to their employees on the proper handling, usage, storage, and disposal of hazardous materials. Training programs for new employees are required, along with yearly training updates for all departmental employees. In medium-sized and larger communities health officials frequently coordinate the implementation of these employee "right-to-know" hazardous materials disclosure programs. Smaller communities frequently use specialized consultants to provide these services. While fire department personnel typically respond to hazardous material spills, it is not uncommon to have cross-departmental response teams respond to these emergency incidents. These teams may consist of health, fire, police, and building personnel. These response teams are frequently headed or assisted by environmental health officials.

Many cities have enacted laws that permit billing these response expenses to the responsible party—typically a building owner, tenant, or contract hauling company. These laws have encouraged private sector compliance with hazardous materials regulations, and have helped to reimburse communities for the costs associated with these responses. Many communities have also undertaken the development of hazardous materials inventories for private companies and industrial plants within their political boundaries. A fee is usually charged to private individuals and corporations for the development of these hazardous materials inventories. These inventories are usually updated annually. The responsibility for this task may rest with health or fire officials, depending upon the expertise available in these departments. If this information is assembled by health officials, it is shared with fire departments to facilitate a proper response to fires and other emergency situations.

The involvement of health officials with all aspects of hazardous materials enforcement and disclosure is on the increase. Because of state and federal mandates, and the increased public awareness of the dangers of hazardous materials, these trends will continue in future years.

Human Resources Management Practices. In their ongoing efforts to hold down departmental costs and increase (or at least maintain) the level of public services they provide to citizens, many health and human service directors have initiated creative measures to achieve both of these goals. These efforts have included ways to leverage public services, cross-train existing employees to perform a greater variety of tasks, and the increased use of contract employees.

Existing public services have been increased through the use of part-time employees and volunteers. Part-time employees save expenses because they do not receive fringe benefits. Volunteers, who are typically used to provide nonprofessional and nonessential public services, donate their time at no expense to their municipal government. These personnel are not used to provide services performed by the regular workforce, but are used to augment existing levels of public services.

The cross-training of personnel has also helped to increase employee productivity. Some departments have sanitary inspectors dedicated to only one program, such as food or milk inspections. Many other departments have adopted the district concept of providing health inspections, where the same inspector has responsibility for all inspection activities within his or her assigned geographic area. This concept eliminates the problems associated with single-task boredom, and keeps personnel fresh and wondering what problem the next phone call will bring. This concept, growing in popularity, permits the greater utilization of staff to perform a wider variety of health inspection services.

Many departments have also increased the use of contract employees to provide specialized health, environmental, and human services. Savings are realized because these employees do not receive fringe benefits, which typically run about one-third of salary expenses. The use of contract employees has also helped to arrange staffing patterns around the public's demand for services. The full-time professional and program staff are usually used to coordinate and monitor the programs provided by contract employees. The hiring of contract personnel—such as doctors, dentists, counselors, and specialized service-providers—is an example of this trend. It should be noted that contract services are very specific and the typically flexibility and spontaneity of reacting to problems may be lost in the process.

Because of requirements imposed by limited budgets, the trend towards the increased use of part-time employees and volunteers, the cross-training of existing employees, and the use of contract employees is on the increase. It should be noted that a municipality's existing labor agreements may place restrictions, sometimes even prohibit, the use of some of these cost-saving practices.

Innovative Public Services. Health and human services departments, because of limited financial resources, and increasing citizen demands for sometimes politically sensitive programs, have been very creative when designing new programs to fit unique community needs. Most of these programs have been designed for special population groups, such as high-risk teenagers, low-income families, senior citizens on fixed incomes, the homeless, and citizens with drug and or alcohol dependencies.

In addition to developing specialized public educational programs to prevent future undesirable and costly conditions from taking place, many positive programs have been designed to assist special groups in need of health and human services programs. Many programs such as treatment centers have been created for problem teenagers and adults with alcohol or drug problems. Successful low-cost day care programs have been developed for working mothers and families with limited incomes. Inexpensive childhood immunization programs have helped to reduce the public health costs of dealing with diseases resulting from lack of inoculations in later years. Many juvenile delinquency and gang-prevention programs are evolving to reduce crime and improve the social fabric of a community.

Many national professional associations have also assisted local elected officials and administrators with their ongoing efforts to properly address the health and social problems in their community. Some of the most recent publications from the National League of Cities (NLC) have been monographs and case studies on how to combat community homelessness. The American Public Health Association (APHA) also has several publications available dealing with health programs for children, AIDS prevention, maternity care, and ways to create a healthier community.

Because of limited funds, public health and human services administrators have worked closely with other public, nonprofit, charitable, and community groups to administer these programs and provide valuable services to needy citizens. The development of specialized programs will continue in the future as these professionals grapple with the health and human service needs and problems in their communities. Limited funds have facilitated interagency coordination and cooperation in the development and provision of these vital public services.

Knowledge of Available Resources. Due to the diverse nature of the responsibilities and programs provided by health and human services departments, the employees in these departments should have a good working knowledge of the "outside" resources available to serve the public. Other government agencies—federal, state, and county—frequently provide related services as well as grant funds for specialized health and human services programs and pilot projects.

A host of nonprofit, charitable, and community organizations, including hospitals, also provide many health and human services, as well as other specialized programs, for children, young adults, families, and senior citizens. Specialized consultants also provide a number of managerial, technical, and computer hardware and software services in the field of public health and human services. A knowledge of the services provided by other governmental agencies—as well as nonprofit, charitable, and community organizations—and specialized management and technical consultants is essential to properly serve those citizens in need of public health and human services.

Because municipal government is the level of government closest to the people, many citizens contact their city hall when they are in trouble or in need of services. An evolving and vital role of public health and human services officials is to refer citizens to the appropriate public and private agencies that provide specialized services in these areas. Many administrators have developed specialized resource manuals and directories to assist their professional and program staff when referring citizens to other agencies for services. The trend to codify information about existing programs and services and to educate employees about these resources is on the increase. Due to the fragmented nature of many health and human services, this trend will no doubt continue in the future.

Organizational Structures. In many states, county governments are required by state statute to provide health services to the citizens of all communities within their political boundaries. In states where counties provide health services, human services have been grafted on to health departments over the years. More progressive counties in these states now provide a wide assortment of health and human services programs to their citizens. Those health and human services provided by counties above the minimum service levels mandated by law have been limited and tailored to fit the unique needs of citizens. Many communities in county-provider states frequently only offer a limited number of programs in the human services area. When these cities have assumed a greater number of human services programs, they have typically been placed in recreation departments. In those states where cities are required to provide health services, as is the case with counties, human service programs have been placed in municipal health departments.

Many local human services–related programs have evolved over the years to fit the needs of a city's poor and disadvantaged residents. In fact, so many human services programs have been assumed by cities in city-provider states that health departments have been renamed the department of health and human services. Regardless of the organizational placement of the human services function, the number of human services have been expanding at a rapid rate over the past decade. As the federal and state governments have reduced both the number and funding of their grant programs in the health and human services areas, counties and cities have assumed the responsibility to provide these needed services.

Local elected officials are in the best position to know the health and human services needs of their constituents. For this reason, they have responded with programs tailored to fit the needs of their communities. Municipal governing bodies face a unique dilemma, however, in that they desire to provide additional services, but since no funds are available from higher levels of government, they must rely on limited local tax dollars to provide these programs. Local elected officials will be grappling with the issue of increasing service demands with limited funding to provide these services for many years to come.

Public Policies and Cost-Effectiveness. Many of the large city problems in this service area, such as unemployment, alcohol and drug abuse, poverty, juvenile delinquency, violence, and communicable diseases such as AIDS, are now spilling over to smaller suburban and rural communities. The typical reaction of elected officials has been to treat the symptoms of these problems by hiring more police officers or health counselors, rather than to initiate programs to treat the causes of these problems.

There is a trend among public officials in many cities to recognize the fact that prevention programs may be less expensive to the taxpayers in the long run when dealing with a community's health and social problems. For this reason, it may be more cost-effective to fund health education programs, child immunization clinics, job training centers, child care facilities, and counseling programs for citizens before the lack of these programs lead to future law enforcement and social problems. For example, sex and drug education programs are less expensive than dealing with the healthcare costs associated with the treatment of AIDS patients and drug addicts. Childhood immunization programs are cheaper to provide than the complications from a preventable disease later in life. Likewise, it may be more fiscally prudent to provide job training programs than to have to pay general assistance costs for unemployable citizens. Also, by providing adequate and affordable child care, parents can work and be productive members of their community.

Local elected officials should be aware that the trend for state governments to provide durational limits on general assistance programs will certainly lead to possible severe and unanticipated health and social problems for cities in the future. Many public health professionals feel that the added costs from increased alcohol and drug abuse, as well as crimes in general, may escalate in the future at the local level because of the actions of state legislative bodies. While states may be saving money and reducing their budgets now, municipal officials will certainly have to confront the local problems resulting from these actions. The possibility of future social problems, coupled with limited funds to tackle these issues, will certainly have negative social consequences at the community-level in future years.

Role of Elected Officials and Advisory Bodies. Many community issues related to public health and human services departments are controversial. It is common for elected officials not to want to fund any new programs, especially those that generate little or no revenue. Many of the needed public health and human services programs for disadvantaged and low-income citizens fall into this category.

When sensitive community issues and problems must be addressed, it is common for a city council to form an advisory body to address these municipal concerns. It is not unusual for cities to have several permanent standing commissions and committees dealing with community issues relating to human rights, affordable housing, senior citizens, children and youth, and persons with disabilities, to name a few. When new, sensitive issues and problems must be addressed, it is not unusual for mayors and city councils to form ad hoc committees and or task forces to address those community concerns that do not fall under the purview of the existing bodies. These issues and problems may include, but are not limited to, juvenile delinquency, substance abuse, gang prevention, youth unemployment, and minority relations.

Rather than get directly involved in sensitive community issues, and in an effort to marshall community support for program recommendations, it is standard practice for members of the governing body to use citizens groups to recommend solutions in these service areas. The astute public health and human services administrator recognizes these municipal political realities. For this reason, department directors may wish to recommend that such citizens advisory groups be formed to address outstanding public health and human services issues. The professional staff can work closely with these groups to form sound recommendations to elected officials. Representatives from these groups, including the governing body, should also be asked to assist with departmental master planning programs.

The trend is for department directors to recommend that such groups be formed by their elected officials to help formulate politically acceptable program recommendations on sensitive community issues. This trend has been facilitated by tight budgets and the need to seek out new revenue sources to fund proposed health and human services programs.

Use of Computers and New Technologies. In recent years, new inexpensive microcomputers, user friendly packaged software applications, medical diagnostic equipment, and other technologies have become available to improve the management and operations of health and human services departments.

As employees have become more computer literate, and the cost of micro-computer systems has decreased, the use of personal computers has become an efficient and effective way to perform routine administrative and technical tasks such as inspection scheduling, conducting clinic registration, perform-ing facilities maintenance, maintaining licensing records, tracking citizen com-plaints, and maintaining citizen immunization records. Departmental budget monitoring and control have also been enhanced with the use of personal com-puters and new easy-to-use financial software. The availability of more user-friendly packaged software applications has served to facilitate these trends. Since health records must be kept on file for a number of years, many depart-ments, in order to save scarce office storage space, have converted their manual records to microfilm, microfiche, and or computer databases. These tech-nologies have greatly enhanced municipal records management and informa-tion retrieval practices. In addition to saving money, these technologies have served to improve the quality of services provided to the public.

New automated cash register and receipting systems are now being used to replace the outdated manual labor–intensive recordkeeping practices of the past. These systems also facilitate making daily bank deposits to increase the amount of interest earned on cash received from over-the-counter transactions. Automated telephone message centers are also being used to better serve the public. It is now possible to program telephones with standard responses to citizen inquiries, such as hours of operation, program offerings, registration information, and health and human services program scheduling procedures. This use of these technologies has freed up the time of existing staff person-nel to perform other essential health and human services functions.

Health and human services professionals have advocated for the use of more sophisticated equipment and technologies to improve their operations and public services. All of these trends have made existing employees more productive and have helped to hold down the need for additional staffing. Since many of these trends improve services and reduce costs their use will be on the increase in the future.

External

Community Resource Centers. A myriad of health and human services programs are provided to citizens by a host of public, private, nonprofit, and charitable organizations. There are frequently so many programs available for certain services that it is difficult for the average individual or family to be aware of their existence. Information about these programs needs to be col-lected, assembled, and made available at one or more central locations for refer-ence by departmental employees, other agencies, and members of the public.

A brief sampling of these agencies and their services are highlighted below. At the federal level, various programs are available from three departments—labor (DOL), housing and urban development (HUD), and health and human services (HHS). State governments usually provide some social services, general assistance programs, job training, and employment counseling As indicated elsewhere in this chapter, municipal governments provide a variety of public health, environmental, and human services. Services are also available from many local nonprofit and charitable organizations such as United Way, YMCAs, YWCAs, Big Brothers, Big Sisters, Boys and Girls Clubs, Salvation Army, Red Cross, and the Legal Aid Society. Some of these community groups provide specialized services for disabled persons, troubled families, substance abusers, as well as operate teen drop-in centers, safe houses, and telephone hotlines. Many local churches and houses of worship also provide various human and social services to their members, as well as to other citizens.

Health and human services administrators should supervise the preparation of community resource directories. The various services and programs need to be brought together for the benefit of program managers, other agencies and, most of all, the citizens being served by these programs. Once prepared, copies of these community resource directories should be distributed to employees, other agencies, as well as placed in the public library for reference by citizens. The trend to prepare community resource directories, due to the importance and fragmented nature of these programs, is on the increase.

Contract and Coproduced Services. Many local agencies are contracting selected public health, environmental, and human services from private sources. Private health professionals such as medical doctors, dentists, and nurses frequently provide citizen clinic services on a contract basis. Private companies may be hired to provide counseling programs, lead-based paint testing, building security services, maintenance functions, and laboratory testing procedures. Some services may be contracted out to local nonprofit, charitable, and community organizations. Many cities are using contract employees to perform selected services since these employees do not receive fringe benefits. Some cities even contract out their animal control services to either their county, another city, or to a local humane society.

All of these trends have assisted administrators in providing the level of staffing needed to fit citizen demands for these services. Also, since many specialized services are provided only periodically, it would make little sense to hire full-time regular employees to perform these tasks. It is generally desirable to contract for services when the service can be provided at a lower cost, performance controls are maintained, legal enforcement is not required, and when these privatization practices do not violate a community's existing labor agreements.

The coproduction of public services occurs when citizens take an active role in helping their municipal government provide the service. It is not uncommon for public officials to ask citizens and community organizations requesting a service to participate in providing the service. The distribution of illness and disease prevention information, and citizen participation in exercise, nutrition, weight loss, smoking cessation, and medical screening programs are examples of this trend. Many state laws prohibit the discarding of hazardous materials with regular household wastes. Rather than using municipal employees to pick up these illegal materials, inexpensive drop-off centers are provided to assist citizens in discarding these materials. Some cities now require private companies, like gasoline stations, automotive garages, and retail stores, to be responsible for disposing of old car batteries, used tires, and household appliances when replacements are purchased by citizens. The coproduction of services between city halls and citizens have helped to provide new programs at minimal expense to the taxpayers.

The use of coproduction service practices is on the increase, as is the use of private companies and contract employees to provide specialized services to citizens. Because of budgetary limitations, these trends will inevitably continue in future years.

Interagency Cooperation. In the area of human services, municipal administrators must cooperate with a host of other public, nonprofit, charitable, and community organizations. When it comes to health services, local public officials must routinely interface with state and county agencies, as well as local hospitals and community clinics. Human and social services require keen coordination because of the expanding number of organizations involved in providing these services.

Municipal governments can perform a valuable service in providing community resource directories, referring citizens to the appropriate agencies for services, coordinating service delivery, and eliminating duplication in the provision of these services. Most importantly, health and human services administrators can identify service needs and inform their city manager and elected officials of the need to provide additional services. The efforts of professional administrators can help reduce the disjointed, fragmented, and incremental nature in which many of these services are provided to citizens. For example, while many cities have already established committees, commissions, councils, and other advisory bodies to deal with these issues, these groups primarily focus their attention and efforts on specific groups and issues (e.g., children, youth, senior citizens, handicapped, affordable housing, discrimination, and human rights, to name a few). Local nonprofit and charitable organizations also have boards of directors that focus on their particular service area.

Because of the many different agencies and organizations involved in addressing service issues, citizens are sometimes confused and do not know how to seek out these services. Likewise, a single problem may involve the resources of several public, nonprofit, charitable, and community organizations. Public health and human services professionals are beginning to serve two important services to address these problems. They are increasingly holding local educational symposiums for service providers so that representatives from each agency can learn what services are being provided by other organizations. They are also forming multiagency task forces to address specific issues and problems. For example, to work on a program to help eliminate juvenile delinquency problems, a multiagency task force may include representatives from municipal government departments, county and state agencies, the school district, as well as local youth service agencies. Because of the diverse and fragmented nature of these services, these two trends will undoubtedly increase in importance in future years.

Private Cosponsorship of Public Programs. In their continuing effort to provide innovative and valuable services with limited budget dollars, many health and human services administrators have reached out to the private sector for financial assistance, services, and donations.

Private sector companies are increasingly being asked to sponsor public health and human services programs, making them available free of charge to citizens. For example, free health clinics and childhood immunization programs may be made available by private companies by paying a community the amount of revenues typically generated by these activities during the "free use" period provided to citizens. Likewise, a private company may wish to sponsor a public health fair, parenting classes, or well-baby clinics at no cost to taxpayers. Many large employers in a community have also provided entry level jobs and job training for public workfare programs designed to employ those citizens receiving general assistance. Local grocery stores and supermarkets have also donated dry goods and canned foods for food pantry programs designed to benefit low-income individuals and families.

Under these public or private service arrangements, companies sponsor these programs financially, provide services, or donate items to their municipal government, while the government provides the service to its taxpayers. This is an inexpensive way for a company to obtain free advertising, helps to promote a company's name in a positive light and, at the same time, provides a valuable free service to the community and its citizens. Many private companies are willing to provide financial support and make donations for these types of community programs. In many cases, all that is needed is for concerned public health and human services administrators to seek out this type of private support. Many of these programs, because they do not involve the use of tax dollars, do not need the typical bureaucratic approvals usually required by publicly financed programs.

The use of these innovative public or private partnerships is on the increase. As public health and human services administrators become more sophisticated at leveraging public services with limited tax dollars, these programs will become more commonplace in the future.

Professional Development. There are several national and state professional associations for municipal employees in the public health, environmental health, and public welfare fields. These organizations provide a vast number of educational programs, conferences, technical resources, publications, and professional networking opportunities. These membership organizations also provide research services on current topics related to these specialized fields. The largest of these organizations is the APHA, which has more than 50,000 members from nearly 80 public health occupations. Specialized training programs and publications are provided in many technical areas such as management and administrative practices, controlling communicable diseases, as well as community health, environmental, and laboratory practices.

Many of the recent publications in these fields focus on specialized programs dealing with children's issues, AIDS prevention, housing standards, helping the mentally ill and homeless, and recommended diagnostic procedures for a host of specific public health issues. Other municipal professional associations, such as the NLC and the International City/County Management Association (ICMA), have published recent case studies on how public officials are successfully coping with numerous public health and human services issues and problems in their communities. The typical urban issues examined include unemployment, substance abuse, homelessness, child care, high-risk youth, and how to provide services with limited financial resources.

Since many cities have reduced the number of personnel in the health and human services area, it makes sense to train employees to make them more knowledgeable and productive. The funds spent for training, conferences, and publications are usually offset by increased levels of employee productivity. Training is especially essential in small communities with limited professional staffs. The trend to spend municipal funds for professional development activities is on the increase.

Public Education and Citizen Empowerment. Public educational programs provide valuable citizen awareness and information on the prevention of illnesses, diseases, and other problems before they become major issues or public expenses. An assortment of health educational programs are now available to hold down the costs associated with health conditions and problems before they reach the point where expensive treatment is required. Communities have also tried to educate and empower their citizens to improve their personal conditions before the social fabric of a community becomes unraveled.

Many of these public education and citizen empowerment programs are geared to young people, adolescents, adults, families, senior citizens, and other special groups. Programs for young people involve drug education projects, immunization clinics, dental hygiene programs, and hearing and eyesight examinations. Services for adolescents include programs on sex and drug education, juvenile delinquency prevention services, and gang prevention assistance. Programs for adults include smoking cessation clinics, weight loss clinics, nutrition and dietary classes, and exercise instruction and workshops. Family programs typically include well-baby clinics, family counseling, and low-cost child care programs. Special services for senior citizens usually include medical screening clinics (e.g., blood pressure, cholesterol, skin cancer) and providing affordable housing to seniors on low and fixed incomes. Job development and employment counseling services are also typically provided to those citizens in need of these services, regardless of their age.

All of these public educational programs help to empower citizens to protect and safeguard themselves against future health and social problems. Citizen empowerment through these types of public educational programs are less expensive than dealing with chronic health problems and negative social conditions in future years. Most health and human services professionals realize that these types of public services are cost-effective, even though a community's health or social conditions have not reached problematic proportions. It is incumbent upon these professionals to educate their city managers and elected officials on the need for these valuable educational and citizen self-help programs.

The trend for health and human services departments to educate and empower citizens on issues and problems relating to these service areas is on the increase, and stands to continue in future years.

Public Health and Human Services Master Planning. Since municipal funds are severely limited and local politicians do not want to increase taxes to raise additional revenues, any additional funding directed towards new health and human services programs must be targeted to high-priority services. Rather than solely relying on the expert judgment of a city's professional staff it makes sense politically for health and human service directors to actively involve the community when developing public service master plans. Such plans, when they involve a cross-section of the community, lend political legitimacy to program and funding recommendations.

To initiate such a planning process, the first step usually involves the formation of a planning committee. This committee is typically composed of a combination of external and internal stakeholders. External stakeholders may include other service providers, members of existing advisory bodies, representatives of advocacy groups, recognized community experts, as well as the users of services. Internal stakeholders usually include representatives from the governing body, advisory groups, other municipal departments, and inhouse departmental resource personnel.

The planning committee's first goal is to assess the external environment to determine program issues and problems that should be addressed. An inventory of existing community resources should then be conducted to determine if service levels are adequate. Those issues and problems that are not being addressed should then be placed in priority, with the planning group focusing their attention on the several most important service issues facing their municipal government. Cost-effectiveness and suggested funding sources must also accompany such a plan. It would serve no useful purpose merely to present the city manager or elected officials with a list of unmet service needs with no sound program recommendations on how to properly finance these services.

The major issues and problems identified should be addressed through a multiyear action plan. This plan will assist elected officials in properly setting health and human services priorities in their community. When the plan is considered by elected officials, representatives of the planning group should be present to advocate for the plan as well as answer any questions on its development. Annual updates to these plans are routine and should be conducted by the planning group that prepared the initial document. Limited revenues and increasing citizen demands for more services have created an environment where the development of service master plans is essential. The use of these planning practices in on the increase.

Sorting Out Responsibilities. Some elected officials and agency directors believe that many health and social problems should not be the responsibility of municipal government. These attitudes generate from one's personal political philosophy and or the belief that municipal taxes should not be increased to provide these services. These public officials believe that these types of problems are best handled by the family, churches, and other community nonprofit organizations. There is a growing belief among public officials to recognize that the services provided by these groups are disjointed, fragmented, and incremental in their nature, and are frequently insufficient to meet the needs of the community.

It is incumbent upon professional health and human service directors to help educate their top management and elected officials on the proper role of their municipal government in dealing with their community's service needs in these areas. The professional staff should determine community needs, inventory available community resources to meet these needs, and make recommendations concerning cost-effective service alternatives to address the unmet health and social needs of a municipality. When they exist, state and federal grants should be sought out to address these service needs. Other non-conventional funding sources may be needed to finance these services, such as funds from philanthropic foundations, private sector companies, as well as contract services from other community service providers.

The problem of sorting out the proper roles and responsibilities rests upon the professional staff, typically the health and human services director, and his or her employees. As previously mentioned, some governing bodies have even established formal advisory commissions and committees to assist them in this effort. Many health and human services directors have successfully used these advisory groups to assist them in preparing health and human services master plans for their municipal organizations.

Since this is a relatively new service area for municipal governments, the development of a community master plan is one of the best ways to address the unmet service needs of a community. The efforts of public health and human services professionals to educate their top management and elected leaders on these needs is essential to properly allocate financial resources to these programs.

State and Federal Grant Programs. The number of federal and state grant programs for public health and human services, as well as their funding levels, have decreased in recent years due to budgetary constraints. This has forced many communities to curtail important programs in these service areas, or to continue these programs using program revenues or limited local tax dollars when grant funds have been discontinued.

A limited number of grant programs are still available from higher levels of government in selective program areas of public health and human services. It is worth exploring the availability of federal and state grant programs, especially for new services that help achieve state and national health priorities. Grant funds may be available for such services as AIDS prevention and counseling, workfare and job development programs, immunization programs for children, and substance abuse treatment services. When planning new programs and services to meet a community's needs, careful attention should be paid by health and human services administrators to design these programs so that they can be financed locally when grant funds are no longer available. Many public officials are wary of developing a dependency on these outside funding sources since most of these programs are only funded on a year-to-year basis.

When a program is not grant funded it is typical to charge a service fee to help offset the cost of providing the service. These service charges are frequently based on one's ability to pay as determined by documented income levels. The days of routinely granting service charge exemptions for all young people and senior citizens are on the decline. The revenues generated by service charges can be used to justify maintaining a program when municipal funding is limited. Many elected officials now have adopted a standard policy that a program must be terminated when grant funds end, unless sufficient program revenues can be generated to continue the service. The trend of having fewer federal and state grant programs is firmly established, as is the practice of charging service fees based on income levels. Because of limited budgets at all levels of government, these trends will no doubt continue in the future.

User Service Charges, Regulatory Fees, and Fines. A different fiscal philosophy is usually used to distinguish between user service charges, regulatory fees, and the imposition of municipal fines.

Regulatory fees are typically charged for the enforcement of health, housing, and environmental laws and regulations. These fees are intended to cover the cost of enforcement and solicit compliance. Fees for inspection services are also cost-covering, while fees for community clinics are intended to offset only a portion of the operating cost of providing these medical services. Municipal fines are assessed to property owners for violations of city codes and regulations. They are usually progressive based on the number of violations, their severity, and the duration of non-compliance. In the area of human services every effort is being made to make these services more (but not totally) cost-covering than in the past. Many other user charges are based on ability to pay, while others are modest charges intended to generate additional program revenues.

Increased revenues from services charges, regulatory fees, and fines are being used to maintain essential and important programs. In the past, many fees for human services have been either waived or reduced for selected segments of the community, such as young people, senior citizens, and those citizens receiving public assistance. The trend is to charge all service users some type of fee, even a modest one based on the user's ability to pay. It should be kept in mind that many of these services indirectly benefit the general public, and in some cases the imposition of totally cost-covering service charges may restrict citizens from participating in needed programs.

Several major trends are evolving with respect to service charges, regulatory fees, and fines. These include the tendency to make regulatory fees and inspection service charges cost-covering, to impose severe fines to ensure prompt compliance with city codes and regulations, and to charge a reasonable fee for human services, granting exceptions and special concessions to certain segments of the community such as those described above. Tight municipal budgets and limited new revenue sources, as well as increasing citizen demand for services, have served to facilitate these trends in recent years.

Working with the Community. Health and human services directors are increasingly seeking input and feedback from citizen advisory bodies, community leaders, and program constituents. In the past, some administrators have arrived at important recommendations and program proposals working in an administrative vacuum. Now, because of the number of agencies and community groups involved in health and human services, major decisions and policy recommendations should not be determined introspectively.

For example, if a health and human services director is working with the chief of police on a new program to combat juvenile delinquency, it should not be presented to elected officials directly from the staff without being discussed first with other interested parties. The astute manager should make a list of the major program stakeholders, including advisory bodies and program constituents, and seek their input and feedback on the program being proposed. Proposed programs and services should be presented to these stakeholders in draft form, and not as a completed work product.

When the final program proposal is presented to the governing body for its consideration it should have been presented to and reviewed by these stakeholders. The report highlighting the proposed program should indicate the various parties that have reviewed and commented on the program in draft form as it was being developed. This advanced political processing should help gain the support of elected officials during the approval process. It should be noted that no single stakeholder or special interest group should be allowed to unduly influence a significant program proposal.

Due to the sensitive nature of many public health and human services programs, and the number of agencies involved with providing related services, it makes good political sense to work with these groups when preparing master service plans, making program recommendations, or merely soliciting feedback on ideas to improve services. The trend for department directors and program managers to work with major stakeholders and community groups is on the increase.

THE FUTURE

Some internal productivity trends, because of their relevance to contemporary and controversial community health and social issues, warrant further examination. Many urban problems like unemployment, alcohol and drug abuse, poverty, juvenile delinquency, violence, homelessness, and diseases such as AIDS are now migrating to suburban and rural communities throughout the United States. Elected officials have usually treated the symptoms of these conditions rather than their root causes. In this respect, many communities have hired more police officers and health counselors, which merely serves to improve the conditions created by these health and social problems rather than to treat their underlying causes. There is a growing awareness among local elected officials that the use of public education and prevention programs may be less expensive in the long run when coping with these problems. Child immunization clinics, job training centers, child care facilities, counseling services, and drug and sex education programs may be less expensive than other municipal service options. These problems will be exacerbated if general assistance payments and health benefits are curtailed by states, forcing those citizens receiving these benefits to fend for themselves. These state government actions will increase the local costs of coping with these municipal issues in the future.

Externally, many communities have been grappling with creative and innovative solutions to these problems by creating low cost programs and by forming partnerships with other local nonprofit health and social service agencies. Additionally, municipalities have been developing public education and citizen empowerment programs to provide self-help initiatives to citizens to minimize the need for additional programs in these service areas. The reduction in the number of federal and state grant programs, as well as the loss of funding under existing programs, have compounded the magnitude and complexity of health and human services issues that local governments must address. When faced with setting budget priorities, health and human services frequently receive less funding than other basic services such as police, fire, and public works. Directors of health and human services departments have sought other funding sources, either from local corporations or from philanthropic organizations, to counteract this budget reality. Even though user fees have been increased for some programs, the total cost of these service can never be totally recovered from their users. Hence, local elected officials will continue to debate the best way to finance municipal health and human services.

One of the major problems confronting this service area is a political one. As Congress grapples with reducing its deficit and balancing the federal budget, many grant programs in these service areas have been eliminated. Those remaining grant programs have reduced funding levels. The federal government has delegated responsibility for health and human service needs of citizens to the states. State legislatures, not wanting to increase their own taxes, have passed these responsibilities on to their cities. City councils must therefore come to grips with addressing the health and social issues in their communities. These actions are being considered in a highly charged political environment where citizens do not want their property taxes increased. For this reason, local legislatures have adopted user fees, many of which are minimal or based on one's ability to pay. These revenues, however, do not generate sufficient funds to finance those services required to address these service needs. Hence the debate in these service areas continue. In those cities where these programs are needed most, a static tax base has exacerbated existing conditions. While states are attempting to solve these financial inequities, they do not have sufficient funds to improve the condition of their communities in these critical service areas.

9

LIBRARY

Public library services rank among the oldest municipal services provided to taxpayers. Many of our nation's older communities had public libraries at the turn of the 20th century. Although traditionally a cultural service, libraries were considered by citizens as essential to the quality of life in their community. Our public libraries have gone from the role of providing written materials to the public to being on the cutting edge of the national information superhighway. Library services, like the services provided by police, fire and public works departments, are almost entirely financed out of property taxes. With the advent of the so-called taxpayers' revolt in the late 1970s, and even continuing to date, some elected officials consider libraries as "soft services" compared to other municipal services. For this reason, library budgets have been under the increased scrutiny of elected officials during the past decade. Strapped with historically limited budgets, library directors have always been innovative and creative in the ways they provide public services. In recent years, libraries have become highly automated, not only to better serve the public, but also in response to limited budgets and static staffing patterns.

When expanding their services, library directors have been careful to tailor their programs to serve the needs of their primary user groups. Adult materials have focused on career guidance, family counseling, lifelong learning, and other materials related to this age group. In communities with a younger population, children's services have been expanded to include such programs as storytelling, reading hours, exhibits, contests, and computer laboratories. In cities with an aging population, many books, periodicals, and related materials have included leisure services, arts and crafts, genealogy, nutrition, and related topics. Many municipal libraries now operate job information centers, provide computer training programs, and have special collections of job and career resource materials. Some libraries even provide job seekers' workshops, where employment counselors and job placement experts periodically address unemployed citizens to increase their job-seeking skills and chances of finding employment. Many of these special programs and resources are even being cosponsored by private companies to help offset library budget costs. Almost every library has a friends of the library support group. These groups help raise funds for library services, provide valuable political advocacy, and offer sound advice on the types of materials and services their library should provide to the public.

In the area of technical services, libraries have led other municipal departments in the automation of their operations and public services. Even the smallest of libraries offers sophisticated services to their users, including online public access, regional interlibrary loan programs, specialized databases, as well as the use of personal computers and printers. Reference librarians now use computer databases rather than manually searching reference books or card catalogs when responding to citizen inquiries for information. Circulation control is now performed by optical scanners linked to automated alarm systems. Late notices and overdue billing statements are also prepared with specialized computer software applications. Nearly all facets of library services are fully automated. In addition to providing access to a greater level and mix of library services, library users receive real-time feedback on their individual search requests for books and periodicals. Many urban libraries have replaced their security guards with anti-theft devices such as computer-readable barcoding labels. This one new technology alone has virtually eliminated theft from U.S. public libraries. Most libraries now have computers at nearly all of their employee workstations, many of which are linked together electronically via local area computer networks to common databases.

The fastest growing area of library services has been the number of community programs offered to citizens. In addition to providing specialized information centers and resource materials, many libraries have opened up their meeting and conference rooms for use by nonprofit community organizations. Virtually all libraries now provide exhibits, educational programs, and a host of special events such as lecture series, discussion groups, demonstrations, guest speakers, and other community-wide activities. Many communities—because they lack a sufficient number of neighborhood branch libraries, their population has expanded beyond their traditional service area, they are sparsely populated, or merely because they are large geographically—provide bookmobile services to their outlying residents. Bookmobiles also serve as an excellent public relations and outreach tool for municipal libraries. Many library directors offer so many diverse programs that they have initiated formal marketing programs to inform citizens about their wide assortment of services. More and more citizens are using library services, not just to obtain reading materials, but for a number of lifelong learning experiences and opportunities.

Figure 9.1 illustrates the six most common programs performed by municipal libraries. One of the newest library services is in the field of adult literacy. A number of innovative programs are examined in this expanding service area. The role of the friends of the library is also examined.

Figure 9.1
Library Major Programs

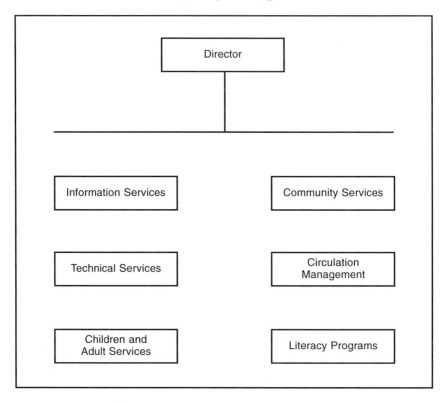

DESCRIPTION OF PROGRAMS

Information Services. One of the most important functions of the municipal public library is to serve as an information resource for the community.
The employees who perform this function, typically called reference librarians, review, select, acquire, and update the most affordable and useful informational resources needed for the community. The type and quantity of reference material available should be determined by the needs of the community.
These staff persons also instruct the public on how to use the library's informational resources—magazines, periodicals, reference and source books,
indices, computer databases, encyclopedias, and other compilations of useful
information. Reference librarians also typically assist the technical staff in
acquisitions and collection development.

Most public libraries are linked together electronically, many smaller
databases are being merged with larger ones, and more access points are

available to better serve the diverse informational needs of the public. In this respect, libraries are on the cutting edge of the evolving national information superhighway. To better serve their community, many municipal libraries now routinely operate community information centers, computer centers, business information centers, and job and career resource centers. Some of these centers may be cosponsored and financed by local private companies, financed by foundation or state grant funds, paid for by revenues generated by friends of the library groups, financed by community donations, or some combination of the above. Tight municipal budgets have forced public libraries to be financially creative depending upon multiple funding sources from a combination of profit, public, and nonprofit organizations.

Technical Services. This service area encompasses automation, systems applications, cataloging, and bibliographic control. Automation includes information processing, networking, storage, telecommunications, electronic document imaging, and workstation locations. Systems applications include those for circulation, cataloging, reference, and acquisitions. Cataloging includes the ordering, classification, cataloging, and physical processing of all library materials. Bibliographic control includes the use of state-of-the-art technologies such as CD-ROM disks, online acquisitions, online public access systems, and other software applications for librarians and library users. Other technical services include database management, filing and indexing, archival services, acquisitions management, collections development, materials preservation, the reproduction of library materials, and staff and public access services.

One recent guide published by the American Library Association (ALA) lists over 2,000 sources for technical library services. Library personnel obtain and maintain computerized information databases that provide public access to all print and nonprint library materials by subject, author, and title. The types of material processed include all reference materials, books, magazines, newspapers, periodicals, journals, audiocassettes, videocassettes, films, records, and compact discs. The technical service staff, in their role as automation coordinators, also train the library staff in the use of new hardware and software applications.

Even a small municipal library may have several thousand items available for circulation. Larger public libraries may have several hundred thousand items available for circulation.

Children and Adult Services. All public libraries carry materials and provide services related to their primary user groups or markets. Typically the largest users of library materials and services in most communities are children and senior citizens.

The goal of many children's programs is to begin the process of creating lifelong readers and users of library services. Children's services include selected learning materials, children's literature, storytelling, reading hours, exhibits, contests, computer laboratories, and special events. Outreach services are also provided to local organizations that serve the needs of children. Adult services may include life and career guidance books, individual and family counseling topics, lifelong learning opportunities, genealogical reference services, parent education materials, aging information, specialized collections, and book discussion groups. These markets and the library services provided to them are determined by the needs of the community. Other special library user groups may include preschool children, young adults, senior citizens, immigrant citizens, minority groups, and the disabled, to name a few. Frequently, library orientation programs are specially designed for each of these user groups.

Most library materials and services are provided free of charge. Sometimes a small fee is charged for checking out audiocassettes, videocassettes, films, records, and compact discs. Similarly, a small fee may be charged for using typewriters or computers. Small fines are commonly assessed against users who return materials after their due date. It has been a longstanding American tradition to keep most library services free, or nearly free, in order to make libraries equally accessible to all segments of a city's population.

Community Services. This function fulfills the municipal library's role as a community activities center. Many libraries contain community meeting and conference rooms, which are frequently made available to local community groups and organizations. Typical uses include community workshops, discussion groups, various exhibits, educational programs, organizational meetings, and other special events.

Many libraries are generating additional revenues by renting out this space to both public and nonprofit groups in the community. Increasingly, libraries are adopting a sliding-scale user fee policy for their space rentals. A three-tiered user fee policy is becoming commonplace. For-profit groups pay the highest user fee. A reduced fee is charged to nonprofit organizations. The fee may be waived entirely if a particular program is provided by a nonprofit organization and is cosponsored by the library. All fees charged must be approved by the local governing body.

These programs may be planned, promoted, and marketed by the library staff to selected local or regional markets. Community services may also provide valuable library services through the use of a bookmobile. The library services provided by a bookmobile reach those citizens who cannot travel to their public library. Portions of the children, young adult, and senior citizens market typically fall into this potential user category. Bookmobiles are also an excellent public relations and outreach tool for libraries—reaching citizens who might not otherwise use library services.

The number of community service activities in local libraries has been increasing in recent years, not only because of the needs, but also because of the public relations and marketing efforts of library directors.

Circulation Management. Library loan services are one of the most important functions performed in public libraries. Circulation personnel ensure the smooth flow of materials in, through, and out of the library. The library staff charge and discharge all written and nonprint materials, place items on reserve, notify users when their materials have arrived, register borrowers, receive overdue fines and charges for lost items, and decide upon resolutions to all disputed charges for late and lost items. Computer applications are commonly used to track overdue items, issue late notices, and mail billing statements.

The physical organization of materials in the library, their location and order on the shelves, and theft detection systems are also the responsibility of circulation management personnel. The magnitude of these tasks is enormous since it is not unusual for one-half of a city's population to hold active library cards, with annual circulations frequently measured in the hundreds of thousands. Computer-read barcoding label technology is now commonplace as a means of enhancing circulation management and control. Detection systems placed at all library exits have virtually eliminated the theft of library materials. Self check-out systems are also now available with these new security and electronic detection devices. New computer software applications also integrate online cataloging with circulation management, enabling library officials to inventory their materials quickly with a high degree of accuracy.

Interlibrary loan programs have made a vast network of library materials available to the public. The use of interlibrary loan programs has increased dramatically during the last few decades due to the use of new computer technologies, more sophisticated and user-friendly software applications, and more comprehensive integrated library databases. A recent longitudinal study conducted by the National Center for Education Statistics revealed that 13.9 million library items were either borrowed or loaned in 1992 compared with 5.4 million in 1974.

Literacy Programs. Many public libraries working with local chapters of Literacy Volunteers of America (LVA) frequently provide instruction and individual tutoring in literacy for people unable to read, speak English, or perform basic math skills. While all of these programs provide individual instruction and tutoring, many programs now offer similar services to family members—with the goal of providing literacy services to the entire family. In recent years, more innovative libraries have expanded their literacy program offerings to include computer literacy, information literacy, and library literacy. Public libraries serve as ideal venues for this training since many already have literacy resources available to the community.

The traditional alliance between public libraries and literacy groups has been expanded to a network of other providers, including other public agencies, schools, nonprofit groups, and other community-based organizations. Literacy program services are determined after conducting a community needs assessment. Individual programs are then designed and tailored to the specific needs of individual groups within a municipality. Literacy programs now provide a continuum of services, ranging from basic reading and math skills to library, computer, and information literacy, and to improving the educational levels of citizens in the community. Some of these programs also assess literacy levels in individual workplaces and provide onsite training in small class settings. These services are frequently provided free or for a nominal charge.

PRODUCTIVITY TRENDS

Library directors in many communities have traditionally had to provide their services with small staffs and limited budgets. Even before other department managers were forced to reduce costs and increase productivity, local public libraries had been the subject of these changes for a number of years. The internal productivity trends examined in the following paragraphs illustrate many of the ways that library directors have increased their department's productivity, held down expenses, and attempted to improve their operations. When libraries have been forced to curtail services, usually the last services to be reduced are those provided to children. Children's services have always received a priority, even when library budgets have been reduced. In recent times, due to the use of computers and specialized application, library organizations have had to be flexible and adaptable to the changing technological trends of the broader society. Municipal libraries usually have an advisory body to serve as a buffer between the library director and the elected officials. Almost all libraries also have a friends of the library group to conduct book sales, help finance services, and provide voluntary support for library programs.

Because of limited funding and a lower priority when compared to other municipal services, library directors have had to seek community support, private cosponsorship of their programs, and outside funding sources for many of their services. The external productivity trends document the efforts of library directors to achieve these goals. Municipal libraries have become the primary information sources for many citizens. Because library services are primarily financed out of property tax revenues, the professional staff has had to seek outside sponsorship and funding for many of their newer programs. Many library directors have worked closely with their formal advisory bodies and citizen support groups to create library service master plans. These plans give political legitimacy to the services provided by many public libraries. In recent years, specialized library services have helped to empower citizens in a number of different ways, from obtaining computer skills to achieving personal literacy. Many libraries provide so many programs that library directors have initiated formal marketing programs to promote their services. An ongoing effort is being made to educate public officials and citizens of the contributions that libraries provide to their community's quality of life.

Table 9.1
Library Productivity Trends

Internal	*External*
Evolving Community Services	Alternative Funding Sources
Evolving Information Services	Community Resource Centers
Evolving Technical Services	Contract Services
Financing Library Services	Library Service Master Planning
Human Resources Management Practices	Library Service Trends
Libraries and Children	Private Cosponsorship and Coproduction of Programs
Management Practices and Organizational Change	Professional Development
Organizational Structure and Advisory Bodies	Specialized Training and Citizen Empowerment
Role of Citizen Support Groups	User Service Charges and Fees
Staff Development and Internal Marketing	Working with the Community
Use of Computers and New Technologies	

Table 9.1 highlights the major internal and external productivity trends taking place in our nation's municipal libraries. Many of these trends relate to the automation of library services, increasing employee productivity, and ways to hold the line on departmental budget expenses.

PRODUCTIVITY TRENDS

Internal

Evolving Community Services. Public library directors have attempted to expand their traditional services and provide outreach programs in an effort to reach more citizens. New programs and services have also been added, frequently at little cost to the taxpayers, to attract a greater number of citizens to use library services.

Bookmobiles have been added to reach children, handicapped citizens, shut-ins, and low-income families that do not traditionally use library services. Bookmobiles are also being used to provide outreach services to housing projects, senior citizen centers, and outlying industrial parks. Many libraries have opened up their meeting rooms to service the community. Space is provided to community groups to hold meetings, for organizations to hold small conferences, for nonprofit agencies to provide specialized educational programs, and to provide a host of exhibits for citizens. The use of public meeting rooms at libraries are so popular that new library facilities are being designed with additional meeting rooms to satisfy the increased citizen demand for this space.

Reader advisory and reference services have also been expanded to improve the quality of services to the public. The use of computers and specialized software applications have facilitated this trend. Library directors have also added important programs to provide computer training, business information, access to job banks, and literacy training programs. Private sponsorship and funding is obtained to provide some of the community programs.

These community outreach programs have served several important purposes. They have generated a need for library personnel to improve marketing and publicity about their services and programs, have been used to generate additional program revenues, and have demonstrated that public libraries are user-friendly to citizens. Attendance and usage records can also be used to justify annual program budget requests. When the number of users of these services increase, the citizen advocacy base for library programs escalates. It is not unusual for program users to attend municipal budget hearings to advocate for the services provided by their library. Many municipalities now use the job title of community service librarian for those librarians who organize and provide these specialized community services.

Evolving Information Services. Many library directors have adopted an open-systems approach to the development of municipal library programs and services. The use of relatively inexpensive computer hardware and specialized software applications have enabled local libraries to go online and network with other libraries, databases, and informational resources throughout the nation. Many public libraries of all sizes have also "connected" to the internet, making available a vast network of informational resources to their citizens.

Traditional reader advisory services and references services have been expanded with the use of these new technologies. Many libraries also hold citizen workshops on how to use these new programs and applications. The use of these computerized databases and such new storage devices as CD-ROM have actually held down the need for libraries to acquire new reference, resource, and reading materials in hard copy form. These new technologies have assisted library directors in expanding the types of community services provided to the public, such as business and economic information centers, access to regional and state job banks, and online reference services. The space requirements necessary to provide these services have also decreased. While it used to take several shelves to place telephone directories from major cities throughout the United States, this same amount of information is now contained on one CD-ROM. The CD-ROMs are also being used to store entire sets of encyclopedias, doing away with the need to acquire volumes of these reference books.

The local public library is now the average citizen's "window to the world," providing nationwide resources to citizens that were unimaginable only a few years ago. This has enhanced the importance of library services in the community, as well as increased citizen usage of library services. The advent of more sophisticated computer hardware and specialized software applications has served to facilitate this trend. Communities of all sizes have taken advantage of these technological advances in the library field.

Evolving Technical Services. Both the types and numbers of computerized services, specialized software applications, and equipment designed specifically for public libraries have greatly increased over the past few years. Technological applications typically encompass the automation of library operations, including cataloging, bibliographic control, and circulation management.

The technical staff are also responsible for department-wide systems development and applications, as well as computer networking with other libraries, including state and national library database networks. Cataloging, while still primarily a manual process, now includes direct online acquisitions and automated cataloging applications. Bibliographic control includes the use of such state-of-the-art computer applications as CD-ROM online public access systems, and other software applications designed for librarians and library users. Other automated library services include computerized database management, online bibliographic information retrieval, and electronic document imaging. The ALA has published one book detailing over 250 inexpensive software packages for public libraries.

The number of sophisticated computer workstations, for both the library staff as well as library patrons, is determined by a library's technical staff. The number of these workstations has expanded exponentially during the past few years. The latest library technologies include automated materials check-out systems, facilities management and financial applications, as well as automated circulation management and inventory control programs. New security devices at library exits safeguard against the possible loss of library materials without the use of security personnel. The technical services provided in libraries are on the cutting edge of technology. This trend has been facilitated by more sophisticated computer hardware, specialized library software applications, and new types of sophisticated library-specific equipment.

Communities of all sizes have automated many of their traditional labor-intensive library operations. The trend towards the increased use of computer hardware, software applications, and new equipment to better serve the public is on the increase. This trend has helped library directors increase the level of services to the public while keeping personnel costs to a minimum. All of these trends, because of these reasons, will inevitably continue in the future.

Financing Library Services. Public libraries are among the oldest cultural institutions in the United States. When cities first built public libraries, many were financed with private grant funds frequently under the condition that library services be provided free of charge to citizens. In the eyes of many early public leaders, free library services were the foundation of a literate population, an educated citizenry, and a free society.

Public libraries have never generated much in the way of revenues from their services. In fact the only service charges are typically for overdue and lost books, rental fees for certain items, fees for making copies, and modest charges for the use of typewriters and computers. Taken together, all of these revenue sources only comprise a minuscule fraction of a library's total annual budget. Some elected officials, wanting to make municipal services cost-covering because of limited finances, have attempted to raise library user fees and charges. It should be kept in mind that while some additional revenues can be obtained by increasing these charges, large increases would undermine the basic purpose of public libraries.

In essence, the greater the amount of fees charged to citizens, the fewer the number of people who will use public library services. Most elected officials now recognize that public libraries enhance the quality of life in their community, and that libraries (much like the public school system) should be financed for the good of all citizens with property tax revenues. While many library directors have been creative in seeking new revenues, most of these new funds have been used to finance new programs and not to fund basic library service. For these reasons, the trend is to charge only modest fees for library services, realizing that the revenues generated from these fees are not designed to offset the cost of library services. When fees are raised special attention must be made to charge lower fees or grant fee exemptions to young people and senior citizens. Another trend is for elected officials to recognize the importance of libraries in contributing to the quality of their community's municipal services. Even though faced with tight budgets and limited new revenue sources, these trends will undoubtedly continue in the future due to the special nature of public libraries.

Human Resources Management Practices. The annual operating budgets for public libraries, like most other municipal departments, consists primarily of salary and fringe benefit costs. Library directors, out of financial necessity, have used a number of innovative and cost-effective methods to hold down their personnel costs. These cost-saving techniques have included ways to leverage library services by cross-training existing employees to perform a greater variety of tasks, the use of part-time employees, contract services, and the increased use of citizen volunteers.

The use of part-time employees, who are professionally qualified but may not wish to work full-time, saves money because they do not receive fringe benefits. Volunteers are used to provide nonprofessional services such as serving as library docents and assisting members of the public in learning how to use library services. Volunteers are normally not used to provide those services performed by regular library employees. The cross-training of personnel has also helped to increase the level of employee productivity. Existing labor agreements may limit or prohibit the use of cross-training and citizen volunteers to perform library services. The use of contract services is also on the increase. Contract services are common for nonprofessional library services such as landscaping, janitorial services, security, and general building maintenance. The full-time professional staff are always used to coordinate and monitor contract services as well as the services provided by part-time employees and volunteers.

In light of the financial constraints that exist in many communities, the use of part-time employees, citizen volunteers, and private contract services is on the increase. All of these trends are likely to grow in popularity in the future since they assist library directors in maintaining services while at the same time holding down departmental budgetary costs.

Libraries and Children. Public libraries have had a special mission and obligation with respect to children over the years. Library directors have worked hard to design special programs to attract children to use their public library. While the traditional focus of public libraries has been on children, recent program efforts have focused on mothers and toddlers, even babies. The use of popular poems, rhymes, picture books, puppet shows, and folktales have been used to acquaint the very young with their public library. Contests, exhibits, and special events are also used to get parents to bring their young children to their public library. All of these programs are aimed at developing the interests of children to use their public library sometimes even before they can read.

Many municipal libraries have specially designed outreach programs to reach children who would not otherwise use library services. Parent education programs are also emerging to inform parents, especially mothers, about the library services available for their children. Many mothers and their young children are involved in these free public library programs. The ALA has recent publications available on how to select library materials not only for children, but also for babies and toddlers. The goal of these children's programs is to begin the process of creating lifelong readers and users of library services. Some of the most recent programs for older children include computer training, the use of computers for children's games, and workshops for children on the many resources available from their library.

These programs not only help educate the young but create lifetime users of library services. Almost without exception, these special children's services are provided free of charge. Many cities have specially trained children's librarians to develop, conduct, and promote these programs within their community. The trend to tailor library services to young people—even the very young—is on the increase and is likely to continue in the future.

Management Practices and Organizational Change. The management of library organizations goes back to ancient times. Throughout the centuries libraries have served one basic purpose. It was, and still is, to acquire and maintain a body of knowledge on some type of medium and to make the medium available to the public when needed. While the body of knowledge has merely expanded over the centuries, the types of storage media have changed drastically in only a few short years. The storage medium is changing from books to interactive digital discs, video recordings, and CD-ROMs. It makes little difference on what form information is recorded so long as it is available and accessible to the public. Managing the body of knowledge through state-of-the-art information storage and retrieval methods now requires library employees to have sophisticated skills in computer systems, software applications, and different database networks.

The basic concern of library directors is to structure their organization to ensure that desired information is stored, retrieved, and made accessible to the public in an efficient and effective manner. This organizational structure requires management processes that facilitate and help achieve this goal. Library directors have had to embrace flexible management styles in order to adapt their organizations to changing technologies. This new management style favors empowering all library employees to develop their skills and apply them to the latest practices to better serve the public. The traditional hierarchical approaches to management are no longer applicable in many municipal libraries. All employees are being trained to work in contemporary flexible and adaptable organizations. Because of the technological revolution, especially as it applies to information storage, retrieval, and public access, these new management styles are essential if library organizations are to be successful.

The use of more adaptive and flexible management styles will become commonplace in future years as library directors adapt their organizations to a changing technological environment.

Organizational Structure and Advisory Bodies. There are several different yet workable organizational arrangements for the provision of library services. Some smaller and medium-sized communities contract with county governments for library services. Many of these cities do not have their own library facility. Some municipalities have special library districts with their own elected board of trustees. These elected officials hire the library director, establish policy, adopt the annual budget, and set their portion of the local property tax rate, which is usually collected by the county tax collector for a small fee.

Many cities have their own library boards, appointed by the city council for fixed terms of office. The board of directors typically has the power to hire the library director, who receives board approval of the library's annual budget before submitting it to the city council for its consideration. In still other communities, the library director is appointed by and reports to the city manager. These cities frequently have library boards that are advisory only. Their job is to make recommendations to the governing body on issues related to library services.

Some city charters insulate their municipal libraries from the politics of the community by requiring a separate board of directors or trustees to oversee library operations. It is not unusual, when a city council considers the library's annual budget request, to have members of the library's board of directors or trustees attend these meetings to serve as advocates for "their" library services. This political support is essential since library budgets are frequently vulnerable because they are not deemed an "essential" public service in the eyes of some local elected officials.

While the organizational arrangement for library services may vary from city to city, almost every community (except those contracting for library services) has some type of council-appointed citizens library board. The trend has been for these groups to become more politically active, especially when the library's annual budget is being considered by the governing body. Because of greater departmental demands for limited city revenues, this trend will assuredly increase in the future.

Role of Citizen Support Groups. The public library is usually the only department in the municipal organization that has a citizen support group not created or endorsed by the elected officials. While many departments have advisory commissions, only the library has a voluntary citizen support group such as a friends of the library. These organizations are separate nonprofit associations with their own constitution, bylaws, and membership requirements. These community support groups typically raise funds to finance library programs, provide volunteer services, and can legally accept private donations because of their tax-exempt status.

When proposed library budgets are considered by elected officials, it is common to have members of the friends of the library in the audience to provide vocal support, if needed, during the annual budget review and approval process. If budget reductions are being considered for library services, these groups have been known to get their entire membership to attend public meetings to support their library's budget proposal and levels of services. Many members of a governing body have not voted to reduce their library's budget due to the lobbying efforts of the members of friends of the library. Some friends of the library groups also organize annual tours of the public library for their elected officials, and use this as an opportunity to stress the importance of their library's services.

Municipal libraries in cities of all sizes and geographic locations have these citizen support groups. Over the past decade, because of budget and financial constraints, these citizen support groups have become more politically active. This trend will continue in the future.

Staff Development and Internal Marketing. Many community libraries now provide a host of innovative and valuable programs to their citizens. Many of these new services have been specifically targeted in recent years to meet the needs of specific user groups in the community. Most library directors now realize the value of externally marketing their programs, not only to increase their usage, but also to improve the image of their library in the community. These programs have been expanding at such a rapid rate that staff development and internal marketing programs are needed before "going public" with a formal marketing campaign.

Educating employees on the mission of their library organization, all aspects of library services, and the fact that these services are designed to meet the needs of the community is essential to the positive development of a library's professional, technical, and rank-and-file employees. Library directors are also empowering their employees to identify new programs and services, and are allowing these employees to work on developing action plans to implement these programs. This trend has improved both employee morale and customer service. These employees are also being taught that they represent and project the image of their library, and that their interface with the public is, at all times, critical to projecting a positive user-friendly image.

All library employees should have a working familiarity with the services their organization provides to citizens, even if they are not directly involved in providing a specific service. The development of a library's staff at all levels, as well as educating all employees on their library's services, is essential before undertaking external image improvement and marketing programs. Since external marketing campaigns are a vital tool in gaining public support for library services, the use of the staff development and internal marketing techniques will unquestionably continue in the future.

Use of Computers and New Technologies. Library directors have taken advantage of inexpensive computer hardware, easy-to-use library software applications, and other types of state-of-the-art equipment to improve the quality of library services to citizens. Since many library employees are already computer literate, the use of personal computers loaded with specially designed library software is becoming commonplace.

New automated applications include information retrieval, records management, book and periodical inventory maintenance, and access to regional and national information databases. Since library records and resources are kept for many years, many libraries have converted their hard copy documents to microfilm, microfiche, or computer database storage. Another example of this trend is the use of optical character recognition (OCR) devices in which documents are scanned, recorded, stored, and retrieved on request from a computer database. New automated cash register and receipting systems are being used to replace the outdated manual recordkeeping procedures of the past. These systems also assist in making daily bank deposits to increase the amount of interest earned on cash received from over-the-counter transactions such as late fees, computer service charges, room rentals, and rental income from videos, tapes, and records. Automated telephone message centers are also being used to program telephones with standard responses to citizen inquiries such as hours of operation, special services, program offerings, and information on exhibits and special events.

The use of these technologies frees up the time of existing staff personnel to perform other essential and more valuable library-related services. These pieces of technology also enhance the quality of services to on-site library users. Library directors are strong advocates of the use of more sophisticated technologies and equipment to improve their operations and public services. All of these trends have made existing employees more productive and have helped to hold down the need for additional staffing. The trend to use advanced technologies to improve services and reduce costs will be on the increase in the future. These trends are firmly entrenched in cities of all sizes and geographic locations.

External

Alternative Funding Sources. Since the amount of general funds monies (those revenues generated by local property taxes) have been limited in recent years, departmental competition for extra funds has been fierce. Many elected officials, if faced with the choice of adding new police officers or expanding library services, almost always favor highly visible and essential services over other municipal programs.

For these reasons, library directors have been forced to seek alternative funding sources for new services. These alternative funding options include federal and state grant programs, as well as other nontraditional financing sources. Since library grant programs from higher levels of government have either been reduced or eliminated entirely in recent years, librarians have focused their fundraising attention on alternative funding sources. These nontraditional funding alternatives include grants from nonprofit organizations, philanthropic foundations, for-profit private companies, and wealthy citizens desiring to fund new and innovative library services. It is also not uncommon for groups of public libraries to form interagency coalitions to collectively seek funding to provide specialized library services to specific user groups. Virtually all libraries now depend upon both municipal and private sector funding support to maintain expand their services.

Fundraising, through lobbying and direct solicitation, has become a way of life for library directors. A library's professional staff has also become innovative and assertive in seeking these outside funding sources. One recent book published by the ALA profiles nearly 1,500 private and corporate foundations, as well as companies, that are receptive to library grant proposals. Another recent ALA publication instructs librarians on how to become successful fundraisers for their public library. The trend of having limited general fund monies to finance new library services, and the increasing scarcity of federal and state library grant programs, is a fact of life for local librarians. Seeking alternative and nontraditional funding sources is becoming commonplace for library directors, regardless of the size of the municipality in which they work.

Community Resource Centers. Many municipal libraries have become important sources of information for many citizens. Library directors have designed and implemented various "resource centers" to improve their public services. Three common examples include business information, employment development, and community resource centers.

Business resource centers assist citizens in seeking census, business, and economic information. Specialized databases and studies featuring the latest economic forecasts, business trends, and statistical and technical information are also available under these programs. Books on how to start and manage a business, how to develop a business plan, and how to locate capital are housed in business resource centers. Employment development resource centers typically include public access to regional and stateside job databases, as well as making the latest position announcements available to residents. Career guidance and résumé preparation publications are also provided. These centers provide valuable one-stop resources for the unemployed, underemployed, or those citizens wishing to change careers. Community resource centers also provide information on the many programs available to citizens from other public, nonprofit, and charitable organizations.

In most cities, there are usually so many different community programs provided that it is difficult for the average citizen to know about their existence. Specialized library personnel are used to compile the material on these programs, prepare resource directories, and make this information available to the citizens as a public reference service. The use of all of these resource centers assists library directors in making their services more relevant to the citizens they serve. The types of centers provided should be geared to the population being served. The trend for municipal libraries to provide these reference centers is on the increase. Additional library personnel may be needed depending upon the size of these community resource centers.

Contract Services. The use of contracts with the private and public sectors to provide specialized services to municipal libraries, or to provide direct library services, is on the increase. The four main types of contact services are usually for professional and technical consulting services, routine non-library related services, specialized training programs, and contracts with other governments for the outright provision of library services.

Computer management consultants are frequently hired to select computer hardware and software, to design local area networks (LANs), and to install computer systems. Hardware and software vendors and consultants may be used to select the appropriate hardware and software applications, or to design or modify existing hardware and software packages to fit the computer and information needs of the library. The use of contracts to provide non-library related programs typically include those for landscaping, janitorial, security, and building maintenance services. Contract employees may be hired to provide unique services, such as to perform specialized training workshops to citizens using available library resources (e.g., computer applications, how to use the internet, and career and job counseling). Smaller cities may contract with larger cities or their county government to provide library services. These cities are usually newly incorporated smaller communities that do not have their own public library facilities.

The full-time professional staff are always used to coordinate and monitor service contract, as well as supervise those services provided by contract employees. Existing labor agreements may place restrictions on or prohibit the use of certain contracts for services. For example, it would not be unusual for a labor agreement to prohibit contracting for those services performed by regular municipal employees, even though a job vacancy may exist in a specific service area. The use of contract services is on the increase, especially in smaller communities with limited library resources, small professional staffs, and minimal technical resources.

Library Service Trends. As the interests of citizens change over the years, so do the types of books, periodicals, and services provided by public libraries. Some of the latest books available to municipal librarians and libraries include topics relating to the changing needs and interests of citizens in general, regardless of their age group.

Recently published books dealing with library services for children include such topics as multiculturalism, serving young people with special needs, educating the gifted, picture books and magazines for children, and serving children in small public libraries. Reading materials for young adults include such diverse subjects as resource-based learning activities, the maturation process, and dealing with diversity. Adult book topics relate to job seekers and career changes, the aging process, personal and family guidance, hobbies and leisure pursuits, family genealogy, the independent learner's sourcebook, library services for off-site education, and family literary projects.

State-of-the-art books for library professionals include how to use the internet, alternative and nontraditional funding sources, financial management, how to conduct fundraising programs, redesigning library services, measuring employee productivity, managing information technologies, library advocacy, using the legislative process, and media and public relations. All of these publications focus on the changing needs and interests of a library's professional and technical employees.

The ALA, the membership association for professional librarians, has virtually scores of books, monographs, and case studies on how to tailor community library services to fit the changing needs of municipal library users. These topics reflect the state-of-the-art interests of library users of all ages, as well as general societal trends dealing with increased multiculturalism, a greater amount of leisure time, citizens wishing to change careers, and the increasing automation of our public libraries. The trend in public libraries is to match their services to the changing needs of users, regardless of the size or geographic location of a municipal library.

Library Service Master Planning. In the past, property tax rates could merely be adjusted by elected officials to provide additional revenues for desired programs. Because of public opposition to increased taxes, especially property taxes, city councils have attempted to hold down expenses, mitigating the need to raise taxes.

Multiple departmental demands on a static revenue base have served to facilitate the need for more focused municipal planning, including library services. Additional library funding requests must be focused on high priority services. Library directors are in unique positions to work with their advisory commissions and citizen support groups to develop service master plans. The astute library director should form a planning committee consisting of representatives of these groups. It is also advantageous to have a representative of the governing body serve on this planning committee. The professional library staff should then assess the community's library needs, inventory available library resources to meet these needs, and make recommendations concerning service alternatives to address unmet library service needs. Because of limited funding, these service needs should be placed in priority order.

Once such a plan has been developed, it should be reviewed by the friends of the library before being submitted to the board of directors or trustees for its consideration. Once adopted, this plan should be forwarded on to the governing body through the city manager for its review and approval. The planning committee, as well as the members of advisory and support groups, usually attend the public meeting during which the plan is considered by the city council. Since these citizen advisory groups usually represent a cross-section of the community, service master plans developed in this manner lend needed political legitimacy and support for future program and funding recommendations. This type of planning process is becoming an important vehicle for identifying and addressing the unmet library service needs of a community.

The efforts of library directors to educate their top management and elected leaders on ways to meet the unmet service demands of citizens is essential. It provides city councils with the information upon which to base difficult decisions in properly allocating a city's limited financial resources.

Private Cosponsorship and Coproduction of Programs. Private sector companies are increasingly being asked to sponsor special library programs or certain services to make them available to the public free of charge. For example, a private company may donate computers to their library for use by the public or may pay for professional trainers to conduct free computer training workshops.

Private companies are also donating funds to their public libraries to finance certain programs such as employment information and career development centers. Local civic and social clubs are also actively involved in funding these special library programs. Private companies have even loaned their employees to provide free employment counseling, job training, or computer education workshops to citizens. This is an inexpensive way for a company to advertise, helps to promote a company's name in a positive light, provides valuable free services to the community and, at the same time, provides a tax writeoff for the sponsoring company. Many community groups are now coproducing services using library facilities. It is not uncommon for library directors to ask these groups to provide the service if the library makes space available for the program. Many community seminars, workshops, and lectures are being provided by community groups using free library facilities and room space.

These public/private/nonprofit partnerships have helped to provide new programs at minimal expense to taxpayers. The efforts of library directors to seek private cosponsorship of library programs, and requests to have community groups coproduce public services, are on the increase. These trends are prevalent in public libraries of all sizes and geographic locations.

Professional Development. Because of the many changes taking place in the public library field, it is essential for professional and support personnel to ensure that their skills reflect state-of-the-art professional library practices. There are several national and many state professional associations for municipal employees working in the municipal library field. These organizations provide many educational programs, conferences, technical resources, publications, and opportunities for professional growth and networking. Some of these membership associations also provide research services on current topics related to library operations and services.

The largest of these organizations is the ALA, which has more than 56,000 members representing professional librarians, library support staffs, library directors and trustees, library students, as well as members of friends of the library. Specialized training programs and publications are provided by the ALA in many technical areas such as management and administration, reference services, technical services, children and adult services, acquisitions and collection development, and facilities management.

In addition to the professional development services available from these associations, many states, as well as public and private universities, now provide structured learning programs leading to professional library designations and certifications. The resources and services available from all of these organizations have helped to increase the level of competency in this field, as well as set standards when hiring professional personnel. The funds spent on job-related training are usually more than offset by the increased level of professionalism, morale, and employee productivity. This is especially true in small public libraries where career advancement may be limited. The trend for library advocates—directors, trustees, friends, and library managers—is to inform and educate elected officials and top management of the need and importance of these professional development programs.

Specialized Training and Citizen Empowerment. Local public libraries serve as excellent training venues for citizens since many technical resources are available, and people already associate libraries with learning. In an ongoing effort to tailor library services to those citizens being served, many library directors have initiated computer, personal literacy, and library training programs.

Since many low- and moderate-income citizens cannot afford to purchase their own computers or pay for needed computer training, many libraries now provide valuable hands-on training on the latest computer hardware and software applications. This training, which may be funded by a sponsoring private-sector company or by using donated hardware and software, provides important and marketable job skills to the public and, in the long run, may help to lower local unemployment levels. Sometimes a modest fee is charged for this training, as well as for renting time on library computers available to the public. Many public libraries, working in conjunction with their local chapter of the Literacy Volunteers of America, frequently provide instruction and individual tutoring in literacy to people unable to read or speak English, or perform basic math. Some of these programs also provide personnel to assess literacy levels in individual workplaces and provide onsite training in small class settings. These services are frequently provided free, or for a nominal charge, sometimes based on income. Libraries are ideal venues for this training since they already have many literacy resources available for public use. Some library directors have started library resource training classes for citizens, acquainting them with how to use reference materials, online services, and new computerized reference resources and databases.

Volunteers or contract employees may be used to provide computer training services. Citizen volunteers are nearly always used to provide literacy training. Library resource training is usually provided by employees but may be performed by volunteers. The use of these specialized training programs specifically designed to serve the needs of a community's citizens are on the increase. All of these programs are designed to empower citizens by providing them with valuable lifelong learning skills.

User Service Charges and Fines. Library directors, and elected officials are very sensitive when it comes to imposing user fee charges and fines for library

services. Virtually all municipal public libraries were founded on the principal that library services should be free to guarantee all citizens equal access,
regardless of their economic status. Notwithstanding this philosophy, fees are
now being charged for a limited number of library services.

Most cities now routinely have service charges for room rentals; video,
tape, and record rentals; charges for duplicating services; and fees for computer usage. Some municipal libraries also charge for computer-generated literature searches. The imposition of new fees should not restrict citizen access
to those library services that benefit the general public. One of the main new
revenue sources for libraries is income from room rentals. Many library directors have recommended a sliding-scale user fee when making their meeting
rooms available to the public. A three-tiered user fee policy is becoming common. For-profit groups typically pay the highest user fee, followed by a reduced
fee for local nonprofit organizations. Frequently the user fee is waived entirely
if a particular program is cosponsored by the municipality or the library.
Because of the equity of this fee structure it has received relatively little political opposition from elected officials. When fines are increased for past-due
materials, they are usually only applicable to adults. Late fines for children
and young adults are usually kept at a modest level so as not to deter these
citizens from using library services.

When user fees and fines are adopted or increased, they typically only
generate a small amount of revenue compared to library's annual operating
budget. Most citizens expect to receive quality library services from the payment
of their property taxes. The trend to charge fees, for computer usage, extensive literature searches, room rentals, and the rental of videos, records, and
tapes are on the increase. These trends will undoubtedly continue in the future.

Working with the Community. For many citizens, their municipal library
is one of the few sources of direct contact with their local government. Library
employees now realize that they represent the image of their city in their dealings with the public. Also, since libraries are available to various community
groups to provide exhibits, meetings, and training workshops, the image projected by library employees to these groups is equally important. Official advisory commissions and citizen support groups should also be educated about
their library's programs and services. These citizens also serve as the library's
ambassadors to the public.

Every effort is being made by library directors to develop positive relations with not only their major stakeholders, but also the rank-and-file users
of library services. The successful library director works closely with its users,
citizen support groups, and advisory bodies when developing new services or
when considering changes to existing service levels. New library service master planning techniques have facilitated these close working relationships. In
the past, some librarians would arrive at important program and policy recommendations working in a political and administrative vacuum, only to

encounter difficulty later when approvals were sought from their advisory body and city council.

The trend is for library directors to value citizen input and feedback, to work closely with their major stakeholders and users, and to plan for future library services in an open and collaborative organizational environment. When the library director and the library's professional and support staff exhibit these personal qualities on the job, there is no need for formal image-improvement programs. Although many of these trends were initiated during tight budget times to solicit support for library services, they stand to continue in the future because it is good management to have employees treat taxpayers like customers.

THE FUTURE

The most significant internal productivity trends in public libraries have been made possible by relatively inexpensive personal computers and software applications. These hardware and software technologies have enabled library directors to automate their operations as well as provide additional information resources to citizens from online computer databases. Operationally, computers have assisted in records management, the inventorying of library resources, making online purchases for library acquisitions, and by facilitating the checkout of library materials by the public. The use of computers has opened up a whole new world of published materials to citizens through numerous subscription databases. If citizens request materials that are not available locally, interlibrary loan programs can fulfill these citizen requests from other libraries within the region. A familiarity with computers and common software applications is so important that many libraries now provide computer rentals to the public, as well as computer workshops and training in using the latest software applications. The most state-of-the-art libraries provide direct online access to their resources for citizens using their personal computers at home.

When reviewing external productivity trends in libraries, the trend that warrants special mention includes the relationship of local libraries to the citizens they serve. While many department managers are preoccupied with their internal operations, library directors have voluntarily sought out community support and funding for their programs. The term "alternative funding sources" is not only a frequently heard phrase, but is also a common practice in many municipal libraries. Private companies are frequently being asked to finance certain library services. These arrangements have proven to be mutually advantageous for a number of reasons. Libraries have been able to provide services without increasing their budgets, citizens have received services that they do not have to pay for, and companies have received valuable recognition for cosponsoring these library programs. Many community groups are also being asked to coproduce certain library services. Under these programs, the library provides the space, and possibly promotes the program, with the community group actually providing the service. Library services have generally been expanded in recent years with only limited budget increases. Most public officials now recognize that libraries can only generate a small amount of their revenues through user fees, and that these fees can only be modestly increased; otherwise, many citizens would be precluded from using historically "free" library services.

Some evolving state-of-the-art practices are helping stabilize the future financial base for many public libraries. Multi-tiered fees systems (e.g., such as those for adults and children) are on the increase. Some library directors are even using "peak-time" charges for adults for checking-out best selling books and other high-demand items. Late fines for these "high-demand" items have also been increased. The acquisition budgets of libraries, in many cases, have remained relatively constant in recent years, while the costs of hard-copy materials has increased dramatically. This trend has served as an impetus for library directors to join regional, state, and multi-state, interlibrary loan programs. This has helped to make more hard-copy resources available to individual library patrons.

Library directors and their professional staffs have worked closely with members of the community to tailor their services to specific user groups, as well as to meet citizen expectations for quality library services. The phrase "external stakeholders" is not new to the municipal library field. In fact it is a common practice for library directors to work with their advisory bodies, support groups, and other community organizations when designing and promoting new library services. Many library directors have conducted external needs assessments of their users, as well as members of the broader community, to determine which programs are necessary to meet the library needs of their community. In this respect, library organizations are open to citizen input, feedback, and criticism about their operations and services. When citizens use public services, one of the most positive encounters they have is when they use library services. Most city departments are only contacted when there is a problem that needs to be resolved, such as police, fire, and public works. One of the few municipal services that helps citizens personally satisfy their service demands in a positive way is through the programs provided by local public libraries. For this reason, many citizens increasingly support the services provided by their community library.

PARKS AND
RECREATION

Historically, most communities have had one or more centrally located public parks, and have provided a basic level of recreational services at these venues for their residents. As communities grew in population, citizens demanded additional parks and recreational services. Today, many municipalities provide specialized playing fields, youth centers, senior citizen centers, and a host of unique programs, depending upon their size and demographic composition. While some larger municipalities may have convention centers, indoor sports arenas, outdoor sports stadium, zoos, golf courses, museums, and other specialized public amenities, most small- and medium-sized communities do not provide these municipal facilities. Passive recreation areas, such as town squares or parks, were even in existence in early New England communities. Parks have generally been considered a part of the basic fabric of community life, even before there were specialized recreation and sporting venues and programs. Many citizens throughout the years have considered these public parks and services to be an essential part of the quality of life in their community.

The largest of the nation's cities have expansive parks to serve the passive and active recreational needs of its citizens. The availability of parks and recreational services are especially critical in urban cities, providing needed services in the midst of highly urbanized and densely populated metropolitan areas. Tot lots, neighborhood parks, playgrounds, and specialized sporting facilities are now considered a critical part of the basic level of public services in many communities. Many public parks now contain playgrounds, tennis courts, basketball courts, handball courts, and baseball and soccer fields for their residents. Now, the number of parks, as well as recreational services and sports venues, are geared to fit the changing needs of citizens. For example, communities with younger populations may have youth centers and a variety of different playing fields to serve the needs of their younger citizens. Parks in these communities typically have active recreational areas and organized

226

recreation and sporting programs to provide activities for young people. Municipalities with aging populations, on the other hand, may provide senior citizen centers, public gardens, and provide parks for passive recreational activities. As a community's demographics change over the years, so does the nature of the parks and recreational services provided to their citizens.

The largest growth in the services provided by parks and recreation departments has been in the number of special community events held at municipal parks, and the facilities contained in these venues, whether they be senior or youth centers, community theaters, municipal bandstands, or related service or entertainment amenities. Most cities now routinely hold annual community events and celebrations for a number of different occasions. Cultural and ethnic celebrations, concerts in the park, holiday activities, municipal orchestras, and special events sponsored by community clubs and organizations are routinely held in most communities throughout the nation. In response to limited budgets, most parks and recreation departments now operate with a small full-time staff, supplemented with a number of contract services, seasonal employees, hourly workers, and community volunteers. Many community events are provided by local nonprofit organizations who pay a fee to use parks and recreational facilities for their special events and programs. Frequently, donations are sought from private companies to sponsor these events. Cities promote the name of the particular company that subsidizes these community activities.

Because of revenue restrictions, many departments have adjusted their existing user fees and service charges, as well as implemented new ones, to help offset their annual operating costs. Faced with budget reductions and a curtailment of their programs and services, many department directors have sought to increase their revenues through a number of different creative methods. Many communities have adopted sliding-scale user fees and service charges, depending upon the type of group or organization that wishes to provide a service or use a facility. Almost without exception, young people and senior citizens receive a discount when fees are raised, or are allowed to use certain services free of charge. These policies have been tailored by elected officials to fit the unique income characteristics of their respective populations. Many governing bodies have adopted development impact fees to help finance new parks, and other public facilities, required by an expanding population. In the past, general obligation bonds would be issued for these facilities, which required all taxpayers to finance their costs. Assessment districts are also being used to finance many parks and recreational facilities when they benefit only a specific segment of a community's population.

One of the newest trends is to finance specialized recreation and sporting venues with revenue bonds with the projected admissions fees generated by these facilities. Many communities now treat golf courses, stadiums, arenas, museums, and zoos as enterprise funds. Local governments use enterprise funds to treat certain services as profit centers. Under this accounting scheme, fees are either adjusted to offset increased operating costs, or operating costs are reduced to equal the level of revenues generated. The philosophy behind this concept is that taxpayers in general should not pay for specialized services that they do not directly use. For example, golfers should pay for the costs of operating golf courses, and spectators should pay for the costs to construct and operate large-scale sporting facilities. A complete listing of the programs provided by parks and recreation departments is shown in Figure 10.1 on page 229.

Description of Programs

Recreation Services. Most municipalities provide a wide range of recreational and sporting activities for their citizens. Many traditional team sports such as softball, baseball, football, and soccer are played on athletic fields. Other sports—such as tennis, volleyball, basketball, golf, ice hockey, bocci ball, and swimming—require more specialized venues.

Many cities also provide both individual and group instruction in areas such as exercise, fitness, aerobics, yoga, swimming, golf, and tennis. The type and level of services provided are determined by the needs of the community as well as its ability and willingness to finance these amenities and services. For example, golf courses and tennis courts generally may be found in greater numbers in more affluent municipalities. Similarly, the type of athletic field amenities, such as bleachers, lighting, concession stands, restrooms, and off-street parking, is also determined by the taxpayers' ability and willingness to pay for these items. Many cities also have a community center, which provides space for many of the programs offered to different segments of the community. Most cities also typically have one or more municipal swimming pools.

Fees are commonly charged to offset some of the cost of providing these services. In many cities, free use periods are also available for low-income citizens. A small number of full-time staff members are usually assisted by part-time employees, seasonal workers, and community volunteers, in order to keep expenses to a minimum. Also, there is a trend to hire contract employees to reduce overhead costs. Some cities are charging development impact fees to finance new community parks and recreational facilities. It is also not unusual for smaller cities to contract with neighboring communities, larger cities, or counties for the use of their recreational venues and services in order to hold down their costs.

Parks Management. Many recreational and sporting activities are provided at municipal facilities located in public parks. Most playgrounds, athletic fields, specialized sports venues, swimming pools, community centers, hiking trails, bike courses, and picnic areas are frequently located in municipal

Figure 10.1
Parks and Recreation Major Programs

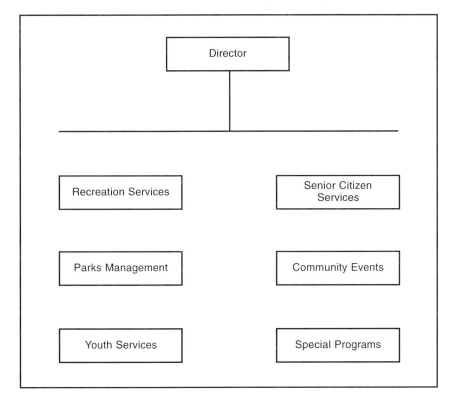

parks. While these improvements are used to provide recreational and sport-ing programs, the larger park areas in which they are located must be contin-ually maintained. Other natural attractions such as rose gardens, open spaces, and greenways also rely on the natural settings provided in public park areas.

Parks must be constantly maintained to retain their natural beauty and attractiveness. Typical parks management activities include landscaping and maintenance. As in recreational services, parks management usually relies on a small cadre of full-time staff members, supplemented with part-time employ-ees, seasonal workers, and community volunteers. One of the main trends in parks management is to contract out parks maintenance. Another trend is for smaller municipalities to contract with larger cities or counties for park main-tenance services.

Federal and state funds are frequently available for cities to acquire open space and parks areas. Because of the expense involved, if grant funds are not available, the acquisition of parks is usually financed by general obligation bonds. Revenue bonds are not used since parks generate little in the way of revenues. Local tax revenues are always required for park maintenance. Some cities now charge development impact fees to pay for new open spaces and parks.

Parks are important to a community since they add public infrastructure that entices businesses to a community. Parks and open space areas, for obvious reasons, are critically important in highly urbanized cities.

Youth Services. Many cities in recent years have been under public pressure to provide a diverse assortment of positive programs for young people. The number of youth-oriented recreational and sporting programs has grown so large that many departments have a separate division of youth services. In addition to the organized sporting programs described above, many of which have preschool and youth leagues, other youth-oriented programs have evolved over the years.

Typical youth programs frequently include courses of instruction (such as for arts and crafts, popular sports, and other creative activities), day camps, preschool programs, after school programs, swimming courses, lifesaving instruction, and toddler-swim classes. Many of these programs are provided at municipal community or youth centers, frequently located in public park areas. These centers are located in parks because of the existence of the specialized playground, sporting, and recreational amenities existing in these areas. The level and type of services provided are determined by assessing the needs of the community, as well as the willingness of citizens to pay for these services. Youth activities may vary slightly from year to year, depending upon the changing local demographics. Youth centers are usually built with local tax dollars since they do not require a large expenditure of capital funds. Staffing is typically provided by full-time recreation supervisors, assisted by part-time employees, seasonal workers, and community volunteers.

A small fee may be charged for these services to offset operating costs and to make these services partially cost-covering. Free use periods may also be available to low-income families. Courses may be taught by contract instructors to hold down overhead expenses. The number of youth services programs available enhances the quality of family life in a community.

Senior Citizen Services. Many cities have aging populations with ample time to pursue leisure activities. Senior citizens, taken as a group, also have a great deal of political clout and they turn out to vote in large numbers. For these reasons, the number of senior citizen programs offered in cities has grown in recent years to keep pace with the demand, as has the willingness of local politicians to provide these services. The number of these programs has expanded to the extent that many departments have a separate division for senior citizen services.

Typical senior citizen programs include courses on aging issues, such as health and nutrition, arts and crafts activities, discount or free lunch programs, educational programs on senior citizen diseases and illnesses, field trips, travel programs, and transportation for the disabled. Referral services are also provided to other public and nonprofit agencies. Many of these programs are provided at community or senior citizen center. As with youth programs, the level and type of services provided are based on community need and willingness to pay. Senior citizen services may increase over the years, depending upon changing local demographics senior centers are usually built with local tax dollars since they do not require a large expenditure of capital funds. Specialized employees work with seniors and are frequently assisted by hourly workers and community volunteers.

A small fee may be charged for these services, depending upon the income levels of the senior citizens using these programs. Courses may be taught by contract instructors to hold down expenses. As with youth services, the number of senior citizen programs provided is directly related to the quality of life for older Americans in any given community.

Community Events. Most cities hold numerous general and specialized community events throughout the year. While the types of events will vary greatly, the number of events is not dependent upon the size of the municipality. Many smaller communities hold a large number of these events. Generally, the more heterogeneous the population of a city the greater the diversity of the events held.

Cities with racially diverse populations typically hold more cultural, multicultural, and ethnic celebrations. Almost all communities typically hold annual community festivals, municipal anniversary celebrations, concerts in the park, holiday celebrations, and Fourth of July attractions, such as fireworks displays. Some cities also contribute funds and sponsor events held by community bands and orchestras, local ballet companies, and community theater groups. While some events may be sponsored and paid for by the municipality and its taxpayers, many more events are held by local community organizations and civic associations. Some cities and community groups seek funding from private companies to sponsor these events. This is an excellent low-cost form of advertising for participating companies. User fees are typically charged for park usage, liability insurance coverage, and janitorial services, as well as for the use of specialized venues such as theaters, concert halls, and bandstands.

When these events are cosponsored by a city, the municipal government may waive their user fees and assume the public liability associated with these events. Typically, full-time employees coordinate these events, assisted by part-time employees, seasonal workers, and community volunteers. These public events generate community pride and contribute significantly to the quality of life in a municipality.

Special Programs. Generally, the larger the city the greater the number of special programs and attractions provided to the public. Many larger municipalities operate their own zoos, museums, public arenas, sports stadiums, municipal piers, ice skating rinks, gymnasiums, meeting and convention facilities, auditoriums, historic sites, golf courses, and lakes with boat houses. The types of special municipal programs and services provided is determined by community preference and willingness to pay. Since the existence of many of these facilities is not based on need, a great amount of public debate and discussion generally surrounds new public improvements of this nature.

Because of the large cost involved, most of these facilities are financed with general obligation bonds. User fees are typically charged for these programs, with discounts provided for students and senior citizens. Free use times or special discounts may also be provided during nonpeak activity or low usage periods. For expensive specialized public venues such as zoos, museums, public arenas, sports stadiums, and golf courses, the trend is to operate these facilities as an enterprise fund or separate profit center. Fees are charged to make these facilities fully cost-covering. Full-time municipal employees, hourly employees, and seasonal workers typically operate these facilities. Hourly employees and seasonal workers are used to hold down overhead costs.

Also, the operation of these facilities may be privatized with a lease agreement to a private sector company. These public facilities must meet the public access requirements mandated by the federal Americans with Disabilities Act (ADA) of 1990. These specialized venues and services also contribute to the quality of life in a community by providing diverse leisure opportunities to its citizens.

PRODUCTIVITY TRENDS

A variety of internal productivity trends are being used to improve services and reduce costs, as well as provide long-term financing for parks and recreational facilities. Most parks and recreation departments are operated by a small professional staff who work to leverage their services through a number of different creative management practices. These include using an increasing number of contract employees, seasonal workers, part-time employees, and community volunteers. Those staffing trends have helped to reduce departmental salary and fringe benefit expenses. The organizational structures of parks and recreation departments have become flexible and adaptable to change. This has allowed the existing full-time staff to procure services without having to hire additional personnel. Larger departments provide so many services that they have to undertake internal marketing programs to educate their own employees on the many programs available to the public. The use of computers and software applications, as well as other technologies and products, has helped to improve operations and public services. These departments, because of the nature of their services, were among the first to feel political pressure to make budget reductions.

Like library directors, parks and recreation managers are no strangers to
the practice of providing alternative delivery systems for their services or seeking out nontraditional funding sources to finance their operations. These
departments have also had to retrofit their facilities to comply with the Americans with Disabilities Act. They have also had to review their operations and
facilities with the goal of reducing their public liability exposure. It is now
common practice for private groups using public facilities to sign contracts
that include special clauses to protect a municipality from these types of lawsuits. User fees and service charges have been adopted to generate additional
program revenues. The general philosophy of elected officials is that while
these services will never be cost covering some fees should be charged to help
offset operation costs and regulate the demand for services. Many departments
have successfully used state-of-the-art coproduction and cosponsorship practices to expand their services. For these reasons, parks and recreation directors have developed a close working relationship with their major external
stakeholders, including the many nonprofit organizations and community
groups that utilize their services.

A listing of the internal and external productivity trends examined in this
chapter are shown in Table 10.1 on page 234. Parks and recreation departments
have demonstrated some of the most sophisticated techniques to expand their
services with limited budgets. These department directors have also adopted
entrepreneurial management styles to adapt their organizations to the changing expectations of elected officials and city managers.

Internal

Cost Containment and Increased Services. Parks and recreation directors
have been using innovative management practices, alternative service delivery arrangements, and cutting-edge financial practices before they became
popular. Most departments are now facilitators or brokers of recreation-related
services in their community. Under this approach, a typical department only
has a small full-time professional staff, augmented by the use of part-time
employees, contract employees, seasonal workers, and citizen volunteers.

Many municipal departments have entered into contract service arrangements with other cities, counties, and regional park and recreation districts to
provide recreational facilities and programs for their citizens. Cities are also
entering into joint facilities arrangements with school districts for ballfields,
swimming pools, and gymnasiums. Under these agreements, these facilities
are constructed next to public schools, with both the construction and operating costs shared by the municipality and the school district. Some cities
have entered into public/private partnerships, whereby recreation services are
provided by private companies on leased public land. Water parks, golf courses,

Table 10.1
Parks and Recreation Productivity Trends

Internal	*External*
Cost Containment and Increased Services	Alternative Funding Sources
Evolving Community Events and Special Services	Alternative Service Delivery Systems
Evolving Parks and Open Spaces	Americans with Disabilities Act Compliance
Evolving Recreational Services	Community Program Information Centers
Financing Parks and Recreational Services	Parks and Recreation Master Planning
Financing Parks, Open Space, and Recreation Facilities	Parks and Recreation Service Trends
Management Practices and Organizational Change	Professional Development
Organizational Structures	Public Liability Reduction Programs
Role of Citizen Support Groups	Service Philosophy of Elected Officials
Staff Development and Internal Marketing	User Fees and Service Charges
Use of Computers, Technologies, and Products	Working with the Community

and other fee-based recreational facilities are examples of this trend. All of these practices assist the department in holding down budget expenses such as salaries, fringe benefits, and operating and capital project costs.

Parks and recreation directors have been leaders in generating additional revenues to offset the cost of their services. Long before it became popular, these departments charged fees for their services, initiated development impact fees for future park and recreation facilities, and actively solicited private funds and cosponsorships for their programs. Department managers and the professional staff have served as leaders in the cost cutting and revenue generating practices of municipal governments over the years. In many cases, what are now considered innovative management practices were first initiated in parks and recreation departments before these trends became popular. Many of these trends have since been adapted by other municipal departments in recent years. The use of these management and financial practices will no doubt continue to increase in popularity in the future.

Evolving Community Events and Special Services. The major growth in the parks and recreation field has been in the area of community events and special services. While community events are viewed as adding to the quality of life in a municipality, special services are often seen as not only increasing the quality of life but also contributing to a city's economic development. In both of these service areas, the city is the facilitator or broker in providing these services once the proper capital facilities are in place.

For community events, these capital improvements may include the construction of public bandstands, theaters, and concert halls. Once these facilities are in place they are made available to event organizers and community groups on a fee basis. The municipality maintains these facilities. For special services, capital projects may include the development of zoos, museums, public arenas, sports stadiums, municipal piers, ice skating rinks, gymnasiums, conference and convention facilities, auditoriums, historical sites, and golf courses. Once these facilities are in place, some of them may be leased to private operators or community groups, who are also required to maintain these facilities. Facilities in the latter category are expensive, and elected officials usually seek voter approval of bond issues to finance these capital projects.

Many of these specialized municipal services can be considered a form of economic development since they promote tourism and attract outside visitors who contribute to the local economy. For example, golf courses, zoos, and museums may contract out cafeteria or restaurant services, reaping a portion of these rental revenues to offset their operating costs. Larger facilities such as arenas, stadiums, and conference and convention facilities attract large numbers of people who spend money on related expenses such as lodging, meals, and transportation. It is easier to win voter approval of special facilities when they generate sufficient income to pay for themselves. The number of community events and celebrations at these facilities is on the increase since they directly contribute to a city's quality of life. The types of special facilities are more controversial but may be justified on the basis of enhancing a city's economic vitality. Generally, the larger the city, the more special facilities available to provide unique public services.

Evolving Parks and Open Spaces. The traditional belief of the first colonists was that every city and town, even small communities, should have a municipal park for citizens to enjoy. This trend started with the early design of municipalities in New England, where nearly every community has a public square, green, or park located in the center of town. Various community events and celebrations are still held in these parks. Early institutions such as city halls, churches, banks, and businesses were located around these central open space areas.

Larger cities usually have one central larger park to serve their citizens, such as San Francisco's Golden Gate Park or Manhattan's Central Park. The number of parks in a community should be determined by citizen need, and financed based on ability to pay. Generally, the trend has been to have more smaller parks in highly urbanized areas, followed by some parks in suburban areas, and few parks in rural areas since plenty of open space already exists for public recreation use. The greatest number of tot lots, small neighborhood parks, and playgrounds are usually found in those communities located in congested metropolitan areas. Many larger parks are resource-based parks, located next to a natural amenity such as beaches, rivers, lakes, ponds, or other unique natural settings.

As the United States becomes more urbanized, citizens recognize the need for more parks, open spaces, and recreation trails. Many local voters have approved bond issues to finance these public amenities. The latest trend is the development of linear parks and recreation areas, which are typically along either natural amenities (e.g., rivers, beaches, or lakes) or man-made settings (e.g., harbors, reservoirs, or large drainage channels). Although parks and open spaces are passive recreation areas, they must still be maintained by a municipality. To help offset their operating costs, many communities have "adopt-a-park" or "adopt-a-trail" programs whereby local community groups agree to maintain these facilities at their own expense.

The development of parks and open spaces is in keeping with the philosophy that cities should provide low-risk activities with limited exposure to public liability. The trend has been to construct a greater number of these parks and open space facilities, since they contribute to a community's overall quality of life.

Evolving Recreational Services. Major service changes are taking place as directors seek to tailor their department's recreational programs to fit the needs of specific user groups within the community. In the areas of children's services, the number of tot lots and playgrounds are increasing. Many playgrounds are specially designed with safe equipment and soft playing surfaces. The number of day camps, preschool programs, and instructional courses are also on the increase. Instructional programs for children focus on field sports, arts and crafts, swimming, and water safety. Youth activities represent the largest growth in services. Many cities cannot build ballfields fast enough to keep up with the demand of youth sporting leagues (i.e., baseball, football, and soccer). Since in many families both parents are now employed, the number of after school programs and drop-in centers have increased to provide a place where children can go after school until the end of the workday. Many cities now provide young people lessons for many sporting activities—particularly swimming, golf, and tennis. Since most adults work, there are fewer services available to these individuals. Special instructional courses are available in aerobics and fitness, and some evening sports leagues are available to adults.

With an aging population, many senior citizen programs have been added in recent years. These services include classes in health and nutrition, disease prevention, and wellness programs. Discount or free lunch programs are also available in many communities. Some of the latest programs include recreation programs for the frail, as well as special therapeutic recreation programs. New programs have also been initiated to serve handicapped citizens as well, such as special swimming lessons and special therapeutic recreational programs. Many cities also have free transportation programs for the disabled. Because of the service demand, many cities now have senior citizen centers as well as youth centers. Smaller communities usually have only one community center to serve all of these program needs.

Many of these programs are provided by contract employees, by nonprofit groups using recreational facilities, or by citizen volunteers. All of these services come under the direct management and supervision of the full-time professional recreation staff. The type of services available typically depends upon the demographics of the community, and political pressure for specific programs, as well as the willingness of citizens to pay for these programs (either from user fees or property taxes). The trend to provide highly specialized services to specific user groups is on the increase.

Financing Parks and Recreational Services. A number of innovative financing techniques, public/private partnerships, and contract service arrangements have emerged in recent years to either generate funds or hold down the cost of providing parks and recreational services. All of these innovative practices have emerged because parks and recreational services are typically financed with local property tax revenues.

User fees and service charges are now routinely adopted and periodically updated to reflect the cost of doing business. Free-use periods and discounts are typically provided to young people, senior citizens, and low-income individuals and families. Many directors have solicited funds from private companies to sponsor these free-use periods and fee discounts. Under these arrangements, the private company pays the revenues typically generated by an activity (for free-use periods), a share of the revenues (for fee discounts), or paying the cost for selected program users (such as children under a certain age).

Many community groups and organizations now provide special services at city-owned facilities. This trend has helped to expand the number of programs available to the public at a minimal expense to taxpayers. When contracting with a private vendor for these services, it is not unusual to charge a basic monthly rent plus a percentage of the program revenues. When services are contracted to the private sector, fee increases usually require the advanced approval of the governing body. Rather than deposit program or donated revenues directly to a city's general fund, it is now common to track these funds and make them available as a financial resource for the department to offset their general fund expenditures.

Some communities are entering into contract service arrangements with other cities, counties, and special park and recreation districts for their residents to use parks and recreational facilities. It is also not uncommon for smaller municipalities to share in the construction costs and operation expenses of such facilities as swimming pools, tennis centers, sporting fields, and community centers. Many cities and school districts have developed joint facilities such as swimming pools, sporting fields, and gymnasiums, and share in the cost of the construction and operation of these facilities.

All of these efforts represent vehicles to increase the level of services to the public while keeping expenses to a minimum. It should be kept in mind that the public expects a basic level of recreational programs, especially for young people, and they sometimes react strongly if admission fees are increased to the point that young people are excluded from using these services. Many taxpayers view parks and recreation services as essential to a community's health and well-being. They can also be used to stimulate economic development by attracting visitors and businesses to a community.

Financing Parks, Open Space, and Recreational Facilities. Most cities cannot afford to finance the acquisition of public parks and open space or the construction of recreational facilities with local tax revenues. This is due to the magnitude of the costs involved with purchasing land and constructing these public amenities.

Several options are available to finance these one-time capital expenses. Some cities have placed local bond issues on ballots to finance parks and open spaces. The electorate can then decide if they wish to finance these community amenities. With citizen approval, general obligation bonds are usually issued to fund these projects. Cities can use revenue bonds when a facility generates a sufficient income stream to satisfy the debt payments over the life of the bonds. Public arenas, stadiums, ice skating rinks, and similar revenue-generating facilities are examples of projects that may qualify for this type of funding. Sometimes states have parks and open space funds available, either from publicly approved bond issues or revenues from state lotteries specifically earmarked for these programs. Sometimes federal and state grant programs may be available for these purposes, but both the number and funding levels of these programs have been greatly reduced in recent years.

Some cities have adopted development impact fees to finance these projects. Under this arrangement, developers are charged a prorated fee on new developments to finance future parks, open space, and community facilities. These revenues are then set aside in special funds to finance these types of projects in future years. Some cities, due to their location or available open space, may enter into lease arrangements with private companies to provide water parks, golf courses, or other fee-based recreational facilities. Under these service agreements, the city typically receives a monthly rental fee plus a percentage of the gross revenues, and the improvements revert to the municipality upon the expiration of the lease. In these cases, the community does not incur any operating expenses associated with providing these services. Parks and recreation directors should explore all of these possible funding options, especially those that have a limited impact on a city's general fund.

Management Practices and Organizational Change. The development of parks and recreational services dates back to around the turn of the century. Since this time, the number of parks, recreational facilities, and related programs and services have increased dramatically. While parks have changed little over the years, what goes in them has evolved to include exercise courses, hiking trails, low-risk playgrounds, concerts, and a host of community events and celebrations. The number of recreational facilities has increased to serve the changing needs of a community to include community, youth, and senior citizen centers. The recreation field has changed most dramatically because of the citizen demand for more services. Traditionally, full-time recreation employees staffed these facilities. It is now common for these employees to only coordinate and supervise the services provided at these locations. The basic goal of parks and recreation directors is to structure their organization to ensure that the desired facilities and services are available to serve the public.

A host of new variables have emerged to make their organizations more complex. These include the greater use of part-time employee, seasonal workers, citizen volunteers, contract service arrangements, joint facilities sharing, and public/private partnerships, to name a few. This organizational structure requires a management process that facilitates and achieves the goal of maintaining, even expanding, services with little in the way of additional funds. Because of the number of venues involved and the constant interaction with a host of community and nonprofit groups, directors have had to embrace a more open and flexible management style to adapt their organization to these changes. This new management style favors empowering employees to develop their skills and allowing them to apply the latest management practices to better serve the public. The traditional hierarchical approaches to management are no longer applicable in many parks and recreation departments.

All employees are being trained to work in contemporary, flexible, constantly changing, and adaptable organizations. Because of the complexity of the contemporary work environment, these new management styles are essential if these organizations are to be successful. The trend towards the use of more adaptive and flexible management styles and methods of employee empowerment will inevitably become commonplace in the future as department managers adapt their organizations to a changing environment.

Organizational Structures. The responsibilities of parks and recreational departments vary greatly between communities, depending upon their size and unique historical development. Maintaining parks, ballfields, and providing sporting and recreational programs at municipal-owned facilities are the traditional roles of this department. Larger cities may have zoos, museums, community centers, and historical sites. Most small- and medium-sized communities do not have these public amenities.

When this department is a provider of services, full-time employees are used to provide services at city-owned facilities. They are usually assisted by part-time, contract, and seasonal employees. Local tax dollars are typically used to finance these services. Under this model, citizens expect that park and recreation services are the responsibility of their city government. When this department is the facilitator of services, the director and his or her staff take a more entrepreneurial approach to service provisions. Using this approach, a small number of full-time employees work with a host of community and nonprofit organizations and organized sporting leagues to provide services using municipal facilities. Under this service model, user fees and charges are kept to a minimum since many of the services provided by these groups are cosponsored by the city government. The staff actively solicits private donations and the sponsorship of municipal programs by private companies.

One example illustrates the difference between these two service models. Under the service provider option, city work crews maintain municipal parks. Using the facilitator approach, a full-time staff person would seek community, civic, and nonprofit groups to volunteer to maintain parks under their "adopt-a-park" program. Under the facilitator model, the municipal government almost always agrees to hold citizens and community groups harmless for the liability arising from their municipal volunteer efforts. This organizational form requires a greater degree of information sharing and joint planning, as well as providing technical assistance to the private sector. When services are provided under this more laissez-faire approach, it is still the responsibility of the government to make sure that fees are reasonable and that the quality of services and programs meet city standards.

While most cities use both organizational structures, the trend is towards the facilitation model due to budgetary limitations. This trend, because of limited tax dollars, is expected to continue in the future.

Role of Citizen Support Groups. Almost every parks and recreation department has a citizens advisory body with the members appointed by the city council. All but the most routine departmental issues are usually passed through this body before being forwarded on to the city manager for the governing body's consideration. For example, the department's annual operating budget would first be reviewed and approved by the members of the advisory body before being submitted to the city manager for the council's consideration. Likewise, capital improvement projects are reviewed and approved by these advisory bodies before being considered by the elected officials.

These advisory bodies are important, since these citizens represent the users of services. Because of this, a department director must work closely with these advisory panels when preparing service master plans, conducting community surveys, analyzing existing resources, and determining the proper mix and level of desirable services. These boards are also effective advocates for the department as well as the public. Members of these groups frequently attend meetings of their local legislative body during their annual deliberations on the parks and recreation department's budget.

Both the elected officials and the professional staff also favor the establishment of other citizen support groups, such as friends of parks and recreation, friends of the zoo, and friends of the museum, to name a few. These support groups frequently take the form of a legal nonprofit organization. Their goal is to actively promote services, conduct fundraising events, solicit private funds, and advocate for these community services. These groups are not a part of government. For this reason, it is sometimes easier for them to solicit funds from other nonprofit, private, and philanthropic organizations.

The trend is for advisory groups to become politically active in supporting departmental services, especially during the annual budget review process. Cities throughout the nation are supporting the formation of "friends of" and similar groups, primarily because of their independent nonprofit status, and their ability to raise funds to support valuable community services.

Staff Development and Internal Marketing. Many parks and recreation departments now provide a host of innovative and valuable programs and services to their citizens. Many of these new programs have been initiated to satisfy the needs of specific user groups and community organizations. Most department managers now realize the value of externally marketing their programs and services, not only to increase their usage, but also to improve the image of their department in the community. Both the number and types of programs have been expanding at such a rapid rate that staff development and internal marketing programs are needed before "going public" with a formal marketing campaign. Educating employees on the mission of the department, on all aspects of departmental services and program offerings, and the fact that these services are designed to meet the needs of citizens is essential to the positive development of the department's employees.

Department managers are also empowering their employees to identify new programs and services, and are allowing these employees to work directly with community groups and nonprofit organizations to implement these programs. This trend has improved both employee morale and customer service. These employees are also being taught that they project the image of their department, and that their interface with the public is, at all times, crucial to projecting a positive user-friendly image. Directors are also spending more time marketing their programs internally to their own employees. All employees should have a working knowledge of the services their organization provides to citizens, even if they are not directly involved in providing a specific service.

The development of employees at all levels, as well as educating them on the services provided by their department, is essential before undertaking external marketing efforts. Since external marketing programs are a vital tool in gaining public support for parks and recreation services, the use of these staff development and internal marketing techniques will no doubt continue in the future.

Use of Computers, Technologies, and Products. In order to keep operating costs to a minimum and improve the quality of services to the public, many innovative computer applications, new technologies, and specialized products are being used in parks and recreation departments. Because of new inexpensive computers and more user-friendly software, personal computers have become an inexpensive way to perform routine administrative and technical tasks such as league scheduling, course registration, facilities management, financial management, the preparation of newsletters, and department mailings to citizen. More sophisticated printers and desktop publishing applications have made the development of courses offering booklets and newsletters a fairly common practice. Recordkeeping practices have also improved with the use of database software applications, as well as with technologies such as microfilm and microfiche. These applications enhance records management and information retrieval.

Many new parks and recreation related products are now on the market, such as safe growth-retardant chemicals, softer playing surfaces, low-risk playground equipment, and more sophisticated lawn mowing equipment. Many departments are also using telephone message centers to answer routine citizen inquiries about program offerings, registration information, community activities, and ballfield scheduling procedures. This technology has freed up the time of existing staff to perform more productive public services. Automated cash register and receipting systems are also being used to account for daily cash transactions and to facilitate making daily bank deposits to increase the amount of interest earned on cash received.

In addition to saving money, the use of computers, state-of-the-art technologies, and other new products have improved the quality and enhanced the level of services to the public. Parks and recreation departments throughout the nation are becoming more sophisticated in the application of these technical resources.

External

Alternative Funding Sources. When additional funds are available to expand municipal services, departmental competition for these funds is fierce. As a rule, city councils favor adding police officers or firefighters over recreation employees. For this reason, parks and recreation directors have been forced to seek alternative funding sources for new services.

These alternative funding sources include federal and state grant programs as well as nontraditional financing sources. Parks and recreation grant programs provided by the federal government have either been reduced or eliminated entirely in recent years. City councils may still allocate a portion of their Community Development Block Grant (CDBG) funds to construct community recreation facilities such as swimming pools, playgrounds, ballfields, and community centers. These facilities must be constructed in qualifying areas, and after they are constructed, maintained with local tax dollars. Some state governments have funds available for the development of parks and open spaces. Funds under these programs are generally made available by allocating a portion of state lottery revenues, or through voter-approved parks and open space bonds. Almost without exception, no federal or state grant funds are available to finance recreational programs.

For these reasons, department directors have been increasingly focusing their attention on seeking nontraditional funding sources for their programs. Nontraditional funding sources include grants from nonprofit companies, and wealthy citizens desiring to fund innovative recreational programs. It is not unusual for parks and recreation departments to join forces with neighboring departments to form coalitions to collectively seek funding for multicity amenities such as parks, open spaces, and recreational facilities. Once acquired, maintenance costs are usually shared among those cities that applied for the grant. Virtually all parks and recreation departments now depend upon both municipal and private sector funding support to expand their services. Fundraising, through lobbying and direct solicitation, has become a way of life for department directors. The department's professional staff has also become innovative and assertive in seeking these outside funding sources.

The trend of having limited general fund monies to finance new services, and the increasing scarcity of federal and state funds, is a fact of life for parks and recreation directors. Seeking alternative and nontraditional funding sources is becoming common for department managers, regardless of the size of the municipality in which they work.

Alternative Service Delivery Systems. Parks and recreation directors have been at the forefront of developing alternative delivery systems for some time. Even before the era of tight budgets, other departments such as police, fire, and public works usually received funding priority over parks and recreation programs. This reality led to the development and use of creative service practices. These alternative approaches to providing services include the use of contract employees, contract services arrangements, joint agreements with other governments, coproduction, private sponsorship, public/private partnerships, and using citizen volunteers to augment existing service levels.

Contract employees can be used to provide special services on demand and do not receive fringe benefits. Typical contract services include parks maintenance, landscaping maintenance, and janitorial services, to name a few. Smaller cities also contract with counties and adjoining cities for parks and recreational services. Cities have also entered into joint agreements with other municipalities for multi-city, or regional, parks and recreation facilities. Since parks and recreation departments can no longer provide all requested services, it is not unusual for the department to provide space, with a community or nonprofit group providing the service. This arrangement, now referred to as coproduction, involves the joint provision of a particular service. Examples of this include the American Red Cross providing swimming instruction, a stroke support group providing therapeutic recreation programs, and a local historical society providing special courses to citizens.

Private sponsorship occurs when a private company donates funds to the department to provide "free" days or "reduced fee" periods to subsidize the cost of selected public services. Public/private partnerships take place when a city leases land to a private corporation to provide a specific service, or when the city and private company share in the profits from a particular public service. Many parks and recreation departments also have active citizen volunteer programs. Under these programs, volunteers are used to augment existing service levels. Volunteers are seldom used to replace regular municipal employees since this practice may violate existing labor agreements.

The use of these nontraditional service delivery methods are now commonly used in other municipal program areas, particularly for library, health, and human services. The use of these alternative services are on the increase.

Americans with Disabilities Act Compliance. The Americans with Disabilities Act (ADA), approved by Congress in 1990, mandates increased responsibility for municipal governments in the areas of providing services to persons with disabilities and for eliminating physical barriers that preclude handicapped individuals from using existing public facilities, playgrounds, and services. While it is fairly easy to retrofit city halls with handicapped restrooms, special parking spaces, and access ramps, it is more difficult and costly to retrofit and update the many park and recreation facilities in a community with these improvements.

Parks and recreation directors have had to inventory their facilities, determining improvements needed to comply with the ADA, and have incorporated these capital improvements into annual municipal capital project plans. In some cases, it has been less expensive to relocate an existing program to another up-to-date facility rather than having to retrofit an outdated facility with these improvements. It is now common to have building officials review proposed plans for parks and recreational facilities to make sure they comply with ADA's handicapped access requirements.

Since Congress mandated these ADA requirements upon city governments without financial reimbursement, most smaller improvements have been financed out of annual departmental capital budgets. Larger capital improvements have been financed by issuing general obligation bonds backed by the full faith and credit of a municipality. In either case, local tax dollars are being used to comply with this federal legislation. All new community facilities and public services must be handicapped accessible. This trend, because it is a federal mandate, will continue in the future.

Community Program Information Centers. A great number of parks and recreational programs are provided to citizens by a host of public, private, nonprofit, and community organizations. There are frequently so many programs available that it is difficult for the average citizen to be aware of their existence. Information about these programs needs to be collected, assembled, and made available at one or more locations for reference by departmental employees, other community groups, and members of the public.

A brief sampling of these agencies and their services are summarized as follows. At the federal and state level, national and state parks, nature preserves, and recreation areas may be located in or near a community. Counties typically also provide parks, open spaces, hiking trails, and special recreational facilities to citizens in cities within their jurisdiction. Special programs are also available from a variety of local nonprofit groups and community organizations such as YMCAs and YWCAs, Big Brothers and Big Sisters, Boys and Girls Clubs, and the American Red Cross, to name a few. Some of these groups provide specialized programs for young people, teenagers, adults, senior citizens, and disabled persons. Many local clubs also provide organized events and specialized instructions for their members as well as the public. Some of these clubs may promote such sports as skiing, mountain climbing, hiking, fishing, camping, canoeing, and sailing. Other clubs and leagues are involved in organizing a number of sports such as football, soccer, baseball, tennis, and basketball.

If they have not already done so, parks and recreation directors should initiate and supervise the development of a community program information center for their municipality. The various services and programs need to be brought together for the benefit of departmental employees, other nonprofit and community groups and, most importantly, for the citizens of all ages who may wish to participate in these organized activities. The trend is for parks and recreation directors to develop community program information centers due to the fragmented nature of these programs. Once this information has been developed, it also serves to eliminate future duplication of services.

Parks and Recreation Master Planning. In the past, when municipal funds were available, existing services could be expanded and new programs could be added to satisfy citizen demands for increased services. Now, competing departmental demands for limited revenues has created the need to prioritize program requests.

More focused municipal planning has evolved to both document and demonstrate the need for high priority programs, especially in parks and recreation departments, since their programs usually receive a lower citywide priority when compared with the program requests of other municipal departments. Department directors are in a unique position to work with their advisory commissions and citizen support groups to develop service master plans. The department director should form a planning committee consisting of representatives of these groups. It is also advantageous to have a representative of the governing body serve on this planning committee. The professional staff should then assess the community's parks and recreation needs, inventory available resources to meet these needs, and make recommendations concerning service alternatives to address these unmet service needs. Because of limited funding, these service needs should be placed in priority order.

Once such a plan has been developed, it should be reviewed by the primary users of parks and recreation services before being submitted to the official advisory commission for its consideration. Once adopted, this plan should be forwarded on to the governing body through the city manager for its review and approval. The planning committee, as well as members of advisory and support groups, usually attend the public meeting during which the proposed plan is considered by the city council. Since these citizen advisory groups usually represent a cross-section of the community, service master plans developed in this manner lend needed political legitimacy and support for future program and funding recommendations. This type of planning process is becoming an important vehicle for identifying and addressing the parks and recreation service needs of a community.

The efforts of parks and recreation directors to educate their top management and elected leaders on ways to meet these service demands of citizens is essential. It provides city councils with the information upon which to make difficult decisions in properly allocating a city's limited financial resources. These master plans also assist the director and his or her advisory commission with long-range departmental programs and financial planning.

Parks and Recreation Service Trends. Parks and recreation programs have evolved over the years to meet changing citizen demands for services. Professionals in this service area keep abreast of the latest developments and issues in their field by joining national professional associations and by reading the latest publications and periodicals available from these organizations. A survey of the most recent books and monographs reveal evolving management and service trends in park and recreation departments. These trends have been divided into administration, parks and recreation, and current issues of interest.

Publications dealing with management include creative programming, long-range planning methods, fundraising programs, alternative service delivery strategies, and leadership styles for the future. Three of the most recent publications include how to promote tourism through leisure services, how to determine the economic impact of parks and recreation programs in a community, and how to initiate a successful public relations program. General parks and recreation trends include using safe playground equipment and playing surfaces, developing programs to unite the community, the value of recreational services for minority groups, special services for older Americans, the use of therapeutic recreation programs, compliance with the ADA, and the use of citizen volunteers. Current topical issues in this field include the use of citizen surveys, how to evaluate service contracts, risk management and public liability, how to reduce sports injury liability, legal issues in the field, and city/county parks and recreation consolidations.

Some of the most recent periodicals available from the National Park and Recreation Association (NPRA) include such topics as management trends, information networking for programmers, therapeutic recreation programs, legal issues in parks and recreation, and cost-effective maintenance techniques. These trends focus on the improved management of services, how to tailor services to meet the needs of the community, ways to hold down costs, and alternative fundraising methods. All of these trends will surely continue in the future.

Professional Development. Due to the entrepreneurial nature of the parks and recreation field, it is imperative that professional administrators as well as parks and recreation specialists acquire state-of-the-art information and training in this changing service area. The primary professional association in this field is the NRPA. Members typically have their own state associations which meet monthly, providing valuable networking opportunities. The NRPA provides many educational programs, conferences, technical resources, and publications on both traditional and topical issues. It also provides a research service on current issues relating to this field. Specialized training programs are provided in many technical areas such as master planning, playground safety, facilities management, therapeutic recreation, as well as the ADA. The National League of Cities (NLC) and International City/County Management Association (ICMA) also provide resources to professionals in this field.

In addition to these professional development services, many states as well as public and private universities now provide structured learning programs leading to professional designations and certifications in this field. The services and resources available from all of these organizations have helped to increase the level of competency and professionalism in the field. They also set standards when hiring new professional personnel. The funds spent on job-related training are usually more than offset by the increased level of professionalism, morale, and employee productivity. This is especially true in small departments where advancement may be limited. The trend for parks and recreation advocates—members of advisory bodies, friends, and department managers—is to inform and educate their elected officials and top management on the need and importance of these professional development programs.

Public Liability Reduction Programs. The number of liability lawsuits against municipalities has increased exponentially in recent years. All department managers, especially parks and recreation directors, are keenly aware of the need to reduce the public liability exposure of their programs and services.

Many cities have hired specialized safety and risk managers to assist department managers in reviewing their facilities, operations, and public services. Smaller communities may use special consultants to perform this function.

Municipal parks and recreation departments usually provide safe, low-risk programs and services to citizens. Existing public facilities are being scrutinized to correct potential hazards and unsafe conditions. Proposed new facilities, especially public playgrounds and tot lots, are routinely reviewed to eliminate any potential hazards and safety problems before construction begins. Many cities have eliminated swings, slides, and merry-go-rounds from their playgrounds to reduce their liability exposure. Specialized manufacturing companies now provide specially designed "user-friendly" and safe playground equipment with softer playing surfaces. This new equipment is frequently constructed with plastic, rubber, or wood products.

High-risk activities, such as skiing, trampolines, scuba diving, sky diving, and mountain climbing are typically not provided directly by cities to the public. When they are provided, cities usually contract these services with private providers, who are required to sign legal contracts relieving the local government from the public liability associated with these activities. Special caution is also being exercised when contracting with private providers of services at public facilities and when allowing community groups and organizations to use public facilities and park areas. Many cities are developing standard contract clauses and hold harmless agreements to reduce their liability exposure for these services and events. The use of all of these safeguards to reduce liability exposure are on the increase in cities of all sizes.

Service Philosophy of Elected Officials. Two distinct service philosophies exist relative to the provision of parks and recreational services. Some elected officials believe that the development of these programs should be the primary responsibility of individuals, families, and organized sporting groups. Those members of a governing body who espouse this viewpoint believe that their city government should provide facilities, but that citizens should provide the services and programs available at these public venues. They also believe that these facilities should be specifically designed to serve the needs of the community. Another popular viewpoint held by elected officials is that parks and recreation services are essential to the health and welfare of the community, and it is the proper role of their municipal government to determine community needs and to provide services to meet these needs.

These two distinct personal philosophies have led to different modes of service delivery in communities. One favors the direct provision of services by municipal government; the other favors municipal government's facilitation of services by the private sector. The more liberal viewpoint is held by those individuals who believe that these services are required to provide opportunities for all citizens to interact and to share common experiences. The more conservative viewpoint, increasing in popularity, has evolved in recent years because of tight budgets and the aversion of elected officials to raise taxes to finance so-called "soft" services. This service philosophy also differs between elected officials in urban and suburban communities. City councils in urban areas typically believe that parks and recreation services are essential for inner-city youth, families, and senior citizens. City councils in suburban communities, with more open space and private recreational options, often favor the facilitation approach in providing public services.

This debate continues in city halls throughout the country. Tight budgets and limited revenues have served to increase the popularity of the service facilitation model of providing community services.

User Fees and Service Charges. Faced with limited budgets and possible service reductions, many parks and recreation directors have been creative when it comes to generating additional program revenues. Many programs now have cost-covering service charges, with special provisions for those citizens who cannot afford to pay. Some cities are now using demand pricing to establish these service fees. Demand pricing is also used to regulate peak activity usage periods. For example, a higher fee may be charged for using municipal swimming pools on weekends when usage is greatest, with a lower fee being charged during "slack" periods on weekdays. This type of service charge also reduces the demand of a community resource during its peak activity period. The same principal would also apply to fees charged in municipal-owned parking lots in public parks. Some cities, depending upon the income levels of their citizens, are also providing "free use" periods during slack times in order to accommodate low-income individuals and families.

Parks and recreation departments, in an effort to raise additional revenues, are also charging for public space rentals. The use of sliding-scale user fees are now common. Under this concept, cities typically use a three-tiered fee policy. For-profit groups pay the highest user fee, followed by a reduced fee for nonprofit organizations, and frequently no user fee is charged when a particular program is co-sponsored by the city. When renting ballfields, in addition to charging the regular maintenance fee, it is now common to charge organized sporting leagues for the cost of the lights used for evening games. Frequently adult leagues are charged the full costs, while children and youth leagues pay a reduced fee. Also, when a program or service only benefits its users, such as specialized lessons and instructional classes, the trend is to charge users the full cost of providing the program.

The trend is to assess some charge to the users of parks and recreational services and facilities, providing avenues for reduced fees for children, young people, and low-income families. All of these trends have helped to generate additional revenues to maintain a community's leisure-related facilities and services.

Working with the Community. For many citizens, parks and recreation departments may be one of the few sources of direct contact with their local government. Parks and recreation employees are increasingly realizing that they represent the image of their city in their dealings with the public. Moreover, since departmental facilities are available to various community groups for meetings, small conferences, and training workshops, the image projected by employees to these groups is equally important. Official advisory commissions and citizen support groups should also be educated about their department's programs and services. These citizens also serve as the department's ambassadors to the public. Every effort is being made by parks and recreation directors to develop positive relations with not only their major stakeholders but also their regular customers—the taxpayers of the community.

The successful department manager works closely with its users, citizen support groups, and advisory bodies when developing new programs or when considering changes to existing services. New park and recreation service master planning practices have enhanced these close working relationships. In the past, some department directors would reach important program and policy recommendations in a vacuum, only to encounter difficulty later on when approvals were sought from their advisory body and city council. The trend is for the department's management staff to value citizen input and feedback, to work closely with their major stakeholders and users, and to plan for future parks and recreation services in an open and collaborative environment. When the director and the department's professional and support staff exhibit these personal qualities on the job, they have already established a positive image in their community.

Although many of these trends were initiated during tough budget times to solicit support for the department's services, they stand to continue in the future because it is good management to have employees treat taxpayers like customers.

THE FUTURE

The most significant internal productivity trend which has developed in response to external financial pressures has been the evolution of the parks and recreation department from a traditional service provider to a contemporary service facilitator. Under the traditional service model, departmental programs were provided by full-time municipal employees. As citizens demanded more services, elected officials approved the expansion of the number of employees in this department. In subsequent years, when these departmental budgets had to be reduced, the number of staff dwindled to the point where the only way to maintain services was to utilize nontraditional service delivery options such as the coproduction, cosponsorship, and facilitation of services. Now, most departments operate under the more contemporary model as a facilitator of public services. This has required department managers and their remaining full-time staffs to develop more entrepreneurial styles of management. Full-time staff now coordinate many programs through private service contracts, seasonal employees, part-time workers, and volunteers. Financial pressures and citizen demands for greater fiscal accountability have resulted in establishing selected services as enterprise funds or profit centers, which are not subsidized by taxpayers in general.

Citizens as well as elected officials have supported two distinctly different political philosophies when it comes to these services. Because of their aversion to increased taxes, many citizens feel that the responsibility for these services should rest with individuals, families, organized sporting leagues, and community groups. This philosophy has led to the belief that a municipality should provide community facilities, such as ballfields, but that the private sector should provide the programs and services available at these public venues. As city populations expanded, increasing service demands coupled with greater property tax revenues changed this philosophy. When funds were available due to expanding property tax revenues, citizens generally believed that these services should be the responsibility of their municipal government. As many cities became fully developed and the growth of property tax revenues became limited, many citizens reverted to the more conservative political philosophy of government being the facilitator—not the provider—of parks and recreational services. Not all citizens and elected officials hold this popular political viewpoint. A dichotomy exists between citizens in highly urbanized metropolitan areas and those citizens living in more suburban and rural areas. Many urban residents realize the contributions made by these services to their quality of life. Citizens living in outlying areas with more open spaces and natural amenities feel less of a need for these services.

The types of parks and recreational programs provided have evolved over the years to fit the demands of those citizens being served by these public services. In the area of parks, communities in congested metropolitan areas now have tot lots and small neighborhood parks with playgrounds. The development of linear parks and recreation areas alongside natural amenities are increasingly being supported by taxpayers. The number of open spaces are expanding as citizens realize the importance of having passive public recreational areas. Recreational programs are also being tailored to the needs of the community. The types of facilities provided, such as youth and or senior citizen centers, as well as the programs provided at these facilities, are geared to the interests of residents. In order to accommodate the needs of working parents, many communities now provide preschool services, day care programs, and after school drop-in centers. Whether a community provides aerobics exercise classes or health and nutrition programs depends upon the ages and needs of its citizens and their service demands. Many specialized services are also being provided for different segments of the population, such as therapeutic recreation programs for senior citizens and handicapped persons. Many taxpayers do not mind subsidizing these special programs because of the unique needs of those citizens being served.

PLANNING AND BUILDING

11

The municipal responsibilities to regulate land uses and improvements to real property are assigned to the staff of the planning and building department. Two related services are also usually provided by this department. They include a city's affordable housing strategy and its economic development program. The organizational arrangement of these programs may vary among communities for a number of reasons, including tradition, charter requirements, the scope of services provided, the size of a municipality, and the alignment of municipal functions. In smaller communities, economic development may be placed in the city manager's office. In very large cities it may have separate departmental status. Also, in very large cities, planning and building services may be divided into two separate departments. Some communities have created community development departments to perform these same functions. Many city managers have assigned compliance with affordable housing requirements to the planning staff, since this program relates to this overall function. In many medium-sized communities, these programs have typically been combined into planning and building departments. Due to budgetary restraints, when these services have been provided by two different departments, the trend has been to combine these departments for reasons of economy.

Every community has a similar planning process. This requirement is nearly always mandated by state law. The process begins with the development of a comprehensive or master plan, which sets forth a community's development goals, separates different land uses, shows existing and proposed roadways, and current and planned community facilities. Future roadways, community facilities, and other components of the municipal infrastructure are projected using the anticipated population trends based on residential land-use densities. The comprehensive plan is implemented through the use of a zoning map and zoning ordinance. The map illustrates permitted land uses, as well as the type of development allowed within each land use. The zoning ordinance sets forth a municipality's minimum development standards and regulations. Every community also has subdivision regulations that require that when land is subdivided the proposed subdivision must be approved by the planning commission. As a part of this approval process, the property owner must dedicate land to the municipality for future roadways and other public improvements. Developers must also provide a performance bond to ensure compliance with these subdivision regulations. Each of these pieces of the planning puzzle require planning commission and governing body approval. The planning staff is responsible for implementing these requirements.

To guide the development of improvements made upon real property, every community has an adopted set of building code regulations which sets forth minimum building construction standards. These code requirements are applicable to all new construction and the rehabilitation of existing structures, as well as building additions and modifications. Municipal building inspectors conduct on-site inspections to ensure compliance with these regulations. Most communities have a host of other specialized codes to control temporary signage, on-site parking, on-site outdoor storage, landscaping requirements, occupancy limits, and housing standards, to name a few. Even though a development received a favorable inspection and the owner is granted an occupancy permit, constant code enforcement is necessary throughout the years to ensure that a community's development standards are maintained. Municipal code enforcement personnel also constantly inspect older structures to make sure that they comply with these standards. While old land uses and improvements may be allowed to continue, when these structures are substantially rehabilitated they must be brought up to current code standards. If a nonconforming structure burns to the ground, the new development standards would apply to future improvements made to this property.

Many communities have approved economic development programs to attract new businesses as well as to retain existing ones. In this respect, many municipalities provide a number of land-based and financial incentives to entice new developments. These programs have been initiated because of the additional jobs and revenues generated by private sector development. Careful attention should be paid to ensure that the economic rewards received from a proposed development exceed the value of the incentives provided by a community's taxpayers. Public officials are now tailoring these incentives to the specific types of companies and industries they desire, and then strategically marketing these incentives to attract these businesses. Increasingly, the quality of life provided by a community is a key factor in attracting private investment. For this reason, the condition of a city's transportation system, community facilities, parks and open spaces, and housing stock are all important variables in the economic development equation. The quality of a city's ongoing code enforcement efforts and how property owners maintain their properties are other important factors.

Figure 11.1 (see page 256) sets forth the typical programs provided by planning and building departments. The development of a community's capital improvements plan is usually the responsibility of the department manager since these projects must be consistent with a city's approved comprehensive plan. Cities receiving federal funds must prepare a Comprehensive Housing Assistance Strategy (CHAS) to increase the availability of affordable housing. This task is almost always assigned to this department.

DESCRIPTION OF PROGRAMS

Planning Services. The community planning process begins with the development of a comprehensive or master plan. This plan is designed to guide all future private and public development in a municipality. This document contains the goals, objectives, and policies concerning a city's future growth and desired quality of life. The plan is usually developed by the planning staff in larger cities and by a planning consultant in small- and medium-sized communities.

The typical plan groups future land uses into major zoning categories such as residential, commercial, industrial, and agricultural, to name a few. It also shows all existing and proposed roadways and public facilities. Future roadways and public improvements are those required to support the projected growth desired by the community. These plans typically include different categories of roadways, land-use distinctions within particular zones, and permitted residential densities, usually expressed in terms of the allowable number of dwelling units per acre. These plans may also show agricultural preserves, special protection areas such as wetlands and nature preserves, and public access to beaches and other natural amenities.

The requirements of these plans are usually mandated by the state. Some states require their advanced approval of these plans before they can be officially adopted and implemented at the local level. These plans are frequently required to be periodically updated, usually every five years. While these plans are developed by staff or consultants, they must be reviewed by planning commissions and adopted by the local governing body. The local review process includes public notices and hearings at all stages of the approval process. These requirements are also set forth by state law.

Once this plan is adopted, all proposed development must be consistent with the requirements set forth in the plan. Receiving approval to build a development before public roadways and facilities are available, for example, may require the developer to pay for these public improvements.

Zoning Controls. The comprehensive or master plan is implemented through the use of an approved zoning map and accompanying zoning ordinance. The zoning map illustrates the land uses and the types of developments

Figure 11.1
Planning and Building Major Programs

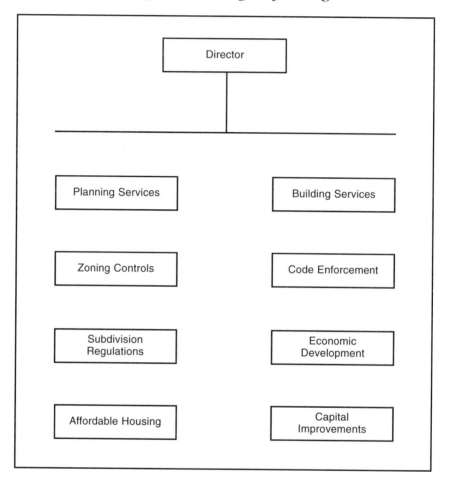

permitted within each zone. This ordinance sets forth the laws that regulate development standards and requirements within each permitted land-use area. Typical regulations include permitted uses, building height limitations, required lot sizes, minimum setback requirements, minimum number of off-street parking spaces, maximum allowable lot coverage, landscaping design and criteria, signage standards, and allowable accessory uses of the property.

The zoning map and ordinance cannot be altered at the staff level; it can only be changed through the local legislative process. This includes planning or zoning commission approval, as well as the required public notices and hearings necessary for this process. If property owners wish a site-specific modification to or exemption from these regulations, they must seek a zoning variance from the required approval body, typically a local board of zoning appeals or adjustment. This body, usually required by state law, may grant individual exceptions to the existing zoning laws. Development conditions may be placed on these approvals.

Planned unit developments (PUDs) may also be authorized by the local legislative body. These regulations relax existing zoning regulations for larger tracks of land proposed for development. The PUD laws may permit mixed land uses, relaxed setback requirements, allow the clustering of buildings, and increase height limitations to create more open space and common areas.

State laws and court decisions severely restrict the use of exclusionary zoning controls and regulations on private property. Spot-zoning is also usually not permitted unless evolving land-use patterns warrant such changes (e.g., older residential lots facing major arterial streets are frequently changed to allow small commercial developments).

Subdivision Regulations. Nearly all municipalities mandate subdivision requirements on property owners. Most states mandate that cities have these laws for the protection of the public. Under these regulations, whenever a property owner subdivides a track of land into two or more parcels for sale or lease, a subdivision map must be filed. The development may also require a dedication of land for public improvements.

This map must be reviewed by the planning staff, approved by the planning commission, and filed with the clerk pursuant to the procedures set forth by state law and local regulations. Private land must be dedicated for all public purposes, including roadways, alleys, utilities, and stormwater facilities. Local subdivision regulations should be consistent with a city's comprehensive plan, and the land must be developed according to the adopted land-use map and zoning ordinance. When a proposed subdivision is in conflict with the comprehensive plan, either the comprehensive plan or the proposed subdivision must be changed. Changing the comprehensive plan is a cumbersome and frequently highly political process, especially if only a single track of land is involved. For example, changing a single-family residential zone to permit a multiple-family residential development may drastically change the character of a neighborhood.

Once subdivided lots are developed, the private and public improvements placed upon them define the character of the area for many years. For this reason, subdivision regulations typically include site design standards and the requirements for the payment of impact fees for future public improvements such as schools, parks, open space, and arterial streets. Once a subdivision map is approved, a city's planning and engineering staff conducts inspections and grants final approvals before individual lots may be sold to the public. Performance bonds are required of developers to ensure compliance with their approved subdivision plans.

Affordable Housing. In many communities, affordable housing is becoming a thing of the past. Many young families, senior citizens, and others on low and fixed incomes cannot find affordable housing in their cities. In many cases, the traditional "American Dream" of home ownership remains just that—merely a dream.

The reasons for this are several: profit margins are greater for more expensive residential development, land acquisition costs have escalated, construction costs have increased, multifamily zoning is scarce, and the cost of public improvements is prohibitive. This has led to two trends. First, the existing affordable housing stock has become more expensive. Second, the market for new affordable housing has not kept pace with the demand. Many affordable housing units are only available in undesirable areas. Hence, many families are forced to rent apartments for many years.

Since the public goal of more affordable housing is not totally being met by the private sector, government has become involved to improve this situation. The federal government, for example, now requires communities receiving federal funds to prepare a CHAS. This report must identify a city's affordable housing needs, barriers to achieving affordable housing goals, and provide a plan to increase the availability of affordable housing units. A number of states now require cities to address housing needs in their comprehensive plans.

Cities are also using a number of planning techniques and financial incentives to achieve affordable housing goals. These include using low-interest loans for housing rehabilitation, offering first-time home buyer loan programs, eliminating expensive regulatory requirements, waiving development and impact fees, subsidizing on- and off-site improvements, streamlining development approvals, granting density bonuses, providing development grants, allowing "granny flat" units on single-family lots, and creating nonprofit housing corporations. Some of these incentives are financed with funds made available from federal and state grant programs.

Building Services. Every municipality has building codes that must be followed by property owners, contractors, and developers when improvements are made to real property. These improvements include initial construction projects, the rehabilitation of existing structures, building additions, and building modifications. Most states require cities to adopt state-approved uniform building codes. For this reason, building codes and regulations do not vary greatly from city to city within a state. While the state may set the minimum standards, a community may approve regulations that exceed these standards.

Building codes are usually administered by a chief building official (CBO) with the assistance of building inspectors. These employees review plans, approve them, and issue building permits to allow construction. After construction begins, on-site inspections are performed to ensure compliance with approved plans. A final inspection is made when a project is completed. After the final inspection the project is approved for occupancy (e.g., in the case of a dwelling) or use (e.g., in the case of a garage). Laws preclude the sale of property until a certificate of occupancy has been issued. Plans for larger developments are typically reviewed by municipal planning, building, fire, and engineering officials. This review process is coordinated by the CBO.

Prior to receiving a building permit, a number of fees must be paid. These include application fees, plan review fees, inspection fees, utility connection fees, and development impact fees. Homeowners are usually charged a small fixed fee to receive a building permit for minor additions and modifications. These fees are usually cost-covering and adjusted periodically to reflect the cost of doing business. Since large projects take more time to review and inspect, fees are usually based as a percentage of the estimated cost of these improvements.

In small- to medium-sized communities the building function may be a part of the planning department. In larger cities it is typically a separate department.

Code Enforcement. Every community has a host of approved municipal codes that require constant enforcement. Typical codes include those for land uses, zoning, subdivisions, building, and housing, as well as more specialized regulations. They set forth the legally allowable uses of property, the type of improvements permitted on property, site design criteria, minimum criteria for building construction, and minimum acceptable community standards for private housing. More specialized regulations cover permanent and temporary signage, on-site parking, on-site outdoor storage, landscaping, and occupancy limitations, to name a few.

Proper code enforcement requires a high degree of interdepartmental cooperation. For example, building and housing inspectors commonly refer violations to other city departments for followup enforcement action. Likewise, health and fire inspectors forward complaints to building and housing inspectors for enforcement. Many complaints are also received from citizens concerning alleged violations of city codes. These violations are referred to the responsible municipal departments. It is typical for the department manager of the planning and building department to coordinate a community's code enforcement program. Computer software applications are now available to track reported violations through to compliance.

When a violation has been verified, the property owner receives a notification of the violation and is given a reasonable time period in which to take corrective action. Failure to correct the violation results in a penalty, with subsequent violations resulting in harsher penalties. Penalties typically include a written warning, fine, restrictions on the use of the property, court action, and even a possible jail sentence. Most violations are routinely corrected by property owners. Every municipality has an approved fine structure for these violations. Fines on selected code violations may be increased periodically to ensure prompt corrective action.

Economic Development. The use of local economic development incentives has expanded in recent years based on the desire of elected officials to hold down taxes and maintain an acceptable level of public services. Recent economic recessions, coupled with high unemployment levels, have facilitated this trend. A large number of incentives are now available to entice private development to a community.

Municipal economic development incentives have evolved over the years from a limited number of inducements to the use of a diverse assortment of high specialized incentives. Typical incentives include financial inducements (e.g., low-cost financing, tax incentives, and tax rebates), land-based incentives (e.g., density bonuses, land subsidies, and relaxed development regulations), as well as other types of incentives (e.g., enterprise zones, business incubators, and business retention programs). In addition to creating new jobs and property taxes, new business and industry generates additional development fees, personal property taxes, business license fees, utility taxes, and sales taxes.

The number and types of incentives provided to a developer must be approved by the governing body. Also, when the staff prepares a development agreement, which usually compares the long-term costs and benefits of these incentives, it must be approved by the elected officials. This approval process usually requires a public hearing. The incentives provided and the benefits received must be justified to the public during this process.

The national trend is towards creating positive and mutually advantageous economic partnerships with private sector companies. These new partnerships have focused attention on the need for municipal planning and building officials to be responsive to the needs of the private sector. One-stop permit processes, streamlined development guidelines, and staff expertise in this new field are an integral part of a city's economic development program. In most small- to medium-sized communities, economic development is a part of the planning and building department. In larger cities it is frequently a separate department.

Capital Improvements. Some cities prepare a capital improvement plan (CIP) because it is required by state law. Other cities prepare a CIP because it is a sound management practice. Capital projects are permanent improvements to public property. Examples include new fire stations, schools, roadways, street improvements, utilities, parks, playgrounds, open spaces, swimming pools, and other municipal facilities and improvements.

The typical CIP is a five-year plan, which is usually consistent with a city's comprehensive or master plan. Project costs include architectural and engineering services, land acquisition, construction, and other improvements to the property such as those for landscaping, parking, lighting, and fencing, to name a few. The anticipated funding source is also listed for each project. Funding sources may include federal and state grants, special revenue funds (e.g., such as those created by development fees, utility connections, or existing sewer and water services), or general funds (e.g., local revenues created through taxation, user fees, or bonding). Because of the large costs involved, general funds are typically raised by issuing general obligation bonds. Revenue bonds may be issued when a project generates sufficient revenues to cover the cost of its debt.

It is common to have the planning director coordinate the preparation of the annual CIP. Sometimes a committee is formed for this purpose, consisting of the planning, public works, and finance directors. The CIP is always reviewed and approved by the city manager. This plan is usually sent to the local planning commission for its review before being sent to the governing body for approval. While the plan goes out five years, usually only the first year is funded. This approval sets a community's capital budget for the fiscal year. Because of the complexity of the CIP, it is usually prepared separately from a city's regular budget.

PRODUCTIVITY TRENDS

In the case of planning and building departments, many of the internal productivity trends examined relate to improving the quality of services to the public. Other productivity trends relate to achieving results from new initiatives such as economic development programs and creative ways to finance capital projects. Many communities on the outskirts of metropolitan areas are trying to manage growth to maintain their image and quality of life. The use of fiscal impact statements and development impact fees have evolved as effective tools to regulate growth. Since many existing municipal codes such as planning, zoning, building, and housing relate to this department, it is not unusual for these department managers to be in charge of citywide interdepartmental code enforcement programs. Under these programs, all complaints are forwarded to this department and subsequently distributed to other departments for appropriate followup action. Feedback from these departments is provided to the staff of the planning and building department, who continually track the status of these code violations. Many communities now have a variety of council-appointed boards and commissions to guide various aspects of development. These groups were designed to remove politics from the development process.

In their role as chief municipal planner, planning and building directors have a primary responsibility for dealing with the public and recommending plans and programs that meet citizen expectations. A host of external forces influence a community's planning process. These include court mandates, state and federal laws, changing demographics, transportation systems, population growth, and greater citizen participation in the decisionmaking process leading

Table 11.1
Planning and Building Productivity Trends

Internal	External
Affordable Housing	Comprehensive Community Code Enforcement
Capital Improvement Plans and Financing	External Forces Influencing Planning
Economic Development Planning	Financial Incentives
Evolving Building and Zoning Controls	General Incentives and Assistance
Evolving Planning Services	Growth Management Techniques
Fiscal Impact Analysis	Land-Based Incentives
Human Resources Management Practices	Marketing Programs and Services
Interdepartmental Code Enforcement Cooperation	Professional Development
Organizational Arrangements	Public/Private Partnerships
Role of Elected Officials and Advisory Bodies	Regional Planning Practices
Use of Computers and Software Applications	Traditional vs. Strategic Planning
Use of Economic Development Incentives	User Fees, Impact Charges, Special Assessments, and Fines
	Working with the Community

to the adoption of new plans. One of the newest and most important programs performed by this department is economic development. Many department directors have carefully crafted incentives to attract selected businesses. Since merely having these programs will not guarantee success, these initiatives must be actively promoted to the private sector. These efforts have led to the formation of public/private partnerships whereby private companies receive public benefits in return for the promise of additional jobs and revenues to the municipality. A strong emphasis has been placed on developing user fees and service charges to make services cost covering. Development impact fees and assessment districts are also being used to finance new municipal improvements. A major shift is also taking place from the use of traditional planning practices to more contemporary techniques such as strategic planning.

These internal and external productivity trends, and others, are highlighted in Table 11.1 above. Some planning issues such as growth management initiatives are so politically sensitive that outside planning consultants may be used for these assignments. All of these measures require advanced approval by the governing body before being implemented. Some approvals are received on a case-by-case basis, such as for economic development proposals.

Internal

Affordable Housing. In many communities the supply of available affordable housing and apartment units does not meet the citizen demand for these types of dwellings. Several factors have exacerbated this trend, namely the high price of available land, increased construction costs, conventional financing costs, and the requirement to pay development impact fees to provide for public infrastructure and community facilities. For these reasons, many young families, senior citizens, disabled persons, as well as citizens on low and fixed incomes cannot find affordable housing in their community. Since the public goal of affordable housing is not being met by the private sector, government—at all levels—has become involved to improve these local housing conditions.

The federal government now requires communities receiving federal funds to develop a CHAS to identify their affordable housing needs, existing barriers to satisfying these needs, as well as a plan and timetable to provide for more affordable housing units. At the state level, some states now require locally approved comprehensive plans to include ways to address the long-range affordable housing needs of a community's residents. Other states have allowed cities to permit the construction of so-called "granny flats" on existing single-family residential properties. A few states make housing trust funds available to local nonprofit housing corporations to develop and or rehabilitate affordable housing units within their city.

Cities have also developed a number of planning and building incentives to achieve their affordable housing goals. These include low interest loans for the construction and the rehabilitation of existing affordable housing units; first-time home buyer low interest loan programs; the elimination of expensive regulatory requirements; streamlining municipal development approvals; waiving user fees, service charges, and development impact fees; subsidizing on-site and off-site improvements; and granting density bonuses for projects with affordable housing units.

These governmental initiatives have served to make more affordable housing units available to citizens who would otherwise be excluded from ever owning their own home. The use of federal and state mandates, as well as innovative local initiatives to provide more affordable housing units, are on the increase. To the extent that communities cannot provide for their own affordable housing needs, additional federal and state mandates can be expected in the future.

Capital Improvement Plans and Financing. Even though they are mandated in many states, communities of all sizes have neglected the preparation of a comprehensive capital improvement plan. This neglect has occurred because elected officials have been preoccupied with raising revenues and reducing costs in balancing their annual municipal operating budgets. For this reason, governing bodies have not wanted to incur the additional long-term debt required to finance infrastructure improvements and community facilities.

In order to finance future capital projects, many planning and building directors are recommending new planning approaches and growth management policies that link future growth to the availability of adequate public infrastructure and community facilities. One of the most popular growth management tools is to require that roadways, utilities, parks, and community facilities be in place prior to or concurrent with the completion of a new development. This can be accomplished through the adoption of a public facilities ordinance. Public facility laws require that these public improvements be in place before a development can take place, unless the developer pays for the cost of these improvements. Development impact fees, on the other hand, require a developer to pay a fee representing a portion of the cost of these community facilities. These revenues are set aside in special funds to finance the construction of these public improvements in future years.

Capital improvement plans typically project a city's capital needs over a five-year period. These plans also link necessary public projects that are critical to a city's economic development goals. The neglect and deterioration of a city's public capital assets may deter new business and industries from locating to a community, may discourage the expansion of existing companies, and may facilitate the decision of a company to leave for a more desirable location. Planning and building directors should educate their top management and city councils that it is usually much less expensive in the long run to maintain pieces of the public infrastructure, rather than have them replaced after they deteriorate. Financing should always be considered from other funding sources first, such as development impact fees and state and federal grants, before approving local funding.

The trend is to have developers pay for their share of the costs of public infrastructure required by their developments, except in cases where the public benefits clearly exceed the costs, such as for certain projects that may help a city achieve its economic development goals. This trend is in keeping with the philosophy that taxpayers should not pay for facilities that they do not directly use.

Economic Development Planning. The extent to which a city is involved in economic development planning and developing incentives to attract private investment is based on the political philosophy of elected officials. With the demise of many federal and state grant programs for municipalities, many city councils have adopted a philosophy of financial self-reliance, acknowledging the need to expand their city's tax base, create jobs, and generate additional revenues without having to raise taxes. This philosophy creates the background against which all economic development planning activities take place in a municipality. This outlook has created a positive climate in which to entice private development to a community. It has also led to the development of positive staff relations between planning and building officials and the private sector. It is the job of city managers and planning and building directors to translate the philosophy of their governing body into an organizational reality.

In addition to developing and proposing various types of economic development incentives for the private sector, one of the initial programs implemented in many communities was the one-stop permit center. Rather than make development applicants go to several locations to obtain the required municipal permits, the issuance of these permits has been centralized at one location to better serve the development community as well as the public. Planning and building department officials have also realized the importance of educating their staffs on the many resources available to serve the development community. This trend is especially valuable since many federal and states agencies, colleges and universities, as well as local economic development corporations, now provide a wide range of economic development services and assistance to the private sector.

Economic development incentives, in the eyes of many elected officials, are now perceived as an important vehicle to raise revenues without increasing taxes. The trend towards the philosophy of financial self-reliance is increasing, and has been facilitated by the public's aversion to increased taxation, as well as fewer funds from higher levels of government. The use of economic development incentives has gained in popularity over the past decade, and is likely to increase in importance in future years.

Evolving Building and Zoning Controls. Many states require cities to adopt uniform building codes, and to follow standard zoning practices. This is not required in all cities, although all cities must meet the minimum state standards by law. They also have the power to exceed these state standards in their community.

The trend in building codes is to permit new and safe building construction technologies in an effort to hold down development costs. New fire prevention requirements such as building sprinklers, smoke detectors, and fire-resistant construction materials are now included in building regulations. The trend is to charge homeowners a flat fee for minor home improvements, and to charge developers a percentage fee on larger projects. One of the largest growth in fees in recent years has been in planning and building departments.

Zoning regulations are being reviewed and revised to help control the character of a community. Zoning changes are continually being made to reduce height limitations, establish minimum and maximum lot coverages, and impose setbacks from the property lines for improvements. Some of the latest zoning controls mandate increased landscaping requirements, greater provisions for off-street parking, a reduction in the size of on-site signage and, on larger projects, requirements for open spaces. Traditional zoning controls are also being relaxed through the use of PUDs, which are applicable to the development of larger tracks of land. The PUD requirements typically provide for mixed land uses (single family, multiple family, and commercial) and greater building densities per acre in exchange for more open space.

The trend in building codes is to permit some flexibility consistent with maintaining strict safety and fire prevention requirements, and to charge developers a percentage fee based upon the estimated cost of their project. The trend in zoning controls is to maintain the character and quality of a community, as well as regulate the consistency of developments in residential, commercial, and industrial areas. All of these trends are on the increase.

Evolving Planning Services. Early municipal planning programs focused on regulating "undesirable" land uses (e.g., bars, pool halls, fortune tellers, and adult entertainment centers) and creating zones to separate dissimilar land uses (e.g., residential, commercial, industrial, and agricultural) in communities. Most states now mandate the development of citywide comprehensive or master plans. These plans are designed to guide all future private and public development in a municipality. They regulate land uses through zoning and show existing and proposed roadways and community facilities.

In the past, all taxpayers paid for these planned roadways and community facilities. Now, it is common for cities to impose development impact fees upon developers and charge them for a pro rata share of these anticipated costs. Not more than a generation ago, municipal planning and building departments created urban renewal programs to revitalize blighted center city areas. Citizen opposition to these major planning efforts gained such momentum that few cities presently engage in such planning practices. During the past few decades, citizens have attempted to control planning practices through such initiatives as development moratoriums, growth management measures, and mandatory referendums on rezonings.

Contemporary planning concerns include preserving the environment, provisions for adequate transportation, providing affordable housing, and ensuring that community facilities are available when development occurs. Rather than the traditional grandiose planning schemes for the entire community, contemporary planning practices are characterized by intense politics, negotiations between conflicting interest groups, and incremental adjustments to existing community plans.

Planning directors are no longer afforded the luxury of working in a vacuum. They now interface with the community on a regular basis. Proposed plans or changes to existing plans are shared with major stakeholders to solicit their input before they are submitted to the planning commission or city council. The use of fiscal impact analyses to show the municipal expenses and revenues associated with development proposals are becoming commonplace. How communities will develop their remaining vacant land areas are frequently determined at "heated" public hearings when these proposals are considered.

The planning environment is increasingly negotiated with a number of special interest groups and change, when it occurs, is incremental in nature. The trend towards citizen activism has facilitated these trends, which are on the increase in most communities.

Fiscal Impact Analysis. Many planning and building departments are using state-of-the-art techniques to calculate the estimated public costs and revenues associated with proposed developments. These calculations are used to determine the costs incurred by a municipality due to the public service demands created by various forms of residential and nonresidential growth. The estimated revenues associated with a proposed development are calculated and compared to municipal service costs to determine the net financial impact of a proposed development upon a community. Many cities now require this information to be prepared and filed as a part of their requirement for an environmental impact statement.

These calculations are based on estimated current costs and current revenues. Since municipal costs and revenues may change over time, these calculations are only valid at the time they are prepared. The expense side of the equation is usually arrived at by determining the per capita costs of public services (i.e., dividing the existing population base into the cost of individual departmental services), and then multiplying these per capita costs by the projected population generated by a proposed development. The final figure represents the estimated municipal costs of servicing the proposed development. The revenue side of the equation should take into consideration both municipal revenues (e.g., real property taxes, personal property taxes, and utility taxes) as well as intergovernmental transfers (e.g., sales taxes, educational assistance grants, gasoline taxes, cigarette taxes, and alcohol taxes). For obvious reasons, the estimated revenues generated by a proposed residential development are easier to calculate than those revenues received from office, commercial, or industrial developments.

Once the public costs and revenues of a proposed development are calculated, an informed decision can then be made by public officials with regard to the merits of new development proposals. Fiscal impact analyses typically do not consider the services provided or revenues received by special districts, county governments, regional authorities, and states. When these figures are calculated by private consultants hired by developers, they need to be carefully checked by the professional staff of the planning and building department for accuracy. Some cities have their own consultants, and require developers to pay the cost of preparing these fiscal impact analyses.

The national trend is for municipalities to use some form of fiscal impact analysis to determine the cost-effectiveness of new development proposals. The rationale for this type of analysis is that public officials do not want existing taxpayers to subsidize the costs associated with new developments. The use of fiscal impact analyses, because they lead to more informed decisionmaking, is on the increase in cities of all sizes.

Human Resources Management Practices. Planning and building directors, like other department managers, have implemented several innovative programs to increase productivity, reduce costs and at the same time increase the level of services to the public. Some small communities now contract with larger neighboring municipalities for technical planning, building, and inspection services. This is a form of privatization since outside contract services are provided to the city lacking the in-house resources to perform these functions.

Many departments have increased their use of part-time and contract employees because of the diminished workload brought about by a sluggish economy and fewer construction projects. It is not unusual as vacancies occur in technical building code inspection areas (e.g., building, plumbing, mechanical, and electrical) to hire part-time and or contract employees to perform these specialized inspection services. In addition to lower salary and fringe benefit costs, the services provided by these employees can be tailored to fit the department's workload. Since many labor agreements preclude laying off full-time employees to hire part-time or contract employees, this is usually done through employee attrition.

The cross-training of personnel has helped to increase employee productivity. Some departments have building inspectors dedicated to perform only one type of plan review and inspection. Many other departments have cross-trained their inspection personnel or have hired employees trained in more than one area to perform multiple plan review and inspection services. The cross-training of employees permits a greater utilization of existing personnel to perform a greater variety of municipal services. It is also not unusual for the planning division of planning and building departments to hire planning interns—typically graduate students in urban planning—to perform special studies during the summer months. Many departments, in order to make more productive use of their employees, have implemented centralized cash management practices. Under these programs, all monies are paid at a single location—usually the finance department—doing away with the need for individual departmental employees to process and account for cash received for user fees, service charges, development impact fees, and fines.

All of these trends have helped to increase productivity, reduce costs, and improve services to citizens. For these reasons, all of these trends are on the increase.

Interdepartmental Code Enforcement Cooperation. Traditionally, each department's inspectors conducted their own code inspections and followed up on those citizen complaints directed to their respective departments. The typical areas of code enforcement in a municipality usually encompass building, fire, housing, public works, zoning, and health. State laws typically require separate certification programs and specialized qualifications for those employees.

In more progressive municipal organizations, these inspection personnel are being cross-trained to the extent that they are made aware of the general code requirements in each of these functional code areas. For example, building inspectors routinely refer other possible code violations to the appropriate departmental inspection employees for follow-up enforcement. Likewise, other departmental inspectors routinely refer building, housing, planning, and zoning code violations to building and zoning inspectors for follow-up inspections and proper enforcement action. While state laws, labor agreements, and job descriptions may restrict the inspectional duties of these employees, the trend is towards greater interdepartmental cooperation in referring possible code violations to other municipal departments.

This trend has served four important purposes. It has increased the work productivity of all municipal inspection employees, has facilitated a more comprehensive approach to the enforcement of city codes, and has enhanced interdepartmental cooperation in this important area of local government. Most importantly, it sends a message to the public that their municipal government is actively concerned and involved in the uniform enforcement of all city codes. Planning and building directors have encouraged this trend since it reflects the efforts of departments to cooperate with the goal of improving services to the public. City managers and elected officials have endorsed these efforts since they hold down the need to hire additional departmental inspection personnel.

In order to place accountability for citizen-reported code violations, it is not unusual for a member of the city manager's staff to be responsible for assigning these complaints to the appropriate department for follow-up action, then tracking the process to make sure that a complaint has been corrected. In smaller and medium-sized communities with limited central staff, this task may be assigned to the director of the planning and building department, who would make periodic reports to the city manager on the status of these citizen complaints.

All of these trends represent greater cooperation between departments, as well as holding departmental personnel accountable for following up on all reported code violations. For these reasons, all of these trends should become common in the future.

Organizational Arrangements. The location of planning, building inspection, code enforcement, and zoning responsibilities may vary from community to community. In many small- and medium-sized communities, planning and building departments usually perform all of these municipal services.

Some small communities contract out some of these services to private planning consultants.

In larger cities, there may be separate planning and building departments as well as other departments such as community and economic development. The trend over the past decade in these cities, primarily due to financial restraints, has been to consolidate these services into a single municipal department. This trend is in keeping with the philosophy of many elected officials and city managers to downsize their municipal organization in an effort to save funds, consolidate services, and make workers more productive. With rare exception, the department director reports directly to the city manager. In some larger communities, the city charter may require that this position be appointed directly by the planning commission. Also, many cities are attempting to cross-train their inspection personnel so these employees may perform more than one type of inspection, reducing the number of inspection personnel in a community.

When new functions such as economic development are taken on by a municipality, they are usually grafted on to planning and building departments. These departments also usually have responsibility for overseeing a city's Community Development Block Grant (CDBG) program, as well as federally mandated affordable housing initiatives. The trend is to consolidate planning and building-related services into one municipal department. Another trend is for planning and building directors to work closely with city managers in the development of proposals submitted to elected officials. This is due to the sensitive political nature of planning and building-related issues and policies. All of these trends are on the increase and should become commonplace in the future.

Role of Elected Officials and Advisory Bodies. Many state laws and municipal charters attempt to restrict the role of elected officials in the planning activities of their community. These laws were designed to take the politics out of the planning process. To accomplish this, almost every community has a legally required planning commission, with its members appointed by the governing body. It is the role of the planning commission to advise the city council on planning issues. Some cities require that a representative of the city council serve as a member of the planning commission. In some larger cities, the planning commission is responsible for hiring the planning director. This is a further attempt to insulate a city's planner from local politics.

Many governing bodies in high growth and environmentally aware communities now take a more active role in setting planning and building policies. In these communities, elected officials and planning commissions work together closely to build a consensus on sensitive development and planning issues. Planning commissions, in their deliberations, hear different viewpoints from citizens and special interest groups and attempt to interpret community values.

Many cities also have conservation commissions, wetlands commissions, zoning boards, and other planning-related advisory bodies, some of which are created by city charter or state law. The trend has been for planning commissions and other planning-related advisory bodies to have a good working relationship with elected officials. This trend has been facilitated by the fact that the city council ultimately approves land-use regulations, and the fact that they must also approve funding requests from these advisory bodies. When governing body support is withheld on these items, the planning process does not work in the best interest of citizens. Also, since members of these advisory bodies are appointed by the elected officials, citizens with extreme viewpoints may not be reappointed to subsequent terms of office. For all of these reasons, the trend between city councils and their advisory bodies is to foster a close and collegial working relationship.

Use of Computers and Software Applications. Planning and building officials have traditionally never worked in a high tech environment. Most of the work done by the professional staff has been based on their personal technical expertise and, for this reason, the services they have provided have been labor intensive. The availability of inexpensive personal computers, more user friendly software, and the development of highly specialized and sophisticated planning-related applications have drastically changed this trend.

In addition to using computers and software applications to perform routine administrative tasks such as database management, word processing, permit issuance, inspection scheduling, project tracking, and records management, new hardware and software has opened up a whole new world of unique planning applications. Specialized software applications are now available to prepare high quality graphics and maps, conduct financial and economic analyses, perform population and employment projections, conduct demographic forecasting, and to perform sophisticated environmental modeling. Computer models are also available to analyze special environmental issues such as water and air quality, stormwater runoff, and hazardous materials disposal. One recent survey of planning-related software applications listed nearly 100 specialized applications. One recently developed piece of software enables the user to explore up to 24 different planning scenarios on any project. Other technologies are also being used for records storage and retrieval. Because building and site plans must be kept on file for a number of years, many departments are converting their traditional records to microfilm and microfiche. In addition to saving space, these storage mediums enhance the quality of services to the public.

The availability of inexpensive computers with large memory capability and easy-to-use specialized software applications have facilitated the trend to apply these technologies to the planning and building fields. These trends show no signs of abatement. All of these trends help make employees more productive, hold down future staffing needs, and improve services to citizens.

Use of Economic Development Incentives. In the truly competitive and free marketplace, government does not get involved in facilitating private real estate transactions. The local economy in some cities is so depressed due to negative market trends such as high unemployment, high crime, lack of parking, outdated and functionally obsolete structures, and a deteriorating public infrastructure that private companies perceive these communities as high risk areas. These trends may also be apparent in portions of cities for the same reasons.

These communities need economic development incentives to arrest these negative market trends and to attract private investment to these areas. By providing enterprise zones and various financial and land-based incentives, these cities can attract companies that will create jobs and generate additional municipal revenues. The rationale for providing these incentives is that these companies would not normally locate in these communities. They would most likely locate in more desirable municipalities.

When all cities get involved in economic development, with similar incentives, it is less likely that private companies will locate in these high-risk cities. Some companies even visit several neighboring communities for the best package of incentives. If these practices continue and companies move from one city to another without any net job creation, public officials and taxpayers will be the losers in the process. Elected officials and economic development specialists must recognize that their incentives must be tailored to specific economic development goals. A community's economic development goals should also include business retention, business expansion, small business development, workforce development, and successfully marketing of the attributes of a community.

When taxpayer incentives are used, public officials should make sure that the value received by citizens exceeds the costs of the incentives provided. The use of targeted incentives is on the increase, as it the objective analysis of the costs and benefits associated with providing these incentives.

External

Comprehensive Community Code Enforcement. Urban blight, traditionally a problem in many major urban centers, has spread to many other medium-sized and smaller communities, both suburban and rural alike. Urban blight is characterized by the existence of abandoned buildings, vacant structures, substandard dwellings, the accumulation of trash and debris, and a deteriorating public infrastructure. While a municipality can improve its public infrastructure and identify the conditions creating blight, code enforcement officials must work with private property owners to correct many of the conditions creating this blight. Some cities are creating their own code enforcement task forces, where all code enforcement personnel jointly walk through blighted neighborhoods to identify violations. Each department is responsible for following up on their respective code violations. Periodic meetings are held by these personnel to make sure that corrective action has or is scheduled to be taken by property owners.

The typical departments cooperating in these efforts include planning and building, police, fire, health, public works, and parks and recreation. Planning and building officials identify building, housing, and zoning code violations. Neighborhood police officers search for abandoned and unregistered vehicles, trailers, and boats. Fire department personnel look for suspected fire code violations. Health inspectors look for possible occupancy violations, unsanitary conditions, and signs of rodent infestation. Public works inspectors identify needed infrastructure improvements such as driveway and sidewalk repairs, and litter and debris in public areas. Public works crews return to clean up these public areas. Park and recreation employees inspect parks and playgrounds for needed repairs and improvements.

In an effort to further reduce those conditions creating urban blight, many communities have adopted new laws restricting the sale of alcohol, placed severe restrictions on adult entertainment businesses, implemented anti-graffiti programs holding property owners responsible for removing graffiti from their buildings, and have adopted housing codes regulating the appearance of residential dwellings and buildings. Some of the more progressive cities have revised their enforcement procedures to permit code personnel to issue citations like the ones issued by police officers.

Elected officials in communities where blight exists have also created neighborhood improvement advisory boards to come up with additional ways to improve the appearance of their community and its neighborhoods, and to hold code enforcement personnel accountable for identifying and following up on violations. It is not unusual to have the planning and building director serve as staff liaison to such advisory groups, providing them with monthly code enforcement updates. Comprehensive code enforcement programs like this are on the increase in communities throughout the nation.

External Forces Influencing Planning. Several major forces have altered the landscape in which communities conduct their municipal planning activities. These forces include court rulings, government mandates, changing demographics, increased concern for open space and the environment, and greater citizen participation in local decisionmaking processes.

Federal and state court rulings have upheld private property rights and have placed limitations on the powers of local governments to severely regulate property to the point that it may not be developable. Cities that adopt rules and regulations that preclude the development of private property may have to compensate property owners for the value of their property. Local elected officials may now be called upon to justify their regulatory decisions.

Many states now closely regulate the planning activities of their local governments. To counteract the "each city doing their own thing" planning practices of the past, most state legislatures have passed laws requiring state approval of local master plans and development regulations. They have also adopted regulations concerning development in sensitive areas such as coastal zones or wetland conservation areas. Changing family demographics have also impacted the traditional planning practices in many communities, especially in the nation's urban cities. Planners are no longer preoccupied with planning for the traditional family structure consisting of two parents with school-age children. Most communities now have single-parent families, two-parent families with one child, childless couples, and poor families, as well as a growing number of elderly couples and disabled persons.

Citizens are now keenly aware of the interrelationships of development and its impact on the environment, especially air and water quality, school systems, the existing transportation network, natural amenities, and the availability of open space. Many citizens get actively involved in shaping the land-use decisions and growth management practices of their communities. Citizens also do not want their taxes spent to subsidize new development. All of these trends are on the increase. For these reasons, the actions of planners increasingly take place in a regulated and negotiated work environment.

Financial Incentives. Several types of financial incentives are being used to attract private investment to communities. Low-cost financing is one of the most common incentives. These loan programs, provided through the use of municipal funds or revenue bonds, save the developer a few percentage points below prevailing market lending rates. The property is used as security for the loan, and funds are given directly to the developer. It is common to make progress payments on these loans at various stages of a new development. Tax increment funds can be used to finance private projects in designated city-created redevelopment areas.

When a redevelopment area is formed, the additional property taxes generated after the base year can be spent within the project area. These funds can be used to provide land subsidies, to purchase property for private development, and to finance both on-site and off-site improvements. On-site improvements usually include surface parking lots or multi-story parking structures. The redevelopment agency's financial participation, ownership rights, and maintenance responsibilities are subject to negotiation. Off-site improvements typically include curbs, gutters, sidewalks, storm drains, sewers, streets, and street lights. An agency's financial participation tends to increase with the desirability of the project. Local tax dollars can also be spent for off-site improvements.

Tax and user fee rebates may also be used as a development incentive. Tax rebates usually involve property taxes, sales taxes, business taxes, and utility taxes. User fees, such as those charged for plan checking, inspections, utility connections, and development impact fees can be lowered or waived. The amount of municipal taxes returned and the duration of the rebate are subject to negotiation, as are the extent to which user fees are reduced or waived. State and federal programs are still available to finance some private projects. The availability of economic development grant funds, state bond bank loans, government sponsored low-interest loans, and special capital funds should be determined in advance of commencing any major development.

Communities compete to attract private development because of the additional jobs and taxes they generate. Some types of financial incentives are usually required for a city to maintain its competitiveness (relative to the incentives provided by other cities) in the regional marketplace. The use of the incentives to help entice private investment is on the increase.

General Incentives and Assistance. A host of general incentive and assistance services are evolving to retain, as well as entice, private development in a community. These services include business retention programs, small business development services, the creation of enterprise zones, the formation of redevelopment project areas, the creation economic development corporations, and providing business assistance programs.

Business retention programs are designed to monitor the economic climate of important businesses and industries in a community. Staff members make contact with faltering enterprises, offering technical and financial assistance when appropriate. These types of programs help maintain a healthy business climate where jobs and revenues are important. Small business development programs, sometimes referred to as "incubator" projects, are being created to attract and foster the growth of small start-up businesses. Low-cost rents, small office spaces, and shared central services (e.g., secretarial, duplicating, telephone, utilities, and computer services) help keep expenses low for new, small businesses.

Many states have created enterprise zones in their cities while some cities have created their own enterprise zone areas. This involves targeting an area, usually blighted, for development or redevelopment in order to create jobs and generate additional municipal revenues. A greater number of economic incentives such as tax reductions, tax abatements, low-interest loans, and job-generation grants are made available to make these areas more attractive to the private sector. States and cities usually offer their own incentives in these areas. Redevelopment project areas may also be formed in blighted areas targeted for economic revitalization. The property tax base is "frozen" upon formation, and the increased property taxes generated in future years (called tax increment funds) are spent in the project area to attract investment. Tax increment funds can be spent for both on-site and off-site improvements, as well as to provide low-interest financing, or outright grants to private developers.

Some cities, either on their own or with other neighboring communities, have also formed nonprofit economic development corporations (EDCs). Funds are provided to these agencies to hire qualified employees that provide technical assistance, to prepare grant applications on behalf of applicants for federal and state programs, and to provide low-cost financing subject to approval of the corporation's board of directors. The EDCs are especially attractive to small communities with limited staff expertise and funds to provide these services on their own. Also, because of the expanding number of economic development services available to the private sector, business assistance programs are being established to centralize this information and make it available at a single location to the business community. These types of incentive and assistance programs being used are being tailored to fit a community's specific development needs.

Growth Management Techniques. Many communities, especially those in the southeast and western portions of the country, have experienced phenomenal residential and population growth rates. When growth management policies are desired by elected officials, the professional planning staff works closely with the city manager to make sure that proper growth management techniques are proposed, consistent with the expectations of elected officials. These proposals are frequently politically controversial and tend to polarize special interest groups. The community's top management and professional staff should not get caught in the middle of citizen debates on alternative growth management practices.

There are four common management practices used in communities to limit future growth. These include growth phasing programs, the use of urban growth boundaries, rate-of-growth programs, and provisions for ensuring that adequate community facilities are available to accommodate new development. The specific planning tools used to implement managed growth programs include zoning designations, subdivision regulations, public facilities ordinances, development impact fees, and user charges for processing development applications, including conducting inspections.

Current trends, primarily due to economic reasons, are against no-growth policies. Instead, elected officials, their top management, and professional planners have favored planned growth strategies along with measures to provide safeguards against the undesirable consequences of new development. Planned growth techniques frequently include preserving open spaces, protecting environmentally sensitive land areas, controlling urban sprawl, and taking steps to make sure that adequate public infrastructure and community facilities are available to support new growth. The department director works closely with a city's legal staff to review proposed growth management regulations since they may be subject to lawsuit by one or more special interest groups. Many cities, especially smaller and medium-sized communities without adequate staff expertise, hire special consultants to develop tailor-made plans that project the desired growth rates and the land-use controls necessary to achieve them. Careful attention should be made to make sure that the growth management techniques used are consistent with a community's desired economic development goals.

Some governing bodies, because of the political sensitivity of proposed growth management initiatives, vote to place such measures on the local ballot for the electorate to decide. Most public officials, however, favor rational, phased approaches to growth as opposed to extreme policy positions such as uncontrolled growth or development moratoriums. This more rational approach to managing urban growth has been facilitated by the desire of elected officials to create more jobs and generate additional revenues to run their municipal government operations. New growth management practices have evolved over the years as more sophisticated planning techniques have been developed to deal with this issue.

Land-Based Incentives. An increasing number of land-based incentives are being used to stimulate private development since they do not require the expenditure of tax funds on the part of the municipality. Some of the more popular of these incentives include the use of zone changes, allowing for mixed land uses, altering development standards, granting density bonuses, and providing land subsidies.

Elected officials have the power to upgrade the zoning applicable to a specific site, thereby permitting a higher land use. Frequently, single-family residential zoning may be upgraded to multiple-residential, industrial, or commercial, depending upon the location of the site and the type of development desired by the community. Land-uses within particular zones are usually standardized to protect property values and to separate different types of structures. A trend is developing to permit commercial uses in residential developments, and vice versa, in order to generate additional revenues and jobs, as well as to promote a "24-hour" community. These mixed land uses have been more popular in densely developed and populated central city areas.

Elected officials also have the power to alter local development standards, such as those for parking space requirements, minimum lot coverages, legal building setbacks, height limitations, and landscaping criteria. These requirements may be either waived or lowered, depending on the type of development and the agreement negotiated with the developer. Some cities have adopted planned unit development guidelines for larger residential projects, allowing for the application of more flexible regulations on selected parcels of land. These changes require the approval of the governing body. Many communities are also offering increased dwelling unit densities in selected areas. The number of residential units permitted may be increased, thereby enhancing the value of the development. Greater building densities can make a project more attractive to private developers.

In redevelopment project areas, tax increment funds may be used to purchase land for private development. This cannot be done outside of legally designated redevelopment areas. The extent of any land subsidy provided, which may be as high as 100 percent, is subject to prior negotiation and agreement. Desirable commercial and industrial developments, generating jobs and revenues frequently receive such land subsidies. The use of land-based incentives are becoming increasingly popular because they do not require taxpayer subsidies through a city's general fund.

Marketing Programs and Services. A planning and building department may have a number of specially designed services and programs, but if the public is not aware of them they will not achieve their goal of improving the community. For example, if business retention and expansion programs are available, they must be marketed to the community's existing businesses. If economic development incentives such as enterprise zones are being offered to the private sector, they should be marketed on a regional or statewide basis to attract new development.

Many municipal departments have services that are designed to provide valuable assistance and information to businesspersons, entrepreneurs, and the development community. Local public libraries frequently have business and economic, as well as job information centers. They also provide the latest demographic, marketing, and advertising information about their community. Some libraries even provide free computer training to the public. Fire departments provide free information and consultations on fire code requirements. Public works departments provide free information on the availability of public utilities. Finance departments, through their assessor, can provide information about existing real and personal property tax abatement programs.

Although these municipal services are available for the asking, if they are not properly marketed few people will know of their existence. For this reason, information about these services and programs needs to be marketed to educate the private sector about the unique services provided by a municipal government. Marketing programs are also being developed to sell a community's quality of life and other attributes, such as available educational institutions and the characteristics of its workforce, to attract private development. Once these programs and services have been developed and are in place, funds must be spent to develop and implement successful marketing programs. Public officials in the most entrepreneurial communities are actively involved in marketing programs of this nature. The trend toward promoting a community through carefully developed marketing programs is on the increase.

Professional Development. There are numerous national professional associations for municipal employees working in the fields of planning, building, and economic development. These professional membership organizations, many of which have state chapters, include the American Planning Association (APA), Building Officials and Code Administrators International (BOCAI), International Conference of Building Officials (ICBO), International Downtown Association (IDA), National Association of Housing and Redevelopment Officials (NAHRO), National Community Development Association (NCDA),

National Council for Urban Economic Development (NCUED), and the National Housing Conference (NHC).

All of these organizations provide a number of educational programs, conferences, technical resources, publications, and professional networking opportunities. Many of these organizations provide research services on current topics related to these specialized fields to their members. Specialized publications and training programs are provided in many technical areas such as growth management, balanced growth, economic development, downtown management, greenways and open space, historic preservation, computer mapping and graphics, strategic planning, urban design, and wetlands management. Some of the most recent publications in these fields focus on financing growth, impact fee programs, community open spaces, planning for capital improvements, strategic economic development, analyzing the fiscal impact of development, permit system improvement programs, nuisance abatement programs, and how to provide housing and business development through community development corporations. Professional certification programs are available through many of these organizations. Other municipal professional associations such as the National League of Cities (NLC) have published recent case studies on how public officials have adopted new planning, building, and economic development programs in their respective communities.

Since many planning and building departments have relatively small professional staffs, some of which have been reduced in recent years, it makes sound management sense to train employees in the latest developments and trends in their professional fields. The funds spent for training, conferences, and publications are usually more than offset by increased levels of professionalism and employee productivity. Training is especially critical in small communities with limited professional staffs. The trend to allocate funds for professional development activities is on the increase, especially for employees in highly technical fields such as these.

Public/Private Partnerships. Many communities, through the use of economic development incentives, have formed positive partnerships with private sector companies. Municipal economic development specialists typically work with local chambers of commerce, economic development corporations, and other departmental officials, making recommendations through the appropriate channels to elected officials concerning the formation of public/private partnerships. Typically, the city government is the key actor in the development of these partnerships, which should be designed to benefit the entire community. These public/private partnerships may take many forms, ranging from technical to financial assistance. Typically, they involve providing technical assistance to determine site location; making grants; providing low-interest loans; reducing or waiving development fees; rebating property, sales and or utility taxes; permitting greater building densities and more flexible zoning; and making various on-site and off-site infrastructure improvements.

City economic development experts also assist private companies in applying for state assistance. Many public/private partnerships include both the municipal and state governments, depending upon the types of incentives provided. When state assistance is provided it usually takes the form of low-interest loans, development grants, job grants, reimbursements to cities for a portion of their real and personal property tax abatements, as well as exemptions and reductions from various state taxes (e.g., real estate conveyance taxes, sales taxes, corporate business taxes, and inventory taxes, to name a few). Before approving any type of public/private partnership, however, municipal economic development officials should perform a cost/benefit analysis to ensure that the cost of the subsidy provided to a private company does not exceed the value of the jobs and revenues generated by a new development. This analysis is crucial since these subsidies are usually financed by the taxpayers of a community. Every public/private partnership arrangement normally requires a public hearing and approval of the elected officials. This holds elected officials accountable for their approval of these partnerships.

The use of public/private partnerships is on the increase, since many city councils desire to create additional jobs for their residents and generate more revenues for their city treasury.

Regional Planning Practices. Many urban and growth-related issues "spill" over the existing artificial political boundaries that define communities. Issues that require the attention of regional planning agencies typically include air and water quality, environmentally sensitive lands such as coastal and wetland areas, adequate transportation systems, regional park and recreation facilities, and open spaces.

Many states have mandated regional planning authorities, the most common of which is a council of governments (COG). Some of these planning agencies include multi-county areas and may include dozens of cities within these counties. Some states have established special planning districts or regional planning commissions. Under all of these arrangements, representatives from county and city governments are appointed to serve on these regional planning agencies. Sometimes representation is based on population, with larger counties and cities having a greater number of representatives. A professional planning staff works for the regional planning agency, which is responsible for planning activities for their member counties and cities. Funding for these agencies is provided through annual assessments made on member governments, typically based on population. While the planning recommendations of COGs are advisory in nature to their members, planning districts and regional planning commissions actually serve as the planning staff for their member communities.

Most regional planning is done through collaboration and consensus. If these joint planning efforts fail, state and federal government legislation is frequently used to adopt regionwide planning policies, such as those for air and water quality. As urban problems worsen it is likely that additional legislation from higher levels of government will be implemented to force acceptable planning solutions on counties and cities, especially in the most urbanized population centers.

Traditional vs. Strategic Planning. Planning in municipalities has traditionally been limited to the development of comprehensive or master plans. These plans focus almost exclusively on desirable land uses for the future, projected population growth based on these land uses, and setting forth the infrastructure and community facilities needed to sustain these projections. This plan, once approved, serves as a guide for future public and private development, typically for a minimum of five years. The only other plan usually developed by a planning department is the capital improvement plan, which is designed to be consistent with the comprehensive plan. There is a growing belief among elected officials, city managers, and even planning directors that the traditional planning practices of the past are antiquated because of their narrow focus and that they merely identify community goals rather than focus on immediate results. Even with approval of master and capital plans, many important community issues remain unresolved.

New forms of community planning have been initiated in recent years, such as strategic planning and issues management. These plans have typically been started by elected officials or city managers, not planning directors. Since community planning is an institutionalized function of planning departments, a city's professional planning staff should organize the development of these plans. New forms of planning involve the identification of community issues, working with stakeholders' committees, and developing results-oriented action plans to resolve these issues. These plans are usually reviewed and updated annually, with resolved issues being removed and new issues being added to address evolving community problems. As information in this new planning field becomes codified, strategic community planning practices will become an integral part of municipal planning departments. Planning directors must be educated to the fact that their department is responsible for planning their community's future, not just designating land-use areas and capital projects.

New results-oriented community planning practices designed to identify and resolve issues and problems are gaining in popularity in many cities. These new planning practices have been facilitated by limited funds, which has forced public officials to identify community priorities so that available funds can be targeted to resolve important issues and problems.

User Fees, Impact Charges, Special Assessments, and Fines. Planning and building departments are making many changes to their user fees, how capital projects are financed, using special assessment districts, and increasing their fines for code violations. This department typically generates more revenues than any other municipal operating department.

While a flat permit fee is usually charged for home improvements and single-family home construction, more and more cities are now charging a percentage permit fee for multiple-family, commercial, industrial, and office projects. Some cities are charging developers for the cost of having a consultant prepare a fiscal impact report for their proposed development, as opposed to having developers pay for and provide these studies themselves. Many cities are updating their community master plans to ensure that proposed roadways, utilities, and community facilities are available to support new development. An increasing number of communities are also charging development impact fees to assess developers their pro rata share of the cost of financing these capital projects. More and more cities are using assessment districts to charge property owners for the cost of improvements that primarily benefit their property. Examples of these projects include sidewalks, stormdrains, utilities, and other property-related improvements. Cities usually bond for these projects over a ten-year period, and charge the benefitting property owner their fair share of these costs (principal and interest) over this period. Many municipalities are also increasing their fines, especially for chronic violators and for those property owners that do not comply in a timely manner.

Concurrent with all of these efforts is the trend to grant user fee waivers and reductions to developers as an economic development incentive. User fees are also being waived or reduced for those projects that benefit the community, such as for affordable housing developments. Some of the most recent publications from planning and building related professional associations focus on alternative development impact fees, how to use special assessment districts to finance property-related public improvements, and how to analyze the fiscal impact of new developments. Planning and building officials recognize their responsibility to make sure that their services are cost-covering and that developers and property owners pay for services that do not benefit the entire community. The use of all of these financial tools is on the increase. Their popularity will no doubt continue to grow in the future.

Working with the Community. Every planning and building department manager should work closely with all major internal and external stakeholders when developing plans and making proposals. Foremost among the internal stakeholders are a city's governing body, the official commissions and advisory bodies, and the top management staff. Since many issues relating to planning and development are politically sensitive, the department should make sure that proposed policies and programs represent the values of the community—not just those of the planning and building staff. To ensure this goal, the department director should work closely with external stakeholders when developing proposals. These external stakeholders include chambers of commerce, merchants' associations, downtown business groups, neighborhood associations, and nonprofit community development corporations.

For example, if a new building facade improvement program is being developed to improve the appearance of an older commercial area, the planning and building staff should work closely with the merchant group for this area, the chamber of commerce, and citizens who may be impacted by the program. Based upon the input solicited from relevant stakeholders, the final proposal can be modified to fit the needs of the community before it is submitted to the appropriate advisory body for its consideration. By the time the proposed plan goes to city council, it would have been reviewed by all major external and internal stakeholders. When proposals are developed in this manner, they usually win the support of the governing body. In the past, some planning and building directors have developed important policies and proposals in a political vacuum, only to encounter difficulty later in the official review and approval process.

The trend is for astute department managers to work with citizens, community groups, and others that are impacted by proposed policies and programs to ensure that their final recommendations reflect the values of the community. This trend, because it results in successful policies and programs on sensitive development and planning issues, stands to continue in the future.

THE FUTURE

The issue of affordable housing has been mandated upon communities by the state and federal governments. While the requirement to expand the number of affordable housing units has been externally imposed, it is through internal policies and regulations that public officials must comply with these mandates. All cities receiving federal funds must identify their affordable housing needs, remove barriers that stand in the way of satisfying these needs, as well as have an approved plan and timetable to create more affordable housing units. This issue has been controversial since some communities, by design, consist primarily of single-family homes on large lots. In these communities, when a family's children move out, the children cannot afford to live in the community in which they were raised. Some of these communities have no apartments, condominiums, townhouses, or inexpensive single-family homes. While most urban communities have more than their fair share of affordable housing, many suburban communities have few, if any, affordable housing units. The purpose of these mandates is to require cities to provide for the current and anticipated affordable housing needs of their own population. Some citizens would argue that there have always been communities where low-income citizens could not afford to live, and that these municipalities should not be required to provide affordable housing. The public debate over this issue will no doubt continue in city halls throughout the country in the years ahead.

The number of external forces influencing local planning policies are on the increase. Likewise, the number of restrictions placed upon elected officials to make planning and land-use decisions has escalated. A community can no longer develop its comprehensive plan in a political, legal, or geographic vacuum.

The number of outside forces impacting this municipal function is expanding at an alarming rate. These forces include state and federal court decisions, mandates from higher levels of government, changing local and regional demographics, pressure to increase development densities, increasing population densities, the location of state and county roadways, and an increasing demand by citizens for more parks and open spaces. Nearly all states have laws that require their advanced approval of a community's comprehensive plan and development regulations. Many states have adopted statewide regulations, imposed upon municipalities, to control development in sensitive land areas such as coastal and wetland regions. Virtually all of these external influences are beyond the control of the actions of local elected officials. Because many planning issues are not limited to the political confines of individual communities, regional planning agencies have evolved to address many issues related to urban growth, such as air and water quality, transportation systems, and regional parks and open spaces. These multicity planning bodies are, for the most part, currently advisory only. As our urban problems escalate and expand over the artificial political boundaries of municipalities, additional state and federal mandates will evolve to mitigate these problems since it is unlikely that local officials can effectively deal with these issues.

Communities still have considerable flexibility when it comes to planning and designing their economic development initiatives and the various incentives available under these programs. This is one of the few remaining ways for public officials to increase the employment and revenue base of their community. States originally initiated these financial incentive programs through the designation of state-approved enterprise zones. The goal of these zones was to relax development regulations and lower taxes to make these areas more economically attractive for private investment. Those areas designated with the enterprise zone status were typically located in less desirable urban areas. While cities cannot waive state development regulations and state taxes, they do have a number of incentives available to attract new business and industry. One of the problems with current economic development policies is that, as more and more desirable communities offer these incentives, private investment is diverted away from the nation's less desirable urban areas. If all cities provided similar incentives, businesses would always make the decision to locate in more desirable geographic areas. This leaves many undesirable urban areas with the same problem of how to attract private investment. This is one planning area where state intervention would be helpful. So long as the number and types of incentives are greater in enterprise zone areas, these areas will maintain their competitive advantage over other suburban communities that provide their own incentives. The trend is for communities to tailor these incentives to target the specific businesses they desire. This effort has helped to reduce the level of competition among cities for private investment.

12

POLICE

Contemporary police departments provide numerous law enforcement–related services. The basic form of service is measured by the number of police patrols. Uniformed police officers patrol certain geographic areas acting as deterrents to crime. They are also on the lookout for criminal activity. These police officers also respond to calls for service from citizens when they report violations of the law. The number of police patrols in a community is dependent upon several variables, including population, demographics, geographic size, building density, the amount of criminal activity, and the ability and willingness of citizens to pay for these services through their property taxes. Generally, the greater the density of a community, the higher the number of police patrols. Walking patrols were initiated in downtown and densely populated neighborhoods, while motorized patrols are provided in outlying areas. Word-of-mouth calls for service subsequently gave way to police callboxes, which were ultimately eliminated as telephone services were obtained in most households. Now, citizens call their police department directly from their home. Over the past two decades special "911" emergency telephone numbers emerged to facilitate and simplify communications between citizens and their police department.

As the size of police departments increased, their operations became more specialized to improve the quality of their services. When it became apparent that individual police officers could not devote the time required to solve the crimes on their patrols, specialized investigative units were developed. Police officers, frequently called detectives, were assigned to perform full-time investigative duties. Minor crimes were solved by field officers, while major offenses were turned over to these permanent investigative units. Depending upon the size of a municipality, there may be several separate investigative units, such as those for juvenile crimes, sex offenses, narcotics, commercial crimes, and the like. Over the years, the number of police officers expanded in an effort to reduce patrol response times. Generally, the number of sworn personnel expanded until citizens became dissatisfied with their increasing property taxes. Concurrent with the pressure to limit the number of police officers, community crime prevention programs emerged to educate citizens on how to assist their police department in reducing crime. The training and development of police officers in specialized areas of law enforcement became necessary because of the division of labor resulting from the expanding size of police organizations.

Today, most municipalities have initiated community policing practices whereby individual police officers are assigned to patrol certain neighborhoods. These patrol assignments are relatively permanent so neighborhood residents and merchants can get to know their police officer and develop a rapport to improve communications between citizens and their police department. Even though state and federal grants have been decreasing in other municipal service areas, the number of grants available to hire new police officers for community policing assignments has been increasing. These programs are politically popular, since few citizens oppose the expansion of law enforcement services and most favor reducing the amount of criminal activity in their community. The prevailing crime rates of a city are an important indicator to the quality of life and image of a municipality. Many police departments have initiated a number of community crime prevention programs. These programs include police reserve and auxiliary units, police cadet programs, citizen police academies, neighborhood watch programs, and a host of related citizen involvement activities. Some police departments even use community volunteers to provide assistance in a number of different areas that do not require professional police training.

Most municipal police departments provide several line and staff programs as a part of their departmental operations. The typical programs provided by municipal police departments are shown in Figure 12.1. While dispatching is shown as a police function, the trend is to centralize police and fire dispatching using civilian dispatchers. Even when these services are centralized, and even though they may use civilian dispatchers, these units are typically located within and are supervised by police department personnel.

DESCRIPTION OF PROGRAMS

Patrol Services. Law enforcement services are typically provided to citizens by using vehicular and walking police patrols. A community is divided into patrol areas based on geography, population, and building densities, or some combination of these factors.

Police walking patrols are used where appropriate, such as in downtown, densely populated, and or high crime areas. Police patrols are provided 24 hours a day throughout the year using three eight-hour shifts. Walking patrols are typically provided to meet the demand for services. The number of police patrol vehicles assigned in any given shift is usually based on the number of calls for service. For example, fewer patrols may be provided on a "graveyard"

Figure 12.1
Police Major Programs

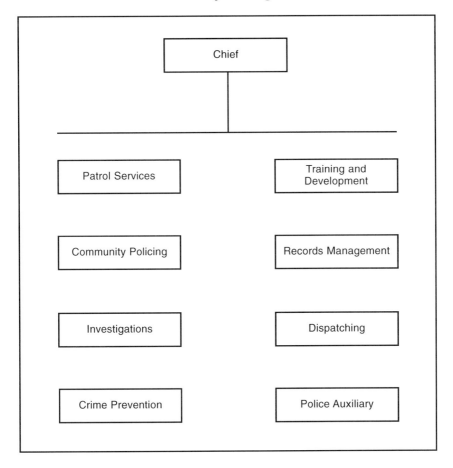

shift due to the decreased number of calls for service. Police patrol, both vehicular and walking, are always equipped with radios.

Police officers may respond to crimes as they take place, but typically respond to a crime scene when they are dispatched to handle a citizen-reported crime. Many departments prioritize their responses, with the highest priority given to more serious incidents. The trend has been to provide a greater number of walking patrols in response to citizen demands for this police service. Police officers perform preventative patrols, traffic control and enforcement, traffic accident investigations, preliminary crime investigations, and investigations on minor incidents. Major crimes are turned over to trained investigators, typically detectives, who conduct full-scale investigations.

With the advent of smaller, more sophisticated and less expensive computers, it is not uncommon for police officers to use such technologies as mobile teleprinters, mobile data terminals, laptop computers, and hand-held computers. Police patrol productivity has been greatly enhanced by these law enforcement technologies. The types of technologies used is based on community need and available funds.

Community Policing. During the past decade, a new policing model has been embraced by many communities throughout the nation. Due to the changing nature of the police workforce, constant high crime rates, citizen demands for safe neighborhoods, more requests for police services, and ongoing financial constraints, many communities have adopted the community policing model of providing police services. Some of the characteristics of this policing model include the greater use of neighborhood walking patrols, treating officers as generalists rather than specialists, a greater emphasis on community problem solving, and a desire to enhance the quality of life in a community starting at the neighborhood level.

This nontraditional style of policing emphasizes greater police-community interaction, actively working with merchants and residents to jointly identify police issues and establish police priorities. Rather than following the strict police chain of command, this model places responsibility on police officers to be decisionmakers. Success of these patrols is based on citizen satisfaction, rather than crime rate statistics or the number of calls for service. Rather than looking for crimes or responding to calls, police officers are encouraged to work with merchants, residents, nonprofit groups, and other government agencies, making referrals for services as they think appropriate. Community policing is more a service philosophy rather than a management style.

Under this model, the duties of police officers are expanded to include code enforcement, conflict resolution, problem solving, and referring issues and problems to other agencies. Some of these job duties contradict the typical hierarchical organizational structure of police departments. For this reason, community policing may be easier to implement in small- and medium-sized communities. Larger cities with huge police bureaucracies may find it more difficult to delegate decisionmaking downward to the lowest levels of their organization.

Investigations. Police operations are typically broken down into patrol and investigative services. Virtually all departments have police officers that conduct investigations for crimes against property, crimes against persons, narcotics violations, vice-related activities, sex crimes, juvenile crimes, and other types of unique crimes. The sworn personnel assigned to this duty usually hold the title of detective or inspector. While patrol officers conduct investigations for traffic accidents, minor incidents, and preliminary investigations, investigations for major and unique crimes are routinely turned over to these full-time trained investigators.

Some departments have special investigative task forces such as for juvenile sex crimes, narcotics violations, homicides, burglaries, and stolen vehicles. If a community has a particularly unique or persistent crime problem, a task force may be formed to more effectively investigate these crimes. Internal affairs officers or units, which investigate complaints against police officers and civilian employees, frequently report their findings directly to the chief of police. These complaints may be made by agency employees or citizens and typically involve alleged misconduct, either on or off duty. This misconduct may involve violations of the law, department rules and regulations, general orders, or written directives. Police investigators also work with fire investigators in suspected arson cases. Even under the community policing model, which attempts to vertically integrate the duties of police officers, major crimes are turned over to the investigations unit.

New technologies such as those for computer imaging, surveillance cameras, automated fingerprint identification systems, DNA print analysis, local access to national crime databases, and computerized sketching applications are used to assist investigators in solving crimes. In small- to medium-sized communities, investigative services are a part of the operations division. In larger cities, investigative services may be a separate division.

Crime Prevention. Crime prevention programs overlap, to some extent, the police services provided by patrols, both vehicular and walking, as well as the efforts of community policing programs. Crime prevention programs, with the above exceptions, have generally remained outside of the scope of traditional police services. These services typically include neighborhood watch programs, commercial watch programs, operation identification projects, crimestopper campaigns, bicycle theft prevention education, citizen police academies, drug free school zones, and the DARE (Drug Abuse Resistance Education) programs, to name a few.

Many of these programs are geared to provide crime prevention education to those groups most vulnerable to criminal activity, such as young people and senior citizens. Under the DARE program, for example, specially trained police officers teach school children how to resist the temptation to use drugs. Special services may also be available to senior citizens, such as burglary and theft prevention education programs. Many of these programs focus on getting citizens to look for suspected criminal activity at the neighborhood level and reporting it to the police. New policing models such as community policing attempt to integrate crime prevention activities into the police officers' regular patrol duties.

There has been a trend among departments to form police explorer posts, police cadet programs, police athletic leagues, and other community-based programs for young people. The police officers assigned to these duties are specially trained in community crime prevention programs. They also work closely with other local social, youth, family, and mental health service agencies.

Small- to medium-sized communities are likely to have one or two crime prevention officers; larger cities may have many.

Training and Development. Traditional police training has focused on instructing rank-and-file employees on how to better perform their basic law enforcement duties. Examples of basic training include firearms training, self-defense tactics, investigative techniques, interrogation strategies, and updates on changes to federal and state laws, as well as departmental policies and procedures. More contemporary police training focuses on the human relations aspect of police work. Human relations training focuses on police-community relations, communication skills, diversity programs, crisis intervention, negotiation techniques, and other important interpersonal skills. Also important is training on the services provided by other local and public and nonprofit agencies.

Recruits receive basic training and once they are on the job receive field training. State laws frequently mandate a minimum number of hours per year for each police officer to receive in-service training. Specialized training is also provided in a number of areas of law enforcement, including the use of new technologies and how to implement modern police practices. Many larger departments also provide supervisory, management, and leadership training.

All of these training programs are designed to develop the human resources of the department and to improve the effectiveness of the organization. Personal development is also provided to police officers in the form of career advancement opportunities, assignments that allow for personal growth and achievement, employee incentive programs, and specialized assignments based on individual desire and departmental needs.

Virtually every department has a training officer. Larger departments may have several highly specialized training officers. The training provided should fit the needs of the community, the department, as well as individual police officers. Training budgets are frequently cut in hard times, but the importance of training should be communicated to top management and elected officials during the budget development and approval process.

Records Management. Managing records is one of the most critical aspects of police support services. Information recording, processing, storage, and retrieval are all equally important in creating an effective police organization. Many aspects of a police officer's daily encounters are recorded in one form or another for future reference. Selected criminal information is sent on the National Crime Information Center (NCIC), which is accessible by all law enforcement agencies throughout the country.

New computer technologies have virtually revolutionized the way police departments handle their paperwork. Many departments have stand-alone computer systems with highly sophisticated police software applications to handle all aspects of records management. Rather than having voluminous files and countless numbers of file cabinets, many departments now have a common computer database, with multiple access points throughout the department.

New technologies include computerized video imaging systems used for book-ings and suspect identification, mobile data terminals that allow information exchange directly with police officers in the field, laptop and hand-held com-puters for report writing and database access, digital dictation equipment that allows police officers to dictate reports over the telephone directly into the com-puter system, and automated fingerprinting identification systems.

The automation of police records has been made possible due to recent trends in the computer field. Smaller, more sophisticated computer systems, most user-friendly software applications, and major hardware and software cost reductions have made the use of state-of-the-art computer systems com-mon in a growing number of departments. These sophisticated systems have also assisted crime analysts in tracking the number, types, and concentration of crimes in the community.

Dispatching. In the past, police and fire departments received calls for service directly from citizens through the telephone operator. Sworn person-nel in both departments usually acted as dispatchers. This increased emergency response times since citizens who contacted the operator did not dial either department directly. Most police and fire departments now use a common dis-patching system with civilian dispatchers that can be reached directly by dial-ing 911 on the telephone.

Many smaller cities now cooperate through interlocal agreements for common police, fire, and ambulance dispatching services. This centralization of services has allowed citizens quick access to all municipal emergency ser-vices. It has also allowed many cities to reduce their operating costs and increase the effectiveness of this important public service. Civilian dispatch-ers typically perform this function, allowing uniformed personnel to perform more important public safety duties. Police and fire emergency call boxes located on the street of many cities throughout the years, have virtually dis-appeared from the municipal landscape. These antiquated systems evolved before virtually every business and household in America had a telephone.

The national trend has been to centralize dispatching services, to use civilian dispatchers, and to dispatch all emergency services—police, fire, and ambulance. The greatest economy for centralized dispatching has been achieved in smaller communities. Most larger communities, while they have combined their police and fire dispatching functions, still dispatch only within their political boundaries.

Dispatchers routinely screen calls, conduct records checks for police officers in the field, verify emergency conditions, prioritize responses, and may provide medical advice to the caller prior to the arrival of emergency person-nel. Dispatchers determine the type and level of service required, coordinate police and fire responses, communicate with on-site personnel, and decide if other municipal resources are required. They also call for police and fire assis-tance from neighboring communities through existing mutual-aid agreements.

Police Auxiliary. Many police departments of all sizes have a police auxiliary or reserve unit. These units consist of citizens in other occupations who provide sworn police services to a municipality on a part-time basis. They usually receive an hourly rate of pay or monthly stipend, and do not receive other municipal fringe benefits. Thus, police auxiliarists and reservists are a cost-effective way for cities to provide a higher level of police services to its citizens. Existing union contracts and employment agreements may place restrictions on the use of these personnel. It is not unusual, for example, to restrict the use of these personnel to primarily providing assistance to members of the regular police force. They usually can never be used by the chief of police or city manager to reduce salary, fringe benefits, overtime, or other departmental expenses. Typically they must be supervised by regular police officers at all times, except when they may be assigned to perform routine nonsworn or civilian duties.

All police auxiliarists and reservists receive some form of basic training and frequently participate in ongoing in-service training programs of a general nature. Their use is usually limited to assisting existing police vehicular and walking patrols. It is not unusual for citizens wanting to be full-time police officers to participate in auxiliary or reserve programs. Because of municipal financial constraints, the number of new positions may be severely limited. Many cities even provide a hiring preference for their own police auxiliarists and reservists.

Some police departments—typically smaller ones—also use citizen volunteers on a limited basis to perform nonsworn duties or routine special assignments. Generally, the smaller the department and the less complex its labor agreements, the greater the flexibility a city has to use citizens to assist in providing municipal police services.

PRODUCTIVITY TRENDS

The main focus of internal productivity trends in police departments has been in maintaining or reducing the number of sworn police officers, the implementation of new community policing concepts, and new techniques in workload scheduling and caseload management. Oftentimes additional police officers have been added to decrease response times. Many governing bodies feel that taxpayers cannot afford to reduce these response times any further. Most departments have started hiring civilians for those positions that do not need the powers of a police officer. Some of these positions include training officers, records supervisors, evidence technicians, front desk officers, and scheduling officers, to name a few. Contemporary community policing practices have helped to improve law enforcement services in neighborhoods and have improved police-community relations. These concepts have also served to empower police officers to assume a greater level of responsibility for their actions. Police officer productivity has also been increased through workload scheduling. Under this practice, the number of police officers on any given shift is matched by the number and types of calls for service. Many chiefs of police are applying caseload management techniques to categorize their criminal cases for investigative purposes. Police chiefs have made great strides in recent years on improving the operations of their departments.

Many external productivity trends have concentrated on community education and citizen empowerment, working with citizens to develop coproduced services, and intergovernmental cooperation and resource sharing. The goal of community education is to inform the public and empower them on ways to safeguard themselves against crime, including how to report crimes and suspicious activities. A variety of citizen-involvement programs have evolved in recent years to improve police services without having to hire additional police officers. Some of these programs include neighborhood watch, commercial crime watch, police reserve and auxiliary units, and the limited use of citizen volunteers. Many small- and medium-sized police departments recognize that they will never have the specialized technical resources available to larger departments. Larger departments are now sharing their resources, upon request, in many specialized areas of law enforcement, including hostage negotiations, SWAT teams, K-9 dog units, police artists, forensic laboratories, and arson investigators, to name a few. The efforts of chiefs of police to work with the community, educate and empower citizens to prevent and report crimes and to share resources with one another have helped to hold the line on police budgets.

These productivity trends are summarized in Table 12.1. Traditionally, police departments have been operationally introspective. They only had public relations programs to minimize bad publicity about the department in the community. The recent efforts to educate, empower, and involve citizens have been highly popular, and will unquestionably continue in the future.

Internal

Budgetary Controls. Police department budgets usually have one of the largest annual appropriations of all municipal departments. The majority of a police department's budget goes to finance salaries and fringe benefits. Salary budget accounts include but are not limited to wages, overtime, longevity pay, and callback pay. Fringe benefit costs typically include expenses for retirement, life insurance, health and dental benefits, and uniform allowances, to name a few. Several types of budgetary controls have evolved over the years to monitor the expenditures of police departments. The most common types of budgetary controls include the monitoring of line-item expenditures,

Table 12.1
Police Productivity Trends

Internal	External
Budgetary Controls	Budget and Service Reductions
Centralized Dispatching Services	Community Education and Citizen Empowerment
Civilianization Practices	Contract Services
Evaluating Police Services	Coproduced Services
Evolving Community Policing Services	Financing Police Services
Evolving Crime Prevention Services	Intergovernmental Cooperation and Resource Sharing
Human Resources Management Practices	Police-Community Relations
Management Information Systems	Police Service Master Planning
Management Practices and Organizational Change	Police Service Trends
Organizational Consolidations	Professional Development
Use of Computers and Technologies	Working with Community Volunteers
Workload Scheduling and Caseload Management	

monthly budget reports, percentage deviation reports, periodic budget allocations, and controls on the filling of authorized and funded positions.

Monthly line-item budget reports compare the annual budget allocation of each individual line item against its expenditures and encumbrances. Monthly budget reports typically show the balance for each line-item budget account. Percentage deviation reports show line-item expenditures and encumbrances as a percentage compared to the annual budgeted appropriation for each line item. Allotment budgeting, although not commonly used, involves making a portion of an annual budget appropriation available on a monthly or quarterly basis. Seasonal differences in expenditure rates are included when making periodic allotment budgets. Management controls are frequently placed on the filling of authorized and funded vacant positions since personnel expenses make up the largest share of any municipal budget, including the police department. By not filling existing vacancies immediately or by delaying the filling of vacancies created by employee attrition throughout the year, considerable savings can be achieved. In tough budget times, a policy not to fill a vacant authorized and funded position for three months can save nearly 25 percent of annual salary and fringe benefit costs.

The development of "tight" departmental budgets and the use of various budgetary controls and monitoring techniques are becoming commonplace. In small departments, the police chief would review these budget reports personally. In medium-sized and larger communities, the chief of police would most likely have a staff member assigned to perform this task. In this case, the chief would only be informed about the budget if a problem exists. The use of these techniques to control departmental expenses, especially salary and fringe benefit costs, will inevitably continue in the future.

Centralized Dispatching Services. Traditionally, police and fire departments had their own dispatching centers handled by their respective uniformed personnel. Many communities have centralized these dispatching services at a single location, typically in police departments since they usually have a greater number of calls for services and dispatching personnel. Rather than have police officers and firefighters serve as dispatchers, which has been the case in the past, civilian dispatchers are now used to provide this service. Civilians are being used for two reasons: they are less expensive to hire than uniformed personnel and their use has freed up the time of uniformed personnel to perform those duties for which they were hired.

Many departments have initiated programs to prioritize their responses to calls for service. Rather than immediately dispatching a police patrol unit in response to a call which may prove routine, calls for service are now analyzed and placed in priority of their importance. A typical priority system may include several categories of calls, such as those requiring an immediate response, those requiring a routine response, and those calls which may be referred to other agencies. Many departments also require dispatchers to take routine reports over the telephone, allowing police officers to perform more important duties.

Many smaller communities now cooperate through interlocal agreements for centralized dispatching services. Under these arrangements, one centralized dispatching center may serve several smaller neighboring communities. Some communities, typically smaller ones, may also contract with their county government for centralized dispatching services. Most larger cities, while they may have centralized their dispatching operations and may use civilians to perform these services, still only dispatch within their own political boundaries. Nearly all cities use a computer-aided dispatching (CAD) system. New CAD systems capture information traditionally maintained in manual logs. This new software has improved dispatching operations by allowing personnel to spend their time dispatching, rather than personally maintaining cumbersome manual logs.

The national trend has been for cities to centralize their dispatching operations and services, to staff this function with civilian employees, to manage citizen calls for service, to use new computer software to track calls and responses as well as provide valuable management information, and to take more routine police reports over the telephone.

Civilianization Practices. The proper mix of sworn and civilian staffing has received increased attention in recent years because of the high cost of police salaries and fringe benefits. Not long ago, almost all of the employees in police departments were uniformed police officers, except possibly at the clerical level. Over the years, the mix of uniformed versus civilian staffing has changed dramatically.

Many positions previously held by police officers are now being performed by civilians for several reasons, the primary of which is related to economics. Many aspects of police operations have become so complex or removed from the daily field operations of the department that they are no longer attractive to the average police officer. Civilian employees are now frequently used to perform specialized work such as crime analysis, dispatching, records management, property and evidence custody, budget preparation and monitoring, planning and research, human resources management, certain training functions, and other functions that do not require the training and authority of a police officer. Some departments have even developed a new paraprofessional position, usually referred to as a police service technician, to perform non-emergency tasks such as conducting vehicle accident investigations, serving as crime scene or evidence technicians, taking routine incident reports, serving as crime and traffic analysts, performing crime prevention tasks, and serving as victim assistance officers, to name a few.

The best use of police officers, because of their specialized training and the fact that they have the power of arrest, is to perform law enforcement-related duties where these qualifications are required. When civilianization practices were originally initiated, the goal was to free up the time of uniformed personnel to fight crime, rather than reduce their numbers for financial reasons. Now, the goal is to hire civilian personnel primarily for reasons of economy, since they usually receive a lower salary and fewer fringe benefits. Existing labor agreements may restrict the use of civilian employees. The use of civilian employees in police departments is on the increase. This trend will continue in the future as attention is focused on additional ways to balance police department budgets.

Smaller communities may have fewer civilian personnel since the typical duties performed by civilians only take a portion of a police officer's time. Civilianization has increased most dramatically in medium-sized and larger cities where the workload is sufficient to justify the use of full-time civilian employees.

Evaluating Police Services. There are several reasons for police chiefs, city managers, and elected officials to want to evaluate their community's existing types and levels of police services. Such baseline information should be developed when conducting a police service master plan, may be desirable when administrations change, or may be conducted by newly appointed police chiefs who wish to "take stock" of what their police department presently provides to the public in the way of municipal police services.

The services and operational factors that should be evaluated include average patrol response times, the level of patrol services compared to the numbers of calls for service, crime and drug prevention services, dispatching services, training and development programs, percentage of crimes solved by the investigations staff, along with the adequacy of administrative support services. Crime rates should also be tracked annually, along with the type and number of citizen complaints received during the year.

Since there are no national standards for a police department's service levels, the results desired must be compared to the funds available to finance these services. The level of services will vary from community to community, depending upon the existing tax base of a city, the service levels desired, and the willingness of taxpayers to pay for these services. The development of this type of baseline information is helpful for both financial and operational planning. Elected officials, for example, when making budget decisions for police services, should want to know the impact of possible budget reductions on public services. This type of information is also essential to keep members of the governing body informed about the quality of their police services.

Once a service evaluation has been completed, it should be periodically updated to reflect any changes that might have taken place since the initial assessment was conducted. Benchmarking techniques are also being used to compare inhouse police programs with those programs provided by other police departments. The Commission on Accreditation for Law Enforcement Agencies, Inc., also requires the development of this type of information for a police agency to qualify for accreditation.

The use of self-assessment practices to evaluate a community's level of police services, as well as the review of internal operating procedures, stand to increase in the future, especially in this era of tight budgets and citizen demands for increased productivity.

Evolving Community Policing Services. The biggest change in police services during the past decade has been the movement toward community policing. Traditional police services were provided by police officers in patrol vehicles. These patrols were provided throughout a community using three eight-hour shifts. If response times were longer than desirable or if crime rates increased, police chiefs would request and city councils would routinely approve additional police officers to provide more vehicular patrol services.

Due to escalating crime rates, severe budgetary constraints, and citizen demands for safer neighborhoods, many cities have initiated community policing patrols. This policing concept involves a greater use of neighborhood police walking patrols, training police officers as generalists rather than specialists, placing greater emphasis on community problemsolving, and making a concerted effort to improve the quality of life in a community starting at the neighborhood level. Unlike traditional police walking patrols, community police officers concentrate on developing personal relationships with merchants and residents to jointly identify problems, issues, and priorities that may vary from neighborhood to neighborhood.

Rather than following the strict chain of command, community police officers are empowered to be decisionmakers. Community police officers are also encouraged to refer complaints to other municipal departments, as well as community nonprofit agencies. To this end, these police officers handle code complaints, resolve conflicts and problems, refer issues and problems to other social agencies, and routinely attend neighborhood association meetings. This model of policing is service-oriented and requires the chief of police and management staff to initiate participative management on a department-wide basis. The most advanced models of community policing embrace a team approach to policing in all of a city's neighborhoods. These teams involve individuals assigned to a particular neighborhood on a permanent basis so citizens can get to know their community police officers.

This policing concept is increasingly being used in cities of all sizes because of its popularity with citizens and elected officials. It also provides a method to improve the quality of police services without substantial budgetary increases.

Evolving Crime Prevention Services. Typically, police departments have focused their attention and resources on reducing crime through regular police patrols, special patrols, undercover operations, and investigations. The goal of these efforts was to apprehend suspects, solve crimes, and reduce a community's crime rate. In recent years, a number of innovative crime prevention programs have been developed to deter and hopefully prevent criminal activity before it takes place. These programs are oriented towards young people in schools, to citizens in their homes, and to businesspersons and merchants in commercial areas.

Some of the more popular school-based programs include DARE, "Take a Bite Out of Crime" and "Officer Friendly." The DARE program is geared towards young people and teaches them how to resist peer pressure to experiment with drugs. The "Take a Bite Out of Crime" program teaches school-aged children how to detect suspicious persons, ways to prevent encounters with strangers, and how to report suspected crimes. Under "Officer Friendly" programs, police officers visit schools and provide orientation courses to acquaint children with the operations of their police department.

Community crime prevention activities involving citizens include neighborhood watch programs, commercial watch programs, citizen radio watch programs, and citizen ride-along programs. Neighborhood watch programs include citizen training so neighbors can watch out for each other, reporting suspected criminal activity to their police department. Commercial watch programs are similar to neighborhood watch programs except they involve businesspersons and merchants in local shopping areas. Citizen radio watch programs involve taxpayers using their personal vehicles, equipped with two-way radios, who patrol their neighborhoods and report suspected criminal activity to their police department for follow-up action. Under citizen ride-along programs, the public is encouraged to ride with police officers on patrol to become familiar with their duties and the services they provide to citizens. Other examples of community crime prevention programs include citizen police academies, operation identification projects, bicycle theft prevention programs, drug-free school zones, and specialized programs for senior citizens. Police officers also receive in-service training in these community crime prevention programs.

The implementation of community crime prevention programs has been an important vehicle to prevent crime without having to hire additional police officers. Because they only require limited budget funds, these programs have served an important role in the community. All of these programs actively involve citizens in assisting their police department. These programs represent ways to expand police services without having to resort to tax increases to pay for more police officers.

Human Resources Management Practices. Police chiefs have implemented a number of state-of-the-art practices in this field. Most of these new programs involve increasing employee productivity, stretching limited budget funds, improving public services, providing specialized training, and making counseling services available to employees.

Most chiefs now assign regular police officers to patrol shifts based on the number of calls for service. Vacant positions are being reviewed with the goal of saving money through the delayed filling of these positions, and by hiring new employees at entry-level salaries. Many departments are now using paraprofessionals and civilians where the authority of a police officer is not needed to perform job duties. This has reduced salary and fringe benefit costs. The movement to community policing has helped to empower police officers to make decisions and solve problems without needing to seek approval from their supervisors. Nearly all departments have implemented police auxiliary and reserve programs to help augment existing service levels. This is an excellent way for civilians who wish to become police officers to receive valuable training and job skills. Young people have become involved in police work through police cadet and police explorer programs. These young people can assist police officers and can be used to perform routine non police-related work.

Many departments have expanded their crime prevention services through the use of neighborhood watch programs, commercial watch programs, neighborhood safe houses, and similar community programs. Also, court trustee–appointed community service workers are frequently being used to maintain police vehicles, provide janitorial services, perform landscape maintenance duties, and to remove graffiti from public places. In the training area, the trend is to provide specialized programs to police officers in such areas as diversity, sensitivity, and stress and burnout. An increasing number of police departments provide professional employee assistance programs, whereby police officers and their families have access to 24-hour hotlines to handle a variety of personal, social, or medical issues and problems. Most cities have initiated pre-employment medical examinations, psychological evaluations, and drug testing for all new police officers.

The trend has been to integrate all of the traditional personnel functions with the evolving human aspects of the workplace. Police departments in cities of all sizes are moving in this direction.

Management Information Systems. Many police departments are on the cutting edge of information processing, management systems, and retrieval technologies. The use of computers and specialized police department software applications have revolutionized the way information is collected, analyzed, and retrieved to make many management and operational decisions.

Specialized software applications are typically used to track calls for service, dispatch the appropriate patrol vehicles and resources to crime scenes, generate reports concerning the number and types of crimes and police incidents, automate police records management, inventory police evidence, maintain equipment maintenance schedules, as well as monitor police department budgets. The reports generated from these software applications help to prioritize responses to calls for service, determine patrol staffing requirements, detect crime patterns by incident as well as geographic area, and provide administrative and operational support for various police functions. By analyzing the number and types of criminal complaints, for example, shift commanders can allocate additional patrols or specialized police resources to combat crime. Police chiefs, when designing their data requirements, should make sure that the data collected is compatible with state and national police data collection systems. The development of these common requirements will lead to statewide and possibly national standards in this field in the future.

Many police departments have stand-alone mainframe computers tied into workstations with remote terminals. The current trend is for departments to be linked into a centralized mainframe "host" computer via a network of microcomputers at individual workstations. The latter approach to configuration of hardware is less expensive since all municipal departments may be networked into a single centralized mainframe computer. The use of microcomputers also serves as a personal productivity system. Efforts are underway to link police officers and patrol units into the central database through the use of mobile teleprinters, mobile data terminals, as well as laptop and hand-held computers. The availability of more sophisticated computer hardware and the development of specialized police software applications have facilitated the trend for departments to automate their management information systems. These technological advances have helped to fight crime and improve the quality of services to the public.

Management Practices and Organizational Change. Although police departments perform many law enforcement-related functions, police patrols are the most visible services provided by city governments to their citizens. Many taxpayers believe that law enforcement is the most essential function of their municipal government. Many elected officials also hold this view.

With increasing citizen demands for police services and limited revenues to expand these services, many police chiefs throughout the country are reviewing their operations and services in an effort to meet the changing expectations of the citizens they serve. Traditionally, as the public demanded more services or as community crime rates increased, police chiefs would merely request more sworn personnel to meet these service demands. In fact, for many years the goals of police chiefs and many elected officials was to reduce police response times. It was not unusual to add more police officers to provide a greater level of patrol services to reduce existing response times. Both the political and fiscal environment in many communities has now changed, and police departments are receiving increased pressure to meet greater service demands without additional funding.

For many years, police chiefs have embraced authoritarian management styles that fit their highly structured bureaucratic organizations. These formal lines of authority centralized decisionmaking at the top levels of the organization, leaving little latitude for rank-and-file police officers to make decisions. Recent trends to increase departmental productivity, reduce operating expenses, use more sophisticated technologies, and improve the level of police services has facilitated the need to empower police officers to assume a greater level of responsibility for making daily decisions without having to constantly check with their supervisors. A more qualified and competent police workforce has been ready to assume a more assertive role on reducing crime.

To meet this challenge, many police chiefs have responded by adopting more flexible styles of management and less bureaucratic organizational structures. Police chiefs that have implemented these changes have not only increased employee morale and productivity, but have also helped to restore citizen trust in their local police agency. As police chiefs continue to meet these challenges, more flexible management styles and streamlined organizational structures will evolve in the future.

Organizational Consolidations. While much publicity has been given to consolidating police and fire departments into a single municipal department, usually called the public safety department, fewer than 50 cities in the nation have actually consolidated these separate functions. Most of these departmental consolidations have occurred in smaller communities.

The more common practice is for communities to contract with their county government or for smaller communities to contract with a larger neighboring municipality for police services. Typical contracts with other governments are generally for animal control services, hazardous materials responses, emergency medical services, code administration and enforcement, and for centralized dispatching services. Many of these services are beyond the financial and operational capability of smaller communities, or the number of incidents is so infrequent as to not justify a full inhouse response capability.

There is a trend towards consolidating police services among smaller cities and police service districts. Some smaller cities in certain areas of the country—primarily in the South and West—have merged two or more police departments to provide multijurisdictional police services. These service consolidations have occurred primarily for economic reasons in high population growth areas. The greatest economies of scale have resulted from regional police service consolidations. These economies have been achieved by centralizing police and fire management functions; centralizing police and fire dispatches and communication networks, as well as support services; and by improving both police and fire services because of increased resource levels and more specialized response capabilities. The primary disadvantage of regional police service consolidations is the perceived loss of local control by citizens over these municipal services. Many local elected officials have opposed regional consolidations for these reasons.

While police and fire consolidations and regional police service consolidations are not a major trend, contract police services between cities and between cities and counties are gaining in popularity. These trends are likely to increase in the future, especially in small- and medium-sized communities with limited staffs and technical resources. Larger cities with a history of having separate police and fire departments and separate police and fire unions are less likely to change their traditional organizational structures and service practices.

Use of Computers and Technologies. The latest developments in mainframe computers, specialized software applications, and other police-related technologies have improved the internal operations of police departments as well as the quality of services to the public. On the department-wide level, rather than have their own mainframe computer, more sophisticated computers with larger storage capacities can be used to serve as a "host" computer for all municipal departments. The number of microcomputers networked into the central computer has increased dramatically. Before long, each workstation will likely have its own microcomputer linked to software on the mainframe.

Police patrol vehicles frequently contain mobile teleprinters, mobile data terminals, as well as laptop and hand-held computers. Mobile teleprinters are used to receive written, as opposed to verbal, information from central dispatchers. Mobile data terminals permit a police officer to access state and national crime databases such as those at the National Crime Information Center. Laptop computers with modems perform the same functions as mobile data terminals. They also permit police officers to write reports in their patrol vehicles and transmit them back to the mainframe computer for storage and reference. Hand-held computers allow police officers in the field to input standard incident reports directly to the mainframe computer.

Some police departments provide digital dictation equipment, providing their police officers in the field with the opportunity to dictate their reports over the telephone and transmit them to a special computer for storage, where they are later typed into the central records database. Centralized dispatching units are using computer-aided dispatching (CAD) applications to provide dispatchers with information on the location and status of patrol vehicles, as well as the address and telephone number of the calling party, permitting a police response to proceed even if the call has not yet been completed. Other non–computer-related technologies commonly used by police officers include video cameras to record crime scenes and arrests, digitized fingerprint identification using special software applications, and video imaging systems to take pictures of suspects when they are booked for arrest.

Many of these technologies have improved communications to police officers in the field, have enabled police officers to spend less time preparing reports, and have enhanced the quality of law enforcement services to the public. The use of all of these technologies is on the increase for these reasons.

Workload Scheduling and Caseload Management. With shrinking municipal revenues, police chiefs have had to review their operations to ensure that employees are being used to the fullest extent possible. Some of the more recent techniques to increase employee productivity include the use of demand patrol scheduling, prioritizing criminal case investigations, and using alternative methods of reporting police incidents.

Many police chiefs are analyzing their calls for services and assigning patrol shifts based on citizen demands for these services by both day of week and shift. For example, if the graveyard shift (midnight to 8:00 A.M.) receives twice as many calls for service as the regular shift (8:00 A.M. to 5:00 P.M.) on Fridays and Saturdays, then fewer patrol units are needed on the regular shift and more on the graveyard shift. This type of analysis should be done for each day of the week, with patrol units assigned to fit the number of calls for service. The number of calls for service should be periodically monitored to ensure that patrol shift assignments continually meet the community's demand for police services.

Many police chiefs are also applying caseload management techniques to categorize their criminal cases for investigative purposes. A typical caseload management system may include three categories of cases—in-custody cases requiring immediate attention, cases with solid workable leads, and non-serious cases with no investigative leads. This type of system is usually administered by the supervisor of the investigations division. By prioritizing cases, the efforts of police investigators are focused on solving the most important cases first. Many departments are now using alternative methods to report police incidents that do not require the personal attention of police officers. Some agencies are mailing out standard report questionnaires directly to citizens; others are taking reports over the telephone; still others are asking citizens to appear in person to report certain types of routine incidents. Civilian employees are used to prepare many of these reports, thereby freeing up the time of police officers for more important law enforcement duties.

All of these management techniques are required due to the need to allocate scarce personnel resources to those police duties with the highest payoff in terms of productivity. Because of increased service demands and fewer human resources, these workload scheduling and caseload management practices are essential. These operating practices reflect sound management principles, notwithstanding the status of an agency's available financial resources.

External

Budget and Service Reductions. When budget and service reductions become necessary, public safety services are usually the last to be spared the budget axe. Police services are typically perceived by elected officials to be one of the highest service priorities. For this reason, chiefs of police have been under increasing political and financial pressure to increase productivity without additional staffing, and to come up with ways to achieve economies without making service reductions. Police chiefs have been able to minimize budgetary and service reductions by controlling the number of uniformed positions, selectively using paraprofessionals and civilians, augmenting existing services through the use of police auxiliaries and reserve units, and by enhancing their department's community crime prevention programs.

Many city councils have already had to reduce budgets and staffing in other municipal departments. For this reason, many elected officials have not approved requests for additional police officers. Additional police officers, when they are added, have typically been financed by federal and state grants. Many elected officials and city managers have required delays when filling uniformed positions in order to save local tax dollars. Each month of delay in filling a vacancy saves nearly one-twelfth of the annual salary and fringe benefit costs. A three-month delay would save up to one-fourth of these costs during the fiscal year. New positions, both sworn and civilian, when they are filled, are usually always filled at the entry salary level.

Many communities are now using civilian police paraprofessionals and are filling selected vacant police officer positions with civilians because of lower salary and fringe benefit costs. Although members of police auxiliary and reserve units cannot be used to replace full-time police officers, many chiefs have expanded their ranks as a way to augment existing police services in the community. Lastly, but no less important, many chiefs of police have enhanced their community crime prevention services and public educational programs in an effort to solicit citizen assistance in reducing crime in their communities.

All of these cost-saving and productivity-enhancement measures have enabled chiefs of police to reduce their operating costs and, at the same time, increase the level of police services to the public. For these reasons, while police agencies have not had their budgets reduced to the extent that other departments have, they have been forced to devise practical ways to hold down their departmental operating expenses. The trend has been for police departments to use techniques such as these for primarily economic reasons.

Community Education and Citizen Empowerment. One of the main purposes of an effective crime prevention program is community education and citizen empowerment. The goal of these programs is to educate the public on how to protect and safeguard themselves against crime, how to conduct themselves when a crime takes place, as well as how to assist their police department by reporting crimes and suspicious activities.

In recent years, a number of innovative crime prevention programs have been developed to deter or prevent criminal activity before it takes place. These programs are specifically tailored to a number of different segments of the community, including children, teenagers, young adults, adults, and senior citizens. In order to properly promote these programs, many local law enforcement agencies have given police officers specialized training in these community crime prevention programs. Many medium-sized and larger cities have created a special job title called community crime prevention officer. Many cities even prepare monthly or quarterly crime prevention newsletters to inform citizens and businesspersons of municipal crime trends as well as ways to reduce these crimes.

Most of these programs have been implemented for several reasons—rising crime rates, fewer police officers, limited budgetary resources, and citizen dissatisfaction with the existing level of police services. All of these crime prevention programs empower citizens to help create safer neighborhoods; to watch out for each others' homes, children, and possessions; to report crimes and suspicious persons; and most importantly, to create an atmosphere in which all of the members of the community—not just the police—are involved in crime prevention. When citizens take an active role in preventing crime, they directly reduce the cost of their municipal police services. The trend for police departments to educate and empower citizens using community crime prevention programs is on the increase, and this will definitely continue in the future.

Contract Services. Although traditionally not a high user of contract services, their use in police departments is on the increase primarily for four reasons. One is the desire for a community to reduce its expenditures for police-related services. Two, smaller police departments, because of their limited size, frequently lack inhouse expertise in some important areas of police services.

Three, the increased use of computers and specialized software has created the need to hire computer hardware and software consultants to perform these services. And four, police management consultants frequently work with chiefs of police to develop police service master plans.

Sometimes smaller communities, especially newly incorporated ones, will contract with neighboring cities or their county for police services for reasons of economy. Sometimes a smaller city will provide a basic level of police services but may, for example, desire additional police patrols on selected shifts. Also, many small police departments lack the necessary technical expertise in specialized areas of police work, such as investigative services, providing various forms of tactical support, and conducting undercover police work. Many police chiefs also use computer hardware and software consultants specializing in police applications to develop their management information systems, as well as to automate their operations. When smaller communities contract with larger cities or counties or form intermunicipal arrangements for dispatching services, they do so for the previously stated reasons. When chiefs of police prepare police service master plans, police management consultants frequently perform organizational assessments, work with major stakeholders, and guide the process of developing these plans.

For all of these reasons, the use of contract services is on the increase, especially in police departments in small- and medium-sized communities with limited inhouse staff capabilities and expertise to perform these services. In larger cities, much of the talent and expertise to perform these services may be found within the department. The only exception may be for the selection of computer hardware and the development of specialized police software applications. Generally, the use of contracts for services in police departments is on the increase.

Coproduced Services. For a number of years, local law enforcement agencies have been at the forefront of the movement to involve citizens in the coproduction of police services. Citizens now work with their police departments in a number of different programmatic areas, primarily serving as the "eyes and ears" of their police department. Police chiefs have made an ongoing effort to make sure that citizen volunteers, regardless of the program in which they are involved, only report suspicious criminal activities to the police department. Citizens should never be allowed to directly confront suspects or take the law into their own hands. Only police officers are trained to perform these duties. Using trained police officers for these duties also reduces the liability exposure of the department.

Some of the programs that involve the use of citizens to report suspicious activities and criminal wrongdoings to their police department include neighborhood crime watch programs, commercial crime watch programs, and radio assistance programs, to name a few. Other programs that require the active involvement of citizens working directly with police officers include police auxiliary and reserve programs (for adults) and police cadet and explorer programs (for youths). Citizens involved in police auxiliary and reserve programs frequently go through the same training as regular police officers and must work alongside a police officer at all times, except when performing nonsworn duties. Police reservists and auxiliarists who work part-time usually receive an hourly rate of pay or monthly stipend. The use of these individuals is often regulated by existing labor agreements with police unions. Police cadet and explorer programs are generally for young people who wish to learn about police work. These young people work with police officers on a voluntary basis but never perform any of the duties of a police officer.

All of these citizen involvement programs expand the level and quality of police services. Because of limited police budgets, these programs serve as excellent vehicles to create safe neighborhoods and commercial areas without having to increase the number of police officers. Local law enforcement agencies have served as fine examples of the national trend to actively involve citizens in the coproduction of municipal services. The use of all of these citizen programs is on the increase.

Financing Police Services. Little attention is given in law enforcement publications on ways to creatively finance police department services. Citizens routinely expect police services—a basic property related service—as a part of paying their annual property taxes.

In recent years, a number of different service charges and fees have been implemented, though taken collectively they raise only a relatively small amount of departmental revenues. Some of the fees charged by police departments include fingerprinting (generally for applicants for state licenses, such as teachers, real estate agents, and other professionals), permits (for concealed weapons, to operate pawn shops, and for taxicab operators, to name a few), vehicle accident reports (for those involved in accidents and their insurance companies), crime reports (for those involved in crimes and their lawyers), duplicating services (copies of local laws and state statutes), and for false alarms (more than the minimum number of false alarms allowed per year). While the number of new services charges has not increased, there is a trend to adjust these fees periodically to ensure that they reflect the cost of doing business.

In many communities, the only new police services added in recent years have been those funded by various state and federal law enforcement grant programs. Because of limited funds at the local level to add additional police officers and the continual need for more law enforcement services, many state legislatures as well as Congress have approved new specialized grant programs to finance the cost of new police officers. These programs are typically limited to hiring police officers only, and only when they will be placed on the street to fight crime. Many communities have taken advantage of these grant programs to expand the number of police officers on their force. Virtually all of these grant programs are based on a funding formula that decreases the grant financing of these positions over a three to five year period. At the end of the grant program, elected officials will either have to fund these positions with local tax dollars or eliminate them from their police department. Only time will reveal the long-range financial impact of these grant programs on an already limited local tax base.

The general trend for cities is to try to maintain the existing staffing size of their police departments and to apply for state and federal grant programs when elected officials desire to expand the number of police officers in their community.

Intergovernmental Cooperation and Resource Sharing. Like fire departments, police departments in neighboring communities have a long tradition of cooperating with one another during a time of crisis. Likewise, local police agencies and county sheriff departments have always cooperated with one another. Similarly, local police departments are increasingly cooperating with state and federal law enforcement agencies on a number of specialized police-related services.

Because political boundaries are artificial and crime can occur at any location, virtually all communities cooperate in providing assistance as requested by the city in which the crime occurred. In the case of "hot pursuit," neighboring communities always cooperate when their jurisdiction is involved. County sheriffs departments, because of their large size, always lend assistance to communities within their boundaries upon request of the city desiring a particular service. Police departments in cities of all sizes now routinely cooperate with state and federal law enforcement on many joint task forces such as those for narcotics, gangs, and organized crime. State and federal law enforcement agencies also provide many specialized services to local police departments, frequently at no charge. The most recent trend is for local police agencies to share their technical expertise, specialized resources, and jail facilities with one another. Examples of these services include hostage negotiating teams, SWAT teams, helicopter patrols, K-9 dog units, police artists, forensic laboratories, arson investigators, and other specialized investigative services.

Many cities have formalized their relationships with neighboring police departments, and as well as with their county sheriffs department, through the use of interlocal service agreements. In some states, county sheriffs departments have taken the lead by creating interlocal service agreements for all municipalities within their boundaries. While all police departments can benefit from these arrangements, police agencies in smaller communities with limited resources benefit the most from these service arrangements. The trend is for cities to formalize their service/resource-sharing relationships with one another through the use of these service agreements. This trend, because it makes sense to cooperate in this specialized service area, is on the increase. Smaller law enforcement agencies also save funds by not having to develop an inhouse capacity in technical police areas where such resources would be infrequently used.

Police-Community Relations. The perceptions of citizens toward their police department in general and members of the police force in particular io critical to a department's image and reputation in the community. A community's police department should be perceived as fair and responsive to the needs of all citizens, regardless of their race, ethnicity, or socioeconomic status. Traditionally, police-community relations programs have been mere public relations efforts designed to put the best "spin" on undesirable incidents after they have taken place. New planning practices that involve major community stakeholders in reviewing existing services and proposed programs will help restore an agency's credibility. These types of planning processes also serve to institutionalize community involvement in a police department's planning process.

Three important police-community issues can be found in most municipalities, regardless of their size or geographic location. These include a commitment that the composition of a department's workforce should represent the community, that all segments of the community should be treated equally by all police officers, and that police officers should strive to maintain high ethical standards. Many departments have formal written recruitment and promotional policies, endorsed by their elected officials, city manager, and chief of police, setting forth their agency's hiring and promotional goals. It is reasonable for citizens to expect that the workforce of their police department should represent the community. The city manager and chief of police should work with their personnel directors to make sure that their hiring and promotional practices reflect these policies. It is incumbent upon the chief of police and the department's management staff to ensure that their police force treats all citizens equally. Citizens also expect their police officers to perform their duties and operate with the highest ethical standards. Written policies in these areas and prompt follow-ups on all citizen complaints—including disciplinary action when appropriate—are essential in maintaining the integrity of a city's police operations.

When police-community issues and problems are handled in a systematic manner, with governing body and top management support, citizens have a higher comfort level knowing that these matters are being properly addressed. Several barometers exist to determine the success of a department's commitment in these sensitive areas. These include the number of lawsuits, complaints, and claims filed by citizens against their department and its police officers. The trend for police chiefs to work with the community in a meaningful way to resolve issues and problems facing their department is on the increase.

Police Service Master Planning. Most local law enforcement agencies are faced with increasing citizen demands for more police services. The growth of revenues has not kept pace with these escalating service demands. For this reason chiefs of police must carefully review their existing levels of police services, prioritize them, and prepare departmental police service master plans to assist policymakers when making budget decisions and planning for the future. These plans are also typically used to develop desired service level standards, analyze possible alternative service operations, and conduct periodic service evaluations to ensure that acceptable service standards are maintained.

It is not unusual for these plans to be prepared in draft form by an internal planning committee consisting of representatives from a cross-section of the department. The draft plan, once it is prepared, is usually presented to internal and external stakeholders. Internal stakeholders may include representatives from the governing body, formal citizen advisory groups, central administration, and police management. External stakeholders may include representatives from the board of education, community support groups, neighborhood organizations, and chambers of commerce, to name a few. The final plan is then prepared based on the comments and suggestions made by these stakeholders. Although politically sensitive, the best master plans also address major police issues and problems facing the department.

While only some chiefs have developed these types of service master plans, it is critical in tight budget times to set forth service priorities and options, especially when they may have widespread community support. These service plans provide valuable information to city managers when they prepare departmental budgets, and also assist city councils in their budget deliberations. This planning trend, because citizen demands for services outstrips available financial resources, is necessary to provide administrative and political legitimacy to existing and proposed service levels.

Police Service Trends. Local law enforcement practices change over time because of new developments in the field, the use of modern technologies to improve services, more sophisticated service models, and research that leads to solutions by other agencies in response to common issues and problems. Most law enforcement professionals continually network with colleagues in their profession and also keep abreast of the latest literature in the police field published by national professional associations.

Some of the latest books and monographs in the police field focus on the ways to improve operations, increase services, reduce crime, and new ways to plan for the future. Recent publications on police management topics include the latest information on the police officer selection (including fitness and drug testing), the financial aspects of police liability, effective police patrol staffing practices, how to use computers, and ways to control false alarms. Subjects related to police services include adapting services to neighborhoods, how to implement community-oriented policing practices, centralized dispatching practices, the use of benchmarking techniques to increase productivity, how to implement police-fire department consolidations, and ways to relieve jail overcrowding. Crime-reduction related topics include how to prepare drug control master plans, as well as how to develop gang prevention and intervention plans. The latest training areas for police officers include multiculturalism, ethics and integrity, and stress and burnout programs. Only a few books and monographs are available on long-range police planning. This is an area of police management that will certainly receive greater attention in future years.

These topics reflect state-of-the-art interests on the part of academians and police managers. In the course of time, this professional literature will ultimately be transformed into modern police practices. In the interim, only the most progressive law enforcement agencies have integrated these police practices into their daily operations. Tight police budgets will facilitate many of these management and service trends.

Professional Development. Numerous national professional and technical associations are available for police personnel. Most of the organizations are professional membership associations; others are nonprofit research organizations. Many professional membership associations have state chapters. Police chiefs usually belong to the International Association of Chiefs of Police (IACP). Police officers involved in crime prevention typically join the National Crime Prevention Council (NCPC). Other national organizations include the National Criminal Justice Association (NCJA), the Police Executive Research Forum, and the Police Foundation.

All of these associations provide a variety of educational programs, conferences, technical resources, publications, research services, and professional networking opportunities for law enforcement personnel from local police agencies. Specialized publications and training programs are provided in such areas as general police agency management, crime and drug prevention, community policing, police-community relations, youth and crime, asset seizure and forfeiture laws, police response strategies, and community and race relations. Professional certification programs are also available through many of these associations. Other municipal professional organizations such as the National League of Cities (NLC) and the International City/Council Management Association (ICMA), have published recent case studies on how cities have implemented successful police department service innovations and organizational consolidations. Police departments have their own nationally recognized professional accreditation program sponsored by the Commission on Accreditation of Law Enforcement Agencies, Inc., based in Fairfax, Virginia.

It is essential that police personnel participate in specialized training sessions, not only to stay on top of the latest developments in their respective fields, but also to improve their personal productivity on the job. Training is especially critical in small communities that lack the personnel to perform many specialized law enforcement services. The trend is to budget funds to properly train police officers in both existing and evolving technical fields.

Working with Community Volunteers. In addition to organizing programs for citizens to assist their police department in reducing crime, many new programs are being developed to familiarize citizens with the operations and services of their department. One common program is the citizen ride-along program, where citizens are encouraged to ride in a police patrol vehicle to find out firsthand what duties are performed by police officers. Some agencies conduct citizen police academies to acquaint citizens with the operations of their department, the responsibilities of police officers, and the proper role of citizens in helping fight crime. These training programs are also being used to recruit citizens to serve in other voluntary police programs. The use of individual citizen volunteers, while not traditionally used in great numbers in police departments, is also on the increase. Citizen volunteers are sometimes used to perform special projects, provide clerical support, type routine documents, perform traffic control, and perform other civilian-related assignments not conducted by regular full-time sworn or civilian employees.

The use of community policing programs has expanded the level of citizen assistance provided by neighborhood walking police. Many municipalities, for example, may use citizens at neighborhood police substations to perform clerical work, take reports from crime victims, act as foreign language interpreters, refer victims who need counseling to social service agencies, and provide other routine support approved by the police department. In some cases, citizens have even donated office space for neighborhood police officers.

All of these programs have improved police-community relations, have served to develop stronger ties between police officers and the citizens they serve, and have helped to make police officers more productive by eliminating some of the more routine duties from their daily workload. For these programs to be successful, they must be supported by the city council, city manager, and the chief of police. Police-community programs such as these are being endorsed by elected officials in communities of all sizes and locations. These trends, notwithstanding budgetary considerations, are gaining in popularity and should increase in future years.

THE FUTURE

While other departmental budgets have been reduced in recent years, police departments have generally been spared the budget axe. They have, however, been the subject of increased scrutiny by elected officials and city managers on ways to reduce crime, increase employee productivity, and educate citizens on methods of community crime prevention. Of the many internal productivity trends discussed, evolving crime prevention services have helped to achieve all three of these goals. Community crime prevention activities appear to be the wave of the future. In recent years, a number of such programs have been developed and implemented by police departments across the country. These programs have been oriented to young school children, teenagers, senior citizens, merchants, and the average homeowner. These educational programs have helped to deter criminal activity, prevent crimes, reduce crime rates, and improve police-community relationships. Since community crime prevention duties are typically assigned to existing police officers, they have only had a minimal budgetary impact. These practices reflect the state-of-the-art citizen educational programs now being provided by other municipal departments such as health and human services departments and fire departments.

In many local law enforcement agencies, police-community relations are at an all-time high because of the recent efforts of chiefs of police to educate and involve citizens in their community's crime-fighting efforts. Citizens of all ages now have opportunities to get involved in a host of different programs, ranging from drug education workshops for young people to crime prevention tips for senior citizens. Teenagers usually have the options of joining police cadet and explorer programs. Homeowners, merchants, and businesspersons can get involved in neighborhood and commercial crime watch programs. Adults can frequently join police reserve and auxiliary units to provide assistance to regular police officers as they perform their duties and participate in the citizen ride-along programs. Some departments have even initiated citizen police academies to train citizens to be the "eyes and ears" of their police department. All of these services have helped to bridge the gap between a community's police department and its citizens.

The practice of consolidating police and fire agencies into public safety departments has received a great deal of publicity in recent years. In reality, only a few smaller communities have actually consolidated these traditionally separate organizational functions. With possible rare exceptions, larger communities have not consolidated these municipal services. In newly incorporated cities, the option to consolidate these services is ideal since existing vested interest groups have not yet formed and political opposition to such service consolidations has not yet developed. The much more popular trend, which has received considerably less media attention, has been for smaller communities to contract with largest cities or counties for selected police services. Typical contracts with other governmental agencies are generally for animal control services, special police patrols, and dispatching services. Elected officials usually do not favor public safety service consolidations because of employee and union opposition to these initiatives. Existing labor agreements in most communities would preclude city officials from undertaking these reorganizations unilaterally. State governments have not mandated these service consolidations, even in smaller communities, because of the political opposition that would develop from local elected officials over the loss of their time honored, and constitutionally guaranteed, home-rule powers.

PUBLIC WORKS

The municipal programs performed by public works departments include both line and staff services. These programs may vary greatly from community to community for a number of different reasons. Line programs typically include the development and maintenance of a city's transportation system, the removal and disposal of a community's solid wastes, provisions for drainage facilities to capture stormwater runoff, transporting sewage to wastewater treatment plants, and the maintenance and landscaping of a city's public buildings and grounds. Staff programs almost always include engineering services for the construction of most municipal projects—regardless of the department in which they were initiated—and central garage services designed to maintain and make repairs to a municipality's vehicle fleet and motorized equipment. Many exceptions exist to these services in smaller communities. For example, larger cities have traditionally had parks maintenance services performed by their parks and recreation departments. Smaller communities are likely to have this service performed by their public works department. Because of budgetary constraints in recent years, the trend has been to consolidate these municipal services into a single department, usually public works.

In many parts of the country, especially in highly urbanized metropolitan areas, separate special districts were formed over the years to provide wastewater treatment and water supply and distribution services. It would serve no practical purpose of each city in these areas to provide their own water supply and wastewater treatment facilities. Economies of scale were achieved for cities in these geographic areas by establishing special districts to consolidate these municipal services. Most of these agencies provide these services to several communities or to all of the municipalities within a county. Some of these agencies even provide these services to users in regional multicounty areas. The provision of these services was ideal for regional consolidation since they are paid for from user fees. The income stream generated by these user fees can also be used to pay for the revenue bonds that finance the construction of these facilities. For this reason, these services do not need to be provided by general purpose local governments with the power of taxation. Special districts

314

do not need the power of taxation since no property tax dollars are needed to finance these facilities or to pay for their ongoing operation and maintenance costs.

Many small- and medium-sized communities contract with private companies for a great number of specialized public works services. These contract services may include engineering, project management, vehicle maintenance, solid waste collection and disposal, janitorial services, and landscaping maintenance, to name a new. In many municipalities, only a portion of certain services are provided by contract. For example, virtually all cities contract for specialized engineering services, such as for the preparation of plans and specifications for bridges and dams, large road projects, and complex public works facilities. In these cases, contract services make sense since it would not be prudent to hire specialized engineering staff for individual projects, only to lay off these employees when these projects have been completed. In fact, since most cities issue general obligation bonds to finance these projects, some cities add engineering costs to the amount of these bonds to pay for contract engineering services. In other communities, the engineering staff keeps track of their time on individual projects and their labor costs are charged to each project's bond account. These practices may vary greatly from community to community.

In recent years, a variety of revenue-generating tools have been developed to finance different components of the municipal infrastructure. The trend is moving away from issuing general obligation bonds since they are paid for by all of a community's taxpayers. Tax increment funds generated from redevelopment project areas are frequently used to finance public improvements in these areas. Revenue bonds can also be obtained by committing the future income stream generated by these funds for the required number of years to satisfy this debt obligation. Many communities are charging development impact fees to developers to finance the future costs of roadways, schools, parks and open spaces, and community facilities. Utility connection fees are also commonly used to finance the extension of sewer and water services. Special assessment districts are being formed with greater frequency to pay for the cost of public projects that only benefit selected property owners. Municipalities also have the option of creating joint power authorities or special districts to provide selected services like wastewater treatment facilities and water supply and distribution systems, since they are financed from the revenues generated by user fees. Governing body approval is required for all of these revenue-generating and financing alternatives.

Of a municipality's operating departments, the department of public works contains the greatest diversity of services provided to the public. In terms of budget size and number of employees, public works departments are always one of the largest municipal agencies, exceeded only by the police and fire departments. Figure 13.1 highlights the major programs performed by the typical municipal public works department.

Figure 13.1
Public Works Major Programs

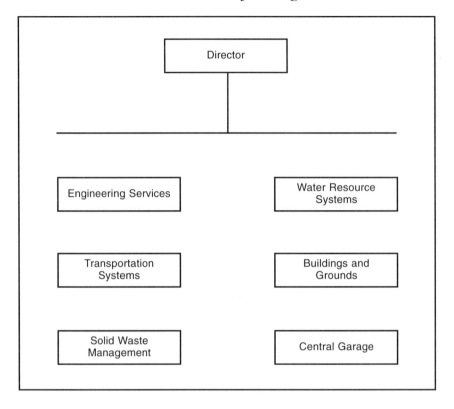

DESCRIPTION OF PROGRAMS

Engineering Services. City engineers design projects and prepare plans and specifications for public improvements made to municipal property. The typical duties performed include the design of public facilities, construction inspection, surveying, and materials testing (e.g., for concrete and asphalt). Smaller cities, because of limited professional staff support, tend to contract for engineering services with private firms.

Larger cities, because they have an inhouse professional staff, perform most of their own engineering services. All cities use consulting engineers for complex and highly specialized projects such as dams, bridges, large road projects, water distribution systems, and sewer treatment plants. All states require that the municipal engineering function be headed by a certified professional engineer (PE). Only a PE can approve municipal construction and design projects and private plans submitted for municipal review and approval. Small cities without a PE must contract out for these services. Consulting engineers usually report to the city engineer, public works director, or in the case of small cities, directly to the city manager.

Municipal engineering consultants are usually hired to provide a service based on a request for proposal, with the contract being awarded to the lowest responsible bidder. In many cases, technical qualifications are more important than the proposed cost. Contracts can be awarded on a project-by-project basis such as for a street project or for ongoing services such as inspection services. A fixed fee is usually charged for permits, such as those for sidewalk construction, curb cuts, and street openings. An hourly rate is typically charged for construction inspection services. These fees are adjusted periodically to reflect the cost of doing business.

Transportation Systems. Municipal transportation systems include arterial, collector, and residential streets, traffic control devices, bridges, tunnels, and city-owned parking facilities. Some cities have their own airports, ports, and small-craft harbors. All of these facilities are publicly maintained. In some states, sidewalks are the responsibility of the property owner, while in others they are the city's responsibility. Most components of the municipal transportation infrastructure must be developed to state-mandated standards. Even traffic control devices are usually regulated by the state.

Transportation construction services include street design and construction; the design, construction, and landscaping of median islands and parkways; traffic signal and intersection design, construction, and installation; and street and traffic control sign manufacturing and installation. Most large public construction projects, by state law, are required to be contracted out to the private sector.

Once these transportation systems are constructed, they must be maintained and repaired by the municipality's public works department. Maintenance activities includes road resurfacing, street cleaning, catch basin and stormdrain cleaning, snow and ice removal, and street striping. Repairs are routinely made to potholes, curb and gutters, stormdrain pipes, and traffic devices. Since the location of streets determines the areas through which utility cables pass, municipal employees work closely with local gas, electric, telephone, and cable television companies when constructing and repairing streets.

A city's comprehensive plan, which includes proposed street projects, is developed in conjunction with the transportation staff of the public works department. Transportation projects are reflected in a city's capital budget, and are usually financed with general obligation bonds. Maintenance and repair costs are reflected in a city's operating budget. The only fees generated by local transportation systems are for toll roads and bridges. These revenues are typically earmarked for replacement and maintenance costs, or to retire the debt associated with their construction.

Solid Waste Management. Solid waste collection and disposal are traditional municipal responsibilities. Now, there is a growing trend for cities to contract out refuse collection services to the private sector. Increasingly, disposal services are being provided primarily by regional agencies, secondarily by private companies. These facilities include landfills and incinerators.

Over the past decade, because of increasing disposal tonnage and transportation costs, transfer stations have been constructed as temporary refuse holding facilities. Transfer stations may also be either public or private. The Resource and Conservation Recovery Act (RCRA) of 1976 regulates the siting, design, operations, and monitoring of groundwater. It also mandates corrective action to minimize groundwater contamination for all public and private landfills. Many old municipal landfills must be closed because they do not meet these new federal standards. Also, the federal Environmental Protection Agency (EPA) required a reduction in the volume of solid waste materials permitted at landfills. Cities have been forced to develop integrated solid waste management plans to comply with these laws.

In order to reduce the volume of solid waste materials generated by a community, public works personnel have had to remove selected materials from their waste streams. They have accomplished this, to a great extent, by developing comprehensive recycling programs. The common items removed from the waste stream—usually through curbside pickup—include aluminum cans, bi-metal cans, glass, plastic containers, newspapers, other paper products, and leaves and grass clippings. Hazardous wastes must also be disposed of separately from other refuse.

For these reasons, many states and cities have undertaken public educational campaigns to promote the reuse of items (e.g., reusable beverage containers), the reduction of solid wastes (e.g., using biodegradable packaging), and improved recycling (e.g., removing selected items from the waste stream). If waste-reduction goals are not met voluntarily, mandatory programs are usually implemented. All of these measures have been taken in order to protect the environment and preserve it for future generations of citizens.

Water Resource Systems. Municipal water resource systems include providing an adequate and safe water supply, a proper distribution system to service users, appropriate stormwater and flood control facilities, an adequate collection system for wastewater, and a proper wastewater treatment facility. It is unusual for smaller cities to provide their own water (supply and distribution) and sewer (collection and treatment) systems and services. Some larger cities and towns in rural areas may provide these services to their citizens. Smaller cities may ban together to create special authorities to provide these services. In some cases, smaller municipalities may contract with a larger city or county for one or both of these services. Many times, especially in highly urbanized areas, special districts are created to provide these service.

Service arrangements vary greatly throughout the country. Under some arrangements, cities own their own water and sewer lines, but the sources of water and wastewater treatment facilities are centrally provided to many cities. Whatever the arrangement, users always pay for sewer and water services— whether to their city hall, a county government, or a regional service agency. Cities frequently provide their own flood control facilities, but this piece of the urban infrastructure may also be provided by a county or state government. Virtually all cities provide their own stormwater facilities. Some smaller cities may have separate sewer and water, or public utility, departments. Many cities, especially larger ones, combine these services under their public works department.

Sewer and water fees are intended to be cost-covering and are adjusted periodically to reflect the cost of doing business. These fees are also designed to generate sufficient revenues to satisfy the debt incurred to construct these public facilities. Revenue bonds may be used to construct water and sewer facilities since future revenues are guaranteed through user fees.

Buildings and Grounds. Public buildings include city hall complexes, library buildings, police and fire stations, public works yards, courthouses, recreation and senior centers, municipal parking lots, and other public facilities. Public grounds include the land upon which these improvements are located, as well as median islands, parking strips, and other publicly owned street-related landscaped areas.

Routine maintenance, minor repairs, simple construction improvements, and janitorial services are provided for public buildings. Landscape maintenance services are provided for all public grounds. The goal of buildings maintenance is to maintain the integrity and appearance of all public facilities. The goal of grounds maintenance is to maintain the appearance and safety of all public grounds.

All cities should maintain replacement funds to rebuild their public facilities at the end of their useful life. Most do not and, for this reason, many public improvements must be maintained beyond their useful life expectancy. When replacement facilities are constructed, general obligation bonds are typically issued to finance these projects. The maintenance of all buildings and grounds is an annual operating expense in the public works budget. Inhouse personnel in the building, janitorial, and landscaping fields provide these services. Economies of scale are achieved by centralizing these services in a single department. State law and city charters usually require that all projects over a certain dollar limit must be bid out to the private sector. Hence, major repairs and rehabilitation projects are typically performed by private construction companies.

Some cities treat their buildings and grounds budget as an intergovernmental service fund, charging individual departments a pro-rated share of the cost of these services. For this reason, the cost of these services should be competitive with similar services provided by the private sector. Some cities contract with private companies for janitorial and landscaping services.

Central Garage. Central garage services include making repairs, performing preventative and general maintenance, overhauling, and rehabilitating all pieces of motorized equipment and vehicles owned by a municipality. Fuel dispensing and management is a critical part of the central garage. All of these activities are a part of what is frequently referred to as fleet management. Inhouse personnel in the mechanical trades provide these services.

The goal of fleet management services is to ensure the sound operating condition and safety of all motorized equipment and vehicles. Computers and special software applications are commonly used to monitor fuel distribution, maintain parts inventories, and for routine maintenance scheduling. All cities should maintain replacement funds to replace equipment and vehicles at the end of their useful life. Most do not, and for this reason, many pieces of equipment and vehicles must be maintained beyond their useful life expectancy. Most pieces of motorized equipment and small vehicles are purchased out of the annual operating budget. Some states allow cities to finance major pieces of equipment and larger vehicles by issuing general obligation bonds. The general rule of thumb is that the life expectancy of the item purchased with bond funds should not exceed the number of years that it takes to retire the debt incurred for its financing.

Economies of scale are achieved by centralizing these services in a single department. Many major and special repairs, including body work, are contracted out to private companies specializing in these areas. For highly specialized items, service agreements may be acquired at the time of purchase. Many smaller cities, with limited inhouse expertise, also contract out portions of their fleet maintenance services. Some cities treat their central garage budget as an intergovernmental service fund, charging individual departments a pro-rated share of the cost of these services. For this reason, the cost of these services should be competitive with similar services provided by the private sector.

PRODUCTIVITY TRENDS

When a community has a well-managed public works department, most citizens take many of their services for granted. Many internal productivity trends have dealt with methods to improve capital planning, the development of creative financing alternatives, and the implementation of real estate asset management programs. Improved capital planning and real estate asset management have helped to reduce the cost of new capital improvements. Local transportation systems are one of the most important and vital components of a city's infrastructure. Existing federal grant programs in this area have forced cities, counties, and states to jointly plan for integrated multimodal transportation networks. Other important facets of public works include the planning and management of a community's solid wastes and water resources. New and innovative ways have been initiated to reduce a municipality's refuse collection and disposal costs. Likewise, new local regulations have facilitated the collection of on-site stormwater runoff. Linking together the many aspects of the public works function are computer systems and specialized software applications that help improve operational control, employee productivity, and the quality of public services.

A public works department has a great deal of interaction with many different segments of the community. Many states require that capital projects over a certain monetary threshold go to public bid. For this reason, the local development community has a close relationship with this facet of public works. Since a number of contracts for engineering services exist, many of these municipal services are provided by private consulting companies. This department, either with its own work crews for smaller projects or with contractors for larger projects, is responsible for retrofitting public facilities for compliance with the Americans with Disabilities Act (ADA). In recent years, public works directors have implemented a number of citizen education and empowerment programs to instruct taxpayers on ways to help their municipality hold down the cost of services. Some highly visible line services may be contracted out to private companies. These programs include everything from comprehensive recycling programs to refuse collection services. While state and federal grant programs for capital construction have been substantially reduced over the past decade, other financing operations have emerged to fund capital projects. Most taxpayers today do not like to pay for public facilities that they do not directly utilize.

Table 13.1 highlights those public works productivity trends examined in this chapter. Because of the great diversity of public works services, many different professional employees are responsible for these operational improvements and cost-saving practices. The technical expertise of engineers, transportation experts, water resource personnel, and maintenance and mechanical employees, have helped to modernize public works practices in recent years.

Internal

Capital Projects Planning and Programming. Historically, many communities have neglected the preparation of comprehensive multiyear capital improvement plans. Since many cities have been preoccupied with balancing their annual operating budgets, their elected officials have not wanted to incur additional municipal debt. It is incumbent upon city managers and public works directors, however, to inform their elected officials that it is cheaper in the long run to maintain a city's capital assets, rather than to have them replaced after they deteriorate. An effective capital projects planning and

Table 13.1
Public Works Productivity Trends

Internal	External
Capital Projects Planning and Programming	Americans with Disabilities Act Compliance
Costs and Benefits of Public Works Services	Bidding Practices
Cost Containment Practices	Contract Services
Human Resources Management Practices	Coproduced and Cofinanced Services
Management Information Systems	Outside Financing of Capital Projects
Municipal Financing of Capital Projects	Professional Development
Organizational Structures and Consolidations	Public Education and Citizen Empowerment
Real Estate Asset Management	Public Infrastructure Issues
Solid Waste Management Planning	Public Works Service Trends
Transportation Management Planning	State and Federal Grant Programs
Use of Computers, Technologies, and Products	User Fees, Service Charges, and other Revenues
Water Resources Management Planning	Working with the Community

programming process includes the establishment of an appropriate organizational structure and administrative procedures.

The typical organizational structure includes the formation of a capital projects committee, usually chaired by the planning director, but which always includes the director of public works as a member. The rationale for this is that capital projects must be consistent with a city's comprehensive plan, which is prepared by the planning department, and the fact that most of a city's capital projects fall under the purview of the public works department. A representative of the finance department is usually a member since it is the responsibility of this department to conduct financial analyses, review the impact of capital projects on a city's operating budget, and recommend possible funding sources for each project.

The proper administrative procedures for the development of a capital projects plan includes a system for assessing the condition of existing capital projects, a formal process for the collection and ranking of capital projects, a requirement to evaluate their impact on departmental operating budgets, making a recommendation on funding sources, and the assignment of responsibility to the appropriate department manager to make sure that approved projects are placed out to bid and completed in a timely manner. Capital project requests are prepared by operating departments following these guidelines and reviewed by the capital projects committee. Planning commissions typically review multiyear capital project plans, making recommendations to the governing body on which projects should be completed during the upcoming fiscal year.

One of the most important goals of this planning process is to educate citizens and elected officials on their government's long-range capital improvement needs. For this reason, these plans also set forth long-range capital financing requirements that go well beyond the typical budget cycle. Another important reason to have an approved capital projects plan is that it gives a community the edge when applying for state and federal grants programs should they become available.

Costs and Benefits of Public Works Services. Public works directors, in cooperation with municipal planning and building departments, are using state-of-the-art financial techniques to calculate the estimated public works operating costs associated with new developments, and comparing these costs against and revenues generated by proposed developments. Many communities now require that this information be prepared and filed as a part of their environmental impact statement for all new development proposals.

The expense side of the equation is usually calculated by determining the per capita costs of public works services (i.e., dividing the existing population base into the cost of all public works department services), and then multiplying these per capita costs by the projected population generated by the proposed development. The revenue side of the equation usually takes into consideration both municipal revenues (e.g., public works fees, development fees, inspection fees, real property taxes, personal property taxes, and utility taxes) as well as intergovernmental transfers (e.g., sales taxes, gasoline taxes, cigarette taxes, and alcoholic beverage taxes). For obvious reasons, the estimated revenues generated by a proposed residential development are easier to calculate than those revenues received from office, commercial, or industrial developments.

Once the public costs and revenues of a proposed development have been determined, an informed decision can than be made by planning commissions and public officials with regard to the financial merits of development proposals. This type of financial analysis compares the operating costs of public works against the anticipated revenues to finance the additional expenses required by a new development. Capital construction costs (e.g., community facilities, utilities, roadways, traffic signal devices, and storm drains) are excluded from these calculations. These expenses are typically financed by utility connection charges and development impact fees. In the past, general obligation bonds, paid for by all taxpayers, were the usual method for financing these public improvements.

The national trend is for communities to use some form of cost/benefit analysis to determine the cost-effectiveness of private sector development proposals. The rationale for this type of analysis is that public officials increasingly do not want existing taxpayers to subsidize the public service costs associated with new developments. The use of cost/benefit analysis leads to more informed decisionmaking by public officials and is on the increase in cities— regardless of their size or geographic location. The trend to finance capital project costs from utility connection charges and development impact fees is also on the increase.

Cost Containment Practices. Public works directors have initiated a number of different measures to reduce their operating costs and increase employee productivity. While the use of computers may not directly reduce operating costs in the short term, the use of computers in the long run may hold down the need for future clerical and midlevel management personnel.

In recent years, inexpensive microcomputers and specialized software applications have been used to implement fuel management, equipment maintenance, energy conservation, sewer maintenance, and street pavement management programs. Computerized fuel management programs have been used to limit access to fuel pumps and to monitor gasoline consumption. Software applications are available to keep track of routine equipment maintenance and are also used to provide preventative maintenance schedules to prolong the life of existing vehicles and equipment. Automated energy management systems are now used to regulate heating and air conditioning in public buildings by turning these units on and off at preprogrammed times to reduce energy consumption and utility costs. Specialized software is available for scheduling routine maintenance of sewer lines and prolonging the life of a city's existing sewer infrastructure. Similar software is being used for street maintenance management programs, placing streets on a routine maintenance schedule, and ranking streets for resurfacing or reconstruction based on their condition.

Other products and practices are also being used to reduce costs. Many departments are using street lights with lower energy consumption costs, such as high-pressure sodium street lamps, as opposed to the more expensive incandescent street lights. Inexpensive growth retardant chemicals are commonly used to reduce the costs of landscaping and park maintenance. Various substances are now used in roadway construction to reduce the costs of snow removal. Similarly, chemicals are being used to facilitate snow removal, reducing the high labor costs traditionally associated with this task. Many smaller communities are sharing seldom used pieces of specialized equipment and machinery on a reciprocal basis, doing away with the need to purchase these capital items. Communities of all sizes have entered into joint purchasing programs with neighboring cities for economies of scale (i.e., the greater the number of items purchased the lower their unit costs). More sophisticated municipalities are using life-cycle purchasing techniques that take into consideration the costs to operate and maintain a particular item, as opposed to merely purchasing items from the lowest bidder.

All of these management practices help to reduce operating costs as well as make the existing public works workforce more productive. While limited municipal budgets have facilitated these trends, they are increasing in popularity because they represent sound management practices.

Human Resources Management Practices. Public works departments have initiated a number of different practices to reduce their personnel costs and increase worker productivity. Many departments have increased their use of part-time employees, especially during the summer months for special projects. These employees save municipal funds because they do not generate fringe benefit expenses or overtime costs.

Workers' compensation costs, especially in public works departments, have skyrocketed in recent years. Safety programs are now routinely used to reduce the number of employee accidents, minimize the damage to public property caused by these accidents, limit the number of employee injuries and downtime due to accidents, and reduce a community's workers' compensation costs. Many cities now have employee safety committees that meet periodically (usually once a month) to review accidents and take preventive measures to ensure that similar accidents do not occur again in the future. Many communities have also implemented claims administration programs to reduce the number of employee accident claims, as well as their financial impact on departmental operating budgets. Prompt accident reporting, employee medical attention, incident investigations, and employee medical evaluations have assisted in promptly returning workers to their jobs. Smaller communities usually contract with private companies for claims administration services. In larger cities, safety and risk managers are usually hired to perform this service inhouse.

Some smaller cities are contracting with larger neighboring communities or private engineering companies for specialized engineering services. The cost of these services may be added on to individual project costs and qualify for bond funding. This is especially cost-effective in small communities when these services are only needed infrequently and not on an ongoing basis. Some public works departments are also using community service workers to perform routine maintenance and for special projects. Community services workers are citizens who have been ordered by the court to perform community service work. All of these trends, because they save money and increase worker productivity, are increasingly being used in cities of all sizes and locations.

Management Information Systems. Public works directors and city engineers have historically never worked in a high-technology work environment. Most of the work done by the professional staff has been based on their personal expertise and, for this reason, the services they provide have been labor intensive. The availability of inexpensive personal computers, more user friendly software, and the development of specialized public works and engineering software applications have changed this trend forever. In addition to using standard software applications to perform routine administrative duties such as database management, word processing, permit issuance, inspection scheduling, project tracking, budget monitoring, and records management, more specialized software has opened up a wide range of engineering public works and applications.

Engineering applications include geographic information systems (GIS) which can store and retrieve information on individual parcels of land, automated drafting and mapping, and project management. Transportation-related applications include maintaining roadway inventories, ranking streets based on their condition, and keeping track of maintenance schedules. Traffic applications include maintaining traffic device inventories and maintenance schedules on these devices. Solid waste, sewer, and water applications include automated billing systems, maintaining facilities maintenance schedules, and tracking service calls. Building and grounds applications include maintaining street tree and capital asset inventories, facility maintenance schedules, and tracking facilities management work requirements. Applications for the central garage include vehicle and equipment inventories, parts inventories, and maintenance schedules.

The use of personal computers and software applications such as these have made the task of management much easier for the various division heads within the public works department. The director of public works can now receive daily computer-generated reports of the work activities and overall performance of the various organization units within the department. The trend in public works departments is to acquire a greater number of personal computers and specialized software applications to improve overall management as well as employee productivity. All of these applications are gaining in popularity, and will no doubt become commonplace in the future.

Municipal Financing of Capital Projects. A number of local financing options exist to fund municipal capital projects. Traditionally, general obligation bonds have been issued, backed by the full faith and credit of the city government, to finance capital improvements that benefit the general public (e.g., city halls, community centers, youth centers, senior citizen centers, parks, and open space). Revenue bonds may be issued for those municipal projects that create a steady income stream (e.g., wastewater treatment plants, water distribution systems, toll roads and bridges, municipal arenas, and sports stadiums). Tax increment funds, or bonds based upon the future income stream generated from these funds, can be used to finance public and private projects in approved redevelopment areas.

Developers can also be made to pay for future municipal infrastructure improvements through the use of development impact fees. Under this plan, developers are charged a pro rata share of the cost of anticipated municipal improvements created by their development. It is also becoming common to charge developers a fee of all sewer and water line connections. These funds, once collected, are set aside in special funds earmarked for capital improve ments. Cities can also issue Industrial Development Bonds (IDBs) for qualifying private projects. Under this plan, the developers receive tax-exempt financing rates for their private projects. Recent federal legislation has restricted the types of qualified projects as well as the amount of funds that may be financed using this funding technique.

Other local funding options for capital projects include placing user fees generated from new developments in capital funding accounts, and using these monies to fund future capital projects. Special assessment bonds may be used for those public projects which only benefit certain property owners, such as wastewater collection systems, water distribution systems, and street improvements. Many communities now consider leasing alternatives as opposed to the outright purchase of certain capital items, such as mainframe computers, large trucks, and expensive pieces of specialized equipment. For larger capital improvements benefitting more than one municipality—such as wastewater treatment plants, regional parks, open spaces, or refuse transfer stations—communities have the option of forming joint powers authorities or creating special districts. Once created, these separate legal entities incur the debt necessary to finance these facilities, with payments made from the revenues generated by users in member local governments' jurisdictions.

The trend is for cities to conserve their general funds, requiring developers to pay either through development impact fees or through user service charges, using special assessment bonds and charging property owners, and leasing alternatives, which are operating expenses as opposed to capital costs. All of these trends are on the increase.

Organizational Structures and Consolidations. The municipal functions assigned to the public works department vary from community to community. The typical public works functions in medium- to large-sized cities usually include municipal engineering services, the development and maintenance of the transportation system, the management of all solid waste and recycling programs, developing and maintaining water resource systems, maintaining all public buildings and grounds, and providing maintenance services through a central garage for all municipal vehicles and equipment. Various exceptions are made to this organizational arrangement, especially in smaller municipalities. Some small communities include planning and building functions, code enforcement, animal control, and parks maintenance in their public works department. It is also not unusual for smaller communities to contract for certain specialized services such as engineering, project management, vehicle maintenance, solid waste collection and disposal, janitorial services and landscaping maintenance.

Of all municipal operating departments, the one with the most diverse functions is the department of public works. While some cities have separate utility departments, the trend is to consolidate these functions under the public works department. During recent times, because of budget constraints, it has become common to consolidate park maintenance with public works maintenance, since the activities performed by workers under these programs is similar. In some areas, special districts have been created to handle wastewater treatment and water supply and distribution. Notwithstanding who performs these services, the users of these services always pay fees to make these services cost-covering. In terms of size, public works is always one of the larger municipal departments, usually only exceeded in terms of budget and staffing by the police and fire departments.

The trend in cities of all sizes is to consolidate all public works–related functions into a single department, headed by a director of public works who is also usually a registered professional civil engineer. This trend has helped to consolidate similar municipal functions, centralize responsibility and accountability for these functions under a single department manager, and reduce the number of department manager positions required to manage these functions.

Real Estate Asset Management. All cities have a large network of improved and unimproved real estate assets. Many of these public assets are not being properly managed. When municipal budgets are reduced, usually the first programs to go are those for capital project construction and the maintenance of existing capital facilities. Also, virtually all state and federal grant programs favor the construction of new capital projects over the restoration and maintenance of existing community facilities.

Capital assets in the private sector, however, are managed quite differently. In most private companies, for example, the useful life of a capital asset would be determined and a replacement fund would be established. Under this practice, funds would be set aside annually to ensure that sufficient monies are available to replace the asset at the end of its useful life. Not even the wealthiest of municipalities properly fund for the replacement of their aging capital assets. In fact, most cities do not even inventory their capital assets, let alone project their useful lives in order to know what asset should be replaced in any given fiscal year. Part of the reason for this is that most politicians would rather fund more visible public services as opposed to budgeting limited funds for capital replacement and maintenance. There are always more votes for hiring new police officers than for setting up capital project replacement accounts.

Nonetheless, it is incumbent upon public works directors and city engineers to have inventories of their community's capital assets prepared, showing the date of construction as well as the projected useful life of each asset. Some cities have initiated this practice for their street replacement programs. This practice needs to be extended to other pieces of the capital infrastructure as well. It is a sound planning practice to know what should be done, even if this cannot be afforded immediately. Some states have mandated that their cities develop inventories of their capital assets, as well as place an estimated value on each asset. City managers should work with their public works directors and city engineers to educate their elected officials on the need to properly maintain their city's physical plant. As additional public pressure is brought by citizens to operate government more like the private sector, the use of these practices will become more commonplace in future years. This trend has been inhibited by tight budgets but, if local revenues improve, real estate assessment management should receive a higher priority.

Solid Waste Management Planning. In the past, when solid waste landfill sites were plentiful and regulations from higher levels of government were minimal, municipal solid waste disposal was not a community issue. The passage of the federal Resource and Conservation Recovery Act (RCRA) in 1976 mandated strict standards for the siting, design, and operation of landfills, including requirements for groundwater monitoring and taking corrective action to mitigate groundwater contamination. The federal Environmental Protection Agency (EPA) adopted guidelines requiring a 25 percent reduction in the volume of refuse materials deposited in municipal landfills by 1992. These two laws have revolutionized existing solid waste disposal practices in cities throughout the nation.

These EPA guidelines in many cases have been exceeded by state mandates to remove a greater percentage of refuse materials from a community's solid waste stream. Cities, regardless of their size or geographic location, have been forced to develop solid waste management plans to comply with these federal and state government requirements. Many cities have complied with these laws by developing and implementing comprehensive municipal recycling programs. Some cities have already achieved over a 50 percent reduction in their solid waste stream by eliminating many traditional refuse items, including aluminum and bi-metal cans, glass and plastic bottles, newspapers and magazines, and other household waste products such as leaf and grass clippings. Federal and state laws also require that many household hazardous wastes be removed from a city's refuse and disposed of separately. Communities have complied with these mandates and achieved these waste-reduction goals by preparing, implementing, and enforcing comprehensive municipal solid waste management plans.

Many communities have undertaken citizen education programs to promote recycling, as well as the reuse of certain waste items (such as reusable beverage containers) and the use of biodegradable packaging (such as paper containers rather than plastic products). These solid waste management practices, while they have required some additional expenses associated with existing municipal landfills, have created budgetary savings because of the reduced tonnage costs created by a decreasing amount of household wastes. They also generate revenues by selling the recyclables. While all levels of government have initiated these programs, citizens should receive the credit for monitoring and managing their individual household wastes. All of these trends, because they help preserve the environment and reduce municipal refuse disposal costs, should increase in popularity in future years.

Transportation Management Planning. The responsibility for a city's transportation network is a very complex web of intergovernmental relationships. Each level of government—federal, state, county, and municipal—has a role in transportation management planning. The primary role of the federal government has been to provide interstate highway systems, to fund some construction and maintenance costs, and to set national safety standards. Federal funds for road construction and maintenance are usually given to the states for distribution to counties and cities. States also make road funds available from special revenues such as gasoline taxes. Depending upon the area, some counties allocate funding to cities within their boundaries to maintain county roadways. Most communities, especially those located in highly urbanized areas, have federal, state, and county designated roads running through their municipality.

The federal government in 1991 passed the Intermodal Surface Transportation Efficiency Act (ISTEA), which reallocated a portion of its funding to include the financing of mass transit–related projects to relieve traffic congestion on national highways. The ISTEA also mandated regional and statewide long-range transportation planning, and requires states to involve cities in this process. In order to relieve local traffic congestion, many communities provide bikeways on their streets, pedestrian walkways through local linear parks, and provide both of these public amenities along rivers, drainage culverts, harbors, and other manmade and natural settings. Communities in most states are required to have a master street plan as a part of their comprehensive land-use plan. Because of these federal funds, transportation options are receiving a high priority in these street master plans.

Cities have received federal and state funds to maintain their roadways for many years. Due to the inability of many cities to raise local revenues, municipal reliance on these outside funding sources is increasing. Federal laws now require municipal participation in the planning of regional and statewide transportation systems. This participation will increase in the future if cities wish to qualify for these funds. Other local transportation options such as bikeways and pedestrian walkways will increase in importance as alternatives to vehicular modes of transportation. Local transportation planning has become an ongoing process that includes multimodal transportation system options.

Use of Computers, Technologies, and Products. Public works departments, because of the diverse functions they perform, have been able to take advantage of a number of specialized computer applications. In addition to the many different software applications available to automate the various divisions of a public works department—engineering, transportation, solid waste management, water resources, buildings and grounds, and central garage—a variety of new computer software applications are now available for highly specialized tasks. Some of these applications include energy monitoring and management, automated water sprinkling, automated fuel management, and employee productivity work measurement.

The public works marketplace is full of creative and innovative products. New pieces of equipment include the one-man pothole filling machines; large snow blowers that remove tons of snow from streets in only minutes; and specialized equipment that trims roadside slopes, parks, playing fields, and golf courses with wider mowing devices. New chemicals include growth-retardant chemicals that may be applied to weeds and lawns to reduce maintenance expenses. Utility costs for street lights have also been reduced through new energy conservation techniques. Many cities have replaced their incandescent street lights with high-pressure sodium lamps and are using light censors to regulate the hours of usage. Many departments are also using telephone message centers to better serve the public. It is not unusual for a dozen different messages to be recorded to inform citizens of public works projects such as snow removal operations, street construction projects, street maintenance and pothole operations, and park maintenance schedules. Many departments are also using automated cash register and receipting systems to keep track of daily transactions and to facilitate making timely bank deposits.

All of these technologies and new products help reduce maintenance expenses, labor costs, increase employee productivity, and improve the level of services to the public. Public works departments throughout the nation are becoming more sophisticated in the application of these sophisticated technical resources. Tight municipal budgets have facilitated these trends.

Water Resources Management Planning. Prior to 1974, regulations concerning drinking water and groundwater quality were regulated by local and state governments. Under these requirements, the quality of drinking water and groundwater were the sole purview of local public officials following local and or state laws. The Safe Drinking Water Act of 1974 authorized the EPA to set forth national regulations for these functions, the majority of which are administered by the states.

In recent years, the cost of municipal and regional water services have been increased, not only to reduce demand and force conservation, but also to set aside special capital funding accounts to replace water distribution systems in the future. Likewise, the cost of municipal and regional wastewater services have increased, primarily to replace aging collection systems and treatment plants. Since water resources are not distributed evenly throughout the country, states, counties, and cities have increased their level of intergovernmental cooperation to ensure that these natural resources are distributed according to legitimate local needs. Water distribution and wastewater collection are frequently performed on a multicity basis through the creation of joint power authorities or special districts. The federal Safe Drinking Water Act was amended in 1986 to include additional water quality standards, including strict regulations governing agricultural and industrial contaminants.

When improvements are made to water collection and distribution systems and wastewater collection and treatment systems, revenue bonds are frequently issued to finance the cost of these capital improvements. Revenue bonds can be used when the revenues created by user service fees generate sufficient funds to pay off the future debt incurred for the construction of these capital projects. Smaller communities that provide these facilities frequently have problems generating sufficient revenues to make legally required improvements, as well as have problems attracting qualified personnel to operate these facilities.

New federal regulations also restrict the disposal of biosolids at municipal landfills, facilitating the creation of suitable disposal facilities such as sludge-to-composting systems and incineration plants. To assist cities in this compliance area, state funds are typically made available, usually in the form of low-interest loans. New federal regulations also impose strict regulations to limit the type and amount of pollutants in stormwater, since it is discharged into lakes, rivers, streams, as well as the ocean. Community governments, in response to these federal regulations, now require private developers to submit plans to contain the stormwater runoff from their proposed developments.

These new federal requirements have fostered the creation of regional water collection and distribution systems, as well as regional wastewater collection treatment plans. Cities, joint powers authorities, and special districts have in turn increased their service charges to cover the costs of these mandated programs. Development regulations have also been imposed on property owners and developers to make it easier for local governments to comply with these new federal requirements. All of these trends will certainly continue in the future.

External

Americans with Disabilities Act Compliance. The Americans with Disabilities Act (ADA), adopted by Congress in 1990, mandates increased responsibility for municipal governments in the areas of providing services to persons with disabilities and for eliminating physical barriers that preclude handicapped citizens from using existing public facilities, parks, and other public services. While individual department managers have been required to review their respective facilities to determine what improvements are necessary for compliance, the engineering divisions of public works departments have usually been given the responsibility of preparing routine plans and specifications for retrofitting existing capital facilities to met these federal guidelines. They are also including these requirements in all new plans and specifications for community facilities and other public improvements, many of which are maintained by the public works department.

While it is fairly simple to retrofit city halls with handicapped restrooms, special parking spaces, and handicapped access ramps, it is more difficult and costly to retrofit and update the many community facilities operated by other departments. In some cases, it has been less expensive to relocate an existing program to another more modern facility rather than having to retrofit an outdated facility with ADA-required improvements. Local building officials also review the actual construction of community facilities to make sure they comply with the ADA's handicapped access requirements.

Since the federal government mandated this program upon communities without financial reimbursement, most smaller improvements have been financed out of annual departmental operating budgets. Larger capital improvement projects are usually financed by issuing general obligations bonds, which are paid for by all of a community's taxpayers whether or not they are handicapped. In either case, local taxpayers are being required to "foot the bill" for their city to comply with this federally imposed mandate. Many taxpayers realize the rationale for these ADA requirements, since citizens are living longer and, therefore, the number of wheelchair-bound and handicapped citizens will undoubtedly increase in future years. Because the ADA is a federal mandate, these trends will certainly continue in future years.

Bidding Practices. When compared to other municipal departments, the public works department coordinates the majority of a city's capital construction projects. Private engineering companies are usually hired to develop plans and specifications for individual projects. Private contractors are almost always hired to construct projects according to these documents. Many larger projects are beyond the scope of the inhouse municipal engineering staff. In many cases, state laws require that construction contracts over a specified amount be performed by the private sector. For these reasons, even the smallest of communities may contract with the private sector for millions of dollars worth of engineering services, roadway improvements, and public facilities.

Nearly all municipalities have, and some states even mandate, formal bidding procedures. The trend is not to award engineering contracts solely on the basis of the lowest competitive bid. In many cases specialized qualifications, successful experience with similar projects, and having the available staff to undertake the project are important factors that must be taken into consideration during the formal selection process. Many communities, rather than issuing a bidding document for engineering services, distribute a request for proposal (RFP) or a request for qualifications (RFQ) and evaluate the responses to the above factors before considering price, which is usually subject to negotiation. Also, contracts for professional services for smaller projects can usually be awarded without using a formal RFP or RFQ process if the cost is below a certain monetary threshold. This limit has been increased over the years because of inflation. The city engineer monitors the work undertaken by private engineering firms to make sure that they perform according to their contract. It is not unusual to continue the services of an engineering company to supervise the actual construction of a project according to their plans and specifications.

In many communities scientific, technical, and professional service contracts are not subject to local competitive bidding practices. When it comes to construction projects, contracts are usually awarded to the lowest "responsible" bidder—not just the lowest bidder—for those reasons outlined above. When a community contracts for private engineering and construction services there are many reasons why public officials would not want to award a contract to the lowest bidder. The use of these qualitative considerations when awarding municipal contracts is on the increase, as is the practice of negotiating fees for scientific, technical, and professional service contracts. These purchasing practices are becoming common in cities of all sizes.

Contract Services. The use of contracts with private sector companies to provide various public works services is on the increase. Private companies such as consulting engineers have always been used to provide specialized services not available from the municipal engineering staff. The use of contract services has been extended to other areas of operation in recent years. Some examples of contract services provided in the various functional areas of public works are highlighted below.

Computer hardware and software consultants are being used to assist directors in selecting the appropriate hardware and software applications for their operations. Contract engineering services include services for special projects such as bridges, dams, large road projects, wastewater treatment plants, water distribution systems, and various community facilities. Private engineering companies are almost always hired to provide specialized services such as traffic engineering, geotechnical analyses, and hydrological studies. Architects are used to design new projects since few public works departments have architects on their staff. When these projects are bond financed, it is not unusual to increase estimated projects by the amount of these services and include them in the bond issue.

In the transportation area, contracts are frequently used for street resurfacing and reconstruction projects, crack and joint sealing, traffic signal maintenance, and snow removal. Many state laws require that street improvement projects over a specific dollar limit must be contracted to private construction companies. For solid waste management services, private companies are frequently used to pick up and dispose of household refuse, recyclable materials, and household appliances. Some cities contract for composting services for their leaf and yard waste. In the area of water resource services, some cities are contracting for the management and operation of their wastewater treatment facilities and water distribution systems. In many regions of the country, these services are provided to communities by joint powers agencies or special districts. Under buildings and grounds programs, many communities contract for janitorial services, landscape maintenance, tree trimming and removal services, as well as the maintenance and repair of heating and air conditioning systems. Many municipal garages contract with private companies for body repair work, specialized repairs services, as well as lube and oil changes.

Many smaller cities contract for certain public works services from larger municipalities as well as their county government. Existing labor agreements may influence the types of contract services used in a community. The use of contract services from private companies and other governments are on the increase. This trend has been facilitated by the search to find additional ways to save money and stretch limited departmental resources.

Coproduced and Cofinanced Services. Property owners, land developers, and citizens in general are knowingly contributing to the provision of public works–related services as well as taking active measures to reduce their costs to the taxpayers. The three major areas of coproduced services include solid wastes, water resources, and buildings and grounds.

Citizens are participating in the reduction of their household waste by recycling portions of their refuse. Recycling programs help a community save money in three ways. They not only reduce the amount of refuse collection and disposal costs, they also generate revenues through the sale of recycled items. Several avenues of citizen participation exists for these programs. They can be mandatory with curbside separation in different containers, or they can be voluntary with municipally owner recycling drop-off centers. Many states in more congested areas of the nation have mandated recycling programs as a form of solid waste reduction. For general refuse collection, citizens can also reduce the cost of this service by placing their refuse and recyclables at the curbside for pickup. Some communities still provide backyard refuse collection pickup, which increases municipal refuse collection costs. In a further effort to reduce their refuse collection and disposal costs, many communities have implemented mandatory or voluntary grass and leaf composting programs. Some communities require that these items be removed from residential waste stream, while other municipalities provide curbside pickup of these items and transport them to citywide composting facilities. These recycling and composting measures have also reduced the amount of materials going to municipal landfills.

In the area of municipal water resources, conservation measures have reduced water consumption and the expenses associated with wastewater treatment. Many local regulations also require property owners and developers to contain their stormwater runoff onsite through a number of approved drainage, as well as retention and detention measures. These programs help reduce the costs of providing additional municipal stormwater collection points and drainage facilities and also help reduce the chances of flooding. When renting space in public buildings, user fees are now commonly being used to offset the cost of maintenance expenses, janitorial fees, as well as utility costs. Other financial actions taken by cities to help pay for future public works infrastructure projects include development impact fees, utility connection charges, and the use of special assessment districts. All of these financial tools require property owners and developers to pay for the cost of public improvements that benefit private property.

By actively involving citizens in helping reduce the cost of public services, by requiring property owners and developers to be responsible for the groundwater displaced by their improvements, and by charging for the costs of public improvements that benefit selected private property owners, public works officials have lowered their operating costs and shifted the burden of financing public works projects to the private sector. The use of measures such as these are on the increase. This trend has been facilitated by limited municipal revenues and a desire of public officials to reduce the cost of their government services.

Outside Financing of Capital Projects. As federal funds for capital projects have steadily decreased over the years, local officials have turned to their state government for grants and other low-cost financing options to construct capital projects. States can no longer rely upon the federal government as a steady source of funds to finance capital projects. Many state governments, notwithstanding limited funds, have implemented several creative programs to assist their communities in financing qualifying capital projects.

Some states have formal economic development assistance programs. These programs typically offer tax abatements, job grants, and low-cost financing for job-creating companies wishing to locate to cities in their state. Many states dedicate a portion of certain taxes—such as gasoline taxes—for selected capital projects like road construction. Some states buy municipal bonds for specific local development projects, providing lower interest rates to these cities. A few states issue their own bonds to finance the construction of qualifying projects, take legal title to land, and sell the improvements back to the company occupying the site over a negotiated time period. Many states are forming infrastructure bond banks where the state sells the bonds needed to finance projects in participating cities, thereby creating lower interest rates for these communities. Lower interest rates are received because these bonds are backed by the credit of the state, and due to the larger bond issues created by financing many capital projects. When state funds are available, they have usually been tied to creating certain types of jobs, such as for manufacturing, biotechnology, and research and development.

Last, but not least, federal funds are still available for capital projects in qualifying areas under the Community Development Block Grant (CDBG) program. Although limited, these funds must be approved for this use by elected officials after a legally required public hearing. Most public works directors explore all of these outside financing alternatives before relying on local funding options to finance capital projects.

Professional Development. There are a variety of professional associations available for employees involved in the various functional areas of public works. These professional membership associations, many of which have active state chapters, include the American Public Power Association (APPA), the American Public Works Association (APWA), the American Water Works Association (AWWA), the Institute of Transportation Engineers (ITE), the National Association of Flood and Stormwater Management Agencies (NAFSMA), the Solid Waste Association of North America (SWANA), and the Water Environment Foundation (WEF). The largest professional organization is the APWA with a worldwide membership of over 27,000 members, primarily from the United States and Canada.

All of these organizations provide a number of educational programs, conferences, technical resources, publications, and networking opportunities for professionals working in these fields. Many of these associations also provide research services on topics of current interest. Although too numerous to mention, most of these associations make available highly specialized publications and training programs to their members on an ongoing basis. Some of these groups have even developed specialized software applications for their respective functional areas, and make them available to their members at a discount.

Also, many of these association provide structured educational programs leading to professional certifications and technical designations. Other municipal professional organizations such as the International City/County Management Association (ICMA) and the American Planning Association (APA) also provide specialized publications, research, and case studies in some of the areas of public works.

Since many public works departments have relatively small professional staffs, some of which have been reduced in recent years, it makes sense to train these employees in the latest developments and trends in their professional fields. The funds spent for training, conferences, and publications are usually more than offset by increased levels of professionalism and worker productivity. Training is especially critical in communities with small professional staffs. The trend to allocate funds for professional development activities is on the increase, especially for employees in highly technical fields such as these.

Public Education and Citizen Empowerment. When city hall educates the public on ways to reduce the cost of their government, they empower citizens to take positive steps to eliminate unnecessary expenses associated with the delivery of their public services. In recent years public works departments have been in the forefront of the movement to empower citizens and encourage them to get actively involved in programs to hold down their taxes. Some of the more successful programs resulting from this effort are described below.

Municipal refuse collection and disposal costs have been substantially reduced through recycling, leaf and grass composting, and removing other yard wastes from residential waste streams. Many communities do not pick up other waste items such as construction debris, rubber tires, and designated household hazardous wastes. Citizens must have construction debris removed separately by private haulers and dispose of hazardous materials and rubber tires at centralized drop-off centers. Cities are even requiring automotive businesses to take old tires when new ones are purchased. Some communities also require citizens to discard yard wastes in biodegradable paper bags, rather than less expensive plastic bags.

Other successful initiatives are common. The cost of water consumption and wastewater treatment have been decreased through conservation and pollution prevention programs. Municipal transportation management costs have been reduced by encouraging citizens to use alternative forms of transportation. Many communities now provide attractive walkways and bikeways for citizens. Property owners in many cities are required to participate in snow removal by clearing sidewalks and driveways adjacent to their property. Even absentee property owners and owners of vacant lots are participating in these programs, frequently under fear of receiving a fine for not complying with these requirements.

A number of programs help reduce the cost of maintaining public buildings and grounds. These include charging refundable deposits when public grounds and buildings are rented for private purposes, and encouraging the user of these facilities to clean up after their events to reduce their rental charge. Many cities require citizen groups to sign hold-harmless contracts prior to using public facilities, relieving their city government from liability claims resulting from the use of these facilities. Many citizens and neighborhood associations request street trees from their municipal government. Some cities have policies where the city will pay for the cost of the initial tree, but the property owner must maintain the tree and replace it if it dies. Anti-litter programs have reduced the cost of street cleaning in public areas.

Since citizen empowerment helps reduce the cost of these services, organized public educational programs are essential to inform citizens of the ways in which they can participate to reduce their taxes. Public education frequently includes the use of program literature, messages on billboards, special programs on cable television, and letters to citizens informing them of cost-saving ideas. These citizen involvement programs have become increasingly popular as positive vehicles to hold down municipal budgets and taxes.

Public Infrastructure Issues. The municipal public works infrastructure provides the essential network of roadways, water distribution systems, waste-water treatment facilities, public buildings, and parks that make a community livable. The condition of a municipality's infrastructure can add significantly to the quality of life in a community, as well as contribute to property values. The quantity and quality of the public infrastructure can also be used to stimulate local economic development through business retention as well as making a city an attractive place for a company to relocate. Notwithstanding these important factors, when municipal budgets are reduced, the first items to be eliminated by elected officials are typically funds for the maintenance of the capital projects, budgets for new public works construction projects, as well as capital project fund reserves set aside to finance future capital improvements. Almost without exception, these reductions are consistent regardless of the size or location of a community.

At the staff level, few cities have inventoried their capital assets, projected their useful live, or have suitable capital project replacement plans. Part of this problem stems from the fact that public works staffs know that in tough budget times, capital maintenance, construction, and future planning give way to the funding of more visible public programs such as police and fire services. Many times, the prevailing mentality among elected officials is to fix something when it breaks. Federal and state grant funds have exacerbated this problem by providing funds, when they are available, for capital construction but not for the maintenance of existing capital improvements. Citizens need to be educated about the important role that the condition of their public facilities contributes to their community and personal lives. Public works directors should help teach their elected officials that it is cheaper to maintain a city's capital assets than to replace them after they deteriorate. Taxpayers should also demand that their city hall adopt the private sector practice of establishing replacement funds for key components of infrastructure. Citizens also need to lobby their state and federal elected representatives of their desire that, when available, funds should be allocated for the maintenance of infrastructure and not just to finance new construction.

Limited municipal budgets have led to deplorable management practices relative to the upkeep of a city's capital assets. Public works directors and city managers should educate elected leaders and citizens about how public works projects contribute to the vitality of a community. Since these conditions have not improved significantly in recent years, municipal capital assets will continue to deteriorate until public pressure is brought to bear on elected officials to correct this condition.

Public Works Service Trends. The work practices in public works departments change over time because of new developments in the field, the application of modern technologies and products to improve services, more sophisticated service delivery systems, and ongoing research that leads to solutions by other agencies in response to common issues and problems. Most public works professionals continually network with their colleagues and keep abreast of the latest research and literature in their field. Some of the latest research, case studies, and publications in the major areas of public works are highlighted below.

Subjects related to engineering include contracting for services, controlling on-site stormwater runoff, improved street designs, and automated mapping and drafting applications. Transportation topics include relieving traffic congestion, traffic control, alternative transportation options, and ways to market public transit. Recent solid waste management topics include research on waste-to-energy facilities, municipal incinerators, radioactive waste disposal, alternative billing systems, leaf and grass composting, landfill management, the handling of hazardous materials, joint refuse collection, and privatization. Water resource topics include water reuse, stormwater management, controlling urban runoff, water and sewer extension policies, charging for wastewater, financing stormwater programs, and water conservation.

Other topics are examined below. Subjects in the buildings and grounds area include energy conservation, underground storage tank regulations, capital facilities planning, street tree programs, measuring worker productivity, contracting for services, compliance with the ADA, automated facilities management, and maintenance management systems. Central garage topics include the use of alternative fuels, automated maintenance scheduling, and how to extend the useful life of vehicles and equipment through preventative maintenance programs. Only a few books are available on long-range planning. This is an area that will receive increased attention in the future since many departments are faced with multiple service demands and limited revenues.

All of these topics reflect the state-of-the-art interests of public works managers. In the course of time, this professional literature will be transformed into modern public works management practices. In the interim, only the most progressive agencies have implemented many of these practices into their daily operations. Limited funds will help facilitate many of these management improvement and cost-reduction trends.

State and Federal Grant Programs. The number of federal grant programs for local public works projects, as well as their funding levels, have been steadily reduced for a number of years. When these grants were available they were earmarked for construction since these types of projects generate additional jobs and help to reduce high unemployment levels. Some federal funds were available to finance wastewater treatment plants, helping cities comply with federal mandates in this service area. These funds have been reduced in recent years. The CDBG funds, although limited, are still available to finance capital projects in qualifying areas. National funding is still available for selected local transportation projects under the ISTEA. These funds are given to states to allocate to their local governments based on transportation priorities determined jointly by a regional planning process. Councils of government have been assigned this planning role in many states since these planning bodies already have municipal representation. Many states distribute a portion of their gasoline taxes and other revenues to cities within their boundaries for roadway projects.

Most public works directors explore state and federal grant funding sources before relying on local funding options to finance individual capital projects. The types of state and federal grants available and their funding levels vary from administration to administration, and with national and state economic conditions. At the national level, conservative administrations usually place a greater emphasis on monetary policies to stimulate the economy, while more liberal administrations favor the use of fiscal policies to invigorate the economy. National fiscal policies typically focus on allocating funds to communities to finance capital construction projects. Grant programs under these policies are used to "pump" money into the local economy for public works projects and, at the same time, create much-needed jobs to alleviate high unemployment rates. Because of the preoccupation of Congress with balancing the budget and eliminating the federal deficit, even the more liberal federal administrations have reduced national public works funding to communities.

These political realities, because of the condition of the federal budget, will not change appreciably in the foreseeable future. This has placed greater responsibilities on states to assist their cities with the financing of their capital improvement needs. Lacking state assistance, public officials are forced to defer needed capital projects or to finance them with funds generated through development impact fees, related revenues, or through the use of general obligation bonds, which requires all taxpayers to pay for these capital improvements. Because of the reluctance of elected officials to issue general obligation bonds, other revenue alternatives are being considered in many cities.

User Fees, Service Charges, and Other Revenues. Public works departments have made many changes to their user fees, are using innovative financing programs to pay for capital projects, are proposing special assessment districts for selected public improvements, and are recommending other revenue-generating programs to offset their operating costs. Even with these efforts, the additional revenues generated by public works department are minimal for several reasons.

Almost without exception, solid waste management, water distribution, and wastewater treatment services are treated as enterprise funds and financed with user service charges. For this reason, these services are almost always financially self-sufficient since user service fees are continually adjusted to pay for the operating costs of these public services. Also, in many communities water and sewer services are frequently provided by joint powers authorities or special districts, which are separate governmental entities. When cities provide sewer and water services, connection fees are increasingly required of developers to pay for these infrastructure costs. Building and grounds and central garage services are usually financed from intergovernmental service funds, which are paid for from funds budgeted in user departments for these services. For this reason, these services should be priced competitively with the private sector; otherwise, department managers will complain that it may be more cost-effective to have these services provided by the private sector. There are usually no user fees associated with the maintenance of roadways and traffic signal devices since taxpayers expect these services as a part of their property taxes.

Some buildings and grounds facility fees, however, such as those charged to private groups when using public facilities, are intended to be cost-covering. These fees are charged for janitorial services, grounds maintenance, and utility consumption. Development impact fees are now commonly assessed to finance the cost of future roadways, community facilities, parks and open spaces, and public schools. Special assessment districts are becoming a popular vehicle to finance those municipal capital projects that only benefit specific property owners. Engineering services include numerous user fees such as permits for sidewalk construction, driveway and street openings, public works inspections, blueprints, sidewalk specifications, and the maintenance of traffic signals serving private property such as regional shopping centers. These fees are now being adjusted annually to reflect the cost of doing business. One innovative revenue generating program being undertaken by many communities involves selling surplus municipal property to place in back on the property tax rolls.

Public works directors were among the first managers to establish enterprise and intergovernmental service funds. When user fees are charged, they are periodically adjusted to make them cost-covering. Development impact fees, utility connection charges, and assessment districts are being advocated to pay for the cost of future public improvements. All of these trends are on the increase.

Working with the Community. Public works directors should take advantage of the opportunity to work with citizens, neighborhood groups, and merchant associations when planning their many programs and services. The administrative staff should work with community groups when preparing long-range capital plans, taking the special needs of older neighborhoods into consideration when preparing these plans. On major projects, informal meetings should be held with citizens affected by the project to explain it as well as to solicit their input on ways to mitigate possible problems. Public study sessions should be routinely held with elected officials on all significant public works projects. The members of the engineering staff should always meet with property owners and merchants on proposed street construction projects. Many public works directors are making the project manager's name and telephone number available to the public to handle citizen inquiries and complaints. In some cases telephone "hotlines" are being used on major projects.

To help reduce traffic congestion, many communities have initiated programs to inform citizens on the importance of using alternative forms of transportation, such as walking, bicycling, and public transportation options. Public works directors are working with citizens and neighborhood groups to develop formal snow and ice removal programs, then educating citizens on the details of these programs, such as the need to concentrate on arterial streets before using resources to clear residential streets. Citizens are also being asked to help hold down solid waste collection and disposal costs through community recycling, reuse, and composting programs. Similar citizen participation programs are being used to reduce the cost of providing drinking water, wastewater treatment, and groundwater management services through conservation plans, anti-pollution programs, and on-site groundwater containment requirements. Lastly, in the areas of buildings and grounds, citizens now realize they can hold down costs by not littering roadways and public facilities, and buy getting their neighborhood or merchant association to take responsibility for cleaning up public areas under municipal "adopt-a-park," "adopt-a-street," and similar programs.

Because of the many services performed by public works departments, directors have a chance to develop positive relationships with citizens in a number of different operational areas. When the public works management staff deals directly with the public in this manner, it makes it easier when seeking approval of programs and projects from their elected officials. While it takes extra time to work with the public, the results far outweigh the costs involved.

THE FUTURE

Two of the largest expenses for any community are the maintenance of its infrastructure and the construction of new capital improvements. Public works directors have typically been lax in managing certain facets of their city's capital assets. Capital planning has been deficient in a number of different areas. For example, many cities do not inventory the different categories of their capital assets, determine their life expectancy, or have replacement funds to reconstruct capital assets at the end of their useful life. Transportation planning has also been lax. Many communities do not rate the condition of their roadways, maintain adequate maintenance schedules, or systematically replace these assets at the end of their useful life. Some cities do not even have multiyear capital improvements plans. Faced with tight budgets and increasing scrutiny from elected officials and city managers, internal management practices are being improved in these areas. Part of this problem has been that various components of the municipal infrastructure have been taken for granted by both elected officials and taxpayers. Elected officials would rather fund more visible public services since these decisions garner more votes at election time. On the other hand, citizens—so long as the condition of their infrastructure is reasonable—do not want their taxes to increase.

The relationship of public works officials to their external environment has changed drastically in recent years. Some of the most innovative cost-reduction programs include educating and empowering citizens to help reduce the cost of their government services. In many cases citizens are actually providing direct assistance to simplify and reduce service delivery expenses. Recycling programs have substantially reduced municipal refuse collection and disposal costs. The cost of water consumption and wastewater treatment have decreased through conservation and pollution reduction programs. Transportation costs have been reduced by encouraging citizens to use alternative means of transportation. Also, anti-litter campaigns have reduced the cost of street cleaning programs. This list goes on and on, and has been increasing as citizens become educated on ways to help their city government hold down their taxes. Citizen education and empowerment initiatives such as these will increase dramatically in the future. This trend fits nicely with the evolving citizen philosophy of reducing the cost of government and lowering taxes.

Public works departments have initiated a number of new financing methods to fund their services. Increasingly, several services such as solid waste management, water supply and distribution, and wastewater treatment are operated as enterprise funds or profit centers. User fees are adjusted to offset the annual operating cost of providing each of these services. User fees may also be increased to establish capital reserve accounts or to generate additional revenues to finance revenue bonds to pay for needed community facilities for enterprise-funded services. Many departments are using intergovernmental service funds to charge user departments for central garage services and buildings and grounds maintenance. Under this accounting practice, user departments only pay for services that they directly use. Development impact fees are being charged to finance future community improvements that benefit certain geographic areas. Likewise, special assessment districts are being formed to fund public projects that only benefit individual property owners. More and more communities are using these two latter funding methods to finance their municipal improvements. All of these practices have helped to reduce costs, enhance financial accountability, and hold down the need to issue general obligation bonds to fund capital projects.

14

CONCLUSION

America's cities have evolved from providing primarily property-related services (e.g., police, fire, and public works) to providing a variety of recreation and cultural programs (e.g., parks, playgrounds, libraries, and museums). The rapid urbanization of the nation during the 19th century placed unprecedented demands on all municipal services. While property taxes increased to finance many basic services, new forms of taxes and user fees evolved over the years to help finance the growing need for many additional municipal services, including cultural and recreational programs. The addition of these new services and the expansion of existing programs created the need for larger and more complex municipal service delivery systems. Recent technological advances in computer hardware and more sophisticated software applications have created the need for highly trained city managers and department directors. All of these trends have brought about the need for the professional management of America's cities in order to properly run the organizations providing these diverse services. Now, with the public's aversion to increased taxation, many communities have either reduced services or eliminated the expansion of existing services. The political environment in which both the mix and level of services are determined is shaped by elected officials as they make decisions to reflect the wishes of their respective constituencies within the community.

Concurrent with the expansion of municipal services throughout the years, America's urban problems increased to the extent that local governments could not finance workable solutions to solve their municipal problems. This was especially true during the Great Depression. The states, because of their inability to raise revenues, were limited in the extent that they could financially assist municipalities in coping with these urban problems. The federal government expanded its programs to fill this service vacuum. Many of our nation's cities during the depression became financially dependent upon federal funds to finance solutions to many of their social programs. Federal assistance continued relatively unabated until the so-called "taxpayers' revolt" in the mid–1970s. Federal aid also fulfilled the economic need to transfer tax

345

revenues from wealthier to poorer communities. This financial assistance balanced the fiscal needs of cities and equalized their ability to address these social problems. The reduction in federal and state assistance in recent years has meant that local officials must cope with and finance solutions to their own municipal problems. Local governing bodies now know that municipal problems must be solved from the financial resources available from within their own communities.

Changing societal values and beliefs over the past century have also served to shape both the structure and process of municipal governments. Many of these values have shaped beliefs that have led to the growth of the council-manager form of government as the predominant form of government now operating in most of the nation's small- and medium-sized communities. Many of the nation's larger cities and counties have also adopted this highly popular form of government. This trend has been facilitated by the belief in the corporate form of organization, the ideals of the progressive political reform movement, and the evolving public administration philosophy that calls for separating the roles of policymakers and professional administrators. While local elected officials have the political legitimacy to set policy in the best interests of their community, city managers have the administrative legitimacy to implement those policies and to run the daily operations of the municipal organization. Local public officials—both elected and appointed—generally feel that strong elective leadership is essential for effective governance and that strong administrative leadership is required to manage the daily operations of municipal organizations.

The council-manager form of municipal government embodies the essence of these requirements in several ways. Just as a private corporation has a board of directors that rely on a professional manager to run their organization, a municipal corporation has a city council that places their trust in a professional manager to operate their organization. The city manager's apolitical qualities qualify him or her to manager the administrative affairs of their community without regard to local partisan political considerations. Under this plan, all citizens are treated equally, regardless of their political affiliation. The council-manager plan also centralizes administrative authority under a professionally trained and competent manager. A community's elected representatives, on the other hand, have centralized political power and policy-making responsibility for their municipality. This form of governance also draws a sharp distinction between the role of policymakers and policy implementors. The professional city manager implements city council policies in an administratively sound and politically neutral manner. The city manager implements all policies adopted by a majority vote of the governing body—notwithstanding the political composition of the vote on these policies. Also, under the council-manager plan, all hiring and promotions are based on merit and competency without regard to political affiliation or loyalty.

Under the strong mayor form of government, for example, both competency and loyalty may have equal importance. While a strong mayor may strive to implement his or her political agenda, the city manager serves all elected officials equally as a single legislative body. While the mayor may strive to serve his or her political constituents, the city manager serves all taxpayers equally. Department managers under the council-manager plan have tenure so long as they are administratively competent. Department managers under the strong mayor form of government may have tenure so long as they support the mayor and his or her political agenda and remain politically loyal. With respect to serving the public, the council-manager plan best serves the need of providing ongoing administrative continuity to a municipal government. While mayors and city council members may come and go, it is the goal of the council-manager plan to provide administrative leadership beyond the tenures of individual elected officials. This generally holds true so long as city managers do not become involved with partisan political leaders and or their personal issues.

City managers also have a healthy respect for members of the governing body, especially mayors. The astute city manager can assist the mayor in a number of different ways that will free up his or her time to devote more attention to the duties of this highest elective office. When a city manager effectively manages the daily operations of the municipal organization, the mayor can devote more attention to being the city's top legislator and chief elected official. The mayor can use this time to rally support in the community around critical municipal issues, do the necessary political brokering among city council members to set public policy, and provide the political leadership necessary to further a community's legislative agenda with higher levels of government. A mayor that has administrative duties does not have the luxury of devoting his or her time solely to these high-profile and demanding political responsibilities. Lastly, while some mayors may have proven administrative abilities, many mayors typically come from many different walks of life. A mayor, although a qualified political leader who holds the trust and respect of the electorate, may have no administrative background or proven management abilities. Under the council-manager plan of governance, a mayor does not have to possess any special managerial abilities since the entire city council appoints a qualified city manager to perform those duties.

The local political arena is constantly changing and is becoming more complex in its nature. Many federal and state laws, as well as court decisions, now limit if not totally usurp the powers of locally elected officials. Citizens are also demanding more services, but do not wish to increase their taxes. This has made it difficult for elected leaders to set program priorities when adopting their annual municipal budgets. Additionally, in many communities there has been a greater demand for minority representation through district elections. Many special and or single issue candidates are elected, but may only serve one term of office, creating discontinuity in local legislative bodies. For these reasons, traditional management practices designed during more stable periods of growth and routine change are being replaced by a host of new management techniques to reduce costs and increase employee productivity. Elected officials should be most concerned with adopting sound policies to solve their pressing community problems and issues. City managers, on the other hand, should be free to implement these policy directives in such a manner as to treat all citizens equally. Since the political environment is becoming more turbulent, elected officials should adopt those policies that establish an acceptable political direction for their community. Management continuity should be provided by city managers and their staffs to ensure the administrative stability desired by the electorate. While the political leadership of a community may change, the administrative leadership of a municipality should provide continuity in these uncertain times.

Municipal program priorities, performance objectives, privatization practices, financial policies, and budget reduction goals should be determined by elected officials as a part of their decisionmaking and policy-setting process. It is incumbent upon city managers and department directors to implement these policy directives in a professional manner. These individuals—city managers and department directors—are specially trained to carefully review their operations, make productivity improvements, recommend new technologies and products, and suggest ways to reduce the costs of their services. During the past decade, governing bodies, city managers, and department directors have worked together closely to achieve these policy goals and to realign their municipal government in keeping with the desires of their elected representatives. It is critical that all of these parties work together to achieve these common community goals. The efforts of elected and appointed public officials to reduce costs, maintain or lower existing tax rates, and improve the productivity of their municipal organizations are highlighted below.

GENERAL PRODUCTIVITY TRENDS

Many of the productivity trends examined in this volume relate to individual municipal departments. Some of these trends cross functional lines and are applicable to other departments as well. A few of these trends are so generic that they apply almost equally to all municipal departments, regardless of their functional responsibilities. These general productivity trends are briefly reviewed in this section. They focus on ways to increase operational productivity, improve the quality of public services, increase revenues without raising taxes, streamline administrative processes, and demonstrate how to confront and resolve community issues and problems using new planning techniques. With few exceptions, most of these contemporary productivity practices are relatively easy and inexpensive to implement. Many of these trends reflect a changing municipal philosophy of working with citizens and community groups to get them involved in reducing the scope and costs of their government. More open management styles, user friendly organizations, public education on the "workings" of city hall, and programs to empower citizens to help themselves are the cornerstones of this new philosophy of municipal government.

Alternative Service Delivery Systems. The more traditional municipal departments like police, fire, and public works primarily use regular full-time employees to provide public services. The three most innovative departments to use alternative service delivery systems include health and human services, library, and parks and recreation. Limited budgets in these departments over the years have led to creative ways to maintain or expand services while holding down expenses. These alternative approaches to service delivery include the use of contract employees, contract service arrangements, joint agreements with other governments, citizen coproduction initiatives, private sponsorship and cosponsorship of programs, public/private partnerships, student internships, and using citizen volunteers to augment existing service levels. Existing labor agreements may restrict the use of some of these alternative delivery systems. These agreements should be thoroughly reviewed before making decisions to select an appropriate alternative service delivery system.

Budgeting Innovations. The type of budget format used in a municipality impacts all departments equally. For many years, most communities used the traditional line-item approach to budgeting. This budget format only contains a listing of anticipated departmental expenses during the fiscal year. Many elected officials and city managers are moving towards program budget formats, with performance measurements for individual programs. Program budgets not only show expenses but also describe the services that citizens are receiving for their tax dollars. The most sophisticated municipal budgets include the development of performance measurements for individual programs. These budgets assist city councils in making more informed funding decisions during their annual budget deliberation process. The development of meaningful municipal budgets is staff-intensive and thus may not exist in many smaller communities. The best budgets are likely to be found in larger cities that have the analytical staff to perform this type of work.

Citizen Advisory Bodies. Many municipal line departments have formal citizen advisory bodies. The most common advisory boards and commissions relate to library, parks and recreation, planning and building, and health and human services departments. Some communities have advisory bodies for their police department. When community issues arise that relate to any of these departments, city councils should routinely refer these issues for review and recommendation by these advisory bodies. Likewise, these department managers should refer all staff recommendations to these groups for their review and endorsement prior to presenting them to the governing body for their consideration. Since these groups are usually appointed by the city council and consist of citizens from the community, they represent the values of the municipality. The use of these citizen groups has helped to streamline the process of dealing with issues and problems relating to these departments. It has also helped to keep the cost of resolving issues and funding staff requests in line with the fiscal expectations of elected officials.

Civilianization Practices. Two municipal departments—police and fire—are affected by this trend. As the salaries and fringe benefits of sworn personnel (i.e. police officers and firefighters) have increased over the years, city councils and city managers have attempted to civilianize those positions for which sworn duties are not essential in performing the job. The use of civilian employees to fill previously sworn positions saves salary and fringe benefit costs. More importantly, highly paid sworn personnel should not be performing those job duties that could be performed by nonsworn employees. The general feeling is that police officers should be fighting crime and firefighters should be responding to emergency situations. This trend has served to make police officers and firefighters more productive. It has also enabled police and fire chiefs to assign nonsworn duties to civilian personnel. Communities of all sizes are using a greater number of civilians in these departments. This practice reflects sound management principles and also saves money.

Community Resource Centers. Two municipal departments either provide or have access to so many services that the available information needs to be assembled and made available to citizens in an abbreviated format. These departments include health and human services and parks and recreation. Health and human services departments typically have access to a variety of programs available from other public agencies as well as a host of nonprofit community organizations. Parks and recreation departments usually have information about different sports leagues, as well as a number of programs available to young people through local community organizations. When this information is assembled, it is usually provided to the municipal library since citizens expect to have easy access to this type of information. The codification of this information has helped to reduce service duplication between municipalities and nonprofit organizations. This is especially important in larger cities that have a diversity of services provided by a number of other public and nonprofit agencies.

Computers and New Technologies. New computer technologies and recent advances in software development have greatly impacted all municipal departments. The use of computer hardware and software has made employees more productive and at the same time increased the quality of services to the public. Not too long ago, each floor of city hall had only one central facsimile machine and photocopier. These "office tools" have become so valuable and inexpensive that it is not unusual for each department to have these pieces of equipment. Other technologies have included such devices as automated checkout systems in libraries, automated voting machines, and new energy monitoring and management systems. Many line departments now have access to an expanding market of new products and services available to improve their operations and programs. While most computers and new technologies do not replace employees, they increase their productivity, improve service quality, and generally hold down the need for future personnel. City councils are approving the use of technologies, products, and services that have a reasonable payback period.

Cost of Municipal Mandates. Cost-conscious city councils are now requiring that proposed legislation and departmental requests contain the estimated cost of implementation. This trend has impacted all municipal departments equally. In the past, many governing bodies would make decisions without knowing their financial impact. Because of limited revenues and greater public scrutiny and accountability, elected officials increasingly desire to know the fiscal impact of their legislative decisions. This has made department managers more conscious of the cost of their requests. It has also placed a greater emphasis on developing user fees to offset these operating costs. Some governing bodies will only consider requests for new programs that are financially self-sufficient. This trend has taken some of the politics out of funding service requests from special interest groups. When elected officials know the financial impact of their decisions on the public, it makes cost an important factor in their decisionmaking process.

Cost Containment. Virtually all department managers are under pressure to either hold the line or reduce their expenditures. While governing bodies may reduce staff departments first, increased scrutiny is being placed on line departments to keep their expenses more reasonable. In many cases, services are being provided by other agencies, community organizations, or even funded by the private sector. In parks and recreation and health and human services departments, for example, some of the full-time staff act as "brokers" or "facilitators" of public services. In the case of recreation services, a community may provide ballfields and lighting, and private sports leagues may get free use of the field for their games, but they may be required to pay for the cost of lighting and clean-up. Similarly, health officials have a knowledge of related services provided by local nonprofit organizations. More timely and frequent computer-generated expenditure reports assist department managers in staying within their approval budget allocations.

Economic Development. The increasing popularity of using economic incentives to attract private investment is having a significant impact on several departments. While elected officials approve these incentives, city managers work closely with planning and building managers to use these inducements to get new companies to locate or existing companies to relocate within their community. Finance directors are frequently involved in making calculations of tax abatements and other municipal concessions. Public works directors are responsible for the development and maintenance of their community's infrastructure. The condition of a city's capital assets is also critical to retaining and attracting companies to a community. City attorneys review these public/private agreements before they are submitted to the governing body. In order to revitalize aging downtown areas, public investment is being directed to these areas to stimulate future private investment. The economic development activities undertaken by a community requires a close working relationship among these municipal departments.

Financial Management. City councils are taking a more assertive role in the financial affairs of their community. It is now common for elected officials to adopt financial policies to guide the future fiscal health of their municipal organization. While many of these policies impact the finance director, others directly influence department managers. For example, the adoption of a debt ceiling policy would affect the public works director and other department managers. A policy that requires all new services to be cost-covering would impact all department managers equally. Finance directors are performing multiyear revenue and expenditure projections to identify future fiscal problems. All department managers now spend more time monitoring their annual budgets and reviewing their user fees to ensure that they are appropriate for the service provided. Special accounting funds such as intergovernmental service funds and enterprise funds are being used to control municipal expenses and revenues. Elected officials, city managers, and finance directors are spending more time than ever dealing with the financial affairs of their community.

Financing Public Services. The ongoing challenge to find equitable ways to finance public services has led to a variety of creative funding techniques and options. Alternative funding sources include possible state and federal grants, private sponsorship of public programs, and private funding from community groups, private foundations, and philanthropic organizations. Some departments with citizen support and advocacy groups—such as libraries and parks and recreation departments—now hold fundraising events to financially support "their" services. Revenue bonds are now being used to finance certain public facilities. Development impact fees are also being charged to the private sector to offset the cost of future municipal improvements and facilities. Utility connection fees and a host of other user fees are now being charged to help finance certain public services. Assessment districts are also being used to finance improvements that benefit only selected property owners. Great progress has been made in recent years to find equitable ways to finance public services.

Human Resources Management. A number of improved management practices in this area have helped to improve services, make employees more productive, and reduce personnel expenditures. Standardized testing, uniform job descriptions, equitable compensation plans, preemployment physical examinations, and drug testing have helped to attract and retain the best qualified employees. Many communities have initiated ongoing training programs to teach both supervisory and functional skills to employees. Because of the cost of salaries and fringe benefits, many cities carefully monitor their vacancies with the goal of pacing the filling of these positions. A position left vacant for three months, for example, usually saves one-fourth of the annual salary and fringe benefit costs budgeted for a particular position. Many cities now routinely use part-time employees, contract employees, student interns, and even volunteers in some departments. Since only full-time employees receive fringe benefits, these efforts have helped to reduce these expenses, which are frequently one-third of salary costs.

Innovative Public Services. Many municipal departments are providing self-help resources to citizens, valuable community educational programs, and are actually involving citizens in the direct provision of their public services. Self-help resources include library services such as job information centers, computer training workshops, and literacy programs. Some of these programs are even being financed and sponsored by community organizations and private companies. Health and human services departments frequently provide resource directories for use by citizens. Parks and recreation departments offer a variety of programs, some of which are provided by private instructors using city facilities. The city usually contracts with these instructors for a flat fee or receives a percentage of the registration revenues. Citizens directly assist in the coproduction of public services through recycling programs, neighborhood watch groups, citizen clean-up projects, adopt-a-park programs, donating through municipal gift ("wish list") catalogs, and other citizen volunteer programs. These types of municipal innovations are only limited by one's imagination.

Infrastructure Issues. Infrastructure issues have become important in recent years due to the past practice of neglecting the maintenance of municipal facilities. Many elected officials would rather fund more visible public services. Hence, issues such as those dealing with the municipal infrastructure have received a low priority over the years. Since city managers and department managers tend to concentrate on those issues important to elected officials, they have not taken the time to educate their governing bodies on the importance of the proper development and maintenance of a community's capital assets. There is a renewed awareness that the condition of a city's capital plant is essential for economic development planning, adds substantially to a community's quality of life, and is less expensive to maintain than to replace after they substantially deteriorate. Elected officials are requiring multiyear capital project plans and are actively exploring equitable ways to finance these community improvements. A variety of new financing tools have been initiated to fund the development of a community's infrastructure.

Interdepartmental Cooperation. Tight budgets and limited staffing have facilitated interdepartmental cooperation and coordination in the provision of municipal services. Pressure from elected officials and city managers have also facilitated this trend. Four primary examples are comprehensive code enforcement programs, emergency management responses, council-initiated budget reduction mandates, and the handling of citizen inquiries and complaints. Municipal code enforcement personnel in several departments now routinely cooperate in the identification, referral, and follow-up action on municipal code enforcement violations. Police, fire, and public works employees routinely cooperate when responding to emergency situations. All departments cooperate with the city manager's staff in processing citizen inquiries and complaints. Also, when asked to reduce their budgets by elected officials or the city manager, department managers work together for the common good of their community. This cooperation is spilling over into other areas of municipal organizations.

Intergovernmental Cooperation and Resource Sharing. The degree of cooperation among governments and the willingness to share their resources have increased in a number of different ways. Many communities have joint purchasing programs with their school district, other municipalities, their county, and even their state government. Economies of scale are being achieved through these joint purchasing programs. Libraries frequently share their written resources through regional and statewide interlibrary loan programs. Larger public works departments may share unique pieces of equipment with smaller neighboring communities. The same spirit of cooperation holds true for police and fire departments. Smaller police departments can call upon the resources of larger neighboring departments. Likewise, fire departments in smaller communities frequently request the use of specialized pieces of equipment from larger neighboring departments. The same spirit of cooperation also holds true for specialized personnel resources. Local, county, and state governments are increasingly cooperating with one another and sharing their resources.

Knowledge of Available Resources. Many municipal departments provide so many programs to citizens, have access to numerous important outside resources, and or have such a vast marketplace of services and products available to them that a working knowledge of these resources is essential to properly serve the public. Libraries, health and human services, and parks and recreation departments often provide so many programs that their staffs must be educated on these diverse assortments of services. City clerk and legal departments have access to a host of new computer software programs and or online services to improve their operations. Planning and building departments need to know about the economic development resources available from other nonprofit, educational, state, and federal sources. Police, fire, and public works departments also have access to new equipment and technologies to improve their operations and services. Department managers and their staffs must be aware of many internal and external resources available to help them improve their operations and services.

Management Styles. The astute department manager must adapt his or her management style to fit the needs of their organization, which must serve the interests of the community. In the past, many department directors managed relatively tranquil organizations, unaffected by the outside environment. Power in these organizations flowed from the top down, and change, when it occurred, was incremental in nature. Citizens, elected officials, and city managers now demand that departments be proactive and strive to serve the needs of their constituents. The most flexible organizations are required in library, health and human services, and parks and recreation departments. Public services in these functional areas are constantly changing based on the demands of citizens and available financial resources. Police chiefs have had to adapt their organizations to graft on new services such as community policing, and to actively use community volunteers, such as those involved in neighborhood watch programs. Traditional management styles were developed for "closed" organizations. More flexible management styles are required for these changing times.

Management Information Systems. Most communities have one or more stand-alone mainframe computer systems, as well as a number of microcomputers. Some of these microcomputers may be connected to the mainframe. The primary user of data processing services in the past has been the finance department. Now, many department managers and their employees are computer literate, are aware of software applications in their respective fields, and desire to fully automate their operations. Communities need to hire management information systems (MIS) directors, replace their aging central computer with an up-to-date mainframe, and "tie in" all user departments. Ideally, a municipality needs one main "host" computer with cables connecting all departmental workstations to this central computer. Departments also need microcomputers to use as stand-alone personal productivity systems. Departments with special needs can be interconnected via local area networks. The important thing is for an MIS director to serve the needs of all departments equitably. Smaller communities may wish to use a computer consultant to develop their computer network.

Management/Union Cooperation. The work environment in all departments is increasingly regulated by complex labor agreements that set forth wages, hours, and working conditions. Many changes to existing working conditions must be negotiated between representatives of management and employee unions. Those communities that have demonstrated positive organizational changes that have made workers more productive, improved services, and reduced costs usually have a good working relationship with all of their employee bargaining units. In fact, many cities, with the support of their governing bodies, have formed joint union/management productivity committees. Also, in many cases labor agreements require the advanced approval of employee unions before decisions to privatize or contract out for services can be made by elected officials. Because of this negotiated work environment, many organizations have reduced the number of their employees through attrition. This has helped to create and foster a positive relationship between a city's management team and employee unions.

Organizational Consolidations. Organizational downsizing can occur in three ways—either through a reduction in the number of employees, by merging programs within or between departments, or by consolidating municipal departments. Programs can be merged if their work activities are similar. For example, the grounds maintenance activities of parks and recreation departments and public works departments can be consolidated. Departments with similar functions can also be integrated. Following this simple guideline, some communities have merged their planning and building departments and health and human services departments. A few cities have even consolidated their police and fire agencies into public safety departments. Larger cities have also consolidated their cultural activities, such as libraries, museums and zoos. It would serve no purpose to consolidate programs or functions unless a positive result is achieved, such as monetary savings, improved services, or a reduction in the number of employees. Any organizational change, because of its potentially explosive impact, should be thoroughly planned in advance before actually being implemented.

Pricing Public Services. Charging for municipal services is frequently a desirable alternative to service reductions. Pricing individual public services is necessary prior to adopting user fees. In the past, many department managers merely calculated their direct labor costs when establishing user fees. City governments have learned a great deal from the private sector when it comes to placing a unit price tag on municipal services. User fees are now frequently based on three types of costs—direct, indirect, and overhead. Direct costs include salaries, materials, and supply expenses. Indirect costs typically encompass fringe benefit, pension, and insurance expenses. Department overhead expenses include administrative costs. Citywide overhead expenses include the cost of central management, finance, personnel, purchasing, and other staff departments. City managers and finance directors should make sure that proper instructions are given to department managers on how to properly price their services. Governing bodies have tended to approve fees for those municipal services that do not directly benefit the general public.

Privatization and Contract Services. While privatization practices have not gained much widespread popularity, almost every community has numerous contracts for services with various private companies. When public officials privatize a service, it means that their municipal government no longer provides the program. Examples of commonly privatized services include refuse collection, recycling, ambulance, transportation, and vehicle towing and storage. Contracts with private companies cover a wide variety of services in virtually all departments. There have been no studies that prove that privatization and contracting out for services are universally less expensive than similar services provided by municipal employees. When considering privatized or contract services, variables other than cost should be considered. Some of these variables include the loss of control, service quality, maintaining public accountability, controlling future cost, and requirements for handling citizen complaints. It is good policy to examine and compare the private versus public costs for municipal services, regardless of the final decision.

Professional Development. Professionalism in local government is on the increase, especially among technical personnel, middle management, department directors, city managers, and elected officials. Nearly all vocations and professions in municipal government have state and national professional associations. Since many communities have been forced to reduce the number of their employees, the professional development of those remaining personnel is essential for them to keep abreast of the latest development in their respective municipal functions. Many functional fields in local government are becoming more complex, and attendance at state and national conferences, as well as training sessions, is one of the best ways to stay current in one's field. Also, many of these professional associations now provide certification programs for their members. These programs not only attest to an employee's competency but also can be used to set a standard when hiring new personnel. These activities also provide valuable opportunities for professional networking and information sharing. The funds spent on professional development are considered a sound investment in a city's municipal workforce.

Public Education and Citizen Empowerment. One of the latest trends in municipal government is public education and citizen empowerment. An increasing number of departments are involved in these activities. Health and human services departments provide information on how to prevent illnesses, courses on wellness and nutrition, and disease prevention or screening clinics. Fire departments are educating young people on how to prevent fires and teaching private employees how to properly evacuate their building in case of an emergency. Police departments are involved in neighborhood watch, drug education for young people, and numerous other community crime prevention programs. Libraries educate and empower citizens on how to properly search for a job, use computers and software applications, and even learn English and mathematical skills. Parks and recreation departments provide courses to enable citizens to stay active and fit through aerobics and exercise classes, as well as develop lifelong interests in a number of different areas. Public works departments have empowered citizens to recycle and reduce their refuse collection and disposal costs. Many of these programs help reduce both the scope and cost of government services.

Public/Private Partnerships. Cooperation between city halls and the private sector is on the increase. Several municipal departments now provide services that are a direct result of joint public/private partnerships. For example, health and human services departments provide numerous medical clinics, some of which are staffed by volunteer doctors, dentists, and other private health professionals who volunteer their time for this purpose. Libraries provide computer training, job information centers, and other programs financed by local civic and nonprofit organizations. Many parks and recreational programs are underwritten by private companies, many of whom sponsor a particular service or event in return for the name recognition that goes along with this sponsorship. Police and fire chiefs also actively solicit contributions for needed equipment from private sector companies. In the area of economic development, local governments are waiving taxes and fees in return for additional municipal revenues and new jobs. All of these are positive trends. These programs, while they do not reduce the scope of government, help to hold down expenses and taxes.

Purchasing Practices. A great deal of government funds each year are spent purchasing goods and services from the private sector. Virtually all municipal departments are impacted by innovative purchasing practices. It is not unusual for smaller communities to ban together to make joint purchases or to have joint purchasing programs with their local school districts. Many smaller cities have also developed joint purchasing programs with larger cities, their county, or even state government. The economies of scale resulting from these joint efforts have achieved considerable savings. Rather than merely awarding contracts to the lowest bidder, lifecycle costing techniques include the costs of maintenance, training, availability of replacement parts, anticipated downtime, and follow-up services. A city may not wish to purchase an item from the lowest bidder if it is selling an inferior product. Rather than using formal bidding procedures for smaller purchases, existing monetary limits have been increased to permit informal price quotes thereby speeding up the purchasing process for smaller items. For scientific, professional, and technical services, a request for proposal is used since qualifications are as important as costs. The use of professionally trained and certified purchasing officers have facilitated these innovative practices.

Revenue Management. This task has taken on new importance in recent years since elected officials desire long-term revenue stability for their community. Many elected officials are now promoting financial self-sufficiency and are not relying on higher levels of government for monetary support. User fees are being used to finance many services that do not directly benefit the general public. User fees are also being updated with greater frequency to reflect the cost of doing business. Property assessments are being updated more frequently and tax collectors are taking a more aggressive approach to collecting their current accounts. Private collection agencies are even being used for past-due accounts. Treasury management practices are being updated to optimize a city's return on its investments. New fees are being implemented to assess private developers for the cost of future public improvements. Enterprise funds are being used to finance certain public services. Elected officials are taking a more assertive role by adopting financial policies that require the use of modern revenue management practices.

Safety and Risk Management. The efforts of elected and appointed officials to reduce their government's liability exposure, from the general public as well as municipal employees, has impacted all departments. While specialized employees like safety and risk managers may be housed in legal departments, their actions permeate all functions and operations within the municipal organization. Legal clauses are now commonly included in all contracts to limit a city's liability exposure. When citizen groups wish to use municipal facilities, they must sign carefully worded hold-harmless agreements. Safety experts are reviewing municipal services and facilities with the goal of eliminating identifiable risks to the public and employees. Employee safety committees review accidents, workplace regulations, and safety procedures to limit the number of employee injuries and lost time from work. The goal of these programs is to reduce the number of workers' compensation claims against a municipality. When a claim is filed against a community, the reason for the claim is investigated and corrected. Claims administration procedures have also been improved to limit a city's monetary loss.

Traditional vs. Strategic Planning. New types of proactive community planning practices have emerged in recent years to enable elected and appointed officials to resolve issues before they become problems and to mitigate problems before they become crises. Unlike the traditional planning techniques of the past, which have concentrated on goal-setting rather than results, strategic planning includes the development of a results-oriented action plan. While traditional planning tended to be top-down in its approach, strategic planning encompasses a more bottoms-up approach. Citizens are even involved in the governmental planning process, a practice unheard of only a few short years ago. Rather than have planners develop plans and then hold public hearings on these plans, working committees are formed around community issues that affect municipal departments. Frequently citizens and department directors work side-by-side to examine issues and problems facing their community. They also work together to develop action plans. In the future, this new planning technique should become institutionalized within the existing municipal planning function.

Working with the Community. In the past, city managers and department managers would make important decisions and develop critical policy recommendations in a political vacuum. Even city councils, on occasion, have made this mistake. Important policy matters should never be resolved in a political vacuum. When a new issue or problem surfaces that needs to be addressed, members of the governing body should routinely refer such items to their citizen advisory bodies. These groups can discuss, debate, and hold hearings on the issue before deciding upon a proposed recommendation for the city council's consideration. The same holds true for staff recommendations. Staff requests should also be sent to these advisory groups before being submitted to the governing body. Important programs and recommendations should never be developed introspectively. When a city manager or department director prepares a major plan, for example, this plan should be presented in a draft form to solicit the comments and views of those individuals and groups affected by the proposed plan. When the staff "politically processes" major plans and projects in this manner, they greatly assist elected officials in their decisionmaking process.

Departmental Productivity Trends

While some of the productivity trends examined in this volume relate generally to all departments, the great majority of these trends are only applicable to individual departments. While some of these concepts and practices may be generic, their actual application may be department-specific. For example, while the use of strategic planning may apply to all municipal departments, recent refinements in transportation planning only relate to the public works department. For this reason, many of the productivity trends examined cannot be applied across the board to all municipal operations but only in selective functional areas. Like general productivity trends, departmental productivity trends focus on ways to increase operational productivity, improve the quality of public services, increase revenue without raising taxes, and streamline administrative processes. While the goals of these efforts may be similar, their applications are not. These trends also reflect the changing political philosophy of working with community groups and program constituents to improve the quality of public services as well as to reduce their costs.

City Council. While members of local governing bodies do not implement these productivity and cost-reduction improvements, they adopt the policies and authorize the funds necessary to approve and finance them. For these reasons, mayors and city councils place a great deal of trust in their city manager and department directors to recommend sound policies consistent with these goals. When it comes to the use of computers and other new technologies, elected officials typically approve their acquisition so long as they have a reasonable payback period or substantially improve the quality of services to the public. Cost/benefit analyses are increasingly being used to justify many productivity improvements. Since one of the basic roles of the city council is to approve the annual budget, they are now demanding more meaningful budget documents, including program descriptions and performance measurements. Citizens are being used to coproduce municipal services and hold down local tax rates. Conversely, economic development incentives are being used to raise revenues without increasing taxes. Because of their large costs, creative ways to finance capital improvements are receiving increased attention by elected officials.

City Manager. The qualifications sought by elected officials in their chief administrators have changed over the years. City managers are expected to be "administrative entrepreneurs" by knowing about ways to stretch scarce budget funds, streamline operations, improve employee productivity, and increase the quality of public services. One of the ways to increase productivity is through the development and implementation of citywide computer-based management information systems. When department managers get immediate feedback on their work activities, it helps them control costs and improve their operations. The use of benchmarking techniques and quality improvement practices are increasing in popularity. While privatization has not dramatically increased, the use of contract services has escalated in most municipal departments. Infrastructure management and creative ways to finance capital projects have received increased attention because of the magnitude of their costs. City managers are also expected to be familiar with economic development incentives as well as ways to revitalize aging downtown areas. Methods to reduce salary and fringe benefit costs have also been essential since they represent the largest components of municipal budgets.

City Clerk. This function, for many citizens, serves as the focal point for their contact with their city government. New computer systems and software applications have helped city clerks to better serve the public as well as improve their internal operations. This is especially true in the areas of automated document storage and retrieval systems. The development of professional certification programs has helped to increase the level of professionalism within this function of city hall. Because of their desire to improve their operations, city clerks are using professional networking to find out about the best ways to automate their services. The number of contracts for services has increased in this department, especially in the areas of elections administration and municipal code codification. Due to the level of public trust placed in this office, city clerks have been given the responsibility for compliance with state "sunshine" laws, financial disclosure requirements, and the administration of ethics regulations. City clerks have been at the forefront of efforts to computerize municipal operations. In this regard, it is not unusual for these departments to have microcomputers at each workstation, share common databases, and link their computers together through local area networks.

Legal. City attorneys have focused in recent years on ways to reduce the public liability associated with the delivery of municipal services provided by their government. Safety and risk management specialists are frequently assigned to these departments to assist with this goal. These personnel are also involved with increasing workplace safety, investigating employee accidents, and reducing the number of on-the-job injuries. Many claims and lawsuits are now settled for reasons of economy rather than their legal merits. Increasingly, elected officials are desiring to know the cost of new legislative mandates. This has served to streamline many laws as well as lower the cost of their ongoing administration. New computer systems and software applications have given legal employees access to statewide and national databases, as well as numerous other legal resources. As opposed to increasing the size of their staff, many specialized legal services are now contracted out to private attorneys. Model ordinance services have facilitated the search and adoption of many municipal laws that have already been legally tested in other communities. The legal staff now routinely reviews proposed legislation and policies prepared by other line and staff departments before they are submitted to elected officials.

Finance. Finance directors have been critical players in the efforts of their municipal governments to increase revenues from a number of different sources. Multiyear expenditure and revenue forecasting has helped to identify future financial problems. The preparation of multiyear capital projects plans have enabled finance personnel to identify revenue sources for these projects. Computer-generated expenditure and revenue reports have helped to monitor departmental expenses and the receipt of municipal revenues. It is not unusual for copies of these reports to be distributed to elected officials. The periodic adjustment of user fees, techniques to increase interest income, and more aggressive tax assessment and collection practices have helped to optimize revenues from these existing sources. New accounting techniques such as special revenue funds, enterprise funds, and internal service funds are increasing in popularity. Contemporary funding techniques like development impact fees, utility connection charges, and special assessment districts are becoming commonplace. New computers and specialized software applications have facilitated these revenue-enhancement practices.

Fire. Fire chiefs have placed increased attention on fire prevention practices through citizen education programs. New building technologies and fire prevention codes have reduced the number of structural fires in many communities. Many fire departments are creating hazardous materials inventories, by specific company and address, to facilitate their firefighting efforts. Measures are also being taken to utilize the latest fire-related technologies and equipment. These efforts assist in emergency responses and also increase employee safety. The use of self-contained breathing apparatus, new fire-retardant clothing, and the removal of diesel exhaust fumes from fire stations, are now typical operating practices. New user fees are also being adopted for false alarms, fire inspections, plan checking, ambulance services, emergency medical services, and hazardous materials responses. Many cities are even charging private companies for the development of city-wide hazardous materials inventories. Some communities have even developed user charges to provide augmented levels of fire services for larger commercials buildings and high-rise residential structures. Because of the size of their budgets, fire chiefs have been under increasing pressure to reduce their costs and increase productivity.

Health and Human Services. Many departments have initiated community education and health-related clinics to reduce the long-term costs of this service area. Public assistance programs are being streamlined to include more rigorous application procedures, workfare requirements, and employment counseling services to reduce the number of citizens receiving general assistance payments. Statewide databases are also being developed to eliminate fraud in this service area of local government. Rather than hire full-time personnel, a number of contract employees—such as medical doctors, dentists, and other healthcare professionals—are being hired. Since a host of nonprofit organizations and other government agencies provide services in this area, many departments are developing community resource directories to assist citizens in seeking services and to eliminate service duplication. Many department managers are seeking foundation funding as well as private cosponsorship for their programs. Because grant funds have been substantially reduced, many communities have initiated user fees, typically based on one's ability to pay. Many governing bodies have formed citizen advisory bodies to assist them in responding to the health and human service needs of their community.

Library. Library directors have been forced to deal with limited budgets and creative service options for a number of years. The use of new technologies and equipment have increased the quality of service delivery and improved operational productivity. Library professionals have made an exemplary attempt to adapt their services to fit the changing needs of their community. Libraries have become valuable information and educational resources to their citizens by providing such resources as computer training, job information, and tutoring in English and mathematical skills, to name a few. Because libraries have been traditionally financed out of property tax revenues, many library professionals have sought private funding and corporate sponsorship for their programs. More library services are now being designed to educate and empower citizens to improve their lives. Some municipal libraries provide so many diverse services that they must educate their own employees on the variety of programs they offer to their citizens. Many library directors have initiated formal marketing programs to educate citizens of the number of programs available to the public. When services have been reduced, every effort has been made to maintain children's services. New technologies are being used to hold down future staffing needs.

Parks and Recreation. Many of these departments are managed by a small professional staff who work to leverage their services through a number of different creative management practices. Foremost in these efforts has been the trend to use a greater number of contract employees, seasonal workers, part-time employees, and community volunteers. These efforts have helped to reduce salary and fringe benefit costs. Department managers have developed flexible management styles and adaptable organizations due to the nature of their relationship with citizens. They have strived to provide alternative service delivery systems—including such initiatives as private funding and corporate sponsorship—for their programs. Because of the many public facilities operated by these departments, the Americans with Disabilities Act had made a significant impact on their operations and finances. Many user fees have also been implemented to generate additional revenues. Young people and senior citizens usually receive special treatment when these fees are implemented and or increased. Citizen coproduction techniques are commonly used to provide services at a minimal cost. Many department directors, out of necessity, have developed entrepreneurial management skills.

Planning and Building. These departments have implemented a number of new practices that increase municipal revenues. The administration of economic development incentives, downtown revitalization efforts, and new ways to finance community facilities are receiving top priority. One of the primary ways to manage growth has been through the use of development impact fees and the requirement that community facilities be in place before development occurs. Under this latter concept, if a developer wishes to construct a project before these facilities are available, these public improvements must be financed by the developer. Many communities have expanded their code enforcement programs to include historic preservation, aesthetic standards, and graffiti abatement, to name a new. An increasing number of court mandates and state and federal laws have served to limit the discretion of public officials in many areas of local planning. Economic development experts have developed and initiated many innovative public/private partnerships for the mutual benefit of a municipality and its corporate citizens. Public officials are increasingly aware that the cost of these partnerships should not exceed the value of the benefits received. This department has a number of citizen advisory bodies to assist elected officials and staff in resolving sensitive land-use and zoning issues.

Police. Even though police departments usually have the largest municipal budget, police chiefs have implemented a number of programs to limit their expenses and the number of police officers needed to protect the community. The greater use of civilian employees, fewer sworn personnel, new community policing practices, and new contemporary management practices to improve patrol scheduling and investigate priorities have also been implemented. A number of community crime prevention programs are being initiated to deter crimes before they occur. Citizen involvement in the coproduction of services have substantially held down the number of police officers needed to protect a community. A host of new citizen-assisted programs—

such as neighborhood watch, commercial crime watch, police reserve and auxiliary units—and the use of civilian volunteers have reduced the need for additional police officers. Community volunteers are typically being used to provide special support services. Many larger departments are also sharing their specialized human and technological resources with smaller neighboring communities. The largest budget expense in police departments is for salaries and fringe benefits. Many of these efforts have helped to hold the line on these cost items.

Public Works. Public works directors have made great strides in recent years to improve capital planning, develop creative financing alternatives, and improve the management of their existing capital assets. Recent mandates in the area of transportation funding have forced cities, counties, and states to jointly plan for integrated multimodal transportation systems to better serve the public. Several citizen oriented coproduction programs have helped to reduce the cost of solid waste collection and disposal. Other coproduction programs have reduced water consumption, the need for public facilities to capture stormwater runoff from private property, and municipal wastewater treatment costs. Most public works departments contract out specialized engineering services rather than increase the size of their staff for infrequent and or unique projects. Some cities are including and charging their engineering services to the general obligation bonds used to finance these projects. Because of the great diversity of public works services, many different employees such as engineers, transportation experts, water resource personnel, and maintenance and mechanical workers have helped to modernize the operations of public works departments. The use of computers and special software applications have improved productivity in all facets of this department.

THE FUTURE

City halls throughout America have undergone a revolution in the manner by which municipal services are financed and provided to citizens. Most public managers are embracing more flexible and adaptive management styles, are creating dynamic and responsive organizations, and are making sincere efforts to improve the quality of their services. Many departments are more open to their external environment than ever before in the history of municipal government. Significant numbers of elected officials and public managers are actively striving to create a "user friendly" interface between their organizations and the citizens they serve. Citizen feedback instruments, process improvement techniques, improved planning practices, and the use of new technologies have all served to facilitate these trends. Above all, since organizations are mere legal entities, the employees that spend their working lives in municipal governments should be recognized for embracing more positive

service philosophies, work attitudes, and operational practices. To have
effective government, roles must be clearly established and followed. Elected
officials must establish prudent public policies, department directors must be
held accountable for implementing these policies, and employees must be
managed to improve their operations and public services.

City managers and department managers have multiple responsibilities—
to the elected officials they serve, to the employees they manage, for the
effective use of organizational resources and, most importantly, to the citizens
they serve. These responsibilities are being effectively carried out along two
distinctly different dimensions. On the one hand, municipal organizations are
becoming more "user friendly" because managers have embraced a more customer orientated management philosophy. On the other hand, employee productivity has been increased through the use of new computer hardware, software application, and other technological innovations. Local government
services have, and will always be, primarily labor-intensive. While technological devices have improved operations and the quality of public services,
they will never replace municipal workers who actually perform services. For
this reason, while technologies may improve services and operations, they are
only a tool to achieve the goal of improved customer satisfaction. While the
use of technologies may reduce the need for additional employees in the future,
few cities have witnessed significant employee layoffs as a result of automation. For this reason, municipal organizations will be more productive in the
future with the same number, or fewer, employees.

The word "manager" is a noun that merely denotes a level of responsibility. The term "managing," on the other hand, is a verb that reflects the
dynamic process of directing employees and organizational resources to achieve
greater level of customer satisfaction. The many productivity trends examined
in this volume can only be realized through the efforts of managers, working
to continuously improve their operations—the process by which public services are provided. Many of these trends reflect ways to empower employees
and citizens, to improve the quality of services or to reduce their costs in light
of static or diminishing organizational resources. When financial resources are
diminished, the number of employees must be reduced since municipal organizations are labor intensive. To a great extent, new technologies have improved
operations to the point where fewer employees may be needed to provide the
same level and quality of services that has been expected by citizens in the
past. This does not mean that every additional piece of technology will result
in fewer and fewer employees. There is a point of diminishing returns, since
technologies are only a tool to serve employees who are responsible for providing public services. Citizens do not blame technologies when they have a
negative encounter with their city government. It is employees—at all levels—
who must be held accountable for the quality of their organization's public
services.

To create a productive and achieving workplace, elected officials must hold their city managers accountable for the effective management of their organizations. City managers in turn must hold department directors accountable for the effective management of their respective operations. The role performed by governing bodies is critical, since elected officials both represent and reflect the values and desires of a community's citizens. Citizens, after all, are the ones that "foot the bill" for the financial resources needed to operate municipal organizations. The ultimate goal of municipal government is to create citizen satisfaction at a reasonable cost. This does not mean pleasing all of the people all of the time. In the democratic process that takes place in local government decisionmaking, the will of the electorate is expressed through the majority. While good government policies attempt to satisfy dissenting options, all citizens and special interest groups cannot be satisfied all of the time. In many instances, regardless of the policies or programs adopted, opposing viewpoints will always exist. Generally, the more homogeneous the population of a community, the less people will feel alienated from their government. Conversely, the more heterogeneous the population of a community, the greater the likelihood of citizen dissatisfaction with their government. While the political environment in which an organization exists may change and the public services may vary, the operating goals of managers should be consistent.

Both the structure and process of municipal government are also changing. From a structural standpoint, more and more communities are changing to the council-manager form of government. This is because citizens have a higher comfort level with the characteristics of this form of municipal government. The separation of policymaking from administration, using highly trained managers, and hiring employees based on qualifications and merit have served to fulfill citizen demands for effective governance. Many citizens have also embraced the corporate model of organization, since it represents the best qualities of private corporations. In this respect, citizens expect their governing body to act like a corporation's board of directors. While more rational administrative structures are evolving, the process by which citizens are elected to public office is being debated in many communities. At-large elections are now the most dominant election process in many smaller and more homogeneously populated communities. The use of district elections, however, is on the increase in larger metropolitan cities with diverse populations. While many citizens may debate the process by which public offices are obtained, few citizens are debating the structure by which their services are being provided under the council-manager plan. As the structure and process of local governments evolve in the future, it is the will of the electorate that is being satisfied by these changes.

The financing of local government has undergone drastic changes in recent years. If the fees charged for the services provided by city halls generated a profit, they would be performed by the private sector. Most municipal services are financed out of local property taxes because they promote the general health and welfare of the community or they generally contribute to a city's quality of life. While service charges have increased, most municipal services will never be totally cost covering. An example is how much a city might charge a citizen for a police car responding to a burglary or a fire apparatus responding to a residential fire. These fees would easily be cost prohibitive to taxpayers, forcing citizens to buy a handgun to protect themselves or to use a garden hose to extinguish a residential fire. This same philosophy holds true for other municipal services. The most dramatic shift in financing has occurred for capital projects. Development impact fees and charges for community facilities have shifted the financial burden for new public improvements from taxpayers to the private development community. Enterprise funds are a step in the right direction for those services that only benefit their users and not the general public. Taxpayers in general should not pay for those services that they do not directly use, especially when they do not benefit the general public or enhance the quality of their lives. The users of these services should pay the cost necessary to make them cost covering.

Change in municipal organizations is invariably incremental. Over the past few decades, these small increments have charted the future path and established trends for the coming years in local government. While the goal of high quality services to the public will not change, the multitude of avenues available to achieve this goal is in a state of transition. And though the interface between a municipal organization and its clients will remain one-on-one (employee to citizen), a variety of processes are available to streamline and improve the manner in which these services are provided. For the most part, public officials in each community are doing their own thing in the dynamic and changing field of municipal government. This volume describes the operations of a typical municipal government and takes stock of the numerous productivity trends being initiated in our city halls. The goal of this work is to codify this information and make it available to others who have an interest in this field—elected officials, professionals, citizens, and students—and to assist them in improving the performance of America's municipal governments. Elected officials will obtain an essential overview of municipal operations and departmental productivity trends. Local government professionals will find the information invaluable to improve their operations and job performance. Citizens will become educated about numerous innovative ways to improve the quality of their services, increase productivity at their city hall, and reduce the cost of their government.

MUNICIPAL RESOURCE DIRECTORY

Major professional associations and research organizations serving municipal government.

City Clerk

Organization: International Institute of Municipal Clerks
Address: 1206 North San Dimas Canyon Road
Sam Dimas, CA 91773
Telephone: (909) 592-4462
FAX: (909) 592-1555
Toll Free: None
Contact: John Devine, Executive Director
Type: Nonprofit membership organization
Members: City clerks in all types of municipal governments
Research: Research service provided for members
Topics: Procedures of local government and the municipal clerk
Resources: Annual conference, educational programs, library, newsletter, directories, surveys, and professional certification program
Mission: To prepare members to meet the challenge of diverse roles of the municipal clerk by providing services and continuing professional development opportunities to benefit members and the government entities they serve
Established: 1947

City Council

Organization: National League of Cities
Address: 1301 Pennsylvania Avenue, N.W. 6th Floor
Washington, DC 20004

Telephone: (202) 626-3000
FAX: (202) 626-3043
Toll Free: None
Contact: Donald J. Borut, Executive Director
Type: Nonprofit membership organization
Members: 49 state municipal leagues and various cities across the United States.
Research: Research service provided for members
Topic: Various issued related to municipal governments of all types, sizes, and geographic locations
Resources: Annual conference, educational programs, newsletter, publications, library, directories, and special reports
Mission: To serve as an advocate for its members in Washington, DC in the legislative, administrative, and judicial processes that affect them; and to develop and pursue a national urban policy that meets the present and future needs of our nation's cities and the people who live in them
Established: 1924

Organization: United States Conference of Mayors
Address: 1620 Eye Street, N.W., 4th Floor
                 Washington, DC 20006
Telephone: (202) 293-7330
FAX: (202) 293-2352
Toll Free: None
Contact: J. Thomas Cochran, Executive Director
Type: Nonprofit membership organization
Members: Mayors of cities with populations over 30,000
Research: Research service provided for members
Topics: Economic development, health, employment and training, criminal justice, housing, and solid waste; and related municipal and regional issues
Resources: Annual conference, educational programs, legislative services, newsletter, sample resolutions, publications, and special reports
Mission: To aid the development of effective national urban policy, strengthen federal-city relationships, ensure that federal policy meets urban needs, and provide mayors with leadership and management tools of value to their cities
Established: 1932

City Manager

Organization:	International City/County Management Association
Address:	777 North Capitol Street, N.E., 5th Floor
	Washington, DC 20002
Telephone:	(202) 289-4262
FAX:	(202) 962-3500
Toll Free:	(800) 745-8780 (Publications)
Contact:	William H. Hansell, Jr., Executive Director
Type:	Nonprofit professional and educational organization
Members:	Administrators serving cities, counties, districts and regions
Research:	Research service provided for members
Topics:	Management, forms of government, community relations, finance, personnel/human resources, police and fire, research resources, public works, environmental management, service delivery management, information systems, technology management, planning and economic development, international management, purchasing, human services; and other municipal, county, and regional government issues
Resources:	Annual conference, educational programs, training institute, job bulletin, newsletter, periodical, library, publications, textbooks, directories, special reports, surveys, videos, and electronic networking
Mission:	To enhance the quality of local government through professional management and to support and assist professional local government administrators internationally
Established:	1914

Organization:	International Personnel Management Association
Address:	1617 Duke Street
	Alexandria, VA 22314
Telephone:	(703) 549-7100
FAX:	(703) 684-0948
Toll Free:	(800) 776-4762
Contact:	Donald K. Tichenor, Executive Director
Type:	Nonprofit membership organization
Members:	Human resource professionals and managers; federal, state, and local government agencies; consultants and teachers
Research:	Research service provided for members
Topics:	Diversity in the workplace, complaint handling, dispute resolution; and other personnel, human resource, labor relations, and legal issues

Resources: Annual conference, library, newsletter, periodical, information packets, publications, books, special reports, and directories

Mission: To promote excellence in human resource management through the ongoing development of professional and ethical standards, and through its publishing and educational training programs

Established: 1973

Organization: National Public Employer Labor Relations Association
Address: 1620 Eye Street, N.W., 4th Floor
Washington, DC 20006
Telephone: (202) 296-2230
FAX: (202) 293-2352
Toll Free: None
Contact: Roger E. Dahl, Executive Director
Type: Nonprofit membership organization
Members: Federal, state, and local governments, and special district professionals involved in labor relations.
Research: Research service provided for members
Topics: Smart bargaining, family and medical leave, drug and alcohol abuse in the workplace, and other issues related to personnel and labor relations
Resources: Annual conference, library publications, newsletter, contract clause reference manual, strike contingency planning manual, computerized information exchange, guidebooks, special reports, and videos
Mission: To provide a voice for public sector management and labor relations professionals in the development of state and national policy affecting personnel and labor relations
Established: 1971

Organization: Public Technology, Inc.
Address: 1301 Pennsylvania Avenue, N.W., Suite 800
Washington, DC 20004
Telephone: (202) 626-2400
FAX: (202) 626-2498
Toll Free: None
Contact: Costis Toregas, President
Type: Nonprofit organization
Members: Municipal, county, and regional governments
Research: Research service provided for members
Topics: Computers, economic development, environment, human services, infrastructure, management, planning techniques, public works, and related municipal, county, and regional government issues

Resources:	Annual meeting, educational programs, seminars, workshops, newsletter, library, information exchange, technical assistance, electronic networking, special reports, the Public Enterprise Program, and the PTI Investment Fund
Mission:	To create and advance new services and products in local governments based on technological progress and the spirit of public enterprise
Established:	1971

Finance

Organization:	Government Finance Officers Association
Address:	180 North Michigan Avenue, Suite 800
	Chicago, IL 60601
Telephone:	(312) 977-9700
FAX:	(312) 977-4806
Toll Free:	None
Contact:	Jeffrey L. Esser, Executive Director
Type:	Nonprofit membership organization
Members:	Finance officers from city, county, state, and federal governments; schools and other special districts; colleges, universities, public accounting firms, and financial institutions
Research:	Research service provided for members
Topics:	Budgeting and financial planning, investments, retirement administration and finance, capital finance, and debt administration
Resources:	Annual conference, educational programs, newsletter, periodical, library, databases, publications, textbooks, and other special and technical reports
Mission:	To enhance members' technical skills, obtain up-to-date information, broaden their knowledge base, provide professional recognition programs, develop leadership abilities, and networking with peers
Established:	1906

Organization:	Institute of Internal Auditors
Address:	249 Maitland Avenue
	Altamonte Springs, FL 32701-4201
Telephone:	(407) 830-7600
FAX:	(407) 831-5171
Toll Free:	None
Contact:	William G. Bishop III, President

Type: Nonprofit membership organization
Members: Internal auditors and accountants from the private, nonprofit, and public sector, including all levels of governments and special districts
Research: Research service provided for members
Topics: Standards and practices for internal auditing and internal control for public, private, and nonprofit sector agencies and organizations
Resources: Annual conference, educational programs, newsletter, periodical, publications, books, technical reports, library, and special activities for officials involved in governmental and public affairs
Mission: To provide comprehensive professional development activities and the standards for the practice of internal auditing and to research, disseminate, and promote knowledge and information about internal auditing and internal control
Established: 1941

Organization: International Association of Assessing Officers
Address: 130 East Randolph Street, Suite 850
                Chicago, IL 60601
Telephone: (312) 819-6100
FAX: (312) 819-6149
Toll Free: None
Contact: John Eckenroad, Executive Director
Type: Nonprofit organization
Members: State and local officials at all levels of government concerned with valuation of property for *ad valorem* property tax purposes
Research: Research service provided for members
Topics: Property appraisal techniques, real estate assessment practices, geographic information systems, and other issued related to state-of-the-art appraisal and assessment practices
Resources: Annual conference, educational programs, newsletter, periodical, publications, library, guidebooks, special reports, and technical assistance
Mission: To provide leadership in accurate property valuation, property tax administration, and tax policy throughout the world
Established: 1934

Organization: Municipal Treasurers Association
Address: 1229—19th Street, N.W.
                Washington, DC 20036
Telephone: (202) 833-1017
FAX: (202) 833-0375

Toll Free:	None
Contact:	Stacey L. Crane, Executive Director
Type:	Nonprofit membership organization
Members:	Treasurers in municipal and county governments
Research:	Research service provided for members
Topics:	Debt management and administration, investing public funds, capital financing, cash management, revenue management, financial management, retirement administration, financial reporting, computer applications, and related local government treasury issues
Resources:	Annual conference, educational programs, newsletter, periodical, library, guidebooks, surveys, technical assistance, legislative services, and professional certification program
Mission:	To enhance local treasury management by providing educational training, technical assistance, legislative services, and a forum for treasurers to exchange ideas and develop policy papers and positions
Established:	1965

Organization:	National Institute of Governmental Purchasing
Address:	11800 Sunrise Valley Drive, Suite 1050
	Reston, VA 22091
Telephone:	(703) 715-9400
FAX:	(703) 715-9897
Toll Free:	None
Contact:	J. E. Brinkman, Executive Vice President
Type:	Nonprofit membership organization
Members:	Government buying agencies of the United States, Canada, and other nations
Research:	Research service provided for members
Topics:	Governmental buying, purchasing laws, procurement management, recycling, negotiating, specification writing, cost-saving programs, and other issues relating to purchasing
Resources:	Annual conference, educational programs, research programs, newsletter, periodical, technical bulletins, technical information exchange, library, dictionary of purchasing terms, guidebooks, surveys, research projects, technical and consulting services, professional certification program, and the Commodities Service Index
Mission:	To establish and maintain professional function and stature for the field of public sector purchasing and materials management
Established:	1944

Fire

Organization: International Association of Fire Chiefs
Address: 4025 Fair Ridge Drive
                Fairfax, VA 22033-2868
Telephone: (703) 273-9011
FAX: (703) 273-9363
Toll Free: None
Contact: Gary L. Briese, Executive Director
Type: Nonprofit membership organization
Members: Fire chiefs in city and state departments, industry, and military installations from 26 countries
Research: Research service provided for members
Topics: Fire rescue, management, risk management, fire prevention, emergency medical services, and related fire prevention and suppression issues
Resources: Annual conference, educational programs, library, newsletter, periodical, publications, books, manuals, special reports, and electronic networking
Mission: To provide members throughout the international community with information, educational programs, services, and representation to enhance their professionalism and capabilities
Established: 1893

Organization: National Fire Protection Association
Address: 1 Batterymarch Park
                Post Office Box 9101
                Quincy, MA 02269-9101
Telephone: (617) 770-3000
FAX: (800) 593-6372
Toll Free: (800) 344-3555
Contact: George D. Miller, President
Type: Nonprofit membership organization
Members: Fire safety professionals and volunteers in city, county, state, and federal government; and special districts
Research: Research service provided for members
Topics: All aspects of fire suppression, prevention, hazardous materials handling and management, emergency response and management, emergency medical services, and related issues
Resources: Seminars, educational programs, newsletter, periodical, publications, textbooks, guidebooks, videos, and electronic networking
Mission: To safeguard people and their environment from destructive

fire using scientific and engineering techniques and education; to develop and publish consensus standards intended to minimize the possibility and effects of fire; and to educate the public in ways to avoid loss of life and property from fire by making fire safety habits a way of life

Established: 1896

Health and Human Services

Organization:	American Public Health Association
Address:	1015—15th Street, N.W., 3rd Floor
	Washington, DC 20005
Telephone:	(202) 789-5600
FAX:	(202) 789-5661
Toll Free:	None
Contact:	William H. McBeath, Executive Director
Type:	Nonprofit professional organization
Members:	Includes physicians, nurses, educators, environmentalists, social workers, pharmacists, dentists, community and mental health specialists, and health administrators in the private, nonprofit, and public sectors
Research:	Research service provided for members
Topics:	Administration and management, communicable diseases, community health practice, environmental health, international health, laboratory practice, public health issues, occupational injury and disease, innovative health programs, and the future of health
Resources:	Annual conference, educational programs, newsletter, periodical, library, publications, textbooks, reference manuals, guidebooks, technical reports, job placement service, and special interest groups
Mission:	To set standards, participate in research and matters concerning the profession, and influence public health policy via committees and coalitions with related groups
Established:	1872
Organization:	American Public Welfare Association
Address:	810 First Street, N.E., Suite 500
	Washington, DC 20002
Telephone:	(202) 682-0100
FAX:	(202) 289-6555
Toll Free:	None

Contact:	A. Sidney Johnson III, Executive Director
Type:	Nonprofit membership organization
Members:	Public welfare agencies and staff members in municipal, county, state, and federal government
Research:	Research services provided for members
Topics:	Management, computer applications, caseload administration, innovative public welfare programs, employment services, health care, and related public welfare issues
Resources:	Regional conferences, educational programs, newsletter, periodical, library, publications, journals, technical reports, directories, and legislative advocacy
Mission:	To develop and advocate for effective public policies that improve the lives of low-income individuals
Established:	1930

Organization:	National Environmental Health Association
Address:	720 South Colorado Boulevard, Suite 970
	South Tower
	Denver, CO 80222
Telephone:	(303) 756-9090
FAX:	(303) 691-9490
Toll Free:	None
Contact:	Nelson E. Fabian, Executive Director
Type:	Nonprofit membership organization
Members:	Environmental health professionals and technical personnel in all levels of government as well as the private and nonprofit sectors
Research:	Research service provided for members
Topics:	Issues related to environmental health and protection
Resources:	Annual conference, educational programs, newsletter, periodicals, library, publications, guidebooks, technical reports, special reports, and directories
Mission:	To promote and encourage research, education, and professional meetings, and the dissemination of information; to publish information relating to environmental health and protection; and to promote professionalism in the field
Established:	1937

Legal

Organization:	National Institute of Municipal Law Officers
Address:	1000 Connecticut Avenue, N.W., Suite 902
	Washington, DC 20036

Telephone:	(202) 466-5424
FAX:	(202) 785-0152
Toll Free:	None
Contact:	Benjamin L. Brown, Executive Director
Type:	Nonprofit professional organization
Members:	Chief legal officers for cities, counties, special districts, and other municipal corporations
Research:	Research service provided for members
Topics:	Laws and ordinances; contracts; court decisions; innovative solutions to perennial problems; latest developments in local, state, and federal laws affecting municipalities; and other municipal-related legal issues
Resources:	Annual conference, educational programs, newsletter, periodical, library, publications, books, sample contracts, model laws and ordinances, surveys, electronic networking, the MuniFax Program, the On-Line System, and professional certification program
Mission:	To provide for the development of municipal law by means of education, publications, research, communications, and mutual cooperation; and to assist its members and others who are interested in the development of municipal law and the effective administration of municipal law departments
Established:	1935

Organization:	Public Risk Management Association
Address:	1815 North Ft. Myer Drive, Suite 1020
	Arlington, VA 22209
Telephone:	(703) 528-7701
FAX:	(703) 528-7966
Toll Free:	None
Contact:	Dennis M. Kirschbaum, Executive Director
Type:	Nonprofit membership organization
Members:	Public agency risk, insurance, and or safety managers from cities, counties, villages, towns, school boards, and other related areas
Research:	Research service provided for members
Topics:	Public sector risk management, tort liability, public officials liability, law enforcement liability, employee assistance programs, workers' compensation case management, risk financing, workplace risks, and related public risk issues
Resources:	Annual conference, educational programs, newsletter, periodical, publications, guidebooks, manuals, surveys, technical reports, special reports, directories, workplace management, and risk management information network

Mission: To advise public agencies on liability and other exposures that affect their operations, and to improve the operation of state and local governments through proven risk management techniques
Established: 1978

Library

Organization: American Library Association
Address: 50 East Hurton Street
          Chicago, IL 60611
Telephone: (312) 944-6780
FAX: (312) 944-2641
Toll Free: (800) 545-2433
Contact: Mary Ghikas, Acting Executive Director
Type: Nonprofit membership organization
Members: Managerial, professional, and technical employees in library agencies and organizations in all levels of government, as well as the private and nonprofit sectors
Research: Research service provided for members
Topics: All aspects of library services, including administration and management, literacy, early reading, facilities management, library science, library trends, reference services, technical services, acquisitions and collections, children and young adult services, and the future of libraries
Resources: Annual conference, educational programs, newsletter, periodicals, publications, textbooks, guidebooks, reference books, and electronic networking
Mission: To assist libraries and librarians in promoting and improving library service and librarianship
Established: 1876

Organization: Special Libraries Association
Address: 1700—18th Street, N.W.
          Washington, DC 20009-2508
Telephone: (202) 234-4700
FAX: (202) 265-9317
Toll Free: None
Contact: David R. Bender, Executive Director
Type: Nonprofit membership organization
Members: Individuals and or organizations having a professional, scientific, or technical interest in library and information science

Research:	Research service provided for members
Topics:	Administration and management, acquisitions and collections, library and information science, recording and retrieval systems, state of the art technologies, methods for the dissemination of knowledge and information, and information management systems
Resources:	Annual conference, educational programs, newsletter, periodical, publications, library, guidebooks, reference books, technical reports, and special reports
Mission:	To promote and improve the communication, dissemination, and use of information and knowledge for the benefit of libraries and other educational organizations
Established:	1909

Parks and Recreation

Organization:	National Recreation and Park Association
Address:	2775 South Quincy Street, Suite 300
	Arlington, VA 22206-2204
Telephone:	(703) 820-4940
FAX:	(703) 671-6772
Toll Free:	None
Contact:	R. Dean Tice, Executive Director
Type:	Nonprofit membership organization
Members:	Professionals in the parks, recreation, and leisure field at the national, state, and local levels of government
Research:	Research service provided for members
Topics:	Management and administration, recreation planning, park planning, maintenance, programming, therapeutic recreation, legal issues, fitness and safety, leisure research and education, facilities management, park and recreation trends, and the future of parks and recreation services
Resources:	Annual conference, educational programs, newsletters, periodicals, publications, textbooks, guidebooks, directories, electronic networking, videos, and professional networking through special interest groups
Mission:	To promote the importance of recreation and parks and to ensure that all people have an opportunity to find the best and most satisfying use of their leisure time in national, state, and municipal parks
Established:	1898

Planning and Building

Organization: American Planning Association
Address:　　122 So. Michigan Avenue, Suite 1600
　　　　　　Chicago, IL 60603
Telephone:　(312) 431-9100
FAX:　　　　(312) 431-9985
Toll Free:　 None
Contact:　　Frank So, Executive Director
Type:　　　 Nonprofit membership organization
Members:　 Public and private planning agency officials, professional planners, planning educators, elected and appointed officials, and other persons involved in urban and rural development
Research:　 Research service provided for members
Topics:　　 Environmental regulations, zoning, land-use planning, open space, growth management, strategic planning, capital facilities planning, wetlands management, economic development, transportation, all levels of planning responsibilities, and related planning issues
Resources:　Annual conference, educational programs, newsletter, publications, textbooks, guidebooks, videos, library, electronic networking, bibliographies, technical and special reports, and professional certification program
Mission:　　To give members systematic ways to work on problems in common and to affect national planning policies
Established: 1909

Organization: Building Officials & Code Administrators International
Address:　　4051 Flossmoor Road
　　　　　　Country Club Hills, IL 60478-5795
Telephone:　(708) 799-2300
FAX:　　　　(708) 799-4981
Toll Free:　 None
Contact:　　Clarence R. Bechtel, Chief Executive Officer
Type:　　　 Nonprofit professional organization
Members:　 Code officials, architects, engineers, contractors and building industry officials
Research:　 Research service provided for members
Topics:　　 Building codes, code enforcement, planning and management, public safety, energy conservation, and other issues related to building and code administration and enforcement
Resources:　Annual conference, educational programs, newsletter, periodical, publications, guidebooks, code handbooks, building code

directories, building code handbooks, model codes, consulting, and technical and special reports

Mission: To provide a forum for the exchange of knowledge and ideas concerning building safety and construction regulation, and to achieve excellence and professionalism in code enforcement

Established: 1915

Organization: International Conference of Building Officials
Address: 5360 South Workman Mill Road
                  Whittier, CA 90601-2258
Telephone: (310) 699-0541
FAX: (310) 692-3853
Toll Free: (800) 336-1963
Contact: John S. Traw, President
Type: Nonprofit membership organization
Members: Code officials, architects, engineers, contractors, and building industry officials
Research: Research service provided for members
Topics: Building codes, code enforcement, administration and management, public safety, energy conservation, fire prevention, building inspection, engineering, plan review, and other issues related to building and code administration and enforcement
Resources: Annual conference, educational programs, newsletter, periodical, publications, textbooks, guidebooks, code handbooks, building code directories, model codes, consulting, Uniform Building Code, related codes (mechanical, plumbing, housing, signs, dangerous buildings, and fire prevention), videos, technical and special reports, professional certification programs, and ICBO Evaluation Service
Mission: To develop and maintain uniform codes, to evaluate new building products and systems, to develop educational and certification programs, to provide management studies of building departments, and to provide consulting services on code matters
Established: 1922

Organization: International Downtown Association
Address: 915—15th Street, N.W., Suite 600
                  Washington, DC 20005
Telephone: (202) 783-4963
FAX: (202) 347-2161
Toll Free: None
Contact: Richard H. Bradley, President

Type: Nonprofit membership organization

Members: Redevelopment agencies and individuals professionally involved in downtown and central city improvement and revitalization

Research: Research service provided for members

Topics: Downtowns of the future, building the framework for the inner-city, downtown development and redevelopment, and related downtown issues

Resources: Annual conference, educational programs, newsletter, periodical, publications, books, handbooks, technical and special reports, directories, videos, technical and special reports, directories, videos, and the Downtown Development Foundation

Mission: To improve downtown and adjacent neighborhoods as attractive places to live, work, shop, and be entertained; to shape appropriate public and private sector policies for the center city; and to communicate the importance of downtowns to the public as the hub of economic activity for the city and the region

Established: 1940

Organization: National Association of Housing & Redevelopment Officials

Address: 1320—18th Street, N.W.
Washington, DC 20036

Telephone: (202) 429-2960

FAX: (202) 429-9684

Toll Free: None

Contact: Richard Y. Nelson, Jr., Executive Director

Type: Nonprofit membership organization

Members: Individuals and public agencies engaged in community rebuilding by community development, public housing, large-scale private or cooperative housing rehabilitation, and the conservation of existing neighborhoods through housing code enforcement, voluntary citizen action, and government action

Research: Research service provided for members

Topics: Management and administration, maintenance, procurement, public and private housing, homeless person assistance, neighborhood commercial rehabilitation, housing vouchers, and related housing and redevelopment issues

Resources: Annual conference, educational programs, library, newsletter, periodical, publications, books, handbooks, directories, dictionary of terms, legislative advocacy, special reports, and technical information

Mission: To provide safe, decent, and affordable housing for low- and moderate-income persons

Established: 1933

Organization: National Community Development Association
Address: 522—21st Street, N.W., Suite 120
                 Washington, DC 20006
Telephone: (202) 293-7587
FAX: (202) 877-5546
Toll Free: None
Contact: Diane Taylor, Director
Type: Nonprofit membership organization
Members: Community development program directors
Research: Research service provided for members
Topics: Management and administration, local community develop-
                 ment, economic development, social development, funding
                 sources, citizen participation, and other issues related to local
                 community development activities and issues
Resources: Annual conference, educational programs, newsletter, periodi-
                 cal, publications, library, books, guidebooks, resource books,
                 directories, and technical and special reports
Mission: To assist local governments to achieve high-quality, locally
                 responsive programs for making communities better places to
                 live and work, particularly for low and moderate income peo-
                 ple
Established: 1970

Organization: National Council for Urban Economic Development
Address: 1730 "K" Street, N.W., Suite 915
                 Washington, DC 20006
Telephone: (202) 223-4735
FAX: (202) 223-4745
Toll Free: None
Contact: Jeffrey A. Finkle, Executive Director
Type: Nonprofit membership organization
Members: Individuals and public, private, and nonprofit agencies involved
                 with national and international economic development projects
                 and activities
Research: Research service provided for members
Topics: General economic development, financing tools and options,
                 neighborhood revitalization, legislative analyses, information
                 on job retention and creation, international economic develop-
                 ment, and other issues related to urban economic development
Resources: Annual conference, educational programs, newsletter, periodi-
                 cal, publications, library, legislative reports, special reports, and
                 technical assistance and information
Mission: To develop policies for local economic development; share

proven techniques to stimulate economic growth; and monitor, analyze, and communicate current legislation affecting urban economic development to members

Established: 1967

Organization:	National Housing Conference
Address:	815—15th Street, N.W., Suite 601
	Washington, DC 20005
Telephone:	(202) 393-5772
FAX:	(202) 393-5656
Toll Free:	None
Contact:	Robert J. Reid, Executive Director
Type:	Nonprofit membership organization
Members:	Professional and technical people employed at the federal, state, county, and municipal levels of government, as well as the private and nonprofit sectors
Research:	Research service provided for members
Topics:	All housing-related issues at all levels of government
Resources:	Annual conference, educational programs, newsletter, periodical, publications, library, technical assistance, legislative advocacy, special reports, and technical information
Mission:	To promote better communities and housing for Americans through legislative action
Established:	1931

Police

Organization:	International Association of Chiefs of Police
Address:	515 North Washington Street
	Alexandria, VA 22314-2357
Telephone:	(703) 836-6767
FAX:	(703) 836-4543
Toll Free:	(800) 843-4227
Contact:	Dan Rosenblatt, Executive Director
Type:	Nonprofit membership organization
Members:	Commissioners, superintendents, chiefs, and directors of national, state, county, and municipal police departments
Research:	Research service provided for members
Topics:	Management and administration, police science, crime prevention, community policing, police-community relations, and other issues related to law enforcement and public safety
Resources:	Annual conference, educational programs, newsletter, periodical,

	policy center, library, assessment centers, guidebooks, surveys, directories, and special reports
Mission:	To develop active partnerships among citizens, private organizations, schools, community groups, and youth to directly address crime in both its cause and effects
Established:	1893

Organization:	National Crime Prevention Council
Address:	1700 "K" Street, N.W., 2nd Floor
	Washington, DC 20006-3817
Telephone:	(202) 466-6272
FAX:	(202) 296-1356
Toll Free:	None
Contact:	John A. Calhoun, Executive Director
Type:	Nonprofit organization
Members:	State law enforcement and crime prevention associations
Research:	General referral service provided for members
Topics:	School-based programs, crime prevention, safe community investment, youth and crime, and drug prevention
Resources:	"Take a Bite Out of Crime" campaign, educational programs, training and technical assistance, newsletter, periodical, publications, library, resource guides, video programs, and largest repository of crime prevention information in the country
Mission:	To help individuals of all ages learn how to reduce their risks of being crime victims and to energize people to look beyond self-protection to build crime-resistant communities that solve problems instead of just addressing symptoms
Established:	1980

Organization:	National Criminal Justice Association
Address:	444 North Capitol Street, N.W., Suite 618
	Washington, DC 20001
Telephone:	(202) 347-4900
FAX:	(202) 508-3859
Toll Free:	None
Contact:	Gwen A. Holden, Executive Director
Type:	Nonprofit membership organization
Members:	Municipal, county, regional, and state criminal prosecutors, defenders, corrections officials, educators, researchers, elected officials, and others employed in the criminal justice field
Research:	Research service provided for members
Topics:	Drug prevention and education, assess seizure and forfeiture,

state laws and procedures affecting drug trafficking control, and treatment options for drug-dependent offenders

Resources: Annual conference, educational programs, newsletter, periodical, publications, technical and special reports, and technical assistance

Mission: To develop and implement national policy in the criminal justice field, and to help states address criminal justice–related problems

Established: 1971

Organization: Police Executive Research Forum
Address: 2300 "M" Street, N.W., Suite 910
Washington, DC 20037
Telephone: (202) 466-7820
FAX: (202) 466-7826
Toll Free: None
Contact: Chuck Wexler, Executive Director
Type: Nonprofit professional membership association
Members: Police executives from large cities, counties, and state law enforcement agencies
Research: Research service provided for members
Topics: Management and administration, drug testing, police response strategies, problem solving, public safety, and other issues related to law enforcement
Resources: Annual conference, educational programs, newsletter, periodical, publications, books, technical and special reports, and informational materials
Mission: To improve the delivery of police services and effectiveness of crime control through the exercise of strong national leadership, research and policy development, and public debate of criminal justice issues
Established: 1977

Organization: Police Foundation
Address: 1001–22nd Street, N.W.
Washington, DC 20037
Telephone: (202) 833-1460
FAX: (202) 659-9149
Toll Free: None
Contact: Hubert Williams, President
Type: Nonprofit research organization
Members: None
Research: Research and technical assistance provided

Topics: Law enforcement, public safety, community policing, strategic planning, civil disorder preparedness, operations and administration, program evaluation, community and race relations, illegal drug control, and other issues related to law enforcement and public safety

Resources: Annual conference, educational programs, newsletter, periodical, publications, police chief selection, research and technical reports, special reports, technical assistance, and the National Center for the Study of Police and Civil Disorder

Mission: To improve policing in America through research and technical assistance

Established: 1970

Public Works

Organization: American Public Power Association
Address: 2301 "M" Street, N.W., 3rd Floor
Washington, DC 20037
Telephone: (202) 467-2900
FAX: (202) 467-2910
Toll Free: None
Contact: Larry Hobart, Executive Director
Type: Nonprofit organization
Members: Municipally owned electric utilities, public utility districts, state and county-owned electric systems, and rural cooperatives
Research: Research service provided for members
Topics: Management and administration, operations, public utilities, conservation, environment, financing, customer service, public relations, engineering, design, construction, and accounting practices
Resources: Annual conference, educational programs, newsletter, periodical, publications, technical reports, manuals, booklets, directories, surveys, research, and special reports
Mission: To advance the public policy interests of its members and their customers; and to provide services to help ensure adequate, reliable electricity at a reasonable price with proper protection of the environment
Established: 1940

Organization: American Public Works Association
Address: 106 West 11th Street, Suite 1800
Kansas City, MO 64105-1806

Telephone:	(816) 472-6100
FAX:	(816) 472-1610
Toll Free:	None
Contact:	William J. Bertera, Executive Director
Type:	Nonprofit membership organization
Members:	Public works chief administrators, commissioners and directors, city engineers, and superintendents; department heads of transportation, water, wastewater, and solid waste; contractors, and utility officials
Research:	Research service provided for members
Topics:	Management and administration, buildings and grounds, equipment, municipal engineering, solid wastes, transportation, utilities, water resources, facilities management, pavement management, and other issues related to public works
Resources:	Annual conference, educational programs, newsletter, periodical, publications, books, manuals, library, electronic networking, technical and special reports, directories, the APWA Education Foundation, the APWA Research Foundation, and the Public Works Historical Society
Mission:	To provide public works–related services with sensitivity to community needs and resources, providing a safe and protected environment and continually aware of their responsibilities to this and future generations
Established:	1894

Organization:	American Water Works Association
Address:	6666 West Quincy Avenue
	Denver, CO 80235
Telephone:	(303) 794-7711
FAX:	(303) 795-1440
Toll Free:	None
Contact:	J. B. Mannion, Executive Director
Type:	Nonprofit membership organization
Members:	Water utility managers, superintendents, chemists, engineers, water departments, boards of health, and manufacturers
Research:	Research service provided for members
Topics:	Management and administration, design and construction, water examination, water quality, public health, safety, purification systems, regulation information, and other issues related to water works processes and systems
Resources:	Annual conference, educational programs, newsletter, periodicals, publications, reference books, manuals, directories, electronic networking, legislative representation, and placement services

Mission: To develop standards and support research programs in water-
               works design and construction
Established: 1881

Organization: Institute of Transportation Engineers
Address: 525 School Street, S.W., Suite 410
               Washington, DC 20024-2797
Telephone: (202) 554-8050
FAX: (202) 863-5486
Toll Free: None
Contact: Thomas W. Brahms, Executive Director
Type: Nonprofit organization
Members: Transportation professionals in all levels of government, as well
               as the private and nonprofit sectors
Research: Research service provided for members
Topics: Management and administration, financing, transportation
               issues (air, railroad, water and highway), facilities design, park-
               ing management, traffic engineering, traffic signal design, reg-
               ulation compliance, maintenance, and other issues related to
               transportation
Resources: Annual conference, educational programs, newsletter, periodi-
               cal, publications, textbooks, handbooks, technical manuals
               and reports, research, special reports, library, and training pro-
               grams
Mission: To provide for the professional development of our members
               and others, assisting them in meeting society's needs for safe,
               efficient, and environmentally compatible transportation
Established: 1930

Organization: National Association of Flood and Stormwater Management
               Agencies
Address: 1225 Eye Street, N.W., Suite 300
               Washington, DC 20005
Telephone: (202) 682-3761
FAX: (202) 842-0621
Toll Free: None
Contact: Susan Gilson, Executive Director
Type: Nonprofit membership organization
Members: States, regions, municipalities, flood control districts, and plan-
               ning and development departments in all levels of government
Research: No research service provided
Topics: Management and administration, financing, development and
               planning, engineering, facilities design, flood control, stormwater

management, stormwater control facilities, and other issues relating to flood and stormwater management

Resources: Annual conference, educational programs, special workshops, newsletter, periodical, publications, books, guidebooks, manuals, and technical and special reports

Mission: To advocate public policy, encourage technologies, and conduct educational programs which facilitate and enhance the achievement of the public service functions of its members

Established: 1982

Organization: Solid Waste Association of North America
Address: Post Office Box 7219
Silver Spring, MD 20910
Telephone: (301) 585-2898
FAX: (301) 589-7068
Toll Free: None
Contact: H. Lanier Hickman, Jr., Executive Director
Type: Nonprofit membership organization
Members: Professionals and technical individuals involved in municipal solid waste management
Research: Research service provided for members
Topics: Management and administration, operation, financing, solid waste management, environmental management issues, hazardous materials handling and disposal, solid waste facilities, solid waste transfer stations, and other issued related to municipal solid waste collection, management, and disposal
Resources: Annual conference, educational programs, newsletter, periodical, publications, library, technical and special reports, and legislative representation
Mission: To advance the practice of environmentally and economically sound municipal solid waste management in North America
Established: 1961

Organization: Water Environment Foundation
Address: 601 Wythe Street
Alexandria, VA 22314-1994
Telephone: (703) 684-2400
FAX: (703) 684-2492
Toll Free: (800) 666-0206
Contact: Quincalee Brown, Executive Director
Type: Nonprofit membership organization
Members: Municipal, consulting and health engineers, water pollution control works superintendents, chemists, ecologists, industrial

wastewater engineers, research personnel, academics, and municipal officials

Research: Research service provided for members

Topics: Management and administration, operations, financing, collection, treatment, disposal, hazardous waste, environmental protection, water pollution control, wastewater operations, new technologies, regulations, legislation, educational materials, and other issues related to water and the environment

Resources: Annual conference, educational programs, special workshops, newsletter, periodical, publications, technical and special reports, training manuals, training materials, library, research program, and suggested water quality curriculum for schoolchildren

Mission: To preserve and enhance the global water environment

Established: 1928

Others

Organization: Academy for State and Local Governments

Address: 444 North Capitol Street, N.W., Suite 345
Washington, DC 20001

Telephone: (202) 434-4850

FAX: (202) 494-4851

Toll Free: None

Contact: Enid Beaumont, Director

Type: Nonprofit public policy organization

Members: None

Research: General referral service provided

Topics: Analysis of programs, issues, policies, and legislation impacting state and local governments, international technology and program information exchange, and other matters related to state and local governments

Resources: Educational programs, training workshops, newsletter, publications, research reports, surveys, government directories, technical and special reports, legislative and legal analyses, research and training programs, joint programs and projects with other national professional associations and organizations, the State and Local Legal Center, and the International Center

Mission: To collaborate with the national organizations of chief elected and appointed officials, and through this partnership, and in cooperation with the private sector and the broader research community, to foster understanding of American government at all levels

Established: 1971

Organization: American Society for Public Administration
Address: 1120 "G" Street, N.W., Suite 700
Washington, DC 20005
Telephone: (202) 393-7878
FAX: (202) 638-4952
Toll Free: None
Contact: John P. Thomas, Executive Director
Type: Nonprofit professional society
Members: Public managers, public officials, educators, and research workers in all levels of government, educational institutions, as well as the nonprofit sector
Research: No research service provided
Topics: Public service issues, leadership, ethics, management, operations, planning, public service history, research, and issues related to public administration in all levels of government and in the nonprofit sector
Resources: Annual conference, educational programs, training workshops, newsletter, periodical, publications, books, and technical and special reports
Mission: To advance the science, art, and processes of public administration, the development and exchange of public administration literature and information, and to advocate on behalf of public service and high ethical standards in government
Established: 1939

Organization: Institute of Public Administration
Address: 55 West 44th Street
New York, NY 10036
Telephone: (212) 730-5480
FAX: (212) 398-9305
Toll Free: None
Contact: David Mammen, President
Type: Nonprofit research organization
Members: None
Research: Research service provided
Topics: Public policy, government structure, public authorities, public enterprises, government procurement, personnel management and training, public-private sector improvements, economic development, charter revision, local government, planning and management, intergovernmental relations, and public ethics
Resources: Educational programs, publications, books, technical and special reports, library, technical advisory and consulting services,

the Gulick Center for Citizenship and Ethics, and the Luther H. Gulick Scholar-in-Residence Program

Mission: To provide research, training, education, consulting, and advisory services in the United States and abroad in the areas of public policy, government structure, public authorities, public enterprises, government procurement, personnel management and training, public-private sector improvements, economic development, charter revisions, local government legislative bodies, planning and management, intergovernmental program responsibilities and relationships, and public ethics

Established: 1906

Organization: National Association of Towns and Townships

Address: 1522 "K" Street, N.W., Suite 600
Washington, DC 20005

Telephone: (202) 737-5200

FAX: (202) 289-7996

Toll Free: None

Contact: Jeffrey H. Schiff, Executive Director

Type: Nonprofit federation

Members: State organizations and individual communities

Research: Research service provided for members

Topics: All local government-related issues, especially those issues related to small towns and communities

Resources: Annual conference, educational programs, training workshops, newsletter, periodical, publications, books, guidebooks, workbooks, audio-visual programs, technical assistance, legislative representation, and the National Center for Small Communities

Mission: To strengthen the effectiveness of towns, townships, and small communities in the United States, and to promote their interests in the public and private sectors

Established: 1963

Organization: National Civic League

Address: 1445 Market Street, Suite 300
Denver, CO 80202-1728

Telephone: (303) 571-4343

FAX: (303) 571-4404

Toll Free: None

Contact: John Parr, President

Type: Nonprofit membership organization

Members: State and local elected office holders, state and local government administrators; and members of nonprofit organizations, academia, businesses, and the media

Research: Research service provided for members

Topics: Model city charter, leadership, civic responsibilities, citizen participation, performance measurements, election processes, healthy communities, governmental structures, governmental processes, and other issues related to local governments

Resources: Annual conference, educational programs, training workshops, publications, periodical, books, technical and special reports, CIVITEX database, clearinghouse for information, All-America City Awards Program, state constitution collection, model laws, research program, and the Civic League Press

Mission: To be a leader in improving local and state governance and helping citizens to participate actively in community problem solving

Established: 1894

Organization: The Urban Institute

Address: 2100 "M" Street, N.W.
Washington, DC 20037

Telephone: (202) 833-7200

FAX: (202) 331-9747

Toll Free: (800) 462-6420 (Publications)

Contact: William Gorham, President

Type: Nonprofit policy research and educational organization

Members: None

Research: Research service provided

Topics: Urban opportunity, discrimination, poverty and income distribution, national priorities, children and families, the elderly, social services, health, housing, public finance, public management, governance, education, the nonprofit sector, employment, microsimulation, immigration and population, and other issues related to America's urban environment

Resources: Educational programs, training workshops, periodical, publications, books, monographs, technical and special reports, library, and the Urban Institute Press

Mission: To respond to needs for objective analyses and basic information regarding social and economic problems confronting the nation and government policies and programs designed to alleviate such problems

Established: 1968

BIBLIOGRAPHY

Administration

Ayres, Richard M. and Paul R. Coble. *Safeguarding Management's Rights.* Dubuque, Iowa: Kendall-Hunt Publishing, 1987.

Banovetz, James M., et al. *Managing Small Cities and Counties: A Practical Guide.* Washington, DC: International City/County Management Association, 1994.

Becker, Christine S. *Performance Evaluation: An Essential Management Tool.* Washington, DC: International City/County Management Association, 1988.

Bennis, Warren. "Transformational Power and Leadership" in Thomas H. Sergiovanni and John E. Corbally. *Leadership and Organizational Culture.* Urbana, Illinois: University of Illinois Press, 1986.

Bens, Charles K. *Measuring City Hall Performance: Finally a How-To Guide.* Denver, Colorado: National Civic League Press, 1991.

Bland, Robert L. *A Revenue Guide for Local Government.* Washington, DC: International City/County Management Association, 1989.

Boxwell, Robert J. *Benchmarking for Competitive Advantage.* New York, New York: McGraw-Hill, 1994.

Burke, Brendan. "Improving Internal Processes: Focus on Quality." *Management Information Service Report,* no. 40699. Washington, DC: International City/County Management Association, 1992.

Campbell, Andrew. *A Sense of Mission.* Reading, Massachusetts: Addison-Wesley, 1992.

Crosby, Philip B. *Quality Without Tears.* New York, New York: McGraw-Hill, 1984.

Crupi, James. "Forces Shaping Local Government in the 1990's." *Public Management,* vol. 72, no. 12. December 1990.

Cunningham, Joy. "Regional Strategies for Local Government Management." *Management Information Service Report,* no. 40718. Washington, DC: International City/County Management Association, 1992.

Davenport, Thomas H. *Process Innovation: Reengineering Work Through Information Technology.* Cambridge, Massachusetts: Harvard Business School Press, 1993.

Davidow, William H. and Bro Uttal. *Total Customer Service: The Ultimate Weapon.* New York, New York: Harper & Row, 1989.

Epstein, Paul D. *Using Performance Measurements in Local Government.* Denver, Colorado: National Civic League Press, 1988.

Everson, Christine. "Local Governments and Schools: Sharing Support Services." *Management Information Service Report,* no. 40919. Washington, DC: International City/County Management Association, 1994.

Frederickson, H. George. *Ideal and Practice in Council-Manager Government.* Washington, DC: International City/County Management Association, 1995.

Gardner, James. *On Leadership.* New York, New York: The Free Press, 1990.

Granthon, Charles. *The Digital Workplace: Designing Groupware Platforms.* New York, New York: Van Nostrand Reinhold, 1993.

Hale, Sandra J. and Mary M. Williams. *Managing Change: A Guide to Producing Innovations from Within.* Washington, DC: The Urban Institute Press, 1989.

Hammer, Michael and James Champy. *Reengineering the Corporation.* Reading, Massachusets: The Free Press, 1993.

Hampden-Turner, Charles. *Creating Corporate Culture: From Discord to Harmony.* Reading, Massachusetts: Addison-Wesley, 1992.

Harney, Donald F. *Service Contracting: A Local Government Guide.* Washington, DC: International City/County Management Association, 1992.

Hatry, Harry P.; Kenneth P. Voytek; and Allen E. Holmes. *Building Innovation Into Program Reviews: Analysis of Service Delivery Alternatives.* Washington, DC: The Urban Institute Press, 1989.

_____; Louis Blair; Donald Fisk; and Wayne Kimmel. *Program Analysis for State and Local Governments.* Washington, DC: The Urban Institute Press, 1988.

_____; Richard E. Winnie; and Donald M. Fisk. *Practical Program Evaluation for State and Local Governments.* Washington, DC: The Urban Institute Press, 1986.

Herrman, Margaret S. *Resolving Conflict: Strategies for Local Government.* Washington, DC: International City/County Management Association, 1994.

International City/County Management Association. *Building Teams and Teamwork: A Foundation for Organizational Success.* Washington, DC: ICMA, 1994.

_____. "Computer Purchasing Practices in Municipalities." *Baseline Data Report,* no. 40933. Washington, DC: ICMA, 1994.

_____. "Computer Services Strategic Plan." *Clearinghouse Report,* no. 40876. Washington, DC: ICMA, 1994.

_____. "Cost/Benefit Analysis for Information Technology Projects." *Clearinghouse Report,* no. 40917. Washington, DC: ICMA, 1994.

_____. *Evaluating Financial Condition: A Handbook for Local Government.* Washington, DC: ICMA, 1994.

_____. "Americans with Disabilities Act: A Guide to Compliance." *Clearinghouse Report,* no. 40799. Washington, DC: ICMA, 1993.

_____. *Software Reference Guide.* Washington, DC: ICMA, 1993.

_____. "Customer Service in Local Government." *Clearinghouse Report,* no. 40721. Washington, DC: ICMA, 1992.

_____. "Employee Attitude Surveys." *Management Information Service Report,* no. 40715. Washington, DC: ICMA, 1992.

_____. "State, Local, and Council Relations: Managers' Perspectives." *Baseline Data Report,* no. 40693. Washington, DC: ICMA, 1992.

_____. "Citizen Surveys: How to Do Them, How to Use Them, What They Mean." *Special Report,* no. 40462. Washington, DC: ICMA, 1991.

_____. "Orientation for Elected Officials: A Guide to Program Development." *Management Information Service Report,* no. 40647. Washington, DC: ICMA, 1991.

_____. "Practical Promotion: Strategies for Improving Services and Image." *Special Report,* no. 40675. Washington, DC: ICMA, 1991.

_____. "Employee Recruitment, Selection, and Affirmative Action Policies in Local Governments." *Special Data Report,* no. 40412. Washington, DC: ICMA, 1990.

_____. "Wellness Programs in Local Government." *Management Information Service Report*, no. 40200. Washington, DC: ICMA, 1988.

_____. "Developing Work Procedures: A Guide for Local Governments." *Special Report*, no. 40059, Washington, DC: ICMA, 1987.

_____. "Recruiting Key Management Personnel: Guidelines for Managers and Department Heads." *Management Information Service Report*, no. 40076. Washington, DC: ICMA, 1987.

_____. "Workers' Compensation: An Employer's Manual for Managing Disability." *Management Information Service Report*, no. 40118. Washington, DC: ICMA, 1987.

_____. "Building Staff Management Capacity in Local Governments." *Management Information Service Report*, no. 38687. Washington, DC: ICMA, 1986.

_____. "Strategic Issues Management: Improving the Council-Manager Relationship." *Management Information Service Report*, no. 37915. Washington, DC: ICMA, 1986.

Keller, Elizabeth K. *Ethical Insight, Ethical Action: Perspectives from the Local Government Manager.* Washington, DC: International City/County Management Association, 1988.

Kotter, John and James L. Heskett. *Corporate Culture and Performance.* New York, New York: The Free Press, 1992.

Kraemer, Kenneth L. and Donald F. Norris. "Computers in Local Government." *The Municipal Year Book.* Washington, DC: International City/County Management Association, 1994.

Linden, Russell. "Re-engineering Local Government." *Management Information Service Report*, no. 40924. Washington, DC: International City/County Management Association, 1994.

Matzer, John, Jr. *Pay and Benefits: New Ideas for Local Governments.* Washington, DC: International City/County Management Association, 1988.

_____. *Productivity Improvement Techniques: Creative Approaches for Local Government.* Washington, DC: International City/County Management Association, 1986.

Merriman, David. *The Control of Municipal Budgets: Towards the Effective Design of Tax & Expenditure Limitations.* Westport, Connecticut: Greenwood Press, 1987.

Mikesell, John. *City Finances, City Futures.* Washington, DC: National League of Cities, 1992.

Miranda, Rowan and Karlyn Anderson. "Alternative Service Delivery in Local Government, 1982–1992." *The Municipal Year Book.* Washington, DC: International City/County Management Association, 1994.

Moore, Barbara H. *The Entrepreneur in Local Government.* Washington, DC: International City/County Management Association, 1983.

Moulder, Evelina. "Use of Volunteers in Local Government Service Delivery." *Baseline Data Report*, no. 40934. Washington, DC: International City/County Management Association, 1994.

Nanus, Burt. *A Visionary Leadership.* San Francisco, California: Jossey-Bass, 1992.

Nathan, Richard A. *A New Agenda for Cities.* Washington, DC: National League of Cities, 1992.

National Civic League. *Governance and Diversity.* Denver, Colorado: NCL Press, 1994.

_____. *The Civic Index: A New Approach to Improving Community Life.* Denver, Colorado: NCL Press, 1993.

_____. *Healthy Communities Handbook.* Denver, Colorado: NCL Press, 1993.

_____. *Healthy Communities Resource Guide.* Denver, Colorado: NCL Press, 1993.

_____. *Model City Charter.* Denver, Colorado: NCL Press, 1992.

National League of Cities. *The State of America's Cities: The 11th Annual Opinion Survey of Municipal Elected Officials.* Washington, DC: NLC, 1995.

_____. *Organizations and Associations: Resource Directory for Local Elected Officials.* Washington, DC: NLC, 1994.

_____. *Rethinking Public Safety.* Washington, DC: NLC, 1994.

_____. *All in It Together: Cities, Suburbs and Local Economic Regions.* Washington, DC: NLC, 1993.

_____. *Dealing Effectively with the Media.* Washington, DC: NLC, 1993.

_____. *Global Dollars, Local Sense: Cities and Towns in the International Economy.* Washington, DC: NLC, 1993.

_____. *Goal Setting: Steps to Progress.* Washington, DC: NLC, 1992.

_____. *Complying with the Americans with Disabilities Act.* Washington, DC: NLC, 1991.

_____. *Diversity & Governance: Changing Populations and the Future of Cities and Towns.* Washington, DC: NLC, 1991.

_____. *Local Officials Guide to Public Real Estate Asset Management.* Washington, DC: NLC, 1990.

_____. *Fighting Poverty in Cities: Transportation Programs as Bridges to Opportunity.* Washington, DC: NLC, 1989.

_____. *Local Officials Guide to the Housing and Community Development Act of 1987.* Washington, DC: NLC, 1988.

_____. *Reducing Urban Unemployment: What Works at the Local Level.* Washington, DC: NLC, 1985.

_____. *Creating Your City's Image.* Washington, DC: NLC, 1982.

Netzer, Dick. *Local Alternatives to the Property Tax: User Charges and Nonproperty Taxes.* Washington, DC: Academy for State and Local Government, 1983.

_____. *Property Tax Issues for the 1980's.* Washington, DC: Academy of State and Local Government, 1983.

Newell, Charldean. *The Effective Local Government Manager.* Washington, DC: International City/County Management Association, 1993.

Norris, Donald F. *Microcomputers and Local Government.* Washington, DC: International City/County Management Association, 1989.

Osborne, David and Ted A. Gaebler. *Reinventing Government.* Reading, Massachusetts: Addison-Wesley, 1992.

Pammer, William J., Jr. *Managing Fiscal Strain in Major American Cities: Understanding Retrenchment in the Public Sector.* Westport, Connecticut: Greenwood Press, 1990.

Salamon, Lester M. *Beyond Privatization: The Tools of Government Action.* Washington, DC: The Urban Institute Press, 1989.

Svara, James H. *A Survey of America's City Councils: Continuity and Change.* Washington, DC: National League of Cities, 1991.

_____. *Official Leadership in the City.* New York, New York: Oxford University Press, 1990.

U.S. Conference of Mayors. *A Status Report on Economic Restructuring and Reemployment Strategies in America's Cities.* Washington, DC: USCM, 1994.

_____. *Impact of Unfunded Federal Mandates on U.S. Cities: A 314-City Survey.* Washington, DC: USCM, October 1993.

_____. *Ending Homelessness in America's Cities: Implementing a National Plan of Action.* Washington, DC: USCM, July 1993.

_____. *Addressing Hunger and Homelessness in America's Cities.* Washington, DC: USCM, June 1993.

_____. *Cities in Recession: The Need for Change, a 125-City Survey.* Washington, DC: USCM, March 1993.

_____. *Community Development Block Grant (CDBG) to America's Cities: Additional Funds Needed to Fight Urban Ills.* Washington, DC: USCM, June 1992.

_____. *Fiscal Stress in America's Cities: The Need for Targeted Fiscal Assistance, a 100-City Survey.* Washington, DC: USCM, May 1992.

_____. *Garbage Solutions: A Public Official's Guide to Recycling and Alternative Solid Waste Management Techniques*. Washington, DC: USCM, 1989.

_____. *How Mayors and City Governments Support the Arts: Innovative Financing Techniques and Strategies*. Washington, DC: USCM, 1988.

West Jonathan P., Evan M. Berman, and Mike E. Milakovich. "Total Quality Management in Local Government." *The Municipal Year Book*. Washington, DC: International City/County Management Association, 1994.

Wheeler, Kenneth M. *Effective Communication: A Local Government Guide*. Washington, DC: International City/County Management Association, 1994.

Whitley, Richard C. *The Customer-Driven Company: Moving from Talk to Action*. Reading, Massachusetts: Addison-Wesley, 1993.

Cities and Society

Baldwin, Deborah. "Creating Community." *Common Cause,* vol. 16, no. 4. July-August 1990.

Bens, Charles K. "Effective Citizen Involvement: How to Make it Happen." *National Civic Review,* vol. 83, no. 1, winter-spring 1994.

Bostian, David B., Jr. "Paradigms for Prosperity: Economic and Political Trends for the 1990s and Early 21st Century." *The Futurist,* vol. 24, no. 4, July-August 1990.

Branscomb, Anne Wells. *Who Owns Information? From Privacy to Public Access*. New York, New York: Basic Books, 1994.

Bray, Paul M. "A New Tool for Renewing the Central City: The Urban Cultural Park." *National Civic Review,* vol. 83, no. 2, spring-summer 1994.

_____. "The New Urbanism: Celebrating the City." *Places,* vol. 8, no. 4, summer 1993.

Burns, Marshall. *Automated Fabrication: Improving Productivity in Manufacturing*. Englewood Cliffs, New Jersey: Prentice Hall, 1993.

Casella, William N., Jr. "The Responsible Executive." *National Civic Review,* vol. 83, no. 4, fall-winter 1994.

Cisneros, Henry G. "Renewing the Bonds of Community." *National Civic Review,* vol. 83, no. 4, fall-winter 1994.

Conway, McKinley. "Tomorrow's Supercities for Land, Sea, and Air." *The Futurist,* vol. 27, no. 3, May-June 1993.

Downs, Anthony. *New Visions for Metropolitan America*. Washington, DC: The Brookings Institution, 1994.

Fishman, Robert. "America's New City—Megalapolis Unbound." *The Wilson Quarterly,* vol. 14, no. 1, winter 1990.

Hale, Sandra J. and Mary M. Williams. *Managing Change: A Guide to Producing Innovation from Within*. Washington, DC: The Urban Institute Press, 1990.

Hanson, Royce. "Cities for the Future." *American City & County,* vol. 99, no. 11, November 1984.

Harper, Charles L. *Exploring Social Change*. Englewood Cliffs, New Jersey: Prentice Hall, 1993.

Henderson, Hazel. "Votes and Prices: The Feedback of Democracy." *The Futurist,* vol. 27, no. 3, May-June 1993.

Kemp, Roger L. *America's Cities: Problems and Prospects*. Aldershot, Hants, England: Avebury Press, 1995.

_____. *Economic Development in Local Government: A Handbook for Public Officials and Citizens*. Jefferson, North Carolina: McFarland, 1995.

_____. *Strategic Planning for Local Government: A Handbook for Officials and Citizens*. Jefferson, North Carolina: McFarland, 1993.

_____. *Strategic Planning in Local Government: A Casebook*. Chicago, Illinois: Planners Press, American Planning Association, 1992.

_____. *Privatization: The Provision of Public Services by the Private Sector.* Jefferson, North Carolina: McFarland, 1991.

_____. *America's Cities: Strategic Planning for the Future.* Danville, Illinois: The Interstate Press, 1986.

_____. *America's Infrastructure: Problems and Prospects.* Danville, Illinois: The Interstate Press, 1986.

_____. *Coping with Proposition 13.* Lexington, Massachusetts: Lexington Books, 1980.

Lowe, Marcia D. "Alternatives to Shaping Tomorrow's Cities." *The Futurist,* vol. 26, no. 4, July-August 1992.

_____. "Out of the Car, Into the Future." *World-Watch,* vol. 3, no. 6, November-December 1990.

Lynch, Alfred F. *What Lies Ahead: Countdown to the 21st Century.* Alexandria, Virginia: Strategic Institute, United Way of America, 1989.

McCoy, Martha L. and Robert F. Sherman. "Bridging the Divide of Race and Ethnicity." *National Civic Review,* vol. 83, no. 2, spring-summer 1994.

Messinger, Ruth. *Diversity & Governance.* Washington, DC: National League of Cities, 1991.

Okubo, Derek, et al. *Governance and Diversity: Findings from Los Angeles.* Denver, Colorado: National Civic League Press, 1993.

Osborne, David and Ted Gaebler. *Reinventing Government: How the Entrepreneurial Spirit Is Transforming the Public Sector.* Reading, Massachusetts: Addison-Wesley, 1992.

Sheffield, Charles, et al. *The World of 2044: Technological Development and the Future Society.* New York, New York: Paragon House, 1994.

Toth, Kalman A. "The Workless Society." *The Futurist,* vol. 24, no. 3, May-June 1990.

Yankelovich, Daniel. "A Conversation About Our Public Priorities." *National Civic Review,* vol. 83, no. 4, fall-winter 1994.

City Clerk

Amy, Douglas J. *Proportional Representation Bibliography.* Washington, DC: The Center for Voting and Democracy, 1994.

Bisheff, Maurice. "Managers: Do You Know Where Your Public Records Are?: Economic and Legal Implications for Local Governments." *IIMC Newsletter,* vol. XLV, no. 8, September 1994.

DeSantis, Victor S. and Tari Renner. "Term Limits and Turnover Among Local Officials." *The Municipal Year Book.* Washington, DC: International City/County Management Association, 1994.

_____. "TQM an Local Government: How Can We Be Better?" *IIMC Newsletter,* vol. XLV, no. 11, December 1993.

Gothard, Erin. "Council Cable Program Relates to Residents." *IIMC Newsletter,* vol. XLIV, no. 4, April 1992.

Guy, Jan. "Welcome to Cyberspace! Or, E-Mail Fever Has Found Me." *IIMC Newsletter,* vol. XLV, no. 10, November 1994.

Haller, Stephen E. *Managing Records on Limited Resources.* Albany, New York: National Association of Government Archives and Records Administrators, 1991.

International City/County Management Association. *Elected Officials Handbooks.* Washington, DC: ICMA, 1994.

_____. *Software Reference Guide.* Washington, DC: ICMA, 1993.

_____. "Orientation for Elected Officials: A Guide to Program Development." *Management Information Service Report,* no. 40647. Washington, DC: ICMA, 1991.

_____. "Records Management Manual." *Clearinghouse Report*, no. 40595. Washington, DC: ICMA, 1990.

_____. "Elections Marketing Plan." *Clearinghouse Report*, no. 40606. Washington, DC: ICMA, 1989.

_____. "Municipal Election Processes: The Impact on Minority Representation." *Base line Data Report*, no. 40082. Washington, DC: ICMA, 1988.

_____. "Records Management." *Management Information Service Report*, no. 37850. Washington, DC, 1986

Johnson, A.K., Jr. *A Guide for the Selection and Development of Local Government Records Storage Facilities*. Albany, New York: National Association of Government Archives and Records Administrators, 1991.

Kemp, Roger L. "Municipal Clerk Services: Beyond Cutback to Creativity." *IIMC Newsletter*, vol. XLV, no. 4, April 1993.

Kraemer, Kenneth L. and Donald F. Norris. "Computers in Local Government." *The Municipal Year Book*. Washington, DC: International City/County Management Association, 1994.

Lyons, W.E. and Malcolm E. Jewell. "Minority Representation and the Drawing of City Council Districts." *Urban Affairs Quarterly*, vol. 23, no 3, March 1988.

Martinez, Elias. "Reinventing Government: Toward an Entrepreneurial Spirit." *IIMC Newsletter*, vol. XLIV, no. 10, December 1992.

Mims, Julian L. *Using Microfilm*. Albany, New York: National Association of Government Archives and Records Administrators, 1992.

National Civic League. *Handbook for Council Members in Council-Manager Cities*. Denver, Colorado: NCL Press, 1992.

_____. *Model City Charter*. Denver, Colorado: NCL Press, 1992.

_____. *Guide for Charter Commissions*. Denver, Colorado: NCL Press, 1991.

National League of Cities. *Organizations and Associations: Resource Directory for Local Elected Officials*. Washington, DC: NLC, 1994.

_____. *Tools for Leadership: A Handbook for Elected Officials*. Washington, DC: NLC, 1980.

Norris, Donald F. *Microcomputers and Local Government*. Washington, DC: International City/County Management Association, 1989.

Pritchard, Robert. "Cutback Management: Continuous Improvement Productivity Study and Implementation." *IIMC Newsletter*, vol. XLIV, no. 8, October 1992.

Renner, Tari. "Municipal Election Processes: The Impact on Minority Representation." *The Municipal Year Book*. Washington, DC: International City/County Management Association, 1988.

Richie, Rob. "Proportional Representation." *National Civic Review*, vol. 83, no. 2, spring-summer 1994.

Rule, Wilma and Joseph F. Zimmerman. *United States Electoral Systems: Their Impact on Women and Minorities*. New York, New York: Praeger, 1992.

Shalby, Chris. "Getting on the Information Highway with IIMC Headquarters (and Everyone Else)." *IIMC Newsletter*, vol. XLV, no. 10, November 1994.

Smith, Gerald W. and Jerry Debenham. "Intelligent Voting Systems." *The Futurist*, vol. 22, no. 5, September-October 1988.

Smith, Harmon. *Protecting Records*. Albany, New York: National Association of Government Archives and Records Administrators, 1993.

Smolka, Richard G. "Alternative Voting Methods." *IIMC Newsletter*, vol. XLV, no. 10, November 1994.

_____. "Redistricting Battles Are Unnecessary." *IIMC Newsletter*, vol. XLV, no. 3, March 1993.

_____. "Major Changes in Election Systems Likely." *IIMC Newsletter*, vol. XLV, no. 2, February 1993.

Spraggins, Pegga A., et al. *The Municipal Clerk's Office in Ohio: A Study of Duties, Professionalism, and Innovation.* Kent, Ohio: Center for Public Administration and Public Policy, Kent State University, 1993.

Stephens, David O. *The Daily Management of Records and Information.* Albany, New York: National Association of Government Archives and Records Administrators, 1991.

Surchik, Joyce. "Bar Codes Used Throughout Shelby Township, MI." *IIMC Newsletter*, vol. XLV, no. 4, April 1993.

The Center for Voting and Democracy. *Voting and Democracy Report.* Washington, DC: TCVD, 1993.

Vedder, Janice. "Bar Coding Election Program Streamlines the Election Process in the Delta Township, Michigan, Clerk's Office." *IIMC Newsletter*, vol. XLV, no. 11, December 1993.

Wallace, Elaine M. *Role Call: Strategy for a Professional Clerk.* San Dimas, California: International Institute of Municipal Clerks, 1990.

White, Kenneth. *Applying Computer Technology to Records Systems.* Albany, New York: National Association of Government Archives and Records Administrators, 1992.

Williams, Darrell. *The Impact of at Large Versus District Electoral Structures on Minority Representation.* Washington, DC: National League of Cities, January 1989.

Wolf, Elliot. "Communicating with Citizens on a Shoestring Budget." *IIMC Newsletter*, vol. XLIV, no. 4, May 1992.

Zeller, Laurie Hirschfeld. *Term Limitations for Local Officials: A Citizens' Guide to Constructive Dialogue.* Denver, Colorado: National Civic League Press, 1992.

Zimmerman, Joseph F. "Alternative Local Electoral Systems." *National Civic Review*, vol. 79, no. 1, January-February 1990.

City Council

Ayres, Richard M. and Paul R. Coble. *Safeguarding Management's Rights.* Dubuque, Iowa: Kendall-Hunt Publishing, 1987.

Bens, Charles K. *Measuring City Hall Performance: Finally a How-to Guide.* Denver, Colorado: National Civic League Press, 1991.

Bennis, Warren. "Transformational Power and Leadership" in Thomas H. Sergiovanni and John E. Corbally, *Leadership and Organizational Culture.* Urbana, Illinois: University of Illinois Press, 1986.

Bland, Robert L. *A Revenue Guide for Local Government.* Washington, DC: International City/County Management Association, 1989.

Crupi, James. "Forces Shaping Local Government in the 1990's." *Public Management*, vol. 72, no. 12, December 1990.

DeGrove, John M. *Balanced Growth: A Planning Guide for Local Government.* Washington, DC: International City/County Management Association, 1991.

Epstein, Paul D. *Using Performance Measurements in Local Government.* Denver, Colorado: National Civic League Press, 1988.

Frederickson, H. George. *Ideal and Practice in Council-Manager Government.* Washington, DC: International City/County Management Association, 1995.

Gardner, James. *On Leadership.* New York, New York: The Free Press, 1990.

Gothard, Erin. "Council Cable Program Relates to Residents." *IIMC Newsletter*, vol. XLIV, no. 4, April 1992.

Herrman, Margaret S. *Resolving Conflict: Strategies for Local Government.* Washington, DC: International City/County Management Association, 1994.

International City/County Management Association. "Community Visioning: Citizen Participation in Strategic Planning." *Management Information Service Report,* no. 40893. Washington, DC: ICMA, 1994.

_____. *Elected Officials Handbooks.* Washington, DC: ICMA, 1994.

_____. *Evaluating Financial Condition: A Handbook for Local Government.* Washington, DC: ICMA, 1994.

_____. "Local Governments and Schools: Sharing Support Services." *Management Information Service Report,* no. 40919. Washington, DC: ICMA, 1994.

_____. "User Fees: Current Practice." *Management Information Service Report,* no. 40775. Washington, DC: ICMA, 1992.

_____. "Orientation for Elected Officials: A Guide to Program Development." *Management Information Service Report,* no. 40647. Washington, DC: ICMA, 1991.

_____. "Practical Promotion: Strategies for Improving Services and Image." *Special Report,* no. 40675. Washington, DC: ICMA, 1991.

_____. "Form and Adaption: A Study of the Formal and Informal Functions of Mayors, City Managers and Chief Administrative Officers." *Baseline Data Report,* no. 40414. Washington, DC: ICMA, 1990.

_____. "Culture, Recreation, and Health: Ensuring the Quality of Life." *Special Data Issue,* no. 40300. Washington, DC: ICMA, 1989.

_____. "Public Officials Liability." *Baseline Data Report,* no. 40312. Washington, DC: ICMA, 1989.

_____. "Solving Community Problems by Consensus." *Management Information Service Report,* no. 40350. Washington, DC: ICMA, 1989.

_____. "Developer Financing: Impact Fees and Negotiated Exactions." *Management Information Service Report,* no. 40140. Washington, DC: ICMA, 1988.

_____. "Taking Charge: How Communities Are Planning Their Futures." *Special Report,* no. 40184. Washington, DC: ICMA, 1988.

_____. "Citizen Advisory Boards: Making Them Effective." *Management Information Service Report,* no. 40101. Washington, DC: ICMA, 1987.

_____. "Strategic Issues Management: Improving the Council-Manager Relationship." *Management Information Service Report,* no. 37915. Washington, DC: ICMA, 1986.

_____. "Streamlining Local Regulations: A Handbook for Reducing Housing and Development Costs." *Special Report,* no. 30643. Washington, DC: ICMA, 1983.

Kraemer, Kenneth L. and Ronald F. Norris. "Computers in Local Government." *The Municipal Year Book.* Washington, DC: International City/County Management Association, 1994.

Linden, Russell. "Re-engineering Local Government." *Management Information Service Report,* no. 40924. Washington, DC: International City/County Management Association, 1994.

Merriman, David. *The Control of Municipal Budgets: Toward the Effective Design of Tax & Expenditure Limitations.* Westport, Connecticut: Greenwood Press, 1987.

Miranda, Rowan and Karlyn Anderson. "Alternative Service Delivery in Local Government, 1982–1992." *The Municipal Year Book.* Washington, DC: International City/County Management Association, 1994.

Moore, Barbara. *The Entrepreneur in Local Government.* Washington, DC: International City/County Management Association, 1983.

Moulder, Evelina. "Use of Volunteers in Local Government Service Delivery." *Baseline Data Report,* no. 40934. Washington, DC: International City/County Management, 1994.

Nathan, Richard. *A New Agenda for Cities.* Washington, DC: National League of Cities, 1992.

National Civic League. *Government and Diversity.* Denver, Colorado: NCL Press, 1994.

_____. *The Civic Index: A New Approach to Improving Community Life.* Denver, Colorado: NCL Press, 1993.

_____. *Healthy Communities Handbook.* Denver, Colorado: NCL Press, 1993.

_____. *Handbook for Council Members in Council-Manager Cities.* Denver, Colorado: NCL Press, 1992.

_____. *Healthy Communities Resource Guide.* Denver, Colorado: NCL Press, 1992.

_____. *Model City Charter.* Denver, Colorado: National Civic League Press, 1992.

_____. *Guide for Charter Commissions.* Denver, Colorado: NCL Press, 1991.

National League of Cities. *Anti-Mandates Strategies: Reimbursement Requirements in States.* Washington, DC: NLC, 1994.

_____. *City Fiscal Conditions in 1994.* Washington, DC: NLC, 1994.

_____. *A Comprehensive Guide to Studies on State and Federal Mandates to Localities: An Annotated Bibliography.* Washington, DC: NLC, 1994.

_____. *Minority Business Programs and Disparity Studies.* Washington, DC: NLC, 1994.

_____. *The 1994 Anti-Crime Law: A Local Officials Guide.* Washington, DC: NLC, 1994.

_____. *Organizations and Associations: Resource Directory for Local Elected Officials.* Washington, DC: NLC, 1994.

_____. *Poverty and Economic Development: Views from City Hall.* Washington, DC: NLC, 1994.

_____. *Rethinking Public Safety.* Washington, DC: NLC, 1994.

_____. *The State of America's Cities: The 11th Annual Opinion Survey of Municipal Elected Officials.* Washington, DC: NLC, 1995.

_____. *All in It Together: Cities, Suburbs and Local Economic Regions.* Washington, DC: NLC, 1993.

_____. *Dealing Effectively with the Media.* Washington, DC: NLC, 1993.

_____. *Global Dollars, Local Sense: Cities and Towns in the International Economy.* Washington, DC: NLC, 1993.

_____. *City Distress, Metropolitan Disparities, and Economic Growth.* Washington, DC: NLC, 1992.

_____. *Goal Setting: Steps to Progress.* Washington, DC: NLC, 1992.

_____. *Local Officials Guide to Defense Economic Adjustments.* Washington, DC: NLC, 1992.

_____. *State Mandates: Fiscal Notes, Reimbursement, and Anti-Mandate Strategies.* Washington, DC: NLC, 1992.

_____. *Complying with the Americans with Disabilities Act.* Washington, DC: NLC, 1991.

_____. *Diversity & Governance: Changing Populations and the Future of Cities and Towns.* Washington, DC: NLC, 1991.

_____. *Local Officials Guide to the Community Reinvestment Act.* Washington, DC: NLC, 1991.

_____. *Local Officials Guide to Dynamic City Commercial Centers.* Washington, DC: NLC, 1990.

_____. *Fighting Poverty in Cities: Transportation Programs As Bridges to Opportunity.* Washington, DC: NLC, 1989.

_____. *Local Officials Guide to Small Business Partnerships.* Washington, DC: NLC, 1989.

_____. *Local Officials Guide to Transit Financial Planning.* Washington, DC: NLC, 1989.

_____. *Local Strategies in the War Against Drugs.* Washington, DC: NLC, 1989.

_____. *Accepting the Challenge: The Rebirth of America's Downtowns.* Washington, DC: NLC, 1988.

_____. *Local Officials Guide to the Housing and Community Development Act of 1987.* Washington, DC: NLC, 1988.

_____. *State Aid to Cities & Towns.* Washington, DC: NLC, 1988.

_____. *Reducing Urban Unemployment: What Works at the Local Level.* Washington, DC: NLC, 1985.

_____ *Creating Your City's Image.* Washington, DC: NLC, 1982.

_____. *Streamlining Your Local Development Process.* Washington, DC: NLC, 1982.

_____. *Monitoring Federal Grants: The Role of the City Council.* Washington, DC: NLC, 1980.

_____. *Tools for Leadership: A Handbook for Elected Officials.* Washington, DC: NLC 1980.

Netzer, Dick. *Local Alternatives to the Property Tax: User Charges and Nonproperty Taxes.* Washington, DC: Academy for State and Local Government, 1983.

_____. *Property Tax Issues for the 1980's.* Washington, DC: Academy of State and Local Government, 1983.

Osborne, David and Ted A. Gaebler. *Reinventing Government.* Reading, Massachusetts: Addison-Wesley, 1992.

_____. "Bringing Government Back to Life." *Governing,* vol. 5, no. 2, February 1992.

Pammer, William J., Jr. *Managing Fiscal Strain in Major American Cities: Understanding Retrenchment in the Public Sector.* Westport, Connecticut: Greenwood Press, 1990.

Rhyne, Charles S. *Mayor: Chief Municipal Executive Law.* Washington, DC: National Institute of Municipal Law Officers, 1985.

Salamon, Lester M. *Beyond Privatization: The Tools of Government Action.* Washington, DC: The Urban Institute Press, 1989.

Svara, James H. *Official Leadership in the City.* New York, New York: Oxford University Press, 1990.

_____. *A Survey of America's City Councils: Continuity and Change.* Washington, DC: National League of Cities, 1991.

U.S. Conference of Mayors. *A Status Report on Economic Restructuring and Reemployment Strategies in America's Cities,* Washington, DC: USCM 1994.

_____. *Immigrant Policy Issues for America's Cities.* Washington, DC: USCM, June 1994.

_____. *Impact of Unfunded Federal Mandates on U.S. Cities: A 314-City Survey.* Washington, DC: USCM, October 1993.

_____. *Ending Homelessness in America's Cities: Implementing a National Plan of Action.* Washington, DC: USCM, July 1993.

_____. *Addressing Hunger and Homelessness in America's Cities.* Washington, DC: USCM, June 1993.

_____. *Cities in Recession: The Need for Change, 125-City Survey.* Washington, DC: USCM, March 1993.

_____. *Mayors and Employment and Training: Partners in Human Investment.* Washington, DC: USCM, 1992.

_____. *A Survey of the United States Conference of Mayors' 1992 Emergency Jobs and Anti-Recessionary Initiatives.* Washington, DC: USCM, 1992.

_____. *Community Development Block Grant (CDBG) To America's Cities: Additional Funds Needed to Fight Urban Ills.* Washington, DC: USCM, June 1992.

_____. *Fiscal Stress in America's Cities: The Need for Targeted Fiscal Assistance, 100-City Survey.* Washington, DC: USCM, May 1992.

_____. *A Compendium of Job Training Programs.* Washington, DC: USCM, April 1992.

_____. *Garbage Solutions: A Public Official's Guide to Recycling and Alternative Solid Waste Management Technologies.* Washington, DC: USCM, 1989.

_____. *How Mayors and City Governments Support the Arts: Innovative Financing Techniques and Strategies.* Washington, DC: USCM, 1988.

Zeller, Laurie Hirschfeld. *Term Limitations for Local Officials: A Citizen's Guide to Constructive Dialogue.* Denver, Colorado: National Civic League Press, 1992.

Economic Development

Arrandale, Tom. "Developing the Contaminated City." *Governing,* vol. 6, no. 3, December 1992.

Baily, John T. *Marketing Cities in the 1980s and Beyond.* Rosemont, Illinois: American Economic Development Council, 1989.

Bamberger, Rita J.; William A. Blazar; and George E. Peterson. "Capital Planning." *Planning Advisory Service Report,* no. 390. Chicago, Illinois: APA, September 1985.

Bartik, Timothy J. *Who Benefits from State and Local Economic Development Policies?* Kalamazoo, Michigan: Upjohn Institute, 1991.

Bendick, Marc, Jr. and David W. Rasmussen. "Enterprise Zones and Inner City Economic Revitalization" in George Peterson and Carol Lewis, *Reagan and the Cities.* Washington, DC: The Urban Institute, 1985.

Berger, Renee. "Building Community Partnerships." *National Civic Review,* vol. 73, no. 2. May 1984.

Blakely, Edward J. *Planning Local Economic Development: Theory and Practice.* Thousand Oaks Park, California: Sage Publications, 1989.

Bleakly, Ken. *Economic Impact Analysis: Assessing a Project's Value to a Community.* Rosemont, Illinois: American Economic Development Council, 1993.

Black, Harry. *Achieving Economic Development Success: Tools That Work.* Washington, DC: International City/County Management Association, 1991.

Black, J. Thomas; Libby Howland; and Stuart L. Rogel. *Downtown Retail Development: Conditions for Success and Project Profiles.* Washington, DC: Urban Land Institute, 1983.

Bonnell, Barbara. "Inner-harbor Development." *Lawyers Title News.* May/June 1986.

Bowman, Ann O. *Tools and Targets: The Mechanics of City Economic Development.* Washington, DC: National League of Cities, 1987.

Coe, Barbara A. "Public/Private Partnerships." *The Western Governmental Researcher,* vol. III, no. 1, summer 1987.

Daniels, Beldon; Nancy Barbe; and Harry Lirtzman. "Small Business and State Economic Development" in Robert Friedman and William Schweke, *Expanding the Opportunity to Produce: Revitalizing the American Economy Through New Enterprise Development.* Washington, DC: The Corporation for Enterprise Development, 1981.

Darling, David L., Jr. "Strategic Planning for Community Development." *Community Development Series,* no. L-830. Manhattan, Kansas: Kansas State University, February 1991.

_____. "Setting Community Economic Goals." *Community Development Series,* no. L-714. Manhattan, Kansas: Kansas State University, February 1988.

_____. "Understanding Your Community's Economy." *Community Development Series,* no. L-776. Manhattan, Kansas: Kansas State University, October 1988.

Doud, Thomas P. "Directing Capital to Small Firms." *Economic Development Review,* vol. 5, no. 3, winter 1987.

Fain, Kenneth P. "Leveraging Private Investment." *National Community Reporter,* no. 40, March 1984.

Farr, Cheryl A. and Lawrence D. Rose. "Encouraging Local Economic Development: The State of the Practice." *The Municipal Year Book.* Washington, DC: International City/County Management Association, 1990.

_____. "Negotiating Business Developments." *Municipal Innovation Series Report.* Washington, DC: International City/County Management Association, no. 34, 1981.

Foundersmith, John. "Downtowns in the Year 2040." *The Futurist*, vol. 22, no. 2, March–April 1988.

Fosler, R. Scott. *Local Economic Development: Strategies for a Changing Economy*. Washington, DC: International City/County Management Association, 1991.

Friedman, Robert and William Schweke. *Expanding the Opportunity to Produce: Revitalizing the American Economy through New Enterprise Development*. Washington, DC: The Corporation for Enterprise Development, 1981.

Gobar, Al. "The Need for Community Self-Evaluation." *Western City*, vol. LXIX, no. 8, August 1993.

Glover, Glenda and J. Paul Brownridge. "Enterprise Zones." *Government Finance Review*, vol. 9, no. 3, June 1993.

Gubala, Timothy W., "The Difference Between Economic Developers and Planners." *Economic Development Review*, vol. 10, no 2, Summer 1992.

Hall, Lawrence; Robert H. Lurcott; Karen LaFrance; and Michael A. Dobbins. "Salvaging Neighborhood Shopping Centers." *Planning*, vol. 49, no. 3, March 1983.

Hatry, Harry; Mark Fall; Thomas Singer; and Blaine Liner. *Monitoring the Outcomes of Economic Development Programs*. Washington, DC: The Urban Institute, 1990.

Henning, Ed. "Business Improvement Districts." *Western City*, vol. LXIX, no. 8, August 1993.

Hoffer, William. "Using Urban Renovation Experts." *Nation's Business*, vol. 77, no. 1, January 1989.

Houstoun, Lawrence O., Jr. "Downtown Managers." *New Jersey Municipalities*, vol. 67, no. 4, April 1990.

Isberg, Gunnar. "Strategic Planning." *Minnesota Cities*, vol. 69, no. 4, April 1984.

Kemp, Roger L. *Economic Development in Local Government: A Handbook for Public Officials and Citizens*. Jefferson, North Carolina: McFarland, 1995.

_____. "Economic Development: Raising Revenues Without Increasing Taxes." *The Privatization Review*, vol. 4, no. 1, Washington, DC: The Privatization Council, 1988.

Knack, Ruth; James J. Bellus; and Patricia Adell. "Setting Up Shop for Economic Development." *Planning*, vol. 49, no. 9, October 1983.

Koepke, Robert L. *Practicing Economic Development*. Rosemont, Illinois: American Economic Development Council, 1993.

Kolzow, David R. *Strategic Planning for Economic Development*. Rosemont, Illinois: American Economic Development Council, 1991.

Kotler, Philip; Donald H. Haider; and Irving Rein. *Marketing Places: Attracting Investment, Industry and Tourism to Cities, States and Nations*. New York, New York: The Free Press, 1993.

Lachman, M. Leanne; Deborah L. Brett; and Lewis Bolan. *Urban Infill Development: Its Potential as a Development Strategy*. Chicago, Illinois: Real Estate Research Corporation, 1981.

Leinberge, Christopher B. and Charles Lockwood. "How Business Is Reshaping America." *The Atlantic*, vol. 258, no 4, October 1986.

Lowe, Marcia D. "Alternatives to Shaping Tomorrow's Cities." *The Futurist*, vol. 26, no. 4, July–August 1992.

Luke, Jeffrey S.; Curtis Ventriss; B.J. Reed; and Christine M. Reed. *Managing Economic Development: A Guide to State and Local Leadership Strategies*. San Francisco, California: Jossey-Bass, 1988.

Mayer, Virginia M.; Marina Sampanes; and James Carras. *Local Officials Guide to the CRA*. Washington, DC: National League of Cities, 1991.

McClendon, Bruce W. "Reforming Zoning Regulations." *Texas City & Town*, vol. 70, no. 8, August 1982.

Meyer, Angela D. and Ronald J. Swager. *A Bibliography of Selected Topics in Economic Development Literature, 1987–1993*. Rosemont, Illinois: American Economic Development Council, 1994.

National Council for Urban Economic Development. *Industrial Development Bonds: A Resource for Financing Economic Development*. Washington, DC: NCUED, 1994.

_____. *Neighborhood Economic Revitalization*. Washington, DC: NCUED, 1994.

_____. *Urban Manufacturing: Dilemma or Opportunity?* Washington, DC: NCUED, 1994.

_____. *Forces in the Economy: Implications for Local Economic Development*. Washington, DC: NCUED, 1993.

_____. *Alternative Approaches to Financing Business Development*. Washington, DC: NCUED, 1989.

_____. *Minority Enterprise Development*. Washington, DC: NCUED, 1988.

_____. *Bank Loan Pools: Financing Structures for Business Development*. Washington, DC: NCUED, 1987.

_____. *Entrepreneurial Development: Formalizing the Process*. Washington, DC: NCUED, 1987.

_____. *The Venture Capital Process: A Guide for Economic Development Practitioners*. Washington, DC: NCUED, 1985.

Palma, Delores. "Ways to Revitalize Your Downtown." *American City & County*, vol. 107, no. 11, November 1992.

Pender, Robert B. and Frank C. Shaw. "Public-Private Partnerships." *Texas Town & City*, vol. 78, no. 6, June 1990.

Perloff, Harvey S. *Planning the Post-Industrial City*. Chicago, Illinois: American Planning Association, 1980.

Ressler, Thomas. "Business Incubators." *Western City*, vol. LXIX, no. 7, July 1993.

Rodne, Kjell. "Diversifying the Local Economy." *Public Management*, vol. 73, no. 3, March 1991.

Roeder, David H. "Organizing for Economic Development." *Planning*, vol. 59, no. 4, April 1993.

Rubin, Herbert J. "Community-based Development Organizations," *Public Administration Review*, vol. 53, no. 5, September-October 1993.

Sinclair, Julie. "Main Street Projects." *Alabama Municipal Journal*, vol. 51, no 3, September 1983.

Snyder, Thomas P. and Michael A. Stegman. *Paying for Growth: Using Development Fees to Finance Infrastructure*. Washington, DC: The Urban Institute, 1987.

Starr, Richard. "Local Roles and Responsibilities." *Journal of Housing*, vol. 39, no. 4, July-August 1982.

Stokley, Jan. "Community-based Economic Development." *Economic Development & Law Center Report*, vol. 15, no. 2/3, March-June 1985.

Swager, Ronald J. *Economic Development Tomorrow: A Report from the Profession*. Rosemont, Illinois: American Economic Development Council, 1991.

_____. *A Bibliography of Recent Literature in Economic Development*. Rosemont, Illinois: American Economic Development Council, 1987.

Thompson, Wilbur R. and Philip R. Thompson. "Rethinking Economic Development Planning." *Commentary*, vol. 9, no. 3, fall 1985.

Urban Institute, The. *Special Districts: A Useful Technique for Financing Infrastructure*. Washington, DC: The Urban Institute, 1992.

Wolf, Virginia L. "General Planning." *Missouri Municipal Review*, vol. 51, no 2, February 1986.

Wollard, E.S., Jr. "An Industry Approach to Sustainable Development." *Issues in Science and Technology*, vol. 8, no. 3, spring 1992.

Finance

Allan, Ian J. *Revenue Collection Administration: A Guide for Smaller Governments.* Chicago, Illinois: Government Finance Officers Association, 1992.

Aronson, J. Richard and Eli Schwartz. *Management Policies in Local Government Finance.* Washington, DC: International City/County Management Association, 1987.

Bean, David R.; Stephen J. Gauthier; and Paul E. Glick. *Governmental Accounting, Auditing and Financial Reporting.* Chicago, Illinois: Government Finance Officers Association, 1988.

Bens, Charles K. *Measuring City Hall Performance: Finally a How-to Guide.* Denver, Colorado: National Civic League Press, 1991.

Blair, John P. and David Nachmias. *Fiscal Retrenchment and Urban Policy.* Thousand Oaks Park, California: Sage Publications, 1979.

Bland, Robert L. *A Revenue Guide for Local Government.* Washington, DC: International City/County Management Association, 1989.

Chapman, Jeffrey I. *Long-term Financial Planning: Creative Strategies for Local Government.* Washington, DC: International City/County Management Association, 1987.

Colvard, James E. "Cutout: The Ultimate Cutback Management." *The Bureaucrat,* vol. 10, no. 2, spring 1986.

Epstein, Paul D. *Using Performance Measurements in Local Government.* Denver, Colorado: National Civic League Press, 1988.

Florestano, Patricia S. "Revenue-Raising Limitations on Local Government: A Focus on Alternative Responses." *Public Administration Review,* vol. 41, no. 1, January-February 1981.

Forrer, John J. *Calculating Growth: Software Used in Financial Analysis in Economic Development.* Chicago, Illinois: Government Finance Officers Association, 1990.

Freeman, Michael A. "Competitive Services: New Revenue Options." *Management Information Service Report,* no. 40459. Washington, DC: International City/County Management Association, 1990.

Gauthier, Stephen J. *Audit Management Handbook.* Chicago, Illinois: Government Finance Officers Association, 1989.

Glassberg, Andrew. "Organizational Responses to Municipal Budget Decreases." *Public Administration Review,* vol. 38, no. 4, July-August 1978.

Glick, Paul E. *A Public Manager's Guide to Government Accounting and Financial Reporting.* Chicago, Illinois: Government Finance Officers Association, 1989.

Government Finance Officers Association. *Best of Budgeting: A Guide to Preparing Budget Documents.* Chicago, Illinois: GFOA, 1993.

_____. *Disclosure Guidelines for State and Local Government Securities.* Chicago, Illinois: GFOA, 1991.

_____. *Building Together: Investing in Community Infrastructure.* Chicago, Illinois: GFOA, 1990.

_____. *Preserving the Federal-State-Local Partnership: The Role of Tax Exempt Financing.* Chicago, Illinois: GFOA, 1989.

_____. *A Debt Management Handbook for Small Cities and Other Governmental Units.* Chicago, Illinois: GFOA, 1978.

Groves, Sanford M. and Maureen Godsey Valente. *Evaluating Financial Condition: A Handbook for Local Government.* Washington, DC: International City/County Management Association, 1994.

Hatry, Harry P.; Kenneth P. Voytek; and Allen E. Holmes. *Building Innovation Into*

Program Reviews: Analysis of Service Delivery Options. Washington, DC: The Urban Institute Press, 1989.

_____; Louis Blair; Donald Fisk; and Wayne Kimmel. *Program Analysis for State and Local Governments.* Washington, DC: The Urban Institute Press, 1988.

_____; Richard E. Winnie; and Donald M. Fisk. *Practical Program Evaluation for State and Local Governments.* Washington, DC: The Urban Institute Press, 1986.

Hirschhorn, L. *Cutting Back.* San Francisco, California: Jossey-Bass, 1983.

Howard, Kyland. "Composition of Municipal Revenues: 1979–1984." *The Municipal Year Book.* Washington, DC: International City/County Management Association, 1987.

International City/County Management Association. "Local Government Infrastructure Financing." *Special Data Issue,* no. 40800. Washington, DC: ICMA, 1993.

_____. *Software Reference Guide.* Washington, DC: ICMA, 1993.

_____. "Tax Rebates and Tax Differentials: Issues and Alternatives." *Clearinghouse Report,* no. 40788. Washington, DC: ICMA, 1993.

_____. "Strategic Budgeting: A Guide to Financial Stability." *Management Information Service Report,* no. 40826. Washington, DC. August 1993.

_____. "Capital Improvement Financing, 1991." *Baseline Data Report,* no. 40760. Washington, DC: ICMA, 1992.

_____. "Five-Year Financial Forecast." *Clearinghouse Report,* no. 40473. Washington, DC: ICMA, 1992.

_____. "User Fees: Current Practice." *Management Information Service Report,* no. 40775. Washington, DC: ICMA, December 1992.

_____. "Analyzing Services to Balance the Budget." *Management Information Service Report,* no. 40666. Washington, DC: ICMA, 1991.

_____. "Impact Fees: Issues and Case Studies." *Management Information Service Report,* no. 40688. Washington, DC: ICMA, 1991.

_____. "Establishing the Cost of Services." *Management Information Service Report,* no. 40425. Washington, DC: ICMA, 1990.

_____. "Municipal Budgeting and Productivity." *Baseline Data Report,* no. 40282. Washington, DC: ICMA, 1989.

_____. "Performance Auditing for Local Government." *Management Information Service Report,* no. 40243. Washington, DC: ICMA, 1989.

_____. "Fundraising by Local Governments." *Special Data Issue,* no. 40121. Washington, DC: ICMA, 1988.

_____. "Developer Financing: Impact Fees and Negotiated Exactions." *Management Information Service Report,* no. 40140. Washington, DC: ICMA, 1988.

_____. "The Budget as a Communication Tool." *Management Information Service Report,* no. 40127. Washington, DC: ICMA, February 1988.

_____. "Financial Trend Monitoring System." *Clearinghouse Report,* no. 40110. Washington, DC: ICMA, 1987.

Kelley, Joseph T. *Costing Government Services: A Guide for Decision Making.* Chicago, Illinois: Government Finance Officers Association, 1984.

Leithe, Joni L. and Matthew Montavon. *Impact Fee Programs: A Survey of Design and Administrative Issues.* Chicago, Illinois: Government Finance Officers Association, 1990.

Levine, Charles H. *Managing Fiscal Stress: The Crisis in the Public Sector.* Chatham, New Jersey: Chatham House Publishers, 1980.

_____. "More on Cutback Management: Hard Questions for Hard Times." *Public Administration Review,* vol. 39. no. 2, March-April 1979.

_____. "Organizational Decline and Cutback Management." *Public Administration Review*, vol. 38, no. 4, July-August 1978.

_____ and Irene S. Rubin. *Fiscal Stress and Public Policy.* Thousand Oaks Park, California: Sage Publications, 1980.

_____; Irene S. Rubin; and George G. Wolohojian. *The Politics of Retrenchment. How Local Governments Manage Fiscal Stress.* Thousand Oaks Park, California: Sage Publications, 1980.

Lewis, Carol W. and Anthony T. Logalbo. "Cutback Principles and Practices: A Checklist for Managers." *Public Administration Review,* vol. 40, no. 2, March-April 1980.

Lynch, Thomas. *Contemporary Public Budgeting.* New Brunswick, New Jersey: Transaction Books. 1981.

Malan, Roland M.; James R. Fountain; Donald S. Arrowsmith; and Robert L. Lockridge. *Performance Auditing in Local Government.* Chicago, Illinois: Government Finance Officers Association, 1984.

Matzer, John, Jr. *Capital Projects: New Strategies for Planning, Management, and Finance.* Washington, DC: International City/County Management Association, 1989.

_____. *Practical Financial Management: New Techniques for Local Government.* Washington, DC: International City/County Management Association, 1984.

Merriman, David. *The Control of Municipal Budgets: Towards the Effective Design of Tax & Expenditure Limitations.* Westport, Connecticut: Greenwood Press, 1987.

Mikesell, John. *City Finances, City Futures.* Washington, DC: National League of Cities, 1992.

Miller, Girard. *Financial Management Handbook for Local Governments.* Chicago, Illinois: Government Finance Officers Association, 1986.

_____. *Investing Public Funds.* Chicago, Illinois: Government Finance Officers Association, 1986.

Moulder, Evelina. "Use of Volunteers in Local Government Service Delivery." *Baseline Data Report,* no. 40934. Washington, DC: ICMA, 1994.

National League of Cities. *Anti-Mandates Strategies: Reimbursement Requirements in the States.* Washington, DC: NLC, 1994.

_____. *City Fiscal Conditions.* Washington, DC: NLC, 1994.

_____. *A Comprehensive Guide to Studies on State and Federal Mandates to Localities: An Annotated Bibliography.* Washington, DC: NLC, 1994.

_____. *Estimating Mandate Costs: Processes and Outcomes.* Washington, DC: NLC, 1993.

_____. *State Mandates: Fiscal Notes, Reimbursement, and Anti-Mandate Strategy.* Washington, DC: NLC, 1992.

_____. *State Aid to Cities & Counties.* Washington, DC: NLC, 1988.

_____. *Financing Infrastructure: Innovations at the Local Level.* Washington, DC: NLC, 1987.

_____. *Local Government Tax Authority and Use.* Washington, DC: NLC, 1987.

Netzer, Dick. *Local Alternatives to the Property Tax: User Charges and Nonproperty Taxes.* Washington, DC: Academy of State and Local Government, 1984.

_____. *Property Tax Issues for the 1980's.* Washington, DC: Academy of State and Local Government, 1983.

O'Toole, Daniel E. and James Marshall. "Managing with Less: What Managers Can Expect." *Public Management,* vol. 66, no. 6, June 1984.

Pammer, William J., Jr. *Managing Fiscal Strain in Major American Cities: Understanding Retrenchment in the Public Sector.* Westport, Connecticut: Greenwood Press, 1990.

Reed, B.J. and John W. Swain. *Public Finance Administration*. Englewood Cliffs, New Jersey: Prentice-Hall, 1990.

Robinson, Susan G. *Financing Growth: Who Benefits? Who Pays? and How Much?* Chicago, Illinois: Government Finance Officers Association, 1990.

Rousmaniere, Peter F. *Local Government Auditing: A Manual for Public Officials*. New York, New York: Council on Municipal Performance, 1979.

Schick, Allen. *Perspectives on Public Budgeting*. Washington, DC: American Society for Public Administration, 1987.

Strachota, Dennis and Bruce Engelbrekt. *Catalog of Public Fees and Charges*. Chicago, Illinois: Government Finance Officers Association, 1992.

Swain, John W. "Budgeting and Financial Management" in James M. Banovetz, Drew A. Doland, and John W. Swain. *Managing Small Cities and Counties: A Practical Guide*. Washington, DC: International City/Council Management Association, 1994.

U.S. Conference of Mayors. *Impact of Unfunded Federal Mandates on U.S. Cities: A 314-City Survey*. Washington, DC: USCM, October 1993.

_____. *Cities in Recession: The Need for Change, A 125-City Survey*. Washington, DC: USCM, March 1993.

_____. *Fiscal Stress in America's Cities: The Need for Targeted Fiscal Assistance, A 100-City Survey*. Washington, DC: USCM, May 1992.

_____. *City Fiscal Conditions: 1980–1990, A 50-City Survey*. Washington, DC: USCM, January 1991.

_____. *How Mayors and City Governments Support the Arts: Innovative Financing Techniques and Strategies*. Washington, DC: USCM, 1988.

Weiss, Barbara. *Public/Private Partnerships: Financing a Common Wealth*. Chicago, Illinois: Government Finance Officers Association, 1985.

Fire

Ayres, Richard M. and Paul R. Coble. *Safeguarding Management's Rights*. Dubuque, Iowa: Kendall-Hunt Publishing, 1987.

Building Officials and Code Administrators International. *Model Disaster Preparedness Program Manual*. Country Club Hills, Illinois: BOCAI, 1975.

Colemen, Ronny J. and John A. Granito. *Managing Fire Services*. Washington, DC: International City/County Management Association, 1988.

Cote, Arthur E. *Fire Protection Handbook*. Quincy, Massachusetts: National Fire Protection Association, 1989.

Drabek, Thomas E. and Gerard J. Hoetmer. *Emergency Management: Principles and Practice for Local Government*. Washington, DC: International City/County Management Association, 1991.

Federal Emergency Management Agency. *Digest of Federal Disaster Assistance Programs*. Report DR & R-21. Washington, DC: FEMA, June 26, 1989.

_____. *Hazard Identification, Capability Assessment, and Multi-Year Development Plans*. Report CPG 1–34. Washington, DC: FEMA, January 1987.

_____. *Guide for Development of State and Local Emergency Operations Plans*. Report CPG 1–8. Washington, DC: FEMA, 1985.

_____. *Objectives for Local Emergency Management*. Report CPG 1–5. Washington, DC: FEMA, July 1984.

Feldstein, Lee M. "Fire Personnel Practices." *The Municipal Year Book*. Washington, DC: International City/County Management Association, 1987.

Fitch, Joseph J.; Rich Keller; and Chris Zalar. *Beyond the Street: A Handbook for EMS Leadership and Management*. Solana Beach, California: JEMS Publishing, 1988.

Fluer, Larry. *Hazardous Materials Classification Guide*. Country Club Hills, Illinois: Building Officials and Code Administrators International, 1993.

Granito, John A. "Fire Personnel Practices." *Baseline Data Report*, vol. 15, no. 2. Washington, DC: International City/County Management Association, February 1983.

Hart, Bob. "Emergency Management" in James M. Banovetz, Drew A. Dolan, and John W. Swain. *Managing Small Cities and Counties: A Practical Guide*. Washington, DC: International City/County Management Association, 1994.

Hoetmer, Gerard J. "Emergency Management." *Baseline Data Report*, vol. 15, no. 4. Washington, DC: International City/County Management Association, April 1983.

International Association of Fire Chiefs. *EEO and Affirmative Action Resource Manual for the Chief Fire Executive*. Fairfax, Virginia: IAFC, 1995.

_____. *Trends in the Ambulance Industry*. Fairfax, Virginia: IAFC, 1995.

_____. *Challenging the Fire Service: EMS in the 1990s*. Fairfax, Virginia: IAFC, 1994.

_____. *Fair Labor Standards Act: A Resource Guide*. Fairfax, Virginia: IAFC, 1994.

_____. *Fire Service Risk Management Implementation Guide*. Fairfax, Virginia: IAFC, 1994.

_____. *Implementation of EMS in the Fire Service: Types, Trends, Funding and Acceptance*. Fairfax, Virginia: IAFC, 1994.

_____. *Drug Testing in the Fire Service: A Guide to Policies and Planning*. Fairfax, Virginia: IAFC, 1993.

_____. *Fire Chief Under Attack: Labor Management Conflict in the Fire Service*. Fairfax, Virginia: IAFC, 1993.

_____. *Improving Fire Department Emergency Medical Services*. Fairfax, Virginia: IAFC, 1993.

_____. *EMS User Fee Survey Results*. Fairfax, Virginia: IAFC, 1988.

International City/County Management Association. "Benchmarking: A Method for Achieving Superior Performance in Fire and Emergency Medical Services." *Management Information Service Report*, no. 40790. Washington, DC: ICMA, 1993.

_____. "Emergency Medical Service System: Analysis and Alternatives for Expansion." *Clearinghouse Report*, no. 40794. Washington, DC: ICMA, 1993.

_____. "Fire Personnel Practices." *Baseline Data Report*, no. 40835. Washington, DC: ICMA, 1993.

_____. "Local Emergency Response Plans." *Special Data Issue*, no. 40831. Washington, DC: ICMA, 1993.

_____. "Planning for Disaster Recovery." *Management Information Service Report*, no. 40834. Washington, DC: ICMA, 1993.

_____. "Fire Department Schedules, Budgets, and Computers." *Special Data Issue*, no. 40712. Washington, DC: ICMA, 1992.

_____. "Fire Personnel Recruitment and Selection." *Special Data Issue*, no. 40711. Washington, DC: ICMA, 1992.

_____. "Fire Personnel Testing and Training." *Special Data Issue*, no. 40713. Washington, DC: ICMA, 1992.

_____. "Emergency Planning and Community Right-to-Know: Local Implementation." *Management Information Service Report*, no. 40503. Washington, DC: ICMA, 1991.

_____. "Forecasting the Outcome of Police/Fire Consolidations." *Management Information Service Report*, no. 40559. Washington, DC: ICMA, 1991.

_____. "Police/Fire Consolidation Case Studies." *Clearinghouse Report*, no. 40563. Washington, DC: ICMA, 1991.

_____. "Consolidation of Public Safety Dispatch Operations." *Clearinghouse Report,* no. 40463. Washington, DC: ICMA, 1990.

_____. "Fire Protection: A Review of Operations, Organization, and Effectiveness." *Clearinghouse Report,* no. 40681. Washington, DC: ICMA, 1990.

_____. "Long-Range Public Safety Plan." *Clearinghouse Report,* no. 40474. Washington, DC: ICMA, 1990.

_____. "A Systematic Approach to Fire Service Consolidation and Merger." *Clearinghouse Report,* no. 40599. Washington, DC: ICMA, 1990.

_____. "Analyzing Present and Future Fire Services." *Clearinghouse Report,* no. 40366. Washington, DC: ICMA, 1989.

_____. "Emergency Medical Services Systems." *Management Information Service Report,* no. 40225. Washington, DC: ICMA, 1988.

_____. "Emergency Planning: An Adaptive Approach." *Baseline Data Report,* no. 40211. Washington, DC: ICMA, 1988.

_____. "Fire Station Location: Analysis and Technology." *Management Information Service Report,* no. 40075. Washington, DC: ICMA, 1987.

_____. "Hazardous Material Control and Emergency Response." *Clearinghouse Report,* no. 37613. Washington, DC: ICMA, 1985.

_____. "Hazardous Materials Incidents: Improving Community Response." *Management Information Service Report,* no. 34568. Washington, DC: ICMA, 1984.

Kemp, Roger L. "Municipal Fire Services: New Techniques for Hard Times." *Journal of Applied Fire Science,* vol. 2, no. 1. Amityville, New York: Baywood Publishing, 1992–93.

_____. "Public Official's Role in Emergency Management." *Hazard Monthly,* vol. IV, no. 12. Rockville, Maryland: Research Alternatives, June 1984.

_____. "The Role of Emergency Management in America's Local Governments." *Hazard Monthly,* vol II, no. 11. Rockville, Maryland: Research Alternatives, May 1982.

Lerner, Ken. "Governmental Negligence Liability Exposure in Disaster Management." *The Urban Lawyer,* vol. 23, no. 3, summer 1991.

National Fire Academy. "The Incident Command System." *National Fire Academy Student Manual.* Emmittsburg, Maryland, NFA, August 1989.

National Fire Protection Association. *Developing Fire Protection Services for the Public.* Quincy, Massachusetts: NFPA, 1989.

National League of Cities. *Developing Alcohol and Drug Testing Programs: A Guide for Local Governments.* Washington, DC: NLC, 1994.

Nudell, Mayer and Norman Antokol. *The Handbook for Effective Emergency and Crisis Management.* Lexington, Massachusetts: Lexington Books, 1988.

O'Leary, Rosemary. *Emergency Planning and the Community Right-to-Know Act.* Washington, DC: International City/County Management Association, 1993.

Rhyne, Charles S. *Police and Firefighters: The Law of Municipal Personnel Regulations.* Washington, DC: National Institute of Municipal Law Offices, 1982.

Scanlon, Raymond D. *Hazardous Materials, Hazardous Waste: Local Management Options.* Washington, DC: International City/County Management Association, 1987.

Swain, John W. "Fire and Emergency Medical Services" in James M. Banovetz, Drew A. Dolan, and John W. Swain. *Managing Small Cities and Counties: A Practical Guide.* Washington, DC: International City/County Management Association, 1994.

Forms of Government

Adrian, Charles R. "Forms of Government in American History." *The Municipal Year Book*. Washington, DC: International City/County Management Association, 1988.

_____. *A History of American City Government*. New York, New York: New York University Press, 1987.

Anderson, Eric. "Two Major Forms of Government: Two Types of Professional Management." *The Municipal Year Book*. Washington, DC: International City/County Management Association, 1985.

Banfield, E.C. and J.Q. Wilson. *City Politics*. New York, New York: Vintage Books, 1963.

Banovetz, James M. *Managing the Modern City*. Washington, DC: International City/County Management Association, 1971.

Boynton, Robert Paul. "The Council-Manager Plan: A Historical Perspective." *Public Management*, vol. 46, no. 10, October 1974.

Cassella, William N., Jr. "The Responsible Executive." *National Civic Review*, vol. 83, no. 4, fall-winter 1994.

Ehrenhalt, Alan. "Good Government, Bad Government." *Governing*, vol. 8, no. 7, April 1995.

Hansell, William. "The C-M Plan: Making Representative Democracy More Effective." *Public Management*, vol. 69, no. 2, February 1987.

Huntley, R.J. and R.J. MacDonald. "Urban Managers: Organizational Preferences, Managerial Styles, and Social Policy Roles." *The Municipal Year Book*. Washington, DC: International City/County Management Association, 1975.

Johnson, Karl F. and C.J. Hein. "Assessment of the Council-Manager Form of Government Today: Managers Meet the Challenge Through Balance." *Public Management*, vol. 67, no. 7, July 1985.

Kincaid, John. *State Laws Governing Local Government Structure and Administration*. Report no. M-186. Washington, DC: Advisory Commission on Intergovernmental Relations, March 1993.

_____. *Residential Community Associations: Private Governments in the Intergovernmental System?* Report no. A-112. Washington, DC: Advisory Commission on Intergovernmental Relations, May 1989.

McGowan, Robert P. and John M. Stevens. "Local Government Initiatives in a Climate of Uncertainty." *Public Administration Review*, vol. 43, no. 2, March-April 1983.

Morgan, D.R. and J.P. Pelissero. "Urban Policy: Does Political Structure Matter?" *American Political Science Review*, vol. 74, no. 12, December 1980.

Newland, Chester A. "Council-Manager Government: Positive Alternative to Separation of Powers." *Public Management*, vol. 67, no. 7, July 1985.

Parr, John. "The Council-Manager Form and the Future." *Public Management*, vol. 69, no. 2, February 1987.

Renner, Tari. "Appointed Local Government Managers: Stability and Change." *The Municipal Year Book*. Washington, DC: International City/County Management Association, 1991.

Rowe, B.J.D. "Theory and Myth vs. Practice." *Public Management*, vol. 69, no. 2. February 1987.

Sanders, H.T. "The Government of American Cities: Continuity and Change in Structure." *The Municipal Year Book*. Washington, DC: International City/County Management Association, 1982.

Stillman, Richard J., II. "Status of the Council-Manager Plan: Continuity in a Changing Society." *Public Management,* vol. 67, no. 7, July 1985.

_____. "Local Public Management in Transition: A Report on the Current State of the Profession." *The Municipal Year Book.* Washington, DC: International City/County Management Association, 1982.

_____. "City Manager—Professional Helping Hand or Political Hired Hand." *Public Administration Review,* vol. 37, no. 6, November-December 1977.

_____. *The Rise of the City Manager.* Albuquerque, New Mexico: University of New Mexico Press, 1974.

Svara, James H. "The Structural Reform Impulse in Local Government." *National Civic Review,* vol. 83, no. 3, summer-fall 1994.

_____. "Sharing the Load of Governance: The Manager's Responsibilities." *Public Management,* vol. 67, no. 7, July 1985.

_____. "Dichotomy and Duality: Reconceptualizing the Relationship Between Policy and Administration in Council-Manager Cities." *Public Administration Review,* vol. 45, no. 1, January-February 1985.

Wallis, Allan D. "Evolving Structures and Challenges of Metropolitan Regions." *National Civic Review,* vol. 83, no. 1, winter-spring 1994.

_____. "Inventing Regionalism: A Two-Phase Approach." *National Civic Review,* vol. 83, no. 4, fall-winter 1994.

Health and Human Services

American Public Health Association. *Healthy Committees 2000: Model Standards.* Washington, DC: APHA, 1991.

Anderson, Wayne F.; Bernard J. Frieden; and Michael J. Murphy. *Managing Human Services.* Washington, DC: International City/County Management Association, 1977.

Agranoff, Robert. *Human Services on a Limited Budget.* Washington, DC: International City/County Management Association, 1983.

_____, et al. *Coping with the Demands for Change Within Human Services Administration.* Washington, DC: American Society for Public Administration, 1977.

Dluhy, Milan J. *Building Coalitions in Human Services.* Thousand Oaks Park, California: Sage Publications, 1990.

Flynn, John P. *Social Agency Policy.* Chicago, Illinois: Nelson-Hall, 1992.

Gans, Sheldon P. and Gerald T. Horton. *Integration of Human Services: The State and Municipal Levels.* New York, New York: Praeger, 1975.

Hasenfeld, Yeheskel. *Human Services as Complex Organizations.* Thousand Oaks Park, California: Sage Publications, 1992.

International City/County Management Association. "Allocating Resources for Human Services." *Management Information Service Report,* no. 40824. Washington, DC: ICMA, 1993.

_____. "Comprehensive Planning to End Homelessness: Four Approaches." *Clearinghouse Report,* no. 40751. Washington, DC: ICMA, 1992.

_____. "Strategies for Youth at Risk." *Management Information Service Report,* no. 40750. Washington, DC: ICMA, 1992.

_____. "Strategies for Reducing Homelessness." *Management Information Service Report,* no. 40501. Washington, DC: ICMA, 1990.

Melaville, Atelia I.; Martin J. Blank; and Gelareh Asayesh. *Together We Can: A Guide for Crafting a Profamily System of Education and Human Services.* Washington, DC: U.S. Department of Education, 1993.

National Association of Counties. *Human Services Integration at the Community Level: A Six County Report.* Washington, DC: NACO, 1974.

National Association of County & City Health Officials. *Blueprint for a Healthy Community: A Guide for Local Health Departments.* Washington, DC: NACCHO, July 1994.

_____. *Providing Culturally Appropriate Services: Local Health Departments & Community-Based Organizations Working Together.* Washington, DC: NACCHO, July 1994.

_____. *Multicultural Resource Guide & Bibliography.* Volume II. Washington, DC: NACCHO, summer 1994.

_____. *Working Together: A Model Strategy Resource Guide for Local Health Departments & Community and Migrant Health Centers.* Washington, DC: NACCHO, January 1994.

_____. *Core Public Health Functions.* Washington, DC: NACCHO, July 1993.

_____. *Multicultural Resource Guide & Bibliography.* Volume I. Washington, DC: NACCHO, Fall 1993.

_____. *Primary Case Assessment: Local Health Department's Role in Service Delivery.* Washington, DC: NACCHO, October 1992.

_____. *Multicultural Health Project Recommendations & Case Study Reports.* Washington, DC: NACCHO, September 1992.

_____. *Current Roles & Future Challenges of Local Health Departments in Environmental Health.* Washington, DC: NACCHO, May 1992.

_____. *Managing & Preventing Environmental Health Controversy: A Communications Approach to Local Public Health.* Washington, DC: NACCHO, May 1992.

_____. *National Profile of Local Health Departments.* Washington, DC: NACCHO, July 1990.

National Conference of State Legislators. *America's Newcomers: Health Care Issues for New Americans.* Washington, DC: NCSL, July 1993.

National League of Cities. *Complying with the Americans with Disabilities Act.* Washington, DC: NLC, 1991.

_____. *Ways and Means for Children and Families.* Washington, DC: NLC, 1991.

_____. *Local Strategies in the War Against Drugs.* Washington, DC: NLC, 1989.

_____. *Children, Families & Cities: Programs That Work at the Local Level.* Washington, DC: NLC, 1987.

Richie, Nicolas D. and Diane E. Alperin. *Innovation and Change in the Human Services.* Springfield, Illinois: Charles C. Thomas, 1992.

Rocheleau, Bruce A. and Thomas K. Mackesey. "Utilization-Focused Evaluation: A Case Study from the Human Services Area." *Policy Studies Journal,* vol. 8, no. 7, July 1980.

_____. "What, Consumer Feedback Surveys Again? A Guide to Improving the Utility of Consumer Evaluation." *Evaluation and the Health Professions,* vol. 3, no. 4, April 1980.

U.S. Conference of Mayors. *HIV Prevention Community Planning Profiles: Assessing Year One.* Washington, DC: USCM, March 1995.

_____. *Language, Culture, and Access to Health Care: Three Local Program Profiles.* Washington, DC: USCM, February 1995.

_____. *Local AIDS Services: The National Directory.* Washington, DC: USCM, March 1994.

_____. *Human Services in City Governments.* Washington, DC: USCM, 1993.

_____. *Local HIV Policies Resource Guide.* Washington, DC: USCM, April 1993.

_____. *Ending Homelessness in America's Cities: Implementing a National Plan of Action.* Washington, DC: USCM, July 1993.

_____. *Address Hunger and Homelessness in America's Cities.* Washington, DC: USCM, June 1993.

_____. *Language and Culture in Health Care—Coping with Linguistic and Cultural Differences: Challenges to Local Health Departments.* Washington, DC: USCM, January, 1993.

_____. *Access to Health Care for Minorities: Profiles of 3 Local Health Departments.* Washington, DC: USCM, 1992.

_____. *Partnerships for Vulnerable Youth: An Annotated Listing of City Programs.* Washington, DC: USCM, October 1992.

_____. *USCM HIV/AIDS Prevention Grants Program Profiles of the 1990–1991 Grantees.* Washington, DC: USCM, October 1992.

_____. *Impact of AIDS on America's Cities: A 26-City Report.* Washington, DC: USCM, 1991.

_____. *Mentally Ill and Homeless: A 22-City Survey.* Washington, DC: USCM, November 1991.

_____. *Directory of Federal Grants for HIV/AIDS Prevention Services.* Washington, DC: USCM, November 1991.

_____. *Local AIDS Policies.* Washington, DC: USCM, 1988.

_____. *Local Responses to the Needs of Homeless Mentally Ill Persons.* Washington, DC: USCM, May 1987.

_____. *Local Policies in Response to AIDS and HTLV III/LAV Infection.* Washington, DC: USCM, 1986.

Wallerstein, Nina and Harriet Rubenstein. *Teaching About Job Hazards: A Guide for Workers and Their Health Providers.* Washington, DC: American Public Health Association, 1993.

Weeks, James L.; Barry S. Levy; and Gregory R. Wagner. *Preventing Occupational Disease and Injury.* Washington, DC: American Public Health Association, 1991.

Infrastructure

American Public Works Association. *Committing to the Cost of Ownership: Maintenance and Repair of Public Buildings.* Chicago, Illinois: APWA, 1990.

_____. *Public Works Today: A Profile of Local Service Organizations and Managers.* Chicago, Illinois: APWA, 1990.

_____. *Revenue Shortfall: The Public Works Challenge of the 1980s.* Chicago, Illinois: APWA, 1981.

Aronson, J. Richard and Eli Schwartz. "Capital Budgeting for Local Governments." *Management Information Service Report,* vol. 14, no. 1, Washington, DC: International City/County Management Association, January 1982.

Bacon, Kevin. "Paying for Public Facilities After Proposition 13." *Western City,* vol. 57, no. 8, August 1981.

Barker, Michael. *Rebuilding America's Infrastructure: An Agenda for the 1980s.* Durham, North Carolina: Duke University Press, 1984.

Beito, David T. and Bruce Smith. "The Formation of Urban Infrastructure Through Nongovernmental Planning: The Private Places in St. Louis." *Journal of Urban History,* vol. 16, no. 3, May 1990.

Bounds, Kenneth R. "Seattle's Renovation and Maintenance Strategy: A Local Approach to the Infrastructure Problem." *Urban Resources,* vol. 1, no. 2, fall 1983.

Chapman, Jeffrey I. *Long-Term Financial Planning: Creative Strategies for Local Government.* Washington, DC: International City/County Management Association, 1987.

Choate, Pat and Susan Walter. "A Capital Budget for the United States." *America in Ruins.* Washington, DC: The Council of State Planning Agencies, 1981, and Durham, North Carolina: Duke University Press, 1983.

Congressional Budget Office. *New Directions for the Nation's Public Works.* Washington, DC: U.S. Government Printing Office, 1988.

Cristofano, Sam M. and William S. Foster. *Management of Local Public Works.* Washington, DC: International City/County Management Association, 1986.

Dew, James Kurt. "Financial Futures for State and Local Governments." *Government Finance Review,* vol. 10, no. 4, December 1981.

Dunlop, John T. "Rebuilding America's Vital Public Facilities." *APWA Reporter,* vol. 51, no. 5, May 1984.

General Accounting Office. *Effective Planning and Budgeting Practices Can Help Arrest the Nation's Deteriorating Public Infrastructure.* Washington, DC: GAO, November, 1982.

Grigg, Neal. *Infrastructure Engineering and Management.* New York, New York: John Wiley and Sons, 1988.

Hamilton, Randy H. "The World Turned Upside Down: The Contemporary Revolution in State and Local Government Capital Financing." *Public Administration Review,* vol. 43, no. 1, January-February 1983.

Hatry, Harry P. *Maintaining the Existing Infrastructure.* Washington, DC: Public Technology, Inc., 1981.

 and Bruce Steinthal. *Selecting Capital Facility Maintenance Strategies.* Washington, DC: The Urban Institute, April 1983.

Houlihan, Barrie. *The Challenge of Public Works Management: A Comparative Study of North America, Japan, and Europe.* Brussels, Belgium: The International Institute of Administrative Sciences, 1992.

Howitt, Arnold M.; Helen F. Ladd; Herman B. Leonard; and Ann B. Weeks. "Physical Infrastructure in Boston." *Urban Resources,* vol. 1, no. 2, fall 1983.

Hudgins. Edward. *How Privatization Can Solve America's Infrastructure Crisis.* Washington, DC: The Heritage Foundation, 1992.

Humphrey, Nancy; George E. Peterson; and Peter Wilson. "The Future of Cleveland's Capital Plant." *America's Urban Capital Stock,* volume II. Washington, DC: The Urban Institute, 1979.

Knorr, Edward L., et al. *Good Practices in Public Works.* Chicago, Illinois: American Public Works Association, 1988.

Matzer, John, Jr. *Capital Projects: New Strategies for Planning, Management, and Finance.* Washington, DC: International City/County Management Association, 1989.

_____. *Practical Financial Management: New Techniques for Local Government.* Washington, DC: International City/County Management Association, 1984.

_____. *Capital Financing Strategies for Local Governments.* Washington, DC: International City/County Management Association, 1983.

Melvin, Eric. *Plan. Predict. Prevent. How to Reinvest in Public Buildings.* Special Report no. 62. Chicago, Illinois: APWA, 1992.

Moehring, Eugene P. *Public Works and Urban History: Recent Trends and New Directions.* Chicago, Illinois: APWA, 1982.

Moskal, Brian S. "America: On the Road to Ruin?" *Industry Week,* vol. 216, no. 5, March 7, 1983.

National Council on Public Works Improvement. *Fragile Foundations: A Report on America's Public Works.* Washington, DC: U.S. Government Printing Office, 1988.

_____. *The Nation's Public Works: Defining the Issues.* Washington, DC: U.S. Government Printing Office, 1988.

National League of Cities and U.S. Conference of Mayors. *Capital Budgeting and Infrastructure in America's Cities: An Initial Assessment.* Washington, DC: NLC/USCM, April 1983.

Odell, Rice. "Can We Afford to Maintain Our Urban Infrastructure?" *Urban Land,* vol. 41, no. 1, January 1982.

Office of Technology Assessment, Congress of the U.S. *Delivering the Goods: Public Works Technologies, Management, and Practices.* Washington, DC: U.S. Government Printing Office, 1991.

_____. *Rebuilding the Foundations: A Special Report on State and Local Public Works Financing and Management.* Washington, DC: U.S. Government Printing Office, 1990.

Olson, Walter T. "To Build Up Greater Cleveland: The Community Investment Strategy." *Urban Resources,* vol. 1, no. 2, fall 1983.

Parent, Phil. *Public Works Guide to Automated Mapping & Facilities Management.* Special Report no. 64. Chicago, Illinois: APWA, 1992.

Penner, Rudolph G. *Public Works Infrastructure: Policy Considerations for the 1980s.* Washington, DC: Congressional Budget Office, April 1983.

Petersen, John E. and Wesley C. Hough. *Creative Capital Financing for State and Local Governments.* Washington, DC: Government Finance Officers Association, March 1983.

Peterson, George. *Financing Public Infrastructure: Policy Options.* Washington, DC: The Urban Institute, March 1982.

_____ and Stephen Godwin. *Infrastructure Inventory and Condition Assessment.* Washington, DC: The Urban Institute, February 1983.

_____ and Mary John Miller. *Financing Options for Urban Infrastructure.* Washington, DC: The Urban Institute, August, 1981.

Pudinski, Walter. "Rialto: A Better Way to Finance Growth." *Western City,* vol. 57, no. 3, March 1982.

Reuss, Henry S. *Hard Choices.* Washington, DC: National Infrastructure Advisory Committee to the Joint Economic Committee of Congress, 1984.

Rosen, Howard and Ann Durkin Keating. *Water and the City: The Next Century.* Chicago, Illinois: Public Works Historical Society, 1991.

Schmandt, Jurgen, et al. *The New Urban Infrastructure: Cities and Telecommunications.* New York, New York: Praeger, 1990.

Stanfield, Rochelle L. "Building Streets and Sewers Is Easy … It's Keeping Them Up That's the Trick." *National Journal,* vol. 12, no. 21, May 24, 1980.

Sundin. H.S. "Can We Afford to Renovate America's Crumbling Infrastructure?" *Illinois Municipal Review,* vol. 62, no. 4, April 1983.

Thompson, Dale. *Infrastructure Sources: A Key to Current Literature for Municipal Officials and Public Managers.* Washington, DC: National League of Cities, 1983.

Vaughn, Roger J. *Rebuilding America: Financing Public Works in the 1980s,* volume 2. Washington, DC: The Council of State Planning Agencies, 1983.

Wiggins. C. Don. "A Case Study in Governmental Capital Budgeting." *Government Finance Review,* vol. 9, no. 2, June 1980.

Woods, Charles. "Introducing Preventative Management." *Illinois Municipal Review,* vol. 61, no. 5, May 1982.

Legal

Adrian, Charles R. *State and Local Governments.* New York, New York: McGraw-Hill, 1976.

Ayres, Richard M. and Paul R. Coble. *Safeguarding Management's Rights.* Dubuque, Iowa: Kendall-Hunt Publishing, 1987.

Bisheff, Maurice. "Managers: Do You Know Where Your Public Records Are? Economic and Legal Implications for Local Governments." *IIMC Newsletter,* vol. XLV, no. 8, September 1994.

Blackman, Lee L. and Erich R. Luschei. "Voting Rights Litigation: A Practical Guide for the 90's." *Municipal Attorney,* vol. 32, nos. 5 & 6, September-December 1991.

Chapple, Stephen. "A Review of Major Federal Judicial Decisions." *The Municipal Year Book.* Washington, DC: International City/County Management Association, 1987.

Dowden, Lisa G. "Municipal Easements, Rights-of-Way, and Public Facilities—Superfund Risks?" *Municipal Attorney,* vol. 35, no. 3, May-June 1994.

Fix, Michael and Daphne Kenyon. *Coping with Mandates: What Are the Alternatives?* Washington, DC: The Urban Institute Press, 1990.

Fleischman, Joel L.; Lance Leibman; and Mark H. Moore. *Public Duties: The Moral Obligations of Government Officials.* Cambridge, Massachusetts: Harvard University Press, 1981.

Geller. Kenneth S. "Municipal Liability Under Section 1983: A Thumbnail Sketch." *Public Management,* vol. 68, no. 11, November 1986.

Hardy, Paul T. and J. Devereux Weeks. *Personal Liability of Public Officials Under Federal Law.* Athens, Georgia: Carl Vinson Institute of Government, University of Georgia, 1988.

Harney, Donald F. *Service Contracting: A Local Government Guide.* Washington, DC: International City/County Management Association, 1992.

Hill, Melvin B., Jr. *State Laws Governing Local Government Structure and Administration.* Athens, Georgia: Carl Vinson Institute of Government, University of Georgia, 1978.

International City/County Management Association. "Americans with Disabilities Act: A Guide to Compliance." *Clearinghouse Report,* no. 40799. Washington, DC: ICMA, 1993.

_____. "Tax Rebates and Tax Differentials: Issues and Alternatives." *Clearinghouse Report,* no. 40788. Washington, DC: ICMA, 1993.

_____. "Public Officials Liability." *Baseline Data Report,* no. 40312. Washington, DC: ICMA, 1989.

_____. "Drug Testing, Sexual Harassment, Smoking: Employee Rights Issues." *Management Information Service Report,* no. 40130. Washington, DC: ICMA, 1988.

_____. "Elected Executives: Authority and Responsibility." *Clearinghouse Report,* no. 40143. Washington, DC: ICMA, 1988.

_____. "Municipal Election Processes: The Impact on Minority Representation." *Baseline Data Report,* no. 40082. Washington, DC: ICMA, 1988.

Kashi, Joseph L. "Designing and Installing Optical Imaging Hardware." *Law Office Computing,* vol. 4, no. 6, December-January 1995.

Kwok-Sze; Richard Wong; and Kathleen Rakestraw. "The ABCs of Risk Management." *Management Information Service Report,* no. 40667. Washington, DC: International City/County Management Association, 1991.

McSpedon, Joseph H. "Standards to Avoid Employer Retaliation Charges." *Labor Law Journal,* vol. 33, no. 1, January 1982.

Merriman, David. *The Control of Municipal Budgets: Towards the Effective Design of Tax & Expenditure Limitations.* Westport, Connecticut: Greenwood Press, 1987.

Miller, Joel C. "Municipal Annexation and Boundary Change." *The Municipal Year Book.* Washington, DC: International City/County Management Association, 1987.

Muzychenko, Jay. "Local Governments at Risk: The Crisis in Liability Insurance." *The*

Municipal Year Book. Washington, DC: International City/County Management Association, 1987.

National Civic League. *Model City Charter.* Denver, Colorado: NCL Press, 1992.

_____. *Guide for Charter Commissions.* Denver, Colorado: NCL Press, 1991.

National League of Cities. *Local Officials Guide to the 1992 Cable Act.* Washington, DC: NLC, 1993.

_____. *Complying with the Americans with Disabilities Act.* Washington, DC: NLC, 1991.

_____. *Choices of the Citizenry: Forms of Municipal Government in the United States.* Washington, DC: NLC, May 1989.

_____. *Municipal Liability and Risk Management: Issues and Answers.* Washington, DC: NLC, May 1989.

O'Conner, Thomas J. "Voice Recognition Systems for the Small Law Office." *Law Office Computing,* vol. 4, no. 16, December-January 1995.

Pellicciotti, Joseph M. *An Analysis of the Age Discrimination in Employment Act.* Alexandria, Virginia: International Personnel Management Association, 1994.

_____. *Title VII Liability for Sexual Harassment in the Workplace.* Alexandria, Virginia: International Personnel Management Association, 1993.

Pine, John C. and Robert C. Bickel. *Tort Liability Today: A Guide for State and Local Governments.* Washington, DC: Public Risk Management Association and National League of Cities, 1992.

Pumpkin, Barry A. "Local Government and Antitrust: A Strategy for Reducing Liability." *Public Management,* vol., 67, no. 4, April 1985.

Reichenberg, Neil. *Family and Medical Leave Act Regulations.* Alexandria, Virginia: International Personnel Management Association, 1995.

Renner, Tari. "Municipal Election Processes: The Impact on Minority Representation." *The Municipal Year Book.* Washington, DC: International City/County Management Association, 1988.

Rhyne, Charles S. *The Law of Local Government Operations Project.* Washington, DC: National Institute of Municipal Law Officers, 1985.

_____. *Mayor: Chief Municipal Executive Law.* Washington, DC: National Institute of Municipal Law Officers, 1985.

_____. *Municipal Attorney Law.* Washington, DC: National Institute of Municipal Law Officers, 1984.

_____. *Police and Firefighters: The Law of Municipal Personnel Regulations.* Washington, DC: National Institute of Municipal Law Officers, 1982.

_____. *Law of Local Government Operations.* Washington, DC: National Institute of Municipal Law Officers, 1980.

Roberts, Jane F. "State Actions Affecting Local Governments: Upheaval for Fiscal Relations." *The Municipal Year Book.* Washington, DC: International City/County Management Association, 1987.

Rohr, John. *Ethics for Bureaucrats: An Essay on Law and Values.* New York, New York: Marcel Dekker, 1978.

Rule, Wilma and Joseph F. Zimmerman. *United States Electoral Systems: Their Impact on Women and Minorities.* New York, New York: Praeger, 1992.

Shafroth, Frank H. "Congressional and Administrative Actions Affecting Municipalities." *The Municipal Year Book.* Washington, DC: International City/County Management Association, 1987.

Svara, James H. *Official Leadership in the City.* New York, New York: Oxford University Press, 1990.

Terry, Nicolas P. "'Tis the Season to Be on the Internet." *Law Office Computing,* vol. 4, no. 6, December-January 1995.

U.S. Advisory Commission on Intergovernmental Relations. *State Laws Governing Local Government Structure and Administration.* Report no. M-186. Washington, DC: U.S. Government Printing Office, March 1993.
_____. *Mandates: Cases in State-Local Relations.* Report no. M-173. Washington, DC: U.S. Government Printing Office, 1990.
_____. *Governments at Risk: Liability Insurance and Tort Reform.* Report no. SR-7. Washington, DC: U.S. Government Printing Office, December 1987.
U.S. Conference of Mayors. *Public Employer Privacy: A Legal and Practical Guide to Issues Affecting the Workplace.* Washington, DC: USCM, 1995.
_____. *Family and Medical Leave: Federal and State Laws.* Washington, DC: USCM, 1993.
_____. *Impact of Unfunded Federal Mandates on U.S. Cities: A 314-City Survey.* Washington, DC: USCM, 1993.
_____. *Smarter Bargaining: A Guide to Contract Language.* Washington, DC: USCM, 1984.
Zeller, Laurie Hirschfeld. *Term Limitations for Local Officials: A Citizens' Guide to Constructive Dialogue.* Denver, Colorado: National Civic League Press, 1992.
Zimmerman, Joseph F. "Alternative Local Electoral Systems." *National Civic Review,* vol. 79, no. 1, January-February 1990.

Library

American Library Association. *Using the Legislative Process.* Chicago, Illinois: ALA, 1993.
Ballard, Thomas. *The Failure of Resource Sharing in Public Libraries and Alternative Strategies for Service.* Chicago, Illinois: American Library Association, 1986.
Baskin, Barbara H. and Karen H. Harris. *The Mainstreamed Library: Issues, Ideas, Innovations.* Chicago, Illinois: American Library Association, 1982.
Bessler, Joanne M. *Putting Service Into Library Staff Training: A Patron-Centered Guide.* Chicago, Illinois: American Library Association, 1994.
Bonnell, Pamela. *Fundraising for the Small Library.* Chicago, Illinois: American Library Association, 1983.
Buckland, Michael. *Redesigning Library Services: A Manifesto.* Chicago, Illinois: American Library Association, 1991.
Cassell, Kay Ann. *Knowing Your Community and Its Needs.* Chicago, Illinois: American Library Association, 1988.
Chelton, Mary K. *Excellence in Library Services to Young Adults: The Nation's Top Programs.* Chicago, Illinois: American Library Association, 1994.
Childers, Thomas A. and Nancy A. Van House. *What's Good? Describing Your Public Library Effectiveness.* Chicago, Illinois: American Library Association, 1993.
Coffman, Steve. *Fiscal Directory of Fee-Based Research and Information Services.* Chicago, Illinois: American Library Association, 1993.
Daubert, Madeline J. *Financial Management for Small and Medium-sized Libraries.* Chicago, Illinois: American Library Association, 1993.
Dewey, Patrick R. *101 Desktop Publishing and Graphics Programs.* Chicago, Illinois: American Library Association, 1993.
_____. *202(+) Software Packages to Use in Your Library: Descriptions, Evaluations, and Practical Advice.* Chicago, Illinois: American Library Association, 1992.
_____. *101 Microcomputer Projects to Do in Your Library: Putting Your Micro to Work.* Chicago, Illinois: American Library Association, 1990.
Durrance, Joan C.; Kathleen Savage; Mary Jo Ryan; and Stephen M. Mallinger. *Serving*

Job Seekers and Career Changers: A Planning Manual for Public Libraries. Chicago, Illinois: American Library Association, 1993.

Eberhart, George M. *The Whole Library Handbook: Current Data, Professional Advice, and Curiosa About Libraries and Library Services.* Chicago, Illinois: American Library Association, 1991.

Fox, Beth Wheeler. *The Dynamic Community Library: Creative, Practical, and Inexpensive Ideas for the Director.* Chicago, Illinois: American Library Association, 1988.

Hill, Malcolm. *Budgeting and Financial Record Keeping in the Small Library.* Chicago, Illinois: American Library Association, 1992.

International City/County Management Association. "Cost/Benefit Analysis for Information Technology Projects." *Clearinghouse Report,* no. 40917. Washington, DC: ICMA, 1994.

_____. *Software Reference Guide.* Washington, DC: ICMA, 1993.

Karp, Rashelle S. *Volunteers in the Small Library.* Chicago, Illinois: American Library Association, 1992.

Kinney, Lisa F. *Lobby for Your Library: Know What Works.* Chicago, Illinois: American Library Association, 1992.

Lazzaro, Joseph J. *Adaptive Technologies for Learning and Work Environments.* Chicago, Illinois: American Library Association, 1993.

Lester, June. *Library and Information Services: The Yearly Chronicle.* Chicago, Illinois: American Library Association, 1991.

Lipow, Anne Grodzins and Deborah A. Carver. *Staff Development: A Practical Guide.* Chicago, Illinois: American Library Association, 1992.

Martin, Ron. *Libraries for the Future: Planning Buildings That Work.* Chicago, Illinois: American Library Association, 1992.

McClure, Charles R.; Amy Owen; Douglas L. Zweizig; Mary Jo Lynch; and Nancy A. Van House. *Planning and Role Setting for Public Libraries: A Manual of Options and Procedures.* Chicago, Illinois: American Library Association, 1987.

Morris, John. *The Library Disaster Preparedness Handbook.* Chicago, Illinois: American Library Association, 1986.

Moulder, Evelina. "Use of Volunteers in Local Government Service Delivery." *Baseline Data Report,* no. 40934. Washington, DC: International City/County Management Association, 1994.

National League of Cities. *The Information Superhighway Game.* Washington, DC: NLC, 1994.

_____. *Dealing Effectively with the Media.* Washington, DC: NLC, 1993.

Norris, Donald F. *Microcomputers and Local Government.* Washington, DC: International City/County Management Association, 1989.

Riggs, Donald E. *Library Communication: The Language of Leadership.* Chicago, Illinois: American Library Association, 1992.

Robinson, Charles W. *Give 'Em What They Want: Managing the Public's Library.* Chicago, Illinois: American Library Association, 1992.

Rosenberg, Philip. *Cost Finding for Public Libraries: A Manager's Handbook.* Chicago, Illinois: American Library Association, 1986.

Rounds, Richard S. *Basic Budgeting Practices for Libraries.* Chicago, Illinois: American Library Association, 1994.

Rowley, Jenny E. and Peter J. Rowley. *Operations Research: A Tool for Library Management.* Chicago, Illinois: American Library Association, 1981.

Saffady, William. *Introduction to Automation for Librarians.* Chicago, Illinois: American Library Association, 1994.

_____. *Automating the Small Library*. Chicago, Illinois: American Library Association, 1991.

Savage, Kathleen M. *Serving Job Seekers and Career Changes: A Critical Bibliography for Public Libraries*. Chicago, Illinois: American Library Association, 1993.

Sheldon, Brooke E. *Leaders and Libraries: Styles and Strategies for Success*. Chicago, Illinois: American Library Association, 1991.

Smith, G. Stevenson. *Managerial Accounting for Libraries and Not-for-Profit Organizations*. Chicago, Illinois: American Library Association, 1991.

Staerkel, Kathleen; Mary Fellows; and Sue McCleaf Nespeca. *Youth Services Librarians as Managers*. Chicago, Illinois: American Library Association, 1994.

Steele, Victoria and Stephen D. Elder. *Becoming a Fundraiser: The Principles and Practice of Library Development*. Chicago, Illinois: American Library Association, 1992.

Taft Group. *The Big Book of Library Grant Money: Profiles of 1,471 Private and Corporate Foundations and Direct Corporate Givers Receptive to Library Grant Proposals*. Chicago, Illinois: American Library Association, 1994.

Van House, Nancy A. and Thomas A. Childers. *The Public Library Effectiveness Study: The Complete Report*. Chicago, Illinois: American Library Association, 1993.

_____; Mary Jo Lynch; Charles R. McClure; Douglas L. Zweizig; and Eleanor Jo Rodger. *Output Measures for Public Libraries: A Manual of Standardized Procedures*. Chicago, Illinois: American Library Association, 1987.

Walter, Virginia A. *Output Measures for Public Library Service to Children: A Manual of Standardized Procedures*. Chicago, Illinois: American Library Association, 1992.

Wedgeworth, Robert. *World Encyclopedia of Library and Information Services*. Chicago, Illinois: American Library Association, 1993.

Weingand, Darlene E. *Administration of the Small Public Library*. Chicago, Illinois: American Library Association, 1992.

Parks and Recreation

Arnold, Henry F. *Trees in Urban Design*. New York, New York: Van Nostrand Reinhold, 1992.

Bannon, Joseph J. *Current Issues in Leisure Services: Looking Ahead in a Time of Transition*. Washington, DC: International City/County Management Association, 1987.

Berry, Jeffrey M.; Kent E. Portnoy; and Ken Thompson. "Empowering and Involving Citizens" in James L. Perry. *Handbook of Public Administration*. San Francisco, California: Jossey-Bass, 1989.

Breen, Ann and Dick Rigby. *Waterfronts: Cities Reclaim Their Edge*. Englewood Cliffs, New Jersey: McGraw-Hill, 1994.

Brock, Barb J. and Lou A. Carver. *Recreation Publicity*. Arlington, Virginia: National Recreation and Park Association, 1994.

Casciotti, Lynn M. *ADA Resource Guide for Parks, Recreation and Leisure Service Agencies*. Arlington, Virginia: National Recreation and Park Association, 1992.

Christiansen, Monty L. *Points About Playgrounds*. Arlington, Virginia: National Recreation and Parks Association, 1993.

_____. *Play It Safe: An Anthology of Playground Safety*. Arlington, Virginia: National Recreation and Park Association, 1992.

Colston, Ladd G. and Pettis Patton. *The Critical Impact of Urban Recreation on the African-American Community: Past and Present*. Arlington, Virginia: National Recreation and Park Association, 1994.

Cryder, Ralph and Sondra Kirsch. *Revenue Policy Manual.* Arlington, Virginia: National Recreation and Park Association, 1990.

Diehl, Janet and Thomas S. Barrett. *The Conservation Easement Handbook.* Washington, DC: Land Trust Alliance, 1988.

Endicott, Eve. *Land Conservation through Public/Private Partnerships.* Washington, DC: Island Press, 1993.

Fogg, George E. and Robert F. Fulton. *Leisure Site Guidelines for People Over 55.* Arlington, Virginia: National Recreation and Park Association, 1994.

_____. *Park Planning Guidelines.* Arlington, Virginia: National Recreation and Park Association, 1990.

_____. *A Site Design Process.* Arlington, Virginia: National Recreation and Park Association, 1986.

_____ and J. William Shiner. *Management Planning for Park and Recreation Areas.* Arlington, Virginia: National Recreation and Park Association, 1982.

Godbey, Geoffrey and Alan Graefe. *The Benefits of Local Recreation and Park Services: A Nationwide Study of the Perceptions of the American Public.* Arlington, Virginia: National Recreation and Park Association, 1992.

Hultsman, John; Richard L. Cottrell; and Wendy Hultsman. *Planning Parks for People.* State College, Pennsylvania: Venture Publishing, 1991.

International City/County Management Association. "Local Governments and Schools: Sharing Support Services." *Management Information Service Report.* no. 40919. Washington, DC: ICMA, 1994.

_____. "Use of Volunteers in Local Government Service Delivery." *Baseline Data Report.* no. 40934. Washington, DC: ICMA, 1994.

_____. "Community Open Space: New Techniques for Acquisition and Financing." *Management Information Service Report,* no. 40868. Washington, DC: ICMA, 1993.

_____. "City and County Parks and Recreation Consolidation." *Clearinghouse Report,* no. 40592. Washington, DC: ICMA, 1989.

_____. "Culture, Recreation, and Health: Ensuring the Quality of Life." *Special Data Issue,* no. 40300. Washington, DC: ICMA, 1988.

_____. "Recreation Task Force Report." *Clearinghouse Report,* no. 40024. Washington, DC: ICMA, 1986.

_____. *Managing Municipal Leisure Services.* Washington, DC: ICMA, 1980.

Keller, M. Jean and Nancy J. Osgood. *Dynamic Leisure Programming with Older Adults.* Arlington, Virginia: National Recreation and Park Association, 1987.

Kelly, Eric Damian. "Planning, Growth, and Public Facilities." *Planning Advisory Service Report,* no. 447. Chicago, Illinois: American Planning Association, 1993.

Kutska, Kenneth S. and Kevin J. Hoffman. *Playground Safety Is No Accident: Developing a Public Playground Safety and Maintenance Program.* Arlington, Virginia: National Recreation and Park Association, 1992.

Mangum, Barry D. and Robert D. Reed. *Successful Parks and Recreation Public Relations.* Arlington, Virginia: National Recreation and Park Association, 1993.

Marcus, Clare Cooper and Carolyn Francis. *People Places: Design Guidelines for Urban Open Space.* New York, New York: Van Nostrand Reinhold, 1990.

March, William M. *Landscape Planning: Environmental Applications.* New York, New York: John Wiley & Sons, 1991.

McGovern, John. *ADA Self-Evaluation Handbook and Checklist.* Arlington, Virginia: National Recreation and Park Association, 1992.

McLean, Janet R.; James Peterson; and Donald Martin. *Recreation and Leisure: The Changing Scene.* New York, New York: John Wiley & Sons, 1985.

Mobley, Tona A. and Robert F. Toalson. *Parks and Recreation in the 21st Century,* Part II. Arlington, Virginia: National Recreation and Park Association, 1993.

_____. *Parks and Recreation in the 21st Century,* Part I. Arlington, Virginia: National Recreation and Park Association, 1992.

Murphy, James F.; William Niepoth; Lynn Jamerson; and John Williams. *Leisure Systems: Critical Concepts and Application.* Champaign, Illinois: Sagamore Publishing, 1991.

National League of Cities. *Families & Communities.* Washington, DC: NLC, 1992.

National Recreation and Park Association. *Abstracts from the 1994 Symposium on Leisure Research.* Arlington, Virginia: NRPA, 1994.

_____. *Best Practice Programs in Leisure and Aging.* Arlington, Virginia: NRPA, 1994.

_____. *Comprehensive Leisure and Aging Study: Final Report.* Arlington, Virginia: NRPA, 1994.

_____. *Leisure Recreation and Aging: A Selected, Annotated Bibliography.* Arlington, Virginia: NRPA, 1993.

_____. *Benefits of Parks and Recreation: A Catalogue.* Arlington, Virginia: NRPA, 1992.

_____. *Playground Equipment for Public Use: Continuum of Skills and Size Differences of Children Age Two to Twelve.* Arlington, Virginia: NRPA, 1992.

_____. *Park Maintenance Standards.* Arlington, Virginia: NRPA, 1986.

_____. *Recreation, Park, and Open Space Standards and Guidelines.* Arlington, Virginia: NRPA, 1983.

O'Sullivan, Ellen L. *Marketing for Parks, Recreation, and Leisure.* State College, Pennsylvania: Venture Publishing, 1991.

Ryan, Karen-Lee. *Trails for the Twenty-First Century.* Washington, DC: Island Press, 1993.

Sessoms, H. Douglas. "Leisure Services" in James M. Banovetz, Drew A. Dolan, and John W. Swain. *Managing Small Cities and Counties: A Practical Guide.* Washington, DC: International City/County Management Association, 1994.

_____. *Eight Decades of Leadership Development: A History of Programs of Professional Preparation in Parks & Recreation.* Arlington, Virginia: National Recreation and Park Association, 1993.

Sims, Millie and Sue Grey. *The Community Connection.* Arlington, Virginia: National Recreation and Park Association, 1992.

Strobell, Adah Parker. *Creative Recreation Programming Handbook.* Arlington, Virginia: National Recreation and Park Association, 1977.

Turco, Douglas M. and Craig Kelsey. *Conducting Economic Impact Studies of Park & Recreation Special Events.* Arlington, Virginia: National Recreation and Park Association, 1992.

Wallach, Frances and Susan Edelstein. *State Regulations Focused on Playgrounds and Their Supervision.* Arlington, Virginia: National Recreation and Park Association, 1992.

Zeiger, Jeffrey B. and Lowell M. Caneday. *Tourism and Leisure: Dynamics and Diversity.* Arlington, Virginia: National Recreation and Park Association, 1991.

Personnel

Ayres, Richard M. and Paul R. Coble. *Safeguarding Management's Rights.* Dubuque, Iowa: Kendall-Hunt Publishing, 1987.

Ban, Carolyn and Norma M. Riccuci. *Public Personnel Management: Current Concerns and Future Challenges.* New York, New York: Longman, 1991.

Becker, Christine S. *Performance Evaluation: An Essential Management Tool.* Washington, DC: International City/County Management Association, 1988.

Bowman, Sarah Y. and Jay M. Shafritz. *Public Personnel Administration: An Annotated Bibliography.* New York, New York: Garland, 1985.

Brock, Jonathan. *Managing People in Public Agencies: Personnel and Labor Relations.* Lanham, Maryland: University Press of America, 1989.

Campbell, John P. *Productivity in Organizations: New Perspectives from Industrial and Organizational Psychology.* Alexandria, Virginia: International Personnel Management Association, 1988.

Cayer, Joseph N. "Local Government Personnel Structure and Policies." *The Municipal Year Book.* Washington, DC: International City/County Management Association, 1991.

Daley, Lorne; Michael Dallard; John Kraft; Mary Ann Nester; and Robert Schneider. *Employment Testing of Persons with Disabling Conditions.* Alexandria, Virginia: International Personnel Management Association, 1988.

Douglas, Joel M. *At the Bargaining Table: The Status of Public Sector Supervisory, Managerial and Confidential Employees.* Alexandria, Virginia: International Personnel Management Association, 1989.

Ellis, Terrence L. and Ralph A. Bailey. "Healthy Police Officers Are Cost-Effective Police Officers." *Western City,* vol. 59, no. 1, January 1983.

Evans, Sara M. and Barbara J. Nelson. *Wage Justice: Comparable Worth and the Paradox of Technocratic Reform.* Chicago, Illinois: University of Chicago Press, 1989.

Feldstein, Lee M. "Fire Personnel Practices." *The Municipal Year Book.* Washington, DC: International City/County Management Association, 1987.

Fyfe, James J. "Police Personnel Practices, 1986." *The Municipal Year Book.* Washington, DC: International City/County Management Association, 1987.

———. "Police Personnel Practices." *Baseline Data Report,* vol. 15, no. 1, January 1983.

Granito, John A. "Fire Personnel Practices." *Baseline Data Report,* Washington, DC: International City/County Management Association, vol. 15, no. 2, February 1983.

Hays, Steven W. and Richard C. Kearney. *Public Personnel Administration: Problems and Prospects.* Englewood Cliffs, New Jersey: Prentice-Hall, 1990.

Huelsberg, Nancy A. and William F. Lincoln. *Successful Negotiating in Local Government.* Washington, DC: International City/County Management Association, 1985.

International City/County Management Association. *Drug and Alcohol Testing for Local Government Transportation Employees.* Washington, DC: ICMA, 1994.

———. *Health Care for Municipal Employees: Plans, Options and Costs.* Washington, DC: ICMA, 1994.

———. "Americans with Disabilities Act: A Guide to Compliance." *Clearinghouse Report,* no. 40799. Washington, DC: ICMA, 1993.

———. "Employee Attitude Surveys." *Management Information Service Report,* no. 40715. Washington, DC: ICMA, 1992.

———. "Helping the Troubled Work Group." *Management Information Service Report,* no. 40737. Washington, DC: ICMA, 1992.

———. "Regional Strategies for Local Government Management." *Management Information Service Report,* no. 40718. Washington, DC: ICMA, 1992.

———. *Assessment Centers for Hiring and Development.* Washington, DC: ICMA, 1990.

———. "Disciplining Difficult Employees: Progressive Approaches." *Management Information Service Report,* no. 40372. Washington, DC: ICMA, 1990.

———. "Employee Recruitment, Selection, and Affirmative Action Policies in Local Governments." *Special Data Issue,* no. 40412. Washington, DC: ICMA, 1990.

_____. "Drug Testing, Sexual Harassment, Smoking: Employee Rights Issues." *Management Information Service Report,* no.40130. Washington, DC: ICMA, 1988.

_____. *Personnel Practices for the 90s: A Local Government Guide.* Washington, DC: ICMA, 1988,

_____. "Wellness Programs in Local Government." *Management Information Service Report,* no. 40200. Washington, DC: ICMA, 1988.

_____. "Controlling Employee Health Care Costs." *Management Information Service Report,* no. 40054. Washington, DC: ICMA, 1987.

_____. "Workers' Compensation: An Employer's Manual for Managing Disability." *Management Information Service Report,* no. 40118. Washington, DC: ICMA, 1987.

_____. "Guidelines for Employee Development and Training Programs." *Management Information Service Report,* no. 37397. Washington, DC: ICMA, 1986.

_____. "Employee Assistance Programs for Local Governments." *Management Information Service Report,* no. 30732. Washington, DC: ICMA, 1982.

Matzer, John, Jr. *Personnel Practices for the '90s: A Local Government Guide.* Washington, DC: International City/County Management Association, 1988.

Moulder, Evelina. "Use of Volunteers in Local Government Service Delivery." *Baseline Data Report,* no. 40934. Washington, DC: ICMA, 1994.

_____. "Affirmative Action in Local Government." *The Municipal Year Book.* Washington, DC: International City/County Management Association, 1991.

National League of Cities. *Developing Alcohol and Drug Testing Programs: A Guide for Local Governments.* Washington, DC: NLC, 1994.

_____. *Complying with the Americans with Disabilities Act.* Washington, DC: NLC, 1991.

Noer, David M. *Healing the Wounds: Overcoming the Trauma of Layoffs and Revitalizing Downsized Organizations.* San Francisco, California: Jossey-Bass, 1993.

Orsburn, Jack D.; Linda Morgan; Ed Musselwhite; and John H. Zenger. *Self-Directed Work Teams: The New American Challenge.* Chicago, Illinois: Irwin Publishers, 1994.

Pellicciotti, Joseph M., *An Analysis of the Age Discrimination in Employment Act.* Alexandria, Virginia: International Personnel Management Association, 1994.

_____. *Title VII Liability for Sexual Harassment in the Workplace.* Alexandria, Virginia: International Personnel Management Association, 1993.

Rhyne, Charles S. *Police and Firefighters: The Law of Municipal Personnel Regulations.* Washington, DC: National Institute of Municipal Law Officers, 1982.

Riccucci, Norma M. *Promoting and Valuing Diversity in Municipal Government Work Forces.* Alexandria, Virginia: International Personnel Management Association, 1992.

Reichenberg, Neil. *Family and Medical Leave Act Regulations.* Alexandria. Virginia: International Personnel Management Association, 1995.

_____. *FLSA Exemptions: An Update.* Alexandria, Virginia: International Personnel Management Association, 1992.

_____. *Employment Discrimination in the Workplace: The Impact of the 1988-89 Supreme Court Term.* Alexandria, Virginia: International Personnel Management Association, 1990.

Shafritz, Jay M.; Albert C. Hyde; and David H. Rosenbloom. *Personnel Management in Government.* New York, New York: Marcel Dekker, 1991.

Sylvia, Ronald D. *Critical Issues in Public Personnel Policy.* Pacific Grove, California: Brooks/Cole, 1989.

U.S. Conference of Mayors. *Public Employer Privacy: A Legal and Practical Guide to Issues Affecting the Workplace.* Washington, DC: USCM, 1995.

_____. *Family and Medical Leave: Federal and State Laws.* Washington, DC: USCM, 1993.

_____. *Local Solutions: Providing Workforce Development Opportunities in America's Cities.* Washington, DC: USCM, 1993.

_____. *A Compendium of Job Training Programs.* Washington, DC: USCM, April 1992.

_____. *On-the-Job Training: A System Facing Change.* Washington, DC: USCM, 1992.

_____. *In Search of the 90's: The Human Capital Connection.* Washington, DC: USCM, January 1990.

_____. *Developing a Supervisor's Labor Relations Guide.* Washington, DC: USCM, 1985.

_____. *Smarter Bargaining: A Guide to Contract Language.* Washington, DC: USCM, 1984.

Van Wart, Montgomery; N. Joseph Cayer; and Steve Cook. *Handbook of Training and Development in the Public Sector.* San Francisco, California: Jossey-Bass, 1993.

Wallerstein, Nina and Harriet Rubenstein. *Teaching About Job Hazards: A Guide for Workers and Their Health Providers.* Washington, DC: American Public Health Association, 1993.

Weeks, James L. and Barry S. Levy. *Preventing Occupational Disease and Injuries.* Washington, DC: American Public Health Association, 1991.

Planning and Building

American Planning Association. "Planning Software Survey, 1990." *Planning Advisory Service Report,* no. 427/428. Chicago, Illinois: APA, 1990.

_____. *The Best of Planning.* Chicago, Illinois: Planners Press, 1989.

_____. "Reaching Consensus in Land-Use Negotiations." *Planning Advisory Service Report,* no. 417. Chicago, Illinois: APA, 1989.

American Council of Building Officials. *Management Manual for Code Administrators.* Country Club Hills, Illinois: Building Officials and Code Administrators International, 1983.

Arendt, Randall. *Rural by Design: Maintaining Small Town Character.* Chicago, Illinois: Planners Press, 1994.

Benveniste, Guy. *Mastering the Politics of Planning.* San Francisco, California: Jossey-Bass, 1989.

Berger, John. *Environmental Restoration.* Washington, DC: Island Press, 1989.

Breen, Ann and Dick Rigby. *Waterfronts: Cities Reclaim Their Edge.* New York, New York: McGraw-Hill, 1994.

Brevard, Joseph H. *Capital Facilities Planning.* Chicago, Illinois: Planners Press, 1985.

Building Officials and Code Administrators International. *Code Enforcement Guidelines for Residential Rehabilitation.* Country Club Hills, Illinois: BOCAI, May 1975.

Burchell, Robert W. *Development Impact Assessment Handbook.* Washington, DC: Urban Land Institute, 1994.

Cevero, Robert. *Suburban Gridlock.* New Brunswick, New Jersey: Center for Urban Policy Research, Rutgers University, 1986.

Cullingsworth, J. Barry. *The Political Culture of Planning.* New York, New York: Routledge, 1993.

DeGrove, John M. *Balanced Growth: A Planning Guide for Local Government.* Washington, DC: International City/County Management Association, 1991.

Diehl, Janet and Thomas S. Barrett. *The Conservation Easement Handbook.* Washington, DC: Land Trust Alliance, 1988.

Downs, Anthony. *New Visions for Metropolitan America.* Washington, DC: Brookings Institution, 1994.

_____. *Stuck in Traffic: Coping with Peak-Hour Traffic Congestion.* Washington, DC: Brookings Institution and the Lincoln Institute for Land Policy, 1992.

Endicott, Eve. *Land Conservation Through Public/Private Partnerships.* Washington, DC: Island Press, 1993.

Forester, John. *Planning in the Face of Power.* Berkeley, California: University of California Press, 1989.

Frank, Karen A. and Sherry Ahrentzen. *New Households, New Housing.* New York, New York: Van Nostrand Reinhold, 1991.

Frank, James E. and Robert M. Rhodes. *Development Exactions.* Chicago, Illinois: Planners Press, 1987.

Girling, Cynthia L. and Kenneth I. Helphand. *Yard, Street, Park.* New York, New York: John Wiley & Sons, 1994.

Gordon, Steven I. *Computer Models in Environmental Planning.* New York, New York: Routledge, 1985.

_____ and Richard F. Anderson. *Microcomputer Applications in City Planning and Management.* New York, New York: Praeger, 1989.

Hanousek, Donna, et al. *Project Infrastructure Development Handbook.* Washington, DC: Urban Land Institute, 1989.

Howe, Elizabeth. *Acting on Ethics in City Planning.* New Brunswick, New Jersey: Center for Urban Policy Research, Rutgers University, 1994.

Hultsman, John; Richard L. Cottrell; and Wendy Zales Hultsman. *Planning Parks for People.* State College, Pennsylvania: Venture Publishing, 1987.

International City/County Management Association. "Community Open Space: New Techniques for Acquisition and Financing." *Management Information Service Report,* no. 40868. Washington, DC: ICMA, 1993.

_____. "Impact Fees: Issues and Case Studies." *Management Information Service Report,* no. 40688. Washington, DC: ICMA, 1991.

_____. "Setting Standards for Community Design and Appearance." *Management Information Service Report,* no. 40685. Washington, DC: ICMA, 1991.

_____. "Water and Sewer Extension Policy." *Clearinghouse Report,* no. 40392. Washington, DC: ICMA, 1990.

_____. "Developer Financing: Impact Fees and Negotiated Exactions." *Management Information Service Report,* no. 40140. Washington, DC: ICMA, 1988.

_____. "Analyzing the Fiscal Impact of Development." *Management Information Service Report,* no. 40173. Washington, DC: ICMA, 1988.

_____. "Permit System Improvement Project." *Clearinghouse Report,* no. 37583. Washington, DC: ICMA, 1985.

Katz, Peter. *The New Urbanism: Toward an Architecture of Community.* New York, New York: McGraw-Hill, 1994.

Kelly, Eric D. "Planning, Growth, and Public Facilities." *Planning Advisory Service Report,* no. 447, Chicago, Illinois: American Planning Association, 1993.

_____. *Managing Community Growth.* New York, New York: Praeger, 1993.

_____. "Enforcing Zoning and Land-Use Controls." *Planning Advisory Service Report,* no. 409. Chicago, Illinois: American Planning Association, 1988.

Klosterman, Richard E.; Richard K. Brail; and Earl G. Brosard. *Spreadsheet Models for Urban and Regional Analysis.* New Brunswick, New Jersey: Center for Urban Policy Research, Rutgers University, 1992.

Lucy, William. *Close to Power: Setting Priorities with Elected Officials.* Chicago, Illinois: Planners Press, 1988.

Lyle, John Tillman. *Regenerative Design for Sustainable Development.* New York, New York: John Wiley & Sons, 1994.

Marcus, Clare Cooper and Carolyn Francis. *People Places: Design Guidelines for Urban Open Space.* New York, New York: Van Nostrand Reinhold, 1990.

McAllister, Donald. *Evaluation in Environmental Planning.* Cambridge, Massachusetts: MIT Press, 1979.

McClendon, Bruce W. *Customer Service in Local Government.* Chicago, Illinois: Planners Press, 1992.

Meck, Stuart. "Planning" in James M. Banovetz, Drew A. Dolan, and John W. Swain. *Managing Small Cities and Counties: A Practical Guide.* Washington, DC: International City/County Management Association, 1994.

Moudon, Anne Vernez. *Public Streets for Public Use.* New York, New York: Columbia University Press, 1987.

Mills, Edwin S. and John E. McDonald. *Sources of Metropolitan Growth.* New Brunswick, New Jersey: Center for Urban Policy Research, Rutgers University, 1992.

National League of Cities. *Complying with the Americans with Disabilities Act.* Washington, DC: NLC, 1991.

_____. *Local Officials Guide to Dynamic City Commercial Centers.* Washington, DC: NLC, 1990.

_____. *Fighting Poverty in Cities: Transportation Programs as Bridges to Opportunity.* Washington, DC: NLC, 1989.

_____. *Intergovernmental Influences on Local Land Use Decision Making.* Washington, DC: NLC, 1989.

_____. *Local Officials Guide to Small Business Partnerships.* Washington, DC: NLC, 1989.

_____. *Accepting the Challenge: The Rebirth of America's Downtowns.* Washington, DC: NLC, 1988.

_____. *Local Officials Guide to the Housing and Community Development Act of 1987.* Washington, DC: NLC, 1988.

_____. *A Time to Build Up: A Survey of Cities About Housing Policies.* Washington, DC: NLC, 1987.

_____. *Creating Your City's Image.* Washington, DC: NLC, 1982.

_____. *Dollars from Design.* Washington, DC: NLC, 1982.

_____. *Streamlining Your Local Development Process.* Washington, DC: NLC, 1982.

Nelson, Arthur C. *Development Impact Fees.* Chicago, Illinois: Planner Press, 1988.

Nicholas, James C.; Arthur C. Nelson; and Julian C. Juergensmeyer. *A Practitioner's Guide to Development Impact Fees.* Chicago, Illinois: Planners Press, 1991.

Perloff, Harvey S. *Planning the Post-Industrial City.* Chicago, Illinois: Planners Press, 1980.

Porter, Douglas R. *Understanding Growth Management.* Washington, DC: Urban Land Institute, 1989.

_____, et al. *Flexible Zoning: How It Works.* Washington, DC: Urban Land Institute, 1988.

Robinson, Susan G. *Financing Growth.* Chicago, Illinois: Government Finance Officers Association, 1990.

Rohe, William M. and Lauren B. Gates. *Planning with Neighborhoods.* Chapel Hill, North Carolina: University of North Carolina Press, 1985.

Rubenstein, Harvey M. *Pedestrian Malls, Streetscapes, and Urban Spaces.* New York, New York: John Wiley & Sons, 1992.

Rusk, David. *Cities Without Suburbs.* Washington, DC: Woodrow Wilson Center Press, 1993.

Ryan, Karen-Lee. *Trails for the Twenty-First Century.* Washington, DC: Island Press, 1993.

Schwab, Jim. "Industrial Performance Standards for a New Century." *Planning Advisory Service Report,* no. 444. Chicago, Illinois: American Planning Association, 1993.

Schwanke, Dean. *Mixed-Use Development Handbook.* Washington, DC: Urban Land Institute, 1987.

Simonds, John Ormsbee. *Garden Cities 21: Creating a Livable Urban Environment.* New York New York; McGraw-Hill, 1994.

Slater, David C. *Management of Local Planning.* Washington, DC: International City/County Management Association, 1984.

Smith, Herbert H. *Planning America's Communities: Paradise Found? Paradise Lost?* Chicago, Illinois: Planners Press, 1991.

Smith, Thomas P. "Flexible Parking Requirements." *Planning Advisory Service Report,* no. 377. Chicago, Illinois: American Planning Association, 1983.

So, Frank S. and Judith Getzels. *The Practice of Local Government Planning.* Washington, DC: International City/County Management Association, 1988.

Stiebel, David. *Resolving Municipal Disputes.* Oakland, California: Association of Bay Area Governments, 1992.

Susskind, Lawrence and Jeffrey Cruikshank. *Breaking the Impasse: Consensual Approaches to Resolving Public Disputes.* New York, New York: Basic Books, 1987.

U.S. Conference of Mayors. *Housing and Community Development Priorities for Local Governments.* Washington, DC: USCM, 1993.

_____. *Community Development Block Grant (CDBG) to America's Cities: Additional Funds Needed to Fight Urban Ills.* Washington, DC: USCM, June 1992.

_____. *Partnerships for Affordable Housing: An Annotated Listing of City Programs.* Washington, DC: USCM, September 1989.

_____. *How Mayors and City Governments Support the Arts: Innovative Financing Techniques and Strategies.* Washington, DC: USCM, 1988.

_____. *Working Towards a Consensus: Final Report of the National Housing Forum.* Washington, DC: USCM, February 1988.

Werth, Joel T. and David Bryant. "A Guide to Neighborhood Planning." *Planning Advisory Service Report,* no. 342. Chicago, Illinois: American Planning Association, 1979.

Police

Ayres, Richard M. and Paul R. Coble. *Safeguarding Management's Rights.* Dubuque, Iowa: Kendall-Hunt Publishing, 1987.

Behan, Cornelius J. "Coping with Fear: Citizen Oriented Police Enforcement in Baltimore County, Maryland." *Public Management,* vol. 68, no. 1, January 1986.

Bowman, Gary W. and Simon Hakim. *Privatizing Correctional Institutions.* New Brunswick, New Jersey: Transaction Books, 1992.

Carlile, Jennifer. "High Tech Alternatives for Public Safety." *American City & County,* vol. 104, no. 6, June 1989.

Chabotar, Kent J. "Financing Alternatives for Prison and Jail Construction." *Government Finance Review,* vol. l, no. 3, August 1985.

Dolan, Drew A. "Police Services" in James M. Banovetz, Drew A. Dolan, and John W. Swain. *Managing Small Cities and Counties: A Practical Guide.* Washington, DC: International City/County Management Association, 1994.

Ellis, Terrence L. and Ralph A. Bailey. "Healthy Police Officers Are Cost-Effective Police Officers." *Western City,* vol. 59, no. 1, January 1983.

Fyfe, James J. *Police Practice in the 90s: Key Management Issues.* Washington, DC: International City/County Management Association, 1989.

_____. "Police Personnel Practices, 1986." *The Municipal Year Book.* Washington, DC: International City/County Management Association, 1987.

_____. "Police Personnel Practices." *Baseline Data Report,* vol. 15, no. 1, Washington, DC: International City/County Management Association, January 1983.

Geller, William A. *Local Government Police Management.* Washington, DC: International City/County Management Association, 1991.

International Association of Chiefs of Police. *Managing the Small Law Enforcement Agency.* Gaithersburg, Maryland: IACP, 1990.

_____. *Operational Issues in the Small Law Enforcement Agency.* Gaithersburg, Maryland: IACP, 1990.

_____. *Criminal Investigation.* Gaithersburg, Maryland: IACP, 1989.

_____. *Police Supervision.* Gaithersburg, Maryland: IACP, 1985.

International City/County Management Association. "Drug Control Master Plan." *Clearinghouse Report,* no. 40872. Washington, DC: ICMA, 1994.

_____. "Gang Prevention and Intervention Plan." *Clearinghouse Report,* no. 40873. Washington, DC: ICMA, 1994.

_____. "Multicultural Training for Police." *Management Information Service Report,* no. 40925. Washington, DC: ICMA, 1994.

_____. "Financial Aspects of Police Liability." *Baseline Data Report,* no. 40773. Washington, DC: ICMA, 1993.

_____. "Police Communication Services Division Staffing Study." *Clearinghouse Report,* no. 40797. Washington, DC: ICMA, 1993.

_____. "Responsive Service Delivery: A Community Orientation to Problem Solving." *Management Information Service Report,* no. 40825. Washington, DC: ICMA, 1993.

_____. "Community-Oriented Policing in Council-Manager Cities." *Management Information Service Report,* no. 40736. Washington, DC: ICMA, 1992.

_____. "Police Personnel Practices, 1990." *Baseline Data Report,* no. 40749. Washington, DC: ICMA, 1992.

_____. "Police Review Systems." *Management Information Service Report,* no. 40748. Washington, DC: ICMA, 1992.

_____. "Probation, Mandatory Retirement, and Budget Cuts in Police Departments." *Special Data Issue,* no. 40652. Washington, DC: ICMA, 1992.

_____. "Forecasting the Outcome of Police/Fire Consolidations." *Management Information Service Report,* no. 40559. Washington, DC: ICMA, 1991.

_____. "Law Enforcement Liability Insurance." *Special Report,* no. 40644. Washington, DC: ICMA, 1991.

_____. "Police/Fire Consolidation Case Studies." *Clearinghouse Report,* no. 40563. Washington, DC: ICMA, 1991.

_____. "Police Personnel Practices: Education, Participation, and Scheduling." *Special Data Issue,* no. 40651. Washington, DC: ICMA, 1991.

_____. "Police Personnel Recruitment and Special Training Programs." *Special Data Issue,* no. 40654. Washington, DC: ICMA, 1991.

_____. "Consolidation of Public Safety Dispatch Operations." *Clearinghouse Report,* no. 40463. Washington, DC: ICMA, 1990.

_____. "Cost-Benefit Analysis of a Take Home Patrol Car Program." *Clearinghouse Report,* no. 40515. Washington, DC: ICMA, 1990.

_____. "Crowded Jails: Options and Alternatives." *Management Information Service Report,* no. 40402. Washington, DC: ICMA, 1990.

_____. "Community-Oriented Policing." *Management Information Service Report,* no. 40337. Washington, DC: ICMA, 1989.

_____. "Juvenile First Offender Peer Jury Project." *Clearinghouse Report,* no. 40381. Washington, DC: ICMA, 1989.

_____. "Police Patrol Staffing." *Clearinghouse Report,* no. 40116. Washington, DC: ICMA, 1986.

_____. "Controlling Private Security System False Alarms." *Management Information Service Report,* no. 35173. Washington, DC: ICMA, 1984.

Keyes, Langley C. *Strategies and Saints: Fighting Drugs in Subsidized Housing.* Washington, DC: The Urban Institute Press, 1992.

Matulia, Kenneth R. *A Balance of Forces.* Gaithersburg, Maryland: International Association of Chiefs of Police, 1985.

Mullen, Joan. *The Privatization of Corrections: Issues and Practices.* Washington, DC: National Institute of Justice, 1985.

Nader, Donald. "New Jail Options Offer More Flexibility." *American City & County.* vol. 104, no. 3, March 1989.

National League of Cities. *School Violence in America's Cities.* Washington, DC: NLC, 1995.

_____. *Developing Alcohol and Drug Testing Programs: A Guide for Local Governments.* Washington, DC: NLC, 1994.

_____. *Exemplary Programs in Criminal Justice: Innovations at the Local Level.* Washington, DC: NLC, 1994.

_____. *The 1994 Anti-Crime Law: A Local Officials Guide.* Washington, DC: NLC, 1994.

_____. *Rethinking Public Safety.* Washington, DC: NLC, 1994.

_____. *Local Officials Guide to Drunk Driving Prevention.* Washington, DC: NLC, 1993.

_____. *Local Officials Guide to Community Traffic Safety Programs.* Washington, DC: NLC, 1990.

_____. *Local Strategies in the War Against Drugs.* Washington, DC: NLC, 1989.

Quinn, Barbara. "Jail Overcrowding: A Systems Problem." *American City & County,* vol. 103, no. 6, June 1988.

Rhyne, Charles S., *Police and Firefighters: The Law of Municipal Personnel Regulations.* Washington, DC: National Institute of Municipal Law Officers, 1982.

Scaglione, Fred. "Jails Without Walls." *American City & County,* vol. 104, no. 1, January 1989.

Swanson, Charles R. and Leonard Territo. *Police Administration: Structures, Processes, and Behavior.* New York, New York: Macmillan, 1983.

Thibault, Edward; Lawrence Lynch; and R. Bruce McBride. *Proactive Police Management.* Englewood Cliffs, New Jersey: Prentice-Hall, 1985.

Toch, Hans and J. Douglas Grant. *Police as Problem Solvers.* New York, New York: Plenum Press, 1991.

U.S. Conference of Mayors. *On the Front Lines: A Directory of Community Policing Programs in America's Cities.* Washington, DC: USCM, 1994.

_____. *A National Action Plan to Combat Violent Crimes: Recommendations of Mayors and Police Chiefs to the President of the United States.* Washington, DC: USCM, 1993.

_____. *Addressing Racial and Ethnic Tensions: Combating Hate Crimes in America's Cities.* Washington, DC: USCM, 1992.

_____. *On the Front Lines: Case Studies of Policing in America's Cities.* Washington, DC: USCM, September 1992.

_____. *Controlling Drug Abuse in American Cities: A 30-City Survey of the Implementation of Anti-Drug Abuse Act Block Grant Programs and on Local Drug Control Efforts.* Washington, DC: USCM, September 1990.

Whitaker, Gordon P. *Understanding Police Agency Performance.* Washington, DC: National Institute of Justice, 1984.

Privatization

Ascher, Kate. "The Business of Local Government—An Alternative View of Privatization." *The Privatization Review*, vol. 3, no. 4, fall, 1987.
Benton, J. Edwin and Donald C. Menzel. "Contracting and Franchising County Services in Florida." *Urban Affairs Quarterly*, vol. 27, no. 3, March 1992.
Blackley, Paul R. and Larry De Boer. "The Structure of State and Local Government Production." *Public Finance Quarterly*, vol. 19, no. 2, April 1991.
Bowman, Gary W. and Simon Hakim. *Privatizing Correctional Institutions.* New Brunswick, New Jersey: Transaction Books, 1992.
Brown, Susan. "Privatization of Public Services—A Cautionary Note." *Policy and Research Report*, vol. 18, no. 1, winter 1988.
Brudney, Jeffrey L. "Coproduction and Local Governments." *Public Management*, vol. 68, no. 12, December 1986.
Carter, Karen B. "Private Contracts for Public Works." *Current Municipal Problems*, vol. 13, 1986-1987.
Chabotar, Kent J. "Financing Alternatives for Prison and Jail Construction." *Government Finance Review*, vol. 1, no. 3, August 1985.
Coleman, William G. *State & Local Government & Public-Private Partnerships: A Policy Issues Handbook.* Westport, Connecticut: Greenwood Press, 1989.
Darr, Thomas B. "Pondering Privatization May Be Good for Your Government." *Governing*, vol. 1, no. 2, November 1987.
Donahue, John D. *The Privatization Decision: Public Ends, Private Means.* New York, New York: Basic Books, 1991.
Ferris, James M. "The Decision to Contract Out: An Empirical Analysis." *Urban Affairs Quarterly*, vol. 22, no. 2, December 1986.
_____ and Elizabeth Graddy. "Contracting Out: For What? With Whom?" *Public Administration Review*, vol. 46, no. 4, July-August 1986.
Finley, Lawrence K. *Public Sector Privatization: Alternative Approaches to Service Delivery.* Westport, Connecticut: Greenwood Press, 1989.
Fixler, Philip E., Jr. "Service Shedding—A New Option for Local Governments." *The Privatization Review*, vol. 2, no. 3, summer 1986.
Florestano, Patricia S. "Considerations for the Future of Privatization." *Urban Resources*, vol. 2, no. 4, summer 1985.
Frug, Jerry. "The Choice Between Privatization and Publicazation." *Current Municipal Problems*, vol. 14, 1987-1988.
Glaus, Barbara. "Weighing Costs and Relative Benefits: Phoenix's Comprehensive Program Budget Review." *Government Finance Review*, vol. 10, no. 2, April 1994.
Goldman, Harvey and Sandra Mokuvos. "Dividing the Pie Between Public and Private." *American City & County*, vol. 99, no. 1, January 1984.
Gormley, William T., Jr. *Privatization & Its Alternatives.* Madison, Wisconsin: University of Wisconsin Press, 1991.
Hatry, Harry P. *Building Innovation Into Program Reviews: Analysis of Service Delivery Options.* Washington, DC: The Urban Institute Press, 1989.
_____. "Privatization Presents Problems." *National Civic Review*, vol. 77, no. 2, March-April 1988.
Hayes, Edward C. "Contracting for Services—The Basic Steps." *The Privatization Review*, vol. 2, no. 1, winter 1986.
Herbst, Douglas and Lanny Katz. "The Privatization of Wastewater Treatment—Three Case Studies." *The Privatization Review*, vol. 2, no. 2, spring 1986.

Hudgins, Edward. *How Privatization Can Solve America's Infrastructure Crisis.* Washington, DC: The Heritage Foundation, 1992.

Jones, Leroy, et al. *Selling Public Enterprise: A Cost-Benefit Methodology.* Cambridge, Massachusetts: MIT Press, 1990.

Kolderie, Ted. "The Two Different Concepts of Privatization." *Public Administration Review,* vol. 46, no. 4, July-August 1986.

_____ and Jody Hauer. "Contracting as an Approach to Public Management." *Municipal Management,* vol. 6, no. 4, spring 1984.

Krings, David and Charles Martin. "Privatizing Information Resources in Government." *The Privatization Review,* vol. 2, no. 2, spring 1986.

Kuttner, Robert. "The Private Market Can't Always Solve Public Problems." *Business Week,* issue no. 2936, March 10, 1986.

Mahtesian, Charles. "Taking Chicago Private." *Governing,* vol. 7, no. 7, April 1994.

Mattson, Gary A. and Philip R. Twogood. "Retrenchment and Municipal Service Priorities: A View from the Sunbelt." *National Civic Review,* vol. 80, no. 2, spring 1991.

Miller, John R. and Christopher R. Tufts. "Privatization Is a Means to 'More with Less'." *National Civic Review,* vol. 77, no. 2, March-April 1988.

Mills, James. "Contract Street Sweeping Is a Viable Alternative." *American City & County,* vol. 99, no. 7, July 1984.

Morris, Joe. "Privatization and the Unions." *American City & County,* vol. 102, no. 7, July 1987.

_____ and Terry Stone. "Private Choices for Public Parks." *American City & County,* vol. 101, no. 5, May 1986.

Perry, James L. and Timlynn T. Babitsky. "Comparative Performance in Urban Bus Transit: Assessing Privatization Strategies." *Public Administration Review,* vol. 46, no. 1, winter 1990.

Peters, Terry. "Public Services and the Private Sector." *Texas City and Town,* vol. LXXI, no. 11, November 1984.

Rehfuss, John. "Contracting Out and Accountability in State and Local Governments—The Importance of Contract Monitoring." *State and Local Government Review,* vol. 22, no. 1, winter 1990.

Roehm, Harper A.; Joseph F. Castellano; and David A. Karns. "Contracting Services to the Private Sector—A Survey of Management Practices." *Government Finance Review,* vol. 4, no. 1, February 1989.

Savas, Emanuel S. *Privatization: The Key to Better Government.* Chatham, New Jersey: Chatham House, 1987.

Salamon, Lester M. and Michael S. Lund. *Beyond Privatization: The Tools of Government Action.* Lanham, Maryland: University Press of America, 1989.

Scully, Larry J. and Lisa A. Cole. "Privatization—Making the Decision." *The Privatization Review,* vol. 2, no. 2, spring 1986.

Seader, David. "Privatization and America's Cities." *Public Management,* vol. 68, no. 12, December 1986.

Stanley, Ralph L. "Time to Get Back on Track—The Need for Competitive Services in Transit." *The Privatization Review,* vol. 2, no. 2, spring 1986.

Suleiman, Ezra N. and John Waterbury. *The Political Economy of Public Sector Reform & Privatization.* Boulder, Colorado: Westview Press, 1990.

Turner, John A. "Privatizing Fire Protection Since 1948—The Rural/Metro Experience." *The Privatization Review,* vol. 3, no. 1, spring 1987.

Valente, C.F. and L.D. Manchester. "Rethinking Local Services: Examining Alternative Delivery Approaches." *ICMA Special Report,* no. 12, March 1984.

Wingerter, Eugene J. "Refuse Collection—The Privatization Alternative." *The Privatization Review*, vol. 2, no. 1, winter 1986.

Winslow, Frances E. "Privatization—The Politics of Advocacy." *Urban Resources*, vol. 2, no. 4, summer 1985.

Public Works

American Public Works Association. *Financing Stormwater Facilities: A Utility Approach.* Kansas City, Missouri: APWA, 1991.

_____. "Public Works Management Practices." *Special Report,* no. 59. Kansas City, Missouri: APWA, 1991.

_____. "Committing to the Cost of Ownership: Maintenance and Repair of Public Buildings." *Special Report,* no. 60. Kansas City, Missouri: APWA, 1990.

_____. "Contracting Maintenance Services." *Special Report,* no. 58. Kansas City, Missouri: APWA, 1990.

_____. "Public Works Today: A Profile of Local Service Organizations and Managers." *Special Report,* no. 57. Kansas City, Missouri: APWA, 1990.

_____. "Managing Public Equipment." *Special Report,* no. 55. Kansas City, Missouri: APWA, 1989.

_____. "Microcomputers in Public Works." *Special Report,* no. 53. Kansas City: Missouri: APWA, 1987.

_____. "Centralized Administration of Public Buildings." *Special Report,* no. 50, Kansas City, Missouri: APWA, 1984.

Barker, Michael. *Rebuilding America's Infrastructure: An Agenda for the 1980's.* Durham, North Carolina: Duke University Press, 1984.

Chertow, Marian R. *Garbage Solutions: A Public Official's Guide to Recycling and Alternative Solid Waste Management Technologies.* Washington, DC: U.S. Conference of Mayors, 1989.

Congressional Budget Office. *New Directions for the Nation's Public Works.* Washington, DC: U.S. Government Printing Office, 1988.

Cristofano, Sam M. and William S. Foster. *Management of Local Public Works.* Washington, DC: International City/County Management Association, 1986.

Felbinger, Claire L. "Public Works" in James M. Banovetz, Drew A. Dolan, and John W. Swain. *Managing Small Cities and Counties: A Practical Guide.* Washington, DC: International City/County Management Association, 1994.

Hartline, Connie, et al. "Tackling Gridlock." *Special Report,* no. 56. Kansas City, Missouri: American Public Works Association, 1991.

International City/County Management Association. "Cost Factors in Local Government Solid Waste Management." *Baseline Data Report,* no. 40901. Washington, DC: ICMA, 1994.

_____. "Drinking Water: Financing and Management." *Management Information Service Report,* no. 40923. Washington, DC: ICMA, 1994.

_____. "Marketing Recyclables." *Management Information Service Report,* no. 40869. Washington, DC: ICMA, 1994.

_____. "Pollution Prevention: A Guide for Local Government." *Special Report,* no. 40951. Washington, DC: ICMA, 1994.

_____. "Local Government Infrastructure Financing." *Special Data Issue,* no. 40800. Washington, DC: ICMA, 1993.

_____. "Capital Improvement Financing, 1991." *Baseline Data Report,* no. 40760. Washington, DC: ICMA, 1992.

_____. "Composting: Solutions for Waste Management." *Special Report*, no. 40689. Washington, DC: ICMA, 1992.

_____. "Trees in the Community: Managing the Urban Forest." *Management Information Service Report*, no. 10716. Washington, DC: ICMA, 1992.

_____. "Community-Based Waste Management Plan." *Clearinghouse Report*, no. 40680. Washington, DC: ICMA, 1991.

_____. "Local Government Materials Recovery and Recycling Centers." *Special Data Issue*, no. 40638. Washington, DC: ICMA, 1991.

_____. "Groundwater Protection: Local Success Stories." *Management Information Service Report*, no. 40408. Washington, DC: ICMA, 1990.

_____. "Landfill Management." *Management Information Service Report*, no. 40488. Washington, DC: ICMA, 1990.

_____. "Making Environmental Partnerships Work." *Management Information Service Report*, no. 40481. Washington, ICMA, 1990.

_____. "Productivity Improvements in Public Works." *Management Information Service Report*, no. 40449. Washington, DC: ICMA, 1990.

_____. "Productivity of City Field Crews." *Clearinghouse Report*, no. 40466. Washington, DC: ICMA, 1990.

_____. "Establishing a Real Estate Asset Management System." *Management Information Service Report*, no. 40288. Washington, DC: ICMA, 1989.

_____. "Leaf Composting Program." *Clearinghouse Report*, no. 40376. Washington, DC: ICMA, 1989.

_____. "Pesticide Management." *Management Information Service Report*, no. 40317. Washington, DC: ICMA, 1989.

_____. "A Productivity Study of Street Cleaning." *Clearinghouse Report*, no. 40397. Washington, DC: ICMA, 1989.

_____. "Promoting a Municipal Recycling Program." *Clearinghouse Report*, no. 40387. Washington, DC: ICMA, 1989.

_____. "Recycling Solid Waste." *Management Information Service Report*, no. 40314. Washington, DC: ICMA, 1989.

_____. "Solid Waste Management Service and Recycling Agreements." *Clearinghouse Report*, no. 40608. Washington, DC: ICMA, 1989.

_____. "Water Pollution Control User Charge System." *Clearinghouse Report*, no. 40390. Washington, DC: ICMA, 1989.

_____. "Developer Financing: Impact Fees and Negotiated Exactions." *Management Information Service Report*, no. 40140. Washington, DC: ICMA, 1988.

_____. "Trends in Urban Forestry Management." *Baseline Data Report*, no. 40141. Washington, DC: ICMA, 1988.

Keller, C.W. *Financing and Charges for Wastewater Systems.* Kansas City, Missouri: American Public Works Association, 1984.

Knorr, Rita E., et al. "Good Practices in Public Works." *Special Report*, no. 54. Kansas City, Missouri: American Public Works Association, 1988.

Maggio, M.E. *Alternative Fuels: What You Need to Know.* Kansas City, Missouri: American Public Works Association, 1990.

Matzer, John, Jr. *Capital Projects: New Strategies for Planning, Management, and Finance.* Washington, DC: International City/County Management Association, 1989.

Melvin, Eric. "Plan. Predict. Prevent. How to Reinvest in Public Buildings." *Special Report*, no. 62. Kansas City, Missouri: American Public Works Association, 1992.

Moehring, Eugene P. "Public Works and Urban History: Recent Trends and New Directions." *Essays in Public Works History*, no. 13. Kansas City, Missouri: American Public Works Association, 1982.

National Council on Public Works Improvement. *Fragile Foundations: A Report on America's Public Works.* Washington, DC: U.S. Government Printing Office, 1988.
_____. *The Nation's Public Works: Defining the Issues.* Washington, DC: U.S. Government Printing Office, 1986.
National League of Cities. *Complying with the Americans with Disabilities Act.* Washington, DC: NLC, 1991.
_____. *Local Officials Guide to Public Real Estate Asset Management.* Washington, DC: NLC, 1990.
_____. *Financing Infrastructure: Innovations at the Local Level.* Washington, DC: NLC, 1987.
_____. *Waste-to-Energy Facilities: A Decision-Makers Guide.* Washington, DC: NLC, 1986.
Parent, Phil. "Public Works Guide to Automated Mapping & Facilities Management." *Special Report,* no. 64. Kansas City, Missouri: American Public Works Association, 1992.
Rosen, Christine M., et al. "Planning and Financing Public Works: Three Historical Cases." *Essays in Public Works History,* no. 15. Kansas City, Missouri: American Public Works Association, September 1987.
Rosen, Howard and Ann Durkin Keating. *Water and the City: The Next Century.* Kansas City, Missouri: American Public Works Association, 1991.
Rush, Sean C. *Managing the Facilities Portfolio: A Practical Approach to Facility Renewal and Deferred Maintenance.* Washington, DC: National Association of College and University Business Officers, 1991.
Scanlon, Raymond D. *Hazardous Materials, Hazardous Waste: Local Management Options.* Washington, DC: International City/County Management Association, 1987.
Schmandt, Jurgen, et al. *The New Urban Infrastructure: Cities and Telecommunications.* New York, New York: Praeger, 1990.
Sullivan, Richard H. "Planning and Evaluating Water Conservation Measures." *Special Report,* no. 48. Kansas City, Missouri: American Public Works Association, 1981.
U.S. Conference of Mayors. *A Report to the Nation on Recycling in America's Cities.* Washington, DC: USCM, 1995.
_____. *Compost Marketing: A Planning Guide for Local Governments.* Washington, DC: USCM, October 1994.
_____. *Negotiating the Optimal Contract for Privatized Waste Processing Facilities.* Washington, DC: USCM, October 1992.
_____. *Recycling in America: Profiles of the Nation's Resourceful Cities.* Washington, DC: USCM, 1991.
U.S. Congress, Office of Technology Assessment. *Delivering the Goods: Public Works Technologies, Management, and Finance.* Washington, DC: U.S. Government Printing Office, 1991.
_____. *Rebuilding the Foundations: A Special Report on State and Local Public Works Financing and Management.* Washington, DC: U.S. Government Printing Office, 1990.

Retrenchment Management

Aronson, J. Richard and Eli Schwartz. *Management Policies in Local Government Finance.* Washington, DC: International City/County Management Association, 1987.
Bachelor, Lynn W. "Bureaucratic Responsiveness and Complaint Resolution: The

Impact of Fiscal Constraints." *Urban Affairs Quarterly*, vol. 22, no. 2, December 1986.

Barbour, George P., Jr.; Thomas W. Fletcher; and George A. Sipel. *Excellence in Local Government Handbook*. Washington, DC: International City/County Management Association, 1984.

Blair, John P. and David Nachmias. *Fiscal Retrenchment and Urban Policy*. Thousand Oaks Park: California: Sage Publications, 1979.

Blais, Andre, and Stephane Dion. *The Budget-Maximizing Bureaucrat: Appraisals & Evidence*. Pittsburgh, Pennsylvania: University of Pittsburgh Press, 1991.

Bolotin, Fredric N. "Distribution of Cutbacks in Local Government Services: A Conceptual Framework." *State and Local Government Review*, vol. 22, no. 3, fall 1990.

Brecher, Charles and Raymond D. Horton. "Retrenchment and Recovery: American Cities and the New York Experience." *Public Administration Review*, vol. 45, no. 2, March-April 1985.

Brewer, Garry D. "Termination: Hard Choices—Hard Questions." *Public Administration Review*, vol. 38, no. 4, July-August 1978.

Browning, Edgar K. and Jacquelene M. *Public Finance & the Price System*. New York, New York: Macmillan, 1994.

Cayer, N. Joseph. "Managerial Implications of Reductions in Force." *Public Administration Quarterly*, vol. 10, no. 1, spring 1986.

Clark, Terry Nichols. *Coping with Urban Austerity*. Greenwich, Connecticut: JAI Press, 1985.

Colvard, James E. "Cutout: The Ultimate Cutback Management." *The Bureaucrat*, vol. 15, no. 1, spring 1986.

Donaldson, William V. "Managing Shrinking Cities: Cincinnati." *The Bureaucrat*, vol. 10, no. 3, fall 1981.

Downing, R.G. "Urban County Fiscal Stress: A Survey of Public Officials' Perceptions and Government Experiences." *Urban Affairs Quarterly*, vol. 27, no. 2, December 1991.

Florestano, Patricia S. "Revenue-Raising Limitations on Local Government: A Focus on Alternative Responses." *Public Administration Review*, vol. 41, no. 1, January-February 1981.

Gist, John R. "Fiscal Austerity, Grant Structures, and Local Expenditure Responses." *Policy Studies Journal*, vol. 16, no. 4, summer 1988.

Glassberg, Andrew. "Organizational Responses to Municipal Budget Decreases." *Public Administration Review*, vol. 38, no. 4, July-August 1978.

Gosling, James J. *Budgetary Politics in American Governments*. White Plains, New York: Longman, 1992.

Gramlich, Edward M. *A Guide to Benefit-Cost Analysis*. Englewood Cliffs, New Jersey: Prentice-Hall, 1990.

Groves, Sanford M. and Maureen Godsey Valente. *Evaluating Financial Condition*. Washington, DC: International City/County Management Association, 1994.

Hayes, Edward C. *The Hidden Wealth of Cities*. Greenwich, Connecticut: JAI Press, 1989.

Hirschorn, L. *Cutting Back*. San Francisco, California: Jossey-Bass, 1983.

Holzer, Marc. "Workforce Reduction and Productivity." *Public Administration Quarterly*, vol. 10, no. 1, spring 1986.

Keller, Elizabeth K. *Managing with Less*. Washington, DC: International City/County Management Association, 1979.

Kemp, Roger L. "Financial Productivity: Beyond Cutback to Creativity." *Municipal Finance Journal*, vol. 7, no. 2, spring 1986.

_____. "More on Managing in Hard Times." *Management Science and Policy Analysis,* vol. L, no. 11, November 1983.

_____. "Managing Government in Hard Times." *Current Municipal Problems,* vol. 9, no. 1, summer 1982.

_____. *Coping with Proposition 13.* Lexington, Massachusetts: Lexington Books, 1980.

_____. "Cutback Management: Coping with Revenue-Reducing Mandates." *Management Information Service Report,* vol. 12, no. 7. Washington, DC: International City/County Management Association, 1980.

Krantz, James. "Group Processes Under Conditions of Organizational Decline." *Journal of Applied Behavioral Science,* vol. 21, no. 1, January 1985.

Levine, Charles H. *Managing Fiscal Stress: The Crisis in the Public Sector.* Chatham, New Jersey: Chatham House, 1980.

_____; Irene S. Rubin; and George G. Wolohojian. *The Politics of Retrenchment: How Local Governments Manage Fiscal Stress.* Thousand Oaks Park: California: Sage Publications, 1980.

_____. "More on Cutback Management: Hard Questions for Hard Times." *Public Administration Review,* vol. 39, no. 2, March-April 1979.

_____. "Organizational Decline and Cutback Management." *Public Administration Review,* vol. 38, no. 4, July-August 1978.

Lewis, Carol W. and Anthony T. Logalbo. "Cutback Principles and Practices: A Checklist for Managers." *Public Administration Review,* vol. 40, no. 2, March-April 1980.

Lewis, Gregory B. "The Consequences of Fiscal Stress: Cutback Management and Municipal Employment." *State and Local Government Review,* vol. 20, no. 2, Spring 1988.

Mattson, Gary A. and Philip R. Twogood. "Retrenchment and Municipal Services Priorities: A View from the Sunbelt." *National Civic Review,* vol. 80, no. 2, Spring 1991.

Merriman, David. *The Control of Municipal Budgets: Toward the Effective Design of Tax & Expenditure Limitations.* Westport, Connecticut: Greenwood Press, 1987.

O'Toole, Daniel E. and James Marshall. "Managing with Less: What Managers Can Expect." *Public Management,* vol. 66, no. 6, June 1984.

Pammer, William J., Jr. *Managing Fiscal Strain in Major American Cities: Understanding Retrenchment in the Public Sector.* Westport, Connecticut: Greenwood Press, 1990.

Pegano, Michael A. "Fiscal Disruptions and City Responses: Stability, Equilibrium, and City Capital Budgeting." *Urban Affairs Quarterly,* vol. 24, no. 1, September 1988.

Reed, Sarah A. "The Impact of Budgetary Roles Upon Perspectives." *Public Budgeting and Finance,* vol. 5, no. 1, spring 1985.

Rich, Wilbur C. "The Political Context of a Reduction-in-Force Policy: On the Misunderstanding of an Important Phenomenon." *Public Administration Quarterly,* vol. 10, no. 1, spring 1986.

Rubin, Irene S. *The Politics of Public Spending: Getting & Spending, Borrowing & Balancing.* Chatham, New Jersey: Chatham House, 1990.

Rutter, Lawrence. *The Essential Community: Local Government in the Year 2000.* Washington, DC: International City/County Management Association, 1980.

Sharp, Elaine B. and David Elkins. "The Impact of Fiscal Limitation: A Tale from Seven Cities." *Public Administration Review,* vol. 47, no. 5, September-October 1988.

Stipak, Brian; Robert P. McGowan; and John M. Stevens. "Effect of Fiscal Stress on

Attitudes of Local Executives." *State and Local Government Review,* vol. 17, no. 1, winter 1985.

Weiner, Richard S. and J.J. Hendricks. "Help During Retrenchment." *The Bureaucrat* vol. 14, no. 2, summer 1985.

Wynne, George G. *Cutback Management: A Trinational Perspective.* New Brunswick, New Jersey: Transaction Books, 1983.

Strategic Planning

Bryson, John M. and William D. Roering. *Strategic Planning for Public and Nonprofit Organizations.* San Francisco, California: Jossey-Bass, 1988.

_____ and R.C. Einsweiler. *Strategic Planning: Threats and Opportunities for Planners.* Chicago, Illinois: Planners Press, 1988.

_____. "Applying Private-Sector Strategic Planning to the Public Sector." *Journal of the American Planning Association,* vol. 53, no. 1, winter 1987.

_____; A.H. Van de Ven; and W.D. Roering. "Strategic Planning and the Revitalization of the Public Service" in R. Denhardt and E. Jennings. *Toward a New Public Service.* Columbia, Missouri: University of Missouri Press, 1987.

_____ and R.C. Einsweiler. *Planning and Decision-Making in a Context of Shared Power.* Lanham, Maryland: University Press of America, 1986.

_____; R.E. Freeman; and W.D. Roering. "Strategic Planning in the Public Sector: Approaches and Direction" in B. Checkoway. *Strategic Perspectives on Planning Practice.* Lexington, Massachusetts: Lexington Books, 1986.

_____ and A.L. Delbecq. "A Contingent Approach to Strategy and Tactics in Project Planning." *Journal of the American Planning Association,* vol. 45, no. 2, spring 1979.

Burchell, R.W. and D. Listokin. *Planning Theory in the 1980s: A Search for Future Directions.* New Brunswick, New Jersey: Center for Urban Policy Research, Rutgers University, 1978.

Byerly, Barbara J. "Charting the Course for Kirkwood's Future." *Missouri Municipal Review,* vol. 54, no. 9, October-November 1989.

Chase, W. Howard. *Issues Management: Origins of the Future.* Stamford, Connecticut: Issues Action Publications, Inc., 1984.

Checkoway, B. *Strategic Perspectives on Planning Practice.* Lexington, Massachusetts: Lexington Books, 1986.

Christensen, K.S. "Coping with Uncertainty in Planning." *Journal of the American Planning Association,* vol. 51, no. 1, winter 1985.

Cramton, Martin R., Jr., and Carol Stealey Morris. "Managing Growth Through Strategic Planning: Charlotte-Mecklenburg's 2005 Plan." *Urban Land,* vol. 45, no. 4, April 1986.

Denhardt, Robert B. "Strategic Planning in Local Government." *Missouri Municipal Review,* vol. 49, no. 10, September 1984.

_____ and E. Jennings. *Toward a New Public Service.* Columbia, Missouri: University of Missouri Press, 1987.

Duff, Jesse H. and John K. Parker. "Duarte Resurgence: Strategic Planning for the Year 2007." *Public Management,* vol. 71, no. 3, March 1989.

Eadie, Douglas C. "Strategic Agenda Management: A Powerful Tool for Government." *National Civic Review,* vol. 74, no. 1, January 1985.

_____. "Putting a Powerful Tool to Practical Use: The Application of Strategic Planning in the Public Sector." *Public Administration Review,* vol. 43, no. 5, September-October 1983.

Eckhert, Philip C.; Kathleen Haines; Timothy J. Delmont; and Ann M. Pflaum. "Strategic Planning in Hennepin County, Minnesota: An Issues Management Approach" in John B. Bryson and Robert C. Einsweiler. *Strategic Planning: Threats and Opportunities for Planners.* Chicago, Illinois: Planners Press, 1988.

Everett, Skip. "Bellingham 2000: An Experiment in Mid-sized Community Planning." *World Future Society Bulletin,* vol. XII, no. 1, January-February 1978.

Ferris, Nancy B. "Developing a Strategic Advantage for Your Community." *Public Management,* vol. 65, no. 7, July 1983.

Fisher, R. and W. Ury. *Getting to Yes: Negotiating Agreement Without Giving In.* New York, New York: Penguin Books, 1981.

Forte, Debra B. "From Reactive to Proactive Fiscal Planning: The Results of Strategic Planning in McKinney, Texas." *Government Finance Review,* vol. 5, no. 4, August 1989.

Fosler, R. Scott. "Strategic Planning for Local Communities." *The Journal/The Institute for Socioeconomic Studies,* vol. IX, no. 4, winter 1985.

Freeman. R.E. *Strategic Management: A Stakeholder Approach.* Boston, Massachusetts: Pitman Books, 1984.

Gargan, John J. "An Overview of Strategic Planning for Officials in Small to Medium Size Communities." *Municipal Management,* vol. 7, no. 5, summer 1985.

Gordon, Gerald L. *Strategic Planning for Local Government.* Washington, DC: International City/County Management Association, 1993.

Hanson, Royce. "Cities for the Future." *American City & County,* vol. 99, no. 11, November 1984.

Hershberg, Theodore and Michael Rubin. "Strategic Planning: Finding Solutions to Future Challenges." *American City & County,* vol. 100, no. 3, March 1985.

Howe, E. "Role Choices of Urban Planners." *Journal of the American Planning Association,* vol. 46, no. 4, fall 1980.

Hudson. B.M. "Comparison of Current Planning Theories: Counterparts and Contradictions." *Journal of the American Planning Association,* vol. 45, no. 4, fall 1979.

Kaufman, J.L. and H.M. Jacobs. "A Public Planning Perspective on Strategic Planning." *Journal of the American Planning Association,* vol. 53, no. 1, winter 1987.

Kemp, Roger L. *Strategic Planning for Local Government: A Handbook for Officials and Citizens.* Jefferson, North Carolina: McFarland & Co., 1993.

_____. *Strategic Planning in Local Government: A Casebook.* Chicago, Illinois: Planners Press, 1992.

_____ and Jonathan D. Kemp. "Cities in the Year 2000: A New Planning Model." *Current Municipal Problems,* vol. 18, no. 3, 1992.

_____. "Cities in the Year 2000: The Forces of Change" in Jeffrey M. Elliott. *Urban Society.* Guilford, Connecticut: The Dushkin Publishing Group, 1991.

_____. "Future Vision Project: Clifton Prepares for the 1990s." *New Jersey Municipalities,* vol. 68, no. 3, March 1991.

_____. *America's Cities: Strategic Planning for the Future.* Danville, Illinois: Interstate Press, 1988.

King, Joseph C. and David A. Johnson. "Oak Ridge, Tennessee: Strategic Planning for a Strategic City" in John M. Bryson and Robert C. Einsweiler. *Strategic Planning: Threats and Opportunities for Planners.* Chicago, Illinois: Planners Press, 1988.

Krumholz, Norman. "A Retrospective View of Equity Planning: Cleveland 1969–1979." *Journal of the American Planning Association,* vol. 48, no. 2, spring 1982.

Kuznik, Robert W. and Roger L. Kemp. "The Placentia 2000 Project: Long-Range Planning in Local Government." *Nevada Government Today,* vol. 10, no. 3, fall-winter 1984.

McGowan, R.P. and J.M. Stevens. "Local Governments' Initiatives in a Climate of Uncertainty." *Public Administration Review,* vol. 43, no. 2, March-April 1983.

Morten, Richard. "Making a Great City Greater: The Unveiling of a Strategic Plan." *San Francisco Business,* vol. 18, no. 2, February 1983.

Morrison, J.L.; W.L. Renfro; and W. I. Boucher. *Applying Methods and Techniques of Futures Research.* San Francisco, California: Jossey-Bass, 1983.

Neufeld. W.P. "Environmental Scanning: Its Use in Forecasting Emerging Trends and Issues in Organizations." *Futures Research Quarterly,* vol. 1, no. 1, January-March 1985.

Olsen, J.B. and D.C. Eadie. *The Game Plan: Governance with Foresight.* Washington, DC: The Council of State Planning Agencies, 1982.

Paulson, Belden. "Scenarios for Greater Milwaukee: Citizen Participation in Projecting Futures." *World Future Society Bulletin,* vol. XVII, no. 3, May-June 1983.

Pflaum, A. and T. Delmont. "External Scanning: A Tool for Planners." *Journal of the American Planning Association,* vol. 53, no. 1, winter 1987.

Rabin, Jack; Gerald Miller; and W. Bartley Hildreth. *Handbook of Strategic Management.* New York, New York: Marcel Dekker, Inc., 1989.

Renfro, William L. "Managing the Issues of the 1980s." *The Futurist,* vol. 16, no. 8, August 1982.

_____ and James L. Morrison. "The Scanning Process: Getting Started" in J.L. Morrison, W.L. Renfro, and W.I. Boucher. *Applying Methods and Techniques of Futures Research.* San Francisco, California: Jossey-Bass, 1983.

Robinson, Richard V. and Douglas C. Eadie. "Putting Strategic Planning to Practical Use in Cleveland Heights, Ohio." *Cities & Villages,* vol. XXXI, no. 10, October 1983.

Russo, Richard and David Penchoff. "Strategic Planning in Local Government: The West Hartford Approach." *Connecticut Government,* vol. 34, no. 2, Spring 1983.

So, Frank S. "Strategic Planning: Reinventing the Wheel?" *Planning,* vol. 50, no. 2, February 1984.

Sorkin, Donna L.; Nancy B. Ferris; and James Hudak. "What Is Strategic Planning?" *Strategies for Cities and Counties.* Washington, DC: Public Technology, Inc., 1984.

Streib, Gregory. "Applying Strategic Decision Making in Local Government: Does the Promise Justify the Challenge?" *Public Productivity Review,* vol. 15, no. 1. National Center for Public Productivity, Newark, New Jersey: Rutgers University, spring 1992.

Walter, Susan and Pat Choate. "The Management Challenges." *Thinking Strategically: A Primer for Public Officials.* Washington, DC: The Council of State Planning Agencies, 1984.

Wier, Sandy. "Strategic Planning in Hampton: Choices and Challenges." *Planning in Virginia,* vol. 2, no. 1, January 1986.

INDEX